DUE PROCESS AND FAIR PROCEDURES

Due Process and Fair Procedures

A Study of Administrative Procedures

D. J. GALLIGAN

Professor of Socio-Legal Studies
Faculty of Law and Director of the Centre
for Socio-Legal Studies, University of Oxford.
Fellow of Wolfson College, Oxford.
Barrister of Gray's Inn

CLARENDON PRESS · OXFORD
1996

Oxford University Press, Walton Street, Oxford OX2 6DP
Oxford New York
Athens Auckland Bangkok Bogota Bombay
Buenos Aires Calcutta Cape Town Dar es Salaam
Delhi Florence Hong Kong Istanbul Karachi
Kuala Lumpur Madras Madrid Melbourne
Mexico City Nairobi Paris Singapore
Taipei Tokyo Toronto
and associated companies in
Berlin Ibadan

Oxford is a trade mark of Oxford University Press

Published in the United States
by Oxford University Press Inc., New York

British Library Cataloguing in Publication Data
Data available

Library of Congress Cataloging in Publication Data
Galligan, D. J. (Denis James), 1947–
Due process and fair procedures / by D. J. Galligan.
p. cm.
Includes bibliographical references.
1. Due process of law—Great Britain. 2. Fair trial—Great Britain.
KD4106.G35 1996
347.41'05—dc20
[344.1075] 96–28113
ISBN 0–19–825676–0

1 3 5 7 9 10 8 6 4 2

Typeset by Vera A. Keep and Theresa M. Murphy, Cheltenham
Printed in Great Britain
on acid-free paper by
Biddles Ltd., Guildford and King's Lynn

To my mother

M.M.G.

Preface

The subject of this book is fair procedures or, as some prefer, procedural due process, with particular reference to administrative contexts. The approach is theoretical in the sense that an analytical framework is devised within which to examine procedural issues. The approach is contextual in that empirical studies are drawn on to give a better understanding of how procedural issues are dealt with in practice (although in the course of the study it became all too clear how many issues there are for which research does not exist). The book is also concerned with doctrine to the extent that a number of important principles of procedural fairness are examined. This mixed approach may not appeal to everyone and runs the risk of pleasing no one, but it reflects a view that all three levels of analysis can, and indeed should, be brought together. Even though this is a long book, I have had to be selective as to both the range of issues dealt with and the depth of analysis of those chosen. At various points in the book, I have indicated areas which would lend themselves to further analysis or with respect to which empirical research would be especially beneficial.

While I hope that this book will stimulate research in the areas of administrative law and administrative government, that is just one amongst several of its objects. Drawing on the literature of political and social theory, I have put forward an account of procedural justice which I hope will be of interest to those of a more speculative turn of mind, particularly at a time when the traditional neglect of procedural justice is starting to be remedied. Procedural justice is also at the heart of the legal process and one of my aims here has been to show practitioners and students of law that issues of natural justice and procedural fairness need not be presented as a mass of decisions, rules, and practices without rhyme or reason. My argument is that this great and expanding body of doctrine can be placed within a coherent framework, where legal principles can be identified, and where the interplay of principle and policy can best be explored. The book is neither a textbook nor a treatise; it should be seen as a study of procedural justice, proceeding at several levels and from various points of view, but offering something to students and practitioners as well as their academic counterparts.

This book may be seen as an extension of Chapter VII of my earlier book, *Discretionary Powers*. In the course of the book, I have drawn heavily on the writings of others and, while that is fully acknowledged in the text, I would like to express my thanks to all those whose work has gone before, even though their views have occasionally attracted critical appraisal. In addition, I would like especially to acknowledge the help and advice received from the following colleagues: Rhonda Andrieux, Paul Craig, David Miller, Genevra Richardson, Deborah Sandler, and Adrian Zuckerman. Work on the book began at the University of Southampton, continued at the University of Sydney, and was completed at the University of Oxford. While all three places were conducive to and understanding of the slow business of writing a book, the Centre for Socio-Legal Studies at Oxford merits special mention. Not only did the Centre pioneer the contextual approach to understanding law and legal institutions, but its multi-disciplinary environment continues to be the ideal place to work.

On the more material side, I am grateful to the President and Fellows of Wolfson College Oxford for a grant to assist with the production of the book. Alison Lampard did most of the typing and her contribution is much appreciated. Oxford University Press has offered its usual high standard of help and advice; Richard Hart has been closely involved and I offer him, together with his editors and staff, my warm thanks. My freelance bibliographer did a fine job and I thank my family for their support throughout the years of this project.

D.J.G.
Wolfson College Oxford
July 1996

Contents

Introduction

If justice is the first virtue of law and politics, then procedural justice is an essential element in its attainment. For no matter how good and just the laws and political principles supporting them may be, without suitable procedures they would fail in their purposes. Some laws will be adopted and acted upon by those to whom they relate as a matter of course and without reference to institutions or officials; others depend on authoritative decisions by authoritative bodies. If the criminal law is to be enforced, if the legal standards regulating and directing an array of activities are to be upheld, if burdens and benefits are to be distributed in accordance with binding norms, and if disputes between parties are to be resolved, then procedures appropriate to each of those tasks must be available.

This book is about the concepts of justice and fairness in relation to procedures. Much has been written in recent years by political and legal theorists about those concepts in general and about substantive theories of justice and fairness. However, relatively little attention has been paid to their close, but neglected, relation, procedural justice or procedural fairness. In the interests of economy of expression, I shall use the term fairness to cover both; sometimes it may be helpful to distinguish between the two, but in the normal course of discussion, they may be used interchangeably. When we move from political theory to practical law, it is soon apparent that procedural fairness occupies a central place. A concern with procedural fairness, whether known under that name or as procedural due process, is the daily fare of courts, tribunals, and administrative bodies. Not only is good time spent determining the meaning of procedural fairness, and its scope and application, but a large share of resources is needed to make sure that practical procedures deliver its promises. Procedural fairness, then, is a serious matter and in this book I endeavour to analyse some of its characteristics.

It may be helpful right at the beginning to state briefly the view of procedures and procedural fairness which I advance in this book. It is in essence quite simple. The key concept is fair treatment. Fair treatment has different meanings in different contexts, but of importance here is the idea that each person should be treated in accordance with the standards which govern the life of the society. These may be referred to as authoritative standards. Legal standards are a major part of authoritative standards and, in general, a person is treated fairly if treated in accordance with the legal standards. But although a major source, legal standards are not the only source of authoritative standards; they must be supplemented by, and in some cases supplanted by, other standards based on values of a moral or social kind. Just what those standards are depends on the values of the society and on the values applying within specific contexts in society. But leaving aside such refinements, the general point is that fair treatment consists in being treated in accordance with authoritative standards whatever they be in each context. This points the way to procedures. The main object of procedures at the general social level is to provide for proper application of the law, to achieve whatever objects the law stipulates, while at the level of the individual person affected, procedures also invoke the additional element of fair treatment. Procedures are instruments to fair treatment; they are inherently neither fair nor unfair, but take on a quality of fairness to the degree that they are conducive to a person being treated properly according to authoritative standards and the values which ground such standards. Around this basic idea, there are complications to explain, modifications to enter, and ambiguities to explore; it is, nevertheless, the hub round which many of the great issues of law and justice revolve.

But why, it may be asked, is legal justice or justice according to law so important? The law, after all, is a set of rules laid down by legislators, judges, and administrators, and there is no guarantee that they are the best rules or even good rules. Is it really so important, is it a question of justice and fairness at all, whether these rules are upheld? The answer, I suggest, is that it matters greatly that authoritative standards are properly upheld, and that, subject to certain qualifications, fair treatment in the sense of treatment according to such standards, constitutes an important and irreducible aspect of justice. Now of course such a claim is not self-evident and, in the following chapters, I seek to explain and defend it. It should be made clear, however, that justice, even in this limited sense of justice according to law, is the exception rather than the rule. Indeed, as an anthropologist of law was recently heard to remark, justice in any sense is the exception, injustice the rule.

That seems as true of legal justice as it is of justice in any more fundamental sense. A society which is able to say with good reason that its citizens are generally treated fairly, in the sense of fairness according to law, is indeed a rare and enlightened society. It is not our society. For the more we know about the great range of legal and administrative authorities making countless decisions each year, affecting individuals and groups in their rights and interests, the more we realize how often they are unjust, not according to some utopian sense of justice but according to the very rules of our own society by which the decisions are meant to be made. That is precisely what fair procedures are about, for the means to fair treatment lie in fair procedures. Fair treatment according to law is not the ultimate in justice, but it is a vital part of any sense of justice. It would be a matter of no small significance if we could say that, in this society or that, people are treated fairly according to law. If a better understanding of procedures helps to achieve that end, these efforts will have been well worthwhile.

The analysis proceeds at a number of levels. At the first the object is to provide an understanding of procedures, with particular attention being paid to the notion of procedural fairness. This involves reference to writings in legal, political, and social theory, although the canon is not extensive. Much of what there is has come from or been generated by discussion of the American doctrine of procedural due process, and although that is a rich and interesting literature, it is not easily loosened from its native soil to provide the seeds for a more general understanding. Guided by these various sources, I therefore propose my own account of procedural fairness, an account which seems to be practical enough to direct the design of procedures, while at the same time being, I hope, theoretically sound. The first part of the book may then be seen as providing a general framework for the understanding of procedures and procedural fairness, a framework within which different types of legal processes can be identified and where notions such as procedural rights, process values, the worth of participation, and the problems of costs can be discussed.

In the second part of the book, the analysis drops from the realms of theory to the applied doctrines of three different traditions of procedural fairness and procedural due process. The English common law is the first and, for one working in that tradition, the most interesting. Even without the space or the expertise to do more than offer a few potted ideas, one can easily become engrossed in the historical evolution of English ideas of procedural fairness, regretting only that it remains largely undiscovered by legal historians. The American tradition serves as an instructive counterpoint, being part of the same family tree and yet in its modern expression a distant cousin. By way of a third tradition, a real comparativist might have chosen a truly continental case but, instead, I take a middle course by offering a very brief introduction to two emerging, related, and partly European traditions, the procedural fairness aspects of the European Convention on Human Rights and the law of the European Union. These are truly brief introductions which do no more than signal the quiet but steady growth of two areas of due process of great future importance.

The third part of the book takes a different tack; working within the theoretical scheme of Part I, my aim here is to identify different types of legal processes. These range across a variety of forms or families, from decisions according to authoritative standards to those of a discretionary kind; they include decisions reached by agreement and those settled by voting; they also extend to variations on the principal types, including investigations and enquiries. Each family is partly a description of how different matters are dealt with in practice, but each also has a distinctive normative character; decision by the application of authoritative standards, for example, being quite different from decisions reached through agreement. The task in this part is to give a reasonably complete picture of the different forms of process, to show how each can be divided further, and to identify the specific issues of procedural fairness with respect to each.

The remaining two parts of the book, Parts IV and V, deal with a number of specific procedural issues. Part IV is devoted to procedural fairness in relation to individualized processes, Part V to collectivized processes in the sense of administrative policy-making. The analysis in both parts is located within the social and theoretical framework already established, but now the focus is on specific issues of procedural fairness and on the way they are handled in English law, with some reference to other jurisdictions, especially Australia and the United States. These two parts are not comprehensive but purport to deal with some of the most interesting and important issues. The question of access to legal processes and its relationship to fair treatment is one glaring omission; the issue of timeliness is another. Both deserve a fuller treatment than I could provide here.

Within that general structure of analysis, my method of approach also proceeds at several levels. The first is theoretical, just in the sense that an account of procedural fairness is given which draws on writings in legal, political, and social theory. The object here is to give a descriptive account of due process and procedural fairness which is sufficiently general to apply across the board of legal processes. At the second level, the object is to examine the application of procedural fairness in administrative processes. The method of approach is partly to examine various doctrines of English law, and partly to analyse those doctrines within the theoretical framework of procedural fairness. Thirdly and finally, my method of approach has also been to understand procedures and notions of fairness in their social context. This has meant taking account of the inter-relationship between law and its context; it has also meant drawing on empirical studies of procedures which, although few in number, have been very helpful in understanding both practical and theoretical issues. Indeed, the writing of this book has heightened my appreciation of the importance of deep empirical research and made me aware of just how much more could be done in this area. It has also confirmed the view that empirical research and theoretical analysis complement each other, indeed, should be seen as components of the one undertaking. For just as empirical research can illuminate theory, a sound theoretical understanding is essential for good empirical work. My emphasis has been on developing the theoretical side, while benefiting where possible from the fruits of empirical work.

Table of Cases

AUSTRALIA

EC Cases

ECHR Cases

NEW ZEALAND

UNITED KINGDOM

USA

Table of Legislation

AUSTRALIA

CANADA

UNITED KINGDOM

Statutes

Statutory Instruments

USA

Conventions and Treaties

PART I

Procedures and Fairness

Introduction

My aim in this first part is to give an analysis of procedures in general and of procedural fairness in particular. A great amount is written about procedures and procedural fairness not only by lawyers and judges but also by social scientists and political theorists. Such issues are at the heart of administrative processes and make heavy demands on the time and energy of administrative officials. And yet, despite the interest in procedures and their centrality to law and legal processes, it is difficult to conceive of a framework or structure sufficiently general to contain procedural issues in their totality. Specific issues are often analysed in great detail and depth, as in the law of evidence or the rules of natural justice, while the broader canvas remains pristine. Similarly, in the traditions of political and social theory, such writers as Rawls and Habermas have much to say about procedures, but usually as incidental to some other major undertaking. The two names which defy such a generalization are Jeremy Bentham and Michael Bayles, the former having devoted a substantial part of a long life to issues of procedure, the latter having come to the subject only towards the end of a short life. Each tried in his own way to expound a comprehensive theory of procedures, with particular but not exclusive reference to law. The importance and influence of both generally and in the writing of this book should be readily apparent.

In this Part, my aim is to build on the work of Bentham and Bayles and to offer a general account of procedures and procedural fairness. The first chapter is meant to be a sort of map of the procedural landscape, noting the main features and contours, dwelling on some, passing by others, and, like any map leaving much of the detail to be inserted when the need arises. In the second chapter, one of the dominant features on the procedural landscape—procedural fairness—is the focus of attention. Having developed a sense of procedural fairness in the second chapter, I proceed in the third to extend the analysis to procedural rights and to confront the difficult question of the relationship between procedural rights and the costs of procedures. The final chapter in this part moves to an analysis of the concept of participation which in its various forms has a major role in legal and political procedures.

1
A Map of Procedures

Without procedures, law and legal institutions would fail in their purposes. And since law is both necessary and desirable in achieving social goals, procedures are also necessary and must be seen as equal partners in that enterprise. For whatever the context, whether the judicial trial, the administrative decision, or any other form of legal process, procedures are necessary to ensure that the issue is channelled to its right conclusion. Whether the object is to apply a legal standard to the facts, to exercise a discretion according to the correct matters, or to settle a dispute by bringing the parties together, procedures have a vital part to play. The first law of procedures may be stated to be that they are instruments for reaching decisions and pursuing processes, and in that way achieving the ends of law. The full scope and significance of that first law lies at the heart of a study of procedures. But there is more to procedures than that: for one thing, the relationship between procedures and outcomes is more complex than a simple instrumental image suggests; for another, procedures serve other ends and values besides outcomes; and for a third, procedures raise questions of fairness. For these reasons, it is wise to begin a study of procedures with a firm understanding of what they do and how they fit into a coherent picture. Accordingly, the object of this Chapter is to map out the main features of the procedural landscape.

1.1 INTRODUCTION

1.1.1 Legal Procedures: a General Outline

Social institutions and social practices can be analysed and understood at different levels. To understand any social activity, we must strip away the layers of meaning, not in order to abandon one in favour of another, but because by grasping the significance of each, the richness and complexity of the whole becomes apparent. In their simplest form, procedures are the steps leading to a decision; they are the means for reaching a decision or other result. In a modern legal system, the range of legal decisions is considerable, but one common feature is that each tries to advance certain ends and goals. Legal decisions are in that sense purposive, and so the main point of procedures is to serve those purposes. The purpose of the criminal trial is ideally to determine whether the accused is guilty or innocent; for the tribunal it is to decide whether the statutory rules for granting a benefit have been met; and for the administrative official, to exercise his discretion wisely and reasonably, taking account of relevant matters. It is tempting to borrow the analogy of science: just as the scientist is able to produce a given result by following certain steps, so the official achieves the required ends and goals by adopting suitable procedures. The analogy certainly has a point; it shows that procedures are purposive and that the primary test in designing or evaluating procedures is whether they lead to the desired outcome in a way which is efficient and effective.

However, the limitations of the scientific analogy are readily apparent. Over the neat simplicity of the idea that legal decisions and processes are purposive, and that procedures are the instruments for achieving those purposes, other frames of meaning must be laid. In the first place, legal decisions have a social dimension. Far from being mechanical processes which, faithfully followed, will lead to certain outcomes, legal decisions are directed towards social goals, and require the exercise of reason and judgment about what those goals are and the best way of achieving them. It is a feature of the social dimension that the ends sought in decision-making do not come clearly defined and neatly labelled. Legal processes, like all social processes, are to some degree open and indeterminate, where currents of meaning and significance compete, and where resolution is achieved by holding a steady course between the authority of the past and the possibilities for the future. The definition and identification of purposes is itself a major task of interpretation and judgment of legal standards, to be made against a background of social and cultural values, where the two dimensions overlap and intermingle. The same decision may serve a number of purposes, and amongst those purposes tension and conflict may prevail. Moreover, there are different points of view from which that judgment of purposes is made: the legislator is likely to see it one way, the judge or administrator another; the professional, whether lawyer, social worker, or police officer, will have his own attitude to it, while the person subject to the decision as accused, litigant, or beneficiary is liable to see it entirely differently. Not all viewpoints carry the same weight, but each may have some influence in settling purposes and designing procedures. Indeed, the more we think about it, the less apt the scientific analogy becomes. For while legal decisions and processes are purposive, procedures are less like steps leading inexorably to outcomes, but more like signposts indicating the direction to take and the issues to consider. Finally, it is not only the purposes of a legal process which sway and bend according to their social context; the procedures themselves, while instruments to ends, are likely to be shaped and influenced by social factors extraneous to those ends.

A second level of meaning to be spread over the simple, instrumental image of procedures is that legal decisions are not only directed to certain social goals, but are made in a context of values. Such values are relevant in a number of ways. The proper application of the law itself is not only a social goal, but is closely linked to values. In particular, it is linked to fair treatment, since proper application of the law usually means that a person has been treated fairly, at least in a special and significant sense. Moreover, the social goals achieved by applying the law may themselves be basic values, values such as non-discrimination or respect for other rights. Values like these are internal to the application of legal standards; other values are external to, but none the less affect, their application. They may relate to outcomes, restricting the possibilities open, or they may relate to procedures, dictating what is to be done or not done in reaching outcomes, or finally they may operate in their own right independently of the nature of the process. The influence of values on the shape and design of procedures can be considerable. Values are seen at work in the criminal trial where restrictions on the conduct of investigations and many of the rules of evidence are best understood partly in relation to outcomes, but also partly as the result of other values restricting the way outcomes are reached. What is seen so dramatically at work in the criminal trial occurs in more muted form across the full range of legal decisions. The ways in which various values are relevant and their significance for procedures constitute another major part of a study of procedures.

The third layer which adds to the richness and complexity of legal processes is fairness. Where decisions are made about the treatment of persons and groups, about the distribution of goods and the allocation of resources, questions of fairness are never far behind. Fairness is itself a complex notion which takes interesting twists and turns when applied to procedures. For whatever the fairness of substantive outcomes, procedures are one step removed and raise their own problems of fairness. They may contribute to fair treatment in the sense that the substance of the decision is just; or they may contribute in the lesser sense that the law is properly applied, even though its content is less than ideal; or they may even raise issues of fair treatment based on other values and standards. Some even suggest that procedures themselves can be fair or unfair without reference to anything further. This, I think, is a mistake, or if not a mistake it at least requires careful elaboration; but enough has been said for the moment to show just how complex and confused ideas of fairness in relation to procedures can be. An attempt to clarify these ideas is made in Chapter 2.

A study of procedures which brought out each of these issues in its fullness would be a grand undertaking. My object is more modest; I hope merely to examine some aspects of these matters, and shall be content if the reader is able to find here some guidance in approaching other procedural issues. But let me here state in a few words the approach to be taken. My approach is that legal decisions and processes associated with those decisions are purposive in the sense that they are directed to ends and goals. The ends and goals are set by the legal system, and are usually linked to important values within the community. The first and primary concern of procedures is to lead to those ends and goals. However, decisions and processes are also influenced and constrained by other values, which may be linked to ends and goals or be separate from them. The second concern of procedures is to ensure that such values are respected in decision-making. Around these two procedural objectives, notions of fairness and rights are developed. Issues of fairness and rights arise when decisions are about how a person is to be treated. One sense of fairness consists in achieving the outcomes required by law. A second sense of fairness is linked to those other values and is satisfied when they are respected. These are the broad themes of the book which will be developed and extended in the following pages.

1.1.2 A Note on Terminology

It may be wise at this early stage to clarify the terminology which will recur throughout the book. To that end, I suggest the following, not as definitions in any theoretical sense, but simply as working meanings. *Procedures* I understand to be the steps taken, the means used in reaching a decision, carrying out a course of action, or settling a matter in some way, within a legal or administrative context. By *process* I mean a distinct legal or administrative act which usually involves a decision, but which need not. An investigation or inquiry into a matter does not normally result in a decision, but it is clearly a legal and administrative act of significance. The expression 'process' is a convenient, generic term for referring to any such legal or administrative acts as well as decisions. Process also includes the aggregate of procedures in relation to that decision or action. The criminal trial, taken as a whole, is a distinct process which includes a number of particular procedures. A general process, such as a trial, can often be divided into several more limited processes.

Legal and administrative processes are different from other kinds of social processes in that they are made under the authority of legal standards which define and set the limits to the scope of authority. It is also characteristic of such processes that other legal standards normally stipulate the criteria for exercising that authority. The degree to which an area of authority is guided by such standards varies. The less a process is governed by guiding standards, then the more discretion there is in the official to decide as he thinks best. Discretion of course is not just a factor of the absence of standards, but may consist in interpreting standards, in choosing between conflicting standards, and in deciding whether to depart from or not apply a standard.[1] Moreover, as we shall see in more detail later in this Chapter, legal standards guiding the use of authority may derive from sources other than the governing statute.

[1] An understanding of discretion is vital to an understanding of fair procedures; for my own account of discretion in its many forms and senses, I refer the reader to *Discretionary Powers: A Legal Study of Official Discretion* (Clarendon Press, Oxford, 1986).

Uncertainty and disagreement may prevail about whether, in a particular context, external social and moral standards have become binding legal standards, or, indeed, whether legal or not, have become authoritative standards in their own right.

The term *process* I also use to include the procedures for rule-making and policy-formation, as well as procedures directed primarily to achieving agreement between the parties. Process may also be given a wider or narrower sense. We talk of the criminal justice process, when in fact it consists of a number of reasonably distinct processes—investigation, questioning, charging, and negotiating over pleas, the trial itself, and finally sentencing. It will also be convenient and economical to use the term 'legal processes' to include administrative and all other forms of legal acts and decisions.

Another term often encountered in discussion of processes and procedures is *process values*. Although not a precise notion, it usually means those values which are relevant to legal processes, but which are not directly related to outcomes. The idea that a process should be timely and intelligible, or that a person should be heard quite apart from any instrumental effect on outcomes, is an example. Process values in that sense are discussed at several points in subsequent chapters, but it is not a precise term and may confuse more than enlighten. However, the term is widely used and further analysis of its meaning and connotations is given in section 2.2.6.

1.1.3 Bentham on Procedures

A good place to start a study of procedures is with the writings of Jeremy Bentham. He wrote at length on the subject and his influence on later writers has been considerable.[2] He left an account of legal procedures which, for its clarity, conviction, and commitment, is unrivalled. Some of the battles he fought are forgotten, some of his views are unacceptable, and his dedication to a particular brand of utilitarianism can be a stumbling block. Nevertheless, Bentham left a cogent theory of procedures, a reference point to which it is instructive time and again to return. For that reason I shall begin with a brief introduction to his general approach and to some of the issues he considered.

A reformer driven by utilitarianism, Bentham examined the law of evidence and procedure of his day with a combination of thoroughness in explaining its detail and passion for exposing its failings.[3] At the heart of an ample and complex work is a fairly simple idea, namely, that the object of procedures at the

[2] The two most illuminating studies of Bentham are: W. Twining, *Theories of Evidence: Bentham and Wigmore* (Weidenfeld, London, 1986) and G. Postema, *Bentham and the Common Law Tradition* (Clarendon Press, Oxford, 1988).

[3] Bentham's writings on evidence and procedure are scattered, but some of his most important ideas are found in *A Treatise on Judicial Evidence* (M. Dumont (ed.), London, 1825), *Principles of Judicial Procedure* (Works 1837, ii), and *Rationale of Judicial Evidence* (Works, 1827, vi).

criminal trial is to produce an accurate outcome, and that the reason for seeking accuracy is utility; not the direct utility in upholding laws which themselves maximize utility, but the utility in the social stability which follows from the accurate and regular application of the laws, even if some of them are less than perfect.

The first point to note about Bentham's approach is the relationship between procedures, outcomes, and values. Procedures are there to produce accurate outcomes; accurate outcomes, or rectitude as Bentham preferred to call it, mean the correct application of the law to the facts. Accurate outcomes are important because they mean upholding social values, the values inherent in the substantive law and the value in stability through regular and consistent application of the law. Bentham found much wanting in the procedural or adjectival law of his day and urged reform. He considered that the law of evidence, with its elaborate restrictions and exclusions, should be replaced by a system of natural proof, meaning roughly that all evidence of probative value should be admitted, subject only to the judge's discretion to exclude. Bentham thought that natural proof would produce more accurate results, which, of course, for him was the yardstick of reform.[4] That the core of a theory of procedures is the relationship between procedures and outcomes, Bentham makes clear and explicit. And whether or not we accept his view of the criminal trial, or indeed his view that social institutions are to be judged by the principles of utilitarianism, his central claim is abundantly clear. Now utilitarianism may have difficulty in explaining all aspects of the criminal trial; in capturing the distinction between mistaken convictions and mistaken acquittals, for example, or in providing adequate protection for the accused at the pre-trial stage. Modern views, moreover, are likely to see the trial as a more complex process serving other ends in addition to accuracy.

Nevertheless, Bentham's insistence on rectitude, on the correct application of the law to an accurate finding of facts, remains a simple but fundamental feature of legal processes. It must be admitted that his ideas are not in favour and that the idea of accuracy of outcome is much too crude to apply sensibly to many legal processes. Indeed, the world is littered with rectitude—sceptics. Bentham had in mind the judicial trial, especially the criminal trial, where accuracy makes good sense. But we should not make too much of the terms accuracy or rectitude, for if we delve deeper, it is easy to translate the idea into terms more acceptable in their own right and more easily applicable outside the criminal trial. For what is at stake is the simple idea that in any legal process, especially those involving action against an individual person, authoritative legal standards are stipulated as to how the matter should be dealt with; the application of standards in turn depends on accurate findings of fact. That

[4] For further discussion of Bentham's approach to evidence W. Twining, *Theories of Evidence: Bentham and Wigmore* and G. Postema, *Bentham and the Common Law Tradition*, n. 2 above.

is the case whether the process is a criminal trial, the decision of a tribunal, or the exercise of discretion by a minister. In each case, there are standards to be applied, not necessarily standards dictating a specific outcome, but at least standards guiding and constraining the reasoning towards an outcome. If rectitude is understood in that way, as the proper application of authoritative legal standards, then it not only applies across the board of legal processes, but also remains as fundamental to them as Bentham held it to be for the criminal trial. This is not to say that rectitude is all that matters in legal processes; it is to say, however, that whatever else we may need to add, rectitude remains a fundamental element.

This leads on to the second matter arising from Bentham's approach. What, if anything, needs to be added to rectitude in order properly to understand the objects of a legal process? Bentham thought rectitude was the overriding object, indeed the sole object. We may applaud his insistence on clarity and simplicity about the objects of the criminal trial, but at the same time doubt that such a complex process can be reduced to one aim. Indeed, without now attempting to define the objects of the trial, we can see that his view is unduly narrow. The use of the jury itself suggests that objects other than accuracy are important. Juries are prone to take account of matters beyond the facts presented in evidence or contrary to the judge's instructions on the law, while their capacity to inject a sense of common justice and popular morality is said to be the main reason for their existence.[5] The adversarial process also appears to serve ends other than accuracy. It may in a roundabout way concern itself with the truth, but it is not obviously the most effective method for doing so, and as Pollock once wrote, it would be a serious mistake to think that the common law trial is solely or primarily about reaching the right result.[6] The active control of the parties and the relatively passive role of the judge suggest a positive value in the trial as a contest between two parties, who are roughly equal, at least in principle, and who control the issues and the way their cases are presented.[7] Another factor is the interrelationship between the trial itself and the processes which both precede and follow it, since it shows that other ends besides accuracy are in play.

Notice what is happening in each of these examples: the legal standards at the core of the process are being supplemented by other normative standards and values—the jury should act according to popular morality, or the trial should be an even contest between the parties. What constitutes the object of a legal process is a normative question; for Bentham the answer to the question was to apply the law properly, but on closer inspection it is clear that other normative standards enter in, that the proper application of the law is one

[5] See the discussion in P. Devlin, *Trial by Jury* (3rd edn., Stevens, London, 1966).

[6] F. Pollock, *Essays in the Law* (Macmillan, London, 1922), 275.

[7] For an attempt to identify the values served by the adversarial process and to explain their development, see M. Damaska, *The Faces of Justice and State Authority* (Yale, Newhaven, Conn., 1986).

important standard but not the only one. We thus catch our first glimpse of the relationship between legal processes and social context, since, in order fully to understand which standards apply and what objects are being pursued, we must examine legal processes in their social and cultural context.

A third point of general interest in Bentham's theory is the claim that rectitude should not be compromised by extraneous considerations, such as the desire to protect the accused from impropriety during the pre-trial process, or to enable the accused to refuse to answer questions. We are familiar with a patchwork of doctrines, such as the right to silence, the privilege against self-incrimination, the rules requiring voluntary confessions, and a general doctrine of fairness. Much of this was undeveloped in Bentham's day, but we can be sure he would have disapproved. By obstructing the discovery and presentation of evidence, such doctrines detract from the likelihood of accurate outcomes; they also protect the guilty, and serve no legitimate object which should be allowed to compete with rectitude, so the argument would go. But here we touch on another central issue in the understanding of procedures: the relationship between the primary objects on the one hand and other values on the other hand. Which values are to be considered, and how they relate to the objects of the process, are again complex issues. Other values sometimes compete with and even compromise primary objects. Bentham was not totally opposed to some such values having a place in the criminal process, although the confidentiality of the confessional was the only one he conceded. To the modern observer, his view of the trial might seem tendentious, for now we are accustomed to a number of limitations stemming from a concern to protect values other than accuracy of outcome. But this is a matter on which widely different views can be held, and much can be learnt from Bentham's vigorous defence of the claim that rectitude should not lightly be tampered with. What Bentham said about the criminal trial can be generalized to apply to other areas: although other values are important, and may even restrict the pursuit of primary goals, their place must be earned by clear and compelling reasons.

Amongst the many matters Bentham dealt with, these three raise issues of special importance in the study of procedures. Bentham concentrated on the criminal trial and to a lesser extent the civil trial, but similar issues occur across the range of legal processes. The relationship between procedures, outcomes, and values, the complexity of legal processes and the difficulty of identifying their primary purposes, and the place of other values, occur and recur throughout the legal process; they also appear and reappear throughout this book. The glaring omission, however, is that Bentham apparently had little to say about procedural fairness. But here we must tread carefully. Recent studies of Bentham's writings, many of which remain unedited, suggest that his views on the fair and equitable treatment of individual persons within a utilitarian framework fluctuated during the course of his life. From a recent analysis by G. Postema, it appears that Bentham was more concerned with the principles of distribution within utilitarianism than his better-known writings suggest.[8] Bentham strove to reconcile the fair treatment of individual persons with general utility, his argument being that at a certain level rectitude serves both. It serves general utility by upholding the ends of the law, which at the same time means treating individual persons according to their expectations under the law. But while this link between the two is important, they do not always coincide and fairness in distribution raises other issues which we need not examine here.

1.2 PROCEDURES AND PURPOSES

1.2.1 The Purposes of Legal Processes

Let us begin with Bentham's idea that the object of procedures is to lead to the accurate application of the law, and in that way to achievement of the purposes of the law. The idea is that for each legal process there are standards to be applied and that the object of procedures is to do just that. For each process, whether the criminal trial, the civil trial, or an area of administration, the task is to identify the legal standards and then to direct procedures to their application. This approach might seem to run into trouble where there is discretion, since discretion in its stronger sense connotes an absence of binding legal standards. The statute itself might give little guidance,[9] and the law developed in judicial review does little more than require that discretion be used reasonably and in good faith and according to whatever objects can be ascertained. The point is, however, that those very matters constitute normative standards so that it might still be said that the object of procedures is to ensure that discretion is exercised in compliance with them.

This general approach to purposes and procedures rests on two assumptions: first, that legal processes are normative processes where decisions are made by applying authoritative standards, and, secondly, that legal processes are distinct normative sub-systems. Those two assumptions are of great importance, for they make clear that while legal processes serve social ends and goods, they do so through a distinct, normative, legal structure. Here a distinction should be drawn between legal purposes and social goals. By legal purpose is meant that, within an area of legal authority, there are authoritative legal standards the application of which constitutes the purpose of the law. That legal purpose will in turn serve some social ends and goals, perhaps to resolve disputes, distribute resources, or punish offenders. The claim is often

[8] These and related matters are well-discussed in G. Postema, *Bentham and the Common Law Tradition*, n. 2 above.

[9] A recent study of regulatory bodies found little guidance in governing statutes as to purposes and standards: see R. Baldwin and C. McCrudden (eds.), *Regulation and Public Law* (Weidenfeld and Nicholson, London, 1987).

made that the primary purpose of a whole range of legal processes is to settle disputes. That may be true, but to express purposes in such broad social terms will never capture the full sense of legal processes. Disputes may be settled in a number of ways, many of which have nothing to do with law. It is only when social goals are pursued through a legal framework that the nature of legal processes can be understood, since the law then provides a normative framework, a set of standards as to how various social functions are to be realized. The ultimate goal may be to settle disputes, but that goal is to be reached by applying the legal standards.

To take another case, the social function of a board or tribunal might be to control access to and conduct within a profession; whatever the possible ways that might be done, the law dictates through its standards how it is to be done. Legal standards, in other words, provide the intermediate means through which social goals, such as the resolution of disputes, are to be reached. The ultimate social goal may be to resolve a dispute, but the intermediate social goal is to resolve the dispute by applying the law. To conclude, after observing a civil trial, that the point was to settle a dispute would be not so much mistaken as incomplete; a fuller description would be that the point was to settle a dispute by applying the law. The distinction between ultimate social purposes and intermediate legal purposes is of fundamental importance for procedures.

At stake here is the recognition of law as constituted by sets of distinct normative sub-systems. Each has its own normative standards, an internal logic and coherence, and a set of legal institutions for its interpretation and development. The relationship between law and the wider society is intricate and complex, but to imagine that the one simply collapses into the other is not only bad law but poor sociology. The starting point, therefore, for an analysis of procedures is the simple point that procedures, and the legal institutions using them, are directed first and foremost to the objects and purposes of the legal system itself. Law has its own purposes which, at least in the first instance, are created and defined by the law, distinct from the wider social system. As a normative order, its first purpose is that the legal standards be applied; that in turn is the first purpose of legal procedures and institutions.

Now that we have clear the idea of legal purposes as a distinct sub-set of social purposes, a keener look should be taken at legal purposes themselves. The idea is that each process has its own set of legal norms to apply and that the main purpose is to apply them properly. But a number of questions arise about the separateness of legal processes: how can a legal process be a sub-set of the wider social context and yet remain distinct; what is the relationship between legal standards and other social standards; indeed what counts as a legal standard in the first place. These questions raise some of the most fundamental issues about the nature of law and its relationship to the social structure, issues which I shall not attempt to analyse here. Instead, I shall propose one general proposition and then offer a number of comments around it.

The general proposition is that each legal process occurs within a framework of distinctively legal standards, that is, standards which are recognized by judges, lawyers, and officials as binding legal standards. This is not to suggest that the standards will necessarily be comprehensive and complete; nor is it to suggest that the only test of whether a standard is a legal standard is some simple master test. The criteria for validity and identity might be more complex, diffuse, and varied, depending as much on the attitudes of officials to their tasks and to the contexts in which they occur as on a recognized rule of recognition.[10] Between those legal standards and the social environment there is a rich and complex relationship. Each legal process is steeped in its social environment and may change in response to it; moreover, while legal processes have legal purposes, they also have wider social tasks to perform. There will be accordingly a certain tension and a constant process of adjustment and re-adjustment between the standards governing a legal process and the demands of the social environment. By adjustment is meant that the legal standards bend and change in response to social considerations.

The underlying idea is that, while each legal process is a normative system, its substantive principles and its decision-processes respond to the conditions of the community. To take an example, we need the rules and processes of civil law and civil trials for various social ends: to adjudicate on and settle disputes between parties, to indicate by authoritative rulings to other members of society what standards will apply in similar cases and how they ought to arrange their affairs; and to maintain a reasonable level of social stability and order.[11] The civil trial is one way of giving effect to these social ends; it does so by creating legal standards and processes. But just as the social needs change from time to time, those changes, if important enough, are likely to be taken up by legal institutions, given a normative legal grounding, and then included in the resulting processes.

The civil trial is again a good example. The conception of the trial as a forum for resolving disputes according to legal standards has to be modified in contemporary practice to accommodate a growing interest in getting the parties to settle. What traditionally was conducted between the parties' lawyers before the trial, in some jurisdictions has now spilt over to the trial itself. The trial is then adjusted to make it more conducive to achieving that end, the judge takes an active role in encouraging settlement, and some of the more confrontational aspects of the adversarial process are modified.[12] There are

[10] See H. L. A. Hart, *The Concept of Law* (Clarendon Press, Oxford, 1961); for modifications to Hart's thesis, see J. R. Lucas, 'The Phenomenon of Law' in P. Hacker and J. Raz (eds.), *Law, Morality, and Society* (Clarendon Press, Oxford, 1977).

[11] See J. A. Jolowicz, 'On the Nature and Purpose of Civil Procedure Law' in I. R. Scott (ed.), *International Perspectives on Civil Justice* (Sweet and Maxwell, London, 1990).

[12] For discussion, see S. R. Scott, 'Two Models of the Civil Process' (1974–5) 27 *Stanford L Rev*. 837; J. Coons, 'Approaches to Court-induced Compromise—The Uses of Doubt and Reason' (1964) 58 *Northwestern UL Rev*. 750.

also drawbacks with this new approach: the rights of the parties might not be properly protected; inequality of bargaining power and unequal pressure on the parties to settle might lead to hasty and oppressive results; and the public interest in upholding legal principles might be sacrificed.[13]

Notwithstanding the drawbacks, however, some jurisdictions, especially in America, have adopted settlement between the parties as an unauthorized goal of the civil process. That is to say, in response to social pressures, some systems have adopted a new normative, legal principle making settlement a legitimate legal purpose, while other jurisdictions are still undecided whether to incorporate settlement into their civil process. The transitionary stage is itself interesting because some judges and other officials unofficially build into their processes a concern for settlement, while others do not. If enough do, the point will come at which we could conclude that a new normative standard has been generally accepted. When precisely that point is reached depends on the internal attitudes of the officials themselves.[14] Many other examples of the relationship between the legal standards within a process and the social context could be given, but enough has been said to show how important and complex the relationship can be, how legal norms are subject to change according to social factors, and that there may be points of transition at which it is difficult to say exactly what the terms of a legal standard are.

There is, however, a second feature of the relationship which is more threatening to the very existence and distinctness of legal standards. The assumption so far has been that, while they may change, legal standards are in general distinct and prevail over other standards. That assumption rests on a reasonably positivist view of the creation, identification, and existence of legal standards. The assumption, however, becomes difficult to sustain when we realize how officials, in the course of their decisions, often make direct reference to a social standard or purpose which is not incorporated into the existing legal standards. This point was touched upon above in noting that sometimes a judge's desire to bring the parties to a settlement can override the duty to apply the law faithfully. Similar cases occur where a jury refuses in the face of the evidence to convict according to the law on the ground that some deeper social or moral norm ought to prevail, or where the official distributing social welfare acts to relieve a clear case of poverty which is not covered by the rules, or the psychiatrist advises against the release of a patient according to the legal criteria on the basis that the public might be put at risk. Each of these examples highlights a common and interesting phenomenon which has many variations, but the essence of which is the pursuit of a purpose or object which is unauthorized, which is to say that a social or moral standard, itself without legal credentials, is used

[13] See O. M. Fiss, 'Against Settlement' (1984) 93 *Yale LJ* 1073; J. Resnik, 'Managerial Judges' (1982) 96 *Harvard L Rev.* 376.

[14] See Hart, *The Concept of Law*, n. 10 above, 50 ff.

to modify or even override a legal standard. This raises both normative and sociological issues.

The normative issue is whether, and under what conditions, an official has legal authority to pursue a purpose by departing from the law and deciding on the basis of an extraneous moral or social standard. This issue is especially important in relation to fair treatment, since the reason for departing may be to bring into the decision a normative standard in addition to those stated by law about how the person should be treated. A link is often created in this way between a deeper theory of justice, of how people ought to be treated, and the practical decisions of officials. This point comes up again later, and the only suggestion to be made now is that just such a link should be seen not as an aberration of law, but as inherent in its nature. Legal standards, apparently separate and distinct, are closely intertwined with moral and social standards and on occasions may give way to them. This is true not only in discretionary contexts where moral and social standards are most obviously relevant, but also in legal processes which are tightly rule-bound. The sociological issue raised by this approach to legal decisions is how, and under what conditions, officials come to perceive certain social goals and purposes as sufficiently pressing to justify bringing them into the legal process without clear authority.

These issues go beyond my present purposes and I shall conclude by summing up the argument of this section. The central proposition is that legal processes are normative processes; that is to say, officials generally act according to standards which they consider authoritative as legal standards. Legal processes are structured by standards, and while they serve the social goals on which the standards are based, they do so through the application of the standards. Legal processes can degenerate into direct and unmediated social engineering, but generally they do not. Secondly, however, legal processes occur in social contexts and there is a constant interaction between process and context. Sometimes a new normative standard will be adopted by officials, reflecting their concern to advance a particular social goal or moral value. Indeed, where there is discretion, the separateness of legal standards from social and moral standards loses much of its point and often vanishes. Finally, it is only through the close study of particular legal processes that we can know what standards are authoritative, whether they are legal standards, and what social goals they serve.

1.2.2 The Multiplicity of Purposes

The distinction in the preceding section between legal purposes and social purposes enables us to understand legal processes as normative sub-systems, while at the same time serving social purposes. But the picture becomes less clear when it is recognized that the same legal process may serve a number of social purposes. Bentham confidently claimed of the criminal trial that its overriding aim was to apply accurately the criminal law and in that way to distinguish between the guilt and innocence of the accused. If, however, the legal standards in operation at the trial are studied, it becomes apparent that other legal purposes are being served and, in turn, other social goals. A moment's reflection, as shown in my earlier comments on Bentham, on the role of the jury, the adversarial process,[15] the relationship between the trial and pre-trial processes, reveals the trial to be a complex matter.[16] Indeed, challenges to an understanding of the trial as a search for truth and accuracy can be even more serious. The need to punish and convict, without scrupulous regard for the niceties of proof, is sometimes said to be the overriding goal, and on occasions that may well be true. The American Supreme Court has been accused of using the criminal process for the ends of crime prevention and control at the expense of accurate determinations of guilt and innocence.[17] A different challenge has come from those who would like to see the criminal process shift from the punitive, with the search for guilt at its heart, towards other more noble aims. Education, rehabilitation, and reconciliation would become the ends of this 'family' model, and the concern for proof and accuracy would be of minor importance.[18] The civil trial lends itself to a similar analysis. On a legal interpretation, the object is to apply the law to the issue and in that way resolve the dispute between the parties; authoritative legal standards are upheld, and the concern for stability and predictability in legal relations enhanced. It is easy, however, to slip from a structured approach based on applying legal standards to a general and unspecific norm to settle the dispute by whatever means.[19] These few examples show well enough that a simple and authoritative statement of the purposes of legal processes is not easily accomplished. The difficulties encountered in the judicial trial have their parallels in other forms of decision. In each of them, it will not always be clear and may be difficult to determine just which social goals have become normative legal purposes. As is often the case, the closer the scrutiny, the more complex the task and the more elusive the answer.

[15] The effect of the adversarial process on the trial is the subject of an extensive literature. On the criminal trial: M. Damaska, 'Evidentiary Barriers to Conviction and Two Models of Criminal Procedure: A Comparative Study' (1973) 121 *U Penn. L Rev*. 506 and 'Structures of Authority and Comparative Criminal Procedure' (1975) 84 *Yale LJ* 480; R. Eggleston, 'What Is Wrong With the Adversary Process' (1974), 49 *Australian LJ* 428. On the civil trial: B. Kaplan, 'Civil Procedure—Reflection on the Comparison of Systems' (1959–60) 9 *Buffalo L Rev*. 409; J. Langbein, 'The German Advantage in Civil Procedure' (1985) 52 *U Chicago L Rev*. 823.

[16] Just how complex the trial can be is shown in W. L. Bennett and M. S. Feldman, *Reconstructing Reality in the Courtroom* (Tavistock, London, 1981).

[17] L. M. Seidman, 'Factual Guilt and the Burger Court: An Examination of Continuity and Change in Criminal Procedure' (1980) 80 *Columbia L Rev*. 436.

[18] J. Griffith, 'Ideology in Criminal Procedure or a Third Model of the Criminal Process' (1970) 79 *Yale LJ* 359.

[19] For discussion, see Scott, 'Two Models of the Civil Process', n. 12 above; Coons, 'Approaches to Court-Induced Compromise—the Uses of Doubt and Reason', n. 12 above.

The task becomes even more problematical if comparisons are made across cultures. The work of early anthropologists of law shows how the attitudes of different cultures towards disputes and the settlement of disputes influence the shape of legal processes. According to Gluckman and Elias in their studies of African law, ideas of compromise and conciliation are embedded in the adjudication of disputes.[20] The parties have to go on living in close relationships and the harmony of community life has to be preserved. Distinctions between justice among the parties and justice across the community, that is, between individual rights and community interests, are difficult to sustain, even where the legal rules are clear and certain. Studies of the Orient portray an even greater concern for peaceful compromise.[21] The dread of open conflict is so powerful that strenuous efforts are made to bring the parties into a sympathetic relationship, where demands can be modified gracefully and solutions accepted honourably. Each case is considered to be unique, and all the circumstances are taken into account in reaching a result. Recourse to legal rules is indeed the last resort which even then brings shame on the parties. Legal processes not only reflect and give normative expression to the cultural environment, but the very concepts used in characterizing and resolving an issue are products of that environment.[22] Different cultural understandings, different conceptions of rationality, and different approaches to the role of law permeate all aspects of legal decisions.

By drawing attention to the complexities in identifying the objects of legal processes with any degree of authority, I do not want to suggest that legal anarchy reigns. In practice, within a community, the standards to be applied within a legal process will be well-settled and uncertainty about their objects will be banished to the margins. Where new processes are created, as in the administrative sphere, some time may elapse before their legal purposes become clear and even more time before practice becomes settled. However, there is nothing mysterious about legal processes, nothing which makes them impervious to analysis. If we enter into the normative understandings of officials, indeed into the cultural understandings of the society, we will normally find that legal processes are rational and purposive. If we go farther and try to make sense of those understandings, we shall in turn come to understand their normative basis and the ends they serve. Such understandings are often best acquired by examining procedures. Procedures are themselves the products of reason; they are attempts to bring about certain ends, and by close attention to procedures, we will often be led to understand the purposes of the process. By

[20] M. Gluckman, *The Judicial Process Among the Barotse* (Manchester, 1955) and N. Elias, *The Nature of African Customary Law* (Manchester University Press, Manchester, 1956).

[21] See F. S. C. Northrop, *The Complexity of Legal and Ethical Experience* (Little, Brown, Boston, Mass., 1959).

[22] For further discussion of this idea, see Bennett and Feldman, *Reconstructing Reality in the Courtroom*, n. 16 above.

tracing procedures through their courses, we may also find that the multiplicity and sometimes incompatibility of purposes are tellingly revealed.

1.2.3 The Shaping of Procedures

While the first task of procedures is to ensure that the legal standards within an area of authority are properly applied, various factors influence their form and shape. The relationship is instrumental, but it is not always driven by a relentless zeal for reason, effectiveness, and economy. Procedures are themselves deeply rooted in a social context and will reflect the beliefs and understandings prevailing in it. In this section, I shall draw attention to some of the ways in which procedures themselves are influenced by such factors.

Bentham saw the design of procedures as a straightforward, rational process, a matter of fitting means to ends. And, while that should be the general goal, the form and shape that procedures finally take is likely to be the product of a more complex environment. What counts as a suitable procedure, and how procedures relate to particular ends, are matters open to different approaches both within and across societies.[23] The American Federal Rules of Procedure were adopted after extensive debate, where various models were proposed, each reflecting subtle differences as to both the objects of the civil trial and the best procedures for achieving them. The final version, with its emphasis on simplicity, efficiency, and a certain amount of discretion in the judge to escape from technical procedures, has been hailed as a victory for the equitable approach over that of the common law.[24] Those who argued that the strength of the common law lay in a close fit between procedures and substantive actions lost the day. The debate was conducted in procedural terms,but it is worth repeating the point that differences expressed in purely procedural terms often reveal differences about the substantive purposes of the trial itself.

What counts as a suitable procedure, and how a procedure relates to a particular purpose, are questions open to different answers. Trial by ordeal has been relied on by many societies at some time in their history. The practices of medieval Europe are typical, where, amid elaborate rituals, the accused's guilt was determined according to how or whether he survived an ordeal. To the modern mind, such procedures appear unrelated to the purpose of determining guilt or innocence, and make no sense. However, according to the understanding of the participants the procedures were justified. Their belief was that one human being should not try to judge another, for, quite apart from the inherent risks in being wrong, judgment is for God. It was believed, more-

[23] See further, Bennett and Feldman, *Reconstructing Reality in the Courtroom*, n. 16 above, ch. 2.

[24] For a study of the emergence of the Federal Rules, see S. N. Subrin, 'How Equity Conquered Common Law: The Federal Rules of Civil Procedure in Historical Perspective' (1987) 135 *U Penn. L Rev*. 909.

over, that if the matter were properly presented, the judgment of God would be revealed.[25] As faith waned in the prospect of God revealing his judgment in this way, men set about trying to decide for themselves whether or not the accused was guilty. The procedures followed were not always effective in achieving that end, and were undoubtedly influenced by other factors. By the time of Bentham, the great reformer, the ground was laid for his insistence that, once the trial was properly understood as being about facts and the application of law to the facts, it was then just a matter of designing the procedures suitable to that end. His own preference was for a system of free proof, unhindered by rules of evidence; but, compelling though it is to some, it has never won the support he hoped for.

Disagreement about the best and most effective procedures to employ in order to achieve a required outcome still prevails. It is now taken for granted that the issue is one of reason and common sense where genuine disagreement is open. Kafka's image of the trial in *Der Prozeß* is so powerful because it strikes at the rational relationship between procedures and outcomes. The procedures in Kafka's pre-trial processes are elaborate, but they bear no relation to purposes and outcomes.[26] For while the medieval culprit could do no more than hope that God was on his side, the worst fear of his modern successor is to have his fate decided without his knowledge and a chance to defend himself.

While the commitment of modern legal systems to the rational design of procedures is unquestioned, the reality can be quite different. Where there is an opportunity to start afresh in a novel area of decisions, or to make sweeping reforms in an existing one, procedures can be designed to be effective and efficient in serving their purposes. More often, however, procedures evolve over time, reflecting not only elements of rational planning, but also legacies and survivals of the past. The historical and social environment, interpreted by each generation in its turn, exerts its influence on the present. Just as views about the objects of legal processes change, so views change as to the procedures most suitable for achieving them. Part of Bentham's complaint was that criminal procedure had become so encrusted with relics of the past, with ideas which bore no clear relation to the objects of the trial, that a fresh start should be made. What he said about the criminal process is equally applicable elsewhere.

Another difficulty in the design of procedures is that the same procedures may serve different ends, and that the same ends may be met by very different

[25] A most interesting account of the ordeal is given in Bloch, *Medieval French Literature and Law* (University of California Press, Berkeley, Cal., 1977). For a similar practice in a very different culture, see R. Linton, *The Le Reva: A Tribe in Madagascar* (University of Chicago, Chicago, 1983), discussed at length in Bennett and Feldman, *Reconstructing Reality in the Courtroom*, n. 16 above, 24–5.

[26] F. Kafka, *The Trial* (originally published as *Der Prozeß*) (Secker and Warburg, London, 1968).

procedures. Italo Calvino tells the tale of a trial which ends in the conviction and execution not of the accused but of the judge himself.[27] The trial took its usual course, following the usual procedures, but to everyone except the judge, it was not the accused who was on trial but the much-hated judge himself. The judge's conduct of proceedings and his attitude to the accused, in the eyes of the other officials and the public, were evidence confirming his guilt. A strange and bitter tale, but it brings home the point that the same procedures may serve very different ends, and that we cannot be sure about which ends are served without entering into the shared understandings of the participants. Without a hermeneutic view, the way is open for conflicting approaches and interpretations, for tension within legal processes, and ultimately for the loss of legitimacy.

Indeed, the widespread acceptance of legal processes and decisions is one of the signs of a stable society. The interesting question then for comparative lawyers is why, amongst relatively stable societies, different and distinctive procedures emerge. A comparison of the civil trial in the common law and the civil trial in continental systems brings out the point.[28] The ends of the civil trial in both cases are professed to be the same—'the just, speedy, and inexpensive determination of every action' as stated in the American Federal Rules—but the procedures are very different. The features of the common law trial are familiar: the extensive control exercised by the parties over the same issues to be settled and the facts to be decided; the role of the judge as an impartial and detached umpire; the sharp division between pre-trial proceedings and the trial itself; and the existence of a complex law of evidence. The trial in continental jurisdictions is strikingly different: the judge has an active role in shaping the issues and in calling for evidence and settling the facts; the parties and their advisers are pushed to the background; and virtually no distinction is drawn between pre-trial proceedings and the trial, while the law of evidence barely exists. Attempts in some common law systems in recent years to encourage a more active involvement of the judge may have blunted the sharper distinctions, but the differences between the two models are still marked. Comparative studies of the criminal trial have found similar disparities: the aims are broadly the same, yet the procedures are markedly different.[29]

The explanation for the disparities, whether at the civil or criminal trial, lies in the social and historical factors which shape laws, institutions, and procedures. M. Damaska, who is a notable scholar in the field, relates the continental approach to centralized government, a rigorous hierarchy of agencies

[27] Italo Calvino, 'A Judgment' in *Adam, One Afternoon* (Picador, London, 1957).

[28] Some of the main works are: Kaplan, 'Civil Procedure—Reflection on the Comparison of Systems'. n. 15 above; Scott, 'Two Models of the Civil Process', n. 12 above; Langbein, 'The German Advantage in Civil Procedure', n. 15 above.

[29] See Damaska, 'Evidentiary Barriers to Conviction and Two Models of Criminal Procedure: A Comparative Study', n. 15 above.

in the administration of justice, and a general style of bureaucratic administration which affects all parts of the legal process, including the courts. The common law on the other hand, can be linked to a liberal tradition distrusting concentrations of power and preferring a fragmentation of authority at all levels. Within the latter tradition, the powers of the state are limited, and the individual is deemed, with the help of his advisers, to know what is best for him. According to Damaska, these ideas help to explain the adversarial trial where the parties engage in a contest which is largely within their own control and where the judge has a limited role.[30]

These are some of the ideas in a theory which is richer and more refined than I can show here. However, the general point is clear: procedural forms and the institutions which administer them are shaped by a range of factors. Some are the dictates of rational planning and reform; others are the consequences of historical events, and the social and cultural ideas which surround them. Procedures are forms of social practice and, like all such practices, they are the fruits of a social environment. In a modern age, however, which tries to be rational in its social practices, we may want to know whether one set of procedures is superior to another in achieving its objects. Comparative studies can help, but caution is needed. Taking the example of the trial, we may be inclined to conclude that the continental approach is superior to the adversarial, since the combination of a more active judicial role and a less adversarial approach seems conducive to more accurate outcomes. But before embarking upon drastic reforms, we should observe two factors. The first is the difficulty of knowing convincingly that, all things considered, one set of procedures is better than another, since the blatant defects in one may be offset by hidden flaws in the other. Whether overall one set of procedures is preferable to another is a complex empirical question which, on the present state of knowledge, cannot be answered. The second note of caution is that, even if the continental system could be shown to be the better, it does not follow that it should be adopted in common law systems.

Here we encounter the problem of legal transplants, of transferring one set of laws or procedures from its cultural context to another, foreign, system.[31] For what takes root and flourishes in one cultural environment in another may wither and die. Linked to this is the general complexity of legal processes, and the way in which they serve various ends and values. One system might be better at achieving accurate outcomes, but less effective in preventing the conviction of the innocent, or in enhancing the accountability of the decision-maker, or in allowing for greater involvement of the parties. Different communities order and value those diverse ends differently and, while one may be

[30] Damaska, *The Faces of Justice and State Authority*, n. 7 above.

[31] For discussion of legal transplants, see A. Watson, *Legal Transplants* (2nd edn., University of Georgia Press, Athens, Ga., 1993) and K. Zweigert and H. Kotz., *An Introduction to Comparative Law* (Clarendon Press, Oxford, 1987).

improved on, it is likely to be at the cost of another. This is not to urge a view which sees social practices as necessarily and inextricably the product of an organic environment where deliberate change becomes harmful meddling; it is only to note that procedures, as the products of a social context, are linked in complex ways to that context; change and reform should be careful and responsive to history and context.

1.2.4 Types of Processes: An Initial Outline

The discussion so far has concentrated on one type of legal process, that is, where a matter is resolved by the application of authoritative standards. This is the characteristically legal mode. It includes a considerable variety of processes ranging from the civil and criminal trials to administrative decisions and actions of great diversity. Across that spectrum, from the criminal trial to routine administrative decisions, the dissimilarities are many, but one common factor is that both are determined by the application of legal standards. Those dissimilarities are important in dividing this rather large family into its members, and that task is undertaken in Part III. For the moment, however, what is of interest is the family characteristic, for that is the basis for distinguishing this group from a number of others. One distinction is between decisions made by the application of standards and decisions of a strong discretionary nature where the official is left to decide as he thinks best. That distinction is often less than clear-cut, more a matter of degree than kind, with only the very strongest cases of discretion clearly outside the family centred on applying standards. Account must also be taken now of the range of processes where outcomes depend on the agreement of the parties. Such processes, often referred to as alternative forms of dispute resolution, alternative, that is, to the judicial trial, have a long history in the law, but attract particular interest at present. This family itself has numerous members, the one uniting characteristic being that the parties should be brought to agreement. The legal objective, that is to say, the mode of resolution and the normative basis, is agreement between the parties.

Processes like these and others can be classified in several ways.[32] My approach here is to separate a number of families according to their legal purposes, that is according to the mode of resolution dictated within the legal system itself. Such modes of resolution, forms of social ordering as Fuller calls them, are a good starting point. Once the different families have been identified, each can be divided into its members according to more specific criteria. To do this comprehensively would be a major undertaking, and in this book I shall concentrate on some at the expense of others. However, the scheme I propose may be useful for more complete analysis in the future. Finally, a

[32] Two of the most helpful attempts at classification are: L. Fuller and M. Eisenberg, *Basic Contract Law* (3rd edn., West, St Paul, Minn., 1972) and M. Bayles, *Procedural Justice* (Kluwer, Deventer, 1990), 168–79.

word of caution. While it is helpful to talk of families of processes, the divisions must not be taken too strictly and too literally. Just as real families intermarry and inter-relate, so families of processes in practice intersect and overlap. The family divisions are useful in highlighting certain prominent features rather than in erecting precise boundaries or definitions. Accordingly, processes are classified according to whether their purpose is: (i) to apply authoritative legal standards; (ii) to decide as the official thinks best; (iii) to reach agreement between the parties; (iv) to decide by voting; (v) to decide by fiat or decree. To these, I add two more which might best be thought of as step-families rather than distinct families: (vi) investigation and inquiry, and (vii) proceduralism and participation.

Application of Authoritative Standards

Decision by the application of authoritative standards is the characteristically legal mode. It is common to the civil trial, the criminal trial, and most administrative processes. The primary purpose in such cases, from a legal point of view, is to deal with a matter according to legal standards. Since the standards are legal standards, made in accordance with constitutional procedures and recognized as authoritative, a decision made in accordance with them is justified and legitimate. The sub-divisions within this family are numerous and can be made on the basis of different criteria. One criterion for creating subdivisions would be to move from a legal standpoint and ask about social purposes. The criminal and civil trials can be distinguished on that basis, since each serves a number of distinct social ends: the former to protect the public, maintain order, and denounce crime; the latter to resolve disputes between parties, to provide guidance for future conduct, and so on. Administrative processes often include elements of both, but they also serve other social purposes, such as distributing welfare and regulating activities. Another method of sub-classification within this family would be according to more formal and analytical criteria. Division into judicial, quasi-judicial, and administrative might be one approach,[33] adjudicative and bureaucratic investigation another.[34] An alternative is to concentrate on the nature of the standards, whether they are full and detailed, or rather open-textured and purposive. Max Weber's famous distinction between formal and substantive legal rationality is based on that idea.[35] Formal legal authority is characterized by 'a separation of law and politics, legal professionalization, a strong (perhaps complete) focus on rules, and the use of deductive logic'.[36] Substantive legal authority, on the other

[33] These distinctions were for a long time popular in administrative law, but have now been discarded.

[34] See Bayles, *Procedural Justice*, n. 32 above, ch. 8; see also sections 8.3 and 8.4 herein.

[35] M. Weber, *Economy and Society* (ed. G. Roth and C. Wittich (University of California Press, Berkeley, Ca., 1978), ii.

[36] M. Herz, 'Parallel Universes: NEPA Lessons for the New Property (1993), 93 *Columbia L Rev*. 1668 at 1689.

hand, connotes more open standards and values to be reached by purposive reasoning.[37] This distinction is in turn reflected in the line drawn by contemporary theorists between autonomous and responsive law.[38] Autonomous law has much in common with Weber's view of law, since both emphasize the detailed and comprehensive nature of the governing rules. Responsive law also echoes Weber's substantive legal authority, although here participation by those affected is a vital element in deciding how to apply the substantive standards in the particular case.[39] Approaches like these are interesting and suggestive, but in general they paint with a brush much too broad to be all that useful in a detailed analysis of legal processes and in the design of suitable procedures. Nevertheless, they provide a useful background on which I shall build in developing a more detailed analysis in Part III.

Discretion, or Deciding as the Official Thinks Best

Discussion of the different kinds of standards and the way they feature in decisions leads on to a second family of legal processes. This family, the discretionary, is closely related to the first; genealogists might even question whether it is a separate entity at all. They could argue that there are always some standards to apply, abstract and indeterminate though they may be. Certainly, we know enough about discretion to reject any suggestion that it is a polar opposite of applying standards; that the two are inter-related, that discretion occurs within and around standards, can now be taken for granted. Nevertheless, the more discretionary a process is, the less easily it fits within the category of standard-applying at all; for the mark of discretion in its strongest sense is that the decision-maker has to determine for himself, to a significant degree, what the standards are to be. The point may come where the standards are so indeterminate, so abstract and so unspecific in their terms, that the process can hardly be described as based on the application of authoritative standards. When the Parole Board is told that it may recommend prisoners for release on parole as it thinks fit, and is given no criteria to guide its judgment, we have surely moved from a decision based on authoritative standards, to one where the only standards are those that the decision-maker might invent for itself.

Opinions may differ on whether the discretionary process is a distinct form of process. On the one hand, even the strongest discretion is subject to some authoritative guidance, even if it be no more than the implied statutory purposes for which the power has been granted. On the other hand, to suggest that strong discretion is really a case of decision by applying legal standards is a distortion, since it neglects the substantial degree to which it depends on the

[37] See my account in *Discretionary Powers*, n. 1 above, section 2.2.

[38] P. Nonet and A. Selznick, *Law and Society in Transition* (University of California Press, Berkeley, Cal., 1995), 53–72.

[39] See also G. Teubner, 'Substantive and Reflexive Elements in Modern Law' (1983) 17 *Law & Society Rev.* 239.

judgment of the official as to what standards should apply. That will sometimes be the main characteristic of discretion. For these reasons, I shall regard the discretionary process as a *second* family of process, but with qualifications. The main qualifications being, first, that the amount of discretion is a matter of degree, and secondly, that it is rare to find a process which is entirely free from the guidance of legal standards. A final point to note about these first two categories of process is that they may involve issues either of an individualized nature, that is, about how a particular person should be treated, or as a collective nature, which is to say of a general policy kind affecting the society as a whole or at least a range of groups and interests within it.

Decision by Agreement

The third family covers processes the object of which is to reach an outcome by agreement between the parties. In everyday life outside the law, the settlement of disputes and other issues through agreement is typical and commonplace, and proceeds according to a variety of forms. Within the law, the sub-categories of process based on agreement are also diverse, but the most usual are negotiation, conciliation, and mediation.[40] Negotiation usually means direct interaction between the parties with a view to reaching agreement, while conciliation and mediation involve a third party who helps to guide and structure the negotiating process, but without imposing an outcome. Within those sub-categories, the procedures can be very different. Now while agreement as a form of process has a long history, its application in law raises a number of problems. One is the difficulty of ensuring that the conditions under which negotiation takes place, and indeed the terms of the agreement itself, are acceptable according to general social standards. Another is the relationship between deciding according to authoritative standards and deciding by agreement. The community has an interest in insisting that it control some issues through authoritative standards, rather than by the choice of the parties, but just how that legitimate sphere should be defined is by no means settled.

Consideration of the relation between decisions based on standards and those based on agreement leads to a further point: within a process, a mixture of both governing standards and elements of agreement is prone to be found. Negotiation and agreement normally occur within a framework of standards, some procedural, others setting substantive limits on what may be agreed and its terms. Alternatively, elements of agreement may encroach on a process which is ostensibly based on the application of standards or the exercise of discretion. Elements of negotiation and agreement may occur in relation to the meaning and application of the standards or as to by whom the discretion should be exercised. Plea-bargaining, which means negotiation between the accused and the prosecutor about how the latter should exercise his

[40] For a full account of the various forms see Pt. III.

discretion, is the best-known case; but there are many others.[41] Finally, one variation on the agreement theme is arbitration, where the parties agree to submit the issue to an independent adjudicator who then has the authority to make a binding decision. Here the agreement is not as to the substantive outcome, but simply as to who should have the power of decision, the procedures which should be followed, and, perhaps, what standards to apply.

The next two categories of process can be dealt with briefly. The fourth, *decisions by voting* speaks for itself: here matters are determined by the vote of those involved. Its most common use is in the political arena, usually to elect governments or other officials. Voting processes might be used to settle a substantive issue, as in the case of a referendum, but their use for such purposes is rare. Composite bodies, such as courts, juries, tribunals, and committees, often resolve disagreement amongst their members by voting.

The fifth category is *decision by fiat*. Its main feature is that the decision is made by the decision-maker as he thinks best according to the standards which he thinks appropriate. The hallmark is that the process is not governed by legal standards at all. The manager of a business is a typical example, since his main objective is to make the decision which he considers best in the interests of the business. Decision by fiat has only a minor role in legal processes, but it is a feature of certain administrative processes which are considered essentially managerial in nature. The tendency to highlight the managerial aspects is a noticeable feature of modern administrative government. To act by fiat is to exercise a type of discretion but, unlike discretions which occur in legal processes, the decision by fiat is constrained by neither legal purposes nor legal principles. Whatever constraints there are derive from the purpose and rationality of the sub-system within which it occurs.[42]

Investigation and Inquiry

The next family includes those processes where the purpose is not to reach a decision, or at least not a final decision, but rather to investigate or enquire into a situation, to report the results, and perhaps to make a recommendation as to what decision ought to be taken. Investigation and enquiry are usually preliminary to a further or final decision to be made by some other authority. Such processes are frequently used in modern legal systems, but just how they should be classified is not clear: in one sense they are part of the process which results in a final decision, either by applying an authoritative standard or by reaching agreement; but since they are often separate from the final decision, they raise their own procedural issues, and are best treated as distinct processes.

[41] Studies of the enforcement of laws in many different contexts show how central to the process negotiation and agreement is; see K. Hawkins, *Environment and Enforcement* (Clarendon Press, Oxford, 1984).

[42] The idea of relatively autonomous sub-systems is developed in G. Teubner, *Law as an Autopoeistic System* (Blackwell, Oxford, 1993).

Proceduralism

While this title is neither precise nor all that instructive, I cannot think of one which is more appropriate and so it may be taken simply as a reference to the ideas I shall now describe. In each of the main forms of process so far considered, the normative basis for reaching an outcome is clear, whether it be the application of standards, agreement between the parties, or decisions by vote. The procedural forms for arriving at each kind of outcome will naturally vary, but we would expect the involvement and participation of the parties to be an important part of the procedures. Procedures generally, and procedures like participation in particular, are instruments for achieving specified, normative outcomes. Suppose, however, that within an area of activity no fixed normative outcome is specified. Suppose that there are no substantive standards to apply and that resolution of the issues by agreement or voting is unsuitable. A number of values may be relevant and a range of interests affected, but no established way of ordering them or deciding amongst them exists; the issue is likely to be complex, with a number of different solutions possible. The suggestion is then sometimes made that issues like these can be resolved only within a special procedural framework, a framework which enables different interests to advance their claims and views through participation or representation, and which encourages each to consider and be responsive to the arguments of others, and so to open the way for a resolution. The procedures should not be adversarial or confrontational, but should foster the softer concepts of discourse, communication, and mutuality.

This idea, which I shall refer to as proceduralism, can be traced to a number of theoretical positions. In Nonet and Selznick's concept of responsive law, abstract, purposive standards are given practical content through the participation of the parties.[43] A solution emerges through participation which is responsive to the conflicting interests and values. The procedural nature of this form of social process is even more marked in the concept of reflexive law developed by Habermas and Teubner.[44] Here the general argument is that in complex contexts, groups, interests, and organizations must curb and simplify their needs and demands so that co-ordination amongst them and coherent solutions to problems can be achieved. In order to bring about those ends, carefully structured procedures are necessary. A connection can be made, moreover, between these strands of theory and ideas of strong democracy. The common principle underlying different versions of strong democracy is that participation enables the parties to arrive at a notion of the common good, a notion which is responsive to private and individual interests, but which goes

[43] Nonet and Selznick, *Law and Society in Transition*, n. 38 above.

[44] J. Habermas' notion of communicative action is discussed in A. Brand, *The Force of Reason* (Allen and Unwin, Sydney, 1990). See also Teubner, 'Substantive and Reflexive Elements in Modern Law', n. 39 above.

beyond them. Participation is then not an instrument leading to a set outcome, but rather through participation the parties are able to see beyond their own interests in order to grasp the possibilities of acting for the common good. The act of participation both heightens the awareness of the parties and leads them to a resolution. The resolution is in a sense agreed on and consensual, but to collapse this mode of action into another form of decision through agreement would be to miss its essential qualities.[45]

These are interesting ideas, but do they constitute a distinct mode of legal process? Strong democracy and the importance of participation are matters to which I return in Chapter 4. But the question may be asked whether the procedural model proposed provides a way of settling issues and reaching outcomes which are both coherent and different from the other forms considered? The answer, I suggest, is yes, with some qualifications; those various theoretical traditions do develop a form of process which is distinctive and separable from other forms. Its focus is on reaching outcomes through a procedural framework, where participation is an essential element, where no precise standards are laid down in advance, where reason, co-ordination, consensus, and a sense of the common good are guiding concepts. This is not to say that the proceduralist mode is entirely self-contained and separate from others. It might occur within an over-arching standard as a way of giving meaning and content to the standard; it might also be that it takes place within an area of authority where an official supervises the process and guides it to a conclusion. Moreover, it clearly relies heavily on an element of agreement. The argument is, nevertheless, that even where those elements are present, the best way of understanding the process is according to the distinctive model of proceduralism.

To sum up this discussion of forms of legal process, the object has been to identify the different ways by which legal issues are settled. The two most familiar to us are of course the first two, decisions made by applying standards or by the exercise of discretion. These two families of process will receive most attention in this book. Legal processes based on agreement are in the ascendency in modern legal systems and deserve a full study of their own. Similarly the proceduralist mode appears to have secured a place in some areas of modern administration, and, according to some, should have a much bigger place. Each of the other modes described also has a significant but often small role in legal processes. Now apart from the inherent interest in an analysis of this kind, my particular purpose here is to link each form of legal process to procedures. Simply put, each form requires a set of procedures which is suitable to its ends, since the primary task of procedures, as we saw at the beginning, is to ensure that each form of process is conducted

[45] Of the various versions of strong democracy, one which brings out these ideas well is B. Barber, *Strong Democracy: Participatory Politics for a New Age* (University of California Press, Berkeley, Cal., 1984).

properly according to its normative structure. Where the normative structure is to apply authoritative standards, then procedures are needed for that purpose; similarly for other objects, whether to exercise discretion, to reach agreement, or to investigate. Now while this is the primary task of procedures, it is not the only task and we must now turn to the role of procedures in upholding other values.

1.3 PROCEDURES AND VALUES

1.3.1 Procedures and the Social Good

The discussion so far has emphasized the relationship between the different types of legal processes, the purposes they serve, and the procedures suited to achieving those purposes. The legal purposes vary for each process: to apply the law, to exercise discretion, to bring the parties to agreement, to resolve an issue by voting and so on. Procedures are the instruments by which each set of purposes is attained; they change from one type of process to another, and the objects of any one form of process may be achieved by any of a number of different procedures. But precisely what procedures are required is not the present issue; the issue in this section is the relationship between procedures and values; for while in one sense legal procedures are simply instruments for achieving legal purposes, they are in another sense value-laden.

Procedures are connected to values in two ways: they advance certain general social values and they protect certain values about the treatment of individuals. As for the first of these, by securing the purposes of legal processes, procedures advance social values. By social values, I mean social goods, that is to say, the social good in achieving legal purposes. Where matters are determined by applying substantive legal standards, the social good is inherent in the standards themselves, and in the fact that society wishes those matters to be settled according to the standards. Where settled legal standards govern the allocation of welfare benefits, we may conclude that the society has decided that welfare ought to be distributed according to those standards. The careful and accurate application of the standards means that welfare is distributed as society wishes, and in that sense the social good is realized. Similarly, in criminal and civil law, and in areas of administration, the social good is upheld when the legal standards are properly applied, when, that is to say, decisions are made by the accurate application of the law to reliable findings of fact. Where, on the contrary, the legal standards are not properly applied, burdens and benefits are distributed wrongly and the social good is to that extent diminished. The same principle applies to other forms of legal process; in some cases the social good is that the parties resolve the matter by agreement, in others that the matter be resolved by a voting procedure. Each process represents the view of society that certain matters should be dealt with by that process. Procedures are in their turn linked to those same social goods; for if procedures are effective instruments in ensuring that the standards are properly applied, that the parties reach agreement, or that a suitable voting process is followed, then they are effective in upholding the social goods.

1.3.2 Legal Processes and the Interests of Persons

Legal processes are also concerned with the way individual persons are treated. A decision can be about the social good in distributing burdens and benefits according to society's wishes, while at the same time deciding whether a particular person should be granted a benefit or have a burden imposed. When a society makes law, it declares through the law how some aspect of the common good is to be achieved. Laws are made in the name and in the interests of the whole; but in making laws, the community does more: it also declares that the laws will govern how individual persons will be treated when their circumstances come within the laws. Once we understand that legal processes can be interpreted in these two different modes, within two different realms, then we can see that the processes are connected directly to values about the treatment of individuals. Once we are concerned with the way individuals are treated, we are concerned with questions of fairness, both substantive and procedural. A person is treated fairly if he is treated in accordance with certain moral and social values; procedures for their part are fair if they ensure fair treatment.

This, however, is to look ahead, and before analysing the ideas of fair treatment and fair procedures, I want to give a more general account of the values involved in legal processes and how they relate to persons affected by them. Let us continue the example of the grant of welfare benefits according to clear and settled legal standards. The person whose case comes squarely within the rules has a good claim to the benefit, indeed has a right to the benefit which it would be wrong to deny. Similarly, the accused in the criminal trial has a right not to be convicted if he is innocent, and the party to a civil action has a right to have the dispute decided according to the law. Rights are in issue in each case, and procedures should be directed to protecting them. The welfare claimant might not have a right to any particular law being laid down, but once society decides how welfare is to be distributed and makes laws to that effect, he has a good claim that they be applied to his case. The proper application of the law not only serves the social good, but also means protecting the rights of persons. A mistaken decision denying benefits where they are due is both detrimental to the social good and a denial of rights. The link between procedures and rights can now be seen, for procedures are needed to guarantee that the legal standards are properly applied. The same idea applies to other forms of process: the person subject to a discretionary decision has a right, not to a particular outcome, but to the discretionary judgment being made according to certain criteria; where the form of process is decision by agreement or by voting, the individual has an entitlement to that form and to the procedures necessary to bring it about. Again, to talk of rights is to look ahead, but it is important at this early stage to catch a glimpse of how rights relate to legal processes.

It can be seen from this discussion that each form of process has a normative basis which not only serves the common good, but also creates rights in individual persons. The normative basis changes from one form of process to another; it may be that certain conclusion-guiding standards should be applied, or that discretion be exercised according to certain principles, or that action be taken on the basis of what is agreed. Now the idea that each form of process has a specific normative basis which creates rights in individuals has caused some confusion amongst writers on procedural fairness. How, it has been asked, can the accurate application of law be related to principles of individual treatment. Accuracy is connected to effectiveness and to the social good in having effective legal regulation; it has nothing to do, the argument goes, with the treatment of individuals.

The answer is that this confuses the two levels of understanding, the social good in having an effective system of law and the individual entitlements which law creates. The foundation of such entitlements is considered later, but it is essential to keep the two levels of understanding apart. Otherwise we shall be unable to grasp that an individual does not appeal to the social good in having the law applied accurately; he appeals rather to his right to have his case determined according to the law, and his right is respected only if the law is properly applied. Now while it is useful to distinguish between the public good or the public interest in, say, properly applying the laws and a person's right under those laws, the distinction in a sense creates a false dichotomy. On closer reflection, we can see both are elements of the public or common good, for the common good represents an organic conception of society where the various elements are integrated into a whole. The common good includes not only the effective application of the laws but also the fair treatment of persons. To neglect one in favour of the other, or to portray them as locked in conflict, would be to distort the relationship between them.

1.3.3 Tiers of Values

Let us now examine more fully the values which apply within legal processes. In a general sense, each form of process has a normative foundation which can be expressed as the social value of deciding by applying authoritative standards, or by the exercise of discretion, or through agreement. This idea is developed further in the next section and may be referred to as the general normative foundation of each such method of social ordering. Within that general normative foundation, more specific values have a role to play, and it is the explication of those values that I shall now consider. This can be done by taking as an illustration the form of process based on applying authoritative standards. Here we find different kinds of values and the standards based on them operating in different ways. One set of standards derives from the general normative foundation: they are the standards of the criminal law, the civil law, or an area of administrative regulation. They dictate the basic legal objective in each arena of decision-making and are directed towards achieving certain outcomes; they are in a sense at the very centre of each decision. It is hard to find an expression which precisely captures the nature of these standards, but perhaps they can be referred to rather clumsily as the first tier of outcome-based standards. Other values and standards based on those values also apply. Neighbouring statutes might impose values affecting outcomes, values based on non-discrimination, for example. The general or common law itself might furnish additional standards, such as the principle of consistency in decision-making, or that the trial should be an even contest between the parties, or that a person should be heard before suffering detriment. Values like these derive from various sources and qualify, modify, or augment the first tier of outcome-based standards, with each adding normative standards which are often directed at protecting in some way those affected by the process. Such standards directly affect outcomes, but are less central than those identified at the first tier; it will be convenient to refer to them as second tier outcome-based standards.

Perhaps another example or two will help to make clear the nature and application of this second tier of standards. An example familiar in the common law world is that the judicial trial, whether civil or criminal, should be an even contest between the parties. The concern that the trial be an even contest might even overshadow the concern for truth and an accurate application of legal standards; instead, the main point of the trial and the procedures appropriate to it becomes the maintenance of an even contest between the parties.[46] Indeed the importance of maintaining a fair contest is sometimes invoked as a reason for disallowing evidence gained from the accused by improper means, even though it might be evidence relevant to an accurate outcome.[47] A similar kind of claim is occasionally made in relation to certain administrative decisions; here it is said that, provided all interested parties have the chance to participate, the process will be fair and legitimate, and the outcome reached will be of lesser consequence. The value of participation, rather than the value of any particular outcome, becomes the controlling

[46] For discussion in a comparative context, see Kaplan, 'Civil Procedure—Reflection on the Comparison of Systems', n. 15 above, and Langbein, 'The German Advantage in Civil Procedure', n. 15 above.

[47] See the discussion in *R.* v. *Cleland* (1982) 43 ALR 619 and *Seymour* v. *Attorney-General* (1984) 53 ALR 513.

factor.[48] Another example is an undertaking, whether by promise, holding-out, or representation, made by an authority which may, in some circumstances, be binding; fair treatment then requires a decision in accordance with it even if it means imposing qualifications on the first tier of outcome values. The idea of legitimate expectations, which has gained ground in administrative law in recent years, is best understood as a distinctive normative standard based on an undertaking from the administrative body that certain actions will be taken or not taken, which may qualify the operation of the first tier principle. The principle of consistency is another example. The strength of the principle varies according to the context, but an authority may be under a duty to decide in a particular way on the ground that those in a similar position have been treated in that way.[49] Consistency derives from a deeper value of equal treatment, which in turn generates a number of subsidiary values: some should not benefit at the expense of others, and all should be treated in accordance with the principles of non-discrimination.[50] Equal treatment may also mean that the parties are treated impartially in the distribution of burdens within a legal process.[51] Principles like these are all about us; some having clearly legal origins, others drawing on deeper moral currents. Their interest for present purposes is their effect on the normative basis of legal processes.

A third tier of values affects more directly the processes leading up to outcomes, and in that way has an indirect effect on the outcomes. In the investigation of crime, a suspect should not be tricked or cajoled into confessing, quite apart from whether the confession obtained would contribute to a more accurate outcome and, therefore, to a correct application of legal standards. The protection of the suspect from abuse, from having rights violated, may count more heavily than the social good in convicting those who are guilty. Bentham held the line against allowing values of these kinds to affect the course of the trial and the quest for rectitude, but his view, although influential, has never prevailed, and each generation argues anew about where the line between rectitude and competing values should be drawn. In this case and many others, there is simply a clash of values, a clash between the social good in having accurate decisions on the one hand, and the social good in protecting certain values for the benefit of individuals on the other hand. The same applies to privacy and confidentiality, which are both values respected in judicial and administrative processes. Another possible source of values is the idea that discretion should be structured

[48] The more emphasis shifts from reaching a given outcome to upholding certain values—fair contest, participation, etc.—the closer we move to Rawls' notion of pure procedures: see J. Rawls, *A Theory of Justice* (Clarendon Press, Oxford, 1971). Note also the connection with proceduralism as earlier outlined.

[49] Consistency is a complicated principle both in theory and practice; for further discussion, see Bayles, *Procedural Justice*, n. 32 above, ch. 5 and D. J. Galligan, *Discretionary Powers*, n. 37 above, 150–2, 157–61.

[50] See further Bayles, n. 32 above.

[51] For an illuminating analysis of this idea in civil process, see A. A. S. Zuckerman, 'Interlocutory Remedies in Quest of Procedural Fairness' (1993) 56 *MLR* 325.

through guidelines; here the value lies in the element of certainty and security in knowing how a power will be used.[52] English law encourages guidelines, but it does not require them as a matter of fairness.[53] This can in turn be linked to a fuller sense of the rule of law and to the idea that legal authority should be exercised through clear and general standards which are prospective and are made known to those affected by them, and with which officials will be required to comply.[54] The example of structuring discretion demonstrates the more general point that opinions may be divided about the worth of a value at the level of principle; and even if that is uncontroversial, the status of a value within a legal system may itself be problematical.

The examples given so far are of values which in some way relate to outcomes; how directly they do, and exactly what effect they have, varies. There are other values which are accepted as binding within legal contexts and yet which are independent of outcomes. These I shall refer to as non-outcome values. Now the difference between values which relate to outcomes and values which do not is not always easy to draw. Some affect the processes leading up to outcomes, while at the same time indirectly affecting outcomes. The rules protecting a suspect from being tricked or cajoled into confessing are based on values about how people should be treated, quite apart from whether the confession would contribute to a more accurate outcome. Some values, however, are clearly separate from outcomes. One is that a person affected by a decision should be heard, independently of any effect the hearing might have on the outcome. The value of being heard is said to flow directly from the principle of respect for persons. Some claim this to be the true basis of the hearing principle, while similar arguments are made for related doctrines, such as the giving of reasons.[55] The soundness of such claims is considered later on, but my present purpose is just to draw attention to the existence of values which have a place in legal processes apart from their impact on outcomes. Several American writers have been imaginative in their suggestions; fraternity, comprehensibility, timeliness, and participation are amongst those put forward, although the precise nature and role of each in legal processes is not always made clear.[56] We need not here examine the range of contenders for inclusion

[52] It might also contribute to equal and consistent treatment. The main exponent of guidelines as a standard of fairness is K. C. Davis in *Discretionary Justice* (Louisiana State University Press, Baton Rouge, Louisiana, 1969); see also section 14.1 herein.

[53] For discussion, see Galligan, *Discretionary Powers*, n. 37 above, 152–61, 284–90.

[54] See L. Fuller, *The Morality of Law* (Yale University Press, New Haven, Conn., 1964), and R. Summers, 'Evaluating and Improving Legal Procedures: A Plea for Process Values' (1974) 60 *Cornell L Rev*. 199–201.

[55] See L. Tribe, *Constitutional Law* (2nd edn., West, New York, 1988) and A. Duff, *Trials and Punishments* (Cambridge University Press, Cambridge, 1986).

[56] See J. L. Mashaw, *Due Process in the Administrative State* (Yale, Newhaven, Conn., 1985), 204; R. B. Saphire, 'Specifying Due Process Values: Towards a More Responsive Approach to Procedural Protection' (1978) 127 *U. Penn. L Rev*. 111; F. Michelman, 'Formal and Associated Aims in Procedural Due Process' in J. Pennock and J. Chapman, *Due Process* (Nomos xvii, New York, 1977).

as values within a legal process; it is enough to observe that legal processes include a number of values, some outcome-based, others separate from outcomes, which have their origins in the moral and social culture of a society and which are binding within those processes.

We now have a framework within which to understand the role and interplay of a host of different values in legal processes. Values generate standards, and shortly I shall show more fully how these values are the basis of the fair treatment of individuals and in turn of fair procedures. In this section, however, my object has been to show how legal processes are value-based, to give an idea of their number and variety, and to make the link between values and the protection of persons. The image of tiers nicely captures the sense of different kinds of values, and standards based on the values, which have a place in legal processes.[57] The first tier consists of the values specific to a particular form of process: that the decision should be made by applying the governing standards, or by exercising discretion, or by agreement. It serves the social good in determining matters according to society's instructions; it serves the good of individual persons in that their entitlements within each area of process are upheld. Around that first tier are other tiers made up of values of various kinds, modifying, influencing, or even on occasions overshadowing the first tier, directly or indirectly, while other values act independently of it. Some values will be established and accepted, others will be more marginal, still to be fully adopted. The tiers may pull in different directions and even be in conflict; a binding representation, for example, might require an outcome different from that indicated by the principle of consistent treatment. Some values will be closely tied to a particular culture; the Anglo-American conception of the trial, with its emphasis on a fair contest, is markedly different from the continental, while the view of the trial found in many traditional systems is radically different.[58] The various tiers together make up the framework of values within which legal processes function. The different values draw on moral and political ideas, but also are shaped in the social and cultural context of each society, and indeed within different parts of the same society. Whether a value applies in a given context is determined by close analysis of the context and its social environment.

My suggestion is, however, that within the Anglo-American context the diversity and richness of the values governing legal processes can be displayed by beginning with the first tier and then adding the different and additional values which apply to legal processes. I have concentrated here on decisions reached by applying legal standards, but the other forms of process can be analysed in a similar way. In each case, it is a matter of first identifying the first tier values,

[57] The term derives from the name of an article by J. Resnick, 'Tiers' (1984) 57 *S Cal. L Rev.* 837.

[58] See the discussion in Bennett and Feldman, *Reconstructing Reality in the Courtroom*, n. 16 above.

which are based on the concept of legal purposes as discussed earlier, and then considering the other tiers which apply and how they affect the first level or whether they are separate from it. The relationship between these values and principles and the fair treatment of person is taken up in Chapter 2.

1.3.4 The Normative Foundation of Legal Processes

Following the discussion of both social (or collective) and individualized values, I now return to the classification of processes and consider more fully the general normative principles distinctive to each of them, that is to say, the first-tier outcome values which govern each one. The order followed earlier is reversed so that we start with the simpler forms and end with the more complex.

Decision by Voting

The distinctive feature of decision by voting is that the law does not specify by authoritative standards what the outcome is to be, but allows it to be determined by vote. The social value lies in letting those involved in an issue decide as they think fit. Rather than applying a set of standards and reaching an outcome on the basis of them, the outcome is chosen by a voting procedure. Various forms of voting procedures are possible, but once a vote has been taken, the outcome is determined, and no further standard is relevant. J. Rawls refers to this as a pure procedure, pure in the sense that the value is in the procedure not the outcome. What that means is that the procedure expresses a value, in this case that people should decide as they think fit. Voting is of course not the only pure procedure; tossing a coin or drawing lots are also pure procedures, although they are unlikely to have a role in legal processes.[59] Voting procedures are most commonly used to elect a government or other official, but they may occasionally be used to settle a substantive issue, often of a serious and controversial kind.

From the individual's point of view, the primary value is simply in being able to vote. But a distinction should be drawn between voting procedures in which the person participates, and voting procedures used by others to determine how the person should be treated and in which he takes no part. In the first case, the value to the person lies in being able to participate by voting and in that way to have a voice in the outcome. Amongst the values served by voting are equality and the need to ensure that the vote of each is of the same value, and perhaps access to information about the issues so that a reasoned decision can be made on how to vote. It is difficult to find examples of issues, other than the election of governments or officials, and an occasional referendum, which should be settled by voting procedures. The most likely context

[59] J. Rawls, n. 48 above. For a critique of pure procedures, see W. M. Nelson, 'The Very Idea of Pure Procedural Justice' (1980) 90 *Ethics* 502.

for greater use of such procedures is in deciding matters of general policy and even in deciding on general laws. Law-making is in practice delegated to parliament, which means in effect the executive, but there is no reason in principle for not submitting more legislative proposals to the electorate. In some areas at least, there is a good case for not just consulting interested parties but letting them decide the issue by vote.

The position is different when voting procedures are used to decide how an individual person should be dealt with. The prospect of an accused's fate being determined by the vote of a group of judges, unguided by substantive standards, is abhorrent. It might be said, however, that this already happens in a jury trial. But the two cases are different since in the first the decision is made in the absence of guiding standards, while in the second the voting procedure is used as a way of coming to a decision when there is disagreement amongst the jurors as to whether the guiding standards have been made out in that case. Voting in this situation is generally acceptable, and it is common for composite bodies, such as juries, courts, and tribunals, to settle disagreements by such procedures.

Here I wish to concentrate on the first case where voting procedures are used as a substitute for authoritative standards; where, in other words, the process is one of pure procedure. The justice of Homer as portrayed in the *Iliad* was pure procedural justice. Conflicts brought to court were argued by the parties in the presence of spectators, who, after witnessing the process, voted for a solution, not on the basis of set principles, but on how they felt about what had been put before them. And whatever agreement the spectators reached was binding.[60] This is a crude and objectionable way of resolving a dispute between two parties or of deciding how a person should be treated. It is objectionable because we generally expect that powers enabling the state to intervene in the life of a citizen will be governed by authoritative standards. To allow such matters to be determined by the vote of officials or other citizens is to allow action to be taken on the basis of subjective and unguided opinions.

The problem with voting as a way of settling issues, a problem common to all forms of pure procedure, is that we do not know in advance what the outcome will be; moreover, the most fair procedures (and equal voting would normally be a fair procedure) may produce unpredictable and unjust results. To put the point another way, the authority gained by a procedure such as voting may be outweighed by the unacceptability of the results it produces. Another, related reason against pure procedures is the lack of congruence between the procedures and the outcomes. A pure procedure, such as voting, represents certain values, but no matter how important they are, they bear no relation to the result that follows from their use. The tendency to look at the

[60] For a modern version of the influence of spectators on legal processes, see J. Resnik, 'Due Process: A Public Dimension' (1987) 39 *Florida L Rev*. 405.

values inherent in procedures and to ignore their outcomes is to be treated with great caution. This is not to reject all reliance on pure procedures in the administrative sphere, but it does raise a strong presumption against them. The question we must consider shortly is whether proceduralism, as described above, is a form of pure procedure, and, if so, whether its use is justified.

Decisions by Agreement

Decisions made by agreement between the parties are attractive in nature and strong in legitimacy. Instead of having an authoritative, external standard imposed on them, the parties come to their own conclusion through negotiation and agreement. The primary value, from the individual's point of view, consists in being able to shape the terms of the agreement and, therefore, of the outcomes as they wish, subject only to the compromises each may have to make in order to reach agreement. The paradigm case of decision by agreement is the freely-entered-into contract. The value to society is that a course of action or decision agreed on is likely to be respected by the parties and normally requires no action on the part of the state. Where the agreement is not honoured and the law intervenes, the object will be to restore the agreement and enforce its terms. The main task for procedures is to provide the conditions under which agreement can be reached.[61] While the paradigm of agreement is a contract between free and equal parties, attempts are sometimes made to transfer the idea to the administrative context. The main problem then is in providing the conditions under which the parties can negotiate and reach agreement on a free and equal basis. This usually occurs on an informal, sometimes unofficial, basis when a government body negotiates with a private person about how the former should exercise its powers in relation to the latter. The risk is that the parties will be neither in positions of equality nor able to bargain freely.[62] The same risk may apply to agreements between private parties, and in the modern trend towards greater reliance on agreement in setting issues and resolving disputes, precautions need to be taken. The problems, however, are acute when the parties are an individual person on the one side and an agency of the state on the other.

Two major problems, therefore, have to be confronted in making decision through agreement a legitimate process. One problem flows from the primary value itself, namely, that the agreement be freely and fairly entered into without coercion or duress, and that the parties be on a reasonably equal footing. Agreements reached between suspects and police or prosecutors are often criticized on the ground that those conditions never exist. The other main

[61] In the terminology of J. Rawls, where agreement is the normative purpose, procedures leading to it are perfect procedures—perfect because we know the outcome sought and because we know whether it has been achieved. See Rawls, *A Theory of Justice*, n. 59 above, 85 and 359 ff.

[62] Although the government body will not always be the more powerful partner; the roles may be reversed when the private party is itself a large and powerful organization.

problem is in the relationship between private agreement and other public values. For while agreements engender legitimacy, there is a public interest in upholding certain standards, whether in the criminal, civil, or administrative spheres, which are beyond bargaining. There are, in other words, other values originating in deeper social principles which place constraints on the way negotiations should be conducted and on the extent to which issues should be resolved by agreement. However, it is often not at all clear just how the relationship between the value in agreement and other values should best be formulated.

Nevertheless, the interest in developing processes based on agreement is strong, especially in settling disputes between two private parties, and in recent years special agencies have been created to encourage the parties in dispute to reach an agreed solution. The courts themselves are beginning to show an interest and may take steps to facilitate settlement by agreement.[63] The Lord Chancellor's Department in the United Kingdom has committed itself to developing alternatives to the existing courts and tribunals, where the emphasis will be on bringing the parties to agreement. The interest of scholars and researchers in such alternatives is also increasing.[64] Various reasons for this interest in developing new processes are apparent. One is the inherent attraction of settling matters by agreement. Another is an impatience with law and the procedures familiar to legal processes, where a case must be brought within established and often unsuitable legal categories, and where there is a high risk that the result will be mistaken. The issue of cost is another reason: since the costs of court proceedings are increasing and the supply of legal aid dwindling, the promise of cheaper and more accessible forms of process is appealing.

Where the relationship is between an administrative body and a private person the issues are different. Negotiation and agreement may be provided for by statute, but are more likely to occur without express statutory authority. Negotiation will often be about how to exercise a power and what conditions to impose or concessions to make. The attractions of an informal agreement are clear: it can be a useful way of securing compliance with regulations; it is often used by prosecutors as a way of gaining a plea of guilty; and it may be the basis on which benefits and concessions are granted. As we learn more about the workings of administrative bodies, the regular reliance on informal agreements becomes apparent.[65] The problems which beset negotiations between private parties are even more serious when one party is an administrative authority. The primary value of free and equal bargaining is more difficult to

[63] See Kaplan, 'Civil Procedure—Reflections on the Comparison of Systems', n. 15 above and Langbein, 'The German Advantage in Civil Procedure', n. 15 above.

[64] See e.g. S. B. Goldfield, E. D. Green, and F. E. A. Sander, *Dispute Resolution* (Little, Brown, London, 1985) and H. Astor and C. Chinkin, *Alternative Dispute Resolution* (Law Book, Australia, 1991).

[65] See for instance, Hawkins, *Environment and Enforcement*, n. 41 above, and J. Baldwin, N. Wikeley, and R. Young, *Judging Social Security* (Clarendon Press, Oxford, 1993).

satisfy, and the relationship between negotiation and other values is more complex. Informal agreements, however, have an important role in administrative processes and, since they cannot easily be removed, it is important that we know more about how they work and that measures should be taken to ensure that they are conducted according to acceptable standards.

Decision by Applying Legal Standards

The most common, diverse, and characteristically legal form of process is decision-making by the application of authoritative standards. Here the social good lies in areas of activity being regulated according to society's standards as expressed in its laws. The primary value, from the point of view of the person subject to the decision, is that the case will be dealt with on the basis of standards laid down in advance. This is conducive to certainty and stability, to enabling people to plan their affairs within a settled normative framework. This idea is developed further in Chapter 2, but for the moment we should note that the principle of treating people in accordance with their normative expectations is at the very foundation of fair treatment and procedural fairness. The main value is in turn supplemented by a range of other values in the way described in earlier sections. The object of procedures within this form of process is to ensure that the legal standards are properly applied and other values are respected. This can be secured by a variety of procedural forms, ranging from the full judicial trial to the hurried decision of an administrative official. The merits of different procedures are examined later, but it may be useful to mention now the main issues which affect the design of procedures in this model of decision-making.

One issue stems from the difficulty of not knowing whether, in a given case, the right outcome has been reached. Fair treatment and general legitimacy depend on the legal standards being properly applied. Yet, again to adopt Rawls' terminology, the procedures here are inherently imperfect: they are imperfect in the sense that, while we know the outcome we want, we cannot be sure that it has been reached.[66] The first issue affecting procedures is, therefore, that of mistakes; the problem is that we have no way of knowing with certainty that the right outcome has been reached. That has a major impact on the design of procedures. A related problem is that of costs. A correct outcome depends on accuracy in finding the facts, interpreting the law, and applying the law to the facts. Better outcomes could often be achieved and mistakes reduced by more exacting procedures, but procedures are expensive; so the costs of procedures have to be weighed against the costs of mistakes. The decision to terminate a welfare payment, for example, is often made by hard-pressed officials on the basis of sketchy evidence and hurried findings. The high risk of error could be reduced by better procedures, but there are limits on how much

[66] Rawls, *A Theory of Justice*, n. 59 above, 85 ff.

should be spent on procedures.[67] Some level of risk of mistaken decisions has to be tolerated, but how that should be calculated is not an easy matter. The type of decision, the rights or interests at stake, and the consequences of mistakes, are all relevant to the issue, as we shall see in Chapter 3.

A further complication is that mistakes can be of different kinds. A mistaken decision incurs social costs, in the sense that the objects of the law have been frustrated.[68] If the object of a licensing system is to provide a service which is effective, economical, and competitive, mistakes in awarding licences mean that those objects fail. That, as we saw earlier, is a social cost and while social costs fall on the community as a whole, the same mistake may also impose costs on the person affected. The mistaken conviction, denial of a benefit, or withdrawal of a licence, all impose a personal cost, a cost which will often be a denial of rights. Once rights are in issue, the balancing process is more complex; rights have a special status and cannot be defeated by just any social cost. It is then necessary in the design of procedures to reflect that special status; in other words, procedures should take account of the different kinds of mistakes and the consequences attached to them, and offer greater protection against some than others. The fact that procedures are imperfect strengthens the case for adjusting them in favour of the person whose rights are at stake, as is commonly the case in the criminal trial where the accused is presumed innocent, where the burden of proof is on the prosecution, and where the standard of proof is beyond reasonable doubt. But the protection cannot be absolute, for as Bentham remarked, to be absolutely sure that an innocent person is not convicted, we must never convict anyone. These are clearly important issues to which we shall return.

Decision by Discretion

As decisions move along the discretionary spectrum, the standards become less settled and more indeterminate, until the point is reached where they do no more than provide a perimeter within which the decision has to be made. It might still be said that the decision is loosely based on the application of standards, but while such an explanation is in a sense correct, it omits the most important feature of the process, namely, the discretionary element.[69] Standards such as the public interest, or educational desirability, or as the minister

[67] This issue is especially acute in areas like social welfare where the cost of procedures absorb the resources available for the substantive relief. See D. J. Galligan, 'Procedural Rights in Social Welfare' in A. Coote (ed.), *The Welfare of Citizens* (Rivers, Oram, London, 1992).

[68] For discussion, see R. Posner, 'An Economic Approach to Legal Procedure and Judicial Administration' (1973) 2 *J of Legal Studies* 399.

[69] I shall not enter into the question whether a clear line can be drawn between applying a standard and exercising discretion. R. M. Dworkin has argued that it can: *Taking Rights Seriously* (Duckworth, London, 1975), ch. 2; my arguments to the contrary can be seen in *Discretionary Powers*, n. 32 above, ch. 1. I assume for the present discussion that no such clear line can be drawn.

thinks fit, give little real guidance on how the decision should be made or the reasoning process which should be followed; and, indeed, some cases lack even the limited guidance of such standards, but allow the decision-maker to decide on what the standards should be. The scale is a sliding scale, but in order to reveal the special features of discretionary procedures, the emphasis here will be on decisions at the more discretionary point of the scale.

What then are the values at issue in discretionary decisions? The social good is that, within a defined context, the public interest should be pursued by officials deciding as they think best. The virtue lies in officials being able to determine issues in the public interest as they understand it from time to time, without the restrictions imposed by general standards attempting to define the public interest in advance. To be able to allocate subsidies, to authorize the release of offenders, or to dictate the safety requirements in a factory as appears best in the circumstances can be a powerful and effective means of advancing the public interest. The role of procedures is to facilitate that purpose by providing officials with the necessary information, and by ensuring that the decision is based on sound evidence and good reasons.

When we come to the standpoint of the person affected by discretion, the values at stake are harder to identify. To begin, it may help to separate three senses of discretion. The first is where the point of the discretion is to enable the official to deal with the circumstances of a particular case, rather than force it into the categories created by general rules. How much compensation is to be awarded, what kind of welfare assistance, or what is in the best interest of the child are each matters of discretion; but the focus is the specific case and the object is to do what is best in that case. The discretion is, in a sense, for the benefit of the person, and the primary value is to have each case fully and properly assessed on its merits.[70]

A second sense of discretion is where a person's situation is in issue, but the point of discretion is to be able to deal with it as seems best according to a wider sense of the public interest. Whether the prisoner be released on parole, or planning permission granted, or an undesirable alien deported are cases where the decision is taken on a view of the public interest which goes beyond the interests and circumstances of the particular case. Here the outcome value is more difficult to define, since the person affected has no good claim to any specific outcome. However, claims of a lesser kind can be justified: that the person's situation be taken into account and genuinely considered; that the process be conducted in good faith; that the decision be based on rational grounds and be reasonable, all things considered. These ideas are sometimes expressed as a right to be treated in a fair and non-arbitrary manner. That is an evocative way of expressing the idea but it rather begs the question of what, in a discretionary context, constitutes unfairness or arbitrariness. Such concepts

[70] Rights are at home here, namely, the right to have one's case properly assessed according to the circumstances; see further Galligan, *Discretionary Powers*, n. 32 above, ch. 7.

have to be given content and the way to do that is to examine the relationship between the individual person and the administrative authority, and ask: what values permeate that relationship; what understandings do the community, or at least those parts of the community involved with such matters, have about the relationship; which values are most compatible with background political principles?

There is no simple answer to these questions. Even within legal systems which respect persons and try to treat them fairly, different ways of understanding the conflict between the common interest and the interests of those directly affected can be seen. The solution normally reached is that the common interest, as interpreted by the deciding authority, prevails and that the fair treatment aspect consists in ensuring that the person's case is considered in good faith and with proper attention to all relevant facts and arguments. The translation of that general solution into detailed legal rules and procedures may itself be done in a variety of ways and result in considerable doctrinal variations. We shall return to this issue at various points in this book.[71]

A third sense of discretion is where the object is to settle an issue of general policy, such as whether to build a new airport, to develop nuclear power stations, or to change an important part of educational policy. By its nature discretion in this sense allows wide scope to the decision-maker to choose one of a number of possible courses of action. The justification for discretion in this sense is that some issues involve complex policy factors to which there is no solution in advance and which are best made by ministers or other officials accountable through the political process. Decisions of general policy also inevitably affect a wide range of people and interests, and so raise questions of fair treatment. Some will be more seriously affected than others, but none has a strong claim that one policy should be chosen rather than another. The question then is what lesser claims are justified, and again no easy answer is available. The policy-maker should take account of the different interests, act in good faith, and reach a reasoned and reasonable conclusion. But is that all; is that all that a person seriously affected by a policy decision can justifiably expect? What about the person whose private interests are not affected, but who is just interested in the broader issues?

The answers to these questions are to be found in drawing out the framework of normative standards and values within which policy decisions are made. Those standards and values will then be the basis of the relationship between a citizen and the state in this context; they will also be the basis for designing the right procedures. Indeed, in trying to identify that normative framework, we are poised on the brink of different models or ways of understanding the relationship. Consider the example of a minister deciding an important issue of educational policy. On one account, the minister would be

[71] See especially sections 9.2 and 13.3.4.

entitled simply to form a view of what is best in the public interest, taking into account whatever he thinks relevant. On a second account, however, the minister would recognize that those affected ought to be given the chance to represent their interests and put their arguments. The minister might even extend representation to those who have no private interest but are concerned as citizens about the general issue. The minister might take the view, in other words, that policy-making should mirror ideas of democracy and participation. Even within this second model, however, different sub-sets can be envisaged: does the minister just listen to the arguments presented and then decide as he thinks best, or is he obligated to deal with each argument, to show why it has been accepted or rejected; is he required to have good evidence and sound facts for his findings and opinions, or is it clear enough that, taken as a whole, his decision is reasonable? In other words, a number of different positions can be conceived, each based on a slightly different view of the citizen–society relationship, each more exacting in its demands on the minister to have good grounds for his decision. We might even imagine a third model which takes up the idea of proceduralism and strong democracy. Here it would be not so much a matter of the minister deciding as he thought best, but of constructing a procedural framework within which a course of action would emerge as rational and consensual.

It is enough for the time being to outline these different normative models and to consider them further in later chapters.[72] We should be clear, however, about what is at issue. Each model is based on a different view of the normative principles which govern the relationship between the citizen and the society in making general policy; each model invokes different understandings of the values which govern that relationship. In one sense they might be seen as procedural issues; whether to hear interested parties, how far to examine the specific consequences for the parties, or whether a reasoned explanation should be given, are all in a sense matters of procedure. But they are much more than that; more fundamentally, they are issues about what values ought to prevail in the context. The task of procedures is to give effect to those values, but first we need to be clear about the values themselves. Again, it might be tempting to think of the values as procedural rather than outcome values, although the validity of that distinction is itself questionable.

What we are trying to do here is to identify the values and the standards of fair treatment based on those values as they apply in discretionary contexts; the standards we decide on will need suitable procedures for their maintenance, but to try to classify some standards as procedural and others as substantive or outcome-based is a poor classification and anyhow beside the point.[73] It should also be noted that, in this context, Rawls' threefold distinction between pure, perfect, and imperfect procedures is of limited help, since

[72] See Chs. 15 and 16.

[73] The procedure-substance point is considered more fully in section 1.4.

elements of each appear in each of the three models. It is not easy, moreover, to identify distinct outcomes and then direct procedures at them. In one sense the correct outcome is what the minister decides, while in another sense it is what the minister decides subject to a number of constraining values, for example, that he take into account the representations of interested parties. Nothing turns on whether such values are thought to be part of the outcome or not, the point of the distinction being to help identify the values relevant to each kind of process, however they might be classified.

Proceduralism

The primary value of proceduralism is the resolution of issues within a special procedural framework, where the involvement of the parties, the high level of rationality, and the element of consensus come together in a compelling whole. The good for society at large is that difficult matters are resolved without resort to standards formulated in advance, and that the solution reached carries great legitimating force. To the individual person, the value is that the outcome is agreed to be the most rational. The person sees it as rational because it properly assimilates his interests within a compelling conception of the common good, while at the same time being partly the product of the person's own involvement. A more perfect form of process is hard to imagine. The real question, then, is not its normative basis, since normatively it is the very apogee of social processes, but whether it can be workable in practice.

Investigation and Inquiry

We might be inclined to think that processes of investigation and inquiry lack a primary principle. Since their object is to gather information, analyse it, and make proposals based on it, they appear to be incomplete processes without a normative basis. Although they are in a way preliminary to something further, it would be wrong to think of investigation and inquiry as outside a normative framework. The very fact that the tasks mentioned should be done in certain ways constitutes a normative principle and creates rights and obligations. The information collected should be accurate, the analysis impartial and objective, and any proposals should be made reasonably and in good faith. A clear sense of the social good is contained in these conditions since there is a general advantage in such tasks being performed properly and in any resulting actions or decisions being based on sound foundations. The person subject to the process also benefits from these conditions and could justifiably insist on them as binding terms in his relationship with the community. A parallel might be drawn between these conditions and those which govern the exercise of discretion. Other values also have a role here. The police investigation is in many ways a special case, but it can be taken as a model illustrating the importance of those additional values—values about how the suspect should be treated, values inherent in the privilege against self-incrimination, and values providing for advice and counsel. Other forms of investigation and inquiry may have their own special conditions, but the police investigation brings out the general importance of various values in this context.

1.4 A THEORETICAL APPROACH TO PROCEDURES

The landscape of legal processes and procedures has proved to be interesting and varied. From the ground traversed in this Chapter, we can see the different forms of legal processes, the role of each as a method of social ordering, and the normative principles upon which each is based. It has been shown how the first tier of normative principles is joined by other tiers of values from which additional normative standards are derived, some relating to outcomes, others standing independently of outcomes, and a third category somewhere in the middle. Our survey of the landscape has demonstrated the importance of dividing the common good into its two elements, one consisting of the collective interest in achieving the objects of law, the other in treating individual persons in accordance with their normative expectations in relation to law. Good government and a just legal system, which are themselves aspects of the common good, require that both elements be advanced and upheld. The concern that persons be treated in accordance with their normative expectations, which is of course another way of saying in accordance with the tiers of values and standards, is the wellspring of rights and fair treatment.

1.4.1 Three Procedural Generalizations

The character and role of procedures within each form of legal process have also featured prominently in our survey of the landscape and it is to those matters I wish to return in concluding this Chapter. Several generalizations about procedures which should hold true across the spectrum of legal processes may be suggested. The *first* generalization is that the normative function of procedures is to provide the means for the practical application in specific cases and instances of the values which pertain within each form of legal process. This applies to all such relevant values, whether they relate to outcomes or are of worth separately from outcomes. The normative function of procedures can be illustrated by a typical legal process based on deciding cases according to authoritative standards. First, procedures should ensure that decisions are made properly and accurately according to first-tier outcome-based standards applicable in each context—the standards of the criminal law, of the civil law, or of an area of administrative regulation. The second task of procedures is to facilitate the application of other relevant standards, including those affecting outcomes and those independent of outcomes. Some examples are: principles of consistency and non-discrimination; principles relating to privacy and confidentiality; and the hearing principle. The question of what normative standards apply within any area of legal process can be answered only by careful study of that process and of the legal and constitutional context in which it occurs.

The *second* generalization is that the design of procedures is a matter of creating institutions and mechanisms which are effective in upholding the full range of normative standards relevant to each process. But the design of procedures itself raises both practical and normative issues. At the practical level, it is necessary to confront such basic issues as how to produce procedures which are not only effective in their purposes but also economical in their costs. The severe limits of our empirical knowledge of the effectiveness of different institutions and mechanisms in achieving their ends is compounded in those areas of process where procedures are imperfect. The design of procedures also has a normative dimension. A mistaken outcome or a transgressed principle are not simply marginal costs to the collective good, but are also likely to be violations of the rights of persons and the standards of fair treatment. Questions of cost and the imperfection of procedures take on an added significance when viewed in this way, and a principled approach must be found in order to reconcile, in the design of procedures, the practical issues of limited effectiveness and the normative issues of rights and fair treatment.

The *third* generalization is that, while the normative function of procedures is to give effect to the tiers of values within legal procedures, it may be sensible and justifiable to develop intermediate procedural standards. By this is meant that, given the need to have procedures which to some degree are generalized, and bearing in mind matters of cost and imperfection, there may be a practical and prescriptive case for creating intermediate procedural standards and rights. The law is full of such intermediate procedural standards: the rules of evidence and procedure and the principles of natural justice are instances in English law, while the constitutional right to counsel is a noteworthy example in American law. Procedural standards and rights deriving from them are of a different order from the tiers of underlying values; the former are contingent and instrumental means for giving effect to the latter, and although certain procedural standards may come to be regarded as permanent and settled, the justification for them is that they serve as practical instruments for achieving the tiers of values within each form of processes. The tendency to develop intermediate procedural standards upon which specific cases can be decided, without having to have recourse to first principles on every occasion, is familiar and convenient in any area of social ordering.

1.4.2 Procedures and Substance

The view of procedures as means, instruments, or mechanisms for giving effect to the values pertinent to each form of process throws some light on the difficult issue of what is procedure and what is substance. The distinction is often made in legal analysis and argument and is sometimes referred to in statutory provisions; yet it is always troublesome, for just what the distinction between the two is, or ought to be, is never clear. In a common-sensical kind of way, the distinction seems straightforward: the substance of a decision refers to the outcome sought, while procedures are the steps leading to the outcome. Bentham found no difficulty in drawing on such practical good sense in making a clear distinction between substantive law on the one hand and adjectival or procedural law on the other hand. Substantive law defined the outcome to be reached and procedural law provided the means for reaching it. If the notion of a correct outcome is defined rather more fully than Bentham's notion of rectitude to mean an outcome which is reached in accordance with all tiers of values, then we are broadly in the Benthamite camp and a clear distinction between procedure and substance (in the sense of outcomes) is possible.[74]

However, the position is not always so clear. Some would wish to distinguish between the various tiers of values with a view to classifying some as substantive or outcome values and others as procedural values. The first tier of values, which expresses an obligation to apply the criminal law or decide administrative matters according to the statutory criteria, for example, is indisputably outcome-based. The second tier, which expresses values such as the principles of consistency and non-discrimination, might seem less unequivocally outcome-based and therefore liable to be thought of as in some sense procedural. At a third tier, where we encounter values such as the need for settled standards of decision-making or that each person be heard and each case properly considered, the move from substance and outcome to means and procedure is more noticeable but still not complete. That the lines between the two are less than obvious is not surprising since there are no settled criteria for classifying primary values at each tier as substantive or procedural. That might itself be a good reason for regarding procedures simply as the mechanisms for achieving values rather than trying to designate certain values as procedural. Indeed, I would suggest that no sound analytical distinction can be made between so-called substantive values and so-called procedural values. Where for practical reasons a legal distinction has to be drawn between the two, the criterion for doing so is likely to be policy-based rather than analytical. The important task in any context of decisions is to identify the values at issue and then ask what mechanisms are effective in leading to them. How we then divide the area between substance and procedure is of secondary significance.

An alternative approach might be to distinguish between outcome values and non-outcome values, and then to claim that the former are substantive

[74] See Bayles, *Procedural Justice*, n. 32 above 3 ff.

while the latter are procedural. The earlier analysis shows that legal processes occur in a context of values many of which originate from sources other than the concern for accurate outcomes, the principles of consistency, privacy, and confidentiality being examples. The idea can be extended to the protections which an accused person has against certain kinds of mistreatment during the investigation by the police. It is certainly desirable to be aware of the existence of such values and to recognize their importance in legal processes, but it seems odd to regard as procedural values which protect certain confidential matters from disclosure or the suspect from being beaten. Values like these are protected because they are important in the life of a society wherever they occur. It is difficult to see what is served or gained by designating them as procedural values, and the same may be said of the modern tendency to call them process values. If the term 'process values' is meant to indicate only that some of the standards governing legal processes are separate from outcomes, no harm is done; if the term means more, then its significance is unclear.

The final point to note is that any attempt to erect a strict division between outcomes and the procedures leading to those outcomes is itself fraught with difficulty. Clear cases can easily be found, but borderline cases are equally numerous: for example, is the principle that a person, subject to a discretionary decision, should have his case properly considered, a matter of substance or procedure? On one view it can be seen as part of what constitutes a proper outcome and, therefore, substantive; but on another it might be regarded as a procedural step leading to a proper outcome. But whether it is one or the other does not matter, or at least at the level of principle it does not matter. What is important is that the proper consideration of a person's case is a value which ought to be respected in legal processes and for which suitable mechanisms should be available. Indeed, as will become clear in the next chapter, it is better to approach procedural issues, especially issues of procedural fairness, by asking, first, what are the values at stake and what standards do they generate in terms of fair treatment of a person, and then, secondly, what procedures are needed to ensure that the standards are upheld in practice.

2
Procedural Fairness

The object of this Chapter is to examine the notion of procedural fairness. The distinction made in the first chapter between the collective interest in having authoritative legal standards properly applied and the interest of the individual person who is affected by them now becomes crucially important. For procedural fairness is very much concerned with the way persons are treated in legal processes. Whenever a question arises about how a person should be treated, about the allocation of burdens and benefits, where rights or interests are affected, fairness is in issue. Fairness is often linked to ideas about giving a person what is due, but it goes further and rests on the general principle that a person is treated fairly if he is treated in a way to which he has a justifiable claim. Since legal processes are about how people are treated, about what they should get or be denied, they raise issues of fairness. The task here is to examine the concept of procedural fairness in relation to legal procedures and to create a framework within which procedural issues can be understood. The discussion begins with a statement of the main features of procedural fairness and then moves on to a fuller analysis in the rest of the Chapter. Procedural fairness is considered in its relationship to standards of fair treatment, and an explanation is given of the sense in which legal standards constitute standards of fair treatment. In the final part of the Chapter, notions of fair treatment and procedural fairness are placed in their social context and a critique is offered of some of the empirical research into common perceptions of procedural fairness.

2.1 THE NATURE OF PROCEDURAL FAIRNESS

2.1.1 A General Outline

The concept of procedural fairness can be expressed in this way. First, legal procedures are fair procedures to the extent that they lead to or constitute fair treatment of the person or persons affected. Secondly, within each type of legal process, there are authoritative standards based on the tiers of values relevant to that process which constitute the standards of fair treatment, so that a person treated in accordance with them is treated fairly. Thirdly, the basis for such treatment being fair treatment is the promise of society as a whole to each of its members that they will be treated in that way. The concept of procedural fairness consists in the relationship between procedures, fair treatment, and authoritative standards. Societies will differ in their conceptions of procedural fairness, which is to say that both the standards of fair treatment and the procedures considered most suitable for applying them will be different.[1]

This approach to fair treatment and procedural fairness applies to each of the forms of legal process discussed in the first chapter. There we saw how the normative foundation of each consists of distinctive tiers of values; it is that combination of values which provides the basis in each case for the standards of fair treatment. It follows that procedures are fair to the extent that they lead to the proper application of the standards of fair treatment. Now while this approach has general application to the various forms of process, the discussion here will concentrate on the most typical legal forms, namely, decision-making by the application of standards and the exercise of discretion. I shall, however, comment briefly on the other main forms, in particular processes based on agreement and the notion of proceduralism.

Before examining the general approach more closely, it may be of help in understanding its practical application to take two examples, one straightforward, the other slightly more complicated. In the straightforward case, suppose that the law provides for the grant of welfare payments on certain criteria being satisfied. The first tier value, therefore, is to decide cases according to those criteria, the principle being that each person's case should be dealt with in that way. Fair treatment requires an accurate finding of fact and the proper application of the statutory criteria to it. In order to ensure that outcome, procedures are needed to provide the necessary information and evidence, and to facilitate a sound and impartial judgment applying the statutory criteria to the facts. Those objectives in turn point to the need for more specific procedures, procedures to enable the applicant to present evidence and argument, and procedures to remove any element of bias or partiality. The same objectives might be achieved by a number of different procedures, while the precise form any particular procedure has, hearing procedures for example, will vary. The guiding test in deciding what procedures are necessary and the precise form they should take is the accurate and proper application of the statutory criteria. But the picture is not complete until values and standards at other tiers also are taken into account. The welfare agency might be prohibited from obtaining information by breach of confidential relationships between the applicant and his doctor; it might also be required to respect certain matters of privacy; and since welfare needs are normally pressing needs, the decision should be made in good time. These are some of the relevant values and there may be others, and each additional value may in turn create a need for further procedures.

[1] Here I am using Rawls' distinction between *concept* and *conception*: J. Rawls, *A Theory of Justice* (Clarendon Press, Oxford, 1972), section 2.

The upshot should be a decision which is made by faithfully applying the statutory criteria, while respecting and giving effect to any other values and standards relevant in that context. A person whose application is dealt with in that way is treated fairly, and the procedures which lead to that result are fair procedures.

In the more complicated case, suppose that an authority has power to grant a licence to carry on certain activities, but is left to decide in its discretion how its power should be used. The first question is what are the values in this context from which standards of fair treatment can be derived. The answer is not immediately clear: the precise terms of the first tier values are unsettled, and the relationships between them and other tiers are complex. However, the first tier principle does at least require that the applicant's case be considered, that issues of fact be determined accurately, that relevant matters be taken into account, and that the decision be reasonable and made in good faith. Once the first tier standards are settled, suitable procedures can be designed to give effect to them. Amongst other possible values, the principle of consistent treatment is clearly important, for while there is no right to or even expectation of a set outcome, each person might reasonably expect to be treated according to general criteria consistently applied from one case to another. Another value which might be argued for is that guidelines should be formulated as to how the discretion will be used and applied in each case. The normative basis for such a principle is arguable, and whether the law requires it varies from one system to another. Other values may also be relevant, but the general approach is now clear: firstly, identify the values governing any context and the standards flowing from them, and then, secondly, design procedures suitable for their application. The person whose case is dealt with according to authoritative standards is treated fairly, and procedures are fair to the degree that they bring about that result.

2.1.2 Procedures as Means to Fair Treatment

Now that we have an outline of the general concept of procedural fairness, the next task is to examine its characteristics. Fundamental to this account of procedural fairness is the relationship between procedures and fair treatment. The relationship may be expressed in this way: procedures are the means by which standards of fair treatment are applied in legal processes; procedures are instrumental to fair treatment and the claim for any particular procedure is contingent on its serving that end. The corollary is that procedures are fair to the extent that they lead to fair treatment. At first sight this might seem an unduly narrow and overly instrumental view of procedures; surely there is more to procedures than that; surely procedures can be fair or unfair in themselves. We do sometimes talk loosely in this way, as if procedural fairness depends on choosing a procedure which is itself fair. But just as procedures are neither effective nor ineffective, efficient nor inefficient, economical nor uneconomical, except with reference to some end or purpose which they serve, so procedures are fair or unfair only by reference to standards of fairness, and standards of fairness are in turn based on values. Hearing a person, allowing him counsel, or giving him reasons, can each be judged to be fair only if we first identify the standards by which to make the judgment. There are often good reasons for having settled rules of procedure, which are then referred to as fair procedures, but we should remember that the justification for those rules is that they serve the standards of fair treatment.

The standards of fair treatment in legal contexts are those authoritative legal standards which govern each form of process. Standards derive from values which, as we have seen, can be grouped loosely in tiers, where their inter-relationships can be complex. The first tier standards of the criminal trial are that an accurate finding of guilt or innocence should be made according to the legal criteria. The suspect is treated fairly if he is judged according to reliable findings of fact and the proper application of the law to the facts. Where second or third tier standards are at stake, the same approach applies, in that fair treatment requires compliance with the standards in question. Examples are that a suspect should not be ill-treated, a person's privacy should not be violated, and certain kinds of confidential material should not be openly revealed. In the exercise of discretion, certain limiting standards, such as consistency and timeliness, should be upheld. In civil actions, authoritative standards include the equal treatment of the parties by ensuring a fair contest and that the risks of error are equally distributed; respect for each of these standards is an element of fair treatment. Some standards have an impact on outcomes, directly or indirectly; others place constraints on the course leading to outcomes; while a few may be entirely independent of outcomes.

The idea that procedures are instrumental and contingent on serving some end, purpose, or value, and therefore are neither fair nor unfair in themselves, needs a little further explanation. It is often said that some procedures are simply good and fair; for example, the idea that the adjudicator who hears both sides acts fairly has at first sight a certain attraction. But on closer scrutiny it is clear that something more is needed for an adequate explanation. For in order to explain why the procedure is fair, we need to invoke some value such as a better outcome, respect for a person, or equal treatment of persons. Otherwise it remains a puzzle why both sides should be heard; once some such value issue is identified, the puzzle disappears. A good test for the worth of any procedure is to ask what value it serves, for unless the answer shows that some significant value is at stake, the procedure is not connected to fair treatment and has no claim on resources. Another claim sometimes made is that listening to both sides, or allowing a person to have his say, is not instrumental to but an expression or instantiation of values. In the same way that tennis can be played to lose weight or because it is enjoyable, procedures can be instrumental to values or the expression of values; or, to quote Italo Calvino, reading books of good quality is simply a good thing to do.[2]

The idea that a procedure can express a value rather than be instrumental to it is true. But all that means for the present analysis is that, when talking of the relation between procedures and values, it is not always the case that one leads to the other, since one might simply be the expression of the other. This does not, however, undermine the argument that procedures are neither good nor fair independently of values; they must still express a value which can be identified and justified as one which ought to be respected and to which resources ought to be dedicated. It then makes no difference whether a procedure leads causally to that value being respected or is itself an expression of the value. What is important is that judgments of fairness or unfairness in relation to procedures depend on their serving values in one way or the other.[3]

2.1.3 The Idea of Fair Treatment

It is sometimes said to be easier to grasp the notions of fairness and fair treatment by considering unfairness and unfair treatment.[4] Indeed in her last book, *The Faces of Injustice*, the late Judith Shklar argued that the concept of injustice has distinctive features which may be lost if study is concentrated on justice.[5] To treat a person unfairly is in some way to do him down, to deny him something to which he is entitled or which is due to him. Fairness, then, in its widest sense, applying to any relationship between persons, refers to what is due within that relationship. Whether the relationship is between two citizens, or between citizen and official, the first question to ask is what is due, and the second, has it been given or denied. The idea is closely related to notions of commutative justice, which in turn can be extended beyond the sense of giving back or restoring to the wider context of distributing or allocating.[6]

Many attempts have been made to isolate the special character of justice and fairness. According to H. L. A. Hart, justice is 'primarily concerned with

[2] I. Calvino, 'Why Read the Classics' in *The Literature Machine* (Picador, London, 1989).

[3] Whether any given value is itself important enough to merit a place in legal processes is of course another question. This point is taken up in Ch. 4 where I examine the hearing principle.

[4] See J. Lucas, *On Justice* (Clarendon Press, Oxford, 1978).

[5] J. Shklar, *The Faces of Injustice* (Yale University Press, New Haven, Conn., 1990).

[6] On the relationship amongst senses of justice, see J. M. Finnis, *Natural Law and Natural Rights* (Clarendon Press, Oxford, 1980), 177–84.

the ways in which *classes* of individuals are treated'.[7] Hart went on to separate two elements in the concept of justice: the constant element expressed in the idea of 'treat like cases alike' and the shifting element according to which likeness or difference are to be judged.[8] Now while this separation of the two elements is vital in understanding the structure of justice, Hart is mistaken, I suggest, in thinking that the idea of treating like cases alike is the constant part. It is a mistake because like treatment is not general enough in its scope. If I promise to treat you in a certain way and then fail, I treat you unfairly, but no question of like treatment arises. Indeed, issues of justice regularly arise in relationships between parties where no question of comparison with how a third party would be treated is relevant. John Finnis' analysis takes us closer to the nature of the constant part of justice:[9] on his approach, justice has to do, first, with relations between persons and, secondly, with what is due to or owed by one to another. Finnis then adds a third element of equality or, more accurately, proportionality, equilibrium, or balance. This third element is not a restatement of Hart's notion of like treatment, but draws attention to the idea that, in making good what is due and in respecting entitlements, a sense of balance between the parties is restored. To these three elements, I suggest that a fourth needs to be added to constitute fully the concept of justice: the fourth is that any course of action must comply with certain fundamental standards of right treatment. For whatever the context, whether it be one of applying rules or working within a relationship between parties, any judgment of fairness or justice is defeasible unless it also meets the most elementary idea of right treatment. There is, in other words, a threshold such that actions falling below it cannot, without perverse distortion, be considered fair or just even though they meet the other three conditions.

These four elements express the constant part of justice. The idea at the core of this constant part is that justice and fairness consist in giving a person his due or entitlement. Does it matter, however, whether we use the term justice or the term fairness? That question is much discussed and disputed,[10] but without entering into the debate, I shall proceed on the following basis. In the first place, I suggest there is no conceptual ground for distinguishing between the two concepts; each fits the analysis above and is characterized by the four elements. Secondly, however, it is conventional and to some extent convenient to use fairness when considering treatment within a context such as law, or within a relationship such as a contract, and to reserve justice for judgments which derive from standards outside that context and

[7] H. L. A. Hart, *The Concept of Law* (Clarendon Press, Oxford, 1961), 163.

[8] Ibid. 156. For further discussion of the distinction, see J. Rawls, *A Theory of Justice*, ch. 1.

[9] J. Finnis, *Natural Law and Natural Rights*, n. 6 above, 161 ff.

[10] See e.g., Rawls, *A Theory of Justice*, n. 1 above, and R. M. Dworkin, *Law's Empire* (Fontana, London, 1986).

which are in some sense fundamental. So we may talk of fair treatment within law, leaving open the possibility that such a judgment might be undermined by some more fundamental sense of just treatment based on standards from outside the law.

2.1.4 Normative Expectations as the Basis of Fair Treatment

If the idea of dues and entitlements is central to the concept of fair treatment, where do such dues and entitlements come from? The answer is that they are created within a context of authoritative standards, standards which create in those to whom they apply normative expectations. An expectation, that is to say, which is not just hope, prediction, or wishful thinking, but has a binding and obligatory character, so that to thwart the expectation would be a breach of obligation. The simplest and most common basis for normative expectations are rules; legal rules, but not only legal rules since any set of rules may be the basis of obligation and entitlement. But while there is a natural association between rules and normative expectations, and therefore between rules and fair treatment, it would be wrong to think that only rules create normative expectations. Normative expectations, and in turn dues and entitlements, spring from many sources: from promises and undertakings, commitments and understandings, even actions and intentions.[11] Normative expectations, moreover, do not depend on the immediacy of a one-to-one relationship or an undertaking of an express kind; they may have a communal basis and derive from longer term understandings and assumptions prevailing within a community. The very idea of a community depends on a high level of settled standards about how people will be dealt with and what dues and entitlements they may expect. The law is one formal and important network of such standards, but it is not the only one.

Reflection on law as a set of normative standards reveals a number of important points about dues, entitlements, and fair treatment. In the first place, the standards of law give rise to normative expectations, the most fundamental of which is that a person will be dealt with in accordance with those standards. That expectation must itself originate outside the law, for the bindingness of law stems from a social principle, prior to the law, to the effect that people will be dealt with in a certain way. Each society naturally develops a whole range of principles about how people should deal with each other and how each should be dealt with by the state. The law is one set of standards, the normative basis of which is the more fundamental principle that people will be treated according to law. In day-to-day affairs, it is enough to point to the law as providing standards of treatment without reference to anything further, since it is taken for granted that the law will be or

[11] See further J. Raz, 'Promises and undertakings' in J. Hacker and J. Raz (eds.), *Law, Morality and Society* (Clarendon Press, Oxford, 1978).

at least should be applied. If we want to know why that is the case and how it comes about, we must move to a different level of discourse and understanding: we must then focus on the relationship between a society and each of its members and ask what are the normative understandings governing that relationship. One basic understanding, but not the only one, is that, subject to certain qualifications, individual persons will be treated in accordance with the law. If the notion of an understanding is not quite strong enough to support such a mighty edifice, then let it be put in the stronger normative terms of an implicit promise or undertaking society gives to its members that, when the occasion arises, each will be treated according to law.

The relationship between the commitment to treat people according to law and other fundamental social principles raises important issues. We tend to assume that society's undertaking to apply the law excludes other normative principles. But why should we make that assumption? There are certainly good reasons for regarding the commitment to deal with people according to law as fundamental to a just society, and one which should not lightly be overridden; but it does not follow that the commitment should be considered absolute or exclusive. In order to reach that conclusion, we would need to decide that, in the relationship between society collectively and its members individually, the most important normative principle is to treat according to law. Not only is such a conclusion intuitively wrong, it is short on reason, since cases occur where to apply the law would be a grave injustice, because to do so would violate some more fundamental principle.

The more rational and defensible approach is to consider the commitment to law as one of a number of principles upon which normative expectations arise about how people will be treated. The principle that people should be treated with concern and respect, as moral agents with autonomy and responsibility, which is itself one of the foundations of the citizen–state relationship, would normally support the commitment to treatment according to law; but not always, for it might on occasions insist on treatment outside or in breach of the law. Respect for persons is an abstract principle, but it is also dynamic, to be made specific and practical within the framework of different cultures and social relationships. The modern tendency is to use that principle to support a core of entitlements, a battery of human rights, without which it is thought there can be no satisfactory respect for persons. The individuation of those rights will naturally be shaped by cultural diversity, and the laws of a society should be an adequate expression of them. But there is good reason for holding that where the law fails to provide some basic right, then the commitment to respect persons may prevail over the commitment to treatment according to law. In other words, while the fundamental normative expectations about how people will be treated in their relations with the state include a high level of commitment to law, they go beyond that and include other principles which may be in conflict with the law.

Connections can be drawn between the idea of basic social standards and part of the discussion in the first chapter. There we saw how social standards often find their way into the law, and how it may be unclear whether a certain standard is a legal standard or not. The relationship between legal standards and deeper social standards was seen to be complex, but open and fluid. The thesis I am now advancing begins with those ideas and suggests that the normative expectations of a citizen, as to how he or she should be treated, draw on social principles which include but go beyond settled legal principles. I shall return to this point again shortly, but the conclusion may now be drawn that, within any legal process, there will always be a complex relationship between settled legal standards and other normative standards originating in deeper social principles. What constitutes fair treatment will be correspondingly complex and sometimes unsettled. This factor has relevance for standards at all tiers, but especially for those which originate in values independent of the first tier outcome-values. Such independent values by their nature draw on deeper social values about how a person should be treated, where those values are often not adopted, or not clearly or fully adopted, into law. That people should be treated according to the principles of consistency and equal treatment might be recognized only partly and imperfectly in legal contexts. And even when such fundamental values are given legal status, their meaning and content in different contexts are likely to demand close reflection on very basic social and moral notions of fair treatment. To take an example, a party to civil litigation might invoke a normative principle that the trial should be a fair contest and that the parties should be treated with equal concern and respect; such principles are indispensable to the common law conception of civil proceedings and yet, in order to apply them, it may be necessary to look to the most fundamental ideas of how people should be treated and what fairness means in such a context.

2.1.5 Justice and Fair Treatment

The sense of fair treatment in dealing with people according to the law is an important and indispensable element in any society purporting to be just. Indeed, to deal with people according to the normative expectations created by law is to accord them fair treatment in a real and significant sense. A society which could genuinely claim that its people are treated fairly in that sense would be both commendable and rare. The even-handed application of the law is not the final yardstick of just treatment, but it is a major achievement in the life of a society. Why this should be so is easily seen. The standards of law are public declarations of the rules governing the relationship between citizen and state; they constitute an undertaking about how some of the most important matters in a society will be dealt with and, like any serious undertaking solemnly made, they create rights and carry with them duties. Fair and just treatment in a range of everyday contexts means no more than that two parties, in the dealings between them, should treat each other in accordance with those normative expectations, with the rights and entitlements thereby created. Fairness consists directly in the upholding of normative standards and expectations, and only indirectly in their substantive content.

There are, nevertheless, cases where treatment according to law is fair in this sense but unjust in some deeper sense. Here we encounter the fourth element in the concept of fair and just treatment: the idea that any specific sense of fair treatment may be indefensible if it violates some deeper standard of justice.[12] The relationship between those two realms is complex and I shall deal briefly with just two matters: one concerns the relationship itself; the other looks to the role of officials applying the law. As to the first, we should begin by being clear about what is meant in saying that the law is unjust: we mean that the standards of the law, that is to say, the conception of justice contained in those standards, are inconsistent with some other set of standards, some other conception of justice, which is more fundamental. But to approach the matter as a direct conflict between two conceptions of how people ought to be dealt with is altogether too crude. Conceptions of justice are many-layered, beginning with a foundation of fundamental principles and ending with a level of detail upon which one opinion may be as good as another. To give an example, while the duty to provide for the weakest members of the community might be a fundamental requirement of justice, rules about how much welfare a claimant should get under the laws of a country are matters of detail. The first point, then, is to be clear that a careful analysis should be made of the level of conflict between law and a deeper conception of justice. If the conflict is truly fundamental, then there can be little virtue in upholding the law; but if, as is often the case, the conflict is within the leaves and branches of the tree of justice rather than an assault on its trunk, the law can then be seen as one reasonable set of interpretations of foundational principles. The case for upholding the expectations created by law is then clear and strong.

The role of officials applying the law can be understood against this background. Here the issue is what should be the officials' approach where a law, or its application in a case, violates a more fundamental standard of justice. Different views are tenable, but I suggest that if, after close analysis, an official concludes that to apply the law would be an injustice at a deep level and of a serious kind, then his duty would be not to apply it. The official's highest duty is, after all, to avoid serious injustice to those subject

[12] See further section 2.1.3.

to his authority. This could be expressed as a discretion to disobey, but to be more accurate it is a duty rather than a discretion, to be exercised when the conditions described above are met; that is, after giving proper consideration to the authority of law as a public conception of justice, it is found seriously wanting. The correlative of the official's duty is an entitlement on the part of the person affected to be treated according to the more fundamental principle and in that way to be treated justly.

The relationship between the individual and the community should now be reformulated. The implied undertaking to treat people according to law is part of a wider commitment to treat them justly or at least to avoid injustice. The undertaking will normally be discharged by faithful application of the law, but on occasions it may be necessary to invoke a principle of justice beyond the law. To express the point in another way, a way which draws on the earlier analysis of laws as sub-systems of normative standards, one standard implicit in and fundamental to all sub-systems is that a person should not be treated in a way which is seriously unjust. Whether such a standard should be regarded as implicit in legal process is a normative issue; whether officials in practice recognize and give effect to it is an empirical matter. No comprehensive study has been undertaken, but in many areas of decision-making the signs are that officials do often subscribe to such a standard.

2.2 PROCEDURES AND FAIR TREATMENT

2.2.1 The Contingent Nature of Procedures

The principle that procedures are fair to the extent that they lead to fair treatment has important consequences for procedures. Since procedures are means for upholding the standards of fair treatment, they should be judged according to how well they achieve those ends. No one procedure or set of procedures is necessarily required, and it will often be that fair treatment could be achieved from a number of different procedures or combinations of procedures. The worth of any procedure depends on its contribution to standards of fair treatment; each procedure is in that sense instrumental to and contingent upon standards of fair treatment. The one qualification which needs to be made to that general proposition is that some procedures may themselves be expressions of standards of fair treatment; in those cases, the language of instrumentalism has to be modified accordingly. Consider some examples. Take the controversy over whether the adversarial nature of the trial at common law is to be preferred to the more inquisitorial procedures of continental Europe. Each may be as effective as the other in leading to fair treatment, that is, in reaching correct outcomes and in maintaining respect for other values; there is no evidence, moreover, to show that one is better than the other in adhering to those ends. The real debate in comparing the two approaches is not about which will lead to more correct outcomes, but rather what values are relevant, with one tradition regarding an equal contest and the autonomy of the parties as important, the other emphasizing the importance of centralized control and unrestricted investigation by the magistrate and judge. The real difference, in other words, between the two traditions is what standards of fair treatment should govern the trial process; and because different answers are given to that question within each tradition, the procedures within them will also naturally vary.

Another example can be taken from the administrative sphere. Suppose the object is to decide whether a licence should be granted, where the decision is to be made according to whether certain conditions have been satisfied and whether it is in the public interest. The proper application of those standards might be achieved through different procedures. One procedural approach would be investigation by the licensing body itself, gathering whatever information it thought relevant, emphasizing informality, and holding discussions with the applicant. An alternative procedural approach would be a judicial-type procedure with all the trappings of a court, including a formal hearing, the calling of evidence and witnesses, and the legal representation of the applicant and other interested parties. The two procedural approaches are very different, but each might be effective in providing information and material on the basis of which a sound decision could be made. The reasons for different societies adopting one or the other are as much cultural and historical as the result of careful deliberation.

This general approach might itself seem questionable. It could be argued that some procedures just are fundamental to any legal process, so that to neglect them would be to act procedurally unfairly. So it might be argued, that procedures to guard against bias and to provide a hearing are necessary elements of fair procedures, without which any process would be tainted. My claim is that even such basic procedures must earn their place and that they do so by their contribution to the upholding of standards of fair treatment. Now exactly what that means and its consequences for the practical design of procedures is a matter to which we shall return shortly. There may also be some doubts which need to be allayed about the consequences that may seem to follow from the contingent and instrumental nature of procedures. These matters are also considered in the next section.

First, however, we should shift our attention from general ideas about procedures to the way they are dealt with in law. Legal institutions develop working rules about what procedures are necessary to achieve their objects: rules of evidence, rules about being heard, rules of legal representation are a few examples among many. All are working rules which, on the basis of reason and experience, have been developed or adopted by the legislature or the courts as the means for attaining the right outcomes, while respecting non-outcome values. But once such rules and principles become settled as legal rules and principles, the justification for them tends to be forgotten, and the temptation is to regard them as complete in themselves and independent of any further justification. It is not surprising that we also come to think of such procedural rules as inherently fair rules, so that decisions reached in accordance with them will be regarded as good decisions, fairly reached, while breach of them will taint the process. The rules come to be seen as ends in themselves and the procedures they import as essential for fairness.[13] Such procedural rules often become the basis of rights—the right to be heard, the right to counsel, the right to cross-examine a witness—and so provide further evidence of the tendency to convert working rules, rules of thumb, rules instrumental to fair treatment, into fixed rules of law, considered fair in themselves.[14] Sometimes procedural rules are even given constitutional status, so that any decision made in breach of them will be open to challenge.[15]

The virtue of having settled rules of procedure is the certainty and stability which result and the guidance decision-makers then have as to the procedures to follow. The cost is that procedural rules, like any rules, both over-include and under-include; they over-include in requiring procedures which, for a particular case, may not be necessary for fair treatment; they under-include in the opposite way by not calling for certain procedures which, in some circumstances, are needed for fair treatment. From time to time, after it becomes clear that they are no longer effective in securing fair treatment, the rules may be reconsidered. Procedural reform is a continuing concern of any legal system, and settled rules need to be re-examined from time to time. New areas may come to light where procedural issues have to be confronted for the first time, as is now the case in administrative law. The general principle that those subject to administrative processes should be treated fairly is now accepted, but it is not yet clear in some contexts what the standards of fair treatment are and what procedures are needed to apply them. Courts, administrators, and legislators are gradually developing a sense of what procedures are needed in these areas, although the process is

[13] Although this may be seen as a general tendency, I do not want to overstate the case. The decision body may try to assess the effect that a breach of the procedural rules has on the outcome, a good example of which is the practice of criminal courts in applying the 'proviso' where there has been a procedural error at the trial, but it is not serious enough to affect the reliability of the outcome.

[14] The close similarity between this tendency and rule utilitarianism is worth noting.

[15] The right to counsel of the American Constitution, Amendments V and VI, are an example. It is interesting to note that, although the Supreme Court is often asked to rule on the scope of that right, it rarely examines the underlying justification: see S. Kadish, 'Methodology and Criteria in Due Process Adjudication: A Survey Criticism' (1957) *Yale LJ* 319. Art. 6 of the European Convention on Human Rights also contains specific procedural requirements.

naturally slow, incremental, and piecemeal. The approach taken by the various legal authorities is first to identify the standards of fair treatment and then to mould the procedural rules accordingly. So, to conclude, we should be careful to draw the right inferences from the fact that legal procedures often become settled rules of law. Despite occasional judicial claims that such rules flow directly from the fountains of justice, in reality they result from good practical reasons for having settled procedural rules. The ultimate justification for such rules is not that they are inherently good or fair, but that they are effective means of upholding the standards of fair treatment relevant to the process.

2.2.2 A Fuller Account of the Relationship

Having seen that the contingent nature of procedures is compatible with settled legal rules of procedure, we can now consider more fully the relationship between procedures and fair treatment. While the core of the relationship is that procedures are the means for upholding standards of fair treatment, a number of other matters need to be considered to produce a fuller account of what is a complex relationship. The fuller account helps us to understand how procedures are instrumental to standards of fair treatment, while at the same time appearing to be self-contained and detached from them. It also helps in showing the influences which shape procedures and why certain procedures appear to be necessary in any context of decision-making. Four factors are especially significant: first, the very process of applying legal standards; secondly, the need to have confidence in procedures; thirdly, the advantages of settled legal procedures; and fourthly, how the principle of respect for persons gives a special focus to legal and administrative processes. In showing how these matters influence procedures, I shall concentrate on processes involving the application of standards and the exercise of discretion.

The first is to explain more fully the process of decision-making in social contexts. We may begin by drawing a contrast between two images. One is the administrator mechanically and bloodlessly applying clear and certain rules to certain facts. This image reflects the methods of science and logic and has its uses as an ideal type of one kind of decision-making;[16] it is sometimes represented as the model of bureaucratic administration.[17] The other image is of decision-making as an unruly social process by which

[16] Max Weber's notion of formal legal authority has been widely used to explain the nature of the modern legal process: see M. Weber, *Economy and Society* (G. Roth and C. Wittich (eds.), UCLA, Berkeley, Cal., 1978). For historical explanation of this idea, see Z. Baumann, *Modernity and the Holocaust* (Polity Press, London, 1989).

[17] J. Mashaw, *Due Process in the Administrative State* (Yale, Newhaven, Conn., 1985), 224–32 and M. Bayles, *Procedural Justice* (Kluwer, London, 1990), 170–2. This issue is discussed further in sections 8.2.3 and 8.2.4.

human agents try to decide on a course of action on the basis of evidence and facts, norms and standards, values and beliefs. This second image reflects the methods of practical judgment within a framework of standards, where the question is what is the best thing to do or what decision is most reasonable and justifiable, where judgments are made under conditions of uncertainty, complexity, and incommensurability. The second image is a more realistic reflection of legal and administrative processes and points the way to procedures, for despite the mechanical connotations that the notion of administration may have, in practice the task is to apply standards which vary in certainty and stability to complex social circumstances. The procedures best suited for that process should encourage inquiry, argument, and deliberation;[18] they should reflect the fact that different ways of viewing an issue are usually available, that interpreting evidence and evaluating facts are open processes, and that knowledge of facts and circumstances is bound to be imperfect. Procedures should recognize the contingency of any one point of view, they should allow for sceptical scrutiny of evidence and material, and they should encourage reasoned judgment. Here is to be found the germ of an argumentative or adversarial procedure, not in the battle-line sense of English law, but in the sense that a sound judgment is likely to be one forged from argument and counter-argument.

The second factor to note is that confidence in a process, confidence that the law has been properly applied or a discretion reasonably exercised, depends to a significant degree on confidence in the procedures as means to those outcomes. In some cases, we know what the outcome should be but cannot be sure whether it has been reached; in others, where discretion is prominent and it makes more sense to think of a good or best outcome rather than a right outcome, we still cannot be sure that, all things considered, the best outcome has resulted. We tend to look, therefore, at the procedures and ask whether they are the sort which, as a matter of our experience of the world, are likely to lead to the right or best outcomes. Procedures are still instrumental to outcomes, but confidence in the outcome is engendered by confidence in the procedures. The notion of confidence is fundamental since legal processes are social processes where the object is to reach a sound practical judgment about the matter in issue; a sound practical judgment for its part is one which can be explained and which can be seen to be rational and reasonable, so that at the end we have confidence in it. That is the final test: can a reasonable person, entering into the circumstances, be confident of the result; not certain but confident. Confidence is gained not only from knowing the result is correct or the best available; it is gained to a large degree by examining the procedures which have led to it. Only then can we see whether, according to common sense

[18] For a fuller account of this idea of an argumentative process, see S. Hampshire, *Innocence and Experience* (Blackwell, Oxford, 1990).

and experience, the procedures followed are the kinds which normally lead to satisfactory outcomes. The test is neither absolute nor relentlessly logical; it depends on a tutored judgment about the world, about the process of practical reasoning, and about when a practical judgment is a sound one. Sometimes we may be painfully aware that our confidence has been misplaced and mistaken outcomes have resulted; procedures can then be changed to remedy the defects for the future. Which procedures are the best and most reliable is a matter of trial and error, so that confidence in any specific case is based on confidence in the procedures in their general application.

The public nature of legal processes adds another element to the notion of confidence. And just as legal processes have a public element, so does fair treatment. The importance of the public element can be seen by contrasting a private moral judgment and a public legal judgment. Let us assume both are judgments about X's behaviour in not supporting his family. I might conclude privately that X is morally culpable, but nothing follows from my judgment; it is private and X need never know about it.[19] Before a court or other official body, the issue is very different; now it carries consequences for X and has a public aspect. It is also important that the practical judgment about X should demonstrably be based on sound foundations, for the judgment, and any consequential treatment of X, has to be justified according to publicly stated criteria. The public element again points to the importance of certain kinds of procedures as ways of showing that the judgment is one in which we can be confident. The trial of Billy Budd, in Melville's story of the same name, is a good illustration. Billy Budd was a sailor tried by a drum-head court for the mutinous killing of an officer. The judgment that Budd killed the man was factually correct, and, in strict law, it may have been a mutinous act warranting capital punishment. Even so, the process was tainted and failed to win the confidence of the other officers and sailors on board. The drum-head court, which meant immediate trial by three officers on board ship, was an unusual procedure to be used only in extreme situations; it was hastily convened and hurriedly conducted; the captain was sole witness to the events, yet lectured the officers constituting the court on the importance of doing their duty to quell rebellion. Most important of all, Budd was struck by an inability to speak under stress, and so was unable and perhaps unwilling to put forward his own defence, or to reveal facts and circumstances about the way he had been persecuted by the dead man. The procedures were tainted and seen to be tainted, so that confidence in the outcome was lacking. As Billy Budd was being put to death, a sense of deep injustice settled over the ship and long haunted it.

[19] Contrast A. R. Duff, who argues that moral judgments provide essential guidance in understanding the criminal trial: *Trials and Punishments* (Cambridge University Press, Cambridge, 1986), ch. 2.

The need for confidence in procedures as a condition of confidence in the result has practical consequences.[20] Given the fallibility of procedures and the paucity of our knowledge about the relationship between procedures and outcomes, the need for confidence is likely to point to great caution in designing procedures. Take the hearing principle. It is important that a person should have the opportunity of being heard, of telling his side of the story, of being free to present evidence and argument. Quite apart from any non-outcome values which might be served by a hearing, we may assume that a hearing contributes to a more accurate finding of facts and a better application of the law. Few would challenge that assumption, but when examined closely, it is full of uncertainties: how far does a hearing enhance the result; does it depend on the issue in question; would the information be better obtained from other sources? But since we do not know the answers to these questions, it is wise to be cautious in designing procedures; a hearing might improve the outcome, and since nothing is lost (beyond increased marginal costs) even if it does not, then the case for a presumption in favour of a hearing is persuasive. In general, confidence is best gained by adopting more demanding and expansive procedures rather than less; in other words, confidence in the result is bolstered by employing procedures which reduce as far as possible the risks of error. It is natural for these reasons to concentrate on developing procedures which, from our experience of social life and the unavoidable uncertainties inherent in it, seem good and effective, without trying to match them too precisely to the process in issue. Considerations of cost and delay must be taken into account, but that is a matter to be considered in the next chapter.

The third matter affecting the form of procedures is the relationship between the person affected by a process and the community in general. The very fact that legal processes are about how a person should be treated by the agencies of the community has implications for procedures: the situation and circumstances of that person are the subject of enquiry and judgment; it is the person's case that must be enquired into, his or her actions that need to be examined, his or her fate that must be decided. This gives a further focus to the process: it adds a set of data to consider, but being a decision about how a person is to be treated, it adds more. For the duty of respect requires that attention be paid to the person's case, that such level of enquiry and consideration should be made as is compatible with the seriousness of the interests at stake and the gravity of the consequences for them, and that the final judgment should take proper account of those factors. Such a decision has a special quality because it is about how a person is to be treated, where misjudgment is not simply a social cost, but is a doing down, a

[20] For a useful case study of the notion of confidence in relation to the law of evidence, see A. A. S. Zuckerman, 'Public Interest Immunity—A Matter of Prime Judicial Responsibility (1994) 57 *MLR* 703.

violation of the collective obligation to that person, an act of injustice. The fact that the treatment of a person is in issue is itself an element of relevance and significance, independent of and in addition to whatever else may be relevant and significant.[21] The image of administration as a matter of bureaucratic engineering misses that core of consideration which flows from the personal factor, from the minimum regard that should be paid to each person. Expressed as rights, the claim to consideration is a component of the general right to have one's case settled in accordance with the law; it is a claim to be considered where the measure of the claim is proportionate to the rights and interests at stake. The claim to consideration is in a sense implicit in the logic of the principle that cases ought to be decided according to authoritative standards; but since the idea of deciding according to law is itself open to different points of emphasis and focus, the claim to consideration draws attention to one point of focus which should not be neglected.[22]

The claim to consideration, as a way of drawing attention to the personal factor in administrative processes, can create problems. The centrality of the personal factor to the merits of a case naturally varies: in the criminal trial its place is central, for here the acts and intentions of the accused are directly in issue, while in the routine issue of a licence it is marginal. The discretionary decision, falling somewhere between the two, causes the greatest problems. Take the prisoner seeking parole: his personal situation is highly relevant, but wider matters of policy should also be considered. But how these incommensurable factors are assessed is a problem at the heart of discretion, the problem being that the very notion of deciding on the merits is problematical, since what counts as the merits can be taken in different ways. *South Australia* v. *O'Shea* is an example.[23] The majority of the Australian High Court thought parole decisions to be mere matters of policy, while the minority, on the contrary, gave the personal factor greater significance. The minority of judges held that the policy at least had to be individualized for each case, and that meant following a process of evidence and argument from which a practical judgment could be drawn; it also meant a process in which the prisoner was involved. The two views represent contrasting understandings of the significance of the personal factor, of the relationship between it and matters of policy. How matters like these are perceived is itself an issue of social construction, of how administrators view different activities, different interests, and different processes. Within a settled legal system a rough ordering normally emerges; we know, for instance, that we must enquire deeply into alleged criminal acts, while the dispensing of

[21] A link can be made between the idea of focusing on a person's case and the concept of adjudication: see sections 8.2 and 8.3.

[22] See the further analysis in section 3.3 and D. J. Galligan, 'Rights, Discretion, and Procedure' in C. Sampford and D. J. Galligan (eds.), *Law, Rights, and the Welfare State* (Croom Helm, London, 1986).

[23] (1987) 73 ALR 1.

licences to drive a motor car may justifiably be a virtually mechanical process. Between the two are many intermediate positions and, as the case of policy-based discretion shows, the best way of characterizing particular cases may be contested.

The need to focus on the situation of the person subject to a decision has practical consequences for procedures. The involvement of the person, the chance to give his account of the matters in issue, is not just a convenient way of obtaining information but often will be a practical necessity. The more deeply the enquiry ventures into personal history and events, the stronger the imperative that the person whose life is under scrutiny be involved. Here, I suggest, is the kernel of the idea that a person should be heard in his defence against a charge or before a decision is made to impose a burden or deny a benefit: the hearing is not just a token of respect which follows from letting the person have a say; it may be that, but it is more. Considering the relationship between the person and the facts in issue, the very truth and integrity of the enquiry are threatened unless he is allowed to contribute.[24] The sense of respect at stake goes well beyond that which might be gained by simply having his say; it is the deeper sense of respect inherent in accepting that an accurate and reliable judgment must be made and yet cannot be made without the person's involvement. For the community to act on a legal judgment about one of its members, knowing or reasonably suspecting it to be flawed, is a violation of rights of great gravity. This idea can be connected to the need for confidence in procedures, since failure to involve the party severely undermines confidence in the outcome. In this very practical way, a good case can be made for the hearing principle; the case is still instrumental and contingent, instrumental in that the point of the hearing is a reliable outcome, contingent in that the degree and level of involvement are dependent on the nature of the issue and of the personal interests in question.

The fourth and final matter affecting the relationship between the contingent nature of procedures and fair treatment may be shown by posing the question: is the contingent and instrumental nature of procedure incompatible with general rules of procedure? We noticed earlier that legal procedures are often expressed as legal rules and that breach of the rules may have serious consequences for the validity of the process. The hearing rule, for example, is well settled in many areas of law and breach of it may lead to the whole process being invalidated. This may create a paradox since, in a particular case, the outcome may be reliable without a hearing. Now the discussion in this section has shown a number of reasons for having general rules and doctrines of procedure, for creating intermediate

[24] This is not to say that the person should be forced to contribute to the process; there may be good reasons of civil rights for allowing refusal. The task of reaching a reliable judgment is then more difficult.

procedural standards, not least because attempts to judge which procedures are needed to produce an accurate outcome in a particular case will often be inconclusive. Moreover, the advantages of having settled procedures are considerable, since the certainty and predictability they create in turn may foster the gains in economy which result from having clear and settled ways of doing things. Bentham's plea for a system of free proof according to which the judge would decide what evidence to admit in each case has never been fully accepted, although in many forms of administrative bodies the modern tendency is to allow procedural informality and a freedom of proof which comes close to Bentham's proposals. If to the advantages of free proof are added the disadvantage of general rules in requiring on occasions that unnecessary procedures be followed, then it is difficult to draw any firm conclusions about the right balance of procedural rules compared with a free approach in each case. These matters are considered again in relation to more specific legal issues, but for the present we may conclude that the debate as to the best balance of rules and discretion in relation to procedures has all the hallmarks of that same debate in other contexts. If we keep clear the image of procedures as intermediate steps towards the proper application of standards of fair treatment, then it should be no surprise to find that the best way of meeting that end is a practical matter which might be achieved in various ways, according to various permutations of rules and discretion. The clear advantages of settled rules might sometimes be outweighed by other matters.

After this lengthy discussion, it may be helpful to summarize the main claims. The first is that, normally, procedures are instrumental to and contingent upon ensuring that a person is treated according to authoritative standards of fair treatment. In some cases, procedures may themselves be the expression of important values. Implicit in this claim is the further idea that procedures are neither good nor fair nor justifiable in themselves. The second claim is that in the practical design of procedures several factors come into play which influence that process and make it more complex than the contingent and instrumental nature of procedures would suggest. The reasons are partly practical, partly epistemological, and partly concerned with the authority and legitimacy which flows from having confidence in the procedures and outcomes of legal processes. The third claim is that, while those ends may best be served by general procedural rules, the precise mix of general rules on the one hand and individualized judgments made in specific contexts on the other hand depends very much on practical factors relevant in each context.

For these reasons, it would be hard to sustain the claim that certain procedures are always necessary in providing the right outcomes; hearing the parties, for instance, would normally be an important element in reaching the right result, since the parties are likely to have information which would not otherwise be available and their version of events is important in forming an accurate account of the situation. But this would not support the strong claim that a hearing is always necessary; whereas such a claim would be empirically insupportable, a more moderate claim might be sustained. The claim would be that it is rational and defensible to adopt certain procedures on the ground that they will normally contribute to better outcomes; the rules requiring impartial decision-makers, to take another example, could be justified on the ground that bias or personal interest creates a risk that extraneous matters will be taken into account and influence the outcome. The difficulty of detecting the influence of such matters is so great that a strict general rule is justified; that risk might even justify a further rule to the effect that actual partiality need not be proved, but that it is enough to bring evidence of a risk of partiality.

2.2.3 Justice Seen to be Done

A maxim often quoted by lawyers is that justice should not only be done, but should be seen to be done. At first sight the idea seems strange and prompts one to ask if justice is done why does it matter whether or not it is seen to be done. Conversely, the appearance of justice has no value in itself if the outcome was a miscarriage of justice. The maxim only applies when the outcome is just, but why do appearances matter if the reality is that justice has been done. The answer is to be found in the practical nature of procedures and in the idea that we must have confidence in them. As the earlier discussion shows, having confidence in procedures depends not on our being sure that they lead in each case to the right outcomes, since such knowledge will rarely be available to us; confidence depends instead on the procedures being of a kind which we have good reason to believe will produce the right results. The value is not in the procedures themselves but in their contribution to the right or best outcomes. Confidence is then a practical standard for deciding whether any set of procedures can be relied on in bringing about that result. But since we are unavoidably labouring under conditions of imperfect knowledge, confidence will sometimes turn out to be misplaced and the procedures should be adjusted accordingly.

The basis of the idea that justice should be seen to be done is now apparent: it suggests that where procedures are laid down, and are tried and tested sufficiently to win our confidence, then compliance with those procedures should be insisted upon. Compliance should be insisted on because it is the only practical guide we have for knowing whether the right or best outcome has been reached and justice actually done. The corollary is that if the procedures followed do engender confidence, then we can be reasonably confident that the right or best outcome has been reached; such confidence, however, is contingent and may on occasions be shown to be misplaced.

This explanation of the maxim can be illustrated with two examples, the hearing principle and principle against bias. Reliance is often placed on a procedural rule that a person should be heard before a decision is made, the basis for the rule being that a hearing is normally an important step in reaching the right outcome, so that the inclusion of such a rule is a necessary step in gaining our confidence. The failure to provide a hearing will undermine our confidence and will normally be an adequate reason for considering the whole process to be tainted. Of course we are unlikely to know whether the failure to hear really did affect the outcome in that case. Generally, however, it will be enough in order to have the process overturned to show that there has been a failure in the appearance of justice. Legal systems may differ in their approach to such matters, with some regarding the breach of such a procedural rule as sufficient to taint the whole process, others allowing for that breach to be compensated for by other procedures. The explanation in the latter case is that, while the breach of procedures might threaten our confidence in the process, other factors might be enough to remove the threat. Bias fits the same pattern, since bias in the decision-maker is likely to cause error or distortion in the outcome. It does not necessarily do so, but considering how hard it would be to detect, confidence demands procedures which depend on proving not actual bias but merely the appearance or suspicion of it. The failure to comply with such procedures would create not only an appearance of justice not being done, but a deep suspicion of justice not actually being done.

2.2.4 Due Process

As the title of this book suggests, due process and procedural fairness go together, but it is not always clear whether they mean the same thing or what the differences between them are. The notion of due process has become associated with certain doctrines, both substantive and procedural, arising under the American constitution, while procedural fairness is more at home in the British context, although even here the term commonly used until recently was natural justice. Natural justice refers to the specific doctrines relating to hearing and bias, while procedural fairness is the more general term, referring to a dynamic principle on the basis of which various procedural doctrines may be based. Although due process now has American connotations, its origins are in the early common law. In its procedural aspects, the doctrine represents a particular interpretation of and a set of doctrines about procedural fairness. Those doctrines are recognizable as particular interpretations of a general principle of procedural fairness, but differ in a number of respects from British doctrines of natural justice and procedural fairness. An account of the American doctrine is given in Chapter 6. The concept of due process has its origins in the early common law, but then usage changed and the term was displaced by the notion of natural justice. Usage is again beginning to change and it is not now so unusual in the British context for reference to be made to ideas of due process. People talk of the due process aspects of criminal justice or the due process side of administrative decisions, while the recent Royal Commission on Criminal Justice has been criticized for not paying enough attention to due process considerations.

Each of the terms due process, natural justice, and procedural fairness can be used in one or other of two senses. In one sense, the terms make reference to specific legal doctrines about procedures within one jurisdiction or another. When we say in English law that all public authorities are now subject to the principles of procedural fairness, reference is being made to a set of procedural doctrines, largely created by the courts, which express fundamental principles about the fair treatment of persons and the procedures needed to give effect to fair treatment. When American lawyers talk about procedural due process they are doing something very similar, except that the primary source of their procedural doctrines is the constitution with its general provisions requiring due process of law whenever life, liberty, or property is in issue, and its more specific doctrines such as the right to a trial by jury and to counsel. Parallels can be drawn with the doctrines of due process and procedural fairness emerging in European law and under the European Convention on Human Rights.

In a second sense, the terms due process, natural justice, and procedural fairness refer not to the legal rules of procedures but to the values which justify those rules. What are then being referred to are the outcome and non-outcome values which apply in legal processes. Some procedural rules when traced to their origins will be seen to be directed at achieving good and accurate outcomes at the first tier, while other procedural rules will draw their final authority from values located within other tiers. Some procedural rules will also be connected to intermediate values, such as the presumption of innocence, the right to silence, to a jury trial, and to counsel. The law is full of intermediate values like these which may come to be seen as free-standing and important in themselves; that may be so, but if we ask why these values are important and try to unearth a sound justification for them, it will normally become clear that they are intermediate stages in realizing one or other set of more basic values. Some intermediate values, the right to silence for example, may be complex, drawing part of their justification as instruments to accurate outcomes and part from other values such as privacy.[25] However, the point of interest is that notions of due process or procedural fairness in their second and looser sense refer to a cluster of such

[25] See further D. J. Galligan, 'The Right to Silence Reconsidered' (1988) *Current Legal Problems* 69.

primary and intermediate values, where precisely which ones are included may be a movable matter.

2.2.5 The Dignitarian Challenge

In writing about procedural fairness, we often encounter the idea that the guiding principle in designing and evaluating procedures is the dignity of the person. Now any idea which starts with a concept as fundamental, but at the same time as abstract, as human dignity is liable to suffer from misunderstanding and misinterpretation. Theories of procedural fairness are no exception, with the result that different interpretations of the dignitarian idea have been put forward, some being rather less persuasive than others. The idea has its provenance in ancient, common law notions of substantive due process, but in its modern form owes much to American constitutional theorists writing about the due process clauses of the Constitution.[26] However, the dignitarian approach is not confined to the problems peculiar to American due process, but is meant to be the basis for a general theory of procedural fairness. The approach has now been adopted by writers outside America, so that it is commonplace to find references to the dignitarian approach included in any account of procedural fairness. Works on administrative law frequently refer to this approach;[27] it appears as an alternative explanation of procedural fairness in a recent work on dismissal from employment,[28] and it is prominent in a study of procedural fairness in prisons and mental institutions.[29]

Since the dignitarian approach is clearly to be taken seriously, let us begin by being clear about what it means. An immediate peculiarity of the approach is that it claims a special connection with the dignity of the person, and yet any theory of procedural fairness is ultimately linked to that notion. Fair procedures are means to fair treatment and fair treatment is important only because each person is recognized as a moral agent who is entitled to be treated with dignity and respect. The relationship between dignity and respect, on the one hand, and procedural fairness, on the other, is not contingent or optional in the sense that some basis other than dignity and respect could be found for fair treatment. On the contrary, the relationship is conceptual, so that if we were to abandon our concern to treat people with dignity and respect, we would also abandon our concern for procedural

[26] The literature is extensive, but amongst the leading exponents of the dignitarian theory are: J. Mashaw, *Due Process in the Administrative State*, n. 17 above; R. Summers, 'Evaluating and Improving Legal Procedure: A Plea for Process Values' (1974) 60 *Cornell L Rev*. and F. Michaelman, 'Formal and Associational Aims in Procedural Due Process' in Pennock and Chapman, *Due Process* , 1.

[27] See e.g. P. P. Craig, *Public Law and Democracy* (Clarendon Press, Oxford, 1990), 160 ff.

[28] H. Collins, *Unfairness in Dismissal* (Clarendon Press, Oxford, 1992).

[29] G. Richardson, *Law, Process and Custody* (Weidenfeld and Nicholson, London, 1993).

fairness. In order, then, to avoid quixotic jousting with non-existent enemies, we must distinguish not between a dignitarian approach and something else, but between different versions of the dignitarian approach itself. When seen in this light, much of the sting is drawn from the dignitarian challenge—to borrow an expression. The more modest claim must then be that some versions of the relationship between procedural fairness and dignity are better than others. This has the good effect of forcing us to be clear about what precisely that relationship is. In being so forced, I shall first explain the nature of the relationship as expressed in the account of procedural fairness in this Chapter; I shall then consider whether that account would be improved by a fuller concern for the dignity of the person.

In the account I have put forward, the dignity of the person is respected in the following way. According to the relationship between the community and each of its members, a number of implicit understandings and undertakings dictate how each should behave towards the other. Here we are especially concerned with those undertakings on the part of the community towards its members; they can perhaps be grouped into three. One set of undertakings relates to the political process and in particular to how laws should be made. The substance of the undertaking is that society will be governed democratically and will respect certain fundamental rights and principles of just treatment. The second undertaking is that once laws are made each person will be dealt with in accordance with them, using laws here not only to mean statutory provisions, but to include the full range of authoritative legal standards. Laws here relate to outcomes, to how each case should ultimately be disposed of. The third undertaking from the community to each citizen is that certain other important values will be respected in legal processes, values that is which are separate from first tier outcome values.

A society which treats its members in accordance with these three sets of undertakings treats each of them with dignity and respect. It is to be expected that in practice each set of undertakings will be honoured to varying degrees: the democratic process will not always work well; laws might be made which are unjust; and precisely what authoritative standards apply within any given legal context may be the subject of genuine dispute. None the less, a society which tries to make reasonable laws, which provides resources, institutions, and personnel to make sure that each person is dealt with properly according to its laws, and which respects such non-outcome values, is a society which treats its members with dignity and respect. Implicit in that commitment to respect its members is a commitment to the procedures necessary to do so. This approach is both powerful and practical. Its power lies in showing how any situation can be analysed in order to identify the terms of fair treatment and, therefore, the basis of respect. Its practical nature consists in recognizing that procedures are costly devices and need to be rooted in objects and values which can be identified and justified. Procedures in the air, procedures good in themselves, and procedures edged with mystery are eliminated. It is also a feature of this approach that statements of grand and abstract principles can be avoided. Nevertheless, the approach may be linked to more fundamental ideas of a foundational right to be treated with dignity and respect, or to a foundational right to fundamental fairness, or to a basic principle of non-arbitrariness.[30]

Against the background of the relationship between dignity and procedural fairness, we must examine the challenge thrown down by the exponents of an alternative account. The unifying idea appears to be that legal procedures are based on a notion of the dignity of the person in a much more direct way than in the account I have given. This general idea can be broken down into several more specific points. One of them amounts to an attack on the importance of accuracy of outcome, on the importance, that is, of deciding cases in accordance with the authoritative standards which derive from first tier values. According to one proponent of the dignitarian challenge, there is more to procedures than the rationality of substantive results. J. Mashaw, who expounds such a view, goes on to say:

> reasonably accurate processes of decision-making may be instrumentally essential to individual security; but these traditional legal forms and intermediate values seem in the end only means for approaching and supporting some more fundamental conception of due process. They do not define the core ideal.[31]

The core ideal proves difficult to pin down, but it seems to be that accurate decision-making is a second-order, instrumental value serving the fundamental, first-order values of privacy, equality, and comprehensibility.[32] The accurate application of law is then a 'prudential or derivative' value serving first-order values.[33]

This account leaves itself open to two critical comments. In the first place, to explain accuracy as a prudential means to privacy, equality, and comprehensibility misses out the connection between accuracy and fair treatment. To treat a person in accordance with authoritative legal standards is to uphold legitimate normative expectations and, therefore, is itself an element of fair treatment. It is not the only element, nor is it absolute, but it is an element which cannot be collapsed into other values like privacy or equality.[34] The second comment is that, quite apart from which explanation of the values served by accuracy is the best explanation, it is difficult to think of a theory of procedures which considers accuracy as somehow a self-contained

[30] See M. P. Golding, 'Comment on Mashaw: Process and Psychology' (1987) 39 *Florida L Rev.* 445.

[31] Mashaw, *Due Process in the Administrative State*, n. 17 above, 158.

[32] Elsewhere first-order values are said to be values 'such as autonomy, self-respect, or equality': ibid. 162.

[33] Ibid. 204.

[34] These values might have an important role in the formation of legal standards as discussed in section 1.3.3.

good in itself. On any account, in order to have any significance, the accurate application of the law has to be interpreted within some normative framework; when seen within such a framework, the role of accuracy in securing respect for rights and, therefore, for the person becomes readily apparent. To miss that dimension of accuracy is to miss its main point. Perhaps the hidden target of the attack on accuracy is Bentham, for Bentham did emphasize that rectitude was the primary goal of legal decisions. If Bentham is the target, then the attack has misfired: for when Bentham extolled the virtue of rectitude he was doing so from the point of view of general utility, that is to say, he was looking at the overall social good, not the fair treatment of individual persons.[35] What best serves the common good and how individuals should be treated are different issues occurring in different realms of discourse.

At a more general level, there is something dubious about an argument for procedural fairness which fails to grasp the importance of upholding the rights and expectations created by law. Accuracy, after all, is just another way of saying that a person's rights and other normative expectations created by law should be respected; to respect them is to respect the right-holder. Accuracy may also 'approach and support' other values, but by upholding rights and normative expectations, it certainly respects persons and the dignity of personhood; but when properly understood, accurate decisions are not a step towards or a signpost indicating or a plank supporting respect for persons; accurate decisions themselves constitute an important element of fair treatment, which in turn constitutes an important element of respect for persons. Conversely, the accurate and proper application of the law is not an optional extra, a mere prudential concern; it is an essential requirement of fair treatment. If there is doubt about that, we might try convincing the prisoner mistakenly convicted of a serious crime, or the welfare claimant wrongly denied a benefit, that the mistake was merely prudential. Now of course fair treatment has more to it than being dealt with properly according to law, but to have one's rights upheld under law is a vital and central element of fair treatment, and any theory of due process or procedural fairness which pushes it to the margins as relatively insignificant, as just a matter of prudence, has gone seriously wrong.

2.2.6 Process Values

A second aspect of the dignitarian challenge takes a different tack. Here the emphasis is on process values and the argument is that process values are important in legal processes in their own right and independently of

[35] Bentham was also concerned with fair treatment but in an ancillary and problematical way: see section 1. 1. 3.

outcomes.[36] Process values are at the heart of the dignitarian challenge and have been defined in this way: 'process values refer to standards of value by which we judge a legal process to be good as a process, apart from any good result efficacy it may have'.[37] Now there is nothing new in the idea that legal processes occur in a context of values about how people should be treated, and that some of those values are worthwhile for reasons independent of their relationship to outcomes. We encountered the idea in Chapter 1 in explaining the tiers of values in legal contexts and the role of non-outcome values within them. The term non-outcome values seems preferable to process values, but nothing of substance hangs on the names and we should accept, as any defensible theory of procedural fairness must accept, that non-outcome values have a significant place in law.

If non-outcome values are accepted as an important part of any account of fair treatment and fair procedures (as they are in the account I have given), then the point of the dignitarian challenge must be some lesser claim. Perhaps the concern is that some important non-outcome values are neglected. Here we need to distinguish between those non-outcome values recognized in legal processes and those which are not, but ought to be. The first can usually be identified by studying the relevant statutes, court decisions, and administrative practices. Whether there is a second set of non-outcome or process values which should be recognized in law is more arguable; views differ and no authoritative yardstick exists to decide between them. The blatant neglect of a value which is widely accepted in the community at large would be inexcusable; typically, however, the argument is about what are the values of the community at large and how they should be translated into practical legal standards. The first takes us deep into the political morality of a society, while the second attests to the inevitable difficulties of reading abstract values into practical standards. Dignitary theorists are inclined to produce lists of values which they would like to see adopted, or more fully adopted, in legal processes: autonomy, privacy, and comprehensibility are bound to be included, with support from a range of other contenders—participatory governance, fraternity, process legitimacy, process peacefulness, humaneness, and procedural legality.[38] The meaning and merits of each of these values need not be examined now, it being enough to note that some disagreement is to be expected about which non-outcome values apply and what they mean. But disagreement about which values ought to apply to legal processes, about what exactly are the standards of fair treatment in a given context, raise practical issues about the design of legal institutions, not theoretical disagreement about the place of non-outcome values.

[36] See Mashaw, *Due Process in the Administrative State*, n. 17 above, 158–60.

[37] Summers, 'Evaluating and Improving Legal Procedure: A Plea for Process Values', n. 26 above, 3.

[38] Ibid. 194–201; F. Michaelman, 'Formal and Associational Aims' in Pennock and Chapman, *Due Process*, n. 26 above.

There is, however, a strand of the dignitarian challenge which makes a stronger claim. It advances the view that a commitment to respect persons carries with it a commitment to certain values which express or directly serve respect and which have direct consequences for procedures. The values in question are being heard (which is sometimes extended to a general principle of participation), lack of bias, and the giving of reasons. The idea is that any role these values have as means to accurate decision-making is incidental, since their real and fundamental role is to express respect for persons in a direct and unmediated manner.[39] The hearing principle is a good example. In a well-known passage, L. Tribe puts the claim for it this way: 'those rights to interchange express the elementary idea that to be a person, rather than a thing, is at least to be consulted about what is to be done with one'.[40] R. A. Duff takes the argument further and gives a vigorous defence of the hearing principle in the criminal trial as being of value independently of its contribution to outcomes.[41] The right to be heard, he writes, 'is the right to respond to charges which are laid against her; and that right is integral to the idea of a criminal trial as a process which calls a defendant to answer to her actions'.[42] There is more than a hint in these claims that the advancement of dignitary values has become the main object of legal processes. Legal processes serve as a forum for discerning the 'values inherent in and intrinsic to our common humanity'; legal processes should be 'independently or directly supporting the citizens' sense of self-worth' and 'we all feel that legal process matters to us irrespective of result'. Although these remarks could be interpreted in several ways, they seem to signal a shift in our understanding of what legal processes are about; instead of legal processes being purposive to the achievement of certain goals through means which are fair to those affected, they become an opportunity to develop dignitary values, with social goals having a minor role. The object of developing dignitary values overshadows the idea that legal processes have definite purposes; substance has given way to process and the distinct social purposes of legal processes have dropped away.

Putting aside that last point for the moment, the main claim being made is that respect for persons generates certain values and that those values justify certain procedures without reference to or reliance upon outcomes. The claim is uncontroversial to the extent that it draws attention to the role of values which are not dependent on outcomes. What is controversial is the idea that this particular value, namely, respect for persons, does in fact generate and justify, directly and without reference to outcomes, certain

[39] Some research by social psychologists has revealed that people's perception of procedural fairness is overwhelmingly based on the importance of procedural values in their own right: T. Tyler, *Why People Obey the Law* (Yale, Newhaven, Conn., 1990). But see my discussion in section 2.3.2.

[40] L. Tribe, *American Constitutional Law* (2nd edn., West, New York, 1988) 503.

[41] Duff, n. 19 above.

[42] Ibid. 118.

standards and procedures. It is controversial because the link between respect for persons and procedures, such as being heard, is assumed to be self-evident; or if it is not self-evident, no reasoned argument is given for it. Many join in the refrain that respect for the person requires certain procedures, but no one attempts to show why. The reason for the silence may be that it is rather difficult to make a case, grounded in sound political theory, for certain procedures as direct requirements of respect for persons. My present purpose, however, is not to consider whether a good case can be made; that is done elsewhere in this book.[43] The general point to be made here is simply that much of the force of the dignitarian challenge rests on showing that there is a direct and compelling relationship between respect for persons and certain procedures. Unless the case for that relationship is established, and the burden of proof must be on its proponents, we have good reasons for remaining sceptical.

On close inspection, then, the dignitarian challenge does not have quite the sting originally suggested. In so far as it asserts the role of non-outcome values in legal processes, it is uncontroversial, since it would be hard to think of a theory of procedural fairness which did not allow for them; even Bentham conceded that rectitude might sometimes be limited by other values. In so far as the dignitarians think too much emphasis is put on procedures as means to outcomes, it may be because they fail to understand that treating a person in accordance with the standards set by law is an important aspect of treating him with respect. And, finally, while there is no difficulty in fitting the dignitarians within the account of procedural fairness offered here, a salutary lesson has been learnt that non-outcome values should be closely scrutinized to see that they really do warrant a place in legal processes and justify the procedures supporting them. At the same time, when stripped of its more outlandish elements, the dignitarian approach serves as a timely reminder that non-outcome values should not be overlooked. There may have been a time when an over-emphasis on the role of procedures as instrumental to outcomes led to neglect of a proper appreciation of non-outcome values.

However, it is possible that something deeper is at stake, that the dignitarian approach rests on a distinct vision of the very nature of legal processes. In concluding this discussion, it may be of interest to contrast two alternative visions. The basic premise of the first is that the law constitutes standards of fair treatment and that the main task of procedures is to ensure that people are dealt with according to those standards. Exactly what the standards are may be a difficult issue, but the claim is that within any context of legal decisions a core of standards, both outcome and non-outcome based, exists upon which rights and normative expectations are based. The role of

[43] On participation and the hearing principle, see Ch. 4; on bias, see section 14.3 and on reason-giving, see section 14.2.

procedures is to uphold those rights. The alternative vision begins with a different premise. The very language used provides the clue: legal processes serve as a forum for discerning 'the values inherent in and intrinsic to our common humanity';[44] they should be 'independently or directly supporting the citizens' sense of self-worth';[45] and 'we feel that legal process matters to us irrespective of result'.[46] The substance of the vision begins to unfold: legal processes are concerned directly with upholding certain basic values—dignity, autonomy, integrity, and so on. Positive legal standards may reflect those values, but they will not necessarily, and if they do not, they are defeasible in favour of the basic values. Between these two visions of legal process a number of intermediate positions can be staked-out, each varying according to how we view the relationship between basic dignitarian values and the positive legal order. One intermediate position would be to place emphasis on upholding legal standards, but supplementing those standards with direct appeal to basic values. F. Michaelman puts forward such an approach: positive legal rights should be upheld, but demands for revelation and participation, which mean being given reasons and having a part in the process, should supplement those rights.[47] The view I have put forward in this Chapter is another variation: legal standards are standards of fair treatment, which are based on tiers of values; the primary object of legal processes is to give effect to those values and standards according to their place within a legal system and not to make direct and unmediated reference to a host of other abstract values. Other variations around those intermediate positions are possible, so that the view one finally takes will be based on the view one holds on much deeper issues about the very nature of legal authority and the relationship between legal authority and deeper moral values.

2.2.7 Procedural Fairness in Other Forms of Process

In the discussion of fair treatment and procedural fairness, I have concentrated on forms of process based on applying authoritative standards and exercising discretion. The same general approach can be applied to each of the other forms of process and can be shortly expressed as a two-stage process: first, to identify the tiers of values and the standards of fair treatment generated; and secondly, to design the procedures needed to apply the standards in practical decisions. I shall not attempt here to provide a detailed analysis of other forms of process, although the general foundation of values and standards with respect to each has already been explained.

[44] Mashaw, *Due Process in the Administrative State*, n. 17 above, 162.
[45] Ibid. 198.
[46] Ibid. 162.
[47] F. Michaelman, 'Formal and Associational Aims' in Pennock and Chapman, *Due Process*, n. 18 above. A useful accompanying essay is T. C. Gray's 'Procedural Fairness and Substantive Rights' also in *Due Process* (see especially the n. at 204).

2.3 PROCEDURAL FAIRNESS IN SOCIAL CONTEXT

The analysis so far in this Chapter has dealt with the theoretical basis of procedural fairness where the approach taken has been analytical and normative. The concept of procedural fairness is also very much a social construct and should be understood in its social setting. Since a full study of social context would require a book of its own, my purpose here is only to give an introductory outline of the social basis of fair treatment and fair procedures. That is the first task in this section; the second task is to examine the way procedural fairness is understood by those who are subject to or caught up in legal processes.

2.3.1 The Social Basis of Procedural Fairness

Since the main object of procedures is to give effect to legal purposes through the application of authoritative standards, my account should begin with the social basis of legal standards. In a long tradition of sociological writing, law is considered to have an important role in maintaining the integration and stability of a society.[48] An early and influential theorist was E. Durkheim who saw law as a vital element in holding together societies which were mixed in composition, interests, and values.[49] Within plural societies, of which modern western societies are good examples, law constitutes a framework of standards which apply generally. Those standards become the basis on which certain relations between people are conducted, the basis indeed of rights and duties. Where disputes arise, they are resolved according to the standards. Provided one part of society is not favoured unduly over others, the standards can be accepted by all and so contribute to the integration of society, or, as Durkheim put it, to its organic solidarity.[50] The laws must reflect certain elementary notions of justice, but within that constraint, the legitimacy of law is tied not so much to its content but to the very fact of having a framework of standards. In a plural society, whose members are divided on many matters and where the threat of fragmentation is always present, laws become a significant unifying force.

To this understanding of the elementary functions of law may be added two further dimensions derived from H. L. A. Hart's descriptive sociology of law.[51] One is the idea that, in order to survive, any society needs certain

[48] See further R. Cotterrell, *The Sociology of Law* (Butterworths, London, 1984) and C. Grace and P. Wilkinson, *Sociological Inquiry and Legal Phenomenon* (Collier Macmillan, London, 1978).

[49] E. Durkheim, *The Division of Labour in Society* (The Free Press, New York, 1964 edn.).

[50] Organic solidarity, which matches a plural society, is contrasted with the mechanical solidarity of a society which is deeply homogenous and uniform in its moral base.

[51] Hart, *The Concept of Law*, n. 7 above.

kinds of legal rules, in particular, rules of forbearance protecting each from the other, recognizing the vulnerability of each, and acknowledging the limited altruism of all. It also needs rules regulating the distribution and use of scarce resources. Precisely what form or content such legal rules have is not so important since the very fact of having the rules means that the social need to ensure survival is met. Ideas of social justice and the content of the law enter at a later stage. The other point of interest in Hart's sociology relates to the nature and social function of rules themselves.[52] Social rules have both an external and an internal character; from an external point of view, they can be used to predict how others are likely to behave, while from an internal stance, they are the reasons for behaviour. The internal point of view is the key to understanding the social functions of rules: rules provide reasons for acting in one way rather than another; they provide both the explanation and the justification for actions. Moreover, rule-governed, normative behaviour is at the centre of social life, much of which makes sense only when it is understood as rule-governed. Legal rules are one kind of social rule and, once recognized within a society as legitimate and binding, recognized, that is, from the internal point of view, are the basis for much social action. Once the rules are effective in regulating social actions, they then contribute to social cohesion. The conditions according to which people will accept legal rules as legitimate and adopt an internal attitude to them, raise an interesting set of questions in themselves; but the lesson to be learnt from Hart's analysis is the need to be aware of the function that rules have in social life. That lesson can only be learnt, however, by first grasping the concept of a rule as a normative standard.[53]

Having established the nature and social role of legal rules, the second step in a social understanding of procedural fairness is to introduce the idea of reciprocity. Reciprocity is fundamental to social relationships and is closely linked to rules. It is most clearly at home in the relationship between two parties where it expresses the idea that, within any such social relationship, there is an 'endless process of exchange of goods, services, and symbols, which creates a dense network of infinite obligations, duties, claims, and expectations'.[54] Within that relationship a balance will be kept, a balance in the sense that a positive benefit conferred or forbearance endured by one in favour of the other will be returned in some form or another.[55] Without reciprocity, social relationships would not exist. The idea has its roots in

[52] Hart, *The Concept of Law*, n. 7 above, ch. 9.

[53] For further analysis of Hart's approach, see J. Hacker, 'Hart's Philosophy of Law' in J. Hacker and J. Raz (eds.), *Law, Morality and Society* (Clarendon Press, Oxford, 1977).

[54] B. S. Turner, 'Prolegomena to a General Theory of Social Order' in B. S. Turner (ed.), *Citizenship, Civil Society and Social Cohesion* (University of Essex, Colchester, 1986).

[55] For an introduction to the anthropological literature on reciprocity, see M. Mauss, *The Gift: Forms and Functions of Exchange in Archaic Societies* (Cohen and West, London: New York, 1954).

one-to-one relationships, but can be transferred to the realm of social rules; I suggest, indeed, that the internal attitude to rules originates in a sense of reciprocity. Here the relationship is between each member of the community and all other members, but it is still founded on creating and maintaining a balance amongst exchanges. Rules express exchanges and balances, they also express the dues and entitlements according to which accounts are kept and reciprocity is maintained. Rules express a relationship of reciprocity just in the sense that they are the standards governing social relationships. They decree how I shall be treated in certain situations and what are my dues, but they decree not just how I, but you, and each other person, should be treated. A sense of reciprocity is maintained only if the dues of each are respected by others. By making a connection between rules and reciprocity, we can explain why the internal attitude to rules, once adopted, makes certain actions obligatory. For to ignore that obligation would be to destroy reciprocity and thus to turn one's back on an elemental aspect of social life. Indeed, Durkheim's notion of organic solidarity consisted in the relations of reciprocity expressed in rules.[56]

It follows that the social origins of justice and fairness are also found in relations of reciprocity. Justice consists, as we have seen, in giving a person his due. To respect dues is to respect the balance within a relationship, while to neglect them is to disrupt the balance. The sentiment of justice then consists in maintaining reciprocity. This is contrary to J. S. Mill's claim that the sentiment of justice derives jointly from the impulse of self-defence and a natural feeling of sympathy for others.[57] Self-defence consists in warding off harms, not only physical harms, but harms to one's life in society, which includes, as fundamental, participation in reciprocal relations. Feelings of sympathy then explain why injustice to another raises the same sense of outrage as injustice to oneself. But as important as these ideas are in isolating the basic sentiments of justice, the account is more complete if those sentiments are mediated through the notion of reciprocity. For we have seen that the failure to respect dues, whether yours or mine, strikes at relations of reciprocity; and since reciprocity is itself a basic element of social life, it provides an adequate account of the sentiment of justice. If, however, we want to look beyond social relationships and locate the sentiment of justice in the individual person set apart from social life, then the impulse of self-defence may offer a plausible explanation. My own inclination is that we need not go so far, but that the idea of justice is rooted in social relations and is adequately accounted for in relationships of reciprocity.

The final stage in this analysis is to make a connection between the account of legal rules and their relationship to ideas of reciprocity and justice

[56] See further N. Abecrombie, S. Hill, and B. S. Turner, *The Dominant Ideology Thesis* (Allen and Unwin, London, 1980).

[57] J. S. Mill, *Utilitarianism* (Fontana edn., London, 1962).

on the one hand, and procedures on the other hand. But first we should restate the view of procedures which prevails in the modern world. They are primarily instruments for applying authoritative legal standards, for ensuring that certain kinds of outcomes are achieved, and that, as a consequence, people are treated in certain ways. Procedures on this view are related to justice not directly, but vicariously through their role in upholding a person's dues under authoritative standards. Other values besides the concern for the accurate application of outcome-based standards have a place, but it is very much subsidiary to, and merely places certain constraints upon, the pursuit of that overriding concern. The strength of this explanation of procedures is that their social role is linked directly to the preservation of normative expectations and in turn to reciprocity. However, the explanation also has a weakness. By advancing an account of procedures as primarily instrumental, as means to ends, subject only to certain marginal constraints, this explanation might appear thin and one-dimensional. We have already encountered the claims of the dignitarians for a sense of procedures as primarily expressing independent values, rather than being mere instruments to one dominant end, albeit the important one of providing fair treatment and maintaining relations of reciprocity.

To the extent that procedures do express directly social sentiments and values, there is no reason for not accepting that as part of their social role. Such sentiments and values will themselves be rooted in social relations, and may express an aspect of those relations which is not reducible to any other, dominant purpose. Indeed, when we look across cultures, many procedural forms appear fuller and more complex, more closely enmeshed in the social and cultural milieu, and more clearly means for expressing its values than an instrumental account would allow.[58] Process itself may even become the element of most significance. A study of the intricate processes of story-telling in Nigerian courts and the incantation of fixed and, to the outsider, apparently irrelevant and disjointed formulae will reveal much about the attitudes of the parties and officials, about the social relationship between them, and how they view each other.[59] Similarly, the study of courts in various parts of the orient shows that matters of honour, integrity, and the preservation of relationships play a central role in legal processes, again to the puzzlement of the western observer. Even the local courts of the late Soviet Union were concerned as much with education and communal solidarity as with applying the law. Compared with such richness and social complexity, the rationalist procedures of western processes appear limited in purpose and prosaic in style.

However, we should be clear about what is at issue. For as strange and

[58] See further S. Falk More, *Law as Process* (Routledge and Kegan Paul, London, 1978).

[59] W. L. Bennet and M. S. Feldman, *Reconstructing Reality in the Courtroom* (Tavistock, London, 1981).

complex as they may appear, there is nothing haphazard or accidental about such processes. They are deeply rooted in the attitudes and values of the society and are public processes for settling serious issues. The sentiments and values expressed in those procedures are exactly the values which, for that society, have to be declared and confirmed. The application of positive legal standards might have a place, but it is only part of the overall process and may be less important than other parts. The preservation of certain relationships, for example, might be much more important than upholding the law. Such processes may be complex and multi-layered, but they are still rational and purposive in expressing and achieving the values of societies. There are clear objectives to be achieved and values to be upheld, which may not be easily discerned by the external observer. We might fail to appreciate them if we begin with the assumption that legal processes are mainly about applying the law; once we have shed that assumption and appreciate that a wider range of values is in issue, the legal processes and their sometimes mysterious procedures become entirely understandable.

When we compare the more familiar terrain of western societies, the differences are marked. Here legal procedures are concerned with the application of legal standards and little more. What has happened to the fuller social context, the richness of values which we would expect to find reflected in procedures? The answer is that we have stripped them away in the cause of rights; for once a society becomes grounded in rights, once the relationship among citizens and between citizens and the state is expressed in rights, a relentless logic takes over.[60] Legal processes are then about rights, about their recognition, scope, and enforcement. Inherent in the logic of rights is an exclusion of other social values, attitudes, or connections; not entirely, but to a significant degree. Whereas ideas of community, of preserving relationships, of securing social integration, are soft ideas capable of adjustment and accommodation, rights are hard-edged. They stake out claims which allow for little adjustment or compromise, and the very idea of rights as trumps expresses that logic simply and perfectly.[61] For the same reasons, notions of justice and fairness are most at home in relation to rights; the same logic which created rights as trumps defines what is due and what fairness requires, since there can be no more clear and central case of unfair treatment than to deny one's rights. It should also be observed that, as we move away from rights to the more fluid values and concepts encountered in the legal processes of different cultures, the less appropriate ascriptions of justice and fairness become.

[60] Interesting parallels can be drawn between the rights-based view and Max Weber's writings on the rationalization of modern societies towards stable rules, where emphasis is on the virtue of rules rather than their content: see L. A. Scaff, *Fleeing the Iron Cage* (UCLA Press, Berkeley, Cal., 1989).

[61] The expression comes from R. M. Dworkin, *Taking Rights Seriously* (Duckworth, London, 1978).

My purpose is not to judge the merits of a right-based system compared with the systems of other cultures. My purpose is only to note the difference, to understand its social basis, and to extract the implications for procedures and fairness. The usefulness of this explanation can be seen by briefly considering two examples. In the first place, we can now better understand the dilemmas of the dignitarian challenge. At the base of that challenge is the search for a deeper set of values in western cultures; values, that is to say, which go beyond the rights-based culture and its expression in positive law. Notions of dignity, fraternity, and participatory involvement, all at first seem promising but ultimately peter out; they do so, I suggest, because the elements within them which we consider important are already expressed well enough in positive laws and practices. In the present state of western culture, there is no social basis for such values which is strong enough to compete with positive individualism and the culture of rights. That is the social reality; it could change, but until it does the dignitarian challenge in its stronger versions remains a romantic vision largely ungrounded in social realities.

The second example is quite different. It relates to the tension between legal processes based on the application of standards and the upholding of rights on the one hand, and alternatives to them on the other hand. Whilst there is a strong movement towards such alternative legal processes, particularly those based on agreement, the opposition is equally strong and determined. At the heart of the conflict are two different visions of the legal process and its supporting culture. The movement for alternative processes resolves around the idea that many issues can be settled by agreement, even between parties in very different positions. That claim must in turn rest on a bed of social values which can guide and legitimate the process of bargaining and argument. The opposite vision is very different.[62] It draws on the paradigm of rights, where, in disputes between parties or in the relations between the citizen and the state, authoritative standards are to be applied. Adherents to this approach draw support from a scepticism about the legitimacy of other forms of process in ordering society's affairs. Negotiation and agreement have their place, but in many contexts they should not be regarded as acceptable alternatives to the application of authoritative standards. It is not my purpose here to enter into a discussion of the merits of those arguments,[63] but just to note that one of the main reasons for that scepticism is the gulf between the normative attractions of forms based on agreement, on the one hand, and the state of cultural development, on the other hand.

[62] See e.g. Fiss, 'Against Settlement' (1984) 93 *Yale LJ* 1073.
[63] That is done in Ch. 9.

2.3.2 Perceptions of Procedural Fairness

The analysis of procedural fairness in this Chapter so far has been analytical, normative, and social. It is analytical in examining the concept of procedural fairness and how it relates to other concepts; normative in that it puts forward a justification for that conception of procedural fairness which is grounded in political morality; and social in that procedural fairness is shown to be steeped in social conditions. A fourth dimension which may further increase our understanding is the way those affected by legal processes perceive issues of procedural fairness. Here we touch on a body of literature and research, written and conducted in the main by social psychologists,[64] the general object of which is to examine the way people perceive fairness and then to draw general conclusions about its nature. There is still scope for further research to augment our understanding of perceptions of fairness, but to report briefly on what has already been done is a fitting conclusion to this examination of procedural fairness.

The pioneers in the field were J. Thibaut and L. Walker. In a series of books and articles, they put forward a view of procedural fairness which is firmly instrumental.[65] Its major premise is that the primary object of legal processes, whatever form they take, is to achieve justice between the parties.[66] Justice between the parties is a matter of substantive outcomes, while the procedural aspects of justice relate to the degree to which each path controls the decision process. No one party can directly control or dictate the outcome, since that is left to the decision-maker. However, the outcome will be determined largely by the procedures followed, particularly as procedures regulate the flow of information to the decision-maker. Control of procedures by the parties is important since the more control each one has the more likely it will be successful in achieving a favourable outcome. Despite a certain strangeness in the concepts and in the language used to express them, the underlying idea is simple: people involved in legal processes want to achieve certain outcomes; their ability to do so depends on their degree of control over procedures; procedures are then judged as fair or unfair according to how well they allow a party to exert that control. The account is instrumental in the sense that procedures are means to achieving certain outcomes; that is their purpose and rationale and the basis on which they should be judged.

[64] For a general review, see T. R. Tyler, 'Procedural Justice Research' (1987) 1 *Social Justice Research* 41.

[65] See J. Thibaut and L. Walker, *Procedural Justice* (Erlbaum, New Jersey, 1975) and 'A Theory of Procedure' (1978) 66 *Calif. Rev.* 540.

[66] The authors have an obtuse view of justice: 'distributive justice is attained when the ultimate outcomes are distributed to contending parties in proportion to their respective contributions of inputs to the transaction underlying the dispute': 'A Theory of Procedure', 541.

It might have been expected that this analysis would soon attract critical scrutiny. According to the critics, two important features are neglected: one is the normative dimension, the other is that part of procedures which is not related to outcomes at all. The desire to remedy those shortcomings stimulated others, so that now we have the benefit of an interesting and wide-ranging body of research into procedural fairness. Amongst the various research projects which may be drawn on, the work of T. R. Tyler is of special interest.[67] Tyler's account is based on extensive research, the centre-piece of which is a study of people's attitudes to fairness in a number of legal situations, including encounters with the police. The research is complex and of considerable interest, but ultimately rests on two simple ideas. The first is that in order to understand legal processes we must grasp their normative nature. By that is meant that a person's perception of the fairness of a process is based on his normative expectations, which in turn derive from the principles and standards which govern, or at least are thought by the person to govern, the process. A distinction should then be drawn between judging a process according to whether or not the outcome is favourable to the party, and whether it satisfies his normative expectations. The two occupy different dimensions: whether or not an outcome is favourable to me is a matter of fact; whether the outcome is one to which I have a justified claim depends on the normative standards applicable. Similarly, whether a set of procedures is fair depends on there being normative criteria by which to judge the matter. In understanding procedural fairness it is essential to have this internal, normative point of view.

The second idea in Tyler's work is that normative standards and expectations in relation to outcomes should be distinguished from those concerning procedures. The normative aspects of procedures of particular note are said to be neutrality, lack of bias, honesty, an effort to be fair, politeness, and respect for rights.[68] This list is by no means complete and might well include matters such as having one's say and having one's views taken into account.[69] But whatever is finally included in the list, the claim is that procedural matters are valued for their own sake and independently of their effect on outcomes.[70] It is claimed, indeed, that where people recount their experiences of legal processes, they put more emphasis and value on procedural matters than on outcomes. Their assessment of the fairness of legal processes is also largely based on whether they consider the procedures themselves to be fair, not on whether fair procedures are likely to produce fair outcomes. The latter position reflects the instrumental approach taken by

[67] The publications I shall rely on especially are T. R. Tyler, 'What Is Procedural Justice' (1988) 22 *Law and Society Rev.* 103, 'Procedural Justice Research' (1987) 1 *Social Justice Research* 41, and *Why People Obey the Law* (Yale University Press, New Haven, Conn., 1990).

[68] *Why People Obey the Law*, n. 67 above, and see also 137 ff.

[69] Ibid. 147–9.

[70] Ibid. 96–7.

Thibaut and Walker, for whom the value of procedures lay in their contribution to outcomes. Tyler and his collaborators for their part have found that people judge procedures to be fair or unfair quite independently of their contribution to outcomes.[71] They support the claim by pointing to the way procedures express values which are irreducibly worthwhile in themselves. To take an example, people like to express their views in legal proceedings for inter-personal reasons.[72] Similarly, people expect an official to be neutral and impartial, to be motivated by fairness, and to consider the views put before him, because such ways of acting are expressions of the values which ought to govern the relationship between them. The grounds for this conclusion are not theoretical speculation but solid empirical analysis of people's attitudes to different legal processes. Through the use of sophisticated methods of analysis, the researchers claim to have isolated people's perceptions of procedural fairness and to have separated those relating to outcomes from those of a non-instrumental nature. What is even more important is that the analysis claims to show how people distinguish sharply between procedures and outcomes, and that attitudes to the fairness of proceedings are determined to a much greater extent by their views of the former than of the latter.[73]

In drawing attention to the perceptions of people subject to legal processes, this research adds a further layer of understanding to our analysis. The analysis I have put forward in this Chapter is based on the point of view of someone attempting to understand the concept of procedural fairness from a position of normative detachment. The assumption made is that such a point of view will not only commend itself to anyone participating in legal processes, whether as official or citizen, but will be an authentic representation of what happens in practice. If, however, the perceptions of procedural fairness of those affected are shown to be different, then it may be necessary to revise the earlier analysis. The research described here appears to provide exactly such a contrary account, that is, it claims to show that people not only distinguish between outcomes and procedures but, in making judgments of fairness, concentrate on procedures as by far the more important part, with outcomes pushed well into the background. Such research lends its support to a strong version of the dignitarian challenge; for if procedures, such as lack of bias, being heard, and having one's case considered, are of value independently of outcomes, then the most likely explanation for their being so is that they express dignitarian values.

However, I wish to suggest that the research described above into people's perceptions of procedural fairness is flawed. It is flawed because it is based on an insupportable theoretical model which I shall now seek to expose. The analysis begins well with its explanation of the normative dimension of procedural fairness. The ascription of procedural fairness, like the ascription

[71] Ibid. 128 ff. [72] Ibid. 128. [73] Ibid. 138–9.

of fairness in any sense, depends on normative standards about how people should be treated and on the normative expectations thereby created. The next, more difficult, task is to identify the different normative standards and show how they relate to each other. Tyler's research is based on distinguishing between normative standards relating to procedures and outcomes respectively; having made that distinction, he then proceeds to show empirically that the standards relating to procedures dictate whether the process is fair. Everything depends, therefore, on the distinction between procedural standards and outcome standards. But Tyler's understanding of that distinction is mistaken. In the first place, the very list of proposed procedural standards should put us on guard, for matters like lack of bias and being heard are generally and rightly considered to be primarily instrumental to outcomes. They may also have a value-expressive function, but as a matter of both common sense and legal practice they are first and foremost directed to outcomes. Bias on the part of the decision-maker is condemned because of the threat it poses to an accurate outcome, while a hearing is important because it is likely to provide relevant and often vital information and to reveal a side of the story which would otherwise remain untold. The combined effect of such procedural standards is the likelihood of their leading to a more accurate outcome.

The competing characterizations can be tested with some examples. Suppose that X is seeking a welfare payment; he takes advice and all the signs are that the case fits squarely within the criteria for a grant. X is then justified in expecting that a grant should be made. Now consider three different cases. In the first, X is awarded a grant with a minimum of procedures and without a hearing. If asked about the fairness of the procedures, the absence of a hearing in particular, any misgivings X might have are likely to be overshadowed by the fact that his normative expectations about the outcome were upheld. At most he may say that, although the procedures were to some degree unfair, the right outcome was reached. However, even that concession on X's part might best be understood to mean that the absence of a hearing created a risk of a mistaken outcome, but in the circumstances the risk was overcome.

The more interesting case would be where X were denied the benefit so that his normative expectations as to the outcome would be unfulfilled. X would now be sure to condemn both the outcome and the procedures, but the basis of his condemnation would be that the procedures were defective in not leading to the right outcome. It would be very odd for him to say that, although the process failed to deliver the benefit to which he was entitled, the really important defect was the failure to express an inter-personal relationship by denying a hearing. It is beyond credulity that anyone could arrive at such an account of the situation. The truth is surely that the inadequate procedures would be condemned because they failed to protect

X's normative expectations about entitlement, with any additional reason for condemning the procedures paling into the background. This conclusion is reinforced by a third case. Here suppose that the wrong outcome was reached and X was denied his benefit, even though apparently sound procedures were followed; the official acted without bias, a hearing was held, and every effort was made to consider the case properly. What would X's reaction be here? Is he likely to praise the fairness of the procedures as the main point of interest, mentioning only as an afterthought that the whole purpose of the process, namely, the proper determination of his entitlement, ended in failure. Such a reaction is implausible: X's response is more likely to be that the procedures failed in their primary purpose and, therefore, despite appearances, are inadequate and defective. In the face of failure to protect his clear entitlement, X would find it very difficult to judge the procedures as fair according to some further criterion. Finally, in order to portray the force of this argument more vividly, imagine that in each case X is not applying for a welfare benefit but is an innocent man on trial for his life.

Something is seriously wrong with an account of procedural fairness which emphasizes the inherent value of procedural rules about hearing and bias to the almost total neglect of their instrumental role in upholding normative expectations relating to outcomes. This is not to deny that the hearing and bias rules may have value independently of outcomes; but it is to insist that whatever non-instrumental value they have is subsidiary to their instrumental role. The error lies in misunderstanding the relationship between procedures and outcomes. The first part of the error is that the researchers have failed to see that the primary significance of procedural notions, like bias, is in relation to outcomes. Such notions help to make sure that the decision-maker is not blighted in a way which will prevent him from reaching the right outcome. That is the primary normative basis for the bias rule. When taken out of that context and made a free-standing value in itself, it is difficult to see what normative justification could be given for it. It is not enough to say it expresses a value in the relationship between citizen and official: it is certainly not self-evidently a value in itself, so we must delve deeper to discover its justification. Once we begin to do so the link with outcomes becomes so obvious that to ignore it in favour of other possible justifications is like saying that the most important thing about Shakespeare is that he was born in Stratford. The second part of the error is that it neglects the process of generalization about procedures by which certain procedures come to be regarded as standard cases of fair procedures. Bias and hearing are good examples; since they have gained recognition as normal and necessary elements in most contexts, it is easy to assume that they are inherently valuable. The justification for them as serving outcomes tends to be overlooked and they are regarded as free-standing. The tendency is buttressed by certain procedures becoming settled within a legal system, even perhaps enshrined in the constitution, so that we rarely have to consider their deeper justification. It is, then, not surprising that ordinary people also adopt a similar attitude, without thinking about why those procedures are important; nor is it surprising to find that the answers people give about their own experiences of legal processes reflect the rules which happen to be settled within their society. But for researchers to accept those conventional attitudes at face value reflects on the adequacy of their own theoretical framework. Had they probed further into why people consider bias, neutrality, the chance to be heard, and so on as procedural values, researchers would have discovered that the reason for valuing such procedures, for having normative expectations in relation to them, is first and foremost that they are the kinds of procedures needed to ensure that the right outcomes are reached and that people are treated fairly.

The tendency to think of certain procedures as settled and valuable in themselves is most acute when normative expectations as to outcomes are uncertain. In the cases considered above, there was no doubt about X's entitlement, but in many processes that is not the case. Where there is discretion, or standards to be interpreted, or complex facts, it might not be clear at all what outcome to expect. That we should then concentrate on certain procedures is understandable, since the right and or best outcome is, in a sense, whatever outcome the procedures lead to. Procedures appear to have an added importance because normative expectations as to outcomes are uncertain. But to interpret that process as making procedures free-standing and valuable independently of outcomes is a misinterpretation of the situation, for procedures are still justified as means to outcomes and an adequate framework for empirical research should take account of that fact. The failure to do so leads to the unwarranted conclusion that procedures have their own normative foundation and that people assess fairness primarily on that basis. The argument presented here points to the conclusion that much of the research by psychologists into people's perceptions of procedural fairness is based on an unsatisfactory theoretical framework. It is unsatisfactory because it is based on a misunderstanding of the relationship between normative expectations in relation to procedures and those in relation to outcomes. The empirical study of people's perceptions is in turn defective and the conclusions concerning the independent basis of procedures must be questioned.

There is a second line of argument which also casts doubt on the persuasiveness of this research into perceptions of fairness. The cause for concern here is the sharp distinction drawn between procedures and outcomes. Indeed, fundamental to this research is the separation of normative expectations in relation to procedures from those in relation to outcomes. We have seen that the separation can be problematical so that any analysis which depends on a sharp separation between the two must be questioned.[74] The alternative is to identify within a given context the standards of fair treatment without insisting on a strict division between those relating to substance and others relating to procedures. Some such standards will in fact be related to outcomes, whether in defining outcomes or placing restraints on them; other standards may relate to non-outcome values. The result is, as much of the discussion in these first two chapters shows, that any legal process is characterized by a cluster of values and standards of different kinds, each of which contributes an element to an overall sense of fair treatment. Attempts to divide the cluster sharply and analytically between outcome values and procedural values are not only likely to fail but are misdirected in the first place. Fair procedures are simply those procedures which lead to fair treatment according to authoritative standards.

[74] See the discussion in section 1.4.2.

3
Rights, Procedures, and Costs

The discussion of procedural fairness in the last chapter leads on naturally to an analysis of procedural rights. The standards of fair treatment applying in each area of process create rights—first-order rights as I shall call them. The question then arises what further rights a person has to legal procedures in order to protect those rights. The general principle is that the claim to have one's first-order rights upheld justifies a further claim to procedural rights. However, the relationship between the two is a little more complex, especially in those types of process where procedures are imperfect and where resources are insufficient to provide the most effective procedures possible.

The object of this Chapter is to explore some of the more important issues relating to procedural rights. The Chapter begins with a brief introduction to rights generally and to procedural rights in particular. The discussion then moves to a more detailed analysis of first-order rights in administrative processes, with particular reference to discretionary contexts; the idea of a right to consideration is proposed as an apt way of expressing the relationship between the citizen and the state in such contexts. The third section of the Chapter examines the issue of mistakes; mistakes, that is, arising either from imperfect procedures or from inadequate procedures, the former being inherent in some forms of process, and the latter usually being attributable to insufficient resources. The Chapter concludes with an outline of various kinds of costs which influence the design of procedures, followed by a brief account of how competing considerations can be dealt with.

3.1 PROCEDURAL RIGHTS

3.1.1 Rights in General

In understanding procedural rights, it is best to begin with a brief introduction to rights in general. Rights are not confined to legal systems and this book is not just about the procedural rights one might have in this or that legal system; it is also about the case for procedural rights in a more general way and in the moral basis of procedures. The claim that the law should be upheld and legal rights enforced is itself a moral claim. For these reasons, we must move between the territory of legal rights and moral rights, although the relationship between the two is intricate and the subject of an extensive literature which can hardly be touched on here.[1] Here I shall give a brief outline of the relationship and then show how it applies in understanding procedural rights.

One way of approaching the general subject of rights is by dividing the field three ways into basic, moral, and legal rights.[2] Basic rights are foundational in the sense that they constitute the philosophical groundwork for any rights at all. They are abstract in nature and are expressed in such terms as the right to equal concern and respect, to pursue one's ends, or to be treated as an autonomous and responsible person. Philosophers have long sought to identify the foundation for basic rights, and the opinion that there is a core of rights, closely tied to the idea of a person as a free, moral agent, has a powerful hold on the modern mind.[3] Basic rights constitute the foundation on which more specific and particular rights can be justified.

Moral rights are just such concrete and specific instances of basic rights. Their justification lies in basic rights and in that respect they share with basic rights a certain universality; they are at the same time prone to be local, the products of the history and culture of different communities. Between universality and cultural autochthon there is a certain tension: some aspects of a basic right might not be embodied in the moral rights of a community, for just as Aquinas noted that the Germans, being at that time a backward people, did not yet recognize the wrongness of robbery, so in modern societies the full significance of basic rights might not be realized. The immorality of discrimination on grounds of race, gender, or religion, so plain to the modern, liberal mind and so fundamental to social change in recent years, was thought within recent memory to be the distorted view of an eccentric minority. Each society develops its moral principles according to its own lights, and even those societies which are serious and conscientious in endeavouring to treat their members properly are likely to find that their conceptions develop and change; moral attitudes, which to one generation seem entirely justifiable, may draw the curses of the next.[4] However, each generation must cope with its own blindness and fallibility, and each is justified in acting according to those moral principles which can be defended according to basic principles as they are understood at the time. Similarly for rights: some moral rights recognized in a society can conscientiously be defended, while others, even at the time, may clearly be out of step with

[1] Two especially helpful articles are: J. Raz, 'On the Nature of Rights' (1984) xciii *Mind* 184 and 'Legal Rights' (1984) 4 *Oxford JLS* 1.

[2] This division is suggested by L. E. Lomasky in his book *Persons, Rights, and the Moral Community* (OUP, Oxford, 1987).

[3] Two of the most interesting works are: L. E. Lomasky, ibid., and A. Gewirth, 'The Epistemology of Human Rights' (1984) 1 *Social Philosophy and Policy* 1.

[4] For an interesting discussion of this theme, see S. Hampshire, *Innocence and Experience* (Blackwell, Oxford, 1990), 51–78.

basic rights; the former, but not the latter, should be the basis for practical action.

Legal rights tend to be specific and concrete,[5] and highly local to a legal system. They should be the product of careful practical judgment, whether legislative, judicial, or administrative, but, being rights within a social institution, their status turns not on their moral force but on compliance with constitutional norms and law-making procedures. Nevertheless, it could reasonably be expected that legal rights should reflect the moral rights of the community and ultimately basic rights. In practice, relationships between them will be contingent, since legal rights may be related only vaguely to moral rights or even be in conflict with them. Where the two are out of step, moral rights are good grounds for criticizing the law and urging change. This feature of moral rights is important in relation to procedural rights.

Now that we have a sketch of the relationship between different kinds of rights, the next step is to make clear what it means to have a right. Let us begin with legal rights. Different ways have been proposed of trying to pin down exactly what it means to have a right, but the simplest and truest is the interest theory: according to the interest theory, to have a right is to have a legally protected interest.[6] The use of the notion of a right is a helpful and commonly adopted way of adverting to the special protection given by law to certain interests of persons. To characterize an interest in terms of rights is to show that, within a legal system, that interest is considered important enough to warrant special protection. The reasons for singling out some interests for recognition in this way can be of several kinds, some being reasons of deep principle, others reasons of policy and expediency.[7] But once the special importance of an interest has been recognized, the grounds exist for providing the necessary legal protection by way of duties on others, together with suitable institutions and procedures for their enforcement. The person whose interests are protected in this way normally, but not invariably, enjoys some control over the claiming, waiving, or enforcing of the right.[8]

Moral rights share some of the features of legal rights; they relate to the interests of persons and they are the grounds for duties on others in respect

[5] But of course they can be highly abstract: see R. M. Dworkin, *Taking Rights Seriously* (Duckworth, London, 1978), ch. 4.

[6] Recent writings of importance on the interest theory are: Dworkin, ibid.; J. Raz, 'On the Nature of Rights', n. 2 above; N. McCormick, 'Rights in Legislation' in A. W. B. Simpson (ed.), *Oxford Essays in Jurisprudence* (Clarendon Press, Oxford, 1973).

[7] J. Raz writes of rights as 'intermediate conclusions in arguments from ultimate values to duties': 'On the Nature of Rights', n. 2 above, at 208. This may be true of moral rights, but legal rights are not necessarily derived from ultimate values.

[8] Adherents to the will theory of rights claim that the control of these matters is the defining feature of a right; the better view is that rights may, but need not, have this characteristic. For discussion of the relationship between the will and the interest theory of rights, see MacCormick, 'Rights in Legislation', n. 6 above. For a helpful discussion of rights generally: J. Finnis, *Natural Law and Natural Rights* (Clarendon Press, Oxford, 1980), ch. 7.

of those interests. But whereas legal rights arise under the laws of a legal system, and disputes about them can be resolved authoritatively by looking to the laws of the system, moral rights derive from moral values. For moral rights, there is no similar positive test of existence, nor an authoritative way of resolving disputes about them; the only appeal is to moral values and ultimately to basic values. Nevertheless, it is often possible to state with reasonable certainty the moral values accepted within a society. Basic rights also relate to interests, but in order to identify and sustain such rights, it is necessary to draw on the most fundamental principles of human society. Approaches to such issues are likely to be conditioned by history and culture, but it is not so unrealistic to suggest that certain fundamental values have come to be recognized in modern, liberal societies, values which are centred around notions of community within which concern and respect are shown for each member.

Now while it is one thing to ascertain what rights a person has within a legal system, it is another to be clear about what follows from having rights. The answer is that to have a right is to have an implicit undertaking from the society that the interest, the content of the right, will be protected. R. Dworkin puts the point in this way: 'Once the content of a right is determined, the community must furnish . . . at least the minimum level of protection against the risk of injustice required by that content, even though the general welfare suffers in consequence'.[9] Legal rights can be changed or removed at the stroke of a legislative pen, but while they stand the community has a duty to protect them. That duty, the 'must' in Dworkin's words, is a moral duty. The basis of that moral duty is the undertaking by the society collectively, to each of its members individually, that rights will be upheld. The undertaking is implicit in the relationship between the collectivity and each individual, and it applies where the rights are created by private agreement between two parties, as well as where they are created by the state. The implicit undertaking is that each person will be treated in accordance with the pattern of distribution represented by rights. This creates normative expectations in the right-holder that rights and the standards on which they are based will be upheld in each case. The failure to protect rights is a failure to give to a person what is due, and that is to treat him unfairly.[10] The provision of suitable institutions and procedures is a vital part of that protection.

[9] R. M. Dworkin, *A Matter of Principle* (Clarendon Press, Oxford, 1985), 89. We should not overlook the fact that the protection of rights is part of the general welfare: see section 1.3.

[10] We cannot here enter into the question whether some legal rights should not be upheld; the duty of enforcement based on fairness may sometimes be overridden by more important moral considerations.

3.1.2 Procedural Rights

Let us begin with a straightforward statement of the nature of procedural rights in legal processes: they are rights to such procedures, that is to say, to the mechanisms and institutions, as are necessary to give effect to the rights arising under the standards of fair treatment applying in a particular process. This may seem a roundabout way of stating that procedural rights are rights to such procedures as will give effect to substantive rights. However, the difficulties with the latter formulation should be clear from the earlier discussion: in the first place, the distinction between procedural and substantive rights is likely to be as elusive and problematical as the distinction between procedures and substance;[11] and in the second place, the notion of substantive rights might be taken mistakenly to refer only to first-tier outcome values to the neglect of the non-outcome values occurring within other tiers. It is better for these reasons not to make the analysis of procedural rights depend on a clear division between substance and procedure; it might also be better not to use either of the terms 'procedural rights' and 'substantive rights', but while the latter may be discarded without loss, I shall continue to use the former. It is neither exact nor precise, but provided we keep in mind what it is that procedural rights refer to, the convenience of using the term 'procedural rights' is considerable.

At their simplest, then, procedural rights are the entitlements a person has to such procedures as are necessary to give effect to the standards of fair treatment and, therefore, to the rights to which they give rise. The standards of fair treatment in legal processes create rights in people in the direct sense that they stipulate how persons should be treated. The rights created under the standards of fair treatment may be rights to outcomes or rights that certain values be respected in reaching outcomes. The question precisely what rights a person has in any legal context is answerable in that context. The discussion in Chapter 1 shows how that should be done and reveals some of the difficulties involved. We saw there that standards of fair treatment may derive from several sources and that, while most will be clear and settled, the status of some might be uncertain. The simple point is that the question of what rights a person has in any legal process can be answered only by first identifying the authoritative standards of fair treatment within it. Rights arising under such standards will be referred to as first-order rights. Procedural rights are then the rights to the necessary procedures for realizing first-order rights.

The idea of procedural rights needs to be explored a little further. First-order rights are the product of laws and any other binding standards, and it

[11] See M. Bayles, *Procedural Justice* (Kluwer, London, 1990), 3 ff. and the discussion in section 1.4.2 herein.

is necessary to have legal mechanisms for acquiring and transferring rights, for resolving conflicts about them, and for ensuring their protection. The enjoyment of rights depends, in short, on a network of institutions and procedures. Here we have the germ of the idea of procedural rights. Once it is recognized that to have a right is to have an undertaking from the community that a certain interest will be protected in a certain way, it is a short step to the conclusion that the undertaking ought to include the procedures and institutions necessary for the purpose. Procedures are part of what is necessary to take rights seriously and so to prevent unfair treatment. Suppose that X is on trial for a serious crime; he is innocent, but there is evidence against him sufficient to warrant a trial. Suppose further that, although the proceedings bear all the trappings of a trial, the verdict is reached by the solemn judicial tossing of a coin. If the toss goes X's way, he is unlikely to complain, except perhaps to note that such serious matters should not be left to luck. If the toss goes against him, X's complaint would be that his right not to be convicted and punished unless guilty, together with other rights which might as a consequence be affected, have not been taken seriously. Society has made no effort to ensure that, when X's rights are under question, suitable procedures are available to determine accurately what exactly has happened. The procedure employed—the tossing of a coin—is not directed to an accurate decision of guilt or innocence, and so it must be concluded that society does not value that right. It has through its laws conferred the right—a right in this case with a direct line to moral and basic rights—but it has failed to provide the procedures necessary for the right to be upheld. A vital element in society's undertaking to X is missing, so that when it really matters, the right proves worthless.

There is clearly a close and interesting relationship between rights and procedures. The procedural aspect is so vital to the protection of a right that it is tempting to see it as part of the first-order right itself, for without procedures for its protection, the right is incomplete and will often be of no value. However, that approach would be too strict. It is perfectly intelligible to say that A has a right to payment by B, and then go on to say that B has fled to Panama and there are no procedures for enforcing the claim against him. The right continues but the procedures are incomplete. The better view is to regard the claim to procedures as a further right which is grounded on and justified by the first-order right. The very existence of the first-order right gives the right-holder a moral claim, based on the undertaking, implicit in the grant of a right, to such procedures. Notice here the interplay between the legal and the moral: the grant of a legal right carries a moral claim based on fairness; that moral claim, which might equally be expressed as a moral right, is that certain legal procedures be made available. This approach fits well with the interest theory of rights: A's interest is in having his right to payment upheld; the justification for having the interest upheld lies in the implicit undertaking that the first-order right will be taken seriously. A right is taken seriously only if there are procedures for its protection.

A general principle can now be formulated: first-order rights within a legal system justify a claim to such procedures as are necessary to protect and uphold those rights. That claim to procedures may itself be expressed in the language of rights: the right-holder does not appeal to decency or to the goodwill of the community to provide suitable procedures; the claim to procedures is itself one of right. Amongst the rights an accused in a criminal trial has is the right to procedures which will result in an accurate verdict of guilt or innocence; the litigant in a civil action has a right to procedures by which the law will be applied accurately to the facts, or at least that the contest between the parties be reasonably equal; in the administrative sphere, the person subject to a decision will often have rights at stake and is entitled to procedures which ensure the rights are upheld. A full analysis of any legal process would of course be more complex than these few examples suggest, and other first-order rights, besides those mentioned, are likely to be in issue. However, the examples are enough to show that, whenever first order rights are in issue, moral claims for certain procedural rights are justified.

This general approach to procedural rights needs some refinements which are considered more fully below. One concerns costs: the costs to the community of providing procedures are substantial and the resources available are limited. How then can the right to procedures be reconciled with the fact that it might not be possible adequately to provide them? Another matter is the problem of mistakes: the procedures based on applying standards are imperfect and do not always produce the correct results; some mistakes might benefit the right-holder but others will be a violation of rights. There is a connection with the question of costs, but the problem of mistakes is more fundamental. It may be impossible to know whether a mistake has occurred —who but the accused really knows whether the verdict of guilt is a true one—because the procedures are inherently imperfect. The problem of mistakes adds an interesting dimension to the understanding of procedures.

3.2 PROCEDURAL RIGHTS IN THE ADMINISTRATIVE PROCESS

3.2.1 Rights in the Administrative Process

In discussing the relationship between procedural rights and first-order rights, there is a tendency to concentrate on the judicial trial, whether civil or criminal, where first-order rights are clearly at stake. The emphasis of this book, however, is on the administrative process and, since that makes up the greater part by far of legal decision-making, we should now consider how well the analysis fits there. Let us begin by distinguishing between two situations: one is where administrative decisions are clearly concerned with first-order rights, while the other concerns administrative powers to act in the public interest, where the public interest goes beyond matters of private right or interest. There are no rights in such cases to any specific outcome, but I shall develop the argument that it is a mistake to conclude that no first-order rights exist at all.

The first situation is not uncommon; powers often are conferred on administrative bodies where the object is to secure certain benefits to individuals. The benefits might include such matters as income support, educational opportunities, medical care, housing, or a licence to follow an activity, trade, or profession. Whether the object of the power is to create rights is a matter to be decided by interpreting the statute, by explicating its terms, and identifying its purposes. In the clearest cases, the provision of benefits will be expressed as rights, with correlative duties on officials, accompanied by suitable procedures. Some cases will be less clear, with the question whether rights are in issue depending on what inferences should be drawn from the terms of the statute and from the fact that benefits are being granted. Other cases may be even more difficult, with little in the statute to indicate whether the matter is one of right or discretion. In all cases, the officials must interpret the statutory scheme as they think best, and often the best interpretation will be that, despite vagueness of wording and indeterminacy of purpose, rights are at stake.[12] If the best interpretation is that the object is to confer benefits on individuals, it is sensible and correct to refer to those benefits as rights.[13]

This is not to deny that whether a grant of power to administrative officials creates rights in those who benefit is often a complex matter. It may be necessary to decide whether a grant of power is to be construed for the benefit of individuals as an individuated social goal and so as a right; or whether the power is to be exercised in the public interest, where the public interest consists in matters other than providing individualized benefits. Even where there is a grant of individualized benefits, and so of rights, the scope and extent of the rights may be left vague and indeterminate. The official may have a substantial degree of discretion, of judgment, and appreciation in deciding the content of the right. Problems of interpretation, however, should not undermine the general point that the best interpretation

[12] This point is discussed further in P. P. Craig, *Public Law and Democracy* (Clarendon Press, Oxford, 1990), 192 ff.; D. J. Galligan, *Discretionary Powers* (Clarendon Press, Oxford, 1986), 188–95.

[13] There are well-known arguments about whether there can be positive rights against the state in this way; we need not enter into that debate here, except to note that there are many positive rights against the state which are analogous in logic and structure to rights as classically conceived. For discussion, see C. Sampford and D. J. Galligan (eds.), *Law, Rights and the Welfare State* (Croom Helm, London, 1986), especially the essays by R. Plant and W. Sadurski.

of a grant of power will often be that it creates rights. Similarly, vagueness and indeterminacy are not incompatible with rights, since the law is full of instances where the precise scope of rights depends on judgment and discretion. There may of course come a point of such indeterminacy that the specification of the right is so dependent on the official's discretion that still to speak of rights would be to debase the currency.

3.2.2 Procedural Rights in Relation to Discretion

However, administrative powers often do not confer rights in the sense of conferring entitlements to certain outcomes. This brings us to the second situation noted above where powers are conferred on public authorities, where those powers allow for discretion, and where in the exercise of the discretion the object to be achieved is the public interest. Many examples could be cited: the power to grant parole or licences of many kinds; whether to build another airport or which route a new road should take; the power to award grants or subsidies, concessions or franchises. The overriding concern in cases like these will often be to act in the way which best serves the public interest, subject only to the boundaries set by the statute and to the proper consideration of relevant matters. What counts as the public interest might be left to the discretion of the decision-maker. To claim that anyone has a right to a defined outcome would be to misunderstand such cases. People might be affected by the way the powers are used; they might benefit or they might suffer a burden, but they do not have rights to a particular result.

Nevertheless, people might be affected in their interests directly and seriously. The public interest is the main concern, but the question arises whether those affected by this kind of decision—let us refer to it as policy-based discretion—have any claim on the way it is made.[14] Consider some examples. The person applying for a licence to carry on a trade or business often has no right that it be granted, since the application, no matter how convincing in itself, might be refused for reasons of public policy. Perhaps there are already enough pubs or taxi-drivers or boxers' managers. The prisoner seeking parole is in a similar position; no matter how well he has behaved or how remorseful he feels, his release is governed by wider notions of public interest. Another case is where a number of parties try to prevent a motorway being built, or to have it follow one route rather than another. Again it is inappropriate to talk of rights, and yet the parties may feel that they have important interests at stake and that they ought to be able to have some impact on the decision.

The issue is whether those affected by the decision have a moral claim to

[14] For an interesting case study of the relationship between policies and rights, see J. Tweedie, 'Rights in Social Programmes: The Case for Parental Choice of School' [1986] *Public Law* 407.

any particular procedures being followed. The statute itself will often set out elaborate procedures for the participation of interested parties, the hearing of evidence, and the giving of reasons; but the question to consider is whether such matters are at the discretion of the legislator, or whether the parties have a moral claim to certain procedures which ought to be translated into a legal right. R. M. Dworkin, who is one of the few jurists to interest himself in these matters, answers the question in the negative.[15] After arguing that procedural rights are generated by substantive rights, Dworkin concludes that, if there is no right to a particular outcome, there is no right to procedures. If, in other words, the decision is one of policy to be settled by the authority as it thinks best, then the procedures to be followed are also matters of policy.[16] Notice that we are not here concerned with whether any specific procedural forms are required, such as the chance to participate or to cross-examine witnesses or that reasons be given. The question rather is one of general principle, namely, whether a person, affected in his interests by a policy decision, has any procedural rights. If there are procedural rights, we would then go on to determine the specific procedures required to discharge them.

The claim that a person has no procedural rights in relation to policy-based discretion needs to be examined more closely. The gist of Dworkin's argument is that procedural rights are parasitic on substantive rights; if there are no substantive rights in relation to policy decisions, then it follows that there are no procedural rights. He then claims that the deprivation of a right consists in two kinds of harm: the bare harm of being denied an advantage or being subjected to an imposition—imprisonment, loss of money, forfeiture of land; and the moral harm or injustice factor which consists in having a right, which is then in some way abused. To be treated in that way is to be treated unfairly, the reason for the unfairness being, as we have seen, the implicit undertaking by the society as to how a right-holder should be treated. Rights are distinctive because of the moral element; interests may be affected by the actions of governments and suffer bare harm in all sorts of ways, but it is only when there is an element of moral harm that fairness makes its entry. The curtailment of a bare interest creates no moral harm, while the deprivation of a right is unfair and so the source of moral harm. The distinction between bare harm and moral harm is important and fits well with my analysis in earlier chapters. However, the next step in Dworkin's argument is questionable: here the claim is that since no substantive rights are at stake in a discretionary decision, there is no risk of moral harm, no risk of unfairness, and so no right to procedural protection. The only restraint is that each person should be treated with the equal concern and respect that we should expect from a good legislator; but that is a weak

[15] See Dworkin, *A Matter of Principle*, n. 9 above, ch. 3. [16] Ibid. 98–103.

restraint, too weak to generate specific procedural rights. And just as the outcome is a matter of policy, so procedures are matters of policy.[17]

This argument, I suggest, is mistaken and the conclusion, being contrary to both common sense and principle, unacceptable. From the premise that a person affected by a policy decision has no right to a particular outcome, the conclusion does not follow that there are no restrictions on the way an outcome should be reached. Consider the prisoner seeking early release: the grant of parole is a discretionary matter to be made as seems best in the public interest; the interests of the prisoner are affected seriously, but there is no right to parole.[18] Does that mean that anything goes; that the decision could be taken by consulting a soothsayer or casting lots; or without having regard to the facts about how the prisoner has behaved in prison, or to the prognosis as to how he might fare on release? Something has gone wrong; surely the prisoner has some moral claims about how the decision is made, about what sort of decision it is. In addition to the bare interests which clearly are at stake, there is a moral dimension, a dimension of fairness and justice. The prisoner who is denied parole by the casting of lots has been treated unfairly, not because the outcome is necessarily wrong, but because it is unjustifiable. The prisoner's claim would be that any decision affecting his interests must be justifiable, and to be justifiable, it must meet certain conditions.[19]

The mistake in Dworkin's argument is in offering too narrow a conception of rights. Rights to certain kinds of outcomes are familiar in civil and criminal trials, but that does not exhaust the range of rights. That it does not becomes obvious as soon as we recall that rights are created by authoritative standards and that the rights so created include but go beyond a simple notion of outcome-rights. Once the concept of authoritative standards of fair treatment is introduced, the full range and variety of rights based on these standards can be seen; some of them are outcome rights, but many are related to outcomes only indirectly and others are quite separate from outcomes. The discussion in section 1.3.4 has shown that certain well-settled standards govern the exercise of discretion, even where it is discretion with a substantial element of policy. If we combine that discussion and the present analysis of rights, it is easy to see that the standards governing the exercise of discretion create first-order rights and constitute the criteria of fair treatment. The rights are not rights to specific outcomes, but rights about the process and reasoning to be followed in reaching an outcome. Such rights

[17] This is the conclusion I draw from Dworkin's discussion in *A Matter of Principle*, n. 9 above, 98–102.

[18] The power could be expressed in rights: the prisoner has a right to parole if it is in the public interest. That does not help, however, since everything turns on what is thought to be in the public interest, and the prisoner has no right that any particular view be taken.

[19] For development of this general argument, see T. Scanlon, 'Due Process' in J. Pennock and J. Chapman, *Due Process* (Nomos xvii, New York University Press, New York, 1977).

are first-order rights in relation to the exercise of discretion; they are in turn the basis for further rights to the procedures necessary for that purpose.

3.2.3 Rights and Values in Relation to Policy

Now that the case has been made for procedural rights in relation to policy-based discretion, the next question to consider is the values and in turn the standards of fair treatment on which procedural rights are based. Questions about what values ought to govern the relations between the citizen and the state in discretionary contexts are bound to be answered in different ways. We could take a clean slate and start at the beginning, devising a set of values which could be defended at every turn; alternatively, we could concentrate on the law as it is, explicating and developing the values that have been incorporated. Neither would be entirely satisfactory and a middle way between the two has much to commend it. Our interest is in law, in revealing and evaluating its underlying values; but we also want to subject law to critical assessment on the basis of more fundamental moral and political values. In this way we keep our feet on the legal ground, while recognizing that that ground is never entirely separate from the neighbouring ground of moral principle. In considering the values that apply in policy decisions, I shall not endeavour to give a complete account or justification; my object is to identify some of those values, to show in brief how they can be supported and how they generate procedural rights.

Before considering what values might apply in discretionary contexts, it may be of help to examine more closely the argument that procedures here are a matter of policy. That argument, as we have just seen, is mistaken, but it is worth examining further its underlying assumptions. One assumption is that a strict division must be made between the realm of legal rights on the one hand, and the sphere of government and administration on the other. According to the division, a community decides which interests are to have the status of rights under law; which rights it creates are matters for its legislative and judicial processes. But once legal rights are created, they should be given proper procedural protection. If, however, matters are left to government and administration, they should be dealt with as seems best in the public interest and the rights of individuals have no place. The argument draws on a certain view of the constitution: each of us, on this view, surrenders to parliament, in a once and for all manner, full and final authority as to what rights we have, and therefore the drawing of the line between law on the one side and politics and policy on the other. The fullness of that authority and the finality of the surrender mean that the individual person holds nothing back; no moral capital is retained on which to found a claim that even the administration must not neglect the person, each with his interests and concerns, and must be conducted according to certain standards of fair treatment.

Any such view of the constitution is unacceptable for a number of reasons. The point has often been made that the actions of government and administration should be responsive to groups and individuals, not just once in the formulation of legal rules, but repeatedly at many levels of administrative activity.[20] The need to have institutions and practices which are responsive to the community through reason, involvement, and explanation is one way of making government more accountable and justifiable. The idea of responsive law captures the point nicely;[21] each institution of government, in making its decisions, should develop ways of responding to the interests and claims of the community. It must act in the public interest where the public interest includes consideration of, but goes beyond, the interests of those affected. The challenge then for both law and politics is to find ways of making government responsive in this manner. Now while this propounds a specific approach to government, it does not tell us precisely how administration can be more responsive to the community. Nor does it tell us where to draw the line between the need for government to govern, to act as it thinks best, positively and decisively, and the need to take account of the personal interests that are affected. There are dangers on both sides: government which is too restricted by the demands of responsiveness may cease to be effective, while government which ignores those demands risks being illegitimate. There has to be a balance between the two, but just where it lies in each area of administration is a matter to be worked out through reason and reflection. The general point, however, is that the legitimacy of modern administration turns in some part on there being a commitment in principle to responsiveness, on recognizing that proper concern for the person affected is a legitimate element of the public interest.

3.2.4 The Right to Consideration

Against that background, let us now consider how to give content to the general principle, to identify the values which should be inserted into it. One idea is often expressed in terms of non-arbitrariness, the claim being that each person has a right to be treated in a way that is non-arbitrary.[22] Now arbitrariness is an elusive concept, but it does convey an idea of what is important in the relationship between citizen and state: the individual with

[20] Amongst the writers who have pursued this theme, see I. Harden and N. Lewis, *The Noble Lie* (Hutchinson, London, 1986); M. Detmold, *Courts and Administrators* (Weidenfeld and Nicolson, London, 1989); and D. J. Galligan, *Discretionary Powers*, n. 12 above.

[21] This expression is used by P. Nonet and P. Selznick in *Law and Society in Transition* (University of California Press, Berkeley, Cal., 1978).

[22] For a discussion on these lines, see T. M. Scanlon, 'Due Process' in Pennock and Chapman, *Due Process*, n. 19 above.

his interests and concerns in some sense counts in the deliberations of the discretionary decision-maker.[23] Individual persons are very much affected by discretionary decisions where the wider public interest is the main concern, and the fact that some of the most fundamental interests in liberty, property, livelihood, and status are vulnerable to administrative action is a sound basis for restraint in pursuit of the public interest. It is then a short step to a normative principle which takes account of that vulnerability and justifies minimum standards of protection.

The principle may be called the principle of consideration, suggesting that the interests of those affected must be taken into account, while allowing that ultimately they may be overridden by wider notions of public interest. But while a sense of public interest may prevail, it does so only after proper account is taken of the interests affected. The principle insists on the official responding to those interests while retaining the decision as to the course of action finally to be followed. The principle of consideration guarantees no result, but it shows that the interests of persons are an element of the public interest and should be taken seriously. The principle of consideration in turn generates a right to consideration.[24] We now have a clear thread running between basic, moral, and legal rights: the basic right to be treated with respect as a person justifies a moral right to consideration in the affairs of government, while that moral right provides the case for a legal right to certain standards of fair treatment governing the exercise of discretion. The standards in turn generate rights to appropriate procedures.

The right to consideration in discretionary decisions might be compelling in principle but seems hopelessly vague in practical application. The sentiment is noble: each person should count and administrators are never justified in simply ignoring the interests of those affected. But how does it help the prisoner seeking parole, the applicant for a licence, or the objectors to the motorway? What is necessary in such cases to satisfy the right to consideration and so to avoid treating the person unfairly? The answers to such questions are unlikely to be clear or simple; since the range of administrative decisions is variable, and the interests that may be affected are diverse, the right balance between the public interest and regard for the individual person is likely also to be variable. This can be illustrated by contrasting an individualized decision, whether to grant parole for example, and the decision as to which route a motorway should follow.[25] In the parole case, it is

[23] One of the difficulties in trying to use arbitrariness as a critical concept is that what amounts to arbitrariness depends on what it means, in different contexts, to take a person into account; arbitrariness is of no help in answering that question.

[24] The argument here is presented in more detail in D. J. Galligan, 'Rights, Discretion and Procedure' in Sampford and Galligan, *Law, Rights and the Welfare State*, n. 13 above.

[25] For the classification of administrative decisions as adjudicative, modified adjudicative, specific policy, and general policy, see my discussion in *Discretionary Powers*, n. 12 above, 114–17.

reasonable to expect close attention to be paid to the situation of the prisoner, even though, finally, the decision might be made to deny parole because of the need to protect the public. But in order for the decision to be justifiable, the parole agency should inquire closely into the facts about the prisoner's case, his record in prison, and the likely risk he would pose to the public. In making the motorway decision, on the other hand, many people, interests, and factors are involved and, while all must be considered, the principle of consideration in respect of any one person or interest would demand less. It might be enough, in justifying the decision, to show that the many claims and arguments put forward have been looked at, that some of them are irreconcilable, and that finally a course has been settled which is rational, reasonable, and in good faith.

It can be seen from these examples that precisely what is required by the right to consideration has to be worked out in different contexts, taking account of the nature and purpose of the power and of the range and importance of the interests affected. Some content can be derived from intermediate standards like purposiveness, rationality, and reasonableness, with each giving some guidance as to how powers are to be used, and with each placing some restrictions on what is permissible. Administrative powers should be exercised for the purposes stated in or capable of being extrapolated from the statute; they should be used rationally in the sense that decisions are intelligible applications of purposes and, at the same time, meet the ordinary canons of reasoning. Powers should be used rationally and reasonably, suggesting that not only are all the relevant matters to be taken into account, but that the outcome is itself reasonable, the product of reflection and reasoned judgment. These notions are the foundations of judicial review of discretionary authority, as we shall see later on. However, standards like these go only a short way towards protecting the person affected; a policy decision can be purposive, rational, and even reasonable without ensuring the required level of consideration of the person.

Take purpose and rationality in relation to parole: the governing statute is unlikely to provide much guidance beyond specifying very general policy goals; decisions of the parole authorities might pursue those goals in ways which are rational and purposive and yet pay scant attention to the situation of the prisoner. If they were to decide that in the interests of public protection, all prisoners whose estimated risk of reconviction is more than ten per cent should be denied parole, it would be difficult to argue that such an approach is beyond purposes or inherently irrational. Now suppose that we insert the principle of consideration, the idea that the prisoner must be treated with respect, that his interests and situation must be taken into account. A new dimension is added: it is itself open and indeterminate, but there is now an additional matter which is required expressly to be put in the balance. What constitutes purpose and what satisfies reason have a sharper focus, since they must now include a concern for the specific circumstances of the prisoner. The grounds of justification have now changed so that a decision will be justifiable only if it adopts a conception of the public interest, which not only advances purposes rationally and reasonably, but also takes proper account of the particular case.

The right to consideration adds to policy decisions a value which must be respected in decision-making. The value remains constant across different decisions, but the practical standards needed to ensure respect for it vary according to the context. The right to consideration in turn justifies rights to procedures, the procedures being those necessary to ensure proper consideration in the discretionary process. They will normally include familiar procedural forms: knowing the issues to be decided and where possible the criteria to be applied; having an opportunity to make one's case, to address the issues, and to respond to others; and being provided with an explanation and justification for the final decision. The right to consideration does not necessarily mean that all or any of these particular procedures are to be followed; for example, the right to consideration does not necessarily include the power to participate. Participation will normally be a part of the right, but participation is an instrument to proper consideration and whether it is needed in a given context will depend on the context. The same applies to other procedures; the justification for each is that it is instrumental to the principle of consideration. Sufficient steps may have been taken at an earlier stage to ensure adequate consideration of those affected, with the result that no special procedures are needed at the administrative level. According to the principle of selective representation it is necessary to ensure only that, taking the policy process as a whole, the interests of groups and individuals are properly considered.[26] The principle of consideration can be satisfied in a number of ways at a number of points in the regulatory process.[27]

To conclude, the starting point in developing the right to consideration was the recognition that important values about the treatment of persons apply to discretionary decision-making even where the overriding concern is the public interest. The basis for those values and the standards based on them is a moral view about the relationship between the citizen and the state. Views may differ about the precise terms of the relationship and therefore about the normative standards governing it. I suggest, however, that there is a central and irreducible principle that, in the discretionary, policy-making functions of the administrative state, the interests, circumstances, and concerns of individuals and groups should be taken into account in making a decision. This right to consideration of course has to be

[26] On the principle of selective representation, see Galligan, *Discretionary Powers*, n. 12 above, section 7.3.2.

[27] A point along these lines is well made by T. M. Scanlon in his essay 'Due Process' in Pennock and Chapman, *Due Process*, n. 19 above.

interpreted in each context, but my suggestion is that it is morally compelling in the sense that it should be included in any set of acceptable principles governing the citizen–state relationship. The right to consideration can be seen at work in notions of non-arbitrariness, purposiveness, and reasonableness; but it goes beyond them and constitutes a dynamic principle of fair treatment. The right to consideration in turn generates and justifies suitable procedural rights. Finally, the right to consideration is not the only right in the discretionary, policy-making context. There may be other standards of fair treatment which ground other rights, principles of consistency and non-discrimination being examples.

3.3 THE PROBLEM OF MISTAKES

3.3.1 The Problem Stated

Anyone witnessing the spectacular miscarriages of justice in the criminal justice system of the United Kingdom in recent years will have been deeply disturbed by them. A number of people had been convicted of serious crimes, and then after years of imprisonment the convictions were shown to have been mistaken or at least seriously unreliable. The long years of unwarranted punishment are bad enough, but worse is the sense that the system has failed and, in failing, worked grave injustice. It is serious enough that fundamental rights of those wrongly convicted and punished have been violated; it is even more serious that society itself has transgressed its own fundamental principles and thereby impoverished itself. To express such a human tragedy in procedural terms may seem pedestrian, but the reasons for the tragedy are themselves pedestrian: the procedures for investigating crime and trying suspects failed; they failed by producing the wrong outcome, by reaching a verdict of guilt without justification.

This is a grave example of a problem which is repeated throughout the legal system, the problem being how to make sure that the procedures lead to the right results. The consequences of failure to do so are several. One set of consequences is to the community in failing to achieve its own objectives as expressed in its laws. Those objectives are frustrated, and the frustration comes at substantial cost in procedures and institutions. Some mistakes go farther and cause moral wrong to members of the community, which is also an additional cost to the community as a whole. The other set of costs is to the person wronged, and that cost has two forms: the bare cost in the sense of hard treatment, and the moral cost in the sense of injustice. The gravity of those costs will vary in each case according to the importance of the rights in issue. Not all mistaken decisions cause wrong to individuals; some will have no effect, others may be windfalls. The guilty suspect who is acquitted, or the welfare claimant mistakenly given benefits, is unlikely to complain;[28] but where the individual person is treated unfairly by being deprived of a right to which he is entitled, injustice results and the integrity of the process is called into question.

The mistakes most often in issue are mistakes as to outcomes. They are mistakes which result when procedures fail to lead to an outcome specified by law. However, not all outcomes are so clearly defined. Where there is discretion, there is likely to be some scope for different decisions, any one of which will be within the scope of powers. Some decisions may be better than others, but they will be mistaken only if they go beyond the range of permissible options or violate the right to consideration or the other standards of fair treatment discussed earlier. A decision which breaches the values relating to consistent treatment, or which fails to take account of a person's interests, affects outcomes and can be dealt with as a mistake which leads to the wrong result. Mistakes may also occur in relation to non-outcome values, when the resulting injustice consists in violating values which ought to be respected. Nevertheless, such mistakes are analogous to mistakes as to outcomes, and where non-outcome values create rights, violation of those values will mean a violation of rights. A mistaken interception of confidential communications, for example, may be a breach of rights. The main issue in such cases is what recourse there should be; whether the violation should be considered to taint the outcome, or whether the remedy should be separate and independent. This problem is familiar in the law of evidence, where the question often arises whether breach of a non-outcome right in gathering evidence should affect the trial; different jurisdictions solve the problem in different ways.

Amongst the various kinds of mistakes possible, I shall concentrate on those relating to outcomes. Although there is clearly a cost to society in failing to achieve its aims, the mistakes which present the most serious problems are those causing harm to individual persons. In order to examine those costs more closely, we should first be clear about precisely what the problem is. Suppose X has a right to a welfare payment when certain conditions are met. The decision is left to a special tribunal, but its procedures are defective and, although X meets the conditions, the tribunal decides otherwise. X's right to the benefit is denied. Had the procedures been better, had the tribunal not acted, say, on unconfirmed hearsay evidence against X, it would have found in his favour. In short, inadequate procedures have led to X being denied his right. From this example, a general formulation of the problem of mistakes can be drawn: society confers a legal right and creates in the right-holder a moral claim that the right be upheld; it then fails to honour the claim by not providing adequate procedures; in being denied the claim, the right-holder is treated unfairly.

[28] M. Bayles gives a full account of the different mistakes in his book *Procedural Justice*, n. 11 above, 115–35.

The ideal solution would be to have procedures which always produce the right results, but that solution is not always available for two reasons. The first is resources. While we can easily imagine how legal and administrative procedures could be improved—by better design, by better training of officials, by more scrutiny and review—the reality is that the resources required would be likely to be more than a society, even an affluent one, could afford. The demands on a society's resources are many and usually outstrip what is available; compromises have to be made and balances have to be struck between competing social goals. The result may be that, because of other pressing social goals, the resources available for legal processes fall short and a less than satisfactory system is accepted. Inadequate procedures will lead to mistakes and at least some of those mistakes will result in the failure to give effect to rights. The second reason why procedures fail is that they are inherently imperfect. The idea of imperfect procedures has been explained;[29] briefly, the point is that in applying standards and finding facts errors occur and, while we know the result being sought, we can never be certain that in any particular case it has been reached.

Procedures which fail for lack of resources will be referred to as inadequate procedures; those which fail because of the inherent imperfection of legal procedures will be called imperfect procedures. The two kinds of defect have more in common than first appears. For while there will always be an element of risk that a mistake has been made because of imperfect procedures, the risk can be greatly reduced by creating procedures which, from past knowledge and experience, we believe to be reliable. We have good reason to believe, for example, that more exacting procedures governing the treatment and questioning of suspects help to reduce the risk of mistaken convictions. Similarly, the better training of officers deciding welfare claims and allowing them more time to consider each case would reduce the high level of mistaken outcomes. The provision of more resources in designing and applying legal procedures and in training officials is the key to reducing mistakes, even though the element of risk due to imperfection cannot be fully removed. The connection between inadequate or misspent resources in legal processes and mistakes will be the main focus in the following discussion.

3.3.2 Rights and Mistakes

The question now to consider is how mistakes due to inadequate procedures can be accommodated in an account of procedural rights. There seems to be a paradox. On the one hand, in creating a right, society commits itself to upholding the right and we would expect its commitment to include provision of the resources and the procedures necessary for the purpose. On the other

[29] See section 1.3.4.

hand, resources are limited so that procedures are likely to be inadequate to a greater or lesser degree, and this will in turn lead to mistaken outcomes and the violation of rights.

In order to resolve the paradox, we should be clear about the relationship between rights and inadequate procedures. In doing so, two different views of rights should be sketched. On one view, the unavoidability of inadequate procedures should be taken into account in the very definition of rights. If I have a right to X—where X is a certain outcome—and there are only enough resources to ensure 70 per cent accuracy, then my right to X is subject to that risk of error. Where the risk eventuates and the result is mistaken, no violation of rights occurs since the risk is part of the definition of the right. It is true that in creating rights, the legislature or other right-creating authority could define them in that way. Parliament could create a welfare right and then provide only a very limited procedure for giving effect to the right, with a high level of mistakes being an inevitable consequence. The right is not to welfare absolutely but to welfare as determined according to the specified procedures. Provided the procedures were followed, an applicant could not complain where a mistake was made that his right to the benefit had been violated; he could not complain because his only right would be to have the claim decided according to the specified procedures.[30] This is a very odd view of rights. [31] An alternative view of the relationship between rights and procedures is illustrated by the claim that the innocent suspect has a right to be acquitted in all cases, not just a certain percentage of them. Similarly for the welfare claimant. On this view, the right to be treated in a certain way should be kept separate from questions of procedure. It is the right, or perhaps more accurately the moral claim on which the right rests, which grounds the claim for certain procedures. The right remains intact whether or not adequate procedures are provided, and where they are not adequate, the right is violated.

The difference between these two views of rights is fundamental. The first suggests that the risk which stems from mistakes is part of the definition of the right; and since the risk is part of the definition of the right, when the risk eventuates, it is justifiable. The Birmingham Six or anyone else wrongly convicted could be told that, although they are probably innocent, their case is one where the risk did eventuate and so there has been no violation of rights. Such a view is clearly unacceptable. The second view makes no such concession; it distinguishes the integrity of rights from the practicalities of procedures. Inadequate procedures lead to the violation of rights and cause unjust treatment; inadequate procedures cannot be justified but they might

[30] Notice that, in making such a claim, we move from procedures as imperfect instruments to certain outcomes to regarding procedures as adequate in themselves; there is, in other words, a subtle shift from imperfect procedures to pure procedures.

[31] It does, however, have some support in one strand of American writings on due process: see F. Easterbrook, 'Substance and Due Process' [1982] *Sup. Ct. Rev.* 85.

in some circumstances be excused as unavoidable for practical reasons, the practical reasons being that procedures are imperfect and society lacks the resources to make them as reliable as possible.[32] The accused mistakenly convicted is unjustly treated, and, should the mistake become known, he has a strong moral claim to have it remedied. The moral harm in failing, through inadequate or imperfect procedures, to respect rights remains, even though in some circumstances the community as a whole may be excused for not providing better procedures. The community might be excused because resources are scarce; but excuses are not justifications and the injustices which result from inadequate procedures remain.

The second view of rights is the more compelling of the two and has practical significance for procedures. It confirms the idea that procedures are means to the protection of rights and to just treatment. At one level they are practical instruments to social goals, but they are more; as the means for upholding rights, they are necessary elements in society's moral commitment to do so. If they fail in the task, moral harm is caused. The extent of the moral harm can be seen in its most brutal form when the innocent are wrongly convicted, but the same idea applies in more muted form in other cases. In the administrative context, the inadequacy of procedures is less dramatic but more pervasive. Empirical research is beginning to show that the decisions of agencies, officials, and tribunals are seriously unreliable, with almost as much chance of being wrong as being right.[33] The procedures are inadequate and serious injustice results.

Now while procedures are an essential means to the upholding of rights, the problem remains how this can be reconciled with the fact that the procedures will often be inadequate. The moral claim to have one's rights respected supports the case for whatever procedures are needed, while the scarcity of resources in practice undermines that claim. It is not clear that there is an entirely satisfactory or principled way of reconciling this conflict. If procedures are inadequate, rights are violated; but we know as a matter of practical knowledge that, because of insufficient resources and inherent imperfections, procedures will often be inadequate and mistakes will result. The best a society can do is to recognize that inadequate and imperfect procedures lead to the denial of rights and the infliction of moral harm. Every effort should be made to devise the best procedures possible within the resources available. If a society uses its best efforts within that constraint to devise adequate procedures, any procedural inadequacy may be excused as unavoidable. But to excuse is not to justify, so that any violation of rights resulting from the inadequacy is still unjustifiable moral harm.

[32] On the distinction between justification and excuse, see H. L. A. Hart, *Punishment and Responsibility* (Clarendon Press, Oxford, 1968), ch. 2.

[33] See the study of social welfare by J. Baldwin, N. Wikely, and R. Young, *Judging Social Security* (Clarendon Press, Oxford, 1993).

3.3.3 An Alternative View of Inadequate Procedures

An alternative way of coping with the problems of inadequate procedures is put forward by R. Dworkin in an important essay on procedural rights.[34] Dworkin begins with the principle that each person has a right not to be convicted for a crime of which he is innocent. To convict mistakenly is to deprive a person of rights and to inflict moral harm upon him. The same principle applies to other rights besides those relating to wrongful conviction and to other types of legal process. The next step in Dworkin's argument is to consider how inadequate resources and the mistakes which sometimes result can be reconciled with respect for rights. He recognizes that because of the many demands made on a society's resources, legal procedures will often be inadequate. That is an unavoidable fact which must be dealt with in considering the extent of procedural rights. This leads to the third step in the argument which is to conclude that a person does not have a right to the most accurate process which can be devised; that would be to impose too great a burden on society, a burden which anyhow it could not bear. A person's procedural rights are something less: first, to have the moral harm in the deprivation of a legal right given a value commensurate with its value in the general morality of the society; secondly, to have that value applied consistently to all cases. The idea behind the first right is that the moral harm or injustice in failing to protect a right varies in its seriousness in accordance with the importance of the right. Any procedures dealing with rights should reflect that importance; the more important the right, the more important it is that questions about it be properly decided. Procedures should reflect that level of importance. Once those procedures have been set, the second moral right requires that they be applied equally to any case which occurs. Dworkin's conclusion is that a person's right to procedures in any context is determined by applying the two moral rights.

While this is an interesting and important analysis, it is not entirely satisfactory. In the first place, the analysis does not make clear the relationship between procedural rights and rights to outcomes. What happens to the innocent person's right to acquittal where procedures are inadequate and lead to conviction? Dworkin is not clear on this point. He does say that, provided the level of risk of a mistake occurring reflects the moral harm in that case in comparison with the moral harm of other kinds of cases, then society's duty, being the duty to make available the procedures for the lesser right, is discharged. Does that mean that the accused's right not to be wrongly convicted is reduced to a lesser right, to a right to an outcome where there is a risk of it being mistaken? Dworkin would undoubtedly wish to maintain the stronger right not to be wrongly convicted without qualification,

[34] Dworkin, *A Matter of Principle*, n. 9 above, ch. 3.

since to suggest that the person who is wrongly convicted, no matter how good the procedures are in general, is not denied his rights and treated with gross injustice, would be preposterous. But one cannot have it both ways: one cannot claim both that the accused has a right not to be wrongly convicted *and* a right to procedures which run the risk of a mistaken conviction. To adhere to both, as Dworkin appears to, is to drive an unwarranted wedge between rights to outcomes and rights to procedures. For a right to outcomes means very little if it does not include as a necessary element of the right itself a justified claim to the procedures necessary to give effect to it. Or, to put it another way, rights to procedures are part of the measure of rights to outcomes, so that to reduce the latter is also to reduce the former.

The reason for the unsatisfactory account of the relationship between rights to outcomes and rights to procedures may be the need to avoid the awful prospect of rights being trumped by policies. But that surely is precisely what is happening; rights to certain outcomes are reduced by moving the emphasis from rights to outcome to rights to procedures. In this way, Dworkin is able to offer a view of procedural rights which, in its very composition, takes account of the necessities of policy (in the sense of scarce resources). Having divorced procedural rights from rights to outcome, Dworkin is free to give a conception of procedural rights which accommodates the problem of scarce resources. But when closely inspected the solution collapses: regardless of how it is presented, the need to take account of insufficient resources in devising procedures has the effect of reducing rights and leading on occasions to injustice. Dworkin's analysis cannot finally cope with the fact that, in procedural matters, policy considerations reduce the value of rights.

The approach advanced earlier is better: it maintains the integrity of the special relationship between rights to outcomes and rights to procedures, while accepting that for unavoidable policy reasons rights will sometimes be sacrificed. It is surely better to admit that that is the true cost of inadequate procedures, rather than to imagine that the two can satisfactorily be reconciled. Here my argument differs from Dworkin's: for while he holds that one's claim and, therefore, one's right is to only such procedures as are required by the principle of proportion, my argument is that one has a right to adequate procedures but that right may have to be compromised for practical reasons. The difference is subtle but important; it is important theoretically because on my view the claim to have one's rights properly protected remains undiminished, while on Dworkin's view that claim is replaced by the weaker one that rights should be protected to the extent required by the principle of proportion. It also matters practically in that my approach gives substantial impetus to the need to devise procedures which do not just meet the demands of the principle of proportion, but which actually lead to the right results. That incentive may lead to a more imaginative approach in designing procedures which, without extra cost, do produce accurate outcomes.

The second problem with Dworkin's analysis (which is not unrelated to the first) is a failure to distinguish between issues relating to rights to outcomes and procedures, on the one hand, and questions relating to the distribution of the risks of mistakes, on the other hand. The real thrust of Dworkin's analysis, I suggest, is in relation to the latter rather than the former. Let me explain this point more fully. Once it is recognized that inadequate procedures create a risk of mistaken outcomes and, therefore, in some cases cause injustice, the question arises how that risk should be distributed among those who might be its victims. To put the point another way, without resiling from the position that parties to legal processes have rights to outcomes, or in discretionary contexts to their cases being considered in a certain way, we may seek a way of distributing the risks of injustice created by inadequate procedures. The issue of distribution can be regarded as distinct and discrete, within which questions of fairness in distribution have to be addressed.[35] Dworkin's two principles of commensurability (or proportionality) and consistency are best understood as a means for dealing with that issue.

Once that unpalatable truth is accepted, we should go on to consider whether the risk of error which flows from inadequate procedures can be distributed in a manner which is fair. The true value of Dworkin's two subsidiary rights lies, I suggest, in distributing fairly that risk. They are not substitutes for or a weakening of the moral claim to have one's first-order legal rights respected.

3.3.4 The Principle of Proportion

Now that we have seen how severely limited resources lead to inadequate procedures, the next matter to consider is how the resulting risk of mistaken outcomes should be distributed. It would be better not to have any risk at all; but if some risk is unavoidable, then it should be distributed fairly amongst those who might be affected.[36] The guiding principle is to treat people with equal concern and respect; what constitutes equal concern and respect in this context should be the relative importance of the substantive rights at issue. A mistaken conviction for a serious crime is a more serious violation of rights than the wrongful denial of a welfare benefit, even though the latter might be very important. Such differences ought to be reflected in the distribution of risk.

[35] An analogy may be drawn with questions of fairness in sentencing.

[36] Hart's distinction between the general justifying aim of a social institution and the principles of distribution within it, is helpful here. See Hart, *Punishment and Responsibility*, n. 32 above, ch. 1.

These ideas can be expressed as a principle of commensurability or proportion. A society should form a judgment on two matters: one is the comparative importance of the moral harm which may result from inadequate procedures, while the other is how those harms compare with other social goals. The first judgment would result in a scale of legal rights according to their comparative importance; the second would provide the basis for allocating resources for procedures. In practice the two parts are likely to be merged into one practical judgment about the kinds of procedures which would reflect the seriousness of the rights at stake and the relative importance of avoiding mistakes. In creating new rights, Parliament should take a view about how important the right is relative to other rights, and then set the procedures, again by comparison with the procedures used in other contexts. Courts and administrators should act in the same way when procedural issues come before them.

The principle of proportionality should be supplemented by the principle of equal treatment or consistency. The second principle means that the weighting attached to different rights should be maintained consistently in each case (although arguably, consistency is already implicit in the principle of proportionality). How different rights are weighted is to be determined by examining the law as a whole.[37] To take a simple example, once the procedures in criminal matters are established, they ought to be made available to all defendants on trial. The principle of equal treatment in allocating risks is not confined to ensuring that established procedures are consistently applied, but is a dynamic principle which guides the formation of procedures. An example of the dynamic quality can be seen in the procedural principle that in a civil trial the contest between the parties ought to be even. As A. A. S. Zuckerman has shown in his studies of civil procedure, the rationale of the fair contest idea is that the risk of mistaken outcomes should be borne equally by the parties.[38]

In explaining the principle of proportion in distributing the risk of error, one problem remains. The account so far has been concerned with ranking rights according to their relative importance and in ensuring that, in applying the ranking, right-holders are treated consistently. But how is the ranking to be made, and will any ranking do? Can society give as little or as much weight to a particular right as it thinks fit, or are there some limits on what it may do? Is society free to hold that, while a mistaken conviction for serious offences is more important than the same for a minor offence, it is not all that troubled by either and, considering the possible social advantages of a high conviction rate, procedures are set which allow for a high degree of

[37] Dworkin, *A Matter of Principle*, n. 9 above, 212.

[38] See the discussion of this point in A. A. S. Zuckerman, 'Interlocutory Remedies in Quest of Procedural Fairness'. Also of interest here is A. A. S. Zuckerman, 'Quality and Economy in Civil Procedure' (1994) 14 *Oxford JLS* 353.

mistakes? Such an approach clearly goes beyond the limits of what might reasonably be excused, but, to see why, the process of ranking must be considered more closely.

Ranking involves two steps: one to decide the relative importance of different rights, the other to decide how seriously society takes rights at all. The first presents fewer problems; opinions may differ as to how rights should be ranked relative to each other, but provided society conscientiously attempts to rank them, it will have discharged its duties. The second step is more contentious: here society must decide the relationship between its almanac of rights and all the other things it values. That step itself involves a double judgment: in creating a right in the first place, society makes an initial decision that a certain interest warrants the protection of rights; but it must then further decide how serious it would be if, on a particular occasion, that right were denied. This may seem curious, but the two decisions are necessary wherever there is a risk of inadequate or imperfect procedures. Indeed, the practical worth of a right is judged on the answer society gives to the second part of the decision, that is, how seriously the protection of the right is valued.[39]

How should the relationship between rights and other things of value be decided? Dworkin suggests it be left to the democratic process; that is to say, the inevitable disagreement about the relationship is best resolved through the fair compromise of the democratic process.[40] That may be the best approach, with the important qualification that, although it might be fair for parliament to decide, parliament ought to decide justly. It would not do for parliament to hold that, although certain rights have been created, they need not be highly valued, and that procedures allowing a high level of mistakes would be tolerable. Parliament is surely bound, not to do what it thinks best where that might mean anything it likes, but to do as the values embedded in the law and morality of the society dictate. Just as the judge is expected to decide a hard case not as he thinks best, all things considered, but according to what he thinks is the best interpretation of the law, so parliament should decide according to its interpretation of the law and morality of the society.[41] To act otherwise would not only convey a lack of integrity,[42] it would violate

[39] The distinction between the two issues is not often noticed; rights are usually discussed as if the only issue is whether an interest has the status of a right. It is assumed that once that status is conferred, the right-holder has a moral right to procedures for its protection, where protection means complete protection. The present account suggests that the moral right is only to such procedures as are proportionate to the seriousness of violating the right. Dworkin in 'Principle, Policy, Procedure' in *A Matter of Principle*, n. 9 above, is the only writer I know of who notices the distinction, but it is a distinction that even he does not note in his work: compare *Taking Rights Seriously*, n. 5 above, ch. 4.

[40] *A Matter of Principle*, n. 9 above, 87–8.

[41] This is, roughly, Dworkin's own approach to adjudication: *Taking Rights Seriously*, n. 5 above, ch. 4.

[42] Here I am using that notion in Dworkin's sense: see *Law's Empire* (Fontana, London, 1986).

the moral rights of members of the community to be treated in accordance with its moral principles. Parliament, in deciding on the law, should be guided by the moral principles of the society.[43]

This point can be linked to another. Some moral rights prevailing in the community will not be just the accidents, as it were, of the history of that community; they will be grounded in basic rights, and for that reason will carry such overriding weight that the law ought to respect them. The values grounding basic rights are not values to be balanced against other considerations; they are absolute, or as close to absolute as a value can be, and the society has a correlative duty of equal gravity to make sure they are not violated by law. The right not to be wrongly convicted and punished for a serious criminal offence is one such basic right and there might be others. The claim which can then justifiably be made against society, in respect of any such right, to lay down procedures which produce accurate outcomes in all cases, is strong indeed. It is tempting to assert that the claim is so strong that society must not ask what level of support is acceptable, all things considered, but what needs to be done to be sure that basic rights are protected completely. But that would be too strong; even here, it could not be insisted that society should remove all possibility of error through inadequate or imperfect procedures. Society can be excused for not dedicating unlimited resources to prevent mistakes, but the scope for excusable error in the case of the most important rights is very narrow. In the ranking process, respect for certain rights must be numbered amongst the most important social values, and, in the design of procedures, the very highest standards of accuracy should be sought.

3.4 DEVISING PROCEDURES AND CALCULATING COSTS

The creation of procedures might seem to be a straightforward, practical matter: if the standards governing decision-making are clear, procedures are needed which apply them accurately; if the process is discretionary, procedures are needed to ensure outcomes which advance rationally and reasonably the objects and purposes for which it has been granted. Various kinds of standards based on the different tiers of values have to be accommodated, but again that is a practical matter; effectiveness and economy can be improved with trial and error as mistakes and shortcomings appear. However, procedures are not only practical matters, but also raise issues of principle. They require resources where resources are limited, and they

[43] A proper explanation of this claim cannot be given here, but the sense of morality I have in mind is the critical rather than the positive or popular morality. See Dworkin, *Taking Rights Seriously*, n. 5 above, ch. 7.

involve competition amongst competing ends and values; we have seen that competition at work in the discussion of mistakes. The design of procedures is, for these reasons, a complicated process. The precise form procedures take and the balance between conflicting values has to be resolved in the context of each area of process, but it may be helpful in this section to sketch a general approach to the design of procedures, taking account of the claims that are made and the costs that occur.[44]

Procedures involve different kinds of costs. In order to illustrate this, let us consider again the criminal trial. First, there are the direct costs of providing courts, judges, lawyers, and related matters. Direct costs may be substantial and procedures should aim generally at keeping them to a minimum. A second category of costs relates to the objectives of each area of process: to determine guilt or innocence, to allocate licences, or to distribute benefits, and in the discretionary context, to advance its general purposes. Since society places value on achieving such objectives, whatever they may be, failure to achieve them, or to achieve them as well as might be, is a cost to society. These I shall refer to as outcome costs. [45] Outcome costs are not confined to the failure to achieve the objects of decisions, but include the costs to people who suffer from mistaken outcomes, such as the innocent who is convicted or the claimant who is refused. The parties bear the brunt of such costs, but the costs to them are also costs to society. Notice also that outcome costs are not confined to final outcomes, but may occur at different points in a process of decision-making: the policeman's mistaken failure to arrest a suspect, the judge's decision to refuse bail where it was warranted, or the minister's decision to grant parole where the risks of reconviction were too great, are all failures in achieving the objectives of legal processes. A second general aim in designing procedures should be to maximize the realization of objects and, therefore, to minimize outcome costs.

The third category of costs is the moral harm or injustice which results from bad decisions. The concept of moral harm, or the injustice factor, as explained earlier, consists in the unfairness of violating rights. The avoidance or at least minimization of moral harm should be a major concern in the design of procedures. The main victim of moral harm is the person whose rights are breached, although the neglect of an important value is also a cost to society. Moral costs are, therefore, both personal costs and social costs. The fourth category of costs is similar to the third, except here it relates to values and standards of a non-outcome kind. The failure to respect non-outcome values creates its own form of moral harm, which is primarily a cost

[44] The best and clearest account of the costs of procedures is Bayles, *Procedural Justice*, n. 11 above, ch. 6.

[45] Outcome costs are, in Bentham's terms, failures in rectitude. R. Posner refers to such costs as error costs: 'An Economic Approach to Legal Procedure and Judicial Administration' (1973) 2 *J of Legal Studies* 399.

to the person for whom the protection is meant, but also has a social dimension. Procedures should aim to minimize both kinds of moral costs; in the case of the moral costs relating to outcomes, that is done by achieving the correct outcomes, while for moral costs relating to non-outcome values, it is done by maximizing compliance with them.

This analysis of costs may sound more complicated than it really is. The approach has been to identify different types of costs, and then to suggest that procedures ought to aim at keeping each of those costs as low as possible. The approach works well for decisions of the more familiar kind, adjudication and modified adjudication, but it also applies more generally. Consider a public inquiry where the object is to make recommendations about the creation of a new town, where the impact on a wide range of interests would be substantial. The inspector is instructed to base his recommendations on a number of factors of an economical, social, and environmental kind, but the decision as to how those matters are to be balanced is left to him. Procedures must be put in train for the inspector to obtain information and to allow him to hear the evidence and arguments of interested parties. The costs in doing so are the direct costs. The inspector has discretion as to what he recommends and no interested party has a right to a particular outcome; but the inspector's recommendations (the outcome) will be judged according to how well they take account of the conflicting factors and reach a balanced view in relation to them. Provided the inspector does not stray beyond his powers, it is unlikely that anyone will suffer moral harm as a consequence of one course of action being recommended rather than another. However, important non-outcome values are likely to be in play: diverse interests ought to be considered and taken into account, and the inspector should respect the principle of consideration. To the extent that he fails to, moral harm will result to those whose concerns are neglected. We could expect arguments to be presented as to what constitutes adequate consideration in this context, but whatever interpretation is adopted, the force of the principle is clear, and if it is breached, moral harm will result. Moral harm might also result from another kind of non-outcome value; if participation is held to be a value in its own right, then the inspector should hear all who come within its scope, and again failure to do so would create moral harm. The greater the respect shown for non-outcome values relevant to the process, the less the moral costs.

Other examples could be given but it is clear that the approach to the design of procedures suggested here fits a wide variety of legal processes. However, the approach is not without its problems which can be seen by taking the criminal trial as an example. Procedures should aim: (i) at an accurate outcome (thereby minimizing outcome costs), but (ii) at the same time tilting the procedures so that, if a mistake occurs, it is more likely to be a wrongful acquittal than a wrongful conviction (thus keeping down the costs of moral harm); (iii) the procedures should make sure that non-outcome values, both at and before the trial, have been respected (again keeping down the costs of moral harm), while throughout (iv) making as little demand as possible on such resources as buildings, judges, and lawyers (and so minimizing direct costs).

An initial problem is the competition between direct and outcome costs, since in order to increase accuracy and therefore reduce outcome costs, it will normally be necessary to increase direct costs. For example the more staff employed in a welfare agency to check the claims made by applicants (increasing direct costs), the more accurate the decisions should be (reducing outcome costs).[46] How is the competition to be resolved? The answer lies in assessing the relative importance of competing public interests: for example, the desire that a decision about creating a new town be well made against the need to keep down the costs of making the decision. The idea of weighing competing factors is familiar in many areas of public activity; it means identifying the goals served by an area of administration and then deciding how much society is prepared to pay for them; or, more precisely, how much society is prepared to pay for procedures to achieve goals which have already been agreed. The balancing will be partly between competing goals, such as better roads versus better education; if more were spent on the procedures for deciding where to build roads, better decisions should result and the road network would be improved. The balancing sometimes occurs within the project itself; the amount available for welfare has to cover both the benefits and the procedures, so that a calculation then has to be made of how much should be spent on each. Poor procedures may reflect a determination to devote the bulk of resources to substantive allocations, at the risk of a high level of misallocation.[47] Calculating the costs and balancing them across social goals and within a defined goal is often a complex matter; it is however, a basic necessity of everyday government and presents no problems of principle.

When the costs of moral harm are inserted, the calculations become more complicated. The underlying problem is that the avoidance or reduction of moral harm is likely to increase both direct costs and outcome costs. The effect on direct costs is easily seen; rights are usually better protected by more exacting procedures which in turn increase direct costs. The relationship between moral costs and outcome costs needs a little more

[46] For a good account of the problems of achieving accurate decisions, see R. Sainsbury, 'Administrative Justice: Discretion and Procedure in Social Security Decision-Making' in K. Hawkins (ed.), *The Uses of Discretion* (Clarendon Press, Oxford, 1993).

[47] This internal balancing is a real problem in areas such as welfare, where the more spent on procedures, the less there is to spend on benefits. For discussion of this issue in welfare, see D. J. Galligan, 'Procedural Rights in Social Welfare' in A. Coote (ed.), *Citizens' Rights in the Modern Welfare State* (R. Oram, London, 1992).

explanation. Consider the following examples. The decisions of a welfare tribunal should make sure that the rights of applicants to benefits are upheld. Since the procedures are imperfect, it may be necessary to design them in such a way as to give the benefit of the doubt to claimants, with the result that benefits will sometimes, perhaps often, be given not only to those who are entitled but also to some who are not. The moral costs of denying benefits to those entitled will be reduced, but more mistaken outcomes in favour of the non-entitled are likely to result. But if the overall level of accurate outcomes is diminished, outcome costs are increased. The same point is illustrated in the criminal trial, where the concern not to convict wrongly and the adoption of procedures directed at that end may result in a higher level of mistaken acquittals. The same analysis can be applied to the moral costs of violating non-outcome values. In order to comply with non-outcome values, the level of accuracy of outcomes might have to be reduced: the rules restricting the admissibility of confessions, for example, or the withholding of confidential information, often mean the loss of probative evidence and a greater chance of a wrong acquittal. In other cases, compliance with non-outcome values might also improve outcomes, as in the case of giving of reasons. The direct costs of meeting non-outcome values are also in general likely to increase.

The competition between moral costs on the one side, and direct and outcome costs on the other side, should not be resolved by simply and expediently balancing the three. To take that course would be to overlook the justified claim a person has not to be deprived of rights and subjected to moral harm. The decision to create a legal right in the first place may be the product of balancing social interests, but once the decision is taken, the right-holder is given a moral commitment which is not open for reconsideration each time the question arises of enforcing the right. However, the commitment is not absolute. We have seen that, generally,[48] legal rights are qualified in the sense that full enforcement is not guaranteed and that society may be excused for allowing some risk of error. In calculating the level of risk, the governing principle is that of proportion, which, as the earlier discussion has shown, is both complex and to some degree contentious. Let it be accepted, however, that rights can be ranked, and that the levels of excusable error can be fixed. Those levels of error can then be translated into outcomes, and outcomes should be produced which are within the margin of error. The fewer the mistakes the better, but, in any event, they should be within that margin, that is to say, within the safety net of proportionality. Notice that only some mistakes cause moral harm, namely, mistakes violating rights; other mistakes are simply outcome costs in the sense that social goals are not achieved. So, the idea is to aim at outcomes

[48] The one qualification is that where legal rights are also basic rights, the commitment is exacting if not absolute; see the discussion in section 3.3.4.

which (a) are within the margins of error allowed by the principle of proportion, and (b) minimize outcome costs. A similar analysis can be made for the moral harm which may result from neglect of non-outcome values. We now have a framework for designing procedures and allocating resources which can be applied to any area of legal and administrative decisions.

4
The Virtues of Participation

Amongst the many procedural forms and doctrines participation stands out as one of the most interesting and important. Its close association with procedural fairness often leads people to conclude that without the one there cannot be the other. If that is putting the case too strongly, there is at least a strong presumption that participation will be included in considerations of procedural fairness. Several reasons can be given for this. One is that the idea of a person being heard before suffering a penalty or disadvantage is deeply embedded in the common law. The idea has long been considered fundamental to civil and criminal trials and has more recently been extended to many areas of administration. Another reason for the prominence of participation as a procedural ideal is its role in political theory and its connection with notions of democracy, since the very idea of democracy turns on citizens participating in the political process.

My main goal in this Chapter is to analyse the notion of participation in its legal and political contexts, and the scheme of the discussion will be along the following lines. In the first part, participation is considered in legal and administrative processes. The analysis follows the two lines of approach developed earlier: according to one, participatory procedures are seen as primarily instrumental to outcomes, while the other views them as serving values independent of outcomes. In the second part, the main ideas on participation found in the literature of political theory will be explored; and in the third part, I shall bring together some of the themes common to both areas. In the final section, the social basis of participation will be briefly considered and some of the practical issues highlighted.

4.1 INTRODUCTION

The contexts in which notions of participation occur are very different and might at first sight seem unrelated. Participation in legal and administrative processes has a narrow and technical meaning. Questions about participation occur in deciding whether a party is entitled to be heard, where that means having the opportunity to put one's case and to answer any opposing claims. The principles behind such matters are usually straightforward, but in practice a great deal of litigation is conducted about precisely what procedures are needed to satisfy the hearing requirements. For Americans these questions arise under the procedural due process clauses of the Constitution or from similar provisions in state laws, while in Britain their vehicle is the common law notion of natural justice. This is not to say that a hearing is automatically required in all legal and administrative processes; some of the fustier corners of administration still escape the light of the hearing principle, although they are gradually being diminished, either by statutory provision or by the courts' developing a general principle of procedural fairness.[1] Ideas of participation in the political process are more complex and varied and have long been the subject of argument and discussion. Political philosophers tend to agree that participation is fundamental to democratic politics, but seriously disagree about why it is important and what form it should take.

Despite the obvious differences between participation in legal processes on the one hand and in political processes on the other hand, certain common ground can be found. In the first place, the justifications given for participation are in principle similar and generally divide into three camps: one is that participation is an instrument to certain kinds of outcomes; another is that participation is an instrument to or in some way serves other values which are held to be important; and the third is that participation is simply a good thing in itself. These justifications can themselves be complex and may be understood in different ways, and the main object of the following discussion is to examine them more closely. A second factor which encourages the search for common ground in understanding participation is that administrative processes often fall between the legal and the political, and incorporate elements of both. This is especially so where administrative processes are directed to general policy matters, but may also be the case where individualized processes involve elements of policy. In order, therefore, to understand its place in administrative processes, we need to draw on ideas of participation in both their legal and political contexts.

A third reason why participation appears to be closely linked to procedural fairness derives from the idea that it enables a person to exert influence over the processes by which he or she is affected. This idea taps a deep spring in modern political theory: it conveys the idea that persons ought to be in charge of their lives and future, and that being involved in any process affecting them is one way of doing so. Whether that involvement has any effect in practice is another matter, just as it is another matter what form the involvement should take. This idea of participation is often associated with a sense of citizenship, that is, of people being actively engaged in shaping their communities in all their aspects. The idea of active citizenship has particular attraction in contemporary societies; its force can be seen in the great revival of interest in theories of participation and in their

[1] For the American position, see Ch. 6; for Britain, see Ch. 5.

implications for democratic theory. The practical reality of active citizenship is again another matter; but what is clear is that the ideal and its association with participation is a major tenet of modern political psychology.

4.2 A NOTE ON THE FORMS OF PARTICIPATION

A preliminary matter in dealing with participation is to be clear about what it means. Participation is one of those general concepts commonly and loosely used as if it had one settled and invariable meaning. The truth is that participation in legal and political processes may take many forms, some involving a person closely in the process, others allowing for only the barest connection. Examples are participation by voting, by being able to express one's opinion, or by full representation through an adversarial procedure; but these are just a few of the innumerable ways of participating, which can vary so much that we may question whether anything is gained by using the concept in a general and undifferentiated way. It may be useful then, before beginning a more detailed examination of the concept, to sketch the main forms it takes.

The adjudicative model is a good starting point. Participation here usually means full involvement of the parties in the sense that they know the issue and are able to present their own cases and respond to the case against them. The parties are free to call witnesses and to present evidence as they wish, subject to relevance and considerations of cost and delay. Participation of this kind is characteristic of the civil and criminal trials. As we move away, then, from the strictly adjudicative model, a host of diverse processes are encountered which are still concerned with how a person should be treated and which are still broadly adjudicative in nature. The mode of participation remains basically the same: the person whose interests are at issue is entitled to be heard in the sense that he knows the case to be made or met and has the chance to put forward evidence and argument. The right to be heard will range in practice from procedures mirroring the adversarial trail to those allowing the barest opportunity to present a statement of facts and perhaps an expression of opinion. The general idea is that, while the right to be heard applies to individualized processes, it is often in an attenuated form with the practical procedures required to satisfy that right varying greatly.

At the next stage along the spectrum of administrative processes, the main aim is to settle matters of general policy rather than decide on the treatment of individuals, although individuals will often be seriously affected by what is decided. Here the mode of participation is consultative, which means that those who will be affected by or who have an interest in the policy usually have the opportunity to present their evidence and arguments. The object is to provide information relevant to the policy and to influence the outcome.

Beyond that common object, however, participation through consultation might again take several forms. In some matters, such as a public inquiry, the proceedings may have many of the trappings of a judicial trial, with the calling of witnesses, examination and cross-examination, and extensive argument and counter-argument. In other areas of policy-making, consultation may mean little more than the chance to make a written submission, without knowing precisely what policy options are being considered or what other information and submissions have been received. However, policy-making does not necessarily mean a policy-maker receiving information and submissions, and then deciding as he thinks best. A genuine attempt might be made to involve interested parties in the decision itself, not just to consult them as a preliminary to it. Consultation between the parties then gives way to a fuller form of participation where agreement between the parties as to the course to follow is the objective. The form of participation for that purpose is clearly more exacting than bare consultation; but again, between the two, different stages can be detected, each pointing to a mode of participation slightly different from the one before it.

At the far end of the spectrum is the political process proper. Participation here takes several forms: it includes the chance to vote, to be involved in meetings and discussions, to express one's views in various forums, and to exploit the media. The object may be to affect the outcome of an election or to influence the way others vote; it may be to make an impact on policy issues or simply to exert one's right to participate as an end in itself. The chance to vote from time to time is the most rudimentary form of political participation which will often be enhanced by other forms and practices.

4.3 PARTICIPATION IN LEGAL AND ADMINISTRATIVE PROCESSES

4.3.1 Participation and Outcomes

The main reason for valuing the participation of the parties in legal processes is the instrumental role it plays in the proper application of authoritative standards and, therefore, in ensuring fair treatment. Without losing sight of the different forms it may have, let us take participation to mean for present purposes that a person affected by a legal process can be involved in it by knowing what is at issue, being able to present evidence and argument, and having the chance to respond to opposing evidence and argument. Participation in this sense is a useful way of gaining information which might not otherwise be easily acquired; it also helps the decision-maker to have a more complete and balanced view of the facts and the issues relating to the facts. But perhaps most importantly, this sense of participation recognizes that legal processes are social processes which are shaped by the parties involved in them and by the contributions they make; participation can also be linked to the rights of parties to be properly considered and to have their circumstances adequately reflected in the outcome.

The instrumental role of participation towards proper and accurate decisions provides the key to its normative justification. Since proper and accurate decisions mean both that social objectives have been achieved and that a person has been treated according to the standards of fair treatment, participatory procedures are fair procedures. Now while that is the general instrumental role of participation, the way it works in practice was explained more fully in section 2.2.2. Several reasons were given there to show why it is an especially important instrument to accurate outcomes and therefore to fair treatment. It may be useful to restate those reasons. First, the person whose situation is being inquired into is often the best source of information and explanation; secondly, it is often difficult to have confidence in the accuracy of a decision where the person whose situation is in issue has not been able to provide his side of the case; and thirdly, the argumentative process which is encouraged by participatory procedures may be an effective means to accurate and proper decisions. The strength of these reasons will vary in different processes, but taken together they constitute a strong case for the value of participation in leading to good decisions. The strength of the case in turn explains why we generally regard participation as an essential element of fair procedures.

4.3.2 Participation and Respect: An Indirect Link

This explanation of participation is not, however, the only one. In dealing with the dignitarian challenge, we saw an alternative approach to participatory procedures: participation is there seen as serving values independently of outcomes, and the value most commonly invoked is a person's dignity and the respect which is owed to him. The argument is that while participation may be useful instrumentally in making the right decision, it has value independently of outcomes; the fact that it might also enhance outcomes is a bonus, but it is not part of the justification. Now if participation can be justified as a direct condition of showing respect for persons, the consequences for procedures are significant. Participation will then have a more secure role in decision-making; it will not depend on its contribution to outcomes; and it may have to be given a more prominent place than otherwise would be warranted. In any event, it is important to understand the proper basis on which participation is justified.

In trying to make the connection between respect for persons and participation in decisions, it is usual for writers to draw on the Kantian notion that a person should be treated as an end in himself, not as a means to an end. This principle is often invoked in contexts far removed from Kant's original philosophical framework, but it does capture with striking effect the idea that each person is a responsible and autonomous being, and that respect for those qualities is a fundamental principle of social organization. But while the principle is clear enough, it is not easy to know what is required in order properly to apply it in practical contexts. It does not prohibit action being taken against a person for breaking the law or other binding standards, although punishing a person in order to deter others would be forbidden. Perhaps the idea of manipulation comes close to capturing the modern sense of the principle, since to manipulate someone is to use him as an instrument towards some ulterior purpose.[2] The difficulty of applying the principle of respect for persons in practical situations has opened the way for two different interpretations. One is that a person is treated with respect if he is dealt with according to the standards of fair treatment within a given context. Participation then serves respect by helping to ensure the proper application of those standards. That I shall call the indirect principle. On the other interpretation, respect for a person is shown simply by allowing him to participate; that I shall call the direct principle. The indirect principle is examined in this section, the direct principle in the next.

The proposal I have put forward in earlier chapters is that the fundamental norm in legal processes is to treat people in accordance with authoritative standards and in that way to show respect for them. Procedures are means to showing respect, but they do so indirectly. The essential element in showing respect for a person is to deal with him fairly and justly according to authoritative standards, of which legal standards are a major part. The indirect principle is well illustrated in Rawls' theory of justice.[3] Rawls sees a connection between the Kantian idea of respect for persons and just treatment: the laws should be made in accordance with the two principles of justice and then applied regularly and impartially. Rawls refers to that process as justice as regularity, it being a legal version of formal justice requiring procedures which are directed towards ascertaining the truth 'in ways which are consistent with the other ends of the legal system'.[4] Little is said about the precise procedures which are required for the regular and impartial application of the law, but it is clear that the object is to produce the right outcomes, and procedures will be appropriate if they achieve that end. The phrase 'consistent with the other ends of the legal system' suggests the existence of other values restricting the procedures that might otherwise be adopted; but within those restrictions, the design of procedures is a matter of instrumental rationality. Participation is likely to be a common feature of procedures, but its place depends on its contribution to outcomes.

[2] See A. R. Duff, *Trials and Punishment* (Cambridge University Press, Cambridge, 1986), ch. 2.

[3] J. Rawls, *A Theory of Justice* (Clarendon Press, Oxford, 1971), 235 ff.

[4] Ibid. 238–9.

Rawls makes no claim that participatory procedures have a protected position in decision-making; nor does he claim that they are in some immanent way a necessary element in showing respect for those subject to it. Respect is shown, and the precept against using a person as a means to an end is honoured, provided that just laws are applied regularly and impartially. Nothing more is needed.

In discussing the relationship between rights and procedures, R. M. Dworkin takes a similar view.[5] On his approach, each person should be treated with equal concern and respect, which means within a legal system upholding the rights of each person. A person whose rights are not respected suffers both the bare harm in losing some advantage or in being subjected to a disadvantage, and the moral harm in being treated unfairly. The unfairness consists in being treated in violation of the undertakings, made by the community to each individual member, which are implicit in the law. Having given undertakings in this way, society is enjoined as a matter of integrity to honour them.[6] Each person has a right not to be treated unfairly in this way, and it is implicit in the right that society should provide the institutions and procedures necessary to protect against it. The nature and form of the procedures will depend on the rights in issue and on the seriousness of the moral harm which might be caused. Notice, however, that the procedures are directed to outcomes; since the moral harm consists in coming to the wrong outcome, the task of procedures is to produce the right one, or at least to produce outcomes at a level of accuracy commensurate with the gravity of the moral harm at stake.[7] When the right outcome is achieved, rights are upheld and the right-holder is treated with concern and respect. The test of good procedures is, accordingly, whether they produce the right outcomes. Participation is again likely to be an important and regular element in designing procedures to that end, but there is no suggestion in Dworkin's writings that it is relevant or required for some reason other than its contribution to outcomes. Dworkin expressly rejects as unhelpful the idea that there is a direct connection between participation and respect.[8]

The approaches of both Rawls and Dworkin emphasize the importance of respect for individuals, and to that extent are broadly within the Kantian tradition. The one approach expresses the issue as the regular and impartial application of just or near just laws, while the other concentrates on rights and the role of procedures in upholding rights. There are clear similarities between the two and it is interesting to see that neither has a place for participatory procedures independently of its role in securing correct

[5] R. M. Dworkin, *Taking Rights Seriously* (Duckworth, London, 1978), ch. 4 and *A Matter of Principle* (Clarendon Press, Oxford, 1985), ch. 3.

[6] On integrity, see R. M. Dworkin, *Law's Empire* (Fontana, London, 1986), chs. 6 and 7.

[7] Dworkin, *A Matter of Principle*, n. 5 above, 211.

[8] Ibid. 101–3.

outcomes; it follows that if the outcomes can be achieved without participation, the principle of respect is not breached.

4.3.3 Participation and Respect: A Direct Link

The fact that two of the leading contemporary political theorists do not claim a direct link between participation and respect does not rule out the possibility that, on closer examination, such a link exists. Indeed, there is a body of opinion to that effect and we must now consider the arguments, which may take a stronger or weaker form. In its stronger form, the claim is that respect for a person provides a reason for participation which is separate from and in addition to any reasons related to outcomes; participation is simply one direct way of showing respect. The claim in its weaker form is that a person, whose interests are likely to be affected by a decision, should be allowed to participate with a view to influencing the decision. Participation is linked to outcomes, but the reason for this person participating is that his interests are at stake.

Exponents of the stronger claim have a heavy onus to discharge. They must show that participation can be justified without including in the justification any reference to its contribution to outcomes. Imagine as an example an agency distributing welfare benefits. Suppose that procedures are followed which produce a high level of accurate outcomes, but without hearing the applicant. This might be difficult to imagine, but suppose in an unusual situation it were possible; it would then be necessary for exponents of the strong version to show that, even so, the absence of hearing procedures constitutes unfair treatment of the claimant. The case is usually put in this way: unless a person is able to participate in the decision, he is not being respected as an end in himself, but is being used as a means to society's purposes. In order to be respected, and thus treated as an end in himself, a person should be consulted about what is to be done to him and given the chance to have his say. The difficulty with this argument is to show how the mere fact of participation constitutes respect for the person. The natural response would be that participation helps to ensure a person is treated in accordance with the law; but since participation has to be shown to be valuable apart from outcomes, that response is not open. E. L. Pincoffs puts the case in this way:[9] treating persons as ends is the condition of self-respect; a person is treated with respect if he is not used by another; the safeguard against being used is that the person enters into consultation about what is to be done to him; participation and reasons are the necessary conditions of consultation.

Despite a certain initial attraction, this approach is finally unconvincing.

[9] E. L. Pincoffs, 'Due Process, Fraternity, and a Kantian Injunction' in J. Pennock and J. Chapman, *Due Process* (Nomos xvii, New York, 1977).

In the first place, participation and consultation are purposive activities, and their primary purpose is to shape outcomes. Here they must also be directly purposive to self respect. But how can that be? If the answer is that consultation is 'about what is to be done to him', as Pincoffs suggests, then we are back to outcomes and the influence consultation might have on outcomes. The reality is that, once the connection between consultation and outcomes is severed, there is no argument left to show how consultation might also be directly linked to respect. The relationship between participation and respect is simply not established. The second problem then is how, independently of any effect on outcomes, consulting a person, hearing him, letting him participate is to show respect. The case seems to rest less on reasoned argument than on an appeal to intuition or self-evidence: we would have to say that consultation and hearing just are expressions of respect for the person. Some might be convinced on the ground that to hear a person just is a good thing, but clearly not all are convinced, and it is difficult to see why we should consider such a contested claim to be a firm basis on which to construct legal procedures.

A third problem is that issues about showing respect are real issues only if they relate to how a person is to be treated. Treatment suggests some action in relation to a person which has genuine consequences. A legal decision has consequences for those subject to it, and the process by which it is reached is judged on its effectiveness in producing the right consequences. But if outcomes are put aside, it is not clear how a person can be 'treated' with disrespect by failing to hear him; there is no action of which he is the subject. The notion of being treated in a particular way makes sense only in respect of the decision and the consequences that follow. If the decision is favourable, the person is unlikely to feel wrongly treated, whether or not he has been heard. If, however, the outcome is unfavourable, whether or not correct, and the person has not been heard, then he has a genuine grievance. The grievance is that a hearing might have made a difference to the outcome. But as soon as that argument is invoked, we are back in the participation as a means to outcomes camp. The point is that as soon as we try to connect participation to treatment the analysis unavoidably becomes instrumental.

These difficulties do not rule out the possibility that there might be a direct link between participation and respect. My claim is only that, on this version of the direct link between participation and respect, the link is missing. But before moving on to a different version, one further problem should be noted: if the direct principle is correct, then presumably participation would be required whenever a person were affected by a decision. In practice that is not the case and it is difficult to accept that the practice should be changed. The truth is that across the spectrum of legal decisions, many are entirely justifiable and made for good reasons even though the procedures do not include participation. The direct principle of participation must either challenge that position and insist on participatory procedures in all cases, or it must provide some way for deciding when it is required and when it is not. The more likely approach is the second, but there is a conspicuous reluctance in the writings of those who espouse the idea of a direct link to address the issue.

One of the most serious attempts to explain the link between participation and respect for persons, again following a broadly Kantian line, is found in the writings of R. A. Duff.[10] In an illuminating study of the criminal process, Duff puts the view that, apart from a correct verdict of guilt or innocence, certain values are intrinsic to a just trial. The right of the accused to be heard, to play his proper role in the trial, is one such value.[11] Appeal is made to the idea that to respect a person and to treat him as a rational and autonomous moral agent is to treat him and to respond to him as one who is able to conduct his life and determine his ends; the person should neither be manipulated nor used as an agent to social ends. When it comes to the criminal trial, the accused should be allowed to participate, not only to affect outcomes, but regardless of the effect on outcomes. Participation:

> is explained neither in instrumental terms as an efficient means towards some further end, nor by reference to independent side constraints on our pursuit of that end, but as being integral to the proper purpose of the trial.[12]

In what way, we might ask, is participation integral to the trial?

One line of explanation is that the trial must be a rational enterprise: it must reach 'a well founded and justified verdict', and there must be good grounds for the verdict.[13] This does not, however, make the case for participation. Participation normally strengthens the grounds for a verdict, but it does not follow that there can be good grounds only if there is participation. It is not difficult to envisage decisions, even ones of guilt, where the outcome has been reached on good, rational grounds and is palpably correct, even though the accused has not participated. Indeed, in so far as the case rests on the claim that participation is a necessary element in having good grounds for a decision, it is an empirical claim which is not only not made out, but is false. Duff takes a further step to strengthen the case: a criminal verdict must not only be reached on good grounds, it must also be 'justified to the defendant on whom it is passed'.[14] The judgment should not only be correct, it must also be communicated and justified to the accused; it can be justified, according to Duff, only if the defendant has participated. But again the conclusion does not follow, for the fact is there may be good, rational grounds for a decision which a defendant can recognize and accept as justifying a particular outcome, without his having participated. Participation might be a factor which encourages a defendant to accept the outcome, but

[10] Duff, *Trials and Punishments*, n. 2 above.
[11] Ibid. 117.
[12] Ibid. 102.
[13] Ibid. 115.
[14] Ibid. 115.

just as participation does not guarantee acceptance, failure to participate does not necessarily destroy it. Acceptance is a complex normative issue which does not stand or fall on participation. Again the case for participation as a necessary element of the trial has not been proved.

There is, however, a further layer of analysis. Here the point is not to deny that a decision-process can be rational and justifiable without participation, but rather to claim that the criminal trial is a special kind of decision. It is special in that it is not just about the defendant, but is a process addressed to the defendant 'as a charge which she must answer'.[15] If the process is addressed to the defendant and she has no chance to reply, then the process ceases to be a trial in the sense defined. This is an interesting way of characterizing the trial, but it is not the only way, and so the question is why should we adopt this view. The answer seems to be that the trial is an occasion of moral criticism which 'seeks to persuade the person whose conduct is under scrutiny of the truth and justice of its conclusions'.[16] Moral criticism is a particular type of criticism; it seeks to persuade the person blamed to understand her mistakes and to modify her behaviour for the future. But not just any form of persuasion will do; the person blamed should not have the truth determined by any external process and then thrust upon her, but must herself engage in the search for it.[17] And since the trial is seen as a form of moral criticism and the guilty verdict a judgment of blame, the defendant should be involved in the process.

This is an interesting account of the criminal trial and of the place of participation within it. Before considering how far the analysis might be extended to other areas of decision-making, there are difficulties to be raised. The first is that the relationship between the two layers of analysis is not made clear. This is crucial, for if the main claim is that the trial must be a rational process and that 'a criminal verdict must be justified to the defendant on whom it is passed', if, that is, it is no more than a process for expressing a judgment on the accused's past conduct, communicating it to him, and showing good grounds for it, then the case for participation as a necessary element fails. Participation then, as we saw above, is contingent, not necessary, since there may well be good grounds for a decision in the absence of participation. However, the position is different if the test as to what are good grounds has to be interpreted against the view of the trial as a form of moral criticism. If participation is a necessary element in ascribing moral blame, then participation must be necessary to a justified verdict. But what is the case for accepting that view of the trial?

As a matter of both history and practice, the trial does not look like an enquiry into moral guilt. In the trial of Billy Budd,[18] the issues of moral guilt gave way to the crude and brutal concern with whether he had in some

[15] Duff, *Trials and Punishments*, n. 2 above, 116. [16] Ibid. 116.
[17] Ibid. 39–54. [18] H. K. Melville, *Billy Budd: Sailor* (Everyman, London, 1993).

objective way been mutinous. And that trial is surely similar to most trials. Only relatively recently has the defendant been allowed to play any role in the trial, and historically the primary concern was to decide whether the evidence was sufficient to support a conviction. The contemporary trial is different and the accused is now able to participate in full. But still the most striking feature is the sense of a contest between two sides, the one bringing evidence to prove that certain acts were done, the other striving to counter that evidence and to show at least a doubt in the minds of the jury; if the truth does emerge, it is through the evidence that the parties choose to bring. There is a moral element in so far as criminal guilt requires a finding of responsibility; but the enquiry into responsibility is of a limited and somewhat crude kind. It is based on drawing inferences from the evidence in a way which bears only vague resemblance to the subtlety and nuance of a moral enquiry. A more realistic approach is to see the trial as an enquiry into whether legal standards have been breached in a manner for which the accused can be held sufficiently responsible for the imposition of punishment. And while the process is in one sense addressed to the defendant, it is also and more significantly addressed to the community to show that legal standards are to be taken seriously.

Now the trial as it is might not be the trial as it should be, but I find it difficult to see that it could, or indeed should, ever be understood primarily as a moral dialogue with the accused. It is not clear why the trial should be regarded as more than an enquiry into whether the accused has broken the law in a manner for which he can be held responsible. Trials and punishments are unavoidable evils conducted for the benefit of the community and in the interests of controlling certain kinds of behaviour. To elevate an intrinsically unfortunate social process into a moral dialogue between the accused and his accusers is to assert a view of law and morals which is unacceptable and unwarranted. Who would not prefer the defiant clansman in Scott's *Waverley* who stood firm throughout his trial and execution for rebellion, where the only justification, if there were one at all, would be the brutal self-interest of a conquering nation,[19] to the anti-hero of *Crime and Punishment*?[20]

That there are various ways of characterizing the criminal trial is not surprising. If the better characterization is the one I suggest, then the main concern should be to have procedures which can be relied on to produce the right outcome, while respecting any important non-outcome values. A verdict reached by that process will be justified. The participation of the accused normally would be guaranteed as a rational and prudential element in reaching a justified outcome, but it would not be guaranteed as a necessary condition of respect for the accused. In other words, the case for

[19] W. Scott, *Waverley* (Penguin, Harmondsworth, 1972).
[20] D. Dostoyevsky, *Crime and Punishment* (Bantam Books, Toronto, 1981).

participation as a requirement of respect for the dignity of a person is not made out. If, as I doubt, there really ought to be the deeper sense of a moral discourse between the prosecutor and the defendant, then the case for a direct link between participation and respect is stronger; but there would be no case for extending that sense of moral dialogue to other types of decisions. Even if, in other words the criminal trial were a special case, the direct relationship between participation and respect for persons in other legal processes would have no foundation.

The conclusion to which we are led is that the claims made for a direct relationship between participation and respect do not withstand close scrutiny. The principle that each person should be respected as autonomous and responsible is not disputed; what is disputed is the claim that, in order to honour that principle, a person must be given the opportunity to participate in decision-making. It is part of the claim that the principle applies independently of the effect participation may have on outcomes; the principle of respect, on this view, is a necessary and sufficient condition for participation. That aspect of the claim also is insupportable. A special case might have to be made for the criminal trial, but even that is contestable. This conclusion does not undermine the importance of participation; it shows only that one ground of justification, namely that it is a good thing in itself, is unconvincing.

4.3.4 Participation and Self-protection: A Modified Claim

The claim that participatory procedures directly express respect for a person fails because it detaches procedures from their purposive role in legal processes, but fails to show in a convincing way what the alternative is. Suppose, however, that we retain the purposive role of procedures and then ask whether, within that framework, participation has some special status and importance for the person involved. The foundations on which such a case can be constructed are twofold: the first is that the person affected has a good claim to his position being properly taken into account, while the second is that the person has a special claim to represent his own position. The first of these draws on the idea, already discussed,[21] that legal processes are social processes and that the result reached will be very much influenced by the contributions made to the process; results will be influenced particularly by the evidence and materials considered, and by the arguments advanced. If we insert into this description of legal processes the normative principle that the circumstances of the person affected are matters to be considered, then the connection is established between the special circumstances of each person and the outcomes reached. This leads to the second part of the case: if the person has a special claim because his interests are at

[21] See section 2.2.2.

stake, then it is a short step to the conclusion that he ought to be able to defend or promote those interests in the process. If that step is warranted, then an additional standard of fair treatment is created which in turn generates a right to be heard. Participating and being heard might have an influence on outcomes, but their justification derives from the separate principle that a person has a right to defend and promote his interests.

An argument for that principle can be made on the following lines. Just as I may lawfully defend myself against physical attack, I may defend myself against the actions of the state which threaten other aspects of well-being. The idea of self-defence can in this way be extended to cover all my legitimate interests. But self-defence is a specific aspect of a more general principle, namely that I am responsible for developing, defending, and advancing those interests. I am not necessarily the best person to look after my own interests, but, in a society which values autonomy and responsibility, I should take primary responsibility for them. Glimpses of this idea can be seen in various places. The principle that the person accused should be able to respond to and to defend himself against accusations runs deep. American law has a principle that the accused in a criminal trial must be allowed to confront the witnesses on whose testimony the prosecution is based. A rather different illustration comes from an Australian case in which a prisoner was denied parole. Early release had been recommended by the parole board, but the state executive refused parole for reasons of public policy. The prisoner was heard by the parole board, but denied the opportunity to make representations to cabinet. In an action for judicial review, the courts upheld the denial of a hearing.[22] The case is troubling. One reason is that the prisoner's representations might have had an affect on cabinet's deliberations; another is simply that O'Shea should have had the chance to defend his interests. He might justly have complained that it was his life that was in issue—his behaviour, his medical condition, and his prospects—and that he was the one to represent and protect them.

The idea that a person ought to be involved in defending and protecting his own interests is an interesting attempt to link participatory procedures directly to respect for a person. It should not be confused with the argument that the person affected will often be the only source of information which is needed to produce the right outcome. Participation on that argument is entirely instrumental to outcomes. The idea of self-defence or self-protection is different; it calls directly on the value of allowing the person affected by a process to participate in it. Support for this idea can be found in various strands of legal and political thought. Here law is seen as not just a system of control imposed from above and external to human relationships, but as a system of regulation occurring within social relationships. Fuller touches on

[22] *South Australia* v. *O'Shea* (1987) 73 ALR 1.

this in his sense of an inner morality of law,[23] where the process of governance occurs in a context of relationships, within which certain principles and understandings are implicit. Detmold seems to have in mind a similar idea when he talks of a compact between the citizen and the state, where the terms of the compact are a set of understandings about how government should be conducted.[24] Indeed, Duff's view of the criminal trial as a moral discourse, where the accused is shown and led to understand the justification for the punishment which is to follow, is a stronger account of a similar idea.[25] Each of these ideas draws on a pre-legal view of social relationships, one element of which is that each person has a basic entitlement to defend and protect himself.

The only remaining question is whether this principle of self-protection really is part of the political morality of a liberal, democratic society. Is it firmly established and important enough to create rights to participate and to justify the procedures needed as a result? The general idea that a person ought to be able to defend and promote his interests does appear to be a foundational principle of political morality. The very notion that people are to be treated as responsible and autonomous includes as an element the principle of self-protection. It is, however, an abstract principle which could be interpreted in various ways, some strict and narrow, others more expansive. While the practical scope of the principle is an arguable matter, a strong case can be made for its application where important interests are seriously threatened. For that reason its application is most apparent in criminal proceedings where the two conditions of importance and seriousness are usually present. How far it extends beyond that to apply to administrative processes is more debatable and should be judged according to contexts and circumstances. The likely conclusion is that it will have considerable force in some cases but not in others.

The conclusion may be drawn that, subject to the conditions discussed, a good case can be made for the principle of participation based on self-protection. The basis of the principle is simply that it is included as an essential element in the pre-legal relationship between persons individually and the community collectively. But before concluding this discussion, two further points should be noted. First, in most legal processes the self-protection principle will have little practical significance. Whenever it applies, there is likely also to be a strong case for participatory procedures based on the instrumental grounds considered in section 4.1.1. In order to take proper account of the person's situation, for example, it will be necessary to allow him to participate. In other words, the instrumental-to-outcomes case for participatory procedures will normally cover the same ground as the self-

[23] L. Fuller, *The Morality of Law* (Yale University Press, New Haven, Conn., 1964).
[24] M. Detmold, *Courts and Administrators* (Weidenfeld and Nicolson, London, 1986).
[25] Duff, *Trials and Punishments*, n. 2 above.

protection principle, the only difference being that the latter has a different justification from the former. Secondly, it is easy to conflate the case for participation as an entitlement based on self-protection with the case based on its civic value. Civic value derives from having procedures which help those involved and the public at large to understand legal processes, where understanding is the basis for critical appraisal and legitimacy. What is at stake is not individual rights but the general social good in that knowledgeable and engaged, yet critical, citizenship is a necessary condition of social cohesion.

To sum up, the discussion in the last three sections has shown that the case for participation in legal and administrative processes can be founded on a number of different grounds. The first and, I suggest, most convincing is that participation is of instrumental value in leading to the right or best outcomes. Its role is contingent on participation being necessary to achieve good outcomes and, being contingent, we should expect it would not be needed in all cases. Whether it is needed, and what form it should take, will then depend on the nature and context of different areas of decision-making. But while participation is instrumental and contingent on outcomes, various factors about the nature of decision-making point to a presumption that those affected should be heard, where the level of involvement should depend on the importance of the interests at stake and the seriousness of the consequences for them. Participation here is related to respect for persons in the indirect sense that it contributes to people being treated properly and accurately according to authoritative standards. The second foundation for participation is through a direct link to respect for persons. I have argued that this account verges on incoherence, but to the extent it is coherent, it is unpersuasive. It depends on showing that the act of participation in legal processes is an expression of respect for persons without reference to outcomes or authoritative standards. My scepticism about this explanation matches common sense and is borne out in practice since there is scant support for it in either law or administrative practice. A more moderate version of the thesis based on the principle of self-protection has more to commend it. Here the idea is that the person whose situation is under scrutiny has a special status in defending himself. The object is still to produce the right or best outcome, but the person affected should be heard as part of that process. The justification is partly instrumental to outcomes, but it is also partly based on the idea that the person subject to a decision has a special status in relation to it. This view highlights a distinct element in legal processes where a person's important interests are seriously in issue, although just how far the principle should have general application in administrative contexts is more arguable.

4.4 PARTICIPATION IN THE POLITICAL PROCESS

Questions about participation in legal decisions have a parallel in the political process. Modern government is based on the assumption of citizens participating, and yet the explanations given for participation are many and varied.[26] Political theorists have been mainly concerned with participation in relation to democracy, and so it is useful to consider a number of themes which emerge from their writings. Comparisons will then be made with participation in legal processes, although in a few pages I shall be able to give little more than an inkling of the range and refinement of the extensive literature.

Between participation in the legal sphere and participation in the political sphere some obvious parallels and connections can be made. Political processes have the same general structure as legal processes: the primary object in both is to produce certain kinds of outcomes in a context where other ends and values also have a part to play. The respective outcomes differ in some aspects; in politics, they are the making of good laws and policies, while in legal decisions the main concern is the application of those laws and policies to specific cases. The guiding principle in the design of procedures in both areas is to produce the best outcomes, subject to the influences and constraints of other values. This close parallel is itself a good reason for examining the political process; but there are also other reasons. Administrative decisions often fall between the legal and the political; their actions may involve matters of policy, whether in dealing with an individualized case or in arriving at general rules or guidelines. Administrative decision-making in policy matters has many of the characteristics of the political process. The parallels are less obvious where administrative decisions veer towards the adjudicative, but even there some connections can be drawn. Historically, theories of participation in politics have taken inspiration from the legal idea that the party whose rights are affected by an action should be summoned to appear and to state his case.[27] However, despite the similarities, legal and political decisions are in many ways different, with the result that an analysis of the concept of participation in politics should be instructive in its application to law.

4.4.1 Participation and Political Outcomes

The first end of government is to produce good laws and policies, and the primary purpose of participation is to contribute to that end. That is the idea

[26] The following gives a good indication of the various examples and justifications: D. W. Klein, 'Participation in Contemporary Democratic Theories' in J. Pennock and J. Chapman (eds.), *Participation in Politics* (Nomos, New York, 1977).

[27] G. Parry, 'The Idea of Political Participation' in G. Parry (ed.), *Participation in Politics* (Manchester University Press, Manchester, 1972), 20.

underlying a wide range of political traditions and is simple enough: politics is largely about having governments which make good laws and policies, and so the point of procedures, including citizen participation, is to produce that end. The working out in practice of the idea is more complicated. The test of good laws and policies is generally taken to be whether they are in some sense in the interests of all. In anything but the simplest community, it is unreasonable to expect laws which cater completely for the interests of all, let alone live up to all their ideals. In large and diverse societies, the aim should be to produce outcomes which at least take into account the interests and concerns of all and are made in accordance with principles acceptable to all. That is the substance of the political process, and, within that process, participation should be a significant means towards its ends.

Beneath this simple outline, various issues need to be considered. One concerns the ends of government itself. If we are to have good laws and policies, then we must have an idea of what is good and desirable. Various ends are possible, but an underlying principle of modern, democratic societies is that laws and policies—the outcomes of the political process—should reflect the diverse interests of society; all should be considered and all count for something. As J. S. Mill put it, 'government should promote the aggregate interests of society'.[28] The idea that a political outcome is good and just if it promotes the aggregate interests of all can mean different things. It might mean simply that in a society composed of diverse interests, the object of government is to find an accommodation amongst them. The political system then resembles a market where each group tries to advance its own interests, while accepting that adjustment and compromise will be necessary. Such an approach allows for no sense of the public good beyond the preferences of the various groups, so that provided an accommodation can be achieved, the public good is satisfied.[29] Participatory procedures are of special importance, for unless persons and groups can participate in the political process, they will not be able to press the claims of their own interests. This version of interest-group pluralism has been much criticized for its impoverished view of government and law, for its lack of a sense of public good, and for the absence of any standard for choosing between competing interests.[30]

The thin sense of interest-group pluralism displayed in this account does not represent the mainstream of democratic theory. On an alternative approach, which runs deep in the traditions of political theory, the diversity of society is accepted but the emphasis falls on achieving an overriding sense

[28] J. S. Mill, *Considerations on Representative Government*, ed. C. V. Shields (New York, 1958), referred to as '*Representative Government*'.

[29] For a full account of this approach, see P. P. Craig, *Public Law and Democracy* (Clarendon Press, Oxford, 1990), 80 ff.

[30] See: R. Stewart, 'The Reformation of American Administrative Law' (1974–5) 88 *Harvard L Rev.* 1667; G. Frug, 'The Ideology of Bureaucracy in American Law' (1984) 97 *Harvard L Rev.* 1276.

of the common good. This is a broad church within which different traditions can be found, some of which have come to be known as republicanism, although the general approach goes well beyond theorists who might claim that title. The main feature of the approach is that government and law should be concerned with the common good. Private and sectional interests are unavoidable, but through education and involvement in public affairs, citizens should be able to stand apart from their personal preferences and develop a sense of the common good. That sense of the common good will ineluctably show through in the decisions and actions of both citizens and officials; conflicts and disputes can be settled in accordance with it and suitable policies and laws can be formulated. Writers in this tradition stress the centrality of participatory structures and the widespread involvement of citizens at all levels of public life.[31]

The idea that the object of politics is to produce just laws and policies, where the guiding standard is the common good, is a sound starting point for political theory. What constitutes the common good is then to be worked out by each society according to its values and its traditions, and just as different conceptions of the common good are to be expected, so societies will differ in their procedures and institutions for achieving them. However, one general characteristic of any tolerable notion of the common good is that the interests of all will be taken into account. And if each person's interests are to count, the conclusion appears to follow that each should be able to participate in politics in order best to represent those interests. According to Mill: 'the only government that can fully satisfy all the exigencies of the social state is one in which the whole people participate'.[32]

However, the case for participation is not so easily made. From the requirement that all interests be taken into account, it does not follow that participation by the bearers of those interests is necessary. Popular participation is clearly one way of projecting interests into the political process and it may be an effective way; but it is one instrument amongst several rather than the only one. We could easily imagine a government which tried conscientiously to identify and take account of the interests of all by means other than popular participation. The idea is neither unusual nor outlandish, although some fairly obvious objections can be raised. As a matter of practicality, a government could never have a proper knowledge and understanding of the great diversity of interests and preferences without widespread participation. Mill claimed that the most benevolent despot could never acquire the knowledge of his subjects necessary to be able properly to take account of their interests. That led him to conclude that each person is the best protector of

[31] The writings in this area are extensive, but the following are especially helpful: C. Sunstein, 'Beyond the Republican Revival' (1988) 97 *Yale LJ* 1539 and Craig, *Public Law and Democracy*, n. 29 above, chs. 10 and 11.

[32] *Representative Government*, n. 28 above, 55.

his own interests, and that those interests are secure only when the person 'is himself able, and habitually disposed, to stand up for them'.[33]

It might be added that the very notion of an interest is partly bound up with a person's subjective perceptions of the matter. In any event, these are empirical claims, not normative principles, and it is difficult to see clear evidence for one position or the other. But in the absence of decisive evidence, it is plausible to accept that a government could make wise and just laws without comprehensive participation. The most that may be concluded is that in discharging its duty to seek the common good, and in doing so to take account of the interests and preferences of all, a government would be wise to make use of popular participation. That provides a case for participation; but it is a contingent case, depending on how effective participation might be compared with other procedures, and considering the relative costs of different procedures. No case has been made for participation as a matter of principle, and it may be that good and just outcomes can sometimes be achieved by other methods.

4.4.2 Participation as Political Principle

That conclusion may seem unacceptable. It is often thought that the opportunity to participate in political decisions is not a matter of contingency or expediency but of principle, and many strands of political theory are based on that idea. One line of support for the idea of participation as a matter of principle might be found in the notion of political equality. The idea that all should be treated with equal concern and respect expresses in a modern way the old principle that government should be in the interests of all.[34] The question then is whether that principle, itself uncontroversial, justifies a principle of equal participation. J. Rawls thinks it does and argues that political equality means equal participation in the political process. The justification for that claim appears to be that political equality is the foundation which 'is more likely than any other to result in a just and effective system of legislation'.[35] Notice that the claim for equal participation, which began as one of principle, has become a matter of practicality, the premise being that participation is the best way of achieving just outcomes.

The point can be illustrated by putting the argument in another way. Rawls' claim seems to be: (i) that the object of politics is to produce just laws; (ii) where just laws means laws responsive to the interests of all; and (iii) that to produce such laws there must be the opportunity for equal participation. The first two steps may be accepted as political principles, but

[33] Ibid. 43. The similarity between Mill's argument and that advanced in section 4.3.4 relating to self-protection should be noted.

[34] The expression in these terms comes from Dworkin, *Taking Rights Seriously*, n. 5 above.

[35] Rawls, *A Theory of Justice*, n. 3 above, 221.

the third follows, in so far as it follows, not as a matter of principle, but as an empirical claim. Accordingly, Rawls fails to show that participation is a foundational political principle, a principle from which basic rights are generated. That does not mean that participation is unimportant; it might be the best way of achieving the best outcomes, or at least of staving off some of the worst. Indeed, if participation is such an important instrument in achieving good laws and policies, then that fact may be a sufficient basis for grounding normative standards and in turn political rights. But there is a significant difference between founding rights to participate on that basis, and claiming the right to be foundational without the need for further justification.

Other attempts besides Rawls' have been made to show that participation is a foundational principle of politics rather than a contingent procedure. Two of these will briefly be considered. The followers of one approach insist that participation in the political process is a thing of value quite apart from any beneficial consequences it might have for laws and policies. The parallel here with participation in legal processes is readily apparent; for according to both, the ultimate foundation for participation is a sense of respect for persons. If persons are to be treated with respect, they should be allowed to have a say in matters affecting them. This argument is redolent of the direct dignitarian argument we saw previously and is beset by the same problems in the political process as in legal processes. We need not go over the arguments again, although I shall return to the point in section 4.4.4.

Another pathway towards establishing participation as a fundamental political principle lies in theories of democracy. Here the idea is that participation is an essential element of democracy, especially versions of strong democracy. The version put forward by B. Barber is striking and well-known.[36] His claim is that communities are capable of arriving at common purposes and mutual action by virtue of their civil attitudes and participatory institutions. While that in itself is orthodox enough, the distinctive part of the claim is the great weight placed on participation as a means to those ends. Participation is held to be the supreme means for allowing a community to resolve conflicts and arrive at common purposes. It is a device which transforms both those who participate and the society itself: private individuals are transformed into free citizens, and partial and private interests are transformed into public goods.[37] It follows that participation is not just one amongst several possible instruments—even to call it an instrument is almost sacrilegious—it is the very centrepiece of political activity: 'public ends are literally forged through the act of public participation' and 'community grows out of participation'.[38] Notice that this is not a theory of pure

[36] B. Barber, *Strong Democracy: Participatory Politics for a New Age* (referred to as *Strong Democracy*) (University of California Press, Berkeley, Cal., 1984).

[37] Ibid. 151.

[38] Ibid. 152.

procedures, that is, a theory which puts all its weight on procedures rather than outcomes.[39] On the contrary, strong democracy is concerned with outcomes, with the belief that the right participatory procedures will produce the transformation of people and society, and in turn good laws and policies.[40] But while participation is a means to outcomes, it is an essential rather than contingent means since the transformation of citizens and society, and the formulation of good laws and policies, will be achieved only through participation.

It would be hard to over-estimate the importance of participatory procedures on this view of democracy. Participation is not only the means for transforming people and society, it takes on almost mystical qualities and makes a strong appeal to deep instincts. If we are to be clear-headed, however, and if we put aside the tinges of romance and the heady idealism which often colour discussions of participation, strong democracy does depend finally on one premise: that it will in practice produce certain good outcomes. This may be a prosaic rendition of a protean theory, but unless participation does produce the right outcomes, the theory collapses. Whether participation does have those consequences is an empirical matter, and whether the empirical evidence to support it exists is problematical. Advocates of strong democracy certainly offer no evidence, and without evidence one way or the other, the general claim of strong democracy, I suggest, is implausible. It is implausible because there is little reason to think that even the best participatory procedures will have the effects claimed for them. Other ingredients are necessary: citizens must already have a sense of moral values, they must be prepared to act on those values even at a cost to their personal interests, and they must have a sense of practical reasonableness. These qualities are essential to good politics, and while participatory institutions might help citizens to make sound judgments, it is difficult to believe that participation really can bear the burdens put upon it. It may be argued, indeed, that effective participation assumes the existence of those other qualities rather than creates them.

One final attempt to raise the status of participation from contingent procedure to political principle should be noted. Again it has several variants, each emphasizing the act of participation rather than the outcome.[41] If no objective standards can be discerned as to what constitutes just outcomes, we are tempted to concentrate on the fairness of the procedures rather than

[39] Barber does sometimes seem to suggest that the theory is one of pure procedures; for example, he refers to the 'politics of process': *Strong Democracy*, n. 36 above, 158. This is a loose use of process, and the general argument puts great emphasis on outcomes.

[40] See the helpful discussion in Craig, *Public Law and Democracy*, n. 29 above, 367 ff.

[41] Dworkin puts the distinction in terms of in-put theories and out-put theories, the former looking only at the procedures, the latter concentrating on outcomes: R. M. Dworkin, 'The Forum of Principle' 56 *NYUL Rev.* 469; see also W. N. Nelson, *Justifying Democracy* (Routledge, London, 1980).

the justice of the outcomes. An argument can then be made that if each person is free to participate in the political process and can do so on an equal footing with others, the results of the process will be legitimate and binding, not because the outcomes are necessarily good, but because the procedures are fair. Participatory procedures are no longer imperfect instruments for achieving specified outcomes; they are now pure procedures where the outcome is unspecified. Some might go further and claim that, if an outcome is reached by fair procedures, the outcome is just. Whichever variant is adopted, however, the argument is insupportable. It is insupportable because the very best participatory procedures can lead to unjustifiable outcomes, and it is hard to see why, in the affairs of politics, we should ignore the poor quality of outcomes just because they have been reached in a particular way. Politics is about producing laws and policies which are good in substance, so that a theory which concentrates only on procedures misses that essential point.[42]

4.2.3 Participation and the Common Good

The conclusion to which we are drawn is that attempts to justify participation as a fundamental political principle do not succeed. As interesting as such attempts are, they are flawed, so that the case for participation remains dependent on its contribution to just outcomes. This is not to devalue its role, but just to be clear about what its role is. As an instrument to just outcomes, participation is likely to be an important and effective way of getting the interests of all into the decision-process. The question now is whether, within this broadly instrumental framework, the case for participation can be strengthened. Theories of strong democracy, by making participation an essential means to good outcomes, offer one approach; but that makes such unrealizable demands on participation that the approach itself is unpersuasive. However, the idea that participation may have a special role in producing good outcomes opens the way, when stated more moderately, for a more convincing case for participation.

The elements of just such a case are to be found in J. S. Mill's writings as expounded and developed by W. N. Nelson in his book, *On Justifying Democracy*.[43] The case begins with the idea that the test of the justice of law and policy is the common good. We have seen that equal concern for all is an element of the common good, and in the discussion so far our attention has been on that aspect. But the common good means more: it embraces what is best for society both as a whole and in all its constituent parts. It must have

[42] The tension between fair procedures and good outcomes is at the base of J. Rawls' theory of justice; but I suggest that the appeal of his principles of justice is not that they were arrived at by fair procedures, but that they are good principles.

[43] (Routledge, London, 1980).

principles for resolving disputes, for allocating resources, and for generally guiding the political process. The disinterested citizen should be able to see that, although laws might not on all occasions be in line with his or her preferences, nevertheless, they serve the common interest. Each person has his or her interests, but each should be able to stand apart from them and accept the idea of a broader conception of the overall good. To take a commonplace example, the restrictions on free speech in the interests of public order will not always suit me; but I should be able to understand and accept that some restrictions are necessary for the common good. In the same way, the paying of taxes is irksome to us all, but we should be able, nevertheless, to see its importance for the common good.

The idea of the common good is fundamental to sound government, especially in diverse and plural societies. In the modern republican tradition, emphasis is put on the pursuit of the common good rather than the good of sectional interests.[44] Theories of strong democracy similarly stress the possibilities of transforming private preferences into universal values and principles.[45] Again, Mill sums it up well. In writing of the ends of government as the advancement of aggregate interests, he means more than literally adding up the sum of private interests; aggregate interests is for him another way of expressing the common good, but the common good as the good of all in a sense which transcends any set of private interests.[46]

How then is the common good arrived at and how is it reconciled with individual interests? In a large and varied society it is unrealistic to expect to find every law to our liking, but it should be reasonable to expect all laws to comply with a body of guiding principles, principles which are constituted from the shared values and culture of the society. The precise laws on particular issues are then matters of practical judgment within the context of principles. It is to be expected that in making such judgments local differences and variations will appear. The existence of such fundamental principles, referred to by Rawls as a fundamental charter, is of considerable importance to both the stability and the tolerability of a society. They represent the shared, critical moral values of a society, and although they may change with time and circumstance, it is important that they be settled and enduring.[47] Rawls refers to the idea of a well-ordered society as a society regulated by a public concept of justice.[48] A public concept of justice means: (i) that everyone accepts and knows that others accept the same principles of justice; and (ii) that the social institutions satisfy and are known to satisfy

[44] See C. Sunstein, 'Beyond the Republican Revival' (1988) 47 *Yale LJ* 1539 and Craig, *Public Law and Democracy*, n. 29 above, 321.

[45] Barber, *Strong Democracy*, n. 36 above, 151.

[46] Mill, *Representative Government*, n. 33 above, 54.

[47] On the idea of a critical morality, see H. L. A. Hart, *Law, Liberty and Morality* (Clarendon Press, Oxford, 1963) and Dworkin, *Taking Rights Seriously*, n. 5 above, ch. 8.

[48] Rawls, *A Theory of Justice*, n. 3 above, 5.

those principles. In a well-ordered society 'while men may put excessive demands on one another, they nevertheless acknowledge a common point of view from which their claims can be adjudicated'.[49] It is to be noted, indeed, that the existence of and reliance on such principles are necessary if a society is to have integrity, that is, a sense of coherence and consistency over time in the way that its laws and policies are made.[50]

The link can now be made between the common good, the charter of principles, and participation. Citizens participating in the processes of government will bring to bear, not only their own personal preferences, but also and more importantly their own sense of moral right. That sense of right will itself to some extent be shaped by the existing charter of principles, but it will also help develop those principles, with the relationship between the two being reciprocal and reflexive. The importance of participation is that it enables citizens to have influence at the various levels of government, in shaping the underlying principles and in ensuring that laws and policies are made in accordance with them. Since the common good consists in governing according to the shared values expressed in the charter of principles, and since those shared values emerge out of social processes, it follows that participation will reinforce those values and help to make sure that laws are made within them. This conclusion is further supported by the need to govern in a way which respects the interests of all.

Now we can see why many theories of participation stress the moral improvement of the citizens themselves. Moral values are shaped by men and women in social situations where decisions have to be made and conflicts resolved. The results of such processes will be no better than the people making them, although the very fact that decisions have to be made, and made according to defensible, public standards, may sharpen the moral faculties of those involved.[51] Nelson sums up the argument in this way: 'democratic institutions promote attitudes in citizens which will in turn lead them to govern themselves in ways consistent with the requirements of morality'.[52] And, it may be added, the more open the process of government is, the more concerned it must be with explanation and justification, and the more successful it is likely to be in making good laws.

We now have a more appealing sense of what it means to govern in the interests of all. Far from requiring a crude accommodation of conflicting interests, government in the interests of all means developing principles which are shared by all, and then making laws within the bounds of those principles. Widespread participation in that process is likely to be conducive to making good laws. Notice that the case for participation is still

[49] Rawls, *A Theory of Justice*, n. 3 above, 51. Shades of Durkheim's notion of organic solidarity can be seen in this approach.

[50] See Dworkin, *Law's Empire*, n. 6 above.

[51] This approach is very much Mill's approach, but for the particular interpretation of Mill, I have benefited greatly from W. N. Nelson's *On Justifying Democracy*, n. 43 above. This book is, in my opinion, the best modern analysis of participation and democracy.

[52] Ibid. 51.

instrumental on outcomes; but understood in this way, the case is more powerful and more convincing. The objection to cruder versions of the instrumental argument, namely, that good government might well be achieved without participation, is now weaker. For on the present account, the very concept of good government is tied to moral concepts, but moral concepts which are developed through social processes and accepted by citizens involved in those processes. However, we must be careful not to overstate the argument. I do not mean to say that whatever laws come out of this process will be good laws; if that were the case we would be in the strong democracy camp with all the difficulties to be encountered there. There is, nevertheless, an objective element to what is a good law, and there is always tension between that objective element and the more subjective values that citizens bring to bear. That tension is in the nature of things. The point argued here is: (i) that good laws should meet that objective element while at the same time reflecting the more positive, variable, and subjective values of the society; and (ii) that participation by citizens at many levels of decision is tied closely to the making of good laws. The claim is still empirical: it depends on such matters as citizens being prepared to look beyond their own narrow interests, on their ability to develop and sustain a sense of critical morality, on their being prepared to participate regularly and vigorously, and to accept the need to justify laws on the basis of the common good. But most importantly, the claim depends on participation having the instrumental effect claimed for it; and that in turn depends on a close study of specific areas of political decision-making.

The writings of Mill are again instructive. He argues along two lines. The first is that participation promotes the virtue and intelligence of the members of the community because the citizen: 'is called upon to weigh interests not his own; to be guided, in cases of conflicting claims, by another rule than his private partialities; to apply, at every turn, principles and maxims which have for their reason of existence the common good'.[53] Secondly, Mill argued, the virtue that flows from participation is good, not just in improving the participant, but also as an instrument towards better laws. Those who participate will improve their character, and people with good characters will tend to produce good laws.[54]

Much more could be said about participation, but we must now draw in the strands of argument. The issue under discussion has been the place of participation in the political process. On the premise that the main concern of politics is to produce good laws and policies, participation is instrumental to that end. The precise nature of its instrumental role can be understood at two levels. At one level, participation is a way of getting diverse interests and opinions into the decision-process; since good government should take

[53] Mill, *Representative Government*, n. 33 above, 54.
[54] See Nelson, *On Justifying Democracy*, n. 43 above, 113.

account of the concerns of all, participation is an effective way of serving that end. At the second level, participation is an instrument serving the common good in its fullest sense; here the common good means, not just taking account of all interests, but making decisions which are good and just and morally sound. Participatory structures are likely to contribute to that end. At both levels, the case for participation is instrumental, and the actual contribution it makes is an empirical matter, but we now have a sound theoretical framework within which to test what happens in practice. In the course of the discussion, various attempts to raise the status of participation by making it a matter of more fundamental principle, were considered and found wanting.

4.4.4 Participation and Other Values

Participation in politics has long been associated not just with outcomes in the form of laws and policies, but also with other ends and values. The idea that by participating in the political process, a person both improves himself and advances various other public ends, is to be found throughout the history of political thought.[55] Such ends are of value quite apart from the effect participation has on outcomes, but the two are naturally interwoven. Modern advocates of strong democracy tend to emphasize the indivisible relationship between social transformation and the laws and policies resulting from it, on the one hand, and the personal transformation which comes to those who participate, on the other.[56]

The benefits, quite apart from good outcomes, which are said to stem from participation can loosely be divided into two kinds. The first is self-improvement of the person participating. We are already familiar with J. S. Mill's idea that participation in public life, no matter how local the issue or lowly the occasion, is a form of moral education. The responsibility that comes with involvement requires the weighing of matters and the evaluation of arguments; it also demands the ability to stand outside one's own station and to make assessments reasonably and objectively. The proper discharge of those duties, argued Mill, leads not only to better outcomes, it also improves one's capacity to make sound judgments, and it opens up avenues of further development which otherwise might have passed unnoticed.[57] Echoes of the same general sentiment can be heard down the years. Among contemporary writers, C. Pateman has put forward the view that participation helps people to develop active, non-servile characters and democratic, non-authoritarian personalities; it also helps people to broaden their

[55] For a survey of non-outcome values, see Parry, 'The Idea of Political Participation', n. 27 above.

[56] See Barber, *Strong Democracy*, n. 36 above.

[57] Mill, *Representative Government*, n. 33 above, 54 ff.

horizons and to appreciate the viewpoints of others.[58] Another writer in this tradition is B. Barber, who sees those who participate in political life transformed from selfish individuals into citizens; and citizens, for Barber, are 'autonomous persons whom participation endows with a capacity for common vision'.[59] The second set of benefits from participation relates more to the public interest than to individuals.[60] These can be various: involvement in political processes may be a way of channelling and containing energy which otherwise would be put to less constructive use; where participants have contributed to the process they might be more inclined to accept outcomes, and in that way social stability will be strengthened; sometimes even stronger claims are made that participation breeds co-operation and a firm sense of community.

Undoubtedly these are but a few of the benefits to be gained from participation, but we need not attempt here to give a complete list. Nor is it necessary for our present purposes to provide a full critique of the personal and public benefits noted above. However, a few comments should be made in passing. In the first place, the claims made for participation are still of an instrumental form: the argument is that in each case participation will lead to, will be instrumental to, certain results, whether the results be improved character, social stability, or something else. The claim then is an empirical one and stands or falls on evidence of what happens in the world. There is no logical or necessary connection between participation and, say, good character; it is plausible that participation might improve character, but whether it does and how much it does depends on circumstance and context.

A second point is that, supposing the claims made for participation to be true, the question is still open how important and desirable it is that political processes should positively pursue those ends. If participation does improve character, the question remains to what extent political processes should be directed to improving character; or if participation does lead people more readily to accept political outcomes, then we may ask whether that is a good thing. Participatory processes do not guarantee good outcomes, and if, by the fact of having participated, people are more inclined to accept bad outcomes, then the value of participation should be questioned. These are interesting issues, but it is enough for the present to note that the claims made for participation are largely of a consequential and instrumental kind, and that those claims must rest, finally, on hard evidence. Whether participation does lead to the benefits claimed, and the value of those benefits, are matters to be examined carefully and closely in any given context.

There is a third matter to note: a claim could be made for participation as

[58] C. Pateman, *Participation and Democratic Theory* (Cambridge University Press, Cambridge, 1970).

[59] Barber, *Strong Democracy*, n. 36 above, 232.

[60] For an account of public ends, see W. N. Nelson, *On Justifying Democracy*, n. 43 above, 48–51.

inherently good. Reference was made earlier to Italo Calvino's claim that he read books because that was a good thing to do and to Bayles' claim that he played tennis because it was enjoyable; so it may be that participation in social and public affairs is a good thing to have. Quite apart from its contribution to better laws and policies, and to other personal or public benefits, participation is simply something to be valued.[61] Some of the stronger theories of democracy totter on the edge of a claim of this kind,[62] and it is perfectly intelligible to hold that widespread participation in a society adds to it an attractive element. [63] Sometimes the claim is value-laden and conceals a causal connection between participation and benefits that flow from participation. That the participants feel good, or less alienated, or better disposed towards each other, are familiar claims made in the name of participation; but really they are instrumental claims, as we have seen. Some would argue, nevertheless, that, rid of such misleading claims, there is still a sense in which participation is simply and irreducibly worthwhile. The difficulty is in knowing quite how to handle a claim like this. Whether participation has that value depends on a particular vision of society, and visions rest finally on faith not proof. Many do not share that vision. Some argue that participation has little value in itself, and even that too much participation has harmful consequences.[64] Others accept some value in participation, but maintain that it has no special priority and must compete with a host of other values; it might beat push-pin but it is no rival for poetry. However, for those who share the vision of a participatory society, the consequence would be that social arrangements should take account of that fact, and in the design of procedures, that would be an added reason for maximizing participation.

4.5 PARTICIPATION IN LEGAL AND POLITICAL PROCESSES: A COMPARISON

The discussion of participation shows substantial common ground between legal and political processes. One feature both have in common is the close and special relationship between participatory procedures and outcomes. In both contexts, participatory procedures are regarded as useful instruments in reaching good outcomes. That is likely to be the case whatever the nature of the process, whether adjudicative, discretionary, or political and policy-

[61] See M. Bayles, 'Commentary on Nagan' (1978) 39 *Florida L Rev.* 491.

[62] Pateman, *Participation and Democratic Theory*, n. 58 above, and Barber, *Strong Democracy*, n. 36 above.

[63] For discussion, see D. Braybrooke, 'The Meaning of Participation and of Demands for It: A Preliminary Survey of the Conceptual Issues' in Pennock and Chapman (eds.), *Participation in Politics*, n. 9 above, 82–5.

[64] M. B. E. Smith, 'The Value of Participation', ibid.

based. In discussing the political process, however, we saw that the role of participation can go beyond giving each person and group the chance to put his or her interests and concerns into the decision-process. It may contribute to the quality of government in the deeper sense that, through participating, citizens may develop a better understanding of what is just and moral, which should in turn be reflected in the mode of participation and the results reached. This approach assumes that participation means more than simply casting a vote or putting an argument; it should be more active and positive, encouraging discussion and argument, the examination of alternatives, and the search for the best and most reasonable solution. Involvement in that sense is often hard to achieve in legal and administrative processes, but the idea is that the accused, the litigant, the claimant of welfare benefits, and the prisoner seeking parole should all be involved in the processes affecting them. In order to put forward evidence and argument, each has to enter into the process, has to understand the rules and principles on which the process is based, and generally should be able to develop a considered and critical attitude towards it.

Participation might also help each party to grasp the normative basis on which things are being done. That understanding is a necessary step towards developing genuine confidence in the decision-process; it is also a condition of the true growth of citizenship and in turn of civic virtue. Quite apart from the effects participation may have on the individual person, it may also help to improve the process, not just in the sense of contributing to better outcomes, but in raising the quality of decision-making in a general way. Participation not only helps to open up the process but also prepares the way for the giving of reasons to explain and justify how the decision has been made. A decision-maker who has to respond to the evidence and arguments advanced may, as a result, be more measured and reflective in his judgment. The quest for transparency of process is also a natural complement to the concern for good outcomes. These arguments for organic and holistic processes should not be pushed too far; the point is simply that in a real sense participation can be effective in heightening the critical understanding of those involved in processes and in improving the processes themselves. That is a lesson we may learn from the traditions of political theory and apply with profit in many areas of legal and administrative process.

A second point of comparison between legal and political processes concerns participation as a value in itself. According to one stream of thought running through the writings in both areas, to let a person participate in processes affecting him is to express respect for him. I have suggested that the stronger versions of such claims are problematical and ultimately unconvincing. However, more moderate versions of the claim, to the effect that a person has a good case for defending and advancing his own interests, has more merit. The notion that people are the best protectors of their own interests is a vital element in J. S. Mill's writings, while a similar assumption appears to lie behind the Rawlsian claim that, for people's interests to be properly considered, they must be allowed to participate. These claims as they stand make a good case for participation as instrumental to and contingent upon that further end; my suggestion is that, in order to give participation a firmer foundation in principle, a normative standard along the lines of self-protection needs to be introduced. The idea then is that each person has a right not only to his or her interests being considered, but also a right to advance and defend those interests whenever they are in issue. The principle of self-protection does not weaken the case for participation as an important means to good outcomes; it merely adds a different kind of justification. The case for the principle of self-protection was considered earlier and opinions as to just how persuasive it is as a foundational principle of law and politics are bound to be mixed. There is in any event an attractive symmetry between ensuring that one is properly treated in the various processes of law and politics, and at the same time being responsible for looking after one's own interests.

4.6 PARTICIPATION IN APPLICATION

4.6.1 The Social Basis of Participation

While the emphasis so far has been on the normative basis of participation, I shall consider briefly its social foundation and draw attention to some of the difficulties in making it effective. Let us begin with the idea of participation as instrumental to outcomes. Here its social basis lies in its role in helping to achieve good outcomes. That means in legal settings outcomes in accordance with authoritative legal standards, while in the political sphere it means outcomes which are wise and rational and within the parameters of the critical moral standards of the community. Participatory procedures are important elements in achieving those outcomes for reasons we noted earlier, in particular, the contribution that interested parties can make through evidence and argument. To this may be added the constitutive role of participatory procedures in developing the very standards by which the process itself is to be judged. A functional account of this kind can be strengthened by reference to the psychology of participation. The psychology of participation offers an explanation of why people value participation, which is itself a complex matter. One aspect, however, is that involvement in a process by which one is affected confers some influence over the outcome. That may then be linked to the instinct of self-protection as well as to an idea of active citizenship.

Support for an explanation of that kind can be seen in the early studies of

Thibaut and Walker which emphasize the importance people attach to participatory procedures.[65] The notion is that involvement in and control over such procedures may lead to influence over and even control of outcomes. This insight into the social importance of participatory procedures sounds right in a general, intuitive way, but would benefit from more detailed research. There is some empirical evidence to show that being heard and having one's views genuinely taken into account are a source of satisfaction to parties and a factor in their perceptions of fairness.[66] That sense of satisfaction might be gained from a variety of forms of participation, and it should not be assumed that some forms are necessarily more conducive to it than others. We should also be aware that, in a study of tort litigants, Lind and others were unable to find any correlation between participation and judgments of procedural justice or satisfaction.[67] This negative conclusion is important in sounding a note of scepticism about the real significance of participation, both in people's perceptions of their influence over processes affecting them, and the reality of that influence quite apart from their perceptions of it. The desire to have influence and control may be elemental, but the relationship between the desire and participatory procedures may be problematical.

The alternative approach to participation, based on the idea that participation directly expresses respect for persons, is more difficult to attach to a sound social basis. According to the views of Tyler and others (views which I have commented on in section 2.3.2 as theoretically questionable), participatory procedures are significant in judgments of fairness, and judgments of fairness are primarily guided by non-instrumental considerations.[68] But why the very expression of one's view is socially significant, independently of any effect on outcomes, is not clear. The explanation appears to be that such procedures express a relationship between the parties: just as A shows respect for B by being polite to him, similarly A shows respect for B by letting him state his case.[69] The argument then would be that mutual respect is fundamental to good social relations. In order to support such an interesting hypothesis, more evidence of the real connection between participatory procedures and mutual respect is needed.

[65] J. Thibaut and L. Walker, *Procedural Justice* (Erebaum, New Jersey, 1975); see also the discussion in section 2.3.2.

[66] See e.g. A. M. Heinz, 'Procedures versus Consequences: Experimental Evidence of Preference for Procedural and Distributive Justice' in S. M. Talarico (ed.), *Courts and Criminal Justice* (8th edn., Butterworth, London, 1985).

[67] E. A. Lind and others, *The Perception of Justice* (Institute for Civil Justice, Rand Corp., Santa Monica, Cal., 1989) 62.

[68] T. Tyler, *Why People Obey the Law* (Yale University Press, New Haven, Conn., 1990).

[69] Ibid. 138 ff.

4.6.2 The Effectiveness of Participation

Since participatory procedures are of great interest and importance, the question should be asked whether they are effective, the primary test of effectiveness being whether they help in producing the right outcomes. Participation serves other ends, as we have noted, but unless it lives up to expectations as an effective instrument to outcomes, much of its appeal will be misplaced. However, effectiveness is not an easy matter to judge. The variety of legal and political processes, and the many methods and degrees of involvement in them, make it difficult to speak with any confidence about the effectiveness of participation in general. A study of the effectiveness of lay participation in a public inquiry is very different, for example, from a study of tribunals and courts, and even within one set of processes, the methodological difficulties in assessing the influence of participation are considerable. Participation connotes such variable practices that the best research strategy may be to isolate specific aspects of it and then try to calculate their impact; we know, for example, that participation with legal representation is more effective in influencing outcomes than without it.[70] Other aspects of participation which could be studied in this way are: the level of knowledge of the opposing case; the extent of access to information relied on by the decision-maker; the scope for calling witnesses and for cross-examining opposing witnesses; and the way in which evidence and argument are dealt with and taken account of in the decision. Other issues could be added, the study of which would help in our understanding of the effects of participation. Existing studies are few and much of the work remains to be done in the future; where research has been conducted on the effectiveness of participation, reference is made to it later in this book.

We may conclude the present introductory discussion with a few more general remarks about the effectiveness of participation. One is the problem of access to participatory procedures. The problem of access occurs at many points in legal processes, but here the point is that the very best forms of participation may fail by default because those affected do not make use of them. This may be through ignorance, or lack of resources, or because the procedures themselves are complex and technical or expressed in arcane language. Various writers have drawn attention to the problems of access to and utilization of participatory procedures, especially in areas of welfare administration, but also in the more formalized processes of the criminal trial.[71]

[70] See the study by H. Genn and Y. Genn, *The Effectiveness of Representation Before Tribunals* (Lord Chancellor's Department, London, 1992).

[71] See e.g. T. Prosser, 'Poverty, Ideology and Legality' (1977) 4 *BJLS* 39 and J. F. Handler, *The Conditions of Discretion* (Russell Sage Foundation, New York, 1986).

Another general point is that the effectiveness of participation in any context will be related to other procedural features of that process. The same point could be made about any procedure, but it has singular force in relation to participation. Where the issues are well-defined and the standards to be applied are settled, as in the paradigm case of adjudication, participation by the parties fits well and its objectives are clear. In more discretionary and policy-based contexts the position is often different. Here the standards may be unsettled and the policy question only loosely defined, so that the object of participation is less clear and an assessment of its efficacy more difficult to judge. Similar problems occur where the aim of a process is to decide a matter of general policy; the effectiveness of participation, whatever form it takes, may be seriously jeopardized because the real issues of policy are not disclosed or the information necessary to make effective representations is not forthcoming. The point in each of these cases is that the form participation takes must fit with other features of the process to form a coherent whole. Reliance on forms of participation which do not conform to the overall procedural context will result in dysfunction, and participation will fail in its objectives. It may be, moreover, that procedural coherence cannot be achieved by tinkering with only the form of participation; other aspects of the process may have to be reshaped in order to open the way for effective participation.

The final point follows nicely from the concern for coherence between the forms of participation and the nature of the process. The normative and symbolic appeal of participation, which is often connected to the idea of its being an irreducible good, is unquestionably powerful. So much attention is then paid to participation itself that questions as to what effects it has are not asked. The danger then is that participatory procedures serve a function which is more ideological and symbolic than real. The danger may apply to other procedures, but it is especially strong in relation to participation. In order to reduce that danger, we should constantly reaffirm the conviction that procedures are primarily instruments to ends and values, that we ought to be clear what those ends and values are, and then be rigorous in testing the effectiveness of procedures in achieving them.

PART II

Three Traditions of Procedural Fairness

Introduction

In the first part of this book, I have given a general account of procedural fairness and due process. The object there was to create a general framework of analysis for notions of procedural fairness, procedural rights, and various other related matters. That framework provides the setting for this second part, but here the purpose is quite different. It is to consider how general ideas about due process and procedural fairness have emerged within three different traditions: the English constitutional and common law system; the American constitutional tradition; and the newer doctrines of the European Union and the European Convention on Human Rights.

Since each of these subjects warrants a full study of its own, I should make clear that my present purpose is only to provide an outline of the way the main aspects of due process and procedural fairness have been developed and refined within the three traditions. The method of approach is to some extent an analysis of doctrine, but doctrine only in a fairly general sense. There is also in each case an historical element, since the precise forms of modern doctrines of due process and procedural fairness are greatly influenced by the social situations within which they arose. It is for that reason of interest to see how ideas developed within each historical context. However, notions of due process and procedural fairness also transcend those particular contexts; they confront common problems and in solving those problems they draw on a common stock of moral and political ideas and values. It is then also of interest to see how that common stock has itself been a major factor in the growth of doctrine.

5

Procedural Fairness in the English Common Law

Notions of due process and procedural fairness have a long and interesting history in the English common law. Some are able to trace an unbroken line through the passages of English history to Magna Carta itself, although whether such claims are valid is a matter of debate. In any case, it is not long after Magna Carta that the expression due process of law begins to appear in statutes and judicial decisions and, from then on, the notions of both substantive and procedural due process are constant themes in the development of the common law. In the masterly hands of figures such as Sir Edward Coke, notions of due process could be put to great effect in times of constitutional crisis.

In the calmer climate of post-Civil War centuries, the procedural aspects of due process appear to have been left to the courts to develop as an element of the rule of law, so that, as we look back, evidence can be found for slowly evolving doctrines of law based on the simple idea that fair treatment requires fair procedures. By the late twentieth century, that simple idea has been transformed into a dynamic principle with special significance in administrative contexts. One object in this Chapter is to convey a sense of the historical background both to the procedural nature of English law and to the special place of procedural fairness. The other object is to sketch the special problems that have been confronted in translating ideas of procedural fairness into administrative contexts.

5.1 THE PROCEDURAL CHARACTER OF ENGLISH COMMON LAW

The study of procedures has never been a major interest of English lawyers, and yet the growth of the common law, indeed the very foundations of the common law, are tied inseparably to procedures. There may be a natural progression in the growth of a legal system, since it is arguable that all early systems of law place great importance on formal procedures, often to the neglect of substantive outcomes; as the system matures, the emphasis shifts from formal procedures to substantive outcomes. The power to think of law apart from its procedure is, as T. F. T. Plucknett has written, a significant step in legal history, a sign of legal maturity.[1] A notable feature of English law, however, is that it has retained throughout its development, and into the modern age, a particular emphasis on procedures.[2] The point can be put in this way: the early growth of the common law (and here I use the term in its widest sense to mean the several branches of English law created by the courts) was characterized not through abstract reflection on what the substantive rules ought to be, but by practical judgments about procedures. By and large, the substantive ends of law were not in doubt: they were to do justice, but justice was beyond human understanding and control; man's task, therefore, was to provide as best he could the mechanisms of justice, the courts, and their procedures, to provide, as Milsom puts it, the channels of justice.[3] Justice was the touchstone, and where the mechanisms for achieving it were defective or non-existent, steps would be taken through new and better procedures. It is only later and gradually that the rules of substantive law were thought of as separate from both justice and the procedures for achieving justice.

The idea of the specifically legal task as procedural is fundamental in understanding the common law. Substantive issues did arise but the emphasis fell on procedures, on how to deliver the ends of justice. The common law, like any social institution, has its foundations and its formative influences, which persist long after they appear to have fallen away. But in this case, the procedural nature of law, the idea of law as a mechanism for achieving abstract principles of justice, is one foundation of continuing importance. For even now, English law retains a special emphasis on remedies, institutions, and mechanisms, all of which taken together can be considered procedural.[4] The procedural orientation of the common law reveals itself in three distinct but related characteristics: first, procedures serve, and are necessary instruments of, justice; secondly, procedures are the vehicles for notions of the due process of law, or, in current terms, procedural fairness; and thirdly, procedures are a vital part of the rule of law. I shall now take each of these in turn.

The first, the instrumental role of procedures as instruments of justice is often stressed.[5] Halsbury's Laws of England states: 'Civil procedure is an

[1] T. F. T. Plucknett, *A Concise History of the Common Law* (Butterworth, London, 1956), 379–83.

[2] See further F. Pollock and F. Maitland, *History of English Law* (Cambridge University Press, Cambridge, 1988), i, 558–63.

[3] S. F. C. Milsom, *Historical Foundations of the Common Law* (2nd edn., Butterworths, London, 1981),76–7.

[4] The procedural emphasis comes out time and again. See e.g. The Committee on Supreme Court Practices and Procedures, *Report* Cmnd. 8573 (1953).

[5] See e.g. J. I. H. Jacob, *The Reform of Civil Procedure Law* (Sweet and Maxwell, London, 1982), 1–2; J. A. Jolowicz, 'On the Nature and Purpose of Civil Procedure' in I. R. Scott

indispensable part of the machinery of justice and operates as an essential tool for enforcing legal rights and claims, for redressing and preventing legal wrongs'.[6] This idea runs through the history of the common law. For the medieval lawyer, legal procedures were the human mechanisms for achieving notions of justice where the abstract principles of justice were settled and beyond dispute. For the modern lawyer, justice has lost its divine and immutable quality, and is now expressed through positive, substantive laws; but the procedural task is undiminished. Procedures are as important as ever in applying the law properly and accurately, and in that way upholding rights and doing justice. As Master Jacob has written: 'The quality of justice, which is the touchstone of a civilized society, depends in large measure on the arrangements provided for its due administration.'[7] What is true of civil procedure is equally true of criminal and administrative procedure.

Now it might be said that this is a truism which applies to any legal system. In what sense is it a distinctive quality of the common law? The answer is that the emphasis on procedures, on being sure that where there are rights and duties there is also the machinery to uphold and enforce them, has been a vital characteristic of the common law from its earliest origins. The earliest forms of action were initiated through writs which were narrow in scope, highly detailed, and emphatically procedural.[8] The concept of an abstract right might have been present, but without a writ specifying the precise nature and scope of the action, and stating the procedure to be followed, any such abstraction was useless. As Pollock and Maitland wrote: 'one could say next to nothing about actions, in general, while one could discourse at length about the mode in which an action of this or that sort was to be pursued and defended'.[9]

The beginnings of equity, similarly, are best explained in procedural terms.[10] Equity did not begin with a set of substantive principles to ameliorate the common law. It began rather as a mechanism, a procedure, through which relief could be sought when it was not available at common law. In the earliest days of English law, there was no body of positive law either in equity or at common law. There was justice, and when the common law failed to provide the procedures for achieving justice, recourse could be had to Chancery to remedy the defect. In Milsom's memorable expression, Chancery was head office for administering justice; its business was procedural,

(ed.), *International Perspectives on Civil Justice* (Sweet and Maxwell, London, 1990) and *Halsbury's Laws of England*, xxxvii, 9–12.

[6] *Halsbury*, xxxvii, 9.

[7] J. Jacob, *The Reform of Civil Procedure Law*, n. 5 above, 1; see also his *The Fabric of English Civil Justice* (Stevens and Sons, London, 1981), 55–65.

[8] See Pollock and Maitland, *History of English Law*, n. 2 above, ch. 9.

[9] Ibid. 562.

[10] See Milsom, *Historical Foundations of the Common Law*, n. 3 above, 74–82.

[11] Milsom, *Historical Foundations of the Common Law*, n. 3 above, 74–82.

and if one set of procedures, one branch of the court system, failed, an alternative had to be found. It is only much later that both equity and common law began to express a conception of justice in rules and principles.[11]

These two examples could be matched with many others. They confirm the picture of English law in which the procedural aspects have a special and prominent place. Questions of substantive law and justice of course arose, but when they did they were approached and resolved through closely defined and well-established procedures. What this means is that the common law as a system has been based from its earliest origins on the centrality of procedures. By way of corollary, statements of principle and claims of right are barren gestures unless they are matched to procedures. This is not to say that the procedures used were always effective, reliable, or even tolerable. Criminal procedures in particular appear crude, ill-conceived, and often ineffective, until late in the nineteenth century when they began to take on some of the features, such as the right of the accused to give evidence and to be represented by counsel, which we now consider indispensable.[12] But the point of general importance is that, however imperfect particular procedures might be in achieving the ends of justice as defined by law, English law had developed a conceptual framework based on the idea that the object of procedure is to achieve those ends. To have arrived at such a conceptualization early in its history, and to have remained constant in pursuit of it, is one of the great strengths of English law, whatever its failings in one or other area of practice may be.

5.2 DUE PROCESS AT COMMON LAW

The concept of due process of law is to modern English lawyers an American doctrine, which is enshrined in the federal and several of the state constitutions, but of no special relevance to English law. Like some of the best families, due process emigrated west in the seventeenth century, leaving only the vaguest folk memory at home that it may have had some part in ancient constitutional conflicts. Procedural fairness is the modern concept, and only on rare occasions is reference made to its predecessor, due process. But on close inspection, it is clear that the two ideas cover the same ground; procedural fairness is a wider concept, but the core idea common to both is that certain procedures are needed to give effect to the ends of justice within legal decisions. There is, moreover, a direct line of development from the

[11] Milsom, *Historical Foundations of the Common Law*, n. 3 above, 74–82.

[12] A good insight into criminal procedure can be gained from J. F. Stephen, *The History of the Criminal Law* (London, 1983), i.

earliest ideas of due process of law to the modern notion of procedural fairness. For just as procedural issues have been one distinguishing mark of the common law, a sense of due process has been another. Its development and its expression have been uneven, but, nevertheless, due process has been an idea of importance from the earliest days of the common law. The relative ease with which principles of procedural fairness are accepted in modern law and extended to the administrative process results from the foundations long since laid.

5.2.1 The History of Due Process in English Law

The history of due process in the common law is a rich and fascinating subject. The best studies I know are those of Faith Thompson, an American historian writing in the middle part of the twentieth century.[13] However, the history of the subject is far from complete and for aspiring legal historians, there are still rich sources to explore.[14] But I shall not here attempt to write a history of due process; my purpose is only to give a brief account of the way the concept has featured in the development of the common law.

It has long been claimed that due process could be traced back to the Magna Carta, and that there, in clause 39 of the Charter of 1215,[15] the basic idea is expressed for the first time: 'No freeman shall be taken and imprisoned or disseised of any tenement or of his liberties or free customs . . . except by the lawful judgment of his peers or by the law of the land.' The important part is the exception, especially the words 'by the law of the land' (*legem terrae*). On first reading it might seem that the significant words are 'judgement of his peers', since they suggest a foundation for trial by jury. Jury trials, however are a long way into the future and have different origins. The more likely meaning of the expression 'judgement of his peers' is the right of a noble to be judged by his equals, which in turn carries some suggestion of a fair trial. This certainly has procedural connotations, but the search for a fuller sense of due process is usually directed at the words 'the law of the land'.

That idea is vague enough to support different meanings, and certainly it is not improbable to suggest, as some have, that it contains at least the kernel of due process.[16] Foremost amongst those who equated the law of the

[13] Her main book is *Magna Carta: Its Role in the Making of the English Constitution 1300–1629* (University of Mineapolis Press, Mineapolis, Minnesota, 1948).

[14] In addition to the standard legal histories which usually have something to say about due process, the following works are of interest: S, Thorne, W. Dunham, P. Kaarland, and I. Jennings, *The Great Charter: Four Essays on Magna Carta and the History of Our Liberty* (Pantheon, New York, 1968).

[15] The original Charter was drawn up in 1215, with a shorter version being promulgated in 1225 by Henry II. Cl. 39 in the original became cl. 29 in the later version.

[16] See the discussion in R. E. Riggs, 'Substantive Due Process in 1791' [1990] *Wisc. L Rev.* 941.

land with due process of law was Edward Coke in the seventeenth century[17] and American constitutionalists of the eighteenth century.[18] While such a view might have been helpful in giving legitimacy and authority to the modern doctrine of due process, it is a matter of debate amongst scholars whether it is a convincing interpretation of the Great Charter itself. Understood in its medieval context, *per legem terrae* appears to have meant by the laws and customs which governed, that is, the 'pious and just laws of King Edward', which were being undermined by the King.[19] Clause 39 was a general reinstatement of those laws, not a statement about process or procedures. The mischief to be remedied was the tendency of the Crown to act against the barons and others without respect for those laws and customs. The issue was less about the procedures for applying the laws, than about the authority of the laws themselves.

Before continuing the discussion of sources, however, a distinction should be drawn between two senses of due process, one substantive, the other procedural. Nowadays we concentrate on the procedural aspects of due process and it is not clear that substantive due process was ever a term with currency in English law, unlike American law where it has had great significance. Nevertheless, much of the early discussion of due process was about its substantive part; indeed I would go farther and suggest that, once due process is understood as having both a substantive and a procedural part, a great deal of the controversy and uncertainty about its place in early English law disappears. My suggestion is that due process as historically conceived had both procedural and substantive elements, that the two are closely connected, and that in later discussions both were subsumed into the English notion of the rule of law.[21] The procedural element refers to certain procedures which came to be regarded as necessary for a fair trial and which later were extended in modified form to administrative processes. The substantive part of due process is not so easily defined, but can perhaps be divided into two elements. One is that the substantive law, which is of course meant to serve the ends of justice, should be upheld and properly applied. This aspect is closely intertwined with the procedural part and might well be included within it. The other element goes further and implies limitations on what laws may be made, by whom they may be made, and what content they

[17] See Sir Edward Coke, *Institutes of the Laws of England* (E. and R. Brooke, London, 1628).

[18] See the account by Justice Harlan in *Hurtado* v. *California*, 110 US 516 (1883).

[19] See C. H. McIlwain, 'Due Process of Law in Magna Carta' (1914) 14 *Columbia L Rev.* 27.

[20] For further discussion: K. Jurow, 'Untimely Thoughts: A Reconsideration of the Origins of Due Process of Law' (1975) 19 *American J of Legal History* 265.

[21] The inter-relationship between the procedural and substantive aspects of due process is not often noticed; but see further W. H. Dunham, 'Magna Carta and British Constitutionalism' in S. Thorne, W. Dunham, P. Kurland, and I. Jennings, *The Great Charter: Four Essays on Magna Carta and the History of Our Liberty*, n. 14 above.

may have. Since the implied limitations for their part derive from deeper constitutional and political values, it is to be expected that they should be the subject of argument and controversy.

With this fuller sense of due process in mind, let us now return to the growth of the notion in English law. The idea in the Great Charter that a person ought to be dealt with according to the law of the land has substantive connotations of the two kinds noted; it means that people are to be dealt with according to settled law and carries the further implication that the Crown is not empowered to change those laws at will. The second part rests on the assumption that what constitutes law is well defined and that acts of the Crown contrary to law are arbitrary and unauthorized. It is more difficult to discern in Magna Carta a coherent sense of procedural due process, although its appearance in a number of statutes from the fourteenth century on is indisputable. A clear and early case is a statute of Edward III passed in 1354 which states:

> That no man of what estate or condition that he be, shall be put out of land or tenement, nor taken, nor imprisoned . . . without being brought in answer by due process of law.[22]

What exactly was meant by due process of law is not clear, but before long it was expressed in this way:

> No one shall be judged or condemned before he has lawful accusers personally present and the opportunity to offer a defence for the purpose of clearing himself of the charges.[23]

The issue is unmistakably procedural and in those early statutes a notion of due process has begun to emerge.[24] The modern concept is a long way off, but the germ of the idea is there: a person should be condemned, or otherwise acted against, only through following certain procedures, procedures which were dictated by the writ in issue. Indeed, until recently, the usual meaning of 'process' was the writ and the procedures of the writ by which an action should be commenced, or by which a further step within an action should be taken.[25]

Again the mischief to which statutes such as the above were directed holds the clue: the King's Council, in exercising judicial powers, was acting against

[22] 28 Edw. III Ch. 3 (1354).

[23] *Leges Henrici Primi* as set out in Jurow, n. 20 above.

[24] Thompson was able to find 6 statutes in the 14th century explicitly directed to procedural issues in this way: *Magna Carta*, n. 13 above, 69.

[25] See Jurow, 'Untimely Thoughts', n. 20 above. It is in this sense that Blackstone used the idea of process: see W. Blackstone, *Commentaries on the Laws of England* (9th edn., London, 1783), bk. 4. According to Blackstone, in criminal law, process meant the procedure by way of the different writs for dealing with a person charged with an offence (318); while in civil matters it meant the method taken by the law to compel compliance with the original writ (279).

individuals without following the procedures of the common law. Chattels were forfeited and lives endangered by decisions of the Council, without the person who was liable being summoned to answer charges according to established procedures. The attack was not on the Council's exercise of judicial powers as such, but on its flouting established procedures, in particular, the procedures of the writs.[26] Whatever the ambiguities of Clause 39 of the Great Charter may be, the statutes of the fourteenth century made clear that *process*, the following of settled procedures, was a distinct element of the legal domain. But the due process of law was not understood as a separate element: to the lawyers of the time, due process and *legem terrae* were the same thing, or to be more accurate *legem terrae* included elements of both substantive law and procedural propriety. The outlook of the fourteenth century is summed up by Faith Thompson in this way:

> The phrase *per legem terrae* was interchanged with the magic formula due process of law; it was made to cover the indicting jury and procedure by original writ; it was believed to limit the jurisdiction of the council, other prerogative courts, and the commissions armed with special powers; and it was supposed to insure trial in common law courts by common law procedures.[27]

Notice in passing how Thompson mixes indiscriminately procedural aspects (the indicting jury and the procedures of the writ) with substantive parts (the limited jurisdiction of the council, etc.); that presumably is also how it was understood at the time of which she writes. The procedural aspects were rather rudimentary, but to insist that the law be administered through settled procedures was a step of great significance upon which the foundations of a fundamental constitutional doctrine could be laid.

When constitutional conflicts again erupted in the seventeenth century, Sir Edward Coke, in a move of great shrewdness, called on Magna Carta as the basis for English law and the protection of liberties.[28] In Coke's hands, *per legem terrae* came to be the fundamental constitutional principle; for it meant: firstly, that all official bodies—the King, the special courts, and the commissions—were subject to the law of the land; secondly, that no one was to be deprived of liberty or property except in accordance with the law of the land; and thirdly, that any deprivation must be in accordance with settled methods and procedures. The law of the land meant the law of Parliament and the common law, and the King himself had no power in his own right to make law. The law of the land also constituted a test of jurisdiction for subordinate judicial and administrative bodies. Such authorities had no powers or jurisdiction beyond those conferred by statute or the common

[26] See Jurow, 'Untimely Thoughts', n. 20 above, 267–71.

[27] Thompson, *Magna Carta*, n. 13 above, 69. (The last part of this quotation must be doubted since trial in the prerogative courts was accepted until much later.)

[28] Coke's view was developed over a long period; a succinct account of his approach to Magna Carta and due process is set out in his *Institutes of the Laws of England*, n. 17 above, 1, i.

law, and the common law courts would determine whether the jurisdiction existed.[29] And if no jurisdiction existed, any deprivation of liberty or property was limited to the normal principles of common law, and according to the settled procedures of common law and, arguably, of chancery.[30]

By drawing together these three elements and claiming for them an unbroken provenance in the *per legem terrae* of the Great Charter, Coke and his followers not only created a powerful weapon in the ideological struggles of the seventeenth century; they also consolidated the place of these ideas in the modern constitution. Later critics may be right in arguing that the law of the land and due process are separate ideas, and that the Great Charter was not concerned with the latter. But historical accuracy often withers in the shadow of ideological necessity, and the two ideas had been persistently conflated from the fourteenth century onwards. In principle, the ideas are related. To the lawyers and parliamentarians of Coke's day, the dominance of law, the idea of jurisdiction, and the principle of due process of law are all inseparably linked. To deprive someone of his goods without trial is as much a violation of the law (the procedural aspect) as it is to usurp an unauthorized power (the substantive aspect). For the very idea of the law of the land translates into the rule of law, and part of the rule of law is that powers will be exercised only to the extent that they are justified by law. Whether they are justified is determined according to whether they follow acceptable procedures, in this case the procedures of the common law courts.

That the point of procedures, of procedural due process, is to ensure proper and justified application of the law was not declared in so many words; such a rationalist, scientific way of putting it had to await the advance of modernism. Gentlemen and lawyers of the seventeenth century, let alone the fourteenth, did not think in that way; but they did grasp the deep connection between the dominance of law, the idea of government through law, and due process. The connection was well seen by one John Ashley, follower of Coke and Reader at the Middle Temple in 1616. In examining the statutes of the fourteenth century, such as 28 Edward III noted above, Ashley explained that they not only secured rights to property, liberty, and the person, but also prevented wrongs, that is, violations of law, by providing for due process; he continued:[31]

> for by virtue hereof no man shall be punished before he be condempned and no man shalbe condempned before he be heard and none shalbe heard but his just deffence shalbe allowed.

[29] See *Case of Marshalsea* (10 Jacobi, 10, Coke Reports 680) where Coke as Chief Justice directly invoked cl. 29 of Magna Carta as establishing a test of jurisdiction. Also *Bagg's Case* (3 Jacobi, 11, Coke Reports 930).

[30] Chancery lawyers argued that cl. 29 (of the 1225 version of the Great Charter) also applied in their courts 'for chancery is intended to correct faulty proceedings in common law': see Thompson, *Magna Carta*, n. 13 above, 284.

[31] From the Middle Temple Records for 1616, quoted in Thompson, *Magna Carta*, n. 13 above, 284.

Procedural due process by now had its own shape and content. John Legate had asked in his petition against charges of heresy in 1612: 'Doth our Laws judge a man before it heare him and now [sic] what he hath done?'[32] Ashley's answer four years later was resoundingly no; due process must be honoured, but it is not honoured by any old procedure; the procedures must be both fair and likely to lead to the right outcome. The right to know and to be heard are thus on the way to being an indispensable core of due process.

Arguments like these were sometimes put in terms of due process, at other times as an emerging notion of the rule of law. Such arguments were heard regularly in the Parliament and the courts of the seventeenth century; but they were not always accepted and there were risks in even putting them. In the parliamentary debates leading to the Petition of Right in 1628, speaker after speaker exulted in the antiquity of these ideas, whilst demonstrating their relevance to the issues of the day. Similar arguments were often put, with mixed success, in the courts; while Coke was Chief Justice of the King's Bench the arguments were well received,[33] but after his dismissal the position was more complex. In the *Five Knights' Case*,[34] for example, the issue was whether certain of the King's prerogative powers could be regarded as *per legem terrae*. Argument for the defence ranged widely, but claimed in essence that the law of the land meant the due process of law. Due process of law, it was argued, in turn meant not only a trial, but also some lawful initial process, such as indictment or writ, the corollary being that commitment by special command of the King, as had occurred here, was not due process.[35] On that point, however, no decision was given. The mixing of substantive and procedural elements of due process can again be seen quite clearly.

5.2.2 The Dominance of the Common Law and the Acceptance of Due Process

The personal fortunes of the protagonists of the seventeenth century ebbed and flowed, but, by the end of the century, the case for due process in its full and double sense was more or less won. The new constitutional order was based on the supremacy of Parliament, the independence and hegemony of the common law courts, and a restricted monarchy. The King could no longer legislate or tax without Parliament; nor could he do justice outside the courts of common law and Chancery.[36] The ideas of Coke and his

[32] *State Trials* (1612) II, 729–34, No. 90.

[33] See e.g. the *Case of Marshalsea* (10, Coke Reports 68v–77) and *Bagg's Case* (13 *Jacobi*, Coke Reports XI, 93v–100), both n. 29 above.

[34] Described in Thompson, *Magna Carta*, pp. 326 ff.

[35] See further Thompson, *Magna Carta*, n. 13 above, 330.

[36] The position is well summarized by Thompson, ibid. 371; see also D. L. Keir, *The Constitutional History of Modern Britain 1485–1951* (6th edn., A. and C. Black, London, 1960), chs. IV and V.

followers, in particular their interpretation of Magna Carta and the course of English law, were now accepted as orthodox. The law was securely in the hands of the common law courts and their lawyers, and whether their interpretation was the right one hardly mattered. For as Thompson wrote: 'Whatever historical errors may have been committed by the Government of the Inns of Court, currently the law was what they made it.'[37] And, it might be added, what they made it became the basis for the new order, the modern constitution.

The essential elements of the new order were few and simple. First, the law of the land meant the statutes of Parliament or the rules of common law (using the terms here to include Chancery). The king remained a powerful force, but by having to govern through Parliament, the course was set for a gradual reduction of those powers, as the authority of Parliament grew and democratic ideas emerged. Secondly, the law of the land meant that subordinate authorities had only those powers which were conferred by statute or which existed at common law. Government and administration had to be conducted within a framework of law, rather than in the open-ended exercise of prerogative. The abolition of the special administrative courts and authorities—the King's Council, the Star Chamber, and the Provincial Councils—marked the end of an alternative system of government and administration based on the King's prerogative and operating independently of Parliament and the common law.[38] Government under law in this sense is now taken for granted, but in the seventeenth century it was a new idea which, although it finally prevailed, was not regarded as an unmitigated good. For the dominance of the common law in Coke's sense meant the loss of those central institutions from which a body of administrative law and regulation might have developed.

The third major element of the new order was the authority of the common law and of the common law courts.[39] Questions of law and of the jurisdiction of executive and subordinate bodies were now settled authoritatively by the courts. The rights and liberties of the subject could be changed by parliamentary statute, but any dispute abut their meaning or scope was settled by the courts. In the many areas where Parliament passed no laws, it was left to the courts to decide what those rights and liberties were and

[37] Thompson, *Magna Carta*, n. 13 above, 373.

[38] It also marked the end of the inquisitorial procedures which were the hallmark of the prerogative courts: with the abolition of the Star Chamber, the common law approach to procedures prevailed in all courts while the inquisitorial approach, with its origins in common law, became the standard form in France and other continental countries: see further Publications of the Selden Society, *Select Cases in the Council of Henry VII*, ed. C. G. Bayne and W. H. Dunham (London, 1958), p. xciv and Pollock and Maitland, *History of English Law*, n. 2 above, 673.

[39] Chancery was the one prerogative court which survived, but probably because by this time it was both independent of the Crown and more like the common law courts than anything else.

under what circumstances they might be curtailed by administrative or executive officials. The law of the land, the *legem terrae*, could now be translated as the rule of law, a notion which depended not only on there being a framework of legal rules, but also on the courts adjudicating upon and upholding those rules. Within the notion of the law of the land, or the rule of law, was a sense of due process in both its substantive and procedural aspects: in its substantive aspect, it meant that rights and liberties would not be affected except by law properly made, while in its procedural sense, it meant that suitable procedures would be available to determine whether any action was justified by law.

5.3 DUE PROCESS AND THE MODERN CONSTITUTION

5.3.1 Dicey, the Rule of Law and Due Process

The constitutional conflicts of the seventeenth century might easily have gone either way, but Coke and his followers were finally so successful that by the late nineteenth century, there was no contest. When A. V. Dicey in 1885 delivered his lectures on the constitution, he could assert with confidence that the rule of law was one of the two central characteristics of the English constitution—the supremacy of central government being the other—which stretched back to the Norman Conquest.[40] Dicey's notion of the rule of law is almost too well-known to warrant repetition, but it is interesting to see how closely it follows views held in the seventeenth century. The first element for Dicey was the absolute supremacy of the law. No one can be punished or otherwise suffer deprivation except for a breach of the law established in the courts. Secondly, no one is above the law, and indeed everyone is subject to the ordinary law and amenable to the jurisdiction of the ordinary courts. No one, not even officials, is exempt from obedience to the ordinary law, at least in the sense that an official has no powers other than those conferred by statute and may be subject to judicial review by the courts to ensure that they have not been exceeded.[41] Between the seventeenth century and the nineteenth, the life of the country may have been transformed, but Dicey's conception of the rule of law could have been written by Coke.

The question of present interest is not so much the merits of Dicey's account,[42] but rather what had happened to due process. It is not mentioned by Dicey in *The Law of the Constitution*: the closest he comes to considering

[40] A. V. Dicey, *The Law of the Constitution* (ed. E. C. S. Wade, Macmillan, London, 1961), 183, 202–3.

[41] Dicey's 3rd point that the general principles of the constitution, e.g., the right to liberty, are the results of judicial decisions in actual cases, is not relevant here; see ibid. 199.

[42] An early critique is I. Jennings, *The Law and the Constitution* (4th edn., Lloyds of London Press, London, 1952); a later one is H. Arthurs, 'Rethinking Administrative Law: A Dicey Business' (1979) 17 *Osgood Hall LR* 1.

it at all is in an article in 1915.[43] I shall return to that shortly, but first let us consider where due process stood at the end of the nineteenth century. One point to note is that the substantive part of due process, that no action should be taken against a person without the authority of law, was by then included in the very idea of the rule of law. A second point is that, once special courts and administrative bodies acting under prerogative were abolished, the problems of arbitrary power were thought to be solved. Any exercise of authority could be brought before the courts, and they would determine its legality. Thirdly, the procedural aspects of due process were enshrined in the procedures of the courts. The rights and liberties of individuals were matters of adjudication for the courts, and since the courts followed their usual procedures, the demands of due process were satisfied. No matter how defective those procedures might appear to the modern eye, they *were* due process; that is to say, the procedures of the ordinary courts were considered to be the embodiment of due process, beyond which there was no further standard to invoke.

The upshot is that, by the time Dicey wrote, due process of law as a substantive idea was contained in the rule of law, while as a procedural notion it meant simply the procedures of the ordinary courts. Those procedure's were by no means perfect, but by this time the influence of Bentham had been felt, the reform movement was well under way, and the Judicature Acts had been passed. The commitment to simplifying the procedures of both the civil and criminal trials had been made; procedures could now be seen for what they are, means to ends, and they could be subjected to scrutiny and criticism if they failed to serve their ends. It is understandable that, by the end of the nineteenth century, due process in its substantive and procedural senses was not an issue of controversy.

5.3.2 Due Process in Administration

The great constitutional conflicts over the supremacy of parliament, the rule of law, and due process had little to say about the administration. For centuries government had depended on a range of administrative bodies to implement its policies, to maintain public services, and to provide relief and welfare of various kinds. A range of officials, boards, and commissions, together with the local justices, has been a familiar part of government since the Conquest. Some acted under the direct authority of the Crown, others under statute, while others still took their powers from the common law.[44] The history of administration, particularly the legal framework of administra-

[43] 'The Development of Administrative Law in England' (1915) 31 *LQR* 148.

[44] The vestiges of common law authority can be seen in the powers of the modern police officer: see L. Lustgarten, *The Governance of Police* (Sweet and Maxwell, London, 1986).

tion remains to be written, but clearly the delegation of extensive authority to administrative bodies has always been a feature of English government. An explosion of administrative government is often thought to be a mark of the twentieth century, but we need only consider the dramatic increase in administration during the first half of the nineteenth century, or indeed the expansion of governmental regulation during the Tudor and Stuart periods, to realize that the delegation of administrative powers to a great range of subordinate bodies has been a regular feature of English government.

The early to middle period of the nineteenth century makes a good case study of the variety and scope of administrative government. The period was one of great social reform, which in most cases was achieved by creating under statute special boards, commissions, and authorities. The task of each was to provide the solution to a pressing social issue, such as the relief of poverty, the exploitation of child labour, the provision of basic public services, or the development of education. The powers given to these authorities were often extensive. A series of Factories Acts, beginning in 1833 inaugurating the Factory Inspectors, and the Poor Law Act of 1834, creating the Poor Law Commissioners, are two leading examples. But they are just examples and, wherever one looks, other statutory bodies abound, from the Turnpike Trusts (of which in 1835 there were over a thousand[45]) to the Improvement Commissioners 'for paving, lighting, cleansing, watching, and otherwise improving the streets';[46] from the Emigration Commissioners,[47] to the Commission of Sewers[48]—to name a few.

What is even more startling than the sheer number of administrative bodies is the breadth of their powers. Inspectors appointed under the Factories Act 1833 had power to make rules, regulations, and orders; to give directions; to enforce against factory owners and others the provisions of the Act; to punish for certain breaches of the Act, where imprisonment was included amongst the punishments which might be imposed; and to summon witnesses to appear and give evidence. The Inspectors had in effect a wide range of legislative, adjudicative, and administrative powers, with no specification of the procedures to be followed and little indication in the statute of how such extensive powers were to be used. The breadth of these powers did not pass without comment, with one mill owner complaining that the only power the Inspectors lacked was 'that of hanging a mill-owner without trial, and leaving his body to the surgeons for dissection'.[49] This may have been the high-water mark of administrative powers, and in later Acts modifications were made; but it was not untypical. The Commission of Sewers, itself

[45] S. and B. Webb, *English Local Government* (Longman, London, 1906), iv, 152.

[46] Ibid. 235 ff.

[47] O. MacDonagh, 'Delegated Legislation and Administrative Discretion in the 1850s: A Particular Study' (1958) *Victorian Studies* 29.

[48] S. and B. Webb, *English Local Government*, n. 45 above, 20 ff.

[49] M. W. Thomas, *The Early Factory Legislation* (Thomas Bank, Leigh-on-Sea, 1948), 7.

of ancient origins, exercised court-like functions, combined with a strong mixture of legislative and administrative powers;[50] the same goes for the Poor Law Commissioners and many others.

What is interesting for our present purposes is whether any concept of procedural due process or procedural fairness prevailed within these administrative bodies. The governing statutes rarely laid down the procedures to follow, and certainly made no reference to due process. Members of the commissions and inspectorates were deeply committed to their work and to achieving the social reforms for which their powers were conferred, and there is no reason to think that procedural niceties were foremost in their minds.[51] Equally, however, there is no reason to assume that they did not extend the rudimentary elements of procedural fairness to those who came within their powers. Procedures varied greatly, but they tended to be informal, unconstrained by the rules of evidence, and altogether unlike those of a court of law.[52] The emphasis on informality has continued to the present day, but whereas we would expect a modern statute to provide some procedural guidelines, in the nineteenth century, procedures were left largely to the administrative body itself. But precisely how they proceeded, and to what extent notions of procedural fairness affected their decisions, is unclear from the evidence I have been able to find and remains a fertile subject for further historical research.

The truth probably is that throughout the history of British administration ideas of the rule of law and due process had little impact on its day-to-day work. The degree of central control in general varied enormously from one period to another and from one kind of authority to another. Local justices, who were for centuries the mainstay of local administration, with a host of powers of an administrative kind, were never subject to any form of regular, legal control as to how they should exercise their powers or as to the procedures they should follow. The recognition that administrative bodies presented particular problems of regulation and control led in France to the separation of law and administration, and to the *droit administratif*.[53] The chances of that happening in England, while real enough in the sixteenth and seventeenth centuries, ended abruptly with the abolition of the special administrative courts in the wake of the Civil War.[54]

The extinction of those central authorities left a major gap in the means of control of administrative bodies. According to constitutional theory the gap

[50] See further C. T. Flower, *Public Works in Medieval Law* (Selden Society, London, 1915 and 1923).

[51] O. MacDonagh, 'The Nineteenth-Century Revolution in Government: A Reappraisal' (1958) 1 *Historical Journal* 52.

[52] Administrative agencies were criticized on that very point: H. Arthurs, *Without the Law* (University of Toronto Press, Toronto, 1985), 141.

[53] See W. Holdsworth, *A History of English Law* (Methuen and Co., London, 1956), 155.

[54] It is often remarked that, although there were abuses, something of considerable importance, both in good government and in developing public law, was lost: see Keir, n. 36 above.

should have been filled by the ideas of parliamentary supremacy and the rule of law. Parliament should specify by statute the terms on which administrative powers were held, with the courts being responsible for enforcing those terms. However, theory and practice were worlds apart. Judging by its enactments of the nineteenth century, Parliament was generally content to confer powers in broad terms and showed little interest in the details or the procedures.

5.3.3 The Role of the Courts

This left the courts. Now judicial review of the actions of administrative bodies, especially of local justices who, it should be recalled, were for centuries vital to local administration, had its origins in medieval law and gradually evolved over the centuries.[55] (We saw earlier how Coke drew from *per legem terrae* the concept of jurisdiction.) The King's judges had developed for that purpose special procedures by way of indictment and presentment and the prerogative writs. But the main object of judicial control was to make sure that a subordinate court or other authority did not go beyond its powers and jurisdiction, the writ of *certiorari* being a well-declared procedure for bringing the matter before the King's Court; on rare occasions an authority would be forced to use its powers by issuing *mandamus*. Judicial review was a limited form of control, carried out in a sporadic and irregular way. It was limited because it was confined to the question whether the subordinate body had legal authority for its actions. The courts were reluctant from the earliest cases to enter into a review of the merits of the decision, or into the way discretion was used.[56]

In practice the position was more complex. In the first place, judicial review developed slowly and haltingly over several centuries, and it was not until well into the seventeenth century with the abolition of the prerogative courts, that the King's Bench was able to begin to create a coherent system of review. Before that, the prerogative courts themselves exercised various forms of control over the administration. Just how tentative, piecemeal, and lacking in cogency judicial review was before that time can be seen in the long history of decisions in relation to the Sewer Commissions.[57] Even Dr. Bonham's case in 1610,[58] which is often said to mark a turning point in judicial review of administrative action, portrays judicial hesitancy and not a little confusion about the role of the court and the scope of its powers.[59] Secondly, the attitude of the courts towards administrative authorities, even after the abolition of the prerogative courts, remained ambivalent. The

[55] Holdsworth, *A History of English Law*, n. 53 above, 155.

[56] Ibid. 252.

[57] See Flower, *Public Works in Medieval Law*, n. 50 above, and L. L. Jaffe and E. G. Henderson, 'Judicial Review and the Rule of Law' (1956) 72 *LQR* 345.

[58] 8 Co. Rep. 107 (C.P. 1610).

merits of an administrative action were considered to be beyond review, but there was no reason in principle for not insisting that such actions, even if discretionary, should be conducted within the terms and scope of the statute. It appears, however, that the courts were not inclined to intervene unless the administrative process was of an adjudicative kind. The precise meaning of adjudication was never clear, but was probably interpreted broadly; certainly where rights or even important privileges were at stake, the courts might exercise review and insist on procedures reminiscent of their own. However, even to express the position in this way is probably to impose a greater neatness and order on judicial practice than history warrants. All that can be said with confidence is that, by the early eighteenth century, judicial review of administrative action by the King's Bench was reasonably firmly established.

The scope of review is one thing, the grounds on which it is founded another, and it is not entirely clear precisely when procedural fairness became firmly established as a ground of review of administrative action. Certainly, by the late nineteenth century, procedural fairness or natural justice, in the sense of the notice and hearing rule and the rule against bias, was a standard ground of review.[60] Working back from that time, cases and statements can be found attesting to the rules of natural justice in the eighteenth century,[61] while the much-cited case of Bagg, the insolent verger,[62] shows that even in 1615 the right to be heard in administrative contexts could be pleaded successfully. However, with the history of natural justice in its application to administrative action still to be written, any attempt at explanation is bound to be speculative and piecemeal. It is not difficult to see that as notions of procedural due process gained acceptance in the context of judicial trials, especially criminal trials, those notions could be transposed naturally enough to administrative contexts which displayed an adjudicative character. The lack of a clear distinction between adjudication and administration, and the tendency to mix functions of both kinds in authorities such as the justices of the peace, would have helped the growth of natural justice in administrative contexts.

Perhaps this explains why some of the prominent early cases involved dismissal from office or loss of a position, for in such cases the notion that the charge should be made known and that the accused should be given the chance to answer it, could be arrived at by direct analogy with the criminal trial. Beyond that, however, all we may conclude in the absence of further historical research is that the rudiments of procedural due process had a

[59] T. F. T. Plucknett, 'Bonham's Case and Judicial Review' (1926) 40 *Harvard L Rev*. 30 and Jaffe and Henderson, 'Judicial Review and the Rule of Law', n. 57 above.

[60] e.g. *Cooper* v. *Wandsworth Board of Works* (1863) 14 CB (NS) 180.

[61] Examples are: *Dr. Bentley's Case* (1723) 1 Stra. 557, *R.* v. *Dyer* (1703) 1 Salk. 181, and *R.* v. *Benn and Church* (1795) 6 TR 198.

[62] *Bagg's Case*, n. 33 above.

foothold in judicial review over a long period. The precise scope of its application and its full significance is hard to judge and it is not at all clear what practical effect an occasionally successful action in the courts had on the vast array of administrative powers.

This brings us back to Dicey and to the paradox that he could extol the virtues of the English constitution as it stood in his day, including doctrines relating to the rule of law, and implicitly due process, while all around administrative government was being conducted through statutory powers of a wide discretionary kind, untrammelled by procedural constraints, and unruffled by any developed notion of administrative propriety. Judicial review might have made an occasional incursion, a restrictive opinion from the Crown Law Officers might have prompted a note of caution, and the rule of law might have been a general idea hovering in the background. But as H. W. Arthurs in his study of nineteenth century administrative law has shown, judicial review and the idea of the rule of law had relatively little impact on the way administrative bodies conducted their affairs.[63] Each authority developed its own objectives, its own ways of doing things, and its own rules; each was subject to the limits set by statute, and to such other principles as the courts might impose. But, in general, administration was marked by diversity and pluralism, and the ordinary law, as a general, controlling principle, had little influence. And what is true of judicial control and administration in the nineteenth century is probably also true of earlier centuries.

The idea that all administrative bodies were subject to law was a grand constitutional principle, which marked off England from its continental neighbours, where administration was outside the ordinary law. To limit the powers of any authority to those conferred by law is indeed a principle of great constitutional importance. However, like many great principles, it was hollow in the middle, for it said nothing about the way administrative bodies ought to make their decisions and conduct their affairs, nor did it provide an effective system of scrutiny and accountability. Most particularly, Dicey's expression of the rule of law says nothing about the procedures to be followed, makes no commitment to a principle of procedural due process. And yet the development of procedural due process in administration is one vital way of extending the general idea of the rule of law beyond the strictly adjudicative sphere. Dicey himself took up the issue in an article published in 1915, to which earlier reference was made. The article consisted of a comment on two recent decisions by the House of Lords where the issue was the extent to which an administrative body exercising judicial functions was required to follow the procedures of English courts.[64] Dicey put the problem with characteristic clarity: should an authority be free to pursue its statutory objectives as it thinks best, acting fairly, but according to such procedures as

[63] Arthurs, n. 52 above.

it thinks fit; or should it adopt the strict procedures of a court of law.[65]

To opt for the former, as the House of Lords did, was to raise again the spectre of an administration largely free of legal controls, while to espouse the latter would have been a futile stand against the tide of modern government. Of course in another way, the issue was about the nature and scope of procedural due process: does procedural due process mean only the procedures of courts, with the result that it has no place in modern administration; or is it a dynamic principle which can be interpreted and re-interpreted in order to fit different contexts, and to have a real place in administration. Dicey gave no clear answer, but he put his finger on the issue which lies at the heart of due process in administration, and which has been a major concern of the twentieth century.

5.3.2 Procedural Fairness in the Twentieth Century

Despite the gloomy predictions of Dicey and others about the state of law and society in the early part of the century, the development of judicial review and, in particular, procedural fairness in the second half of the century is considered to be a story of success. But progress was neither even nor unhindered. Whatever confidence the courts had gained in reviewing administrative actions in the nineteenth century amid a fresh cycle of increased governmental activity and regulation, seemed to be lost in the opening years of the twentieth. Without recounting here a story which is now familiar, we may briefly advert to the tendency of the courts to restrict the scope of judicial review to administrative actions which were judicial in character.[66] While it was never clear exactly what that meant, the upshot was that a wide range of administrative actions, especially those of ministers and those of a discretionary nature, were regarded as beyond the scope of review, except as to the most fundamental errors of jurisdiction or the most blatant cases of abuse.[67] That attitude, however, did not endure for long and in the post-war years the courts began gradually to respond to modern administrative government by removing some of the barriers to judicial review, both as to the range of decisions and the types of authorities.

Of interest for our present purposes, however, is not just the scope of review in that sense, but also the grounds of review, particularly those based on procedural fairness. Since abandoning the idea that, in the absence of statutory provision, administrative bodies should be left to devise their own

[64] *Board of Education* v. *Rice* [1911] AC 179; *Local Government Board* v. *Arlidge* [1915] AC 120.

[65] Dicey, *The Law of the Constitution*, n. 40 above, App., 496–7.

[66] See S. A. de Smith and T. M. Evans, *de Smith's Judicial Review of Administrative Action* (4th edn., Sweet and Maxwell, London, 1980); 162 ff.

[67] For an analysis of the ideas which informed the judicial approach at that time, see D. J. Galligan, *Discretionary Powers* (Clarendon Press, Oxford, 1986), sect. 5.2.

procedures, the courts have made considerable progress towards adopting a general principle of procedural fairness.[68] The term 'natural justice', which has connotations of a judicial process, has been replaced by the more general term 'procedural fairness'. The idea is that procedural fairness is a general principle which applies across the spectrum of administrative processes, with its precise content to be determined in each context. The general principle is now regarded as a distinct ground for the judicial scrutiny of administrative actions.[69] The old rules of natural justice are also now seen as specific applications to judicial processes of the deeper principle, the idea being that in other contexts the requirements of procedural fairness may be different. The growth of the notion of procedural fairness as a general principle matches, and indeed is partly the consequence of, the courts being willing to regard a wide range of administrative processes as generally subject to procedural principles. It is a mark of the courts' success in developing the principle and extending its application that we now expect Parliament to include the principle in its statutory enactments.

However, it would be over-generous to conclude with the impression that procedural fairness has reached the peak of perfection and that nothing more needs to be done. Without distracting from the advances which have been made in bringing administrative actions within an acceptable framework of fairness, there are still weaknesses to be remedied and deficiencies to be made good. One is the need to recognize that, without detracting from the importance of the two classic requirements of procedural fairness—hearing and lack of bias—the concept can be extended to other issues, such as the giving of reasons, the setting of standards, and the issue of fettering. In other words, once procedural fairness is seen to be a general, dynamic principle, wider questions arise about the standards of fair treatment and the procedures needed for them. Indeed, once the connection is made between standards of fair treatment and procedures, the ground is laid for a full flowering of the procedural principle. The other comment relates to the areas of administration covered by procedural fairness. While great progress has been made in extending the principle to areas such as prisons and other closed institutions, pockets of administration still remain beyond the pale of review.

[68] The current state of judicial review for procedural fairness is explained more fully in Chs. 11 and 12.

[69] See the classic statement by Lord Diplock in the GCHQ case: *Council for Civil Service Unions* v. *Minister for the Civil Service* [1983] AC 374.

6

The American Doctrine of Procedural Due Process

The American doctrine of procedural due process of law, the second tradition to be considered here, has some affinity with the ideas from English common law as examined in the preceding chapter. Indeed, in the early days the American courts often looked to the English common law tradition for assistance in interpreting principles of due process. One major difference between the two systems is that the American doctrine is contained in the Constitution while the English approach has been the offspring of the common law. Since the American doctrine is expressed in the constitution simply as 'due process of law', the scope for judicial interpretation is substantial. In performing that task, the courts have to some degree drawn on the English common law as it was in the late eighteenth century, but they have long since created a distinctive American approach. One of the first points to note in understanding that approach is that the due process clauses have been taken to support doctrines not only of procedural but also substantive due process. While that distinction itself derives from English constitutional history, it has never had the same continuing importance here as in the United States. For while in the United Kingdom substantive due process has been subsumed in doctrines of the rule of law, the sovereignty of Parliament, and the concept of jurisdiction, in the United States substantive due process creates a possible point of entry into the constitutional sphere for values which are not otherwise provided for in the constitution. In this Chapter, I shall be concerned mainly with procedural due process, but a short introduction to the substantive doctrine is also given.

The plan of the Chapter is as follows. First, a brief outline is made of the general doctrine of due process, including both parts; secondly, an explanation of the substantive doctrine is given, while the third section examines the threshold requirement that procedural due process applies only when life, liberty, or property is affected. In the fourth section, an analysis is made of the procedures required by due process once the threshold test is met. The fifth section considers the values behind procedural due process, and the Chapter concludes with a short account of how the doctrine is applied in administrative contexts.

6.1 THE DOCTRINE OF DUE PROCESS IN GENERAL

Procedural fairness in American law is based around the doctrine of due process of law. Amongst the amendments to the draft Constitution adopted in 1791, two of them, the fifth and the fourteenth, stipulate that a person shall not be deprived of life, liberty, or property without due process of law.[1] The fifth amendment applies to the laws and actions of federal government, while the fourteenth amendment extends due process to the states. The provenance of the due process clauses is itself interesting.[2] The immediate sources were a number of the existing colonies which already had due process clauses in their constitutions; amongst them were Virginia, Maryland and North Carolina, and Massachusetts. The colonial constitutions for their part took inspiration from the rights and liberties enjoyed under English law. The Congress of Colonies, meeting in New York in 1765, declared that the colonies were entitled to all the rights and liberties confirmed by Magna Carta to the subjects of Great Britain. Around the same time, delegates of the Colonies and Plantations in Congress declared their people to be entitled to the rights secured by the immutable laws of nature and the principles of the English Constitution.

Due process was one such right with its own long and glorious history. Coke's *Institutes*,[3] written in the seventeenth century, were a source of authority for the colonists of the eighteenth century. And, as we saw in the last chapter, according to Coke, the due process of law principle could be traced back to Magna Carta itself. Coke claimed that the expression *per legem terrae* of Magna Carta meant due process of law; he then assumed that where the idea of due process was used, as for example in a statute of Edward III in 1354,[4] it meant the *lex terrae* of Magna Carta. Whether Coke was correct in equating the two is a matter much debated,[5] but whatever the historical merits of his claim, the founding fathers of the Colonies, and later of the federal Constitution, found advantage in being able to invoke an unbroken line of authority for due process, originating in the foundations of English law.

The history of due process in the United States is a subject of great interest, but not one I am able to pursue here. We must be content for

[1] Amendment V: '[N]or shall any person . . . be deprived of life, liberty, or property, without due process of law.' Amendment XIV: '[N]or shall any state deprive a person of life, liberty, or property, without due process of law.'

[2] For the background to the 14th Amendment, see W. N. Nelson, *The Fourteenth Amendment* (Yale UP, 1990).

[3] E. Coke, *Institutes*, especially *Institute II*, i (E. and R. Brooke, London, 1629).

[4] 28 Edw. III Ch. 3 (1354). The expression was used only rarely in English statutes; see also *Leges Henrici Primi*.

[5] For further discussion, see C. H. McIlwain, 'Due Process of Law in Magna Carta' (1914) 14 *Columbia L Rev.* 27 and K. Jurow, 'Untimely Thoughts: A Reconsideration of the Origins of Due Process of Law' (1975) 19 *American J of Legal History* 265.

present purposes to consider the main lines of interpretation of the due process clauses and to understand how they relate to procedural fairness. The discussion begins with a number of general points and then considers some of them in more detail. The first point is to note how the due process clauses work in practice. All federal and states authorities, including the legislatures, executives, and administrations, are subject to the due process clauses. Claims of violation of due process are adjudicated by the courts and may go to the Supreme Court for final determination. Such actions usually arise where a person is affected by a legal or administrative decision and claims that the procedures do not meet the requirements of due process.

The next point to note is that the due process clauses themselves make no reference to procedural fairness. The principle is expressed as the due process of law, which has been interpreted to include substantive and procedural parts. The procedural part covers much the same ground as procedural fairness in English law, but we must not assume that the one is simply another way of expressing the other. Procedural due process has a narrower and more specific meaning than procedural fairness; moreover, the American doctrine is limited to actions which affect life, liberty, or property. It is not enough to show that an interest is affected; the interest must be one in life, liberty, or property. This threshold requirement, which has to be met before the right to procedural due process comes into effect, restricts the application of the doctrine. In summary, the logic of the due process clause is clear: where a person has an interest in life, liberty, or property, which is affected by a legal or administrative action, certain procedures must be followed.

No specific conditions are laid down in the Constitution to cover administrative decisions and actions, but the general right to due process will apply if the threshold test of life, liberty, or property is met. Some of the most difficult and arguable cases decided by the Supreme Court are about whether particular administrative decisions do affect liberty or property. This issue is taken up in section 6.3, where it is shown that, for the purposes of due process, liberty and property are given a narrow meaning, with the result that areas of administrative actions fall outside the due process clauses. Moreover, a distinction is drawn between administrative action, which connotes a decision about how a particular person is to be treated, and rule-making, which is about how people in general will be dealt with. The distinction is important because rule-making by administrative authorities falls outside the due process clauses.[6]

Another point to note is that the constitutional doctrine of due process guarantees a minimum of process and procedure to which federal or state law may add further requirements. Provided the constitutional standards are met, state and federal legislatures have the authority to dictate procedures

[6] Rule-making is treated in Ch. 16.

which may be more exacting than those required by constitutional due process. The Administrative Procedure Act, for example, states the procedures for administrative decision-making which go well beyond the bare constitutional demands. Moreover, the due process clauses are not the only parts of the constitution dealing with procedural fairness; procedures dealing with the investigation and adjudication of criminal charges, for example, are provided for in a number of clauses. The investigation is subject to numerous conditions,[7] while the rights to trial by jury, to a speedy and public trial, to be informed of the charge, to confront and cross-examine witnesses, and to have legal representation, all derive from Amendments V and VI.[8] Similarly, the right to a jury trial in civil matters is guaranteed by Amendment VII.[9]

The final introductory point is that the application of due process has two stages. First it is necessary to show that a person is affected in his life, liberty, or property by a legal or administrative decision or action; if that condition is satisfied, the second stage is to consider what process is then required. The point about the first stage is that not all interests which a person has are entitled to the protection of due process. For example, an applicant for a governmental position or a welfare payment may have an interest, but may be held not to have a property interest. There is no right in that case to procedural due process. The threshold requirement of life, liberty or property has been the subject of much litigation, with continuing argument about what amounts to liberty or property; it has also provided the occasion for shifts and changes from one generation of Supreme Court Justices to another in interpreting its scope. The threshold condition can be used to give a wider or narrower scope to procedural due process, and it is clear that, in recent years, it has been used to narrow rather than widen.

Once the first stage is satisfied, the second stage is to ask what process is due. The constitution gives some guidance, especially for criminal trials; but in general and particularly in the administrative context, it is for the courts to determine what procedures are necessary. This is another area of interesting and difficult cases where courts often take different views and where the doctrine is liable to fluctuation. The judicial trial is regarded as the paradigm of due process, and the courts' approach usually amounts to asking in what ways, if at all, the full procedures of the trial ought to be relaxed in the particular case. Due process usually means some form of notice and hearing, some opportunity to call and cross-examine witnesses, the giving of reasons, and an impartial decision-maker. The real issue for the courts is usually about the precise content these procedures should have in the cases in hand. That in turn is settled by examining the nature of the decision, the

[7] Amendments IV, V, VI, and VIII.

[8] These provisions generally apply to both federal and state matters, except that the right to indictment by a Grand Jury does not apply to state trials. See *Hurtado* v. *California*, 110 US 516 (1883).

[9] But this does not apply to state civil trials.

importance of the interests at stake, and the costs of providing the procedure. At a deeper level of principle, the main concern is that the procedures should lead to accurate decisions, that is to a correct finding of facts and to the proper application of the law to the facts. Other principles may also have a role. Openness, participation, and reason-giving are sometimes put forward as values independently of outcomes; but although the case for such values is often made by constitutional theorists, there is little support for them in the cases.

6.2 SUBSTANTIVE DUE PROCESS

The procedural part of due process is my main concern here. It means that whenever a government authority takes action against a person, affecting life, liberty, or property, it must do so according to certain procedures. Procedural due process itself expresses and protects certain values, the main one being that the person subject to the decision should be treated fairly, where the primary element of fairness consists in treating him in accordance with authoritative standards. That in turn means treating the person as the law has held out that he should be treated. By applying the law properly, the person's legal rights are also upheld. Fair treatment may have other aspects which will in turn influence the procedures to be adopted; other values may come into play and they will also affect procedures.

The substantive sense of due process is quite different. It refers to the limitations on the powers of the state and federal legislatures, and of any other legal or administrative body, to deprive a person of life, liberty, or property. Substantive due process refers, in other words, to the substantive limits of governmental power and is not directly concerned with procedures. The idea of substantive due process can be clarified by identifying two senses or areas of operation. The first sense is where an administrative body, say, makes a decision which violates a right protected under the Constitution, the right to free speech for example. The decision violates the First Amendment which protects free speech and could be struck down on that basis; but it also violates due process because it purports to take away a liberty where there is no legal authority to do so. If there is no legal authority for the decision, then its enactment and enforcement are without due process of law. But since the decision is unconstitutional anyhow for breach of the First Amendment, in this case the added breach of substantive due process has no practical significance.[10]

The second and important sense of substantive due process—substantive

[10] For an historical analysis see R. E. Riggs, 'Substantive Due Process in 1791' (1990) 6 *Wisconsin L Rev.* 941 and F. Strong, *Substantive Due Process* (Carolina Academic Press, Durham, N.C., 1986).

due process proper—is where the due process clause is the vehicle for incorporating into the constitution certain values which are not expressly protected within it. Values admitted in this way acquire constitutional status and limit the powers of legislatures and other authorities. Needless to say, whether a particular value is enshrined in substantive due process is likely to be a disputed matter.[11] There is, however, a long tradition, beginning with the earliest cases, of extending constitutional protection in this way. In one case it was said that due process 'protects those fundamental principles of liberty and justice which lie at the base of our civil and political institutions'.[12] In the *Dred Scott* case,[13] action by Congress in agreeing to the Missouri Compromise was held to violate substantive due process because it interfered with vested property rights—in that case, the owners' rights to their slaves. The argument was that the powers of the legislature were subject to certain fundamental values, and that action taken in violation of those values must also be in violation of due process; property taken without legal authority is property taken without due process of law. Arguments based on the claim to vested property rights, of whatever kind, are unlikely to succeed today, but values of contemporary importance, such as the protection of privacy, which includes a woman's right to have an abortion, rest on substantive due process.[14]

Having outlined some of the general features of the American doctrine of due process, I shall now consider the more specific issues listed above. The substantive due process doctrine will not be examined further, except to note that the relationship between it and procedural due process is itself an interesting and somewhat tangled issue.

6.3 LIFE, LIBERTY, OR PROPERTY

Let us now turn to consider the threshold requirements of life, liberty, or property. If that threshold is met, the authority has a duty to act with due process, which usually means some form of hearing and the absence of bias. The converse is that other interests, which do not constitute life, liberty, or property, may be affected without violating the due process clause. In addition to the constitutional requirements, there may be other procedural rights under state and federal law. It has been suggested that in the earlier part of the century, life, liberty, and property was taken as an inclusionary concept, 'embracing all interests valued by sensible men',[15] the implication being that, whenever a significant interest was affected, due process would apply. The

[11] Further discussion can be seen in R. S. Myers, 'The End of Substantive Due Process' (1988) 45 *Washington and Lee L Rev.* 557.

[12] *Hurtado* v. *California*, n. 8 above, at 535.

[13] 60 US 393 (19 How) (1857).

[14] *Roe* v. *Wade*, 410 US 113 (1943).

[15] H. D. Monaghan, 'Of "Liberty" and "Property" ' (1977) 62 *Cornell L Rev.* 405.

older distinction was between rights and privileges, with due process applying only to rights; that distinction was always problematical and has been gradually abandoned in favour of a single test of significant interest. In more recent years, however, the significant interest test has in turn given way to the notion of entitlement. The upshot is that it is necessary to show the existence of a precise liberty or property interest and that one has a legal entitlement to it. So in *Board of Regents* v. *Roth*,[16] a university professor, who was denied renewal of his contract without notice or hearing, was held not to have a liberty or property interest affected. His interest in continuing the employment was undoubted, but that, said the court, was not a liberty or property interest, and accordingly due process was not required. The threshold question has in this way become a serious hurdle, with the Supreme Court now taking a rather narrow view of what constitutes liberty or property.[17]

Although the Supreme Court naturally has a keen interest in the meaning of life, liberty, and property, it has not tried to offer any general definitions. However, from a study of the cases, of which there are many dealing with the issue, it is possible to gain some idea of what the concepts mean. Life creates the fewest problems, although it has been of major importance to questions of abortion and to the use of the death penalty. With regard to the former, an unborn child is thought not to be sufficiently a person to warrant due process protection, while, in the case of the latter, the death penalty clearly affects life and may be imposed only after due process—small protection though it may be against such barbarism.

The liberty interest has a much wider application. Laws violate liberty if they take away or curtail physical freedom, by such means as arrest, imprisonment, or corporal punishment. Laws also violate liberty if they restrict a person's freedom to do things or to make choices; the sources of liberty in this sense may be twofold. One source is the general freedom a person enjoys to do or enter into a range of things or activities—to enter into contracts, engage in business, acquire property. The other source is the liberty to enjoy the rights guaranteed by the Constitution, free speech and privacy, for example. But while the families of liberty are easily identified, whether a particular liberty is a member of one or other family is often difficult to decide. A prisoner who was transferred against his wishes to a mental hospital was held to have a liberty interest at stake on the ground that, as a result of the transfer, he was more strictly confined and subject to compulsory treatment.[18] On the other hand, while each statute had to be interpreted according to its terms, no liberty interest is at stake where a

[16] 408 US 564 (1972).

[17] For discussion and background, see L. Tribe, *American Constitutional Law* (2nd edn., West, New York, 1988), 663 ff.

[18] *Vitek* v. *Jones*, 445 US 480 (1980).

prisoner merely hopes that he may be given parole;[19] once granted parole, however, the prisoner would have a liberty interest in it not being revoked. Where constitutional rights are at stake, the liberty interest is to enjoy those rights; the right to free speech, for example, is protected by the Constitution and so each person has a liberty to enjoy it in all its aspects. However, the right to free speech is not absolute, but may legitimately be restricted by government in certain circumstances; a licensing system for television producers affects free speech, but in a legitimate way. But since such laws affect the liberty interest in free speech, the application of such a licensing system is subject to due process. The object is to make sure the restrictions are properly applied in each case, and normally notice and hearing will be required.

While the examples given so far are clear cases of liberty interests, other cases will be more borderline and judgments may be divided.[20] Liberty is a broad and residual concept, suggesting that a person is free to engage in a diverse and indefinable range of activities. The widest connotation would be that, in a system governed by law, we are free to do whatever the law does not forbid. On that approach, liberty would be at stake whenever the law restricts an activity. But it seems that in recent years the Supreme Court has not taken such a wide view. In *Meacham* v. *Fano*,[21] the Court held by a majority of six to three that a prisoner who was transferred from a less restrictive to a more restrictive prison had lost no liberty interest. The line may shift from one generation to another, but the underlying principle is that liberty is at issue 'whenever action is designed to deprive an individual, or a limited group of individuals, of the freedom to engage in some significant area of human activity'.[22] However, there are some signs that, although it is a broad notion, the courts may be moving towards a narrower concept based on entitlement to a specific liberty under state or federal law. The entitlement doctrine is discussed in the following pages.[23]

Property for the purposes of due process includes, but goes beyond, the usual forms of real and personal property. Claims, rights, or entitlements, which are created by state or federal law may amount to property; the closer interests are to the more traditional senses of property, the stronger their claim under the due process clauses to be property interests. But the range of interests which might constitute property is indeed wide; in addition to the usual forms of property interest, property may be taken to include

[19] *Greenholtz* v. *Nebraska Penal Complex*, 442 US 1 (1979).

[20] For further discussion see H. D. Monaghan, 'Of "Liberty" and "Property" ', n. 15 above.

[21] 96 SCt. 2532 (1976).

[22] J. Novak, R. Rotunda, and J. Young, *Constitutional Law* (3rd edn., West, St Paul, Minn., 1986), 468. See also W. Van Alstyne, 'Cracks in the "New Property"; Adjudicative Due Process in the Administrative State' (1977) 62 *Cornell L Rev.* 445.

[23] For a narrower approach to liberty along these lines see *Kentucky Department of Corrections* v. *Thompson*, 490 US 454 (1988), *Paul* v. *Davis*, 424 US 693 (1976); but compare *Ingraham* v. *Wright*, 430 US 651 (1977).

benefits conferred by government, positions of employment under government, public education, and reputation. Welfare benefits are a good example: state laws often provide for the grant and withdrawal of benefits under certain conditions; the question then is whether a person's interest in receiving or retaining such benefits is a property interest. If it is, due process applies, and some form of notice and hearing must be part of any decision to grant or withdraw the benefit; if the interests are not property, due process does not apply.

Claims of these kinds have been contentious. A wide range of interests of a financial or economic kind is affected by the modern state, but whether they are property is not easy to decide. It is not easy to decide because no suitable conceptual framework has been devised for analysing the issue. The connection with traditional forms of property is often tenuous; and, as an alternative, a notion of entitlement is now normally invoked as a way of distinguishing property and non-property interests; whether or not there is an entitlement will then depend on the legislative framework under which the claim is made. But that seems to revive the old rights–privilege distinction, according to which legal rights were protected by due process while privileges were not. The trouble with the distinction is that many important interests which appear to require due-process protection are neither rights nor entitlements. Some, like R. Reich, have argued that many of the benefits which government confers on individuals, government largesse as he called it, should be considered a form of property, indeed, the new property.[24] This rather daring leap of the imagination has its own problems, but it has the advantage of attracting the protection of due process to a wide range of important interests.

This wider sense of property found support in the leading case of *Goldberg* v. *Kelly*,[25] where a recipient of state welfare was held to be entitled to due process before his benefits were terminated. The Court treated the claim to state benefits as a property interest rather than as simply a privilege or as the conferment of largesse by the state as an act of charity. By recognizing that welfare benefits could be a property interest in the claimant, the Court opened the way for a wide variety of claims to benefits and services to attract the protection of procedural due process.[26]

However, it still remains to decide in each case whether a claim to benefits or services constitutes a property interest. The question could be approached in different ways. One way would be to analyse the interest at issue according to its importance in the culture of the society; another would be to look at its importance to the claimant. The interest in being able to practise one's trade or profession, for example, might be considered so basic to a person's life

[24] R. Reich, 'The New Property (1964) 73 *Yale LJ* 733.

[25] 397 US 254 (1970). See also *Board of Regents* v. *Roth*, 408 US 564 (1972).

[26] See e.g. *Godd* v. *Lopez*, 419 US 565 (1975); *Cleveland Board of Education* v. *Londermill*, 470 US 532 (1985); *Bell* v. *Burson*, 402 US 535 (1971); *Barry* v. *Barchi*, 443 US 35 (1979).

and well-being that it should be considered a property interest. However, that is not the way the courts have gone. They have taken the view that the claimant must show a legal entitlement to the benefit under state or federal law; whether there is such an entitlement depends, in other words, on positive law which may create and define entitlements as it wishes. And just when positive law does create entitlements is not settled. Where the statute sets out reasonably clear criteria for award of the benefit, the position is straightforward and an entitlement to the benefit will normally be accepted. But an expectation that an interest will be treated in a certain manner is not enough to create an entitlement. So, in *Bishop* v. *Wood*,[27] a policeman who might reasonably have expected that his employment would continue was held to have no entitlement to his office. Moreover, the more discretionary the decision is, the more difficult it will be to show an entitlement. Each statutory scheme has to be analysed and whether there is discretion, and how much discretion there is, are matters of interpretation. The mere fact of some discretion does not automatically remove the claim to entitlement, but the point is that according to the entitlement principle, a state or federal legislature can decide through its legislation whether or not an interest, affected by the legislation, attracts due process.

This way of deciding whether the procedural protections of due process are required does not seem entirely satisfactory to the outside observer. By making the question depend on how each state frames its statute, the scope for disparity from one jurisdiction to another is considerable. On such a localized and positivist approach, it is difficult to develop any general jurisprudence about when procedural protections should apply. The approach appears, moreover, to be blind to the nature of the modern state where discretionary powers are prevalent, and where the most important interests may be subject to discretionary action. It is clearly more difficult to devise a satisfactory doctrine about what constitutes due process in discretionary contexts; but that, surely, is one of the challenges to be met. And, finally, it is difficult to see how the entitlement doctrine is different from the old and (for this purpose) discredited rights–privilege distinction: to require an entitlement under positive law is to require a right under positive law. However, we should be careful not to assume that the law is more settled than it really is. The Supreme Court appears to have taken a narrow view of entitlements and property, but its own approach is variable and changeable, with more recent cases suggesting that the Court might be more willing to find entitlements under state law than *Bishop* v. *Wood* allows. The courts might also be more prepared to look beyond positive state law and to discover property interests arising from background constitutional principles.[28]

[27] 426 US 341 (1976).

[28] See Rubin, 'Due Process and the Administrative State', 1076–82. For an example see *Logan* v. *Zimmerman*, 442 US 1 (1979) (property interest in a cause of action).

To sum up, the constitutional limitation on due process to life, liberty, or property has been the source of litigation and controversy. That is understandable since the condition that life, liberty, or property should be affected has to be given some meaning and cannot be ignored by the courts. The tendency in recent years is to require an interest which is 'grounded in substantive legal relationships defined by explicit constitutional provisions or by specific state or federal rules of law'.[29] The argument is often made, however, that the interpretation adopted, especially the entitlement doctrine in relation to property interests, is unduly restrictive and prevents the full development of procedural protections for those affected by government action.[30] Due process of law is a narrower concept than procedural fairness, but it is vitally important in helping to bring about fair treatment of groups and individuals—fair treatment in applying the law properly and in upholding other values. Fair treatment, and in turn respect for persons, is the foundation of due process, and ought to be the guiding standard in deciding its nature and scope. American courts are stuck with the threshold condition of life, liberty, or property, but the interpretation of that condition could be brought more into line with the underlying principle of fair treatment than current doctrine allows.[31]

6.4 WHAT PROCESS IS DUE?

Once it has been shown that an interest in life, liberty, or property is at stake, the next question is what procedures are needed for the due process of law. Due process is not an end in itself and as Justice Blackmum has remarked: 'its constitutional purpose is to protect a substantive interest to which the individual has a legitimate claim of entitlement'.[32] The question is, then, what procedures are necessary to guarantee that an interest in life, liberty or property is dealt with according to the due process of law. Notice that the protected interest has a double role: it triggers due process in the first place and is then the point of focus in deciding on procedures. For due process, as developed by the Supreme Court, does not mean a general duty to treat the person fairly; it means only that decisions about certain, protected interests be in accordance with the law. This symmetry between the interest which triggers due process and the procedures which are dictated by due process is not a requirement of general principle. An alternative approach would be to regard the two as separate: due process would be triggered by certain kinds of interests, but then the object would be to ensure compliance with a wider

[29] Tribe, *Constitutional Law*, 677.

[30] For critical analysis, see ibid.

[31] See further discussion in Rubin, 'Due Process and the Administrative State', n. 28 above, 1095 ff.

[32] *Olim* v. *Wakinekona*, 103 SCt. 1741 at 1748 (1983).

notion of fair treatment of the person in that context. Fair treatment would then draw on other standards besides accurate application of the law. But that is not the approach of the American courts, for according to them the interest which triggers due process also largely determines the process that is due.

Before it can be decided what procedures are required, the very point of due process should be made clear. After all, if the demands of due process vary according to the context and to the interests at stake, we need to have some criteria for deciding what the procedures should be. The principal criterion is that the decision should be made in accordance with the law; that is to say, the law should be applied accurately and properly.[33] The accurate and proper application of the law is of course a basic tenet of fair treatment. Consider some examples. Suppose that under the law of a state private property may be requisitioned by an agency when certain conditions are met; the first task of procedures would be to ensure that in the case of a requisition those conditions are made out. Suppose in another case that a state agency has power to award contracts, but there is a distinct risk that the tenders of certain groups will not be properly considered, and that the contracts always go to members from other groups. Here the disappointed parties might claim that the constitutional principle of equal protection is being violated. It would then be for the agency to adopt procedures preventing a property interest in government contracts being denied in breach of the Constitution. Constitutional standards might be express, as in the equal protection example, or they might be implied under substantive due process. Privacy is a good example of the latter; action under state law must respect privacy, and procedural due process directs that procedures suited to that end be adopted. Whether the proper application of state or federal law and respect for constitutional principles are the only ends of procedural due process is debatable, with some commentators arguing for various process values of the kind mentioned earlier. In the next section I shall consider what place those wider values have. All we need note here is that process values, to the extent they are recognized by the courts, inject another set of values into the notion of due process and may point to the need for procedures which would not otherwise be required.

6.4.1 In the Shadow of the Trial

Let us now consider in more detail what procedures are required by due process and how the case for particular procedures is made out. The object of properly applying legal and constitutional standards can be achieved

[33] This is well established in the cases. For recent examples see *Walters* v. *National Association of Radiation Survivors*, 473 US 305 (1985); *Mathews* v. *Eldridge*, 424 US 315 (1976); *Greenholz* v. *Nebraska Penal Complex*, n. 19 above.

through different procedures, and the approach adopted within any system is influenced by its cultural context and its historical background. Once certain procedures are established, they tend to acquire an autonomous status within the law and are then perpetuated with only occasional reference to the underlying principles. In their early decisions, the American courts were keen to maintain continuity between the due process clause of the Constitution and the 'immutable laws of nature' which, happily, were revealed in the principles of English law.[34] English law in turn was considered to have had a long and glorious history which could be traced without serious disruption to Magna Carta itself.[35] With such an impressive genealogy, the procedures of English law were thought to be the very embodiment of due process. But of course local factors also had to be accommodated. Since each state was responsible for its own laws and procedures, variations were inevitable and understandable. So in *Hurtado* v. *California*,[36] a convicted murderer failed in his bid to challenge the criminal procedures of California on the ground that they did not include arraignment before a grand jury, as required by English law at the time of the Constitution. The reasoning of the Court was that, provided the procedures were fair in securing the right outcome, due process was satisfied and need not be tied inflexibly to certain procedures. As law expanded beyond the criminal and civil trials to the administrative process in all its forms, and as local differences became more pronounced, the immutable principles of English law faded away.

In place of the laws of nature as revealed in the English common law, the American courts substituted a more general idea that, whatever the context, due process consisted in some form of notice and hearing,[37] which in turn normally means a right to present evidence and to cross-examine adverse witnesses. The hearing principle is not only central to the criminal trial, but serves equally well in other contexts where other interests in life, liberty, or property are threatened. The right to be heard before suffering loss of any kind 'even though it may not involve the stigma and hardships of criminal conviction, is a principle basic to our society'.[38] Around the notion of a hearing, flexibility has become the guiding beacon; flexibility in the sense that while there has to be a hearing 'at a meaningful time and in a meaningful manner',[39] exactly what that means is to be judged according to the situation.[40] The courts look closely at the procedures in question to decide whether they suit the context. The procedures suitable for the criminal process might not be needed in other types of decisions and, similarly, the denial of a benefit will not attract the same level of procedures as a decision

[34] Quoted by Harlan J in *Hurtado* v. *California*, n. 8 above.

[35] See *Murray's Leasing* v. *Hoboken*, 18 How 272 (1855).

[36] N. 8 above.

[37] This idea is repeated time and again; see e.g. *Wolff* v. *McDonnell*, 418 US 539 (1974).

[38] *Joint Anti-Fascist League* v. *McGrath*, 341 US 123 (1951); see also *Armstrong* v. *Manzo*, 380 US 545 (1968).

[39] *Armstrong* v. *Manzo*, n. 38 above.

[40] See *Morrissey* v. *Brewer*, 408 US 471 (1972).

to remove a property right of a more traditional kind. Both in turn will differ from the appropriate procedures for committing a person to a mental institution.[41] A clearer picture of the general approach can be gained from *Goldberg* v. *Kelly*,[42] where the issue was what procedures had to be provided for welfare claimants facing a termination of benefits. The Supreme Court held, first, that considering the important interests at stake, due process required some form of pre-termination hearing; secondly, that the function of the hearing should be to determine whether the grounds for valid termination were made out; and, thirdly, that in order to ensure an accurate determination of that issue, there should be a trial-type, oral process with adequate opportunities for the claimant to produce evidence, challenge opposing witnesses, and generally make the case.[43]

The idea of flexibility in setting procedures should not, however, be pushed too far since the adversarial trial remains the paradigm of due process. It is deeply entrenched in the American legal mind and, whatever the context, is the lens through which process is viewed. Ideas deriving from the trial permeate the legal and administrative process, so that when courts speak of flexibility they are referring to the degree of variation on the procedures of the judicial trial. To take an example, due process in the involuntary transfer of a prisoner to a mental hospital requires the following procedures: notice to the prisoner of the intended transfer; notice of his rights to contest it; time for the prisoner to prepare his case; a hearing which includes the right to call and cross-examine witnesses; an independent adjudicator; and a written statement of reasons.[44] Procedures in other contexts may be less exacting, but they still bear the marks of a judicial process. It has been suggested that one of the reasons for insisting on a high threshold of life, liberty, or property before due process applies is that when it does apply some version of a trial will be required and the procedures will be exacting.[45]

The hegemony of the trial as the model for procedural due process is reinforced by the line between individualized decisions and rule-making. Due process is tied to, is only relevant to, decisions about how to treat an individual, while rule-making, as a form of law-making, belongs to the political process and has no place for ideas of due process.[46] The procedures of rule-making are discussed elsewhere,[47] but the reason for not extending due process seems to be that it does not carry the same risks of mistreatment and

[41] It is interesting to note that the courts have not put anything like the same emphasis on the impartiality of the decision-maker as a fundamental requirement of due process: see further M. H. Redish and L. C. Marshall, 'Adjudicatory Independence and the Values of Procedural Due Process' (1986) 95 *Yale LJ* 455.

[42] N. 25 above.

[43] See further B. Brudno, 'Fairness and Bureaucracy: The Demise of Procedural Due Process for Welfare Claimants' (1979) 25 *Hastings LJ* 813.

[44] See *Vitek* v. *Jones*, 445 US 480 (1980).

[45] See further Rubin, 'Due Process and the Administrative State', n. 28 above.

[46] *Bi-Metallic* v. *State Board of Equalization* 239 US 441 (1915); *US* v. *Florida East Coast Railway*, 410 US 224 (1973).

[47] See Ch. 16.

abuse of particular persons. Since that risk is most acute in decisions about how to deal with individuals, it is there that the need for due process is greatest. American law allows no room for intermediate positions between the two, and that perhaps is another reason why the adjudicative model is so prominent.[48]

6.4.2 The Balancing Process

Against this background, we can now look more closely at the way procedures are judged against the standard of due process. Each context is like a magnetic field with different poles exerting different influences. One pole is the paradigm of the judicial trial with its immanent view of good procedures; another is the need for clear and settled procedural rules; while a third is the concern for flexibility in moulding procedures according to context. The more recent tendency to stress flexibility does not mean that each case is considered afresh and in isolation from other cases. Patterns emerge within specific contexts and across contexts and the variations are often marginal, while notice and hearing, reasons and impartiality, are always the fixed stars of the due process universe around which lesser constellations revolve.[49] I shall not here attempt to describe the procedures for different contexts, since that is well done elsewhere;[50] what is of more general interest is the reasoning process by which the Supreme Court determines the adequacy of procedures.

Within this field of competing forces, the contemporary approach of the Supreme Court is to emphasize responsiveness to context and flexibility in balancing different factors.[51] The approach is especially relevant in extending procedural due process to administrative contexts which have elements of an adjudicative process and yet are often very different from the judicial trial. The Court has given some guidance as to the factors to consider in deciding whether particular procedures satisfy due process. The leading case is *Mathews* v. *Eldridge*,[52] where the three factors to be balanced are stated: first, the private interest affected; secondly, the risk of a mistaken deprivation of that interest through the procedures followed; and thirdly, the state's interest. The last of these takes account of the governmental function involved, and the costs and administrative burdens of more exacting procedures. The first two factors go together. They follow directly from the principle that the law should be properly applied and that the rights and

[48] There is discussion in the literature of possible intermediate forms of decision-making.

[49] See further L. Tribe, *Constitutional Law*, n. 17 above.

[50] See Nowak, Rotunda, and Young, *Constitutional Law*, n. 22 above, 493–520.

[51] For a reflective essay on balancing public goods in relation to due process, see J. Hazard, 'Rationing Justice' [1965] *J of Law & Econ.* I.

[52] N. 33 above. For discussion of balancing, see: L. Tribe, *Constitutional Law*, n. 17 above; Nowak, Rotunda, and Young, *Constitutional Law*, n. 22 above, 489–93.

recognized interests of the person be upheld. But interests vary in their importance and it is right that procedures should be more exacting and the risks of mistake reduced according to the value of different interests.[53] The nature of the interest might affect procedures in other ways; for example, the termination of a benefit before a hearing might have severe consequences for a claimant; fair treatment would then point to the hearing taking place before termination, rather than after termination, even though it might be more convenient for the administrative body to follow the latter course.

It follows that the first stage in deciding whether due process is satisfied is to ask whether the procedures are likely to lead to the correct application of the law, bearing in mind the nature and weight of the interest at stake, and the consequences for those interests of different procedures. The suspect being tried for a criminal offence and the prisoner whose parole is revoked have a right to the relevant legal standards being properly applied. But the liberty interests in each case are significantly different, the accused having a stronger interest in not being wrongly convicted in the first place than the prisoner in having parole wrongly revoked. Procedural due process reflects the distinction and the procedures suited to each should also be different.[54] Practical judgments applying the procedural standards might come to different conclusions, but disagreements are usually at the margins, about precisely what form the hearing should take, rather than whether there should be a hearing at all.

The third factor to be weighed under the *Mathews* v. *Eldridge* test is the governmental interest. At one level, the government's interest and the individual's interests coincide. Both have an interest in the case being properly decided, the government because that means achieving the social good intended by its legislation, the individual for the reasons given. At another level, balancing the governmental interest means adopting procedures which are as economical as possible. There is still no necessary incompatibility between the two interests; provided the procedures lead to the correct outcomes, the individual can have no objection to their being as economical as possible. If a decision can be made just as accurately by written representations as by an oral hearing, then it is in the governmental interest to adopt the former, and no harm is done to the individual's interest.

However, the idea of balancing the two sets of interests goes farther. It appears to mean that, even though certain procedures are the minimum needed to protect the individual's interest by achieving an accurate result (or at least a result where the risks of error are minimized), those procedures can then be reduced by considerations of governmental interest. This sense of balancing can be illustrated with two examples. One example is where the

[53] This approach fits well within the analytical framework given earlier: see Ch. 3.

[54] For the judicial approach to procedures for revoking parole see *Morrisey* v. *Brewer*, n. 40 above.

procedures required to protect the individual's interest are reduced simply on grounds of cost. A welfare agency might acknowledge that an oral hearing would be needed in order for it to be reasonably sure that claims were properly decided, but nevertheless substitute written representations as the form of hearing in order to save costs. The other example is where the government agency has policy reasons, other than sheer cost-saving, for reducing the procedures otherwise required. A parole board might consider that the public interest in not releasing offenders with a record of recidivism is a strong reason for restricting parole; it might, therefore, adopt procedures which are directed more to restricting parole than genuinely trying to decide whether an offender meets the criteria for release. The public interest in not having recidivists released is used to outweigh each prisoner's interest in having his case properly considered on its merits.[55]

These two cases raise questions about the application of the balancing test which are not fully resolved in American law and which I shall not attempt to analyse in detail here. The general point should be made, however, that balancing in this sense can undermine the right to procedural due process. Once balancing goes beyond ensuring economy of procedures, it means taking into account policy factors which compete with the concern to reach an accurate outcome. The fixing of procedures is then akin to a calculation of the best result, all things considered. This approach raises certain difficulties. The first is in finding any basis for weighing the interest of the individual against those of the state. Once the person's claim to certain procedures is regarded as just one interest among several, it is hard to see what criteria can be called on to assess the importance of that interest in relation to those of the state. A second problem is that balancing is not only difficult to do in practice, but raises issues of principle.[56] It is wrong in principle to accept that there is a right to procedural due process and then to determine the context of the right by balancing competing interests. These matters are dealt with in Chapter 3 and the discussion need not be repeated beyond noting three general points. The first is that interests of state might properly enter into consideration in determining what entitlements a person has under the law. In the parole case, for example, the state interest might be that the risks of recidivism of parolees should be minimized. Parole might then be conceived as a highly discretionary matter where the only entitlement of the prisoner is that his case be considered according to the usual standards governing discretion. Such bare entitlements might be contrasted with an alternative system where there is a right to parole on certain conditions being met. The example demonstrates well how the interests of

[55] For discussion, see 'Specifying the Procedures Required by Due Process: Towards Limits on the Use of Interest Balancing' (1978) 88 *Harvard L Rev.* 1510.

[56] See the discussion of procedural rights in Ch. 3; see also R. M. Dworkin, *A Matter of Principle* (Clarendon Press, Oxford, 1985), ch. 3.

the state determine what entitlements a person has and, provided no constitutional principles are breached, the determination of entitlements is a matter for state and federal legislatures.

The second point is that, once those entitlements are set, the right to procedural due process comes into effect. It carries the commitment on the part of the state to such procedures as are necessary to ensure that authoritative legal standards are properly applied and entitlements upheld. Procedural due process does not in principle require any particular procedures so long as entitlements are honoured. The balancing of interests has no place at this level. The third point is that if by balancing is meant that, for policy reasons, the procedures adopted are less than are required to protect entitlements, then balancing is hard to justify. The only legitimate state interests here are, first, that the procedures be as economical as is possible and, secondly, that they be designed in a way which, without undermining entitlements, respects other legitimate policy concerns. Investigatory procedures, for instance, should take account of the state's interest in not losing relevant evidence. If that means precluding certain procedures, advance notice for example, then it is necessary to introduce other procedures which will ensure that, nevertheless, entitlements are protected.

The fourth point is that the concern to achieve proper application of the law may have to be compromised for practical reasons of cost. This does not change or reduce a person's entitlements, but merely limits the resources that should be dedicated to procedures. It is still not a matter of directly balancing state and personal interests; we have seen that there is a principled way of designing procedures according to the relative importance of the rights and interests at stake. The state has the authority, within certain limits, to decide what resources are available for procedures. But the state's interests end there and the distribution of the resources should be according to the principle of proportion.

6.5 THE VALUES OF PROCEDURAL DUE PROCESS

Although the American courts do not often examine the values underlying procedural due process, the very point of the doctrine is to impose on the government and its agencies constraints in the way they treat citizens. Procedural due process is in one sense a procedural doctrine, but it makes no sense unless it is understood to imply a commitment to substantive values. To put the point another way, if the purpose of due process is, as Justice Blackmum has remarked, to protect an interest in life, liberty, or property, the question we might ask is, protect it against what? Since a state or federal legislature usually has power, subject to constitutional limits, to pass laws which affect liberty or property, the point of procedural due process is not to grant those interests immunity from governmental interference. The protection is something less; it is to make sure that decisions and actions affecting those interests comply with certain values. The basic value is fair treatment through proper application of the law; legal rights are then respected and the rule of law is upheld. But while the connection between procedural due process and respect for rights is fundamental, it is not necessarily the only value served by the doctrine. Procedural due process may also be a vehicle for other values, which in turn will influence the formation of procedures.

The early approach of American courts in giving effect to procedural due process was to apply the procedures settled at common law without enquiring too deeply into them. In later cases, the question tends to be what variation on the notice and hearing principle will be suitable in different contexts. In order to answer those questions, the courts needed to have in mind some further standard or standards against which to make their judgments. The emphasis on the flexibility of process, on the idea that different forms of process are suited to different contexts, suggest an instrumental approach where the end is the accurate application of the law. That that was the underlying standard was made explicit in *Mathews* v. *Eldridge*,[57] where the question was whether a hearing was required before rather than after the termination of benefits. The guiding standard in providing an answer was considered to be the need for an accurate determination of the merits. The balancing approach of the courts might suggest that other goals of a more public policy kind are also relevant, but to the extent that such goals are properly taken into account, they are constraints on procedural due process rather than an expression of the values served by it.

However, a long line of academic writers and judges (often writing in dissent) has argued that other values, besides fair treatment through application of the law, are fundamental in determining what processes are due.[58] Now, as the discussion in Chapter 2 shows, a range of values informs and constrains any area of legal process. Values about how criminal suspects should be treated in pre-trial and trial processes, values of privacy and confidentiality, and values relating to intelligibility and timeliness are just a few examples. Values like these are generally recognized by federal and state laws, and, to the extent that they are, they apply to legal processes. Some are compatible with the object of accurate decision-making, but others are not, and to the degree that they are not some accommodation between them has to be found. But amongst the general category of non-outcome

[57] N. 33 above.

[58] From a vast literature the following are good examples: H. K. Kadish, 'Methodology and Criteria in Due Process Adjudication' (1957) 66 *Yale LJ* 319; F. Michaelman, 'Formal and Associational Aims in Procedural Due Process' in J. Pennock and J. Chapman, *Due Process* (Nomos xvii, New York University Press, New York, 1977); J. Mashaw, *Due Process in the Administrative State* (Yale University Press, New Haven, Conn., 1983); R. Summers, 'A Plea for Process Values' (1974) 60 *Cornell LR* 199.

values, some are designated as process values and it is those whose place in legal processes is rather less secure. In a well-known statement of process values, F. Michaelman distinguishes between formal and non-formal procedures.[59] Formal procedures are directed to upholding the law and legal rights created under it, while non-formal procedures are concerned with 'prudence, morality, fairness, or whatever'. Non-formal procedures 'seem responsive to demands for *representation* and *participation*. They attach value to the individual's being told *why* the agent is treating him unfavourably and to his having a part in the decision'.[60] J. Mashaw, whose views were considered earlier, is another leading exponent of process values,[61] while according to L. Tribe, the specific process values are: the right not to be singled out without a chance to talk; the right to be told why one is being dealt with in a particular way; and the right to public participation as an aspect of self-government.[62] The point about process values in these senses is that they derive from sources independent of the concern for accurate outcomes, although in their application they might contribute incidentally to accuracy. The argument is that they are based on values which are inherent in the concept of procedural due process and, therefore, should be reflected in the design of procedures.

It is not always clear how process values find their way into the Constitution. One explanation would be simply that they are included in the values which give meaning and content to procedural due process: in order to answer the question what process is due, it is necessary to determine what values are relevant. Since the due process clauses do not say what those values are, the courts have to decide and, therefore, must draw, as they have historically, on whatever values seem most appropriate. There is no reason in principle why they should regard the proper application of the law as the only value relevant. A different explanation would be to consider process values as part of substantive due process; on that account, process values would be read into the Constitution as substantive values which should be respected by governments. The two explanations are not all that different since both depend on reading into the due process clauses values which are not stated explicitly. And to read in additional values would be to raise the familiar fears about courts finding new constitutional values through due process.

The theoretical basis of process values is considered in a general way in Chapter 2 and I shall not add to it here. Whether or not the theoretical case for process values is convincing, they have not in general been embraced by the courts. Traces of process values can be found, and well-settled

[59] Michaelman, 'Formal and Associational Aims', n. 58 above, 126–9. [60] Ibid.

[61] Mashaw, *Due Process in the Administrative State*, n. 58 above. See also the discussion in sect. 2.2 herein.

[62] Tribe, *Constitutional Law*, n. 17 above, 503 ff.

procedural doctrines, such as the hearing rule, can often be justified in different ways, parts of which might be attributable to process values in the sense of non-outcome values. Since the courts do not often delve into the foundational principles of due process, there is room for speculation about the most satisfactory explanation of their decisions.[63] However, the main tendency of Supreme Court decisions in recent years is towards procedures as instrumental to correct outcomes and the proper application of the law. That explanation fits well with the entitlement thesis, according to which the point of due process is to make sure that legal entitlements are not removed or denied except in accordance with the relevant legal standards. To admit process values would be not only to add to the content of what process is due, but to invite serious questioning of the entitlement thesis itself;[64] for if the due process clauses include process values, it is hard to see why they should not apply to a wider conception of interests to liberty and property than allowed under the current interpretation of the entitlement doctrine. Nevertheless, the pendulum of judicial opinion is never still and it might be that future courts will embrace the idea of process values more firmly than has so far been the case. What ultimately lies behind the case for process values is the sense that, once procedural due process is triggered, certain values automatically come into play. They are not confined to making sure that the law in a narrow and positive sense is properly applied, but also include other values such as the hearing principle as independent and worthwhile in themselves. The quest is, then, for a fuller sense of what constitutes the standards of fair treatment in the relationship between the citizen and the state, whatever form that relationship may take.

Three final and general points should be made about the claims for process values. One is that some accommodation would have to be found between the procedures which are required by process values and the government interest in cost. This is a difficult enough issue when due process is confined to upholding the law; it would be even more difficult to devise a principled relationship with process values. Another point is the tendency amongst some American commentators to draw too strict a line between process values and proper application of the law. The very characterization of procedures under the latter as instrumental, while seeing those under process values as inherently worthwhile, bears this out. The reality is that all procedures are instrumental to or expressions of values, and process values, in so far as they have a moral content, are aspects of a more general principle of fair treatment, which is also the basis for proper application of the law. The final point is that the very nature and status of process values is deeply arguable.[65] Some are moral values about how individuals and groups

[63] See Tribe's discussion in ibid.

[64] For a most perceptive account of some of these issues, see M. Herz, 'Parallel Universes: NEPA Lessons for the New Property' (1993) 93 *Columbia LR* 1668.

[65] See the fuller discussion in Ch. 2.

ought to be treated, where failure results in unfair treatment. Others, however, are based on the personal and psychological satisfactions which are said to result from certain procedures. For example, 'a participatory opportunity may also be psychologically important to the individual'.[66] Claims like these need proper argument and support if they are to be convincing, and it is interesting that those who espouse process values appear to have missed the work done by psychologists and other social scientists on procedural values.[67]

6.6 DUE PROCESS IN ADMINISTRATION

The due process clauses of the Constitution apply to individualized administrative processes, and the reader will have noticed that many of the issues discussed earlier in this Chapter either have arisen in administrative contexts or would apply to them. It is in administrative contexts, indeed, that some of the most difficult questions appear about the scope and meaning of procedural due process. With regard to scope, the question often arises whether administrative powers affect a person's liberty or property in such a way as to attract procedural due process. With regard to the requirements of due process, the range and variety of administrative proceedings mean that it will often not be clear precisely what procedures are needed. The courts have grappled with these issues on many occasions, but in two cases in particular the Supreme Court marked out the boundaries of procedural due process in administration.

The first case is *Goldberg* v. *Kelly*,[68] where the essential question was what procedures were required to be followed by an agency in terminating the payment of welfare benefits under a federal scheme for the relief of poverty of families with children. In a judgment which has often been hailed as a transformation of procedural due process in administrative contexts, the Supreme Court held that a pre-termination hearing with the following elements was required: the giving of notice, an oral hearing, an impartial adjudicator, the calling of witnesses and cross-examination, the right to counsel, the compiling of a record, the basing of the decision on the record, and the giving of reasons.[69] These are exacting procedures which, although specific in their detail to the facts in *Goldberg*, have set the tone for administrative contexts generally. They have been criticized as too exacting, as imposing a trial-type procedure on a great array of administrative acts and decisions. However, the case still stands as the guiding beacon on what process

[66] F. Michaelman, 'Formal and Associational Aims', n. 58 above, 126.

[67] See the discussion above, in sect. 2.3.2.

[68] N. 25 above.

[69] A good account of the impact of *Goldberg* on administrative law is given in W. F. Fox, *Understanding Administrative Law* (2nd edn., M. Binder, New York, 1992), ch. 5.

is due in such matters. It is also an important case in extending the notion of property, for the purpose of the due process clauses, to welfare benefits. This has in turn opened the way for the due process clauses to be applied to wider conceptions of liberty and property than those traditionally recognized.

The second landmark case in applying procedural due process to administration is *Mathews* v. *Eldridge*.[70] The termination of welfare benefits was again in issue, but the approach was different. While *Goldberg* insists that, once due process is triggered, certain defined and exacting procedures come into effect, *Mathews* holds that what procedures are due is to be determined by weighing three factors: the private interest affected, the risk of error, and the state's interest in minimizing costs and additional burdens. My earlier discussion of this balancing approach shows that it has its difficulties, both in being clear about what it means and in its practical application.[71] The general object of the approach appears to be to apply accurately and properly the relevant legal standards to the facts, while a subsidiary goal is to keep the costs to a minimum. The trouble is the two pull in different directions and the courts have so far given little guidance on just how the balancing is to be done in practice. However, despite those difficulties, the idea that procedures are to be settled by balancing competing factors remains the dominant approach to administrative due process. The balancing approach is not fully compatible with *Goldberg* and to that extent the former must be regarded as a modification of the latter.

The due process clauses of the Constitution set minimum standards of procedural fairness which are often supplemented by federal and state laws and by administrative practice within agencies and departments. The federal Administrative Procedure Act 1946 and its state equivalents make extensive provision for administrative decisions which are required by the parent statute to be determined on the record after a hearing. This does not apply to all administrative agencies, nor to all kinds of individualized administrative processes; but where it does apply, a trial-type hearing is required and it must be conducted according to detailed and exacting procedures. The great bulk of administrative actions and decisions, often referred to as informal agency action or informal adjudication, fall outside the trial-type hearing provisions and are not dealt with to any significant extent by the Administrative Procedure Act (APA). Since informal agency actions take many forms, the appropriate procedures also greatly vary. They are subject to constitutional due process, to any relevant parts of the APA, and to the specific provisions of the parent statute in each area; beyond that the agencies themselves usually develop their own more detailed and sometimes more demanding procedures than would be otherwise required.[72]

[70] N. 33 above.

[71] See sect. 6.4.2.

[72] For further discussion see P. Verkuil, 'A Study of Informal Adjudication Procedures' (1976) 43 *U of Chicago L Rev.* 739.

Considering its variety and often low visibility, informal agency action may be the most fertile ground for procedural injustice. It was informal agency action which caught K. C. Davis' eye and sparked off the guidelines movement; it is also informal agency action which has led to some of the landmark decisions of the Supreme Court. But the question to what extent informal agency action remains beyond the pale of adequate standards of procedural fairness could be answered only after undertaking more detailed studies than now exist.

One issue deserving special mention is where informal agency action depends on the exercise of discretion.[73] In deciding on the application of procedural due process, the usual two questions must be posed: is life, liberty, or property at stake, and, if so, what procedures are required? In answering the first part, it is not enough to assume that whenever a person is affected by a discretionary decision some interest in liberty or property is inevitably affected. According to the entitlement thesis, it must be shown that the interest affected already has some status in law; that there is already some legal entitlement to it. Entitlements are sometimes discovered through ingenious argument in the most unlikely places, but in general a basis has to be found either in the Constitution itself or in the relevant state or federal legislation.[74] Legislation is the most likely source, but the position in relation to discretion is paradoxical: an entitlement is likely to be made out only on the basis of clear and certain standards in the statute, yet by its very nature discretion suggests the absence of such standards. What is the best interpretation of a statutory power is of course arguable and the presence of some discretion does not necessarily exclude entitlements.[75] Whether standards create entitlements can be a complex matter. The reality is that, in typical cases of broad discretion, entitlements to liberty or property are not created and the due process clauses do not apply.[76]

The justification for this attitude is that the legislature should be responsible for deciding whether to protect or give advantage to interests in liberty or property. If the legislature decides to make the matter discretionary, that is a legitimate choice and the due process clauses should not be used to impose added procedures. The contrary view is that discretionary decisions about how a person is to be treated should be subject to due process; it might be argued, indeed, that the risks of abuse, of not exercising the power properly according to law, are greatest in the case of discretion. As a consequence of the entitlement thesis, however, many areas of discretion will be excluded from due process. The threshold requirement that liberty or

[73] See T. Searchinger, 'The Procedural Due Process Approach to Administrative Discretion: the Courts' Inverted Analysis' (1986) 95 *Yale LR* 1017.

[74] It might be easier to make out an entitlement to liberty than to property.

[75] See the discussion in sect. 3.2.

[76] A good, recent example of this problem is *Kentucky Department of Corrections* v. *Thompson*, n. 23 above.

property be affected has to be given some reasonable meaning, but it need not be the current meaning. One alternative would be to begin with the principle that no one should be subject to the arbitrary decisions of an administrative official. That itself could be considered a liberty interest which would attract the procedural protections of due process. This is a moderate proposal which goes to the very essence of due process as a way of protecting against arbitrary actions.[77] However, the only port of entry into the Constitution for such a principle would be through substantive due process, and for that very reason it is unlikely to gain much ground, at least under the present judicial approach. An alternative would be to understand the due process clause as essentially concerned with the procedural fairness of governmental action.[78] Procedural fairness is then said to consist in properly applying authoritative legal standards, and doing so by following certain minimum procedures. There is again a good sense in such an attitude which fits well with the theory of procedural fairness propounded in this book; but whether the Supreme Court is prepared to adopt it is another matter.

A final issue to comment on briefly is the procedural approach to general policy decisions. The object of general policy decisions is to reach a substantive outcome which is the best, all things considered. The governing statute typically leaves the substantive issue to be settled by the administrative body, often subject to only the most general guidance. The procedural mode is consultative; that is to say, interested parties should have the chance to put and substantiate their views through participatory procedures. The final decision, however, should be made by the government agency, taking full account of the issues, the evidence, and the arguments. The procedures vary in detail, but the general pattern is constant; the National Environmental Protection Authority, for example, makes major policy decisions only after preparing an environmental impact statement. The statement must include a statement of the changes that will result from the proposed decision which include economic and social effects. Possible courses of action must be displayed and explained, and the reasons for the preferred action given. The preparation of the statement is made through extensive procedures allowing for consultation, argument, and scrutiny. Part of the underlying rationale is the need to reach the most satisfactory outcome by considering and taking into account the complexities of the issue; the other part is to satisfy the principles of procedural fairness through allowing the participation and involvement of interested parties.[79]

[77] For a more theoretical analysis of the idea, see T. Scanlon, 'Due Process' in Pennock and Chapman, *Due Process*, n. 58 above.

[78] Rubin, 'Administrative Due Process', n. 25 above, 1179.

[79] An analysis of the procedures in this context is: M. Herz, 'Parallel Universes; NEPA Lessons for the New Property', n. 64 above.

7

Procedural Fairness in Europe: The European Convention on Human Rights and the European Union

The third tradition of procedural principles is to be found in the new European order. The two areas of interest here are the European Convention on Human Rights and the law of the European Union. The two are distinct but related, with the European Convention being a source of guidance for the development of European law. Indeed, to talk of a tradition here may be premature since both parts are creations of the post-war period; they are, however, two dynamic centres of law-making, which consists in the one case in drawing from the general principles of the Convention detailed doctrines of procedural fairness, and in the other case building a set of doctrines based on various sources, including the doctrines of national legal systems. This is an interesting area which deserves a full study of its own; my present intention, however, is merely to give an outline of the approach taken to procedural fairness within the two systems.

7.1 THE NEW EUROPEAN ORDER

The new European order consists of three parts: the European Union, the Council of Europe and its statements of principles contained in the European Convention on Human rights (ECHR), and the Member States.[1] We are not here concerned with the last of these except to note that some Member States belong to both the European Union and the Council of Europe, while others are members only of the latter. The significance of belonging to either one is that each state becomes subject to a system of legal standards originating from outside the national sphere but potentially having a major impact within it. However, it is not the Member States on

[1] For a fuller discussion of the nature of the new European order, see K. Lenaerts, 'Fundamental Rights to be Included in a Community Catalogue' (1991) 16 *EL Rev*. 367.

which I wish to concentrate here, but the new European systems themselves. Both systems have the capacity to develop principles of procedural fairness which not only create rights in citizens but also greatly influence the law of each Member State.

The European Convention on Human Rights consists of a statement of fundamental rights which are to be respected by Member States of the Council of Europe.[2] The statement of rights was formulated by the Council of Europe, which was itself created in the post-war years by a small group of western European states whose numbers have steadily increased since then and now include several of the states of central and eastern Europe.[3] The original statement of rights is added to from time to time in the form of protocols to the Convention. All Member States are bound by international law to ensure that the principles of the Convention are respected in their national legal systems. Some Member States have incorporated the terms of the convention into their national law so that national courts have the primary responsibility for ensuring that it is respected. Other states, of which the United Kingdom is a notable example, have not ratified the international Convention in national law, but have agreed to citizens within the state being able to bring complaints of violation of the Convention directly before the Commission and the Court at Strasbourg. The somewhat ironic result is that, while the British courts have no jurisdiction to apply directly the principles of the Convention, a significant number of actions have been taken directly before the Strasbourg authorities. The point of particular interest for our present purposes is that the ECHR contains in Article 6 a statement of procedural due process.

The European Union is rather different in nature. Whereas the ECHR constitutes a set of standards to be respected by Member States, with the Commission and Court at Strasbourg providing supervisory support, the European Union is itself a distinct legal order, with its own law-making, adjudicative, and law-enforcing procedures and institutions.[4] The constitution of the Union is the Treaty of Rome and several other treaties which were agreed to by the original Member States in 1961 and which have been added to since.[5] The Union is distinctive in creating a new and separate legal order, the laws of which apply directly within the domestic systems of the Member States. The Treaty of Rome created the institutions of the Union and allocated powers, duties, and obligations to them. Later constituent

[2] At present there are 34 members with several other states seeking membership.

[3] The background to the Council of Europe and the ECHR is provided in D. Feldman, *Civil Liberties and Civil Rights* (Clarendon Press, Oxford, 1993).

[4] See further T. Hartley, *The Foundations of European Community Law* (3rd edn., Clarendon Press, Oxford, 1993).

[5] The basic treaties are now: EEC Treaty, ECSC Treaty, Euratom Treaty, Merger Treaty, and the Single European Act.

treaties have added to the original structure and in a number of areas have created rights in citizens. In general, however, the more fundamental principles governing European law are not stipulated in the Treaties but are developed by the Court of Justice. In discharging its duty to generate general principles, the Court of Justice draws on both the constitutional traditions of Member States and the fundamental rights declared in international treaties, including the ECHR. In this way a vital link is created between the ECHR and the dynamic legal principles of the European Union. The role of the Court of Justice in creating general principles of European law is vital to the emergence of sound procedural principles. For while the constituent documents of the Union deal only marginally with procedural principles, the Court of Justice has taken steps towards formulating a general jurisprudence of procedural due process.

7.2 THE EUROPEAN CONVENTION ON HUMAN RIGHTS

7.2.1 Introduction and Background

Provision for procedural fairness is made in Article 6(1) of the ECHR, which states as follows: 'In the determination of his civil rights and obligations or of any criminal charge against him, everyone is entitled to a fair and public hearing within a reasonable time by an independent and impartial tribunal established by law'. The approach expressed in this Article has the same logical pattern as English and American law: the first part imposes a threshold test which must be met in order to attract certain procedures, while the second part states what those procedures are. The logical pattern may be familiar, but both the threshold test and the procedural requirements are distinctive: the former is satisfied when civil rights or obligations or a criminal charge are being determined, while the latter calls for a fair and public hearing which is timely, independent, and impartial. The right to procedural fairness created by the ECHR is a right to procedures of that kind, subject to the threshold test first being met. The following analysis will consider the meaning and scope of the threshold test and the procedures required once it is passed.

7.2.2 The Threshold Test

The threshold test itself has two parts; one is that civil rights or obligations are being determined, the other is that a criminal charge is in process. The right to certain procedures takes effect if either part is satisfied. The second part is the more clearly defined of the two and introduces a notion of procedural fairness suited to processes of a criminal nature. Whether a criminal charge is in issue is not usually too difficult to determine, although questions can arise as to how far the concept extends and whether it includes certain penalty-imposing processes.[6] The more serious difficulties occur in relation to the first part of the threshold test, namely, whether civil rights or obligations are being determined. Questions about obligations do not often arise, but what constitutes civil rights has been the subject of extensive discussion and litigation.[7]

This part of the threshold test is important as the gateway through which all non-criminal, that is to say civil and administrative, processes must pass in order to attract the procedural standards expressed in Article 6(1). It is the basis for ensuring compliance with standards of procedural fairness, not only in the settlement of issues between two private parties, but also in administrative processes where decisions are made by officials about private parties. The procedural standards of the Convention apply to administrative processes only if civil rights are in issue.

The difficulty is that the concept of civil rights has no clear or precise meaning either at international law or in the legal systems of Member States. In English law, 'civil rights' is a term loosely used to connote rights associated with basic liberties and can be used interchangeably with civil liberties. However, there is nothing in Article 6(1) or in the discussions preparatory to its adoption to justify restricting the expression to rights in that sense. Nor is there positive evidence from which to gain a clear idea of what was intended. Article 6 of ECHR is based on Article 14 of the International Convention on Civil and Political Rights (ICCPR). The French version in each case uses the expression 'droits de caractère civil', while the English version, which was originally 'rights and obligations in a suit at law', was changed to 'civil rights and obligations'.[8] The reasons for the change in the English version are unclear, but it has been argued persuasively that there is no reason to suppose that the drafters of Article 6 intended to set a narrow or restrictive threshold test for procedural fairness.[9] Nevertheless, the expression 'civil rights' appears in the Article and must be given some meaning; many cases have come before the Commission and the Court, but precisely how the expression should be interpreted still causes difficulty and is the subject of disagreement.[10]

[6] For discussion, see R. Beddard, *Human Rights in Europe* (Sweet and Maxwell, London, 1992).

[7] See M. Janis and R. Kay, *European Human Rights Law* (University of Connecticut Law School Foundation Press, Connecticut, 1990) and S. Stravos, *The Guarantees for Accused Persons Under Article 6 of the European Convention on Human Rights* (Martinus Nijhoff, Dordrecht, 1992).

[8] For further analysis of the background, see P. van Dijk, 'Access to Court' in R. St Macdonald (ed.), *The European System for the Protection of Human Rights* (Martinus Nijhoff, Dordrecht: London, 1993).

[9] Ibid., 350.

[10] See, further, H. Schermers, 'The Right to a Fair Trial under the European Convention

Once again we have the spectacle of great efforts and substantial resources being devoted to determining whether legal and administrative processes satisfy the threshold test and attract fair procedures. On the numerous occasions that the Commission and the Court have been asked to rule on the meaning of civil rights, their response has been piecemeal and variable, with a clear and defensible sense of civil rights, particularly in relation to administrative processes, not yet having emerged. Indeed, the court has deliberately adopted a piecemeal approach, rather than attempt a comprehensive definition.[11] It is not my purpose here to offer a detailed analysis of the decisions of the Strasbourg authorities, but perhaps their general approach can be summarized in the following propositions. First, civil rights are sometimes equated with private rights as opposed to public rights, although quite what the criterion is for distinguishing between the two is not clear.[12] The distinction is said to derive from continental legal systems, while for English lawyers it has not traditionally been of great significance.[13] The Court often makes reference to the distinction between private rights and public rights, but it has never explicitly defined civil rights as private rights.[14] Secondly, while civil rights are most likely to be at issue in disputes between private parties, they may also be present where a public authority takes action in relation to a private party. The application of Article 6(1) depends on neither the character of the legislation governing how the matter is to be decided, nor the character of the authority deciding; its application turns entirely on the nature of the right.[15]

Thirdly, it seems that where a person is subject to the actions or decisions of a public body which affect an existing right under national law, the right is likely to be regarded as a civil right.[16] What constitutes an existing right may itself be a difficult matter to determine, but it need not be a legal right in a precise sense. In *Benthem*, the general right to engage in commercial activities was considered adequate; while similarly in *Kraska* the Court concluded that the right to practise medicine was sufficiently recognized under Swiss law to constitute a civil right.[17] The result of this approach appears to be that, once a right is found to exist under the law of a Member State, no additional feature is needed in order for it to be characterized as a civil right. The tentative conclusion to be drawn is that virtually any right which has some legal basis in national law, and which is subject to or affected by a legal

on Human Rights' in R. Blackburn and J. Taylor (eds.), *Human Rights for the 1990s* (Mansell, London, 1992).

[11] *Benthem*, 23 Oct. 1985, Series A No. 97; *Ringeisen*, 16 July 1971, Series A No. 13.

[12] *Feldbrugge*, 29 June 1986, Series A No. 99.

[13] Although it should be noted that the distinction between the private and the public is now much discussed.

[14] *König*, 28 June 1978, Series A, No. 27, 30; *Benthem*, 23 Oct. 1985, n. 11 above, 16.

[15] *König*, n. 14 above, 30.

[16] *Ringeisen*, n. 11 above; *Deumeland*, 21 May 1986, Series A, No. 100.

[17] 19 April 1993, Series A, No. 255B.

or administrative process, will be a civil right for the purposes of Article 6(1).[18]

The question of special interest for our present purposes is the extent to which Article 6(1) applies to administrative processes. The simple answer is that it applies whenever such processes affect civil rights. Since the threshold test looks to the consequences of a process rather than to its nature or function, administrative processes may be subject to Article 6(1). Where clearly existing rights are affected, particularly if their origins lie in private law, the qualifying test will be met. It will also be met where the administrative process restricts or curtails rights more broadly conceived, such as the right to conduct commercial activities or to engage in some other form of legitimate activity. Procedural standards will probably also apply where rights created under one statute are subject to administrative powers conferred under another; similarly, the standards should apply where the point of the process is to give effect to positive rights created under statute. On this view, administrative processes for determining whether the statutory criteria for the grant of a welfare right are satisfied would be subject to Article 6(1). The main reservation in these cases is whether some further quality must be detected to warrant such rights being considered civil rights. The earlier discussion shows the uncertainties surrounding that issue, although the conclusion was that to be able to point to a clearly existing right might be enough.

The one situation where Article 6(1) might seem clearly not to apply is where the administrative process involves the use of discretion, for in some situations discretion connotes the absence of rights. However, even here the position is neither clear nor simple, for it should be kept in mind that, in some of its senses, discretion is compatible with rights.[19] The best example is where rights are defined by standards which need to be interpreted; the element of discretion in interpretation may be necessary in defining the precise content of the right but without in any way undermining it. In cases of strong discretion, however, there is no right in the sense that there is entitlement to a defined outcome, and that may seem conclusive against the application of Article 6(1). The only counter-argument that can be offered is that there is still a right to certain processes in the way the discretion is exercised, an idea expressed in the right to consideration as described in earlier chapters. Whether the right to consideration, first, will be recognized by the Strasbourg institutions as a genuine right and, secondly, if so, will be regarded as a civil right, are matters for future determination.

Two final points should be noted. One is that much of the anxiety over the meaning of civil rights would be dispelled by interpreting the expression in a

[18] The Commission may be more restrictive in its view of the scope of civil rights than the Court: see van Dijk, n. 8 above, 357–9.

[19] See the analysis in Ch. 3.

way which seems most obvious. The text of Article 6(1) contrasts civil and criminal, suggesting simply that civil rights and obligations are all those rights and obligations which are not of a criminal character. Nothing in the text itself suggests that, within the category of non-criminal rights and obligations, further divisions should be drawn between those which are civil and those which are something else. The second point is that the right to procedural fairness or to procedural due process might itself be considered a civil right in the same way as a right to free speech or a right to conduct certain activities are civil rights. If there were a right to procedural due process in this general sense, it would mean that Article 6(1) is triggered whenever a party is affected in a significant manner by an administrative process. As the notion of a general right to procedural due process gains acceptance in national legal systems, the Strasbourg institutions may in time adopt a similar approach.

7.2.3 The Procedural Standards

Once the threshold test is satisfied so that Article 6(1) comes into effect, the question is what procedural standards are to be applied. The answer provided is that anyone so affected 'is entitled to a fair and public hearing within a reasonable time by an independent and impartial tribunal established by law'. Unlike the American Constitution, which states simply that in similar circumstances there shall be due process of law, leaving it to the courts to decide what standards are necessary, the Convention goes a step further in stipulating what the standards are. For civil rights and obligations, the procedural standards are those stated above, while more detailed provision is made for criminal charges. Here I shall concentrate on civil rights, particularly those subject to administrative processes.[20] The central idea is that there should be a hearing and that the hearing should have certain features; it must be fair, public, timely, independent, impartial, and established by law. Each of these features has to be interpreted and made more concrete, but it is of great interest and importance to have expressed in an international convention the fundamental principles of procedural fairness. Member States may add to the principles, but they must not fall below them. At the same time, the generality of the principles allows for considerable variation within Member States as to the precise procedures necessary to satisfy them. Different approaches within national states can be tolerated provided that, taken as a whole, they comply with the general standards of Article 6(1).[21]

Without attempting a comprehensive review of the many decisions of the Commission and the Council, I shall offer a few brief comments on the

[20] See further, A. Boyle, 'Sovereignty, Accountability and the Reform of Administrative Law', in G. Richardson and H. Genn (eds.), *Administrative Law and Government Action* (Clarendon Press, Oxford, 1994).

[21] This approach is illustrated in many cases, a good example being *Borgers* v. *Belgium* (1991), Series A No. 214A.

progress which has been made towards a body of detailed rules and doctrines within the framework of Article 6(1). It is convenient in doing so to adopt the threefold division of legal processes into access, the decision itself, and recourse from the decision. As to the first, the right of a party to have access to a court, tribunal, or other kind of authority is inherent in Article 6(1).[22] To have access means to be able to apply to a court or tribunal in order to have one's rights and obligations determined.[23] Member States have a duty not only not to obstruct access but positively to ensure that it is practical and effective, although limited resources may necessarily impose limitations.[24] The negative prohibition is well illustrated in the *Golder* case where restrictions on prisoners corresponding with their legal advisers were held to be invalid.[25] The positive duties on Member States are more problematical. Their duty to make access practical and effective would seem to include such positive help as may be necessary to have one's case properly presented; that in turn might require some form of legal aid. The Court has stopped short of holding that the right of access includes a right to legal aid; its approach appears to be that the interests of justice may in some cases require that legal aid be available.[26] In *Airey*,[27] the Court stated that in fulfilment of its obligations under Article 6(1), a state may have to take positive measures to make the right of access effective. What constitutes the necessary positive action depends on what is necessary in the circumstances.

At the second stage, the issue is what procedures are required in order to constitute a fair and public hearing. The first point to note is that Article 6(1) provides a right to a hearing. Considering the amount of energy spent in national systems in deciding whether, in a given context, a hearing is needed as an element of procedural fairness, it is noteworthy that a hearing is here declared to be a fundamental attribute of fairness. The second point to note is that the hearing must be fair. Member States must take initial responsibility for devising procedures and considerable scope is left to them to decide what constitutes fairness. National variations are likely to be extensive, and the Court has emphasized that, in judging fairness, it will take careful note of local procedures. Nevertheless, it must on occasions judge, and in doing so has substantial scope for stipulating the conditions of fairness, although Article 6(1) does go on to state characteristics, such as independence, impartiality, and timeliness, which could be regarded as aspects of a fair hearing.

A fair hearing includes the opportunity to put one's case, to call witnesses, and to question witnesses called by the opposing party. The right to call

[22] *Golder* v. *U.K.* (1975), Series A, No. 18.

[23] See the discussion in van Dijk, n. 8 above.

[24] *Ashingdane* v. *U.K.* (1985), Series A No. 93; see also *Philis* v. *Greece* (1991), Series A No. 221.

[25] (1975), Series A No. 18.

[26] *Grainger* v. *U.K.* (1990), Series A, No. 174.

[27] (1979), Series A No. 32.

witnesses is not unlimited and may be restricted for reasons of efficiency and economy,[28] although the Court has left open just how the balancing of the two is to be done. From the right to a fair hearing the Court has developed the principle of equality of arms. The basis of the principle is that each party, whether in criminal or civil proceedings, should be on an equal footing, or at least that one should not be disadvantaged in relation to the other.[29] The principle is strongly reminiscent of the doctrine of English law that there should be a fair contest between the parties to an action.

Specific doctrines like these are drawn from the notion of fairness, but they by no means exhaust its capacity.[30] The concept of a fair hearing remains open and dynamic; it may be used to generate other doctrines, or it may be seen as a general standard for judging whether a certain hearing process is fair all things considered. Examples of the issues which may need to be considered according to the general standard of fairness are questions of evidence, whether the parties should be allowed to appear in person, and the extent to which one party is entitled to reply to the opposing case. Of special importance is the use of the general standard in justifying the duty on the deciding body to give reasons. The duty to give reasons as an aspect of a fair hearing is now settled doctrine.[31]

The other procedural standards specified in Article 6(1)—independence, impartiality, and timeliness—have been much discussed in the decisions of the Commission and the Court. Although the standards might be seen as implicit in the idea of a fair hearing, by being provided for expressly, each is given an added importance. The independence of a court or tribunal means independence from the executive and from the parties; it has been suggested that it should also mean independence from the legislature and from interest groups.[32] Impartiality has connotations similar to those of English law and emphasizes the need to dispel the appearance of bias as well as actual bias.[33] The need for timeliness in resolving an issue has attracted more litigation than any other part of Article 6(1). Considering that delays of several years are common place in Member States, it is not surprising that the Court should attach great weight to the right of a party to obtain a judgment within a reasonable time.[34] What constitutes a reasonable time is judged according to the circumstances of the case, with special emphasis on complexity, the conduct of the party, and the behaviour of the authorities.[35] Timeliness is

[28] *Schuler-Zgraggen* (1993), Series A No. 63; *Brandstetter* (App. Nos. 1170/84, 12876/87, 13468/87).

[29] Illustrated in *Bönisch* v. *Austria* (1990–) Series A No. 92; *Borgers* v. *Belgium*, n. 20 above.

[30] See *Monell and Morris* (1987), Series A No. 115.

[31] *H* v. *Belgium* (1987), Series A No. 127; *Kaufman* v. *Belgium* (1987), 50 ECHR 98.

[32] See O. Jacot-Guillamod, 'Rights Related to Good Administration of Justice' in Macdonald, n. 8 above.

[33] Often referred to as an objective approach to bias: see *Piersack* (1982), Series A No. 53; *Borgers* v. *Belgium* n. 20 above; *Demicoli* v. *Malta* (1991), Series A No. 220.

especially important in criminal cases, but applies equally in civil cases.[36] The claim that the national courts and tribunals have a heavy backlog of cases is no defence to a claim under Article 6(1).

A final and important point concerns the relationship between primary decisions and appeal processes. Article 6(1) requires that a person whose civil rights are affected be given a fair and public hearing; it does not specify, however, that the hearing should be provided at the primary level.[37] It follows that the terms of the Article may be satisfied by a suitable appeal procedure. This does not mean that an appeal procedure is an essential element of Article 6(1);[38] it means rather that the process by which rights are determined, taken as a whole, must satisfy the due process standards. The relationship between primary and appeal processes is governed by the principle of adequacy: if the standards are not met at the primary level, an appeal procedure should be available to make up the loss.[39]

It may be concluded from this survey that a framework of procedural fairness has been created in Article 6(1) which has many similarities with both English and American law. In each case, certain conditions must be met to attract procedural fairness but, once having been met, a set of procedural principles comes into play. The condition that civil rights be in issue bears some similarity to the entitlement test under American law, although the former is potentially narrower than the latter. Whether there is much difference in practice is more arguable. It is hard to think of good reasons for restricting the due process provisions of the European Convention to civil rights, rather than making them applicable to all legal and administrative processes which affect rights or significant interests. Once the threshold has been surmounted, the procedures required under Article 6(1) are very similar to those in other national systems. It is important that there should be a statement of procedural principles which all Member States should respect; it is also important that in developing and refining those principles, the Court and the Commission should draw on the ideas and doctrines emerging in the jurisprudence of Member States.

7.2.4 Two Contextual Factors

Having seen in outline the basis for procedural fairness under the ECHR, we may conclude the discussion with two points of a more contextual kind. One point concerns the extent to which the procedural regime created under Article 6(1) applies to administrative processes. The very wording of the Article and the need to show that civil rights are at issue suggest that it was

[34] *Guincho* (1984), Series A No. 81. [35] *Buchholz* (1981), Series A No. 42.

[36] *Jesso* v. *Austria* (1987), 50 ECHR 55; *C* v. *Italy* (1987), 50 ECHR 168.

[37] *Brigandi* v. *Italy* (1991), Series A No. 7; *Editions Periscope* (1992), Series A No. 234; *R.* v. *France* (1992), Series A No. 236.

[38] See *Belgian Linguistic Case* (1968), Series A No. 33.

not meant to be a comprehensive statement of procedural due process. No matter how broad an interpretation is given to the concept of civil rights, many areas of administrative decision-making will still be excluded from its scope. It is not clear why Article 6 was conceived in this narrow way, especially if we consider how important questions of procedural fairness in administration are in the national systems of the Member States, both in western and eastern Europe. The result is that the Convention not only provides inadequate guidance on procedural matters in the administrative field, but also lags behind progress made within Member States. The Council of Europe has been closely involved in developing standards, including procedural standards, in administrative law and it may now be timely for Article 6(1) to be revised to take account of those advances and to reinstate the Convention as a source of foundational principles in this area of such importance. The second point is simply to note how little is known about the practical operation and effect of the procedural principles of Article 6(1). The dearth of empirical research and the absence of a comprehensive study of the types of process covered by Article 6(1) make generalizations about its strengths and weaknesses difficult to sustain.

7.3 PROCEDURAL FAIRNESS IN EUROPEAN LAW

7.3.1 The Sources of Procedural Principles

In the constitutional documents of the European Union, little is said about procedures and even less about procedural fairness. Apart from the duty on the Commission to give reasons for certain of its actions pursuant to the EEC Treaty,[40] procedural matters are left largely to be dealt with either in subordinate legislation by way of regulations or directives, or by the European Court in developing the legal principles of the Union. Regulations and directives made by the Commission often specify the procedure to be followed by itself, by other authorities of the European Union, or by Member States in discharging their obligations under European law. The Commission is concerned mainly to specify procedures which are effective in achieving the aims of a particular area of regulation, but of course it may on occasions be guided by general considerations of procedural fairness. In the area of competition law, for example, the regulations provide for a range of procedures which derive from the right to be heard (or the rights of the defence as it has come to be known).[41] It would be interesting to know more about the extent to which subordinate law-making by the Commission adopts

[39] See *Albert* (1983), Series A No. 58.
[40] Art. 149 EEC.
[41] See the discussion of L. Ritter, W. Braun, and F. Rawlinson, *EEC Competition Law*

general principles of procedural fairness, but so far no comprehensive study has been conducted.

Whatever contribution the Commission may make, the main impetus for generating principles of law in general and procedural principles in particular comes from the European Court. Taking its mandate from Article 164 of the Treaty of Rome, which instructs it to ensure that, in the interpretation and application of the Treaty, the law is observed, the Court of Justice has created a body of legal principles of general application within Community law. The main sources of the *principes généraux* are the constitutional and legal traditions of Member States and the provisions of international treaties, with special emphasis on the ECHR.[42] While the Court is expected to respect the principles expressed in the ECHR, it may go beyond them and draw on other sources.[43] The Court is not bound to adopt every general principle which may be found in the law of a Member State; but where fundamental rights are at issue, careful attention should be paid to the protections available under national laws.[44]

7.3.2 The Rights of the Defence

The main principle of procedural fairness so far adopted by the Court of Justice is that a party affected by a decision or action of the Commission or other institution of the Community should be given a fair hearing.[45] The principle was stated by Advocate-General Warner as follows: 'It is a fundamental principle of Community law that, before an individual measure or decision was taken, of such a nature as to affect directly the interests of a particular person, that person has a right to be heard by the responsible authority . . .'.[46] The principle protecting the rights of the defence applies not only to administrative procedures which may lead to the imposition of a penalty, but also in other contexts, such as a preliminary inquiry or investigation into a party's affairs.[47] The Court of Justice has not dealt at any length with the nature of the interest which party must have in order to attract the hearing principle; it appears to be sufficient that the party is the direct subject of the decision or action or is affected by it in some other significant and tangible way.[48]

The approach of the Court of Justice appears to be similar to that of the English courts. According to that approach, the precise procedures required

(Klewer, 1991), 648 ff.

[42] *Hoechst* v. *Commission* [1989] ECR 2859.

[43] See further, Lenaerts, 'Fundamental Rights to Be Included in a Community Catalogue' and *Orken* [1988] ECR 3283.

[44] *Al-Jubail* v. *Council* [1991] ECR 3187.

[45] *Transocean Marine Paint* v. *Commission* [1974] 2 CMLR 459 and *British Leyland* [1987] CMLR 185.

[46] *Japanese Ballbearings* [1979] ECR 1363.

[47] *Hoechst* v. *Commission*, n. 41 above, and *Michelin* v. *Commission* [1983] ECR 3461.

by the hearing principle depend on what is needed for fair treatment in the circumstances. A hearing is an essential element, although the form it should take may range from a full oral proceeding to simpler procedures of consultation.[49] The rights of the defence, however, go beyond the hearing itself and include certain conditions which are necessary if the hearing is to be effective. One essential condition is that the party be 'informed of the facts and considerations on the basis of which the authority is minded to act'.[50] The duty to give notice to the parties of the proposed decision or action, and to disclose documents and other evidence which may be relied on, has become an especially important part of the rights of the defence in investigative processes conducted by the Commission.[51]

The notice, disclosure, and hearing elements comprising the rights of the defence are the core of procedural fairness, but it is a dynamic principle which may extend to other procedures. Legal representation is one such addition for which some support has been expressed by the Court of Justice.[52] The duty to give reasons for the regulations, directives, and decisions of the Council and the Commission is stated in Article 190 of the EEC Treaty itself.[53] This is an interesting provision which extends beyond individualized decisions to include the legislative acts of the Council and Commission. The form in which reasons should be given and the level of detail they should contain varies according to several factors, but legislative acts will not normally warrant the degree of detail that would be expected for an individualized decision.[54]

It may be concluded from this outline that the approach to procedural fairness emerging in the decisions of the Court of Justice, while still in its early stages, has many similarities with that of English law and the British courts. A jurisprudence is gradually being forged by the Court which is guided by the more mature doctrines of national law, while retaining the authority to depart from or add to those doctrines. At the same time, the Court has adopted the ECHR as a foundational document expressing principles to be applied across Europe; but it is neither perfect nor complete, and again the Court has the authority to extend and develop those principles as it considers fit. The positive and dynamic approach the Court has taken so far towards the *principes généraux*, and towards procedural due process in particular, are clear signs that it may have a major part in creating a distinctively European sense of procedural principles.

[48] See Ritter, Braun, and Rawlinson, n. 40 above, 648 ff.

[49] *Hoechst* v. *Commission*, n. 41 above.

[50] Warner, A.-G. in *Japanese Ballbearings*, n. 45 above.

[51] See V. Korah, 'The Rights of the Defence in Administrative Proceedings Under Community Law' [1980] *Current Legal Prob.* 73 and *Hoechst* v. *Commission*, n. 45 above.

[52] *Demont* v. *Commission* [1981] ECR 3147.

[53] Similar provision is made in the Euratom and the ECSC treaties.

[54] For a fuller discussion of the adequacy of reasons, see Hartley, n. 4 above, ch. 5.

PART III

Forms of Process

Introduction

It is not only lawyers who, given occasion to think about legal processes, conjure up an image of the judicial trial, with distinctive personnel, specialized procedures, and a script as tight as a Greek tragedy. And yet, if we survey the field, it is apparent that such an image bears no relation to most decisions within it. Not only is there the variety of administrative decisions, from the public inquiry to the routine application of rules, there is also a galaxy of institutions, including tribunals and specialist courts, arbitrations, mediations, and conciliations. It has often been remarked, moreover, that the procedures suitable for this array of processes are likely to be far removed from those of the judicial trial. But the pull of the trial, especially its adversarial aspects, is not easily thrown off, and the threat is constant that decisions, designed to be settled in other ways, will be drawn within it.

In the modern world, however, the adversarial trial has a relatively minor role. Many court processes bear little resemblance to the model of an adversarial contest, especially in the lower courts where parties are often unrepresented and where matters are as much concerned with speed and turnover as with accuracy and justice. Quite apart from the courts, a great range of bodies and institutions exercises legal or administrative authority according to an equally great variety of methods and procedures. Examples are the many varieties of administrative process, the various forms of policy-making, and the diverse ways of bringing parties together through negotiation and mediation. The most cursory view of a modern legal system would suggest a mass of procedural forms which overlap at many points and which as a whole do not seem to fit into clear patterns of logic and reason. The judge sitting in a civil trial appears to be doing much the same thing as many administrative bodies—settling disputes, allocating resources, or just imposing the will of the government—and yet the procedures of each are fundamentally different. It is also obvious that the form and shape of procedures are very much the product of a society and its culture, of accident as well as design, and that any attempt to impose order and system upon them is fraught with difficulty.

While all that is true, it is nevertheless useful to try to unearth some pattern and purpose in the ways different social tasks are performed by legal processes. In the performance of those tasks, social institutions are purposive and, in their essentials, substantially rational. A commitment to economy and efficiency also runs deep and the appearance of chaos may be due more to our misunderstanding than to reality. The object of this part is, then, to enquire into some of the questions of classification and of how different processes and procedures can serve different ends and values. An initial attempt at classifying legal processes according to family groups was made in Chapter 1; the task now is to build on that preliminary analysis by looking more closely at their internal composition. Special attention will be given to those based on the application of standards and the exercise of discretion, while a less detailed analysis will be offered for decisions based on agreement and for processes of investigation and inquiry.

8
Forms of Process I

The object of this Chapter is to begin an examination of forms of process based on the application of authoritative standards. This is a large family which includes a number of more specific types of administrative process, including those of a discretionary kind, for although discretion is sometimes thought of as the absence of standards, it is more accurately characterized as a matter of degree ranging through various positions from the interpretation of standards at one end to their virtual absence at the other end. The emphasis in this Chapter, however, is not on discretion as an analytical concept but rather on a number of general issues which arise in the application of authoritative standards to individual cases.

The main issue is to develop a notion of administrative adjudication within which certain principles of fair treatment are applied and respected. In the course of doing so, a distinction is drawn between an adjudicative mode where fair treatment of the individual party is the foremost concern, and a bureaucratic mode which stresses expedition and regularity. Although the two modes have certain common features, each has a different dynamic and draws on different assumptions about the nature of administrative decision-making. The result is that elements of both can be detected within administrative processes; indeed, the tension between the two is itself a feature of those processes. It should also be noted that the classification of processes, and in particular the notion of adjudication, is partly a matter of logical analysis and partly a question of values. The discussion in this Chapter amply demonstrates the combination of the two elements in relation to adjudication. The connection between different versions of the concept and different values is explained and clarified. The link between adjudication and fair treatment is examined at length. In the final part of the Chapter, the limitations of adjudication as a means for ensuring fair treatment are identified and suggestions are made as to how failure may be achieved through alternative procedures.

8.1 THE PROBLEM OF CLASSIFICATION

Since many attempts have been made to classify legal processes and the procedures to match them, it may be wise to begin by considering exactly what the issue is and the difficulties likely to be encountered. Let us begin with the initial classification of Chapter 1; the family groups identified there are as follows:

- processes based on voting procedures
- processes based on managerial fiat
- processes based on pure procedures with an emphasis on participation
- processes based on applying standards and exercising discretion
- processes of investigation and inquiry.

Each of these families represents a way of doing things, a way of achieving social goals and performing social functions. What distinguishes each family is its normative foundation, that is to say, each is based on a set of values about how particular matters ought to be dealt with. Some issues are dealt with by the application of authoritative standards, others by an official's discretionary choice; some are settled by agreement, others by voting; and so on. Each may be a justifiable way of settling issues in certain circumstances and each is a distinct and legitimate way of exercising authority.

One question to ponder is when one form of process should be used rather than another. What criteria should be relied on in deciding whether to deal with an issue by laying down authoritative standards or by allocating discretion or by trying to bring the parties to agreement? In the discussion of Chapter 1, the suggestion was made that no very definite criteria could be formulated. The best that can be done is to be clear about the values served by each family of process, and then ask which is most suitable in a given set of circumstances. That is itself a complex social issue which will be much influenced by the values and attitudes of the society and to which no answer will easily be found. Sometimes an analysis of the situation might point firmly to one form of process as most suitable; for instance, we normally take the view that certain relations between persons, particularly those involving criminal actions, ought to be governed by clear, authoritative standards. On other occasions, the answer might be more equivocal; where the goal is to settle disputes, the choice between having authoritative standards and getting the parties to agree may be very real. Similarly, there can be real disagreement as to whether a matter should be governed by authoritative standards or left to official discretion.

What is clear is that the same social goals often can be achieved through more than one form of process. The choice of one rather than another will then turn partly on its being more effective in achieving the desired ends and partly on other values and considerations. These matters will not always point in the same direction; strict rules might be effective in settling certain disputes, the custody of children after divorce, for example, but at the same time cause a level of antagonism between the parties which could be reduced by processes directed towards agreement. In practice, the position will be even more complicated with the potential for such reasoned appraisal buried beneath convention and the accidents of history. We live, however, in an age of reform which looks beyond historical practices in order to make informed and reasoned judgments about the best form of process for such contexts as family breakdown, the compensation of victims, the allocation of welfare, and the use of land. The point should also be noted that the different families of process inter-relate and overlap; the categories are not watertight and it is not unusual to find elements of one creeping into another. In an area governed by standards, we may find elements of negotiation and agreement about how the standards or some part of them should be applied. And we need hardly be reminded that the relationship between applying standards and exercising discretion is always in practice one of degree and emphasis. Each family of process represents a theoretical model of a certain coherence and purity which may well be dented and tarnished in practical application.

Moving now to the second level of analysis, let us suppose that a form of process to deal with a set of issues has been settled; the decision might be to apply authoritative standards, or to adopt a highly discretionary regime, or to seek agreement. The next task is to look inside each family of processes to determine whether it in turn can be divided into more specific procedural forms. To take some examples, in the context of standard-application, a sharp distinction is often drawn between adversarial adjudication and bureaucratic investigation.[1] Both are ways of deciding on the basis of authoritative standards, yet on closer inspection each displays quite different qualities. Similarly, where the object is to reach agreement, a choice might have to be made between leaving the parties to negotiate on their own and requiring them to be guided by a mediator. And finally, in a matter of high discretion, it might be a case of choosing between one set of procedures which provides a structured basis for intensive public involvement and another which leaves it to the official to proceed as seems best.

While these examples are clear enough, the difficulties of identifying the individual members within each family of processes are considerable. One difficulty is that we might have quite different conceptions of what is in issue. According to one conception, the idea might be to identify distinct procedural forms—adversarial adjudication, for example—and then show that each is especially suited to certain tasks. The alternative conception is more sceptical and perhaps more realistic. It eschews the possibility of finding distinct procedural forms which can be matched to equally distinct tasks, and then proceeds on the basis that, for any specific task, a choice of procedures is usually open, and that whatever arrangement one finally adopts will rest on a judgment about effectiveness and values. Such a judgment will try to isolate a number of factors which are pertinent to the issue and on the basis of which suitable procedures can be designed. The modern

[1] See M. Bayles, *Procedural Justice* (Kluwer, London, 1990) and J. Mashaw, *Due Process in the Administrative State* (Yale University Press, New Haven, Conn., 1985).

trend is towards the latter approach, although the influence of well-established forms, especially adversarial adjudication, can be powerful.

Two other difficulties in defining distinct procedural forms and then matching them to particular tasks should be mentioned. One is that the objects and purposes of legal and administrative processes are not always clear or settled. It is easy to state an idealized view of processes based on standard-application or discretion, for example; but when we look closely at specific instances, the objects to be sought and the values to be respected in doing so may vary significantly. Discretion is a good case in point. In some cases, the main object will be to allow the official to decide as he thinks fit, in others it will be to act more like an arbitrator trying to reconcile disputing parties, while in a third category of cases, the real object will be to decide an individualized issue in a judicial manner. The design of procedures will be greatly influenced by which view is taken. The other difficulty is that an analytical approach to procedural design can take us only part of the way, with the rest of the way being a product of social and historical factors, of values as well as analysis; for how things have been done in the past shapes our expectations about how they should be done now. Social attitudes to prisoners and the penal system, for example, have been a major influence on the approach taken to procedures affecting them. Procedural design and reform do not begin with a clean slate, but must work within the attitudes and values already settled in a society.

Despite these difficulties, however, it is well worth while examining some of the procedural forms which have emerged and the claims made for them. Indeed, a sound analytical and critical perspective is of importance in changing existing procedures. It is also of considerable interest to try to extract the different values which lie just below the surface.

8.2 APPLYING STANDARDS AND EXERCISING DISCRETION

8.2.1 Criteria for the Design of Procedures

The two families of process to be considered in this section are those based on applying standards and exercising discretion. Considering their close relationship and the natural overlap between them, it is sensible to treat them together and the object will be to examine some of the issues relating to the design of procedures with respect to each. Practical decisions are being made all the time by legislatures, administrative bodies, and courts about the procedures to be followed in performing particular tasks. Parliament may decide to regulate an activity through detailed rules, which can then be applied by an administrative body in a fairly mechanical way with a minimum of procedural formality; alternatively, Parliament might resort to looser standards, appoint a semi-judicial body to apply them, and impose procedures based around an oral hearing. For the courts' part, they might be called on to decide, where Parliament has left the matter open, whether a hearing or some other procedure is required. Their role is subsidiary, but on many procedural issues they take the lead in developing notions of fairness. The administrators themselves also make a major contribution to procedures in filling in the many gaps left by legislation or judicial rulings.

The design of procedures is not just a practical matter, since all practical matters stand on the shoulders of some view of the world, some theoretical stance; the issue, then, is to unearth whatever principles there may be to guide those practical decisions. It is not enough just to describe what Parliament or the courts are doing; an approach needs to be developed which is acceptable and coherent in principle as well as sound in practice. Again, expectations should not be too high; decision-making is enormously variable, and the forms it takes bend with the task in hand. We should not expect that the underlying principles will all hold together in a coherent whole; on the contrary, the guiding factors are likely to be in a state of tension, partly compatible, but partly pulling in different directions. We can, however, at least make a start and begin to build a theory of procedural forms and understand the tensions within it.

We should begin by being clear about the criteria for designing procedures.[2] The first criterion is that the procedures should be effective means for realizing the social goals being sought. The first step, then, is to identify the objects and purposes to be achieved, and to adopt procedures suitable for attaining them. The objects may be in the one case to determine issues by the application of authoritative standards, in another case to decide by discretionary judgment, where some guidance will be given by authoritative standards. The procedures at this stage will be directed to achieving those ends. This will usually require: procedures about who is to decide; procedures to provide information to the decision-maker; procedures to test the accuracy and cogency of the information; and procedures for forming a judgment about the information according to the relevant objects.

The variety of procedures at this stage can be considerable. What sort of person or body of persons should have power to decide can be settled in many ways, ranging from the independent judge to the board of committed policy-makers. The facts and materials on which the decision is based might be obtained by the authority itself, they might derive entirely from the parties directly affected, or they might be gathered by a mixture of the two. The sifting and analysing of the information might also be done in different ways: by scrutiny and reflection on the part of the authority itself, by discussion and argument in an open forum, or by some variable combination of the

[2] Reference should be made to the discussion in sect. 3.5.

two. The making of the final judgment also lends itself to different approaches: it might be the detached weighing-up of the judge, the policy preferences of a committee, or the vote of a jury—to mention just a few. The final procedural question will usually be whether the original decision should be final or subject to review by another body. In answering any of these questions, the guiding policy should be in each case to realize the objects effectively and economically.

The next stage in the design of procedures is to take account of considerations of fair treatment which arise whenever the interests of individuals or groups are at issue. What precisely is required by fairness then depends on the standards of fair treatment in the specific context. The standards relating to outcomes will normally be that the person be treated in accordance with authoritative standards, or, in the case of strong discretion, that his interests be properly considered and various standards be complied with. Fair treatment in relation to outcomes largely coincides with effective realization of ends at the first stage, but with some variations. First, other standards besides those based on accurate and proper outcomes must be included; this means standards such as those based on equal, consistent, and non-discriminatory treatment. It might also include standards based on values such as privacy and confidentiality. Secondly, the very fact that important interests of a person are in issue gives a special focus to the process, a focus which would not be required by the simple concern for effectiveness.[3] Thirdly, and closely connected to the second, the fact that important personal interests are in issue, indeed that rights are at stake, may tilt the process so that a greater effort than otherwise would be warranted should be made to avoid mistaken decisions to the detriment of the person.

We now have a scheme for the design of procedures. At both stages economy should be a major concern and the most significant factor in achieving economy is to keep the direct costs to a minimum. A certain tension may exist between stages one and two, since the factors relating to fairness to some degree compete with the effective realization of social goals. The resolution of that tension was considered earlier.[4] With this framework of design in mind, we should now examine the different procedural forms within it. It will become clear in doing so that the classes of decisions based on applying authoritative standards and exercising discretion contain within their boundaries considerable diversity. They include the great mass of decisions made by courts, tribunals, and a variety of administrative officials. The routine application of a clear rule to clear facts by an official, as seen in many areas of administration, is different from the application by a superior court judge of a complex area of law to a complex set of facts, while both differ from the decision of a minister of state to deport a foreign alien on the

[3] See the discussion in sect. 2.2.2. [4] See Ch. 3.

grounds of public interest. Each is recognizably in the same family, but each has a character and identity of its own. The interplay between these two factors, family membership and personal identity, is the key to any attempt at classifying decisions. Since all belong to the same family, we must not expect the divisions between different forms to be too strict; and yet each member has its own character which is worth trying to identify.

8.2.2 Two Categories: Individualized and Collectivized

An initial distinction should be drawn between individualized and collectivized decisions. Individualized decisions are about how one person or perhaps a few people should be treated, while collectivized decisions are about a course of action to be taken in the public interest where a range of people and interests are affected. The distinction should not be taken too strictly, since cases may occur which involve elements of both; nevertheless, different procedural issues tend to follow the distinction.

Collectivized decisions can in turn be divided into two types. In general, collectivized decisions allow substantial discretion and affect a range of parties and interests; the issue might be to solve a specific problem, whether to build another airport, or it might be to draw up rules for general application to individualized cases in the future. The common element is that general policy is made on an issue of collective interest. The differences are that one case relates to a specific issue, while in the other policies have to be settled for the purpose of rule-making. Decisions of collective interest might involve the application of standards—arguably all legal decisions are made according to authoritative standards at some level of generality—but they are usually background standards of such indeterminacy, offering such little guidance, that the decision is better characterized as policy-making rather than standard-application. Moreover, such decisions look to the political process and should respond to the currents of public opinion; they reflect the values common to the political process and attract procedures suited to it. The procedural issues relating to collectivized decisions are considered in Chapters 15 and 16.

8.2.3 Three Groupings: Routine Administration; Basic Adjudication; Policy-based Discretion

The great range of administrative processes based on the application of standards can be divided into three groups: processes of a routine nature, decisions requiring distinct elements of enquiry and judgment, and discretionary processes of a policy kind. The main features of each are as follows.

Routine administration involves the almost mechanical application of a set of criteria to a simple and easily established set of facts. Amongst many examples which could be cited, one which well captures the idea is a university admissions procedure based entirely on obtaining a certain score in the qualifying examination. The decision is made in each case simply according to whether or not the score has been achieved. A similar process applies in areas of licensing and the allocation of benefits. The basis of routine administration is that the decision criteria are clear and precise, that the facts are easily determined and uncontested, and that the application of one to the other requires judgment in only the most elementary sense. Considerations of accuracy and fairness coincide, and since the level of accuracy will be virtually perfect, the level of fairness will be high. The only question is the normative one as to which matters should be settled by routine administration.

At the other end of the spectrum are cases of strong discretion where the decision about how to treat a person is substantially governed by broad policy considerations. The way the parole of prisoners is decided is often a good example: no settled criteria are laid down, and in each case a loose and unspecified notion of what is in the public interest is the determining factor. The process is heavily policy-laden and the prisoner has no claim to a particular outcome, but only that his case be properly considered. Precisely what that means we shall consider later, but the important point is that the decision-maker must decide the individual case as seems best to serve the public interest. That the person should be properly treated is a matter of concern, but is subject to wider policy factors. The object of the process is to advance the public interest in each case, while fair treatment consists in having each person's situation and circumstances enquired into and taken into account in the decision. Again, the normative question is for what sort of cases policy-based discretion should be used.[5]

Between routine administration and policy-based discretion lies the great mass of administrative processes based on the application of authoritative standards. Here decisions are made by the application of standards which require a greater degree of enquiry and judgment, even discretion, than is provided by routine administration, but fall short of strong policy-based discretion. Processes falling within this middle range might be concerned with the allocation of benefits and advantages, the regulation and licensing of activities, or the imposition of penalties. In each case, the decision is made by an enquiry into the facts and a judgment applying authoritative standards to them. Each decision is part of a statutory scheme for the advancement of a certain sense of the common good, but each is also a decision about how a person should be treated. It is in this middle ground that the encounter between the citizen and the administration is most common.

[5] Policy-based discretion is considered more fully in sect. 9.1.

8.2.4 The Middle Ground of Administration: Bureaucratic Administration and Administrative Justice

Within this middle ground, of individualized, adjudicative decisions, two models of how decisions ought to be made compete with each other. One we may call bureaucratic administration, the other administrative justice. The first looks primarily to the need to administer an area of activity, whether through allocation, regulation, or imposition, effectively and efficiently within the scope of available resources. The goal is to maximize the common good as expressed through the statutory scheme, a matter to be achieved by an aggregate of accurate and proper decision-making. Individual cases are significant only as elements in achieving acceptable aggregates. The second model, the administrative justice model, shares some of these features but has a different emphasis. Here the main concern is to treat each person fairly by upholding the standards of fair treatment expressed in the statutory scheme, together with standards deriving from other sources. The primary object is still an accurate and proper application of authoritative standards, but the emphasis now is on accuracy and propriety in each case, not just in the aggregate. In addition, fair treatment may require compliance with standards besides those relating to accurate and proper application of outcome-based standards. Although there is much common ground between the two models, each marches to a different tune, with a different emphasis and a competing normative basis.[6] It is important to consider these two models in more detail in order to draw out the implications for procedures.

The model of bureaucratic administration as a distinct and dominant form of process owes much to Max Weber's notion of formal legal authority and its close association with the workings of modern bureaucracies.[7] Many will be familiar with Weber's image of officials applying rules according to logical analysis, where the rules are comprehensive, largely self-contained, and separated in their application from ethical and political principles. The virtues of bureaucratic decision-making are efficiency and calculability, with analogies to the formal processes of accounting and the efficiency of market capitalism. The overall impression is of rules being applied in a bloodless and logical way to the facts that come before them. Now we must be careful not to over-simplify a theory which does much to illustrate the features of law in modern societies;[8] the point of present interest, however, is not the

[6] Some might wish to add a third model which acquires part of this middle ground, namely professional judgment; see J. Mashaw, *Bureaucratic Justice* (Yale University Press, New Haven, Conn., 1983). This is dealt with in sect. 9.1, not as a separate model, but as a sub-set of the above models.

[7] See M. Weber, *Economy and Society*, ed. by G. Roth and C. Wittich (University of California Press, Berkeley, Cal., 1978), i, pt. 1, ch. 111 and ii, 654–8, 809–15.

[8] For a fuller account see D. J. Galligan, *Discretionary Powers* (Clarendon Press, Oxford, 1986), 65–85.

merits of the theory itself, but its legacy in the modern understanding of administrative authority. Formal legal authority can be modified to take account of the rich texture of administrative decisions, of the open-ended nature of standards, and of the prevalence of discretion and policy. Nevertheless, the idea that the primary concern of administrative decision-making is to achieve certain clearly defined ends remains the foundation. According to M. Bayles: 'The goal of bureaucratic investigation [that is, administration] is to implement a purpose or policy set by others';[9] J. Mashaw writes in a similar vein: 'Administration—the accurate application of rules—appeals not to the impersonality of a conflict-resolving process, but to the impersonality of the rules'.[10] To these ideas must be added the pressure on officials within organizations to achieve demanding goals and targets under stress and often with inadequate resources.

This model of administration is one of the major organizing principles of modern government. It reflects the ethos of bureaucratic institutions and expresses a commitment to effectiveness and efficiency to the maximum levels possible with limited time and resources. In a curious way, it suggests the absence of a relationship between the official and the citizen. The official, whose responsibility is fully discharged by applying the rules, has no obligation to the person affected, who in turn has no special claim on the official, so that even the herding of people into cattle-trains for deportation and death can be characterized as the meeting of targets and the fulfilment of quotas—a mere matter of routine administration.[11]

What is missing from the administrative model is the simple point that individualized processes are not only about efficient and effective decisions, but are also about the treatment of persons. Such processes occur within a relationship between the official and the person, a relationship grounded in understandings which draw on basic moral and political values. We have seen how this framework of understandings affects individualized processes.[12] It recognizes that each person's case has to be properly considered, thereby giving a direction and emphasis which is missing in the administrative model. Indeed, we have here the germ of the administrative justice model, or, as I would prefer, the fair treatment model. Its major premise is that each administrative process is an exercise of authority over a person or group, thus creating a relationship which by its very nature introduces values and considerations quite different from pure administration. We have, in other words, to take notice of a set of normative considerations on the basis of which an alternative and competing model of administration can be constructed.

[9] *Procedural Justice*, n. 1 above, 170.

[10] For fuller explanation of the notion of bureaucratic investigation, see Mashaw, *Due Process in the Administrative State*, n. 1 above, 227.

[11] For the development of this idea, see Z. Baumann, *Modernity and the Holocaust* (Polity Press, London, 1989).

[12] See sect. 2.2.2.

This may seem paradoxical. Surely the primary object within each model is to achieve accurate outcomes and, after all, the argument running through this book is that the core of fairness is treatment according to authoritative standards. Indeed, it might be thought that, in distinguishing between the two models, I am in danger of falling back on a soft dignitarian theory of the very kind earlier rejected. The paradox is easily resolved. The fair treatment model retains the proper and accurate application of authoritative standards at its centre, but draws on a wider range of standards than that required to achieve the statutory objects. Inherent in the model is the idea that the very process of applying standards requires an enquiry into the position of the person, into the facts and circumstances of each person's case. It builds on the idea of decision-making as a social process rather than a purely logical activity, on the inherent indeterminacy and contingency of standards, and on the need to construct facts from inadequate evidence. These factors, normative, logical, and social, taken as a whole, provide a distinct model of individualized decision-making with fair treatment at its centre.

The competition between the two models of administration has consequences for procedures. The main task for bureaucratic administration is to devise procedures which lead to accurate and proper outcomes, tempered by the need for economy and efficiency. On this approach, the direct costs of procedures are set against the social good in the effective realization of social goals. The set-off might take various forms, depending on the level of achievement of social goals; the higher the level, the more exacting the procedures. What the level of achievement should be is a matter of policy. The fair treatment model, with its emphasis on each case and on doing justice in that case through the proper application of authoritative standards, is likely to need even more exacting procedures. A mistaken outcome on this model is not just a failure to achieve a social good, but has the moral connotations of treating a person unfairly. The need to take adequate measures against such mistakes is likely to increase direct costs. It may also be necessary to tilt procedures in such a way as to reduce the risks of mistakes which are to the detriment of the person concerned, with a consequential reduction in the level of achievement of general social goals. Procedures to protect non-outcome values will also have to be adopted.

Having seen the differences, how do we choose between the two models? Do we characterize administrative processes as primarily directed to social goals, or do we see them as the expression of a relationship of authority between officials and citizens? This is the classic question which has appeared in many forms and to which different answers have been given. In criminal justice, Herbert Packer's famous distinction between the crime control and due process models is one instance of it.[13] Amongst public

[13] H. Packer, *The Criminal Sanction* (Stanford University Press, Stanford, Conn., 1969).

lawyers, it lies behind such distinctions as green and red light theories,[14] and has long divided the field between those who see public law as directed towards facilitating the achievement of governmental purposes, and others who think it is to do with protecting the rights and interests of individuals or groups.[15] These questions, however, are somewhat artificial since the choice is already determined for us: a society which respects the individuals and groups within it is committed to the fair treatment model, and that commitment follows from the recognition that people have rights about the way they are treated by government. To insist on fair treatment of persons by administrative bodies is to draw on those implicit commitments and understandings at the very base of the relationship between the citizen and the state.

The choice, in other words, is no real choice, since the issue is already settled at a deeper level of principle; at that level, the achievement of social goals is mediated through the fair treatment of persons. This can be brought out even more forcefully by considering the consequences of adopting the bureaucratic administration model; it would amount to claiming that administrative processes are simply about achieving social goals, and that the rights and interests of persons affected do not count, except to the extent that they coincide with such goals; fair treatment and individualized justice would not then enter into consideration. Such a view is palpably unacceptable.[16] This is not to say that the fair treatment model applies to all administrative processes; but it is to claim that wherever those processes affect persons in significant ways it should be the dominant model.

The practical problem in devising procedures is that the bureaucratic administration model, because it better matches the internal dynamics of administrative bodies, will be the natural and dominant model. The result is that special efforts will be needed to curb that natural hegemony in order to support the fair treatment model. Perfect realization of the fair treatment model may never be possible, but the aim should be to devise procedures which guarantee proper treatment according to authoritative standards, at least to the levels required by the principles discussed in Chapter 3. To achieve even those levels is no small task.

[14] C. Harlow and R. Rawlings, *Public Law and Administration* (Weidenfeld and Nicholson, London, 1984).

[15] Compare H. W. R. Wade, *Administrative Law* (6th edn., Clarendon Press, Oxford, 1992) with Harlow and Rawlings, *Public Law and Administration*, n. 14 above.

[16] Of course the difficulties of making the fair treatment model effective in protecting rights and interests are considerable: see the critique by D. J. McBarnett in *Conviction* (Macmillan, London, 1983). But that is a second-order problem; the first-order issue is to understand that, at the level of principle, the normative case for the fair treatment model is compelling.

8.3 ADJUDICATION AND FAIR TREATMENT

The thesis I wish to put forward in this section has two parts. The first is that a natural affinity exists between the fair treatment or administrative justice model of administration and an adjudicative mode of procedures. In order to support this thesis, it will be necessary to spend some time unravelling the notion of adjudication. The second part of the thesis qualifies the first, the claim being that the adjudicative mode is unsuitable for various kinds of administrative processes. In order to provide for fair treatment in these contexts, it is necessary to think imaginatively about alternative procedures which respond to contextual factors, while at the same time leading to the proper application of authoritative standards.

8.3.1 The Adjudicative Mode

We should begin by untangling the terminology and identifying different senses of adjudication. First, a distinction may be drawn between a broad concept and a narrow one. In a broad sense, all standard-application decisions are adjudicative, in that they require judgment in applying standards to facts. Most administrative decisions involve the application of standards and are adjudicative in that sense. In a narrow sense, adjudication represents only a small segment of decisions based on the application of standards and generally is confined to those processes used by civil and criminal courts. The narrow sense can in turn be divided into adversarial adjudication, as associated with common law courts, and the more inquisitorial approval which is characteristic of continental European court processes.[17] Before considering the narrower, more specialized sense, let us identify the character of adjudication in its broad, generic sense.

In its generic sense, adjudication is a combination of language, logic, and values. As a matter of language, we use the term 'adjudication' in association with the idea of judging. Judging in its focal sense connotes the determination of an issue according to settled standards. The more indeterminate and abstract the standard, so that a decision becomes more a matter of choosing between different possibilities, the less appropriate is the notion of adjudication. But language is never so precise that the term will not be used loosely and in ways which are analogous to, rather than central instances of, judging.

Once language has staked the context of adjudication as the determination of an issue according to standards, a certain logic takes over. The very process of judgment according to standards points to a distinct mode of reasoning, a mode which requires the identification and interpretation of

[17] The term 'non-adversarial adjudication' is best avoided because the inquisitorial form is still to a degree adversarial.

standards, the gathering of evidence and the marshalling of facts, and a judgment on those facts according to the standards. These elements taken together constitute a frame within which to view adjudication and to devise distinct sets of procedures. But it does not take us far enough; without more, all standard-application decisions would have to be considered adjudication. There would be nothing to distinguish the procedures suited to bureaucratic administration from those appropriate to individualized justice. If the two modes are to be separated procedurally, some additional element is needed to define adjudication.

The additional element is to be found not in logic but in values. In order to characterize adjudication as a distinctive procedural mode, it must be linked to a foundation of values. The concept of adjudication is prescriptive and value-laden, and various attempts have been made to capture the precise values at issue. Some have found the distinctiveness of adjudication in the nature of the standards. The standards characteristic of adjudication, it is said, are measures of fault and blame, unlike those of bureaucratic administration which are clear and precise rules. According to Bayles: 'the common law has traditionally involved judgments of fault-violation of a contract, commission of a crime or tort. . . . In making judgments of fault, the norms used are moral norms'.[18] Those norms, however, may be buried in social values, awaiting extrapolation by the courts, and requiring judgment and discretion. The question is not so much who did what, but who is to be preferred 'when specific interests and the public values on which they are connected conflict. This entitlement-awarding goal gives a distinctive cast to adjudication.'[19]

These arguments are interesting but confused. In the first place, attempts to distinguish adjudication from administration according to the nature of the standards applied by the courts is unpromising. Whatever the position might have been at common law, the courts are now regularly required to apply standards of all kinds, ranging from those clearly based on moral notions to those, such as many of the rules of taxation, where the issue is simply what do they mean and do certain facts fall within them. Whatever differences there might be between the standards, the judicial processes for applying them is constant and it would be difficult to classify some processes as adjudicative, others not. A second problem with Bayles' analysis is that it slips from classifying adjudication on the basis of certain kinds of standards to characterizing it as 'entitlement awarding'. The two are not the same. Entitlements can arise under standards of various kinds besides those which are 'moral norms'; indeed, in a modern legal system it is commonplace for rights to be created by rules which are far removed from moral norms. Rights may be created under the most technical-looking set of administrative rules.

[18] Bayles, *Procedural Justice*, n. 1 above, 169.
[19] Mashaw, *Due Process in the Administrative State*, n. 1 above, 231.

Bayles is right in suggesting a connection between adjudication and rights, but wrong in thinking that either is joined in some special way to standards based on fault or moral notions more generally.

Another attempt to catch the distinctiveness of adjudication is based on the independence of the decision-maker.[20] The argument is that adjudication requires a body, typically a court or tribunal, which is able to judge the matter from a position of detachment and impartiality in relation to both the parties and the issue. In the administrative context this means that a tribunal to which an appeal lies acts in an adjudicative manner, but that the primary decision-maker does not, at least not when he is an official within a government department or administrative body. But now, while impartiality is a vital element of adjudication, it is not clear that independence in this sense is also necessary. Institutional independence might be one element which helps to secure impartiality, but it does not follow that an official is barred from impartiality by mere membership of an institution. There is no reason to assume that a welfare officer within a government department, or even the minister himself, cannot act impartially and, therefore, in an adjudicative way in deciding specific issues.

It depends on exactly what lack of independence means. If it means that the official must toe a certain line or that his decisions are subject to intervention by other officials, then lack of independence in that sense will destroy impartiality. But whether impartiality is undermined by one's institutional commitments is a question of fact which has to be determined by close examination of the context. The influence a department or other institution can exert over an official is certainly a major factor to consider in allocating adjudicative tasks, and in practice a separation of officials exercising adjudicative authority from departmental structures may be a wise strategy. But such independence, while an incident of adjudication, does not capture its primary sense or express the values at its centre.

8.3.2 Adversarial Adjudication: The Importance of Participation

A third attempt to identify the core sense of adjudication has been of such influence that it should be considered more fully. This is the account of adversarial adjudication put forward by L. L. Fuller,[21] which follows closely the mode of procedure developed by the courts in common law countries. The claim is that adversarial adjudication has the following elements. First, the parties participate in a special way which consists in each being able to present arguments and proof towards a decision in its favour. Secondly, the parties and the adjudicator are in a special relationship which requires

[20] The case is well expressed in G. Richardson, *Prisoners, Patients and Process* (Weidenfeld and Nicholson, London, 1993), 64–5.

[21] L. L. Fuller, 'The Forms and Limits of Adjudication' (1978) 92 *Harvard L Rev.* 353.

the latter to base decisions on the proofs and argument which have been presented by the parties. The adjudicator is not free to seek out additional material, and impartiality between the parties is of course fundamental. The third element is that the dispute must be settled on the basis of standards which are acknowledged by the parties as appropriate. The standards need not have the precision of rules but may well be of a more abstract nature.[22]

These elements combine to form a coherent whole, the distinctive mark of which is, according to Fuller, the mode of participation of the parties. Each is able to present proofs and reasoned arguments in its favour, and the decision must be founded on that basis. The adversarial nature of the procedure is its hallmark. However, despite hints of timelessness made on its behalf, this conception of adjudication is tied closely to the way courts proceed in common law jurisdictions. The emphasis there falls on the special nature of the relationship between the judge and the parties: the judge's role in fact-finding is essentially passive; the evidence and the arguments come from the parties; and the judge must decide on the basis of that alone. The particularity of this approach becomes clear when we compare it with continental legal systems, where adjudication has a more inquisitorial character and where it is not uncommon for the judge to direct the collection of evidence and to stimulate lines of enquiry.[23] An active role in fact-finding is part of a more active role generally: in defining the issues, in bringing the parties towards settlement, and in being involved at each stage of the proceedings. The story of how such important differences between the two came about is well told in the writings of M. Damaska,[24] whose thesis is that different attitudes to politics and authority, different approaches to the judicial system and the legal profession, and different historical experiences are all part of the explanation.

The point of sharpest contrast between adversarial adjudication and its inquisitorial counterpart is that, while the civil law judge controls the proceedings in several ways, that control in the common law trial is largely in the hands of the parties. Arguments can be waged as to exactly how different the two systems really are (and the divisions may be less sharply defined than is often suggested) and as to which system is better.[25] The disadvantages of

[22] Fuller, 'The Forms and Limits of Adjudication', n. 21 above. For further discussion, see P. Weiler, 'Two Models of Judicial Decision-making' (1968) 46 *Canadian B Rev.* 406.

[23] See B. Kaplan, 'Civil Procedure—Reflection on the Comparison of Systems' (1959–60) 9 *Buffalo L Rev.* 409 and J. Langbein, 'The German Advantage in Civil Procedure' (1985) 52 *U of Chicago L Rev.* 823.

[24] His main ideas are collected together in *The Faces of Justice and State Authority* (Yale University Press, New Haven, Conn., 1986).

[25] For defence of the common law approach to adversary adjudication, see M. R. Gross, 'The American Advantage: The Value of Inefficient Litigation' (1987) 85 *Michigan L Rev.* 734 and J. Resnick, 'Managerial Judges' (1982) 96 *Harvard L Rev.* 376.

the common law approach are well documented,[26] but the important point is this: the control which the parties hold over the proceedings, and the manner in which the trial is a contest between the parties, suggest that the real value of adversarial adjudication is not its effectiveness in fairly and accurately applying the law, nor even in resolving a dispute; the real value lies in the quite different idea that each party should have control of the conduct and resolution of its own disputes. The parties shape the issues, address the evidence, and present their arguments, where the test of success is almost entirely whether or not they win the contest.

That last idea is reflected in Fuller's account where the most striking feature of adjudication is said to be the importance given to the participation of the parties and to the control they then exert over the proceedings. That is a bold claim which makes participation the normative base from which all else follows.[27] Fuller is right to the extent that any conception of adjudication rests on values, the foundational value for him being participation. As Fiss has remarked, Fuller saw participation in the curial process as being on the same plane as participation in politics and bargaining;[28] in each context, participation constitutes an essential element in the idea of citizenship. But while the method of approach is right, Fuller's conclusions are strange, for two main reasons. The first reason is that the strict adversarial form on which Fuller relies is both highly particularistic to certain historical circumstances and deeply unstable. Indeed, there is good reason to think that, even within the trial itself, adversarial adjudication will in time give way to more active judges and a more concerted effort to get at the truth. Already there are signs to that effect in the jurisdictions most closely associated with the adversarial model.[29] Some argue even that in any case the common law trial has never conformed to a strict adversarial model.[30] Judges and courts, it is claimed, have often gone well beyond the passive and circumscribed role marked out for them in adversarial adjudication.

The second reason for doubting Fuller's analysis is revealed by asking why participation should be regarded as the most important value at issue? Participation, I suggest, is most potent as an instrumental value, as a means to ends, besides which any role it may have as an end in itself is secondary. Fuller never really asks why participation is so important; he sees it as somehow linked to protection of the individual, but never explains exactly how. The result is a beguiling but hollow analysis. Had he followed the chain

[26] They are summarized in R. Eggleston, 'What Is Wrong with the Adversary Process?' (1974) 49 *Australian LJ* 428.

[27] For further discussion, see O. Fiss, 'The Forms of Justice' (1979) 93 *Harvard L Rev.* 1.

[28] Ibid.

[29] See A. Chayes, 'The Role of the Judge in Public Law Litigation' (1976) 89 *Harvard L Rev.* 1281 and J. Resnick, 'Managerial Judges', n. 25 above.

[30] T. Eisenberg and S. L. Yeazell, 'The Ordinary and the Extraordinary in Institutional Litigation' (1980) 93 *Harvard L Rev.* 465.

of reasoning, of which there are hints in his account, and explained why participation is so important, his conclusion might have been different. For the real importance of participation, in the trial as in administrative processes, is to lead to proper and accurate treatment according to authoritative standards. That is the end towards which participation is a means; it is also the real basis for individual protection and for the upholding of rights. It is indeed the end earlier described as individualized justice, and an appropriate procedural form for producing that end is adjudication.

Fuller's account led him not only to an odd view of adjudication, but also to extol as timeless what is really a transient historical form. We need only take the short step from the adversarial model to the inquisitional sense of adjudication to realize that participation by the parties is one element in adjudication, not its defining feature. Inquisitorial procedures show that the fundamental object of adjudication is to provide a means for achieving proper and accurate outcomes, not to provide a closed contest within which the parties have control. We can then also see why the absence of a contest between parties does not necessarily remove the very notion of adjudication; for again a contest is an instance of adjudicative processes, not its defining element. Adjudication is a suitable mode of procedure even when the only question is how a particular case should be dealt with according to a set of standards. Indeed, reflection on the nature of inquisitorial adjudication brings home the affinity between it and administrative processes;[31] to the extent that they are about the treatment of individuals according to standards, administrative processes fit neatly into the mould of inquisitorial adjudication.

8.3.3 Adjudication and Fair Treatment: A Synthesis

The various attempts considered above to find the normative basis of adjudication are instructive, but none is entirely satisfactory. Each recognizes that the idea of adjudication as a distinct procedural form is based on certain values, but none succeeds in showing satisfactorily what the values are. The true position is, I suggest, both simpler and more general than the above accounts allow. My suggestion is that the value which gives the adjudicative process an identity and significance is the fair treatment of the person whose interests are at stake; the value, in other words, of individualized justice. Fair treatment in such contexts consists in treatment according to authoritative standards, and adjudication connotes a mode of process especially suited to that end. It does not dictate the precise procedures, for even within the adjudicative framework different procedures might serve equally well. But the close match with fair treatment is borne out in the standard

[31] See further G. Osborne, 'Inquisitorial Procedure in the Administrative Appeals Tribunal—A Comparative Perspective' (1982) 13 *Fed. L Rev.* 151.

conception of adjudication which has the following features: an issue to be resolved, which includes but is not confined to a dispute between two or more parties and which may concern the affairs of only one; where the issue will be determined according to settled standards; which itself requires impartiality on the part of a decision-maker; where in order to apply the standards, an inquiry must be made into the relevant facts; and where the party or parties will usually be able to present their cases. The force and coherence of this conception of adjudication derives from the importance of dealing with the party or parties fairly according to authoritative standards. Adjudication is functionally effective in determining particular cases according to authoritative standards, while it is normatively compelling in thereby doing justice in each case.[32] In making the standards concrete in the particular case, the person's situation must be inquired into, not as a thing to be administered where error is merely a social cost, but in order to determine what rights are at issue and what treatment should be meted out. This special concern for individualized justice is the hallmark of the adjudicative process.

Having established the affinity between fair treatment and adjudication, we may now draw together the conclusions for administrative processes. One is that the adjudicative mode is particularly apt whenever administrative processes are concerned with individualized justice. A second conclusion is that the adoption of an adjudicative mode does not mean a commitment to complex, court-like procedures; the adjudicative mode provides a framework within which quite simple procedures may be adequate to secure the proper application of authoritative standards. And finally, the mere fact that we tend not to think of administrative processes in this way, that we tend to distinguish sharply between court-like procedures and administrative, is not an argument against the close association between adjudication and fair treatment. The tendency within administrative law towards requiring a more adjudicative mode of procedures in standard areas of administration is a recognition of that association.

8.3.4 Variables in Applying Standards

Within the framework of adjudication, several variables affect the precise form that procedures ought to have. Here the following are considered briefly: the nature of the standards; the facts; the personal interests in issue; the element of dispute; and the nature of the administrative body.

Standards

The standards governing administrative processes can be grouped according to several features, from amongst which I shall deal with just three. The first

[32] For further discussion, see P. Robardet, 'Should We Abandon the Adversarial Model in Favour of the Inquisitorial Model' in 12 *Dalhousie LJ, Commissions of Inquiry*.

is the degree of determinacy. How precise the standards are is a matter of degree, and beyond the virtually mechanical standards of routine administration, the level of precision varies greatly. Standards may be fixed but still be in need of interpretation; or they may just specify the matters to take into account, or state the guiding policies and values, leaving it to the official to decide on more precise meanings and applications. The degrees of determinacy are often expressed in the language of discretion. The level of determinacy of standards should influence the design of procedures: where rules can be applied without difficulty and problems of interpretation are rare, simple procedures will do, unless other factors point to the contrary; where the standards call for an element of judgment, even discretion, not just in understanding the standards but also in relating them to the facts, then the process becomes more open to argument and discussion. More careful consideration and deliberation are then integral to the process, and the party affected has a stronger claim to involvement in issues both of interpretation and fact-finding. If the discretionary element expands to such a level that the process would be better characterized as policy-based discretion rather than standard-application, the procedural mode will also be different.

Another method of classification of standards is based on their substantive content, especially where elements of moral judgment are involved. Such elements are likely to be present when the standards turn on assessments of personal action, whether in determining responsibility, blame, merits, or deserts. Judgments of these kinds have a special character and are very different from the decision that a transaction is liable to tax, or that one's examination marks are not high enough for the award of a scholarship. The application of standards which have moral connotations means delving closely into the actions and situation of the person, and so has important implications for the design of procedures.

A third method of classification is whether the standards depend for their application on expert or professional knowledge. Perhaps the most familiar area is the standards of professional judgment in medical matters; whether a patient needs treatment and what form it should take are decisions for the medical doctor, to be made by applying specialized knowledge and training and with which anyone lacking that expert experience would be loath to interfere. Decisions based on specialized knowledge occur across a wide range of activities, including science, technology, and engineering. In some cases the expert is used as a witness with the final decision being left to someone else, while in other cases the expert makes the decision. The procedural approach to standards based on expert knowledge can vary greatly; in judicial trials, expert knowledge and its application are often keenly contested, while in administrative contexts they are normally accepted without question. The tradition overall has been to allow autonomy to experts and professionals and to treat their judgments with great respect, not only in the case of a doctor's clinical judgment, but also in relation to others, whether they be social workers, clinical psychologists, or penologists. It seems, however, that the tradition of respect is being eroded, with a certain scepticism about expert judgments and professional knowledge taking its place. As a consequence, interest is growing in procedural formality as a way of guarding against inaccuracy and misjudgment. One way forward is to insist on more extensive procedures at the point of decision, but it is also worth considering whether procedural strategies, other than a greater reliance on adjudication, could be more successful.[33] From this brief discussion it should at least be clear that the substantive nature of standards is a significant variable in the design of procedures.

Facts

While questions of fact and the interpretation of facts are closely connected to interpreting and applying standards, the fact-finding element is itself a major variable in procedural design. In the adversarial trial, responsibility for proving the facts falls to the parties; but what there seems in the nature of things is really rather exceptional, the more natural and usual course being that the state, through its agencies and officials, should be involved in collecting evidence and establishing the facts, usually in co-operation with or at least with some contribution from the parties. Administrative bodies are typical in this regard and usually have powers to enquire into an issue in order to acquire evidence, sometimes from the party affected, sometimes from other sources. The approach of each authority to fact-finding and the nature of the facts to be found are themselves major variables in procedural design. Most authorities will have to make some enquiry into the evidence, but their capacity to do so will vary, with some empowered to investigate fully and reliably, others forced to settle for cursory enquiries and incomplete evidence.[34] In some matters, the authority's own enquiries will be adequate, while in others it will depend on the party affected supplying the information. The nature of the facts themselves adds another set of variables. The simpler the facts and the easier they are to ascertain, the simpler the procedures needed; the more complex they are, the greater the need for more exacting procedures for gathering and testing the evidence. And, finally, the shape of procedures will be influenced by the extent to which evidence is linked to the affairs of the parties and can be provided only by them, rather than obtained by the authority from other sources.

[33] See sect. 8.5.

[34] G. Ganz in her book *Administrative Procedures* (Sweet and Maxwell, London, 1974) gives examples of the different methods of investigation and offers some explanation of why one method rather than another is chosen.

The Impact on Rights and Interests

The guiding principle is that the more important the rights and interests at stake, the stronger the person's claim to a high level of accuracy and propriety in applying the standards, and in turn the stronger the claim to more exacting procedures. This principle explains why the procedures of the criminal trial and the resources available for them differ so much from those allowed in deciding welfare benefits. We would not normally expect administrative processes to attract the procedural bounty of the criminal trial, but we should insist that the comparative importance of the interests dealt with by administrative bodies be reflected in procedures. The decision whether to license ramblers to enter a special nature reserve is logically little different from a decision allocating welfare benefits, but because the personal interests are different and more important in the latter case, it would be reasonable to expect a more exacting process than in the former. This general point can be applied across the spectrum of personal interests.

The relative importance of the interests, although of major concern, is not the only factor affecting procedures; their nature and the consequences for them are also relevant. This can be illustrated through the example of moral interests mentioned above, the point being that where a party's interests are linked to moral factors, special considerations come into play.[35] Condemnation through the criminal trial is the most striking example, while a lesser but none the less real degree of opprobrium can be seen in a range of other cases. That one has acted unreasonably, unfairly, or unconscionably, or is not fit to carry on a profession or vocation, are all judgments spiced with moral condemnation. Each calls for an investigation into the life of the person, into his knowledge and understanding, his motives and purposes, in a manner which goes well beyond an objective enquiry into facts. The presence of that moral element in the criminal trial provides much of the explanation for the high level of procedures adopted there. One of the strengths, indeed, of the adversarial trial is that the parties are unrestricted in the lengths to which they may go in putting before the court the whole picture and in a sense the whole person.[36] The same idea in a modified form may be introduced into administrative processes which have an element of moral assessment and condemnation. From these examples the general point can be extrapolated that the nature of interests, and the kinds of judgments which may be made about them, is a relevant variable in settling procedures.

[35] For further discussion of this idea, see Bayles, *Procedural Justice*, n. 1 above, 169 and J. Mashaw, *Bureaucratic Justice* (Yale U.P., Newhaven, Conn., 1983), 29–31.

[36] The early jurisdiction of the Chancery Court is, perhaps, the best example of this idea. See S. F. C. Milsom, *Historical Foundations of the Common Law* (2nd edn., Butterworths, London: Boston, 1981).

Where the judgment has a moral dimension, the procedures should ensure that any judgment is properly formed and rigorously tested.

The Element of Dispute

Most individualized administrative processes do not initially involve a dispute between two parties. They are more likely to be bilateral processes in which the official decides how a party should be treated. That may change when an appeal is made to a tribunal or other body, since an element of contest between the party and the primary authority is likely then to be created. However, first-level decisions do sometimes involve two or more parties, and so we should consider to what extent an element of dispute between them influences procedures. It is clear that a readiness to characterize appeal processes as adjudicative and therefore suited to adversarial procedures stems partly from the element of dispute. The reason is that the existence of a dispute means a contest about the facts, about the existence and characterization of evidence, or over the interpretation of standards. Once there is a contest, the case for allowing each party to present its case and to counter that of its opponent is compelling. This does not mean adopting a full adversarial procedure and a power of independent enquiry by the deciding authority will still be important. It does mean, however, that an element of dispute is a significant factor in having procedures which allow the parties a fuller involvement than might otherwise be warranted.

The Nature of the Authority

A final variable in the setting of procedures within an adjudicative framework is the character of the authority itself. A number of factors are relevant. One is whether the authority has the capacity to conduct its own enquiries in obtaining evidence or whether it is largely confined to the material put before it by the party. Where the authority gathers the evidence itself, procedures are needed to allow some scope for testing by the party. In the opposite case, where the material comes mainly from the party, the authority itself needs the opportunity to scrutinize it; as result, the procedural emphasis in each case will be different. Another factor is the level of training and expertise of the decision-makers, a matter on which the levels of competence can be strikingly variable. The more expert and better trained officials, as members of tribunals typically are, can be trusted with a substantial element of judgment and discretion, with an appraisal of the specific case, and can be relied on to reach a sound conclusion. Officials entrusted with primary decisions are often in a different position because of poor education and training. So, while it may be useful at the appeal level to have procedures which allow for a more adversarial exploration of the case, decision-making at the primary levels will often be better served by a carefully structured and somewhat simplified approach. This may indicate a need for simple procedures which are easy to follow and as uncontentious as possible; that need will in turn often be reinforced by pressures of time and scarcity of resources.

The aim of this section has been to show how various factors can influence the design of procedures within a broadly adjudicative framework. The factors considered here are of particular importance, but there may be others which have a role. The idea behind the analysis is that the adjudicative mode requires only that a certain approach be taken, namely, that each case should be considered and properly determined according to authoritative standards. Within that approach different procedural sets may be suitable and, even with respect to the same context, there is no reason to think that a unique arrangement has to be found, since the same end might be achieved equally well by different procedures. It is also to be expected that the different variables might themselves point in opposing directions and that some compromise amongst them might have to be found. However, it should not normally be too difficult to order the variables according to their relative importance in a given context and on that basis to devise a suitable procedural regime.

8.4 BEYOND ADJUDICATION

The discussion so far may appear to rest on the tacit assumption that adjudicative procedures are uniquely suited to the fair treatment of persons according to authoritative standards. While that assumption does indeed hold true in many cases it is not always the case, and in this section I shall show how it may need to be modified. Despite a natural fit between fair treatment in individualized processes and adjudication, adjudicative procedures have their shortcomings and in some contexts quite different procedures may be more effective in securing fair treatment and respect for rights. The first step, therefore, is to consider the drawbacks of adjudication, while the second is to suggest a more imaginative approach in developing alternative procedural forms.

8.4.1 The Shortcomings of Adjudication

The first shortcoming relates to time and resources. The adjudicative mode does not necessarily require elaborate procedures, let alone anything like a judicial trial, but it does require a careful examination of each case. Evidence has to be gathered and facts determined; standards must be understood and properly interpreted; and the elements of discretion and open texture need to be reflected upon. And yet in many administrative contexts, the time and resources needed to pursue an adjudicative approach are unavailable. The pressures on officials to act quickly and to decide a large number of matters in a short time is a constant theme in studies of primary decision-making; speed and volume, however, are the natural enemies of accuracy and individualized justice. In a recent study of social security, the researchers stated that: 'The difficulties of achieving accuracy when under pressure to process claims quickly was perhaps the strongest point to emerge from our own survey of adjudication officers.'[37] The research found that, although officers distributing income support were meant to adjudicate, their own descriptions of their work suggest that it would be more accurately described as routine administration.[38] For however good their intentions might be, the officers were overborne by administrative pressures and found themselves lapsing from adjudication into routine administration. The tension shown there between the need for speed and the shortage of resources, on the one hand, and the concern for accurate individualized judgments, on the other hand, is endemic in administrative decision-making, especially at the primary level. The result often is poor decision-making, with the administrative justice model giving way to bureaucratic administration, and the level of protection of rights accordingly reduced.

It might be thought that this does not matter, since provision will normally be made for appeal to a tribunal or similar body which can then properly examine the case in an adjudicative manner. A glance through the statute book offers support for such a view, for it will be seen that statutory schemes typically say little if anything about procedures at the primary level, while providing elaborate arrangements for appeal or review. The trouble is that only a tiny fraction of cases go on appeal, so that for most parties the primary decision is also the final decision. This is not to deny the importance of appeals, nor to dampen attempts to create more effective and accessible forms of appeal and review; but however creditable such attempts may be, better appeals will never be an adequate substitute for a proper and accurate decision at the primary level.

The need for cheap and fast decision-making is a major obstacle to sustaining an adjudicative mode in administrative processes, but it is not the only obstacle. Another factor is the internal dynamics of organizations which propel decisions towards the mode of bureaucratic administration. Even small organizations are prone to such tendencies, so that the fragmentation of government and administration into small, specialist agencies, noticeable in a number of countries, offers no great promise of change.[39] There is, moreover, an ambivalence at the political and legal levels about the very

[37] J. Baldwin, N. Wikeley, and R. Young, *Judging Social Security* (Clarendon Press, Oxford, 1993), 39.

[38] Ibid. 52.

[39] On this trend towards fragmentation, see N. Lewis, 'Reviewing Change in Government: New Public Management and Next Steps' [1994] *Public Law* 105 and P. Dunleavy, 'The Architecture of the British Central State' (1989) 67 *Public Admin.* 249.

nature and goals of administrative processes. On the one hand, concepts of efficiency, good management, and routine orderliness, each traceable to the Weberian model of formal, rational authority, resonate deeply in modern societies.[40] Despite the dire warnings of post-modernism, these classic features of modern society stubbornly persist. On the other hand, however, the concern to respect individuals and groups, to grant and uphold rights, and to translate ideas won in the high theatre of political philosophy to the low levels of administration, is one of the powerful currents of the age. That ambivalence, which expresses itself in law as well as in politics, is an important part of the explanation for the tension in administration between bureaucratic rationality and adjudicative deliberation.

A second difficulty in maintaining an adjudicative mode in administration is that some processes are unsuitable for it. The reasons for which they might be unsuitable can be illustrated by examples. Take pre-trial processes in criminal justice where police officers have to make a number of decisions ranging from caution and arrest, through detention and questioning, to charge and bail. The standards governing each step are laid down, important rights are at issue, and yet adjudicative procedures do not easily fit. Another example occurs where standards based on expert or specialized knowledge are being applied. This situation is not entirely inhospitable to an adjudicative approach, but the match is not perfect. An expert judgment can be tested for the reliability of the evidence on which it turns, but the judgment itself, the application of expert knowledge to the facts, is reliable according to how advanced the body of knowledge is and how skilful the expert is in applying it. These matters are not easily brought within an adjudicative approach. Other examples could be added, but these two are enough to show the difficulties which can be encountered in casting an adjudicative mode around some administrative processes.

Another set of difficulties derives from aspects of the social context of administration. This can be shown by first considering the debate over welfare rights and the new property solution, and then by noting the problems it failed to solve. In a series of influential writings, R. Reich argued that claims to welfare, using welfare in a broad sense to include a wide range of benefits, ought to be regarded as rights and should be supported by adjudicative procedures.[41] These ideas were based on a conception of welfare as the new property according to which claims to welfare would be taken out of the discretionary sphere and given the status and protection of entitlements. Adjudicative procedures based on settled standards, a proper enquiry into each case, and the right to be heard were thought to be the natural guardians of rights. The doctrines of procedural due process, which were

[40] To pursue these ideas, see Z. Bauman, *Modernity and the Holocaust*, n. 11 above.

[41] R. Reich, 'The New Property' (1964) 73 *Yale LJ* 733, and 'Individual Rights and Social Welfare: the Emerging Legal Issues' (1965) 74 *Yale LJ* 1245.

well-developed in relation to conventional property interests, could easily be extended to this new conception of property. The new property movement was influential in the United States and elsewhere in leading to the judicialization for the first time of many administrative processes dealing with the distribution of welfare benefits.

The new conception of welfare as property and the reliance on adjudicative procedures was not without its critics. According to one critic, a regime of rights and a set of adjudicative procedures to back it will only ever be partially successful in directing and regulating administrative processes.[42] One reason for this derives from the organizational context. Administrative organizations are complex, multi-dimensional, and subject to many influences and processes, whereas adjudicative procedures are simplified and in a sense one-dimensional. The statutory framework is only ever part of the full reality and cannot assimilate the attitudes of officials, their relationships, the informal norms on which they rely, and various other features of an organizational context. At another level, the analysis concentrates on the informal factors which exert great influence over the making of administrative decisions. Many issues will be settled according to informal and unspecified rules; others will be open to bargaining and unofficial understandings between officials and claimants. What went before and what is likely to come later may be as important as any specific, once-and-for-all decision, with the result that procedures which concentrate on the decision itself may be ineffectual in controlling administrative behaviour in a more continuing sense. And, finally, a relationship between the administrative authority and the parties often develops and continues beyond any one decision. The relationship is likely to be complex and accumulative, based on past understandings and future expectations, and at risk of being disrupted in an unhelpful way by attempts at judicialization.

This is a powerful critique, not least in reinforcing the need to understand the social and organizational context of administrative processes in devising procedures. The failure to do so may result in a mismatch between the two, with the result that procedures will fail in their purposes.[43] However, we should be careful not to draw the wrong conclusions. The difficulty of fitting some areas of administration into an adjudicative mode does not mean that all attempts will fail; the close general connection between rights and adjudication remains intact, but may have to be modified or abandoned in some contexts. Where the adjudicative mode has to be abandoned the case for rights remains powerful. The battle for rights has been hard-fought and ought not to be lightly surrendered; nor should it be forgotten that in any

[42] J. Handler, 'Controlling Official Behaviour in Welfare Administration' (1966) 54 *Calif. L Rev.* 479 and *The Conditions of Discretion* (Russel Sage, New York, 1986).

[43] See further T. Prosser, 'Poverty, Ideology and Legality' (1966) 4 *Brit. J of Law and Society* 39.

area of individualized administration, rights and fair treatment are in issue. Rather than returning to a view of administration and government as the conferring of discretionary privileges according to a bureaucratic mode, the conclusion should be that, in some areas at least, alternatives to adjudication need to be devised in order to protect rights and guarantee fair treatment. The task then is to find procedures and methods which are suitable for that purpose.

8.4.2 Alternatives to Adjudication

How then is it possible to design administrative procedures which guarantee fair treatment and the protection of rights, while being responsive to the dynamics of administrative regimes, and while taking account of the organizational structure and the influences and variables at work within it.[44] The place to start is with the first level of decisions, for if administrative justice is not done at the primary level, it is unlikely to be done at all. Lawyers naturally think of appeals and reviews as a solution to poor decisions at the primary levels and willingly devote effort and resources to developing forms of recourse, including appeals to courts, review by tribunals, and investigation by ombudsmen. These are important but fairly much incidental to the real problem of regulating primary decisions. Forms of recourse may have an effect on the attitudes of primary decision-makers, both from the very existence of such forms and from the educational effect of specific rulings. But since little evidence exists to show what that impact is, it would be prudent to assume that it is marginal.[45]

One way of approaching this problem is to analyse carefully the administrative context and then to think imaginatively about the methods and procedures suited to it. At this point, legal procedures and the study of organizations come together, for it is only through understanding both the theory of organizations and the empirical evidence about them that suitable and effective procedures can be devised. Procedural issues then merge into matters covering the training of officials and the building of administrative structures. Officials who are well trained and who have the time and resources to consider each case properly are often the best guarantors of sound decisions. Similarly, the most significant factor in good professional judgment is that the person making the judgment be well trained and that his decisions be tested from time to time by peer review. In these and other cases, decisions depend on attributes more fundamental than procedures: a commitment to sound training, to imaginative methods of quality control,

[44] See further, N. Lacey, 'The Jurisprudence of Discretion: Escaping the Legal Paradigm' in K. Hawkins, *The Uses of Discretion* (Clarendon Press, Oxford, 1992).

[45] This matter is considered at more length in Ch. 13.

and to creating appropriate organizational structures, are amongst the strategies that can be pursued.

However, not all can be left to structure and training, for procedures themselves still have an important role to play. This is well illustrated by the example of pre-trial processes in criminal justice.[46] Decisions in this context, decisions, that is, of police and prosecutors, throw into sharp relief the difficulty of respecting rights within administrative processes. The standards of fair treatment and the rights they generate are clear enough; the difficulty has always been to find ways of making the practice match the principle, that is to say, protecting suspects in an environment which is insulated from the public gaze, where one party holds great power over the other, and where retrospective recourse is notoriously ineffective. At the same time, attempts to introduce an adjudicative mode would be largely inappropriate. The challenge to find alternative procedures has been met in an interesting way by the Parliament of the United Kingdom in legislation and codes of practice, originally passed in 1984 and modified a number of times since.[47] The interesting feature of the statute and codes is that they create procedures which have transformed the relations between the police and the suspect, first by making clear the suspect's rights through clear standards, and secondly by devising elaborate procedures to ensure compliance. The procedures are based on explaining to the suspect each step that is taken and giving reasons for it, recording actions and the reasons for them, making the records available, allowing proper legal representation, recording and sometimes video-taping interviews. These are buttressed by an extensive system of internal checks and reviews of one officer by another, supported by a special body to investigate complaints.

The system is far from perfect, but it has made progress in devising procedures which really do protect the suspect's rights while maintaining respect for authoritative standards. Its success lies in bringing together the dynamics of policing and the culture of the police station, on the one hand, and acceptable normative standards, on the other hand. The procedures are responsive to the police culture itself and, as a result, are not viewed as external constraints imposed from above; indeed the police may come to see the procedures as not only protecting the suspect but also providing a shield for themselves. Now of course, this model cannot easily be transplanted elsewhere, but it does show that, with careful analysis and imaginative thinking, procedural systems can be devised which protect rights and maintain standards of fair treatment, without having to resort to the standard model of adjudication.

[46] See also D. J. Galligan, 'Regulating Pre-Trial Decisions' in I. Dennis (ed.), *Criminal Law and Justice* (Sweet and Maxwell, London, 1987).

[47] Police and Criminal Evidence Act 1984.

9
Forms of Process II

This Chapter continues the analysis of different types of processes. The first section deals with the application of standards which are based on expert or specialist knowledge. Decisions of that kind belong to the family of processes based on applying authoritative standards but raise important issues of their own. In the second section, the object of analysis is policy-based discretion occurring in individualized contexts. This warrants special attention because it combines two objectives which are not easily reconciled: the concern to exercise the discretion according to the public interest, and at the same time, to treat fairly those affected by it. The third section examines the procedural issues which arise in processes of investigation and enquiry. A great variety of special authorities now have powers of investigation and inquiry, and while they are usually preliminary to some further and more final decision, they should also be seen as discrete processes which give rise to special procedural problems. The final section, which occupies a large part of the Chapter, introduces a quite different set of issues, for here we move from cases based on authoritative standards to processes directed at reaching agreement through negotiation and mediation. That is itself a large subject which calls for a full study of its own, but considering the growing interest in this family of process, and taking into account the way in which standard-application cases often adopt elements of negotiation and agreement, a strong case can be made for examining here some of the procedural issues.

9.1 DISCRETION AS PROFESSIONAL JUDGMENT

Administrative decisions are often based on the judgment of an expert or specialist.[1] Doctors and social workers, engineers and architects, to name just a few among many, all have a form of specialist knowledge which can be the decisive factor in an administrative process. In some cases, the decision itself will be made by the specialist applying expert knowledge, the doctor in a mental hospital deciding that a patient requires a certain form of treatment, for example. In other cases, the decision will be made by a non-specialist, such as a judge or tribunal, but with the specialist providing expert

[1] See also sect. 8.4.4.

evidence on which the outcome is likely to turn. Since in both cases the professional judgment based on specialist knowledge will always be influential and often decisive, the questions to consider are, first, what are the specific problems, and, secondly, what kinds of procedures would be suitable for dealing with them.

Professional judgments pose a problem because by their nature they constitute an opinion based on the application of specialist knowledge and training, the implication being that anyone lacking that knowledge and training is unable to assess the merits of the judgment.[2] But while professional judgment is in one sense simply the application of specialist knowledge, in another sense it contains a large element of opinion which might well be characterized as discretion. For expert knowledge has to be applied by reason and judgment, and the process of applying it is of a holistic kind which cannot easily be broken down into more discrete elements. The doctor's judgment that a patient needs treatment of a certain kind, or a social worker's judgment that the emotional welfare of the child requires it to be removed from its environment, are complex assessments of complex situations. They are reached partly by the straightforward application of knowledge, but also partly by a more subjective judgment about the best way of applying that knowledge under conditions of uncertainty, where rival judgments might be equally justified. The expert, when pressed, has to fall back on his claim to special knowledge and experience in making judgments.

What then are the procedural issues in making professional judgments? The primary object is to have accurate judgments, or if accuracy is not quite the right term, to have judgments based on an accurate foundation of facts, to which specialist knowledge can be applied in a reasonable and reliable manner. If professional judgment is accurate in that sense, a party subject to it will be treated properly and fairly according to legal standards. The procedural arrangements for achieving that result will vary according to the context, but a number of interesting problems in relation to professional judgments are of general application. But let us first be clear that a professional judgment has the same elements, the same structure, as any other practical judgment: facts, standards, and the application of standards to the facts. It differs only in the nature of the standards, for it is the standards and their application which invoke expert knowledge. The danger to be guarded against is that the element of expert knowledge will overshadow other elements of the judgment so that the whole appears impervious to scrutiny. Indeed, attempts at scrutiny of any kind will often be regarded as threats to the integrity of the specialist. But without proper understanding and adequate scrutinizing, the potential consequences of unrestrained professional

[2] See M. Bayles, *Procedural Justice* (Kluwer, London, 1990), 175–7.

judgments are alarming: the element of expert opinion may be inflated beyond its proper role; the concern for accurate facts may be obscured; and the usual canons of reasoned scrutiny are at risk of being suspended.[3] Decisions may then be made and actions taken which are unjustifiable according to the basic principles of fair treatment.

This suggests the need to look closely at three aspects of professional judgments: first, the facts; secondly, the standards; and thirdly, the expert opinion itself. As for the first, it is important that doctors, social workers, and experts of other kinds base their opinions on accurate evidence and facts. The decision to take a child into care on the ground that he is at risk of serious emotional damage ought to be based on evidence and facts. Here we may distinguish between ordinary facts, that is, what exactly is going on in the child's home, and a clinical judgment about those facts. The clinical judgment is a matter for the expert, but the ordinary facts are not, and they should be subject to the usual requirements of evidence, proof, and scrutiny. When a clinical judgement is the basis for taking action against a person, the hearing principle should apply to the fact-finding part of the judgment to the same extent as it applies in other contexts. The precise form of hearing will be influenced by the context, but it should allow for disclosure of the evidence on which the professional judgment will be based, the opportunity for the party affected to question that evidence and to put forward other evidence, and the clear articulation by the expert of his assumptions of ordinary fact. The distinction between ordinary facts and a clinical judgment based on those facts is fundamental to good decision-making, but in practice is often overlooked. The risk, then, is of clinical judgments proceeding on the most flimsy evidence, with guesses and suspicions being substituted for hard evidence.[4] The distinction between the facts and an interpretation and judgment about those facts is not always clear or easy to draw; but difficulties at the margin should not obscure the importance of the separation in principle. For here, as elsewhere, the first condition of fair treatment is that a decision be founded on good evidence and sound conclusions of fact. It is understand-able that professional judgments emphasize the element of expert opinion, especially when the overriding concern is for the welfare of the person affected, sometimes at the cost of factual accuracy. But fair treatment is not necessarily the same as treatment which someone else considers in my best interests, and here we are concerned with the conditions of fair treatment.

[3] For a useful study of the expert or specialist perspective, see: W. Carlton, *In Our Professional Opinion: The Primacy of Clinical Judgments in Our Moral Choice* (Notre Dame, Indiana, 1978).

[4] See the wider discussion in P. Bean, *Rehabilitation and Deviance* (Routledge and Kegan Paul, London, 1976) and J. Floud and G. Young, *Dangerousness and Criminal Justice* (Heinemann, London, 1981).

The second element to consider is the standards applied in professional judgment. The first task is to distinguish between truly diagnostic standards, and standards which are of a moral or social kind. The point of the distinction is that the specialist is qualified to apply the standards of his expertise, but not standards which go beyond that and encroach on the moral and social sphere. The psychiatrist may offer expert advice as to whether a patient is suffering from a particular mental disorder, but this expertise does not extend to deciding whether people suffering from that disorder should have treatment forced on them. Similarly, a social worker might be able to judge whether abusive treatment of a child in the home is likely to have serious and lasting effects, but he has no special qualification for deciding that such a child should be removed from the home. In practice, professional experts are often required by statute to make both kinds of judgments, with the risk that the two sets of standards will be run together and the distinctions between them lost. It is wise, however, to keep the two tasks separate and to entrust the second, the decision about moral and social standards, to a separate, independent authority. That is a matter for the design of procedures, but the hearing principle may be effective in directing attention to the existence of the different kinds of standards, differences which are easily lost in the haze of professionalism.

A related problem is that professional standards are often cast in such loose and general terms that they hardly operate as standards at all, but rather indicate a grant of discretion. The concept of 'dangerousness' in the criminal justice system is one example, while the 'welfare' of the child and the 'need' for treatment are others. None of these is itself a workable standard, but must be divided into more specific guidelines and directives. Nevertheless, in practice, the professional may be left to apply such indeterminate standards as a matter of expert judgment. This not only allows reference to non-expert considerations as noted above, but also weakens the scientific nature of the judgment. For loose concepts of that kind are not scientific in the sense that they are fully contained within the discourse and logic of a specialist discipline. They may be given a scientific face and analysed in scientific terms, but the result will be a misuse of science. The over-extending of specialist knowledge through loose standards is common practice in administrative processes. There is no easy solution to this problem, but much can be done in the design of procedures to formulate standards which properly distinguish between genuinely specialist knowledge, on the one hand, and social values, on the other. The hearing principle can be an effective way of demonstrating the real nature of the standards, and of encouraging both the professional expert and the independent decision-maker (if the two are separate) to reduce holistic standards to manageable parts. That will in turn help to distinguish the specialist element of a judgment from the non-specialist.

The third aspect of a professional judgment is the specialist element itself, and here the issue is about its reliability. The main risks of unreliability are twofold: one is slovenly diagnosis, the other is the worth of the diagnosis and subsequent judgment, no matter how well made. Let us consider the latter point first.[5] A specialist judgment may be unsound because its theoretical assumptions and the basis of its knowledge are unsound. In court proceedings, it is possible to challenge the very basis of expert knowledge, but the same opportunity is less likely in administrative processes. Another problem arises where an area of expertise is established beyond doubt, but its application in the specific case is questioned. Conflicts of expert evidence are common enough before courts and tribunals, and may well be encouraged by the adversary system. The law is that the court must decide for itself which opinion to accept; the choice is not entirely arbitrary since some experts will be better and more convincing than others, but nevertheless it is a choice, the grounds for which do not always inspire confidence.[6] In the administrative sphere, where the process is likely to be less adversarial, the problem of rival judgments is less acute. Where a second opinion is sought, it will often be in order to reinforce the first, rather than to challenge it. Notions of professional loyalty, together with a generous margin of tolerance of what is a reasonable judgment, mean that a second opinion or review of an original opinion are often not effective means for ensuring high standards of professional judgment. Where, for example, one doctor decides that treatment is desirable even without the consent of the patient, the second doctor, whose opinion must be sought, will normally agree.[7] The practice by which one professional reviews the judgment of another professional is not in general conducive to fair treatment.

At this point the problem of experts conflicting in their judgments merges with the issue of poor diagnosis. The basic point is that expert judgments should not be seen as beyond scrutiny; like other practical judgments, they can be badly made, through ignorance, error, or simple incompetence, resulting in wrong decisions and injustice. This is not to deny that there is an irreducible core which is beyond articulate scrutiny and which must finally be left to the expert. While that may be conceded, the right to ensure that the judgment is properly made remains intact, and in order to satisfy that right, obvious sources of misjudgment should be closely watched. Here procedures have their part to play and a number of measures can be suggested. One is to separate the expert from the decision-maker; that is

[5] For discussion, see P. C. Davis, 'Law, Science and History' (1988) 86 *Michigan L Rev.* 1096.

[6] On expert witnesses in the courts, see C. F. H. Tapper, *Cross and Tapper on Evidence* (8th edn., Butterworths, London, 1995), ch. xii.

[7] See the discussion by G. Richardson in *Law, Process, and Custody* (Weidenfeld and Nicholson, London, 1993), 245–6 and J. Peay in *Tribunals on Trial* (Clarendon, Oxford, 1989).

to say, it is generally conducive to better decisions if the expert offers his judgment, while any decision based on it is taken by another. If such a separation is not always practicable, at least at first instance, then there should be easy access to review or appeal by an independent body. A second practical measure would be to allow the party affected access to independent expert advice. Despite the misgivings already mentioned, the very process of allowing one expert to examine the opinion of another is likely to be conducive to a more careful diagnosis. This may mean introducing an adversarial element where it is not welcome; indeed, research on the Mental Health Review Tribunal shows that both the tribunal and the medical officers whose judgments are in question will resist any such tendency.[8] But to introduce an adversarial element is not the same as adopting an adversarial process in its totality, and while the latter would be inappropriate in many administrative processes, the former often has much to commend it. For our present purposes, the ability to question professional judgments, to know the grounds on which they are based, and to be able to propose alternatives are all steps towards better diagnosis and more accurate outcomes. The third measure to mention in bringing professional judgments under scrutiny is procedures allowing the party to question the case against him and, where appropriate, to present an opposing view. This is foreshadowed in the discussion above, but the temptation to think that a hearing of any sort in the face of a professional judgment is of no use is so great that the point should be emphasized. The apparent inscrutability of such judgments to reasoned assessment is often taken as a good reason for denying rights to notice, disclosure, and hearing, which would be taken for grantedin other contexts. The very opposite should be the case, since some formof hearing may be an effective means for enabling a satisfactory level of questioning and scrutiny.

The burden of the argument in this section has been to show how procedural fairness applies to processes based on professional judgment. Once professional judgments are dissected into their various elements, the requirements of procedural fairness become clearer and the case for a hearing becomes stronger. It might seem, however, that there is at the same time a deep tension between professional judgment and fair treatment, between the concern to act for a person's welfare and the concern to treat him fairly; or, as the point has been nicely expressed, between beneficence and autonomy.[9] Now while there is at one level a certain tension between the two, it can be resolved if we move to a deeper level of principle. The fundamental principle is the autonomy of the person and the rights which go with it; those

[8] See H. and Y. Genn, *Representation Before Tribunals* (Lord Chancellor's Dept., London, 1992).

[9] Richardson, *Law, Process and Custody*, n. 7 above, 238.

rights, which are often the classic liberal rights simply to be left alone, to be able to decide for oneself, may sometimes be restricted, but only for good reasons. Any such curtailment, which might be either for the good of the person or for the general good, must be exceptional. To reverse the order and begin with the good of the person, let alone the good of the society, as judged by someone else, as the fundamental principle, is unacceptable. Once the fundamental principle is recognized, it follows that intervention and any consequent curtailment of rights will only be justified if there are good grounds for it. Professional judgments come within the general principle, and in order then to justify intervention, it must be shown that there really are good and supportable grounds, that the intervention is the minimum necessary, and that other, less invasive courses are not available. This approach in turn supports a procedural framework which allows for the questioning and scrutinizing of action based on professional judgment. Here, as elsewhere, fair procedures are not optional extras; they are fundamental to the most basic respect for autonomy and rights. When seen in this way against the background of principle, the tension between fairness and professionalism is greatly eased.

9.2 POLICY-BASED DISCRETION

Policy-based discretion occurs where, in deciding how a person is to be treated, the authority is obligated to act as appears best in the public interest. It involves an uneasy combination of an individualized process on the one hand and a policy-based process on the other hand.[10] This sense of discretion should be distinguished from various others: one is where the element of discretion consists in judging what is best for the person in this case,[11] the other is where the decision is predominantly concerned with general policy and no question arises as to how a particular person should be treated.[12] Examples of the discretion now under consideration are where authorities may release a prisoner on parole or depart an alien, or where the local authority may grant planning permission. The decision in each case turns partly on the merits of the individual case and partly on a sense of the wider public interest.

The first step in deciding on procedures in such contexts is to clarify the objects of individualized, policy-based decisions. The general object is that the official should determine the matter according to the purposes underlying the grant of authority, taking guidance from whatever standards the statute may provide or which derive from other sources. The statute is

[10] See the related discussion in sects. 1.2.4, 1.3.4 and 3.2.2.

[11] This is regarded as a case of individualized adjudication and is dealt with in the preceding Chapter.

[12] This is considered in Chapters 15 and 16 under policy-making.

likely to offer only limited guidance, with the official being left to determine what constitutes the public interest. The policy-making element should be settled according to the normal procedures for that purpose, with the result that, by the time the official comes to decide individual cases, he ought to have a fairly clear sense of the criteria to be applied. The criteria may in some cases be so clear and settled that the individualized decision really becomes one of adjudication. In other cases, however, the official may already have some sense of the criteria to be applied, while retaining a substantial element of discretion as to how to apply it in each case. It is the need to apply a relatively open sense of the public interest to specific situations that gives this form of decision-making its special character.

At the procedural level, two different and potentially conflicting modes of adjudication and policy-making are in play. Both the public interest and the rights of the party require that the particular case be properly considered, which means that the evidence should be collected, facts determined, and a judgment made which accurately reflects them. The adjudicative mode is suitable for that part, but the absence of a settled and authoritative standard means, however, that adjudication is imperfectly present. At this point the policy mode enters; it means that the official must decide what is the best course of action in this case considering the public interest on the one hand and the interests of the party on the other. The consequence is that the relationship between the official and the party, while including elements suitable for an adjudicative approach, is better characterized as one in which the official may decide as seems best while at the same time being responsive to the claims of the party. Consultation captures the sense of that relationship between official and party; it connotes the presentation of arguments and evidence in order to influence the way issues are to be settled, where the official has a duty to hear and consider, but may decide for reasons which go beyond those submissions.[13]

That sense of the public interest is made more firm and precise when we consider it from the standpoint of the person affected. The focus is now on fair treatment and the standards which constitute fair treatment in policy-based contexts. Fair treatment is bound to be attenuated since the interests of individuals are subordinated to the public interest. There are no rights to given outcomes, but only rights to have those outcomes reached according to certain procedures and processes. Rights in this latter sense are still important, but severely limited.[14] Such rights in turn depend on whatever standards are applicable in discretionary contexts, but the precise definition of those standards is not easily made. The standards are not easily defined because

[13] On consultation, see further D. J. Galligan, *Discretionary Powers* (Clarendon Press, Oxford, 1986) 341 ff.

[14] See further on rights in this sense the discussion in sect. 3.2.

the individualized part of the process and the policy element are in a state of tension, with no clear point of equilibrium between them yet having been established. Legislation and judicial decisions provide only limited guidance, and even at the level of political principles, it is not clear how the tension between the two parts should be resolved. In this shadowland between adjudication and policy, the very understandings governing the citizen-state relationship are unsettled.

Subject to these reservations, three fairly well settled standards of fair treatment can be formulated: first, that the facts of the case be inquired into and properly assessed; secondly, that in making the discretionary judgment, the official properly consider the circumstances of the case and the consequences of it; and thirdly, that the party affected should have the chance to make a case directed at influencing the discretionary part. The first principle is straightforward in insisting that the facts of the case be properly established. The second principle is the principle of consideration: it recognizes that the exercise of discretionary judgments is not just a matter of applying a policy to the case, but requires a bringing together of the two and a decision as to what is the best course of action in the case. This principle also imports notions of good faith on the part of the official, and a concern to act rationally and reasonably. The third principle is the most speculative of the three. It introduces the idea that the party affected ought to be able to address the policy element with a view to influencing its application in that case.[15] The principle points to involvement and participation by or on behalf of the party affected. The justification for involvement and participation is that the party has a special interest in the way the policy element is made specific in that case, an interest which goes beyond that of interest groups or of the public generally. Both will normally have had opportunities at other points in the policy-making process to exert their influence, and, in accordance with the principle of selective representation, their involvement in individualized decisions will not be justified.[16]

We now have a picture of policy-based discretion in individualized cases as a distinct form of legal process. The distinctiveness consists in the combination of individualized adjudication and policy-based discretion; indeed part of its distinctiveness consists in the tension between the two elements. Can it be said that any particular set of procedures is especially appropriate? The answer lies in the notions of adjudication and consultation. The adjudicative element points to procedures for gathering evidence and finding facts, a task typically done by a mixture of investigation by the authority itself and the presentation of evidence by the party. The adjudicative element should

[15] Some might argue that the third principle is better understood as implicit in the second principle of proper consideration. On balance, however, I suggest it is right to recognize it as a distinct principle.

[16] On selective representation, see Galligan, *Discretionary Powers*, n. 13 above, sect. 7.3.2.

also include an opportunity to comment on and even contest the evidence and facts found by the authority. The precise procedures for discharging the adjudicative part will be much influenced by context, conception, and preference, as in other areas. As for the discretionary parts, consultative procedures are appropriate, since the object of this part is to ensure proper consideration of the specific case and to allow the party to present arguments in relation to the policy part. In order to be effective, consultation should include procedures requiring disclosure by the authority of its proposals and the materials on which it proposes to act; for the making of submissions by the party; and for proper consideration of those submissions by the authority. The degree of formality, whether submissions should be oral or written, the forms of representation and participation are very much practical matters to be settled according to the specific context.

9.3 INVESTIGATION AND INQUIRY

Not all administrative processes end in a decision being made or definite action being taken. Amongst various processes which do not, investigations and inquiries are both commonplace and present interesting procedural issues. The most common forms of investigation are those conducted by the police into suspected crime and, if we add the activities of other police-like agents, such as customs or immigration officials, such investigations make up a large part of administrative action. Investigations of these kinds raise fundamental issues of values and procedures, for here some of the most basic civil rights are at stake and may be in direct conflict with the need to detect crime and other forms of illegality. Such issues have long been the subject of discussion and are well covered in the literature on criminal justice and police powers. Here I shall concentrate on forms of investigation and inquiry which are civil in nature rather than criminal, but which nevertheless raise important issues of procedure and fair treatment, and which have received much less attention than their criminal counterparts.

The kinds of investigations I have in mind are those directed at a specific problem, occurrence, or issue, where the object is, first, to find out what happened and, secondly, to report on the matter to some higher authority, often with a recommendation that certain action should be taken. Such investigations are often conducted by special bodies appointed for the task, a Royal Commission for example; alternatively, forms of investigation might be on a more permanent footing with a roving commission to inquire into an area of activity. The Commission for Racial Equality in the United Kingdom is an example of the latter.[17] We need not here attempt to make a detailed

[17] See A. Pardoe, 'Investigation by the Commission for Racial Equality' [1982] *New LJ* 670.

classification of the different kinds of bodies that might be created or their precise legal status, but examples chosen at random from the United Kingdom include: inquiries into the Profumo affair where alleged liaisons between a cabinet minister, a call-girl and a Soviet official were the subject-matter; enquiries into the conduct of medical staff and social workers in removing children from their homes in the west of Scotland after allegations of abuse by a group of parents; and the Scott enquiry into the behaviour of ministers and civil servants in relation to the alleged supply to Iraq of components for making arms. In Australia, where special forms of investigation and inquiry are much used, the subjects covered in recent years include: malpractice in various trades unions: bribery and graft amongst meat inspectors; corruption in the government and administration of the state of Queensland; and the financial and speculative dealings of the state of Western Australia. While inquiries like these tend to catch the limelight, there has been in recent years a steady growth in the number and variety of investigative bodies spread across a wide range of activities from insider trading to unfair commercial practices. The powers of such bodies are normally conferred by statute and are often extensive, and while many of them relate to commercial and financial activities, it is not now unusual to find initiatives being taken in a great variety of contexts.

Investigatory bodies of these various kinds are usually required to investigate a matter causing public concern. The objective in each case is to investigate the matter and to report on it, with a view to action being taken by that same authority to remove the concern or to guard against its recurrence in the future. In order to discharge its public duties, however, the investigative body may need to question people, to pry into their affairs, and to reveal information personal and confidential to them. The problem then is to devise procedures which enable the objectives of the investigation to be met, while making sure that people bearing the brunt of the inquiry are adequately protected. These are major issues which warrant a full study of their own, but in this brief analysis, I shall deal with three issues: first, the classification of investigatory bodies; secondly, the issue of fair treatment of people affected, and thirdly, the design of procedures.

9.3.1 A Classification of Investigative Bodies

Amongst the various kinds of investigative bodies, a standard case can be identified with the following characteristics: it inquires into the facts of an event or issue; it analyses the material; and then makes recommendations about what should be done for the future.[18] Authorities coming within the standard case are hybrid in that they offer advice as well as investigate, and

[18] A fuller analysis can be found in C. Rhodes, *Committees of Inquiry*, (Allen and Unwin, London, 1975), ch. 2.

in that sense they are linked to the policy process. They should be distinguished, nevertheless, from governmental bodies which are solely or primarily concerned with providing advice to government.[19] These latter kinds may also be involved in investigation, but in so far as they are it is incidental to their primary task of giving advice. Indeed, the investigative element in such cases is only one source from which knowledge and information will be sought; the members of the authority may also draw heavily on their own expert knowledge, or they may open the process to wider forms of consultation with interested parties.

The precise distinction between investigative and advisory bodies has caused difficulty. A report by the Law Reform Commission of Canada suggested a sharp distinction between the two, but then went on to say that both often investigate and offer advice.[20] However, we need not here dwell on these problems of difference and similarity; the distinction of present relevance is between those which are primarily concerned with investigation, and others which are primarily concerned with policy-making, or at least with giving advice on which policy can then be made. Authorities in the latter categories are best seen as part of the policy process and are dealt with in Chapters 15 and 16, while the following discussions will concentrate on those primarily concerned with investigation: to the extent that investigative bodies have a role in advising on policy, they are included in the discussion in those later chapters.

In order to perform their functions, investigatory bodies generally need extensive powers, which often include the powers: to compel witnesses to give evidence, usually under oath; to require the production of information and documents, to search premises, and to seize documents and other materials; and sometimes the power to punish for contempt. Not all investigatory bodies have all these powers, but most have some or other part of them. The procedural model which is required to enable an authority to perform its functions is fairly simple: each body needs such a combination of the above powers as is necessary to obtain whatever information is needed for the proper discharge of its public function. The authority should be able to investigate as widely and as deeply as it thinks necessary, and the less it is hindered in doing so, the more effectively it can perform its functions. But of course there is more to good government than one-dimensional pursuit of a public goal, and two kinds of constraints are immediately applicable. One flows from the canons of good government and civic education and requires: that the investigative process be as open and public as possible; that there be procedures for the bringing of evidence by parties independently of the

[19] See further, K. C. Wheare, *Government by Committee* (Clarendon Press, Oxford, 1955), 43, 68–9.

[20] Canadian Law Reform Commission, *Working Paper on Commissions of Inquiry* (1977); see the Foreword, 5.

investigative body itself; that all evidence be open to question and scrutiny in an open forum; and that the authority publish its findings and recommendations with reasons. The other constraint also derives from good government, but emphasizes the position of the person who is subject to investigation; that in turn raises questions of rights and fair treatment.

9.3.2 Investigation, Inquiry, and Fair Treatment

It might seem at first sight that, since investigations and inquiries do not really decide anything but are preliminary to some further decisions being made, the need for procedural protection is slight. That view used to carry weight with Parliament and the English courts, but it has little merit and now has been largely abandoned. It is not hard to see that the very process of the inquiry affects interests and values, of which privacy and confidentiality are the two most notable, while the ensuing report and recommendations might themselves have a detrimental effect on the person under investigation, not least to reputation but also in other ways. Since the results of the inquiry will often be the basis for a further or final decision which may affect seriously the person's interests, it is important that the facts and conclusions be properly grounded. Considerations of fair treatment are relevant at each of these points. However, the fair treatment of those subject to investigation appears to be incompatible with the very object of the inquiry, which is to elicit information and to propose a course of action where the public good is the guiding principle. However, just as we have seen in other contexts that the public good includes as one of its necessary elements the fair treatment of persons, the same applies here. The true realization of the public good consists in fulfilling the objects of an investigation or inquiry while at the same time treating fairly those subject to it. The task is then to elucidate the constraints that ought to be imposed on investigations and inquiries in the interests of fairness, but without unduly hampering the very point of the process.[21] Here I shall consider the three main areas which raise questions of fair treatment: conducting the investigation; testing the evidence; and formulating conclusions and recommendations.

Conducting the Investigation

The effective conduct of an investigation usually depends on parties being required to produce documents and materials, and to give oral evidence, often under oath. In some jurisdictions, such powers are standard;[22] in others, the powers of investigative bodies may be tailored to fit each case.

[21] For discussion of some of these issues, use P. Robardet, 'Should we Abandon Adversarial Model in Favour of the Inquisitorial Model in *Commissions of Inquiry*?' and A. W. MacKay, 'Mandates, Legal Foundations, Powers and Conduct of Commissions of Inquiry' both in *Commissions of Inquiry* (special issue) 12 *Dalhousie LJ*.

[22] See the Canadian Inquiries Act, s. 17.

Whatever the approach, the tension between the two opposing factors is clear: without the power to compel evidence and witnesses, an investigation is often likely to fail in its purpose; while the countervailing argument is that a person should not be required to disclose information which is private and confidential, and sometimes incriminating. With an increasing reliance by governments on special bodies having wide investigative powers, this latter argument is sometimes put with vigour. In such a stark form, however, it claims more than can be justified, for if a clear and strong public interest can be shown for the investigation, it is surely justifiable that ordinary claims to privacy and confidentiality should be overriden. An analogy can be drawn with the civil trial where a third party may be required to produce information and give evidence at the initiative of one of the parties in order to help in the proper resolution of the issue. The two provisos which should be added are that the public interest at issue in the investigation must be a serious one, and the information should not be readily available from other sources, such as official records.

The position is different if the production of information or the giving of evidence would reveal misconduct of a criminal kind. Here the analogy is with criminal proceedings, where the principle is that a person should not be required to incriminate himself. However, the analogy is not perfect since investigations raise the additional and stronger interest in understanding and resolving a problem of public concern, which goes beyond the very real but often lesser public interest in the criminal prosecution. It is often the case, moreover, that the investigation can be properly conducted and the public interest served only if otherwise privileged information is disclosed. This dilemma has been resolved in some jurisdictions by compelling disclosure, while allowing the person disclosing an immunity from prosecution on the basis of the disclosure.

Testing the Evidence

The second procedural issue is whether people whose interests are under scrutiny by the investigative body should be able to test the evidence gathered by it. Practice varies, as can be seen in the following examples. Commissions of inquiry operating under the Canadian federal statute allow any person whose interests are adversely affected by the evidence to be heard on the matter; and the person may be allowed by the commission to question witnesses.[23] The British Commission for Racial Equality, however, must allow a party being investigated to be heard and to be represented by counsel, but it need not allow the examination or cross-examination of witnesses.[24] In other contexts, it is not uncommon for parties to be denied

[23] Inquiries Act (Canada), s. 11. For another, similar case, consider the powers of the New South Wales Independent Commission Against Corruption under the ICAC Act (1988).

[24] See the analysis by A. Pardoe, 'Investigation by the Commission for Racial Equality', n. 17 above.

rights to be heard or represented, let alone to question witnesses; the Scott inquiry into the sale of arms to Iraq has been criticized on this ground by some of those affected by its investigation. Where a right to be heard is provided for it is normally accompanied by a duty on the investigating body to disclose the evidence and materials on which it proposes to act.

Is there a clear standard of fair treatment to govern this situation? The risk is that untested evidence might be accepted as the basis for later recommendations and possible action against a party. If the evidence is unreliable, it would be unfair to those adversely affected for the authority to act on it. Fairness requires that the evidence be reliable, which means that procedures are needed to test it; and the only question then is what procedures are adequate for that purpose. Fairness does not dictate that the procedures should necessarily include involvement by the parties; it requires only that the evidence be properly tested by whatever procedures. The principle of adequacy also applies here; according to its terms, an investigative body might be justified in not hearing the parties at this stage, provided that its procedures for testing the evidence in other ways are satisfactory and possibly that the opportunity to be heard is provided at a later stage. Consideration of time and cost will often make non-hearing procedures attractive to the investigator, since procedures for allowing the parties to be involved in testing the evidence can be laborious and costly. The spectre of a public inquiry slowly grinding on under the weight of lawyers, with their endless cross-examinations and ingenious legal arguments, haunts the most experienced investigator.

However, within this framework of principle, where practical judgments have to be made whether the parties affected should be involved in testing the evidence, several lines of guidance can be suggested. The first is that time and cost are not decisive arguments against hearing the parties at this stage. According to first principles, time and cost should be linked to the importance of the issues at stake, including the importance of the personal interests which might be adversely affected. Some issues warrant at this stage the investment in an inquiry of time and resources, others less so, and in all cases the issue should be settled according to the principles of proportionality and adequacy. Secondly, account should be taken of the idea that the scrutiny of evidence by those with an interest in it can be an effective method of testing. This is not to say that an argumentative, to some degree adversarial, approach is necessarily the only or the most reliable method of testing; empirically it is hard to know whether one way is better than another. Our faith in the argumentative approach, however, is reinforced in many forms of social practices. A third and most important point to consider is that those whose interests are in question may have additional evidence to contribute, or may be able to provide explanations and interpretations which would not otherwise be available; that material might be highly relevant to a proper understanding of the situation. Finally, for those who favour a conception of the hearing principle as inherently desirable, this may be one context in which involvement by the parties being investigated is an obvious requirement of fairness, both as good in itself and under the principle of self-protection.

Formulating Reports and Recommendations

Once the evidence has been gathered and tested, an investigatory body usually has to draw its conclusions of fact and formulate its recommendations as to what course of action should be taken. The possibilities here are many, but we are mainly concerned with recommendations which adversely affect a party: that a prosecution be brought, a licence forfeited, or some other serious disadvantage be imposed. A less obvious but nevertheless damaging effect is where criticisms of a party are made by the investigator, even though no further action is recommended; the loss of reputation may be as serious as more blatantly punitive action.

Again we must ask what is the standard of fair treatment here and what procedures are needed to maintain it. The basic standard is that any conclusions of fact in the report be accurate and that any judgmental conclusions or recommendations of further action be properly informed, made in good faith, and reasonable in their terms. The procedures for reaching these ends might vary, ranging from the Royal Commission and the judicial inquiry, with all the trappings of a trial, to the informality of an inspector looking into the affairs of a company or a suspected tax-avoider. But whether formal or informal, there should be at the centre of such procedures suitable mechanisms to guarantee compliance with the basic standard. For reasons similar to those set out above for testing evidence, procedures here should include: notice of what is being concluded and proposed; disclosure of the materials on which it is based; and the opportunity to be heard in relation to it. The extent of the notice and disclosure and the form of the hearing will depend on the principle of proportionality, but generally a reasonably exacting combination of the three will be helpful in identifying errors and in providing a more balanced and reasonable set of conclusions and recommendations.

9.4 NEGOTIATION, MEDIATION AND AGREEMENT

The idea that conflicts should be settled by agreement between the parties has a long history in the law.[25] Outside the law most conflicts are resolved by agreement, and for that reason relatively few come to law. Agreement might be brought about by simple discussions between the parties, or it might be the climax of arduous negotiation conducted through the intercession of an

[25] In relation to decision by agreement, see also sects. 1.2.4 and 1.3.4.

impartial third party. The possibilities are several. When the parties finally come to agreement, it may be for a mixture of reasons; genuine agreement will sometimes be reached, but more often the result will reflect the need to seek accommodation and compromise. The need to compromise can itself be influenced by a host of factors; the parties might be in unequal bargaining positions so that one feels there is no real alternative, or the alternatives may be so unappealing that compromise is the lesser evil. One such alternative is that the matter will otherwise go to litigation with the attendant expense, vexation, and delay. That is one reason why lawyers and policy-makers have in recent years shown a renewed interest in settling disputes by agreement. Cheaper and more informal forms of decision-making offer an attractive solution to congestion in both the civil and criminal courts. If, for example, the prosecution and defence can agree on a compromise resulting in a plea of guilty, the prospect of a long and costly trial is replaced by the briefer and cheaper process of sentencing. However, the move to informal processes based on achieving consent also has an ideological edge. Conflict is seen as a bad thing, something to be reduced and neutralized, rather than aggravated; the restoration of harmony through agreement, accordingly, is both pleasing and socially desirable.[26] The parties' ability to participate in the decision and to shape the outcome as they think best is another advantage of decision processes aimed at agreement.

For these reasons, informal processes are a common feature of modern legal systems, and negotiation, conciliation, and mediation are all enlisted in the cause of peaceful settlement through agreement. Around that cause has grown a movement in its own right known as alternative dispute resolution, alternative, that is, or in addition to, litigation before the courts or court-like bodies. In its various forms, alternative dispute resolution can be seen at work across the spectrum of legal decision-making, embracing labour relations, family matters, commercial disputes, and many others.[27] Some of these alternative forms are entirely consensual, others take place (to borrow the hackneyed but still memorable expression) in the shadow of the law,[28] which is to say that, if negotiations fail, recourse may be had to the full force of the law, including possibly a court trial. The fall of that shadow often creates irresistible pressure on the parties in both civil and criminal matters to settle, while in other areas, attempts to reach agreement are sometimes mandatory measures to be taken before some other form of action is initiated. But quite apart from the hovering threat of the law, informal procedures directed

[26] For an extended discussion of the ends and ideals served by such informal processes, see R. L. Abel, *The Contradictions of Informal Justice* (Academic Press, New York, 1982), i.

[27] A comprehensive account of the use of alternative dispute resolution in Australia can be seen in H. Astor and C. M. Chinkin, *Dispute Resolution in Australia* (Butterworths, Sydney, 1990).

[28] R. Mnookin and L. Kornhauser, 'Bargaining in the Shadow of the Law: the Case of Divorce' (1979) 88 *Yale LJ* 950.

towards reaching agreement might be adopted deliberately as the best way of resolving certain kinds of disputes.

9.4.1 Classification of Processes Based on Agreement

Once informal negotiations are entered into, the forms such proceedings take can be divided broadly into two: direct and unassisted negotiations between the parties leading to agreement, and negotiations where the parties are assisted by a third person towards agreement. The first can be referred to simply as direct negotiation, while the second is a form of mediation.[29] The significant difference between the two is that, while the parties in the first case are left to themselves in reaching agreement, in the second a mediator is called on to help define the issues in dispute, identify options, and propose lines of agreement. It is essential that the mediator be impartial between the parties, and that the object be to bring them to agreement, rather than impose a settlement. Mediation is the more sophisticated process and could be expected to have a better rate of success than bilateral negotiations.

9.4.2 The Use of Direct Negotiation and Mediation

While it is easy enough to describe direct negotiation and mediation, and while both display features of undoubted attraction in resolving conflict, it is more difficult to say when they should be used. The problems are naturally fewer where the process and the outcome are generally consensual. In general, the law should encourage settlement through agreement, although some forms of agreement may need to be controlled on the grounds of public interest or community values. Since agreements reached through the processes of negotiation or mediation are a species of contract, they should be subject to restrictions at least as exacting as those imposed by the general law. Subject to that, the principal test in deciding whether to provide for negotiation or mediation is the practical one of whether agreement is likely to result. That will in turn depend on factors like the level of goodwill between the parties and whether they have to continue to deal with each other in the future; it also depends on the nature of the dispute and the consequences of not agreeing.

The attractiveness of informal proceedings is to some extent sullied when resort to mediation takes on a compulsory aspect and the pressure to reach agreement is severe. Its most common use is as a preliminary to other

[29] Amongst the extensive literature on these forms, the following are especially helpful: S. Roberts, 'Mediation in Family Matters' (1983) 46 *MLR* 537; C. Menkel-Meadow, 'Towards Another View of Legal Negotiation: the Structure of Problem Solving' (1983–4) 31 *UCLA Rev.* 754. Mediation might have a subtly different meaning from conciliation, but I shall not go into that here; see Astor and Chinkin, *Dispute Resolution in Australia*, n. 27 above, 60–4.

processes, where participation of the parties is either mandatory or at least strongly encouraged. Mandatory mediation has advantages and might on occasions lead to genuine agreement: the very fact of being forced to enter into negotiations may reveal unexpected common ground and open the way for common cause. The problem is not so much that mediation is mandatory, but that, once having entered into mediation for whatever reason, the parties will be pushed into agreement. Some pressure on quarrelling parties to settle their differences rather than go to law has long been a common feature of legal systems and is not necessarily to be condemned. The imperial Chinese combined an elaborate code of strict law with a mediatory system where the pressures to settle, and thus to avoid the horrors of a legal suit, were intense. This may seem paradoxical and contradictory, but it has been pointed out that it is 'a natural combination. It is the strict law that cures the overclaiming problem and thus makes split-the-difference work'.[30]

However, the dangers are real. For unless agreement is genuinely consensual, negotiation and mediation become a means of coercion and injustice. A severe form of that injustice occurs when the suspect is persuaded to sign a false confession or enter a plea of guilty for a crime of which he is innocent. That these are extreme cases should not hide the fact that a multitude of lesser injustices can result from negotiation and mediation. Such informal processes may be less consensual than they appear, with the parties having no real choice whether to participate or to accept a particular outcome.[31] And if, in addition, the parties are in positions of inequality, the pressures on the weaker party to settle for compromise will be compounded.

Some have gone further and argued that there are contradictions within the very processes of negotiation and mediation. One prominent critic is R. Abel who claims that, on the one hand, such processes appeal to important values such as harmony; to easy, cheap, and quick access to the processes for settling disputes; and to wider participation.[32] On the other hand, negotiation and mediation tend to neutralize disputes by channelling them into consensual forms; they can be coercive in that the participants often have no real choice; and, since they look to agreement rather than the enforcement of standards, rights and the procedural protections which flow from rights may be jeopardized. Indeed the protection of rights is not the driving force behind mediation; on the contrary, it is often the case that agreement can be reached only by one or even both parties compromising or even surrendering

[30] M. Shapiro, 'Compromise and Litigation' in J. R. Pennock and J. T. W. Chapman (eds.), *Compromise in Ethics, Law and Politics* (Nomos xxi, New York University Press, New York, 1979).

[31] A substantial critical literature has grown up around informal procedures of this kind: see the two-volume survey edited by R. L. Abel, *The Politics of Informal Justice* (Academic Press, New York, 1982).

[32] R. L. Abel, 'The Contradictions of Informal Justice' in Abel, *The Politics of Informal Justice*, ibid., i.

their rights.[33] To enter into negotiation is to surrender the right to have one's particular rights and duties determined according to authoritative standards, in favour of more subjective and elusive notions of agreement. For these reasons, and despite their obvious strengths, negotiation and mediation are processes to be handled with great care and should not be seen as the ideal forum for all disputes.

The disparity between adjudication as a formal process directed to upholding authoritative standards, and the informality of mediation directed to agreements, should be noted.[34] Adjudication, with all its imperfections, is still in principle an open process for the enforcement of public standards, where accuracy of outcome is the primary object, with procedures to ensure that the parties participate from positions of equality. The judge is not just a stranger looking in on someone else's dispute; in a sense he is that, but he is more importantly a public official whose task is to 'explicate and give force to the values embodied in authoritative texts'. Moreover, the risk of inequality between the parties will often undermine the legitimacy of agreement. And, it might be added, if adjudication is not working properly, the solution to imperfection is not to abandon it in favour of unregulated informality, but to try to improve it.

To this critical and sceptical line of argument regarding procedures based on agreement, several responses can be made. It has been said that direct negotiation and mediation are possible only if there is no real dispute in the first place.[35] The idea is that, once properly explored, common ground between the disputants can be found and many apparent conflicts shown to lack substance. The difficulty is, however, that it is not normally possible to know in advance which disputes are real and which are only apparent, and by pushing into mediation disputes which are genuine, harm may be done. An alternative response is to identify deeper values, shared by the community, which will then be the basis for agreement. This approach is strongest where societies do retain a sense of shared values which can be called on to settle disputes. Attention was drawn in Chapter 1 to societies in which there is a marked division between the formal legal rules (sometimes imposed or inherited from a colonial power, at other times native to the indigenous culture), and the informal community standards which really govern. Just as in such societies adjudication itself may be based largely on unwritten community standards and the values supporting them, mediation may draw on similar standards. It is perhaps characteristic of such community values that

[33] O. Fiss, 'Against Settlement' (1984) 93 *Yale LJ* 1073.

[34] For further discussion, see B. Garth, 'The Movement Towards Procedural Informalism in North America and Western Europe: A Critical Survey' in Abel, *The Politics of Informal Justice*, n. 31 above, and T. P. Terrel, 'Rights and Wrongs in the Rush to Response: On the Jurisprudence Dangers of Authoritative Dispute Resolution' (1987) 36 *Emory LJ* 541.

[35] F. E. Snyder, 'Crime and Community Mediation' [1978] *Wisconsin L Rev.* 737.

they make appeal, not to the rights or interests of the parties, but to the good of the community; indeed, the very point of such values often is that the good of individuals is submerged in the good of the whole. Difficulties in relying on such organic standards arise when we move from pre-modern societies, which retain elements of collective solidarity, to modern societies where the emphasis falls on the rights and interests of individuals. It is less likely in the case of the latter that a sufficient foundation of collective values will exist; indeed, in a culture which encourages each to pursue his or her own ends, the chances of agreement through shared values are slender.

The reality is that in most situations agreement can be reached between two disputing parties only if one or both are prepared to compromise. Compromise here means resiling from a position or claim which one has under law and settling for something less. It often means surrendering the chance to have rights and duties determined in a court or court-like forum according to formal procedures. The couple in the maelstrom of divorce trying to agree on children and property, the parties settling at the door of the court, and the suspect bargaining over pleas are all engaged in compromise. The significance of compromise is that the formal procedures accompanying the application of authoritative standards, of which adjudication is the primary instance, are given up for the prospect of agreement which is reached informally, and which may in its result mean sacrificing entitlements. Once we recognize compromise as a central element in reaching agreement, negotiation and mediation can be effective instruments towards that end, even where the dispute is real and serious. This enables us to avoid the thankless task of trying to determine whether apparent disputes are real or not, for the very idea of compromise is that, even in the case of a genuine dispute, the parties are prepared to surrender some ground in order to reach agreement.

Compromise, moreover, can be the most rational and justifiable course of action to take.[36] Even where the dispute is real and no shared standards are available to draw on, it may be in the interests of each party to agree to a solution which is less than ideal. The reasons for compromising can vary, but the common feature is that the parties accept an outcome which, although not perfect, is preferable to the alternatives likely to follow from failure to agree. It is here that negotiation and mediation find their most common uses and, provided they are conducted within certain boundaries, they can be both fair and legitimate processes. What then are the boundaries within which compromise through agreement can be fair and legitimate? The first point is to suggest some modifications to the sharp contrast drawn above between decision by agreement and decisions by authoritative standards. Decisions in the latter class often themselves contain elements of negotiation

[36] For further analysis of compromise, see Pennock and Chapman, *Compromise in Ethics, Law and Politics*, n. 30 above.

and compromise. At one end of the spectrum, solutions are imposed by a purely objective exercise of authority by a judge or other official, but that is not the typical case. Civil and criminal trials regularly include elements of negotiation and compromise on such matters as the issues to be determined, the evidence, and the facts, and even on the law to be applied. The same can be said of administrative officials applying standards to specific cases. Indeed, as M. Shapiro has suggested, an accurate portrayal of the relationship between applying standards and reaching agreement would not be one of sharp contrast, but as end points along a continuum, between which several intermediate stages could be plotted.[37] On this view, 'the existence of an elaborate code of strict law side by side with an essentially mediatory system of conflict resolution constitutes not a contradiction or paradox but a natural combination'.[38]

The second, related point is that, far from excluding the role of authoritative standards, negotiation consists very much in the 'invocation, elaboration, and distinguishing of principles, rules, and precedents'.[39] This is most likely to be the case when negotiating parties are legally represented or when negotiations are conducted through a professional mediator. The view advanced by Eisenberg complements Shapiro's thesis; for just as Shapiro emphasizes the element of negotiation in applying standards, Eisenberg sees standards having an important role in negotiations. What this means in practice is that the parties will employ standards, both legal and moral, to support their own positions and to contest those of their opponents. And of course the tactic of last resort is to stand on one's rights and to abort the negotiating process.

We may conclude from this discussion that, while important concerns have been raised about the resolution of issues through agreement between the parties, it may also be a legitimate and effective form of process. Just as it is widely used and accepted in civil disputes between parties, so it can be used with justification in contexts involving administrative or judicial authorities. The course often taken in such cases is to require the parties to go through a form of mediation and, if that fails to produce an agreement, the matter will then be settled by applying authoritative standards. Whether mediation should become a normal part of civil litigation, and if so, whether the court itself should be involved, are matters for discussion.[40] For our present purposes, however, we may conclude with two general suggestions about the use of mediation. The first is that mediation is not appropriate where there are reasons of public policy for insisting on a proper adjudication of the issue.

[37] M. Shapiro, 'Compromise and Litigation', in Pennock and Chapman, *Compromise in Ethics, Law and Politics*.

[38] Ibid. 171.

[39] M. A. Eisenberg, 'Private Ordering Through Negotiation: Dispute-Settlements and Rule-Making' (1976) 89 *Harvard L. Rev.* 637.

[40] See J. Resnick, 'Managerial Judges' (1982) 96 *Harvard L Rev.* 376.

From the point of view of the community as well as the parties, not everything is negotiable for, as Fuller has remarked, some signposts and boundary markers as to what is tolerable should be preserved.[41] In the second place, because mediation generally means compromise, it is important that parties have the procedural protections necessary to ensure that their agreement to compromise is voluntary and informed.

9.4.3 Procedures in Mediation: A Note

The last two general suggestions provide guidance as to the kinds of procedures which should be suitable in mediation. Procedural design can in turn be divided into three stages: (i) procedures for deciding whether to allocate a dispute to mediation; (ii) procedures for reaching agreement; and (iii) procedures to maintain other values relevant to the process. At the first stage, mediation should not be entered into unless certain criteria are satisfied, especially where mediation is compulsory or semi-compulsory. It is not easy to detect the criteria being applied in current practice, but some guidance can be taken from the earlier discussion of principle. The starting point should be to formulate standards which take account of the following matters: the public interest in having certain issues openly adjudicated; the concern that mediation should not be a vehicle for the loss of important rights; and the need to be reasonably satisfied that a genuine and uncoerced agreement can be reached. Once the content of standards along these lines has been settled, procedures for their implementation should be adopted.

The second stage in mediation is to ensure agreement, and here the very nature of the process gives some guidance to the form procedures should take. Two features are fundamental. First, the parties must be able to participate to the extent necessary to enter into negotiations, to present their arguments, and to respond to the other side. A good case can usually be made for representation, legal or otherwise, to see that the bargaining process is effective and that the party's side is properly protected. Access to information, knowledge of the consequences of possible outcomes, and understanding of the implications if agreement fails, are all part of a satisfactory bargaining position. Secondly, the mediator must not only be impartial between the parties, but must also bring the parties to agreement rather than impose agreement on them. But just how far he should be neutral as to what the agreement is and the values it reflects is more problematic.

The degree of involvement of the mediator varies greatly in practice as to the level of activism, the determination to achieve an agreement, and concern to base the agreement around legal values.[42] The mediator is crucial

[41] L. L. Fuller, 'Mediation' (1970–1) 44 *S Calif. L Rev.* 305.

[42] For more detailed discussions of the role of the mediator in practice, see Astor and Chinkin, *Dispute Resolution in Australia*, n. 27 above, ch. 5.

vulnerable; the chances of agreement depend on his skills, while at the same time he should have responsibility for ensuring that the process is fair, fair, that is, in the sense that some level of equality is maintained between the parties so that the outcome is genuinely voluntary, but also in the sense that the parties are kept informed as options emerge, and that important values are not violated.[43] Impartial adjudication is itself hard enough, but the role of the mediator is even more daunting; for having been denied the refuge of an authoritative standard, the mediator must guide the parties along a path not only uncertain in its direction, but perilous in its course. The object of procedures is to ensure that the parties participate in a suitable way and that the mediator maintains his role of impartial guide, with the result that an agreement can be reached which is legitimate and binding.

The third and final stage in devising procedures in mediation is to identify and adopt other relevant values. The nature of mediation is such that any relevant values are caught up in the process of arriving at agreement. The importance of being informed, of knowing the possibilities and the consequences, has already been covered. Another matter which is not often touched on is the need for mediation to be open to scrutiny. The suggestion might seem contrary to the very idea of informality, but there is no doubt that the proper recording of the bargaining process and the possibility of independent scrutiny should be essential measures in ensuring that the process is fair and the resulting agreement acceptable. The review process need not be elaborate and can itself be informal; but its importance in ensuring against some of the worst dangers of mediation is undoubted.

9.4.4 Bargaining in Administrative Contexts

Amongst the many contexts in which negotiation and agreement take place, their occurrence within administrative processes is of special interest. Even here the variety is extensive. Mediation might be provided for in some contexts, direct negotiation in others. In the first case, the administrative body is likely to be the mediator between disputing parties, while in the second, the negotiations are likely to be between the authority itself and a party over whom it has some power. In that case, the object is not to settle a dispute, since none exists; it is rather to determine how the power or some element of it should be used. Such direct negotiations may be expressly provided for by the governing statute but, more typically, they are entered into unofficially. An example of the first case is where a licensing authority is required to negotiate with the licensee the conditions of the licence. Examples of the second case abound: water inspectors negotiate with polluters about the levels of pollution which will be tolerated;[44] a housing authority bargains with a homeless person

[43] It might be noted in passing that it is the absence of a mediator with these responsibilities which make processes such as plea-bargaining so open to abuse.

[44] See the studies by K. Hawkins, *Environment and Enforcement* (Clarendon Press,

about the kind of housing to be provided;[45] a parole authority might negotiate with a prisoner the terms of his release on licence. Although few empirical studies have been done, there is good reason to think that bargaining is a common part of administrative processes.[46] Here I shall concentrate on the more informal and unofficial processes, but the analysis will apply equally well where express authority is given.

The reasons for unofficial bargaining between an administrative agent and the parties under its authority are several. The main reasons from the agent's point of view is likely to be that without agreement its actions will be futile. This point is well demonstrated in studies of pollution control.[47] The inspectors knew that, with inadequate resources at their disposal, attempts at full enforcement of statutory standards would be piecemeal and only partially effective. The result is likely to be that, if agreement can be reached with each polluter, the chances of compliance may be improved. In order to secure compliance, the statutory standards may have to be unofficially lowered. A similar pattern can be seen in other areas; licensing conditions agreed to by the licensee may have a better chance of being upheld than those imposed; similarly for the prisoner on parole or the offender on probation. The same concern for costs and effectiveness underlines bargaining over pleas and charges in the sphere of criminal law: if the accused pleads guilty to a lesser charge than might otherwise be brought, costs are saved and conviction rates maintained, while the fact that they are for lesser offences hardly matters. Compromise and agreement have advantages for the parties affected by administrative action. The polluter knows that, although prosecution is selective, he could be the one singled out and made an example of; the prisoner knows that by agreeing to proposed parole conditions it might increase the chances of early release; and the accused knows that by pleading guilty he trades the certainty of a lesser sentence for the uncertain risk of a heavier one. For both officials and parties there is also the further idea that negotiation followed by agreement has a special legitimacy as a form of social ordering.[48]

Although the practice appears to be widespread, the legal basis of informal negotiation and agreement in administrative contexts is problematical. The official has a duty to exercise his powers according to their

Oxford, 1984) and G. Richardson, A. Ogus and P. Burrows, *Policing Pollution* (Clarendon Press, Oxford, 1984).

[45] See I. Loveland, *Housing Homeless Persons* (Clarendon Press, Oxford, 1995).

[46] See further, R. Lempert, 'Discretion in a Behavioural Perspective: The Case of the Housing Eviction Board' in Hawkins, *The Uses of Discretion* (Clarendon Press, Oxford, 1992).

[47] See Richardson, *Policing Pollution*, n. 44 above, and Hawkins, *Environment and Enforcement*, n. 44 above.

[48] Informal negotiation in administrative decisions is positively encouraged by the Administrative Conference of the United States; see *Sourcebook: Federal Agency Use of Alternative Means of Dispute Resolution* (Office of Chairman, Washington, D.C., 1987).

statutory objectives, and in doing so to act reasonably and in good faith, taking account of relevant matters and ignoring those which are not. The parties affected should be heard and listened to, but the official is supposed to weigh up the pros and cons and come to his own decision about the best course of action. Doctrines against fettering a power or contracting it away are based on the idea that the official considers all matters and then, with an open mind, decides what is best. That image of decision-making is of course much too pure to reflect properly what happens in practice; all sorts of influences bear on the way powers are exercised, especially where there is an element of discretion, and amongst such influences is the concern that decisions should be realistic and effective. The way is then open for informal negotiations with the party affected. In short, hearing and consultation easily spill over into bargaining and negotiation.

What then are the implications of informal negotiation for the design of procedures and notions of fairness? Let us first be reminded of the standards of fair treatment: where there are rules creating substantive entitlements, fair treatment consists in having each case properly judged according to the rules; where the process is more discretionary and without substantive entitlements, fairness consists in having one's case considered reasonably and in good faith according to the relevant factors. Informal negotiation and agreement change the position in both cases, with treatment according to authoritative standards being replaced to a significant degree by treatment according to agreement. The governing standards are still likely to have a prominent place in both the negotiations and the agreement, but the point is that the standards are modified or even abandoned in favour of a different and agreed course of action.

Whether treatment meted out in accordance with an informal agreement reached in this way is fair treatment is questionable. The polluter, the prisoner, and the accused, in the examples given above, might all have good reasons for thinking they have been coerced into formal bargaining, that they have had to surrender their rights to be treated according to settled standards, and that, as a result, the arrangements agreed to are not entirely legitimate. This is an interesting issue which needs a more thorough analysis than I can give it here, but I suggest that, provided certain conditions are met, treatment on the basis of informal agreements in administrative contexts can be fair. The guiding principle should be that the agreement be real and that it be voluntarily entered into; the task of procedures is then to create suitable ways of achieving that end. But before considering the procedures, mention should be made of several factors which contribute to a real and voluntary agreement. The factors are: knowledge of the options open; willingness to enter negotiations; and a genuine decision to accept a compromise. The first, knowledge of the options, is a prerequisite for legitimate negotiation between the official and a party affected. What this means is that the party should know what would happen if negotiations were not entered into or an agreement not reached. The incentive for agreeing, for accepting a compromise, is normally the risk that the alternative could be worse; the prisoner might get a longer sentence, the claimant less money, the polluter a heavy fine.

While such consequences might follow, it should not be assumed that they will; the prosecution, for instance, might not have the evidence to prove any offence against the suspect, let alone a more serious one. The element of uncertainty inherent in any context is especially pronounced when the decision is discretionary, since until the discretion is exercised, it is a matter of speculation as to what the outcome will be. The point has been made that the parties to divorce proceedings will often not know what information the judge will rely on or what criteria he will apply in matters such as the best interests of the child.[49] In an administrative process, where negotiations are between a citizen and an official, the citizen should at least know the criteria to be applied and the official should be required to indicate the most likely outcome in the absence of negotiation and agreement. The extent to which this can be done in practice will vary, but, none the less, the first rung on the ladder of procedural fairness is to have procedures requiring the authority to make clear the criteria of judgment and the likely alternatives. Such procedures are particularly important in the light of evidence that negotiations tend to be of low intensity, that is to say, that little real bargaining goes on, the main question being whether one party will accept an offer from the other.[50] The temptation to accept what is on the table, while always strong, is even greater in the administrative context where the official is not only a party to negotiations, but has the power to impose a less appealing outcome.[51]

A second factor relevant to fair negotiation and agreement is that the process be entered into willingly. The party who negotiates gives up something: the suspect surrenders his right to a full trial, while the party subject to a discretionary power has a right to the decision being made in a certain way and to his being treated accordingly. It may be that the broader the discretion the less there is any sense of entitlement to be surrendered in negotiation; but it means, nevertheless, losing the right to have one's situation dealt with according to certain normative principles. Indeed, some see this abnegation of publicly declared standards as a major criticism of bargaining processes.[52] At the base of such criticisms is the important and complex issue of

[49] Mnookin and Kornhauser, 'Bargaining in the Shadow of the Law', n. 28 above.

[50] See H. Genn, *Hard Bargaining* (Oxford Socio-Legal Studies, Oxford, 1990); also H. Kritzer, *Let's Make a Real Bargain: Understanding the Negotiation Process in Ordinary Litigation* (University of Wisconsin Press, Madison, Wisc., 1990).

[51] See further C. Menkel-Meadow, 'Towards Another View of Legal Negotiation: The Structure of Problem Solving', n. 29 above, at 833 ff.

[52] See O. Fiss, 'Against Settlement', n. 33 above, and J. Resnik, 'Managerial Judges', n. 40 above.

the public interest in having the law applied and discretion exercised as laid down by the community, rather than as agreed between the parties. There is, however, no one clear resolution of this issue and each area of decision-making has to be closely examined to determine the public interest.

It is important also to take account of third-party interests, for an agreement between the official and one party may have serious consequences for another party; it might also have unacceptable results for the public at large.[53] However, in general, neither the public interest nor third-party interests rule out negotiation and agreement as a legitimate way of exercising discretion,[54] although it would be contrary to both the public interest and fair treatment to force a party to negotiate. The liberty to choose whether or not to negotiate is fundamental, although what it means willingly to enter negotiations is itself somewhat opaque. One element is to know what the options are, as discussed above; another element is the capacity to evaluate the options; while the third is the ability to decide on the basis of the evaluation to choose to enter negotiations rather than pursue some alternative course. This is not to say the alternative need be especially attractive or one which the party would choose under ideal conditions; it means only that in the specific case the party can make a reasoned choice between having the issue decided by the exercise of discretion, or giving up that entitlement in favour of negotiation. One of the tasks for procedures is to provide the conditions under which a real choice can be made.

The third factor in fair treatment is that the negotiations be genuine. Precisely what this means is not entirely clear, but the idea is that there must be some real process of negotiation. The prosecutor who offers a lesser charge in return for a plea of guilty on a take-it-or-leave-it basis is not entering into negotiations; he is offering a choice between two courses, but he is not negotiating with a view to agreement. The process is one of negotiation only if a number of possible courses, or variations on courses, are open. The idea of negotiation also suggests that the parties are open to persuasion and prepared to compromise. When we apply these ideas to discretionary contexts, it is clear that what often passes for negotiation is not negotiation at all; indeed, the difficulties of fostering real negotiations are considerable. One problem is that parties tend not to be experienced in such skills and are inclined to accept any compromise without question; where, however, the parties do engage in vigorous negotiation or hard bargaining, the gains are likely to be considerable.[55] Negotiations are also likely to be more productive

[53] On this point in relation to patients detained under the Mental Health Act, see Richardson, *Law, Process and Custody*, n. 7 above.

[54] The issue has many aspects: see C. Menkel-Meadow, 'Towards Another View of Legal Negotiation' n. 29 above, and 'Lawyer Negotiations: Theories and Realities' (1993), 56 *MLR* 366.

[55] See H. Genn, *Hard Bargaining* (Oxford Socio-Legal Studies, Clarendon Press, Oxford, 1990).

if the approach of the parties is one of identifying and solving a problem, rather than regarding it as an adversarial contest.[56] The problem-solving approach concentrates on identifying the parties' needs and objectives, and then posing possible solutions; adversarial strategies and tactics are subordinate to finding solutions.[57]

Another problem in fostering genuine negotiations is the imbalance between the official and the citizen. Since the official may decide finally as he thinks best he holds the trump cards. But while that is true, it does not negate the possibility of genuine negotiations. The official's powers are limited, and within those powers there may be good reasons for seeking agreement. So, although the prosecutor has power over the suspect in that a more or less serious charge may be brought, it is in the prosecutor's interest not to have to go to trial; that fact may then be the basis on which genuine negotiations can be conducted. Overall inequality between the parties does not preclude the possibility of real and principled negotiations with respect to some matters within their relationship. The first task of negotiation is to determine what those aspects are; the second is to initiate discussions within them.[58]

Several conclusions about informal negotiations may be drawn from this discussion. The first is that, provided the three conditions of knowledge, willingness, and genuineness are met, discretionary negotiations can be fair. The second conclusion is that a party treated in accordance with the resulting agreement is treated fairly. But while fair negotiation and agreement might be open in principle, it will not often be achieved in practice. Some parties subject to discretion—large companies, firms, and interest groups—may be experienced and expert in securing favourable results; indeed, in some cases the imbalance of power will favour them rather than the authority. Across the spectrum of administrative decisions, however, the likelihood of the three conditions being met is small; what is presented as a negotiated agreement is often a sham and should be regarded by courts and tribunals as unfair and an abuse of power. Nevertheless, the imperfections of the existing system should not lead us to reject informal administrative agreements as illegitimate. Informal agreements are clearly a fact of administrative life and no point would be served by pretending to the contrary.

The better approach is to work towards creating an administrative culture in which the requirement of fairness in negotiation and agreement are immanent. The creation of such a culture can be helped by devising suitable procedures to uphold the standards of fairness. It is not hard to imagine a procedural framework which would enable a party to know the options,

[56] Menkel-Meadow has written extensively on this theme of problem-solving: see 'Towards Another View of Legal Negotiation', n. 29 above.

[57] Ibid., 795 ff.

[58] For further discussion: R. Fisher and W. Ury, *Getting to Yes* (Penguin, London, 1981).

which would make sure that the party is able to decide on good grounds whether to enter negotiations, and which would provide the party with the capacity to conduct negotiations. These objectives can be achieved by developing the hearing principle in this context, by insisting on criteria in exercising discretion, by greater use of specialized advisers, including but by no means limited to lawyers, and by a much bolder approach to the giving of reasons. Through these measures, the practical necessity of discretionary negotiations could be matched by the principled requirement of procedural fairness.

PART IV

Individualized Processes: Principles, Doctrines, and Practices

Introduction

In the first and second parts of this book, my objective was to establish a sense of procedural fairness and to show the relationship between fair treatment and fair procedures. In the third part, the discussion turned to an analysis of the different forms of processes by which individualized decisions are made. There the object was to identify different kinds of decisions and processes, to distil the standards of fair treatment within each, and to outline the main issues in designing procedures. In this Part, the emphasis moves to the procedural principles and doctrines which legislatures, administrators, and courts apply across a wide range of decisions. The idea is to take at least the main principles and doctrines and to examine both their rationale and their application. The emphasis will be on English law, but reference will be made from time to time to other jurisdictions.

The emphasis will also be on administrative processes and on the doctrines of procedural fairness most relevant to them. Administrative due process, as it might be called, is an area of great activity and enormous interest. As I suggested at the beginning of this book, the experience most people have of government and their encounters with the state occur in administrative contexts, in the welfare agencies, the licensing authorities, and a myriad of other boards and bodies. The real test of procedures and of notions of fairness is how people are treated in these contexts, which are often complex, disorganized, and hidden from the outside eye. To protect against unfair treatment here is no mean task. Parliament, administrators, and courts have all been active in building a culture of due process, and some of the most interesting developments are in the most mundane aspects of administration. The way in which the prison has been transformed in a few years from a closed and lawless institution to one which is reasonably open to scrutiny and subject to basic ideas of due process is an outstanding example.[1]

But although important progress has been made in this and other areas, administrative processes are vast in quantity and enormously variable in nature. New bodies and agencies are being created almost daily, often without proper statutory provision for procedures. The courts have certainly played their part in recent years in extending ideas of procedural fairness to many areas of administration. Their decisions in relation to one area can often be extrapolated to other areas, but judicial review is invoked on a

[1] The transformation is well documented by M. Loughlin and P. Quinn in 'Prisons, Rules and Courts: A Study in Administrative Law' (1993) 56 *MLR* 497.

somewhat haphazard basis, and some areas of administration still seem to escape judicial notice. There is no reason to think that the administrative officials themselves are unconcerned with fair treatment; as empirical studies consistently show, they clearly are. Their difficulty is that they often work under such constraints of time and resources that regard for fairness is overshadowed by other, more pressing concerns.

Against this background, the matters to be considered in this part are as follows. In Chapter 10 an outline is given of the sources of procedures and procedural principles, and of the different influences and controls over them. This provides the opportunity for a brief review of the role of Parliament and other bodies involved in designing procedures. This leads on in Chapter 11 to discussion of the general legal approach to procedural fairness in administrative contexts and of the more specific issues to be discussed. Doctrines relating to notice, disclosure, and hearing occupy Chapter 12, while the setting of standards, the giving of reasons, and the idea of impartiality in administrative contexts are analysed in Chapter 13. The final chapter in this part offers a brief account of the various forms of recourse available from primary decisions, together with an assessment of their importance and their effect on the quality of primary decisions.

While my primary aim in this Part is to examine the doctrines and principles in this area, I also introduce, where possible, another level of analysis, namely, the empirical. The empirical study of administrative processes is now well-established and adds an important dimension of understanding. Many issues still await investigation, but such studies as exist are invaluable, not only in showing what happens in practice, but also in reflecting back on the doctrines and theories themselves. Theory guides practice, but practice may also point to better theory.

10
The Sources of Procedures

The object of this Chapter is to give an account of the sources of procedures in administrative contexts. Amongst the various sources available, Parliament has the final say and it is now generally expected that, in creating administrative bodies, Parliament will make provision for the procedures to be followed. Just how procedural approaches emerge within statutory schemes and the influences which shape them are important matters which await empirical study. While the role of Parliament in settling procedures has developed in recent years, it is by no means comprehensive. The result is that gaps are left to be filled by other sources—by the administrative agencies themselves, by the courts, and by special bodies such as the Council on Tribunals and the various ombudsmen. Indeed, as the discussion in this Chapter shows, a whole range of administrative institutions plays a part in creating a procedural environment.

While much of the Chapter is devoted to a brief examination of the main sources of procedures, towards the end of the Chapter the issue of a code of administrative procedures of general application is raised. With the recent publication by the Council on Tribunals of a procedural model to guide the creation of procedures in tribunals, the idea of a general code of procedures for administrative processes, which surfaces from time to time only to be quietly dropped shortly after, has once again attracted attention. The case for such a code is reviewed and, although arguments can be seen both for and against, the Chapter concludes on a somewhat negative note as to how useful a code really would be.

10.1 SOURCES IN GENERAL

The sources from which the procedures of administration derive, and the institutions responsible for them, are several. In most legal systems, the first place to look for guidance is the constitution, with the pattern set by the American Constitution now familiar: a general due process clause (or clauses) is followed by a number of more specific procedural principles. The general clauses in the American Constitution mean that administrative decisions must comply with the due process of law principle whenever life, liberty, or property is affected.[1] Precisely what procedures are required in

[1] The American due process doctrine is discussed more fully in Ch. 6.

the administrative sphere, once the due process clause is triggered, is likely to vary from one context to another and is often a matter of dispute and the subject of much litigation. The more specific procedural guarantees of the Constitution relate to the right to counsel and the right to trial by jury. The Constitution is of course only a starting point, with a wealth of procedural matters being left to legislators, administrators, and courts.

Since the United Kingdom does not have a written constitution, the sources of procedures are more diverse. The main source is parliamentary statute and we should now expect that whenever new powers are conferred or authorities created, procedural provisions will be included in the statute. Parliament may also enact a statute which stipulates procedural principles of general application. The most notable example is the Tribunals and Enquiries Act 1948 which contains a number of general procedural principles applying to tribunals. Often the responsibility for procedures is delegated by Parliament through statutory provision to a minister or other official. Procedural rules might then take the form of delegated legislation with the usual requirement that they be laid before Parliament. The procedures for making rules are sometimes less formal and proposed rules may escape parliamentary scrutiny altogether. The administrative body itself usually has some role in designing procedures, or at least in adding to and making workable the more general provisions contained in statute for delegated legislation. There are also special bodies like the Council on Tribunals, which has responsibility for the procedures of tribunals, and various Ombudsmen who may discover procedural defects in the course of an investigation into alleged maladministration or other impropriety. The role of the courts in developing principles of procedural fairness has already been touched on and is considered more fully in later chapters. Their task divides broadly into two parts: one is to fill in the gaps which escape statutory regulation or where statutory procedures are considered inadequate; the other is to formulate principles of more general application. Since both tasks have to be performed in the context of applications for judicial review in specific cases, the opportunities for the courts to develop general procedural principles are limited. Finally, brief mention should be made of the European Convention on Human Rights with its due process clause which is beginning to have an impact on the law of the United Kingdom.[2] A brief account of these main sources of procedures and of the institutions responsible for them will be given in the following pages.

The division amongst so many authorities of responsibility for procedures can hardly be efficient or effective, so that the case for a general code or even a set of general procedural principles may seem powerful. The Franks Committee, however, rejected the idea of a code of procedure even for

[2] See the discussion in Ch. 7.

tribunals, let alone for administrative processes in general.[3] The Tribunals and Enquiries Act 1948, which originated in the Franks Committee Report, deals with some procedural issues, the right to be heard and the giving of reasons in particular, but it does not purport to be in any sense a code of fair procedures. The Committee's objective was to improve the levels of procedural fairness in administrative tribunals, but it considered that, rather than have a general code, each statute should specify the procedures suited to the particular tribunal. Following the Committee's report, Parliament created the Council on Tribunals and gave it a general brief to advise ministers and departments on the procedures of tribunals; it is also required to comment on such matters in its annual report. The Council, whose role is considered in section 10.3, has been active in developing procedural principles and recently published a model code of procedures for tribunals. This undoubtedly will strengthen the mounting support for a code of administrative procedures in the United Kingdom, but it is by no means certain that any major reforms will follow.

Outside the United Kingdom, it is not unusual to find the statutory enactment of general procedural principles. The American Administrative Procedure Act 1944, which applies to the agencies and departments of federal government, states the procedural principles governing rule-making[4] and individualized decisions of an adjudicative nature.[5] Matters such as access to information, participation at the hearing, and the giving of reasons are dealt with in detail in the legislation. A Model State Act, which is broadly based on the Federal Act, has been adopted in whole or part by most of the states.[6] Now while both sets of legislation are important in stating general procedural principles for rule-making and adjudication, neither applies to administrative processes which fall outside those categories. Adjudication, moreover, is narrowly defined and does not include the mass of decisions, sometimes called informal adjudication, which are estimated to constitute 90 per cent of the total of administrative decisions.[7] Informal decisions are subject to constitutional due process and to common law notions developed by the courts, but otherwise the procedures applicable to them are left to the specific statute and to the informal actions of administrative agencies. The result is that the procedural requirement for large areas of administrative action differ from one jurisdiction to another and even within jurisdictions.

[3] *Report of the Committee on Administrative Tribunals and Enquiries* (Cmnd. 218, 1957), para. 63.

[4] See the discussion in Ch. 16.

[5] Administrative Procedures Act, s. 554 ff.

[6] Model State Administrative Procedures Act, 1982.

[7] See further W. F. Fox, *Understanding Administrative Law* (2nd edn., Bender, New York, 1992), ch. 9.

10.2 PARLIAMENT AND THE ADMINISTRATION AS SOURCES OF PROCEDURE

10.2.1 Parliament and Procedures

The main argument against attempting to stipulate a general code of procedures is the diversity of administrative processes and the need to design procedures to fit each context. This puts the onus on Parliament to direct its attention to procedural matters each time it confers powers and creates new authorities. Its record in this regard is mixed; on the one hand, some of the earliest statutes incorporate principles of due process, which on the other hand Parliaments in the nineteenth century were profligate in granting the widest powers without a hint at procedures.[8] Parliament's record has improved in recent years, so that now new statutory schemes usually include procedural issues. This may be because politicians have become more aware of the importance of procedural matters, but is probably due in greater part to the influence of bodies like the Council of Tribunals, the Parliamentary Commissioner for Administration, and various other Ombudsmen; it is also partly due to the courts in developing judicial review, and not least owes much to the professionalism of Parliamentary Counsel in drafting legislation in the first place. The contribution from Parliament may take a number of forms. One is to insert procedural principles into the statute itself; a second is to delegate to the minister or official the power to make procedural rules, while retaining some scope for parliamentary scrutiny; a third is to invest special authorities like the Council on Tribunals with responsibility for supervising procedural issues and reporting on them to Parliament. Each of these will be considered in turn.

As to the first, since it is common practice for Parliament, when conferring powers on an authority, to make provision for the procedures to be followed, primary legislation is now a major source of procedural principles.[9] Amongst the many examples to be found in recent studies, the following are typical. The powers of the Local Government Commission to review the electoral boundaries of local government are subject to detailed statutory procedures relating to representation, consultation, and the provision of information.[10] Similarly, the procedures to be followed by port authorities in proposing schemes for the transfer of certain port functions to private companies, and those governing the setting of standards of performance by the Director of Telecommunications for broadcasting bodies, are set out in detail.[11] While

[8] See the discussion in sect. 5.3.1.

[9] For an extended analysis of the various statutory approaches to procedures, see K. J. Keith, *A Code of Procedures for Administrative Tribunals* (Legal Research Foundation, NZ, 1974).

[10] Local Government Act 1992, s. 15.

[11] Competition and Service (Utilities) Act 1992, s. 27B.

examples like these relate to policy- and rule-making, a similar approach applies in relation to decisions of a more clearly individualized nature, although here Parliament often delegates responsibility for the detailed procedures to the Secretary of State or other official. Under the Child Support Act 1991, for example, provision is made for the Secretary of State to order a revision of maintenance payments, and, while the statute sets out the general procedural framework, power is given to the Secretary of State to make regulations filling in the procedural details. It is also noticeable in this context that, while statutes often deal with the procedures for appeal from or review of a decision, they tend to be silent on the procedures to be followed by the primary decision-maker. Within the framework established for social security payments, for example, provision is made for appeals to the tribunal and from the tribunal to the commission, but nothing is said about the primary decision of the adjudication officers who initially determine claims to welfare.[12] Procedures in that case are more likely to be dealt with in delegated rules or left to the discretion of the administrative agency.

From the study of recent statutory schemes, it is difficult to discern any clear pattern as to which procedural issues are considered important enough to be dealt with by Parliament in the statute. Where a procedural framework has to be created in order to achieve the very objects of the statute, this will normally be found in the statute itself. Similarly, questions of appeal and review of the primary decision are usually provided for by statute. Beyond these cases, however, generalization becomes difficult: procedures for notice and hearing are sometimes decreed, at other times not; rights of participation and consultation occur frequently in statutes conferring general policy- or rule-making powers, while the position with regard to individualized decisions tends to be haphazard. Generalizations like these are not all that helpful and it is difficult to resist the conclusion that Parliament as a collective body and its professional advisers have no clear view about what should be included in the statute and what not.

Whatever provision is made in the statute, it is often supplemented by more detailed rules made under delegated authority. Examples are plentiful. The Secretary of State for Social Security has power to make regulations on procedural matters relating to the determination of claims and appeals from them. Some of these are rules for the efficient and orderly conduct of the system, while others deal with issues of access to information, and with the right to be heard, to be represented, and to be given reasons. Similarly, the Treasury is given power to make procedural rules for appeals from decisions of the Friendly Societies' Commissioner to a tribunal, although interestingly that power does not extend to the procedures of the Commission at first instance.[13] In the broadcasting field, the procedures to be followed by the

[12] Social Security Act 1991. [13] Friendly Societies Act 1992.

Director of Telecommunications in settling a dispute between the operator of a service and a complainant are to be laid down by the Director himself.[14] However, it is again difficult to say whether any pattern emerges as to when Parliament will delegate procedural rule-making to a minister or other official. The common practice in modern statutes is for procedural matters to be expressly delegated in this way, subject to more important matters being dealt with in the statute itself. Extensive delegation generally makes good sense, since the minister or other authority responsible for the oversight or implementation of a statutory scheme is in a good position to decide on the details of procedures. Not only are such officials aware of the practical issues likely to arise, but they can keep the procedures under review and make changes as necessary. The codes of practice for police investigation and the questioning of suspects, and the immigration rules governing entry and deportation, are good examples; both are much concerned with procedural matters and both are kept under regular review by ministers and their advisers. Since procedural rules are normally (but not always) required to be laid before Parliament,[15] there is a chance that they will be scrutinized by the Merits Committee or even by Members in the House itself.

10.2.2 Procedural Rule-making by Administrative Bodies

Many procedural matters escape the attention of Parliament or the minister and are left to be settled by the administrative bodies themselves. Where the statute is silent or the procedural regime it creates incomplete, or where procedural matters are not covered in delegated legislation, it is for the administrative body to settle its own procedures. This might be done under express statutory authority, an example being the powers of the Director of Telecommunications to devise the procedures his office will follow in settling certain disputes. More often, however, the administrative body simply is left with a gap in the procedures which must be filled in order for it to carry out its statutory tasks. It must then not only settle the procedures for the effective and economical discharge of its powers, but also determine such matters as whether people affected should be heard, what information should be provided, and whether reasons should be given. Procedural rule-making by administrative authorities will usually be part of their general rule-making powers, although amongst the many studies of rule-making, I do not know of any which deal specifically with the making of procedural rules.

[14] Competition and Service (Utilities) Act 1992.

[15] Whether they are so required depends on the parent statute and there are clearly exceptions: see e.g. the Friendly Societies Act 1992.

10.3 THE COUNCIL ON TRIBUNALS AND ITS MODEL PROCEDURES

10.3.1 The Role of the Council on Tribunals

The Council on Tribunals is a body created by Parliament with direct responsibility for procedural issues. Its main task is, in its own words, to keep 'under review the constitution, working and procedures of a large number of tribunals, and the procedures of certain inquiries'.[16] This task is carried out in several ways. In the first place, the Council must be consulted about the procedural rules to be made by a minister or other official for use in a tribunal or public inquiry.[17] Secondly, the Council must be consulted before a tribunal can be exempted from the duty to give reasons for its decisions.[18] Thirdly, in addition to its statutory entitlement to be consulted, the Council urges ministers and departments to consult it about procedural matters which may be included in primary legislation. Finally, the Council keeps a close watch over the practical operation of tribunals and regularly offers advice to ministers, departments, and other officials, about shortcomings and how they might be remedied. It also takes an active interest in the creation of new tribunals, and may recommend from time to time that the adjudicative functions of administrative bodies should be constituted as tribunals and brought under the control of the Tribunals and Inquiries Act.

In a recent and typical year,[19] the Council expressed concern about the delay in hearing appeals to the Mental Health Appeal Tribunal; it investigated problems of the impartiality of the Education Appeal Tribunals; and it urged the General and Special Commissioners of Income Tax to adopt proper procedural rules. The Council recommended that tribunals should be created to hear appeals from housing benefit decisions, and it argued that some of the powers of the directors of new regulatory bodies, especially those relating to recently privatized industries, were adjudicative in nature and should be brought under the Council's supervision. In the same year, the Council reaffirmed the importance of the right to a full and fair appeal from any administrative decision which affects important rights and interests. On that score, it found certain of the government's proposals to change the right of asylum seekers and prisoners to be cause for concern.

These examples are typical of the matters with which the Council concerns itself. On the basis of these cases and other comments by the Council, a number of general procedural principles, which it has consistently pursued,

[16] *Annual Report 1983–4*, 1.

[17] Tribunals and Inquiries Act 1992, s. 8. The duty to consult is limited to tribunals listed in the schedule to the Act, but the list is fairly comprehensive.

[18] Ibid., ss. 9 and 110.

[19] These examples are taken from the *1990–1 Annual Report.*

can be identified. The most important of these are: that the person affected by an administrative decision should generally have the right to appeal to a tribunal; that tribunals should be independent of ministers and departments and impartial in their decisions; that administrative bodies exercising adjudicative functions should be regarded as tribunals and made subject to the Council's supervision on procedural matters; that there should be a right of appeal on matters of law from a tribunal to the courts.[20]

10.3.2 The Council's Model Rules of Procedure

One indication that the Council has consolidated its position and established itself as a major source of procedural principles is the recent publication of a model set of procedural rules to be adopted by tribunals throughout the country.[21] The model is not intended as a code of procedures to be applied rigidly by all tribunals, but is meant to express in the form of detailed procedures the general ideals of openness, fairness, and impartiality put forward by the Franks Committee. It also reflects the Council's own experience of procedural issues over a long period and its commitment to a number of basic principles. The idea is that, while the precise procedures for each tribunal will vary according to its own circumstances, the model rules should be both the starting point and a common measure.

It is unnecessary here to examine the model rules in any detail, but several features are noteworthy. One is that much attention is paid to the procedures to be followed by tribunals in making their decisions and to the values underlying those procedures. These include the opportunity for a person to put his case and to know the opponent's case; the availability of documents and information; the importance of expedition and efficiency in deciding cases; and the giving of reasons. The model rules also emphasize other significant values. One is that people should know of their rights of appeal and have easy access in pursuing them. Another is that a person should not be prejudiced by ignorance and fear of the tribunal's procedures. A tribunal's duty is to reach the right decision, that is, the decision which properly judges the appellant's claim according to an accurate finding of facts and the correct application of legal standards. That duty and the applicant's right to its performance should not be compromised by the lack of representation, nor by the inability of a claimant to argue the case properly. Tribunals are expressly exhorted to adjust their procedures to ensure that the issues are adequately clarified and that the proceedings are justly conducted in all respects. This is not to say that a tribunal should

[20] These general themes are gleaned from Annual Reports of the Council, from its *Model Rules of Procedures of Tribunals* (Cm 1434, 1991) and *The Function of the Council on Tribunals* (Cm 7805, 1980).

[21] *Model Rules of Procedure for Tribunals*, n. 20 above.

adopt a relentlessly investigatory and inquisitorial demeanour; the general assumption, indeed, is that the proceedings should be broadly adversarial.[22] Within an adversarial framework, however, duties are cast on tribunals to reach the right outcome and to provide the applicant with whatever assistance is needed for that purpose.[23] It is too early to tell what effect the model of procedural rules will have on the future procedures of tribunals, but the very fact that a detailed model has been formulated and that the values at stake have been identified, is itself significant. Final assessment of the impact of the model on tribunals, and more broadly, must wait, but one or two observations can be made about the general effect of the Council on Tribunals on the procedural landscape.

The role of the Council on Tribunals is consultative and advisory; it must be consulted about the procedures of tribunals and it may give advice, but it has no power to require that one set of procedures rather than another be adopted. Nevertheless, having been created by Parliament following the report of the Franks Committee, the Council on Tribunals has established itself as a significant institution in developing administrative procedures and as the guardian of certain important principles. Its advice to ministers and departments is not always acted on, but the very fact that it exists, that it keeps a close watch over tribunals, that its views must be considered, and that it can publicly criticize, is important.[24] A tolerable society needs intermediate bodies of that kind, bodies which do not make final decisions, let alone govern, but which are engaged in an activity and in acquiring knowledge and experience within it, and which must be listened to by government. It is also characteristic of such bodies that their precise impact on tribunals, and to a lesser extent inquiries, occupies a large part of the administrative process. The Council has more than eighty different kinds of tribunals under its supervision, which amongst them deal with more than a million cases each year.[25] Since almost every year sees the creation of new tribunals and an increasing number of decisions made by them, the need for a body like the Council to supervise and monitor procedures is all too clear. A strong case can also be made for a body committed to developing a stock of general procedural principles, which become accepted as standards, to be adhered to not only by tribunals but possibly throughout the adjudicative process.

[22] The tension between the two procedural models has also arisen in the context of the Australian Administrative Appeals Tribunal and has been much discussed by courts and commentators. See further D. J. Galligan, 'Tribunals' in Galligan, *Laws of Australia: Administrative Law* (Law Book Co., Sydney, 1993).

[23] See *Model Rules*, n. 21 above.

[24] For a fuller assessment of the Council see C. Harlow and R. Rawlings, *Law and Administration* (Weidenfeld and Nicholson, London, 1984), ch. 6. For an earlier analysis see R. Wraith and P. Hutchinson, *Administrative Tribunals* (Allen and Unwin, London, 1973).

[25] Some of these bodies are not designated as tribunals but are brought under the Council's supervision because they exercise adjudicative functions, either at first instance or by way of appeal.

The practical impact of the Council on Tribunals, however, awaits proper empirical investigation. It is a small organization, working on very limited resources, a matter which undoubtedly hampers its activities. Its lack of power to insist that procedural reforms be adopted by tribunals is also a drawback, for no matter how convincing the Council's prospects may be, the final decision as to their practical application rests with ministers and their departments. That the Council does not always have its way but may be thwarted by ministers and advisers is clear from its annual reports. It is also important to bear in mind that the supervisory role of the Council extends only to tribunals, which usually means appellate bodies exercising adjudicative functions.[26] Primary decisions, whether made by ministers, departmental officials, agencies, or statutory authorities, are beyond the direct scrutiny of the Council. General principles expounded by the Council might have some influence on administrative processes other than those directly under its supervision, especially primary decisions of various kinds, but any influence will be indirect and piecemeal. The Council may recommend to a minister that an area of decision-making is really of an adjudicative nature and ought to be brought within the provisions of the Tribunals and Inquiries Act; it is sometimes successful in this, but again the final decision rests with the minister who may be more influenced by other factors.

10.4 OMBUDSMEN AND THEIR INFLUENCE ON PROCEDURES

10.4.1 The Role of Ombudsmen

Since the creation in the United Kingdom of the office of Parliamentary Commissioner for Administration (PCA) in 1967, the idea of the ombudsman as an independent investigator of administrative malpractice has spread in both the public and the private sectors. The PCA's powers in relation to central government were soon matched by a similar body, the Commission for Local Administration (CLA), whose task is to investigate complaints at the level of local government. This was followed by the creation of the Health Service Commission, the Police Complaints Authority, Ombudsmen for Wales and Scotland respectively, the Adjudicator for taxation and other matters, and most recently the Ombudsman for Prisons.[27] While the precise powers of each office differ, the task common to all is to receive complaints from individual persons about their treatment by a department or other public authority, to investigate the complaints which have substance, and to

[26] Not all tribunals are subject to the Council's supervision, which applies only to those listed in the Schedule to the Tribunals and Inquiries Act 1992.

[27] Various ombudsmen have also been created in a number of private spheres, including banking, insurance, and building societies.

recommend suitable remedies where maladministration or other impropriety is made out.

A detailed discussion of each office is beyond my present purpose,[28] the main point of interest here being the role of each ombudsman in relation to procedural matters. Even on that issue the discussion must be brief. However, two general statements may be made with confidence. The first is that procedural issues, that is to say, the procedures followed by administrative bodies, are central to the ombudsmen's concerns. A high percentage of complaints relates to procedures, but because the procedural points are not always expressed as such, it is difficult to state exactly what the percentage is. The second general statement is that very little evidence is available to show what impact the investigations of ombudsmen have on administrative procedures. In the absence of extensive empirical research on the matter, we can only guess at what the impact might be.[29] It is still worthwhile considering how ombudsmen become involved in procedural issues and I shall deal mainly with the PCA and CLA, although the various other offices are similar in many respects.

The main task of ombudsmen is to consider and to investigate complaints made by individuals about the way they have been treated by administrative authorities.[30] Ombudsmen provide one avenue of recourse which, like other forms of appeal or review, depends on someone lodging a complaint. The original rationale, that the ombudsman's powers should be based on the investigation of specific complaints, has since been confirmed from time to time. In investigating a complaint, an ombudsman generally has ample powers to inquire into the affairs of the agency or department, but it has no roving commission to investigate matters beyond what is necessary for that purpose, nor to undertake an investigation on its own initiative.

While the investigation of complaints is the primary function of ombudsmen, to regard it as the sole function would be to miss an important second aspect. In the course of an investigation, an ombudsman will often have the opportunity of scrutinizing in a more general way the practices and procedures of the administrative body.[31] Where flaws are uncovered, it is only sensible that the ombudsman should be able to report on them. A recent writer has expressed the relationship between the individualized aspects and the general in this way: 'As well as obtaining redress for the

28 For a recent and helpful account, see M. Seneviratne, *Ombudsmen in the Public Sector* (Open UP, Milton Keynes, 1994).

29 In general very little empirical research has been carried out into the workings of ombudsmen; for a review of the work to 1986, see R. Rawlings, *The Complaints Industry: A Review of Socio-Legal Research on Aspects of Administration Justice* (Economic and Social Research Council, 1986).

30 See the discussion in K. Friedman, 'Realization of Ombudsmen Recommendations', *4th International Ombudsmen Conference* (1988).

31 See *Justice—All Souls Review of Administrative Law in the United Kingdom* (Clarendon Press, Oxford, 1985).

individual complaint, ombudsmen are concerned with improving public administration in general, so that future injustice and maladministration will be prevented.[32] It seems that the various ombudsmen regard this as part of their function, but no research has yet been done to show how much effort is being put into the more general aspects, nor what impact it has had on general administration. Recent reports from the PCA do not give the impression that improving public administration in a general sense is a major aim. Indeed, since the number of complaints to the PCA is small, the opportunities for a more systematic appraisal of general administration are few.[33] Where suggestions for general improvement are made, it is not clear that the PCA monitors their implementation. The PCA does make reference from time to time to the wider aim and suggestions for improving this part of its work have been included in its management plan.[34] The CLA takes a more positive approach and regularly reports on its efforts to improve the general practices and procedures of local government.[35] It has published a code of practice on complaints procedures for local government and gives guidance on setting them up; it consistently emphasizes the importance of good practices and procedures and regularly comments in its annual reports on its success in securing improvements. The CLA appears to be diligent in monitoring any changes introduced following its suggestions, and in the housing area local authorities now have a statutory duty to notify the CLA of the steps taken to implement the latter's recommendations.[36]

10.4.2 The Influence of Ombudsmen on Procedures

Both aspects of an ombudsman's role, the individualized and the generalized, are likely to involve procedural issues. Complaints made to ombudsmen are often, perhaps mainly, about procedural errors, while at the level of general administration, the matters which come to their attention are also predominantly procedural. Since the powers of ombudsmen are normally limited to or based on notions of maladministration, it is understandable that procedural errors should be one of the main reasons for complaint. Parliament has tended not to try to define maladministration, but leaves it to the ombudsmen and occasionally the courts to develop the concept. A recent list compiled by the PCA of matters amounting to maladministration includes: neglecting to inform a person of his rights; offering no redress or disproportionate redress; showing bias; not informing people of their rights

[32] M. Seneviratne, *Ombudsmen in the Public Sector*, n. 28 above, 12; see also 57–8. Some argue that this wider task ought to be given greater prominence: see Harlow and Rawlings, *Law and Administration*, n. 24 above, ch. 7.

[33] Fewer than 200 complaints are investigated each year.

[34] *Annual Report 1991*.

[35] See e.g. the *Annual Report 1992–3*.

[36] See further M. Seneviratne, *Ombudsmen in the Public Sector*, n. 28 above, 116–20.

of appeal; faulty procedures; failure to monitor compliance with procedures.[37] Matters of impropriety like these and others of a similar kind have a strongly procedural nature. The PCA went on to say that the main errors encountered in investigations are delay, mistaken outcomes, failure to follow procedures, and bad advice. If we keep in mind that the point of good procedures is primarily to ensure that people are treated in accordance with law, that they get what is due to them, then these four heads are strikingly procedural or have procedural implications. Similar patterns appear in the work of the CLA. To take a recent annual report as an example, reference is made to: the failure to make adequate enquiries into the circumstances of a homeless person; the failure properly to consider relevant information in making a decision; the absence of clear standards for providing a service, such as home help; neglecting to inform a person of his rights of appeal; not treating people consistently; and delay.[38] The work of the Health Service Commission suggests the position there is similar.[39]

At the level of general administration, procedural issues are equally prominent. Although we do not have the evidence on which to base a full and accurate account, it seems that when the investigation of a complaint concerns a more general malpractice it is likely to be procedural. Since the ombudsman's job is to counter maladministration rather than pass judgment on the wisdom of substantive policies, it is to be expected that procedural matters should be prominent. We noted earlier the limited role of the PCA in improving administration at the general level in contrast to that of the CLA; we also noted the positive interest the latter has taken in improving procedures in local government. In the field of housing benefit, for example, the CLA has made recommendations about general procedures in almost half the cases investigated.[40] It has also made a significant contribution to procedures both at the level of primary decisions and in relation to appeals and reviews from them. The CLA has been particularly active in helping local authorities set up their own internal complaints procedures. It has a statutory duty to encourage local authorities to develop and publicize their own procedures for the fair settlement of complaints and to settle as many as possible.[41]

The role of ombudsmen in improving general administrative procedures may be bolstered in the future by the adoption of the Citizen's Charter.[42] The Charter has not directly affected the functions of ombudsmen, but the duties imposed on departments, agencies, and local authorities may have implications for ombudsmen.[43] The Charter works at two levels. At the first,

[37] *Annual Report 1992–3*, 4.

[38] See *Annual Reports 1991–2* and *1992–3*.

[39] See D. Longley, *Public Law and Health Service Accountability* (Open UP, Milton Keynes, 1993).

[40] *Annual Report 1992–3*.

[41] *Annual Report 1991–2*.

[42] *The Citizen's Charter; Raising the Standard* (Cm. 1599).

[43] The relationship is examined in *The Implications of the Citizen's Charter for the work of*

authorities and agencies are requested to formulate and publicize their standards (performance targets as they are now called) in providing services; they must also publish a full account of the standards which they in fact achieve. At the second level, steps should be taken by the agency to make sure that the standards are met. Such steps include the introduction of more effective complaints procedures, the creation of more inspectorates to monitor the level of performance by the institution, and the adoption of better means of redress for people affected by poor service.[44] The standards of performance are required to have several qualities: they should be explicit; they should ensure courtesy and helpfulness on the part of the agency; they should aim at producing accurate decisions in accordance with the statutory standards; and they should encourage promptness.

The Charter standards do not bind the various ombudsmen, nor are they definitive as to what constitutes good and bad administration. The very idea of the Charter has been met with scepticism in some quarters, but the duty on the public authorities to set standards of performance may prove to have advantages. Much of course depends on what the standards are and whether they are genuinely directed at improvements in the quality of service and performance. Subject to such rather exacting provisos, the idea that an authority should declare the standards by which it will function, and by which members of the public may expect to be treated, is commendable. If the Charter idea survives and develops, the standards laid down will undoubtedly become important considerations in any investigation by ombudsmen. The implications for procedures are also significant, since the very formulation of standards of performance and the importance put on accurate decision-making according to them raise procedural issues. Both the setting of standards and compliance with them in individualized decisions are basic elements of fair treatment. The various mechanisms required to ensure compliance with the standards and to provide means of redress are explicitly procedural. We may conclude from this brief account that while the Charter is in its early stages, the relationship between it and ombudsmen will be an interesting development to follow in the future.[45]

10.5 OTHER BODIES CREATING AND INFLUENCING PROCEDURES

This survey of the institutions and authorities involved in the creation and supervision of administrative procedures is by no means complete, since a

the PCA (Select Committee Report on PCA, 2nd Report, HMSO, 1992). See also A. W. Bradley, 'Sachsenhausen, Barlow Clowes and Then' [1992] *Public Law* 353.

[44] See *The Citizen's Charter*, n. 42 above, 5.

[45] See further A. Barron and C. Scott, 'The Citizen's Charter Programme' (1992) 55 *MLR* 526.

host of others are likely to become involved in procedural issues in a variety of ways. The object here has been to mention just a few of the more important ones, as well as to note the changes and upheavals which have swept through British government and administration in recent years. Noteworthy amongst such changes and upheavals have been the adoption of the Citizen's Charter and the creation of ever more boards, commissioners, and inspectorates, to supervise and scrutinize primary decision-making institutions. Another manifestation of the changes has been the idea of the ombudsman as a form of supervision which has spread in one guise or another to many areas of government and administration.[46] Provision is made in the Citizen's Charter for a system of lay adjudicators who will complement the ombudsmen and provide recourse at the most basic levels of administration. The Audit Commission has been given added powers to examine and report on the financial management of administrative bodies, including local government.[47] In the intermediate world of the public or recently privatized utilities, regulatory bodies have been created to monitor and give directions with respect to certain activities of privatized corporations.[48] If we add to this list the increasing interest in the idea that administrative authorities should have their own informal procedures of review and scrutiny, then the range of institutions and processes is extensive.[49] The fragmentation of central government through the creation of specialized agencies (Next Steps Agencies as they are called) with relatively autonomous powers, will add to the need for additional bodies to watch over them.[50] Many of the authorities mentioned have no direct control over procedural matters, but considering the close relationship between procedure and substance, each is likely unavoidably to have an influence on procedures. These, however, are matters which are hardly touched in the literature and are fertile areas for further enquiry.

[46] For a fuller account of recent changes in administrative government, see D. J Galligan, *Introduction* in D. J. Galligan (ed.), *Socio-Legal Readings in Administrative Law* (Clarendon Press, Oxford, 1996).

[47] See M. Loughlin, *Local Government in the Modern State* (Sweet and Maxwell, London, 1986).

[48] See T. Prosser, *Nationalized Industries and Public Control* (Blackwell, Oxford, 1986), and C. Graham and T. Prosser, 'Rolling Back the Frontier: The Privatization of State Enterprises' in C. Graham and T. Prosser (eds.), *Waiving the Rules* (Open UP, Milton Keynes, 1988).

[49] For discussion of the merits and demerits of internal review, see R. Sainsbury, 'Internal Reviews and the Weakening of Social Security Claimants' Rights of Appeal' in G. Richardson and H. Genn, *Administrative Law and Government Action* (Clarendon Press, Oxford, 1994).

[50] On the fragmentation of central government: Efficiency Unit, *Making the Most of Next Steps* (HMSO, 1991); N. Lewis, 'Change in Government: New Public Management and Next Steps' [1994] *Public Law* 105; G. Flynn and others, 'Symposium on Improving Management in Government' (1980) 66 *Public Administration* 429.

10.6 A CODE OF ADMINISTRATIVE PROCEDURES?

The model procedures recently formulated to guide tribunals in the exercise of their powers draws on the experience of the Council on Tribunals over many years. The question may be asked whether that or some other model ought to be the basis for a code of procedures to apply across the board of administrative processes. The discussion in the preceding sections has given an indication of the different authorities, from Parliament to ombudsmen to administrators themselves, which are responsible for creating and developing procedures and ideas of procedural fairness, or which at least have some influence on such matters. If the contribution of the courts in setting procedural standards is added, the range of approaches may seem so diverse that it is timely to adopt a general procedural code.

10.6.1 Current Trends

Although a code of anything is distinctly un-British, signs of change are beginning to appear. The Council on Tribunal's model procedure is likely to be influential in both the creation and operation of tribunals. The different ombudsmen have become involved to one degree or another in general principles of good administration, a major part of which relates to good procedures. The CLA has been especially influential in procedural matters and has begun work on devising a code of good administration for local government.[51] The Justice–All Souls review of administration recently proposed the adoption of a code of good administration and recommended that the PCA should be responsible for drawing it up.[52] The PCA has been less than enthusiastic at the idea, but there is some evidence to suggest that its interest in general principles of administration is increasing. In an earlier report, Justice proposed a set of principles of good administration which would be binding on all administrative bodies and which included the right to be heard, non-retrospectivity, accurate fact-finding, the provision of information, timeliness, the giving of reasons, and the notification of decisions.[53] The Council of Europe has also taken an interest in the matter and in 1977 the Committee of Ministers adopted a resolution that member states should be guided by five principles, similar to those of Justice, but with two important additions: one was to provide for assistance and representation to a party affected by an administrative process, while the other dealt with recourse and the importance of a party being informed of the avenues of

[51] See M. Seneviratne, *Ombudsmen in the Public Sector*, n. 28 above, 57–8.
[52] Justice–All Souls, n. 31 above, ch. 2.
[53] Justice, *Administration Under Law* (Justice, London, 1971).

recourse available.[54] Shortly after, the Council added principles to deal specifically with administrative discretion. In addition to the standard requirement that discretion be used for the purposes for which it was conferred and that only relevant matters should be taken into account, the new principles dealt with equality before the law, proportionality, timeliness, the consistent application of guidelines, and the giving of reasons for departing from them.[55] It is interesting to note in passing that the proposals did not include a duty to formulate guidelines.

The Justice proposals were never made statutory and appear to have had little impact. The resolution of the Committee of Ministers also came to nothing, even though the United Kingdom government participated in its formulation and agreed to its terms. The British genius for muddling through has prevailed once again and administrative practice remains as diverse and uncoordinated as ever. When it came to formulating the Citizen's Charter, the government and its advisers appeared either not to know of or to have forgotten about those earlier efforts and made no reference to them. With respect to the Charter, the government's motives and purposes were different, for although the Charter is permeated by notions of good administration, no attempt was made to say how it might be achieved. The Charter implicitly recognizes that the accurate application of statutory standards is fundamental to raising the quality of administration, but its emphasis remains on providing recourse when mistakes are made, rather than on improving the quality of primary decisions.[56] This is very much in step with the general trend of British administrative reform, where complaints procedures, forms of appeal, and lines of review of various kinds are the main object of attention. It is important to have adequate means for redressing grievances, but to concentrate on recourse while largely ignoring the basic issues of effectiveness and fairness at the primary level is to mistake the tip for the iceberg.

10.6.2 The Case for a Code

In order to judge the strength of the case for a code of procedures, we ought first to be clear about what it might mean.[57] A procedural code could be drawn at different levels of detail, ranging from rather general standards, such as that a person ought to be heard, to very detailed rules, such as

[54] Resolution of the Committee of Ministers, *On the Protection of the Individual in Relation to the Acts of Administrative Authorities* (Resol. (77) 31 of 28 Sept. 1977).

[55] Resolution of the Committee of Ministers, *Concerning the Exercise of Discretionary Powers by Administrative Authorities* (No. R. (80) 2, 11 Mar. 1980).

[56] See *The Citizen's Charter*, n. 42 above, 5.

[57] For a useful study of a code of practice in the area of mental health, see M. Cavadino, 'Commissions and Codes: A Case Study in Law and Public Administration' [1993] *Public Law* 333.

precisely what sort of hearing it should be. The proposals put forward by Justice are broadly in the first category, while some of the provisions of the American Administrative Procedure Act, such as those specifying what constitutes a hearing, fit the second category.[58] The case for a code pitched at a high level of detail is likely to be unconvincing and a few of the more obvious difficulties should be mentioned. First, it would be difficult to draft a code which would be both generally applied and yet highly detailed. The procedures suitable for individualized adjudication are unlikely to be right for routine administration or policy-based discretion; and even within the confines of individualized adjudication, the procedural variations will be substantial. Secondly, since procedures are very much instruments to ends and values, they need to be malleable and changeable, able to respond to new ideas and improved methods. To bind the future with detailed procedures seemingly appropriate at one time may be an unfortunate hindrance at a later time. Thirdly, inflexible procedures, which are ill-matched to the task in hand, run the risk of being ignored and replaced in practice by informal arrangements and agreements. This apparently happens in some of the areas where a hearing is required under the American Administrative Procedure Act, with respect to which it has been remarked that, if the official procedures were followed in all cases, administration would soon come to a halt.[59] In practice, the formalities are regularly avoided, sometimes by informal agreement between the parties, at other times by unilateral agency action. It might even be suggested that one of the laws of a modern organization is that unsuitable procedures will be ignored and that means will be moulded to ends in the most reasonable and economical manner possible.

The alternative to a detailed, highly specific code of procedures is one based on middle-order standards. The case for a procedural code of that kind is stronger. The proposals put forward by both Justice and the Council of Europe are examples of such middle-order standards. They are general in their terms and apply across the full range of individualized processes. They specify procedures which are normally effective in achieving accurate and proper outcomes, while at the same time being responsive to other relevant values. On close inspection the proposed standards turn out to be a mixture of those two different things: some are a means to accurate and proper outcomes, for example, the provision of information, the right to legal representation and to accurate facts; while others are statements of values, such as non-retrospectivity, proportionality, and consistency, with the right to be heard having a foot in both camps. The distinction is important. In respect of the first group, the implicit claim is that, although each is an

[58] Administrative Procedure Act 1946, s. 5.

[59] See the analysis by J. A. Farmer, 'A Model Code of Procedure for Administrative Tribunals—An Illusory Concept' (1970) 4 *NZUL Rev.* 105.

instrument towards achieving certain outcomes, and in that way is contingent, nevertheless, experience suggests that each will tend always to be a useful and effective instrument to those ends. The weakness in such a claim is that it is not hard to think of cases where one or other procedure will not be needed; legal representation, for example, may not be necessary in many areas of primary decision-making, and a hearing in any real sense of the term is not needed in cases of routine administration. So, even at this level of middle-order generality, unwarranted costs would be incurred by a code of procedural standards. It may be that, all things considered, the costs of over-inclusion in some cases would be justified by the advantages they would bring overall, although such a calculation would be difficult to make.

The second group of procedural standards listed by Justice and the Council of Europe are quite different. They are themselves statements of values, some outcome-based, others independent of outcomes but values to be respected in administrative processes. It may be misleading to think of such values as procedural, since they simply state basic values about how people should be treated in any context. The principle of consistency, for instance, derives from deeper notions of equal treatment, while other values like non-retrospectivity and proportionality are of a similar nature. Each is important enough to justify modifying the main outcome-based standards and to include them in a procedural code would be something of a misclassification. However, the name we give to them should not matter too much; the important thing is, first, to recognize that they are serious social values and then, secondly, to ask whether they are of such enduring importance that they should be stated in a code of good administrative practice. Which values ought to constrain administrative processes is a serious question which deserves proper analysis and discussion; it should not be answered by assuming that such values are procedural and therefore either value-neutral or self-evidently worthwhile. To put the point another way, what values and standards of fair treatment are appropriate is a matter for debate in different contexts; once the case for a particular set of standards is made out, the next step is to devise the procedures needed to ensure their application in administrative processes. This is not to argue against the values contained in the proposals by Justice and the Council of Europe; indeed, they are the very kind of values which we should want to adopt, provided the case for each is properly made.

The question whether to adopt a general code of administrative procedures turns out to be more complicated than might have been expected. The case for attempting a highly detailed code is unconvincing and its value in the longer term is questionable. The case for a middle-order code which is more general and less detailed offers more promise. The main advantage would be the recognition that all administrative processes should be conducted within a defined framework of values and procedures. The values and procedures might have to be adjusted to take account of the different forms of process, but the same common values are likely to be in the background. The shortcoming of a middle-order code is its very generality, so that more detailed procedures would have to be formulated for each area of administrative action, although that might be a strength rather than a shortcoming.

Against this general background, I shall conclude with three final observations. The first is to suggest that the practical formulation of a code should be approached through a two-stage process. The first stage would be to consider what are the values which do or ought to apply in administrative contexts, while the second stage would involve specifying the procedures which are needed to ensure respect for those values and which are general enough to merit a place in the code. Amongst the values to consider would be the main outcome-based value, the accurate and proper application of authoritative standards, and such other surrounding values as consistency, non-retrospectivity, and timeliness. At the second stage, the issue would be whether certain procedures, instrumental to or expressive of those values, are important and constant enough to warrant inclusion in a general code. Examples of the procedures at this level would be the giving of notice, access to information, the hearing, impartiality, reasons, and recourse.

A second point to note here is that, whatever the virtues of a code of values and procedures at the normative level, their application in administrative practice is another matter altogether. The point that the mere statement of normative standards will not lead automatically and naturally to their application in the daily work of administrators is obvious, but worth repeating. The evidence is that even the most basic legal principles are often either not known about or ignored at the lower levels of administrative action. This should not be taken as a counsel of despair. Administrative officials work within a normative context and try to act for reasons which, from their point of view, are both sound and practical. The task is to introduce external normative standards into that working environment so that they shape and influence each official's view of the world. The task, in other words, is to cultivate an administrative ethos which includes the standards of fair treatment to which the society subscribes. That is a difficult task, in the discharge of which we may draw on the fuller understanding socio-legal research has provided of how administrators work and of how their normative environment is constructed.

The final point is to reaffirm the need to improve the quality of administrative processes at the primary level. At that level, which covers the great mass of administrative action, the quality of decisions is generally poor and often abysmal, and it is there that the case for administrative reform is most powerful. One of the merits of a code of procedures would be that it could be directed mainly at improving the quality of primary decisions; we should not, however, expect too much. While a code of procedures may have some influence in bringing decisions up to acceptable standards, in the absence of more fundamental change, its impact is likely to be small. The real obstacles to higher standards of first level decisions and actions are related to the structure of organizations, the training and competence of personnel, and the amount of resources available.[60] In the face of obstacles like that, a code of procedures will be marginal in its effect. Again, this is not an argument against a code; it is merely an attempt to be clear that the source of resistance to justice in administration is more deep-rooted than an absence of sufficiently clear normative standards.

[60] See T. Carney, 'Cloaking the Bureaucratic Dagger: Administrative Law in the Welfare State' (1989) *Canberra B. of PA* 123.

11
The Legal Approach to Procedural Fairness

Amongst the several sources of procedures, the courts have a special and distinctive place. Although the volume of cases they consider is small, the courts have a special significance for a number of reasons. The first is that they are concerned primarily, if not exclusively, with questions of fairness in relation to procedures; secondly, they give reasoned explanations for their decisions; and thirdly, their rulings, although directed at the case in hand, can often be regarded as laying down general principles for application in other cases. The courts have made good use in recent years of their standard-setting role with the result that they have been able to cast off certain restrictions on their own doctrines of procedural fairness; by articulating a number of fundamental, general principles, they also have given guidance to Parliament and the administration. It is true that the precise extent and effect of that guidance is not always clear and requires further study; it is also the case that the courts have not always made the most of opportunities to develop more complete standards of procedural fairness. Nevertheless, they have been a major force in opening up administrative processes to basic notions of due process and fair procedures, and for that reason they occupy a special place in a study of those notions. The role of judicial review as a source of principles of procedural fairness is a major theme running through this and succeeding chapters.

The aim of this Chapter is to describe and analyse the general judicial approach to procedural fairness. That aim is achieved by examining a number of issues: the tests developed by English law as to who is entitled to fair treatment and fair procedures; the standards of fair treatment and fair procedures; the extent to which abstract principles are translated into more detailed procedural rules; and the general judicial approach to exactly what procedural fairness requires and how those requirements are reconciled by the courts with competing considerations, especially costs.

GENERAL LEGAL APPROACH

and courts are all concerned with procedural
me should make provision for procedures, but
t to follow and the variety of approaches found
Procedural issues will only rarely attract the
hemselves, being left in most cases to the profes-
mental lawyers and parliamentary draftsmen.
etween such professional advisers and policy-
hile subject for study, since at present little is
ators also are involved in procedures. They are
ural details, either by the express direction of
case with tribunals, or by necessary implication

The third estate in procedural matters is the courts. Their role, which normally is exercised in the context of judicial review, is not to design primary procedures, but to determine whether those laid down by other authorities meet the standards of procedural fairness. The emphasis lawyers place on the courts may seem out of proportion to their actual role in procedural issues, but it is to some extent justified on the ground that, on many fundamental issues of fairness, the initiative is often taken by the courts. Judicial rulings in cases brought before them lay a foundation of principles which in turn influence Parliament and administrators. It was shown in the preceding chapter how in recent years other bodies have been created which have special interests in procedures, the proliferation of ombudsmen and similar investigatory bodies being notable examples. The work of the Parliamentary Commissioner for Administration (PCA) is concerned with whether government departments have followed good and fair procedures, and the same can be said of the work of other, more specialized ombudsmen. Another example of a different kind is the Council on Tribunals which has a special obligation to oversee procedural matters in relation to tribunals.

An initial question which may be raised is whether, despite the particular concerns of each of those authorities, we may talk of a general legal approach to procedural fairness, especially in administrative matters. Certainly, at a practical level, the same issues arise whatever the authority involved and whatever the context: should the person affected by the process be heard; what sort of hearing should it be; what information should be disclosed; should reasons be given; what does impartiality mean; when is an appeal required; and so on. The answers to such questions depend to a great degree on the context, but not entirely; they also have a more general dimension and can be seen as particular issues within a common framework. The framework itself can be understood at different levels. At an abstract level, the common concern is to devise procedures which in each context lead to fair treatment. At a lower level, the abstract issue can be translated into more precise questions: who is entitled to fair procedures in that context; what are the standards of fair treatment; and what practical procedures are needed to satisfy the standards. These three issues constitute the elements of a legal approach to procedural fairness and each will now be considered in a little more detail.

11.1.1 Who is Entitled to Fair Procedures?

Fair procedures follow fair treatment, so that whenever there is a right to fair treatment by legal authorities, there is also a right to fair procedures. To put the matter at its simplest, whenever a person is involved with the state through its agencies, there is an entitlement to be treated fairly, and, therefore, according to fair procedures. This follows from the discussion in earlier chapters, but it may be of help to restate the gist of the argument. Questions of fair treatment usually arise within a relationship where one party is able to affect the other in a significant way. The relationship may be contractual, where A agrees with B to do Y; or it can arise from social status, as in the case of the parent–child relationship; or it may derive from the relations of power between the community and each citizen. The last of these is marked by the state having power and control: power to impose penalties and disadvantages, control over the distribution of goods and resources. The relationship between citizen and state is governed by implicit normative understandings shared by the members of the community. One such understanding, which is fundamental to the relationship, is that the state's powers and control will be used fairly with respect to each citizen. The concept of fairness in turn means that each person will be given his due, that is, treated as he is entitled to be treated as expressed in authoritative legal standards. In order to be treated according to those standards, a person is entitled to the necessary procedures, and in that sense the right to fair procedures follows the right to fair treatment.

The practical expression of these ideas is that the duty to provide fair procedures comes into play whenever a person is affected by an administrative process. It might be the denial of a benefit, the imposition of a penalty, or the loss of some advantage. Other cases may be less direct and final, but nevertheless real; after an investigation and report, one's reputation might be tarnished; or, as is the case of an arrest or prosecution, a suspect is taken just one step closer to a final outcome, possibly disadvantageous to his interests. In these cases, the person affected is the direct subject of the decision or process, but that need not be the case: I may be put at a disadvantage by a decision granting planning permission to my neighbour; similarly, I may be a member of a group all the members of which are affected by a decision or process.

There are many ways in which a person can be affected tangibly by the actions of officials, some direct and obvious, others indirect and less obvious. Each situation must be examined to see precisely how a person is affected and how society views the consequences. That itself can be problematical since there may be no clear consensus: for example, strongly held but conflicting views are likely to be expressed on whether an alien seeking admission to the country is owed a duty of fair treatment. In other cases, the same consequences may be viewed very differently by those who suffer them compared with the community at large. There are, moreover, bound to be cases of difficulty: is an interest group such as those dedicated to the protection of children, cats, or ancient monuments, owed a duty of fair treatment, or is it just the representatives of those whose interests are affected? Cases like these warrant closer examination than I can give here, but enough has been said to show that, while the principle of fair treatment is easily stated, it is not so easy to decide how it applies in particular cases.

When we move from these general questions of political morality to legal processes, it is usual to find that the range of interests and consequences which attract a right to fair procedures is narrowed. The law tends to ask not just whether a person is affected by a legal process in a general way, but whether certain definable interests are in issue. We have seen how the American doctrine of due process limits interests to life, liberty, or property. This has been taken to mean that, in order to attract due process, it is necessary not only to make out an interest in life, liberty or property, but also to show an entitlement to it under the Constitution or pursuant to state or federal law.[1] The range of interests attracting procedural fairness under the European Convention on Human Rights is even narrower, applying only when the interests are the subject of criminal proceedings or constitute civil rights.[2] English law has its own restrictions on the kinds of interests warranting procedural protection.

Any legal test based on a limited range of interests has certain disadvantages. At the level of principle, such restrictions may be hard to justify, since anyone who is affected by a legal decision has a right that it be made properly according to the law; that in turn is another way of saying that the person is owed a duty of fair treatment, and fair treatment requires fair procedures. Apart from that general point of principle, there are also practical disadvantages. One is the waste of time and resources in deciding whether an interest is protected or not. Another is that some interests valued by the community are likely to be excluded. A familiar criticism of the American doctrine of due process is that certain interests generally considered important do not qualify for due process. Another consequence is that the legal recognition of what constitutes a significant interest is likely to lag behind the views of the wider community. Interests in welfare, using the

[1] See Ch. 6. [2] See Ch. 7.

term in its widest sense of personal well-being, interests in personal liberty in its many forms, interests in being able to pursue opportunities, all offer a wider and more diffuse conception of interests than is easily translated into law. The need for a filter against any old claim being made is obvious, but the cost often is an unduly narrow version of what interests ought to attract procedural protection.

Reflection on the interests approach soon leads to the theoretical point of whether the very concept of an interest is the best way of allocating and restricting procedural protection. The idea of each person as the bearer of a bundle of interests may be useful for practical purposes, but it is less suitable as a defining characterization of the person and of what is important to him. Human personality may be constituted by more intangible senses of well-being, which carry moral significance as to how the person should be treated, in addition to any number of tangible and definable interests. The principle, for example, that the expectations of one person aroused by the undertaking of another should not be lightly frustrated is compelling in itself and need not be reduced to a notion of harmed interests. This is not to argue against a threshold for procedural protection based on interests; such an approach is morally justifiable and has practical advantages. But it is not the only way, nor is it comprehensive, for the rights to fair treatment and procedural protection go beyond the notion of harmed interests.

11.1.2 The Threshold Test of English Law

It is often said by the highest courts that in English law any official who decides anything has a duty to act fairly and in particular to listen to both sides.[3] Since duties of fairness are not owed in the abstract, this can be taken to mean that a duty is owed to anyone affected in a significant way by an official's decision or action. English law is then brought squarely within the general principle of fair treatment and it is not normally difficult to determine whether a person is so affected. Once the duty of fair treatment comes into effect, it brings with it the duty to follow fair procedures.

Although a general principle along these lines is now established in English law, recent history and practice have shown its application to be uneven. Other factors besides the interest affected have weighed in the decision whether or not in a given context a duty of procedural fairness was owed. A review of statutes over the last several years does not reveal a clear or consistent pattern; rights to procedural fairness are sometimes amply conferred, at other times no provision is made at all. Much is left to administrative practice, but we do not know enough about what happens across the range of processes to draw any conclusions. Even in the courts, where

[3] Lord Loreburn in *Board of Education* v. *Rice* [1911] AC 179 at 182.

decisions are important in setting general standards, approaches have been less than consistent. The general duty to act fairly was at one time restricted to administrative processes of a judicial nature,[4] at another time to decisions where legal rights were affected.[5] Both restrictions have now been replaced by the idea that the duty to act fairly applies whenever interests are at stake.[6] What counts as an interest can be problematical, but the tendency has been to broaden the concept beyond economic and property interests to include interests in liberty and welfare.

It is not beyond belief, however, that a court might still consider some interests unimportant enough to attract procedural protection. The alien seeking entry or resisting removal is a case in point; although an interest is at stake, it may not be an interest recognized by English law. Moreover, the interest test is not the only factor to consider. The context of administrative power is relevant, with some areas considered outside judicial protection. The prisons and other closed institutions used to be ignominious examples of where the writ of procedural fairness did not run; that is no longer the case, although some processes within the prison are still not subject to procedural fairness. This is sometimes achieved by their being characterized as managerial discretion or as incidental to maintaining good order.[7] Considerations like these can be legitimate grounds for overriding the general duty of fairness, but the concern is that they are rather crude notions and that their relationship to procedural fairness needs careful examination. Examples like these also raise a wider issue. The principles of fair treatment and fair procedures are general principles which, like any general principles, are likely to conflict with other aspects of the common good. I do not mean just the costs and inconveniences which are implicit in a commitment to principles of fair treatment; I refer rather to those other aspects of the common good which genuinely compete with fairness, so that some accommodation between the two has to be worked out. In some cases fairness may have to give way to other considerations, as in the case of national security;[8] in other cases, a fuller analysis may show that a genuine accommodation can be reached. The good management of a prison, for example, might be arranged in such a way as to include certain elements of procedural fairness. The need to be free of procedural restrictions might be justified in some matters, but such a conclusion should be reached only after careful and imaginative analysis; it should not be, as it often is, an assumption made at the beginning and rigidly applied.

[4] *R.* v. *Leman Street Police Station Inspector, ex parte Venicoff* [1920] 3 KB 72.

[5] *Ridge* v. *Baldwin* [1964] AC 40.

[6] See Lord Diplock in *Bushell* v. *Secretary of State for the Environment* [1981] AC 75.

[7] See M. Loughlin and P. Quinn, 'Prisons, Rules and Courts' (1993) 56 *MLR* 497, 521 ff and G. Richardson, *Law, Process and Custody* (Weidenfeld and Nicholson, London, 1993), ch. 16.

[8] As in *Council of Civil Service Unions* v. *Minister for the Civil Service* [1985] AC 374.

11.1.3 Legitimate Expectations

The principle of procedural fairness may also be triggered by the notion of legitimate expectations, and although it is usually only relevant in relation to hearings, it is convenient to consider the issue here. In one sense legitimate expectations is an extension of the idea of an interest. The duty of procedural fairness is owed, it has been said, when a person's rights, interests, or legitimate expectations are in issue.[9] One might have no right or interest at stake, but, because of something said or done by the authority, an expectation may be raised which should not be disappointed without following certain procedures. An example is an alien seeking an extension of a visa to stay in the United Kingdom. Under English law, he has no right or legitimate interest in being allowed to stay; but he might acquire a legitimate expectation from an undertaking or holding-out that he will be allowed to stay.[10] The expectation becomes a kind of interest which should not be prejudiced without a hearing.

A truer and more satisfactory basis for the link between legitimate expectations and procedural fairness is rather different. On this alternative basis, the principle of fair treatment behind legitimate expectations derives from an undertaking, explicit or implicit, given by an administrative body that, in the exercise of its powers, certain things will be done or not done.[11] Once such an undertaking is given, it would be unfair for the authority not to honour it, or at least not to do so without first following certain procedures. The undertakings which create an expectation may be of different kinds. One is a direct undertaking that certain procedures will be followed. In one case an express undertaking was given that each person's situation would be looked at on its merits before a deportation order was imposed;[12] this was taken to mean that each person would be heard before being deported. In other cases the undertaking is implied. In the *GCHQ* case,[13] an undertaking that the unions would be consulted was implied from the practice of consulting them on other occasions when conditions of service were in question.[14] Lord Fraser put the point in this way:

> prior consultation has been the invariable rule when conditions of service were to be significantly altered . . . in my opinion even if there had been no question of national security involved, the appellants would have had a legitimate expectation that the minister would consult them before issuing the instruction.[15]

[9] Deane J in *Hoaucher* v. *Minister for Immigration and Ethnic Affairs* (1980) 169 CLR 648.

[10] *Schmidt* v. *Home Office* [1969] 2 Ch. 149.

[11] Legitimate expectations arise from the undertaking and it is the undertaking not the expectation which grounds the duty of fairness. See further P. P. Craig, 'Legitimate Expectations and Procedural Fairness: A Conceptual Analysis' (1992) *LQR* 79.

[12] *A.G. of Hong Kong* v. *Ng Yuen Shiu* [1983] 2 AC 629.

[13] N. 8 above.

[14] See Lords Fraser and Roskill, ibid.

[15] Ibid. 322.

The underlying principle is that when a minister or other authority gives an undertaking that certain procedures will be followed before or in the course of a decision, it would be unfair to go back on that undertaking.[16]

A second situation occurs where the expectation is based on an undertaking not as to procedures, but that a certain decision will be made or that a power will be exercised in a particular way. The extent to which an authority can be bound by undertakings of this kind is a matter of difficulty because of two conflicting principles. One is the principle of fair treatment which points to an authority being bound by its undertakings; the other is a principle of public law according to which an authority must use its powers as it considers best at the time. Since the general doctrine is that the public law principle prevails, an authority cannot be bound by prior undertakings which relate to the substance of its powers. However, in practice the courts do not simply apply the public law principle to the exclusion of fair treatment. A compromise is reached by requiring that, before the authority departs from its earlier undertaking, the party should be heard. The legal consequences of a commitment as to substance is that certain procedures must be followed before the authority may resort to its power to act or decide as it considers best at the time.[17] The rationale for this compromise approach is not entirely clear, but rests, presumably, on the idea that before an undertaking is overridden, it is fair to give notice and to let the party make a case against the change.

While legitimate expectations as a source of procedures depend on an undertaking of some sort, it is not always clear whether an undertaking is made out. This is particularly so where the undertaking is not given expressly but has to be inferred from the circumstances. The most problematical case is where the inference is that an existing state of affairs will continue or that a certain state of affairs will be brought into being. The point is brought out in *GCHQ* where, after stating that a civil servant had no right that any term in his employment would continue, Lord Diplock concluded:

> civil servants employed at GCHQ who were members of the national trade union had, at best, . . . a legitimate expectation that they would continue to enjoy the benefits of such membership. . . . So, . . . they were entitled, as a matter of public law under the head 'procedural propriety', before administrative action was taken on a decision to withdraw that benefit, to have communicated to the national trade unions . . . the reason for such withdrawal, and for such unions to be given the opportunity to comment on it.[18]

[16] See also *R.* v. *Liverpool Corporation, ex parte Liverpool Taxi Fleet Operators' Association* [1972] 2 QB 299.

[17] The clearest judicial survey of this issue is that of Justice Gummow in *Kurtovic* v. *Minister for Immigration and Ethnic Affairs* (1990) 92 ALR 93. See also Craig in 'Legitimate Expectations and Procedural Fairness', n. 11 above and the discussion in *R.* v. *Secretary of State, ex parte Ruddock* [1987] 2 QB 299.

[18] N. 8 above.

The logic of the argument is: (i) the fact that a state of affairs has persisted may give rise to an expectation that it will continue; (ii) the expectation is based, presumably, on an implicit undertaking from the authority; (iii) the undertaking gives rise to a duty of fair treatment; (iv) the duty of fair treatment does not require that the state of affairs actually continue, but that certain procedures will be followed before it is altered and expectations disappointed; (v) the procedures usually required are that reasons for the proposed alterations be given and that a chance to comment be extended to the party.

I shall not attempt here to examine all the points of interest arising from the logic of the first argument, but shall conclude with two brief comments.[19] The first concerns the nature of the undertaking which usually takes the form that a state of affairs will happen or continue; that a licence will be renewed, that membership of a trade union will continue, or that a state policy will be applied. In order to discover whether an undertaking has been made and precisely what its content is, it is necessary to examine the power being exercised and the relationship between the official and the person affected. The question then is what is the best interpretation of the relationship, what understandings are there within it, and are they firm enough to create duties on the authority. Whether an undertaking is made out will depend very much on the context; and while every case of administrative power is likely to raise hopes that it will be used in one way rather than another, the point at which mere hope becomes a legitimate expectation may be hard to discern. The second comment is that once the notion of legitimate expectations is linked to an undertaking of some kind on the part of the authority, an apparently new and potentially rich source of standards of fair treatment is revealed. The source is only apparently novel because a similar notion of an implied undertaking or understanding lies behind the idea that rights and interests trigger the right to fair treatment and fair procedures. The person with a right has a legitimate expectation based on the undertaking or understanding that, when the right is under threat in any way, certain duties on administrative bodies come into play. The legitimate expectations movement is less a new source of duties of fair treatment than an extension of an old one.

11.1.4 What are the Standards of Fair Treatment

Once the duty of fair treatment is held to apply in a given context, the next task is to identify the standards which constitute fair treatment. Since much

[19] A fuller but by no means complete analysis is contained in D. J. Galligan, 'Procedural Fairness' in P. B. H. Birks (ed.), *The Frontiers of Liability* (Clarendon Press, Oxford, 1994). For further judicial discussion, see *R.* v. *Panel on Takeovers and Mergers, ex parte Fayed* [1993] ALR 337.

has already been said about this, we may here be brief. The general idea is that each administrative process should be understood as a sphere of authority within which an official may do certain things, examine certain matters, or make certain decisions. Within that sphere of authority, normative standards govern the way an official should behave. Fair treatment then consists in each person's case being decided, examined, or acted upon in accordance with the standards. The standards may relate to outcomes or to values independent of outcomes. They may be standards laid down by statute or delegated legislation; they may derive from the informal rules of the administrative authority; or they may be standards based on the common law or on a looser sense of social understandings. The richness and complexity of such standards have been described in earlier chapters where we saw how spheres of administrative authority are anchored in context and culture and steeped in moral and social conventions and understandings. It has also been made clear that this does not mean that anything goes; on the contrary, spheres of authority, even when discretionary, are typically closely structured by authoritative standards. And, moreover, it is not usually too difficult in each context to identify the governing legal standards constituting the basis of fair treatment, even though at the margins questions may arise as to their place, scope, and interpretation.

The identification of the standards of fair treatment depends then on a close analysis of each context of authority. But it would be wrong to convey the impression that this is always a difficult or complex matter. On the contrary, the governing statute will often be clear, providing a simple standard for the determination of cases, as portrayed in the model of routine administration. Things become more complex in cases of standard adjudication, for here elements of interpretation and discretion appear; moreover, the statutory provisions may now be supplemented by further standards of interpretation and consideration, deriving sometimes from the courts but more commonly from the administrative officials themselves. Such standards may include not only rules to apply but also matters to take into account, factors to consider and weigh up, so that fair treatment becomes bound up with the process by which the outcome is reached, as well as with the quality of the outcome itself. The position becomes even more fluid and open-ended when we move to policy-based discretion. Here the standards of fair treatment, while still linked to outcomes, become predominantly standards about what kinds of matters are to be taken into account and about the process for doing so. The principle that each case be properly considered is at the centre of the discretionary process and provides a powerful constraint on otherwise largely unconstrained processes; but that principle is directed at means and methods rather than given outcomes.

11.1.5 Developing Procedural Principles

Once the duty of fair treatment has been made out and the standards of fair treatment identified, the final step is to settle the procedures. The three models of individualized decision-making developed earlier give some guidance. Routine administration requires little procedural formality other than providing the authority with the information needed for a decision. Standard adjudication and modifications around it point to the need for procedures of a broadly adjudicative kind, based on notice, the provision of evidence and materials, fact-finding, consideration of standards, and reasons. Policy-based discretion, for its part, while emphasizing the consultative process, also needs procedures relating to notice, evidence, fact-finding, due consideration, and reasons.

Each of these models provides a context within which more detailed procedures can be developed. That task can normally be divided into three elements: first, to enable access to the process; secondly, to provide for the proper determination of or dealing with the issue; and thirdly, to allow for recourse by way of appeal, review, or some other form of scrutiny. This procedural model does not always fit perfectly, but generally it nicely captures the three stages in individualized processes. To take a practical case, the welfare claimant, in order to be treated fairly, ought to be able to get his claim before the authority; it ought to be decided according to authoritative standards; and avenues of recourse by way of appeal or review should be open. The emphasis tends to fall on the middle level, the decision itself, but access and recourse are also vital elements. However, not always since in some processes, particularly those where the authority takes the initiative, such as an inquiry or investigation into a person's affairs, access is not an element. In other cases, appeal or recourse from the initial process might not be appropriate. The role and importance of access and recourse are to be judged, not as separate and independent elements of procedural fairness, but according to their contribution to ensuring that people are dealt with in compliance with the standards of fair treatment. Questions of access to administrative processes require a study of their own and are not dealt with in this book, while issues of recourse are dealt with in Chapter 14.

The main emphasis in settling procedures is usually placed on the middle stage: the making of the decision, the determination to take action, the conduct of the inquiry, or the drawing of a conclusion. It is here that the basic questions of procedure arise: questions of notice and access to information; questions about the hearing, the gathering of evidence, and giving of reasons. Some guidance can be taken from the threefold classification of routine administration, standard adjudication, and policy-based discretion, but within each category considerable variation is possible. The gathering of evidence, for example, might be done by the administrator's own investigation or left in the main to the parties. The need for a hearing might be accepted, but what form it takes contested: should it be oral with witnesses and cross-examination, or the chance to present oral argument, or nothing more than the presentation of written submissions? Each procedural step—notice, information, hearing, and reasons—can be handled in different ways and the precise procedural set finally adopted will depend heavily on what is most suitable in the context. The guiding objective should be fair treatment according to authoritative standards, but the connection between any specific procedure and fair treatment might be to some degree indirect. The resolution of one procedural issue may be intertwined with the resolution of others; the form of hearing might depend on how precise the standards of decision-making are, while both matters will affect the nature of the reasons that should be given. The ultimate aim is to be confident that, taken as a whole, the procedures satisfy the outcome and non-outcome based standards of fair treatment.

The design of procedures is a matter of practical judgment to be made by legislators, administrators, and courts in very specific contexts. However, several general points of guidance may be noted. In the first place, the major component of fair treatment will always be to have procedures which lead to the accurate and proper application of authoritative standards. Whatever the context, facts have to be found and standards applied to them, and Bentham's firm but simple approach should be endorsed: identify what facts need to be ascertained and what standards to be applied, and then design suitable procedures, bearing in mind considerations of time, cost, and convenience. As to the facts, different approaches are open. The adversarial approach might be preferred where the parties themselves are responsible for presenting evidence; alternatively, the onus might be on the administrative body to gather evidence and draw conclusions; or possibly these might be some combination of the two. A more inquisitorial approach generally prevails at the primary decision—whether to grant welfare benefits, or a licence, or parole—where it is not a case of two parties in dispute, but rather one deciding an issue about a party. That will be especially so where the main purpose is to inquire into or investigate an issue, and then form a judgment about it. At the level of appeals, a more adversarial approach is typically used, since here the primary decision-maker becomes more like a party to a dispute who must defend the action he has taken before an independent authority. Tribunals tend for that reason to encourage an adversarial approach, although they normally have some power to gather evidence themselves and to conduct their own enquiries.

Another main variable in setting procedures is the nature of the legal standards. Are they straightforward and easily applied, or do they give rise to complex issues requiring skilled legal argument? Interpreting the revenue statutes, for example, will be rather different from deciding whether the conditions for awarding a driving licence are satisfied. The nature and extent of discretion will also be an important factor. Where there is discretion, the shape of procedures will depend on whether it is a judgment about the person's situation—does he need a welfare supplement, or is he fit for release—or whether it is more clearly a matter of policy—what course is best followed, when should subsidies be granted, or what should the policy be as to the size of schools. Indeed the various factors discussed in section 8.4.4 will be important in matching procedures to the standards particular to each context. A third guiding factor in the practical design of procedures is the principle of proportion.[20] Considerations of fair treatment have to be reconciled with matters of efficiency and cost. The two will coincide to a large extent, but there may be points where the concern for fair treatment would require more extensive procedures than can reasonably be borne by the society. In the earlier discussion, we saw that this is a difficult issue to which there is no completely satisfactory solution. The best approach is to invoke a principle of proportion between the relative importance of the interests at stake and the level of procedural protection. This will have direct, practical application in the design of procedures.

A further factor of special relevance is the context. The context is relevant in a functional sense. The police officer considering whether to exercise his power of arrest in the heat of an incident is clearly different from the magistrate deciding in the quiet of the court what sentence to impose. The fair treatment of the suspect by the police officer is no less important than his treatment by the magistrate, but the procedures suitable to ensure fair treatment in each case are very different. The police officer cannot be expected to hold a judicial-like hearing about whether he should arrest or not. Nevertheless, it is important that the suspect be treated fairly and alternative procedures for that purpose need to be in place. The criteria for arrest should be clear and public; where unofficial guidelines as well as official rules are laid down, they should be known; the scope for review after arrest to ensure a proper exercise of powers is important; and indeed the very education and training of the officer will be a key factor. The magistrate, on the other hand, should proceed differently, for here we expect a judicial process based on evidence and argument from the parties, a careful weighting of factors, and a reasoned judgment. A similar analysis can be applied to other contexts.

The context of an administrative power is also relevant in a social sense. Our perceptions of different areas of authority are greatly influenced by social understandings, which are in turn the products of history and education. An example is the attitude of the public to closed institutions like prisons and hospitals for the mentally handicapped. Perceptions of such institutions

[20] See the analysis in Ch. 3.

have changed in recent years, and as those perceptions have changed, our view of fair treatment and fair procedures has also changed. Bargaining at pre-trial stages between the prosecution and the defence is another case in point. After refusing to believe it went on at all, we now recognize its existence, but without so far accepting that this practice, which appears to be widespread, raises important questions of procedural fairness. Legislators, lawyers, and courts are content that such procedures should be left to the discretion of the prosecuting authority. Such an approach is unsatisfactory and the next step will be to realize that this pocket of potential arbitrariness and unfairness must be brought into line with general principles of fair treatment. Other examples are not hard to find, but enough has been said to demonstrate that the practical design of procedures is influenced by social attitudes which will often impede the full development of a sense of fairness.

A final factor to mention in the practical design of fair procedures is methodological, that is, whether to have general procedural rules or to leave the matter to be determined on a case-by-case basis. An example is the representation of prisoners in disciplinary proceedings within the prison. The present position is that the governor should decide in each case whether representation is necessary to ensure fair treatment; representation is then sometimes considered necessary, at other times not. An alternative would be to adopt a general rule that representation be allowed, without having to justify it in each set of circumstances, as is the case with criminal charges before a court. Each approach has advantages and disadvantages. On the one hand, a piecemeal, incremental approach would seem most suitable in extending procedural fairness to varied, administrative contexts. On the other hand, general procedural rules provide greater certainty and security, and avoid the difficult task of judging procedural needs in specific cases. General rules also help to boost confidence in the procedural regime by showing that people are being treated consistently. In the end, there is no necessarily best method, but the advantages of moving towards more general procedural rules outweigh those of a more particularized approach.

11.2 PROCEDURAL FAIRNESS IN THE COURTS

The courts in the United Kingdom and other common law jurisdictions have developed a general principle of procedural fairness independently of statute. The principle is that any administrative authority, exercising powers which affect the rights or interests of particular persons, must do so according to fair procedures. The precise requirements of the principle depend very much on the circumstances and the context. The principle is usually invoked by an aggrieved person by way of judicial review of an administrative act or decision. It may be used to supplement statutory procedures, or to generate procedures where the statute or regulations made under statute are silent. Traditionally, the demands of procedural fairness were thought to be adequately provided for in the rule that one ought to be heard before being prejudiced and the rule against a biased decision-maker. It is now recognized that those rules are expressions of a more fundamental principle of procedural fairness.

The object of this section is to give a general account of the judicial approach to procedural fairness. The role of the courts on the procedural landscape may seem rather limited compared with Parliament, administrators, ombudsmen, and various other bodies. Judicial review is sporadic and unsystematic, responding to complaints in particular cases rather than designing general structures. Nevertheless, the number of cases going to the courts is significant and the judicial influence over doctrine is substantial.[21] Specific cases offer the courts an opportunity to formulate more general principles and it seems that many of the ideas about procedural fairness now taken for granted by Parliament and administrative bodies owe their origins to judicial decisions. Now doctrine is one thing and administrative practice another, and just what impact judicial review and judicial doctrine have had on the administration is hard to judge. Whatever the answer (and I shall return to this point), the courts are closely involved in procedural matters.[22] The task in this section is to sketch the general nature and basis of that involvement, while more specific doctrines will be considered in later chapters.

11.2.1 The General Judicial Approach

The history of judicial review of administrative bodies is still rather sketchy, but we know that the English courts have exercised some supervisory jurisdiction from the earliest times. The two aspects of natural justice referred to above, hearing and bias, are amongst the earliest grounds of judicial review. They owe their origins to the common law courts, and have long been regarded as the two main pillars of due process and procedural fairness. In more recent years, the courts have made two major advances. For the one part, they have moved from the two rules of natural justice to a general principle of procedural fairness; while for the other part, they have extended that principle to apply generally to administrative processes. These advances have not come easily. The courts resisted for some years the idea that natural justice should extend beyond judicial or quasi-judicial processes. In *Ridge* v. *Baldwin*,[23] however, the emphasis shifted from whether the process was

[21] A recent analysis of the statistics for the UK is M. Sunkin, L. Bridges, and G. Mazeros, *Judicial Review in Perspective* (Public Law Project, London, 1993).

[22] See sect. 10.2.6.

[23] N. 5 above.

judicial, using the term in a rather technical sense, to whether it affected a person's interests. Once that step was taken the way was open for natural justice to apply to the many different forms of administrative process. The issue then centred on what kinds of interests were to count in attracting the protections of natural justice. The general approach to that issue has been to define interests broadly but not without limits.[24]

With the extension of procedural fairness to a wider range of administrative processes, it was soon evident that the rules of natural justice as traditionally stated were not always suitable. What suits in judicial, trial-like proceedings, might not fit in many administrative contexts. One course open to the courts would have been to adjust the two rules to fit the special features of administrative processes. To some degree that has happened, but more importantly the courts began to talk about a general principle of procedural fairness, to apply in all cases, with the content to be determined according to the circumstances.[25] If the question were whether a prisoner should be heard by the parole board, or the residents of an old people's home should be consulted before the council closed it down, or whether there should be an oral hearing rather than written representations, the answer should be found by considering what procedures would be necessary in each situation to ensure fair treatment. The approach can be expressed in different ways: the authority must perform its duties fairly;[26] the procedure must be sufficient to achieve justice;[27] or there must be such procedural safeguards as will ensure the attainment of fairness.[28] Expressions like these suggest a substantive part and a procedural part: the substantive part is that the decision be made properly according to legal standards, while the procedural part is that procedures suited to that end be adopted.

An obvious strength of this approach is that all areas of administration are now, in principle, subject to the requirements of procedural fairness. It is no longer an excuse to say that an authority is exercising discretionary powers, or that it is the decision of a minister, or that it occurs in a context, such as a prison, which is exempt from procedural principles. Exceptions to the principle might still be made, but only where there are strong reasons for doing so; indeed, the presumption is that the general duty to follow fair procedures will apply unless exceptions can be justified. The practical application of the principle can still be uneven, with various factors influencing a court's appraisal of what procedures are needed. However, problems of application should not be allowed to undermine the general normative principle of procedural fairness. A second strength of the contemporary approach is that

[24] See sect. 11.1.1.

[25] Amongst the leading cases are: *Wiseman* v. *Borneman* [1971] AC 297, *Lloyd* v. *McMahon* [1987] AC 628.

[26] Woolf LJ in *Lloyd* v. *McMahon* [1987] AC at 663.

[27] Lord Reid in *Wiseman* v. *Borneman*, n. 25 above, at 308.

[28] Lord Bridge in *Lloyd* v. *McMahon*, n. 25 above, at 703.

it rightly sees the traditional rules of natural justice as specific applications of a general duty of procedural fairness rather than its essence. It is now acknowledged that procedural fairness is a dynamic principle from which other doctrines, besides the hearing and bias rules, can be derived. Procedural fairness, in other words, far from being exhausted by those rules, embraces any procedural issue which is relevant to treating a person fairly. The third feature of this approach is that it allows procedures to be judged in their context and according to how important and effective they really are in securing fair treatment. This in turn should allow a more accurate assessment of whether the procedures followed by an administrative body are sufficient to ensure fair treatment. Instead of the duty of procedural fairness triggering specific rules of natural justice, it now initiates an inquiry into whether the procedures followed by an authority were adequate in the circumstances.

Within this general approach, let us now consider a number of more specific issues: (i) the relationship between fair treatment and fair procedures: (ii) the tension between having detailed procedural rules and approaching each case on a discretionary basis; (iii) the judicial construction of procedures; (iv) the competition between costs and fair treatment; (v) statutory procedures; and finally (vi) the impact of judicial review on administrative procedures.

11.2.2 The Relationship between Fair Treatment and Fair Procedures

The first of these, the relationship between fair treatment and fair procedures, is implicit in what has already been said. The courts begin with the notion of fair treatment as treatment according to the legal standards prevailing in an administrative context. They recognize that the legal standards will be a mixture of outcome-based and non-outcome-based; the question then is what procedures are necessary to secure treatment according to those standards. Procedures are fair to the extent that they contribute to that end. This approach can be seen running through the modern, as well as many of the ancient, cases. It is not often made explicit but, I suggest, is the best way of understanding the judicial approach. Just such an approach appears to have been in the mind of Earle CJ when, considering the advantages of a local authority's hearing the applicant before acting against him, he said: 'I am conscious of a great many advantages which might arise in the way of public order, in the way of doing substantive justice, and in the way of fulfilling the purposes of the statute.'[29]

The court's approach can be illustrated further through the following examples. In *R.* v. *Board of Visitors of H.M. Prison, ex parte Hone*,[30] the

[29] *Cooper* v. *Wandsworth Board of Works* (1863) 14 CB (NS) 100. See also the interesting discussion in *R.* v. *Leicester City Justices, ex parte Barrow* [1991] 3 WLR 374.

[30] [1988] 2 WLR 177.

question was whether a prisoner appearing on a charge before a Board of Visitors was entitled to legal representation.[31] The House of Lords held that, although the duty of natural justice applied, in the circumstances there was no established legal right to have a solicitor. The accused's right to counsel in a criminal trial had not been extended to the present situation and, therefore, the claim had to be judged on whether legal representation was needed in these circumstances. That in turn was to be judged on whether representation was necessary to ensure the right outcome, namely, that the rules were properly applied to an accurate finding of the facts. The reasoning was that, as there was no dispute about the law, and as the prisoner was able to present his own case, there was no need for a solicitor; the Board of Visitors could reach the right outcome on the law and facts without the assistance of a lawyer. And if it could reasonably be concluded that the right outcome would be reached, then the prisoner had been treated fairly. The practical judgment that the prisoner was capable of properly presenting his own case might be questioned on empirical grounds, but the general approach is correct. If the prisoner were judged accurately in accordance with the rules relating to disciplinary offences, then he would be treated fairly under the law; provided the procedures lead to that result (and subject to other relevant values), the principle of procedural fairness would be met.

Once it is realised that the test of fair procedures is whether they lead to fair treatment, the approach of the courts in *Hone* and many other cases makes good sense. The enquiry in each case is whether, as a matter of practical judgment, the procedures lead to fair treatment. Indeed, the courts have a better grasp of the issue than many of their critics; for while the former regularly affirm that the object of procedures is to ensure fair treatment according to law, it is hard to find a critic who makes clear what he or she thinks is, or should be, the test of procedures.[32] But let us consider one or two more cases. In *Hone* the legal standards were clear and settled so that it made sense to talk of a correct result or an accurate outcome. The same general approach applies when the standards are less settled and the decision is discretionary. It is then less appropriate to think of a correct outcome, since discretion usually indicates a certain amount of choice in the decision-maker as to what should be done. Nevertheless, the law has developed standards about how discretionary decisions should be made: the authority must consider the merits of the case; it must address itself to relevant matters and exclude the irrelevant; it must not act arbitrarily or with prejudice; it must act in good faith and for the right purposes; and its decision must be

[31] The disciplinary powers of the Board of Visitors have now been abolished.

[32] Consider C. Harlow and R. Rawlings, *Public Law and Administration* (Weidenfeld and Nicholson, London, 1984), 78 ff and M. Loughlin, 'Procedural Fairness' (1978) 28 *U. of Toronto LJ* 215. A cogent and convincing understanding can be seen in D. J. Mullan, 'Procedural Fairness: The New Natural Justice' (1975) 25 *U. Toronto LJ.*

reasonable.[33] These are the standards of fair treatment in discretionary contexts. They do not say what the outcome should be, but a person whose case is dealt with in this way is treated fairly. *Ridge* v. *Baldwin* illustrates the point well.[34] There the Watch Committee had a number of options open in deciding what action to take against the Chief Constable. Its duty was to examine and decide on the merits; provided that was done, the Chief Constable would have been treated fairly. The question for the courts was whether a hearing was necessary to ensure that the merits were properly considered.[35]

The point is further illustrated by the case of *McInnes* v. *Onslow-Fane*,[36] a case which has had its share of criticism. The issue was whether the procedures followed in refusing the grant of a boxing manager's licence were fair. Megarry V-C asked, first, what conditions had to be met for the proper exercise of discretion and, secondly, whether the procedures followed were appropriate to that end. The discretion here was wide and unstructured; it was properly exercised, he thought, if the decision on the merits was honestly taken, without bias, and not in pursuit of a capricious policy. These conditions had been met by the procedures followed and the claim that there should have been a hearing was rejected. Not all aspects of the judge's reasoning are convincing. How, we might ask, could the merits have been properly considered without a hearing of some sort which would have enabled the claimant to put his side of the story. More importantly, the judge's conception of a proper exercise of discretion may be drawn too loosely, it being arguable that the licensing committee should have examined the merits more closely than would be required by the above conditions.[37] Discretion does raise a number of problems about precisely what is required for its valid exercise; notice, however, that they are problems about what constitutes fair treatment, that is to say what are the standards of fair treatment in such cases; only when they have been resolved can the question of

[33] It is arguable that these different standards can all be included in a general principle against arbitrary treatment: see T. Scanlon, 'Due Process' in J. Pennock and J. Chapman (eds.), *Due Process* (Nomos, New York, 1977).

[34] N. 5 above.

[35] For other examples, see *Lloyd* v. *McMahon*, n. 25 above, and *Hoaucher* v. *Minister for Immigration and Ethnic Affairs*, n. 9 above.

[36] [1978] 1 WLR 1520.

[37] Compare the approach in *Re HK* [1967] 2 QB 617, especially Blain J who referred to 'applying his mind dispassionately to a fair analysis of the particular problem and the information available to him in analysing it'. See also D. J. Mullan, 'Procedural Fairness: The New Natural Justice', n. 32 above, 504–5.

It should be noted that I have chosen as an example an unpopular case. Apart from the possible criticisms I have suggested, it is said that there is a confusion of procedures and merits. The merits, in the sense of what should the outcome of the application be, are of course for the original decision-maker. But it is perfectly legitimate for a reviewing court to ask whether the procedures followed are of the kind that are likely to lead to a proper consideration of the merits by the authority. The latter is in the realm of procedure and process which is just where a reviewing court should be.

procedures be considered. I shall return to this point about discretion; I wish to suggest, however, that Megarry's general approach of dividing the issue of fair procedures into two stages, as set out above, cannot be faulted.

Courts do not often theorize about what they are doing, nor when deciding particular cases should they be unduly concerned with the overall scheme of things. Nevertheless, their approach to procedural fairness fits closely the theoretical outline developed earlier in this book. Their understanding of the relationship between procedures, fairness, and authoritative standards is coherent and compelling. They recognize that fair treatment of persons is at the heart of government and administration, while at the same time accepting that Parliament to a large extent dictates the standards of fair treatment. Not entirely, however, for the courts also have a significant role in their creation and development. The standards of judicial review, such as the principles against unreasonableness and irrationality (or arbitrariness), and the principle of relevance, are to a large extent both judge-made and important elements of fair treatment. We might quibble about whether these are standards of substance or procedure, the orthodox view being that courts in exercising review are concerned with process and procedure rather than substance.[38] Such concerns, however, are both confused and largely pointless, since the distinction between substance and procedure has been shown to be elusive and unhelpful.[39] The better approach is to ask, first, what are the standards of fair treatment and, secondly, what procedures (institutions, mechanisms) are necessary to give them effect.

This is not to say that the courts in judicial review are licensed to decide whether the original decision was fair in some full and more complete sense. Lord Denning's view that a probationer police constable, who was dismissed by the Chief Constable, should not only be given a fair hearing but was entitled also to a fair and reasonable decision, was firmly rejected by the House of Lords.[40] Judicial review, it was said, is concerned with the decision-process not the substance of the decision itself. However, as T. R. S. Allan has remarked, that is only partly true,[41] the full truth being that any strict distinction between procedure and substance is conceptually insupportable. In practice, the courts may and do concern themselves quite legitimately with some aspects of substance but not others. The real issue is how far the courts should involve themselves in the merits of administrative decisions, and they have created doctrines which help to define the boundaries. Ultimately, the proper role of the court in exercising review is a matter of constitutional debate; within that debate, the distinction between substance and procedure has a minor role.

[38] For further discussion on this point, see T. R. S. Allan, *Law, Liberty and Justice* (Clarendon Press, Oxford, 1993), ch. 8.

[39] See sect. 1.4.2.

[40] *Chief Constable* v. *Evans* [1982] 3 All ER 141.

[41] *Law, Liberty and Justice*, n. 38 above, 192.

We need not enter into that debate here, except to note two senses in which courts may legitimately be concerned with substantive matters, and, in particular, substantive issues of fairness. The first is that indicated above, they may be responsible for creating and developing certain standards which bind administrative officials in the exercise of their powers. That already happens to some degree and some jurists would like to see it happen more. It has been suggested that the courts ought to be more active in creating standards of equal and consistent treatment, proportionality, and certainty.[42] The second sense is that, when judicial review is brought, the courts have the final decision as to what the standards of decision-making are or ought to be in that area of administration. That task is implicit in deciding procedural issues, for unless the courts have a view as to what the standards of fair treatment are, they cannot decide questions of procedural fairness. This is not to say that the courts are exclusively responsible for creating the standards, since some will be stipulated by statute. It is true, nevertheless, that many of the more general standards determining the grounds and scope of review are the creation of the courts. This unavoidably involves the courts in substantive matters and in a sense of substantive fairness, not a complete sense of total fairness, but the middle-order sense by which people should be dealt with according to authoritative standards. However described, their responsibility in judicial review takes the courts far beyond a thin sense of procedural fairness.

11.2.3 Rules, Principles, or Discretion?

One drawback of current judicial attitudes is that the courts have to assess the adequacy of procedures according to the context of each administrative process, with the old certainties of natural justice having been put aside in favour of a more individualized and discretionary approach. Some new rules have become settled, but in the main the courts have to decide as they judge best what procedures are necessary for fair treatment. Amongst commentators this has caused concern.[43] It seems to allow some interests to have better procedural protection than others, with some types of power being subjected to stringent procedures and others escaping more or less unrestricted. Extraneous factors may then be influential and a lack of even-handedness from one context to another may appear. Moreover, the nature of the enquiry tends to be highly contextual and particularized and does not encourage the formulation of general procedural rules. Some critics even talk of a crisis in the judicial approach, with rampant discretion, threats to the autonomy of law, and crippling procedural costs on administrators.[44]

[42] See J. Jowell and A. Lester, 'Beyond Wednesbury: Substantive Principles of Administrative Law' [1987] *Public Law* 368.

[43] See Harlow and Rawlings, *Law and Administration* n. 32 above, 78 ff.

[44] M. Loughlin, 'Procedural Fairness: A Study of the Crisis in Administrative Law', n. 32 above, 215.

While such cries of alarm can be exaggerated, there is a need to look closely at the way the courts interpret the principle of procedural fairness. The direction judicial discretion has taken is a matter of concern, but unfortunately no comprehensive study of judicial review in this area has yet been made.[45] Some of the influences on judicial discretion are considered in the next section, but here one or two general points about the judicial role should be considered. In the first place, while the courts exercise discretion, it is not discretion in the strong sense that the judges simply choose whatever procedure they think desirable. It is discretion only in the weaker sense that the court has a principle to apply and it must judge what the principle requires in the circumstances.[46] The principle is that the decision should be made according to such procedures as will lead to fair treatment of the person affected. Fair treatment in turn means treatment in accordance with legal standards. We have seen what that means: that the facts will be accurately determined, the legal standards properly interpreted and applied, and, where there is discretion, that the case will be properly considered according to relevant factors. The task of a reviewing court is to assess the procedures against those standards of fair treatment, and to decide whether the procedures followed are likely to have led to fair treatment in the case in point. Judgment has to be exercised, but it is judgment guided by principle and directed at clear purposes. The courts fail on occasions; they may be mistaken, or one might disagree with them, but that is the nature of a practical judgment and should not be mistaken for unfettered discretion. Indeed, far from being unfettered, the discretionary element here should be, and in the main is, highly principled, being concerned with the application of standards and the upholding of rights to fair treatment.

The second point of concern is that the approach of the courts undermines the rule of law which, it is supposed, means decision-making by applying general rules. Arguments based on the rule of law in this narrow sense are not only quaint, but beg a number of jurisprudential questions, such as how different rules are from principles and whether decisions can ever be made just by applying rules. Quite apart from the difficulties of distinguishing rules and principles, there is no reason to think that a decision based on principle is any less compatible with the rule of law than one based on rules. The rules of natural justice themselves have to be interpreted and applied according to the context: what sort of hearing is required, what does bias mean in this situation? And we need only glance at the American case law on the meaning of the notice and hearing rule to see that such questions are anything but straightforward.[47] In any event, the difference between applying

[45] The best account is D. J. Mullan, n. 32 above.

[46] Some deny that this is discretion at all: see R. M. Dworkin, *Taking Rights Seriously* (Duckworth, London, 1978), ch. 1; but compare D. J. Galligan, *Discretionary Powers* (Clarendon Press, Oxford, 1986), ch. 1.

[47] See Ch. 15.

rules and deciding on principle is at best methodological, and it should not be taken for granted that one leads to fairer procedures than the other. The well-known debate in other areas of discretion over the relative advantages and disadvantages of precise rules and open-textured principles is applicable here. Any conclusion that fixed procedural rules produce higher levels of fairness than a discretionary judgment guided by principle could be justified only after extensive empirical study of the cases; such a study has not yet been undertaken. In any event, the very dichotomy is flawed, since no clear distinction exists between having rules on the one hand and something else on the other hand. Rules have to be interpreted and often contain open-textured standards; they may be departed from, selectively applied, or be subject to exceptions. Finally, it is typical of any changing area of law that rules give way to principles, but then, after a period of transition, new rules begin to emerge.[48] That is the very method of the common law and there is no reason to doubt that, over time, settled procedural standards will emerge in various contexts. Some such standards can already be seen: for example, it is an established standard that a person whose affairs are being investigated is entitled to know the general findings and to make representations in relation to them.[49] Many other examples could be cited, but there is no reason to think that the overriding objective should be to develop comprehensive and detailed procedural rules. The strengths of a piecemeal approach are not to be overlooked and, here as elsewhere, a continuing flux between constancy and change should be welcomed.

When judicial review of procedural fairness is understood in this way, some of the qualms about judicial discretion should be allayed. But not all, for when the space between the general principle and a specific judgment is large, even a principled process can appear to be arbitrary and subjective. Several solutions are possible. The courts could defer more to the judgment of Parliament and administrators on procedural matters and intervene only in extreme cases. Such deference would have advantages and disadvantages, but in general there is no reason to think that either Parliament or administrators have a better or more measured view of procedural fairness. Recent history would suggest that the courts have often taken the lead in raising the standards in areas where Parliament showed no interest and administrators feared to tread. The position would be different if Parliament were to provide more complete schemes of statutory procedures, or indeed even if administrative bodies themselves were required to produce procedural codes for their respective areas. Neither is generally the case, although reflection of the issue raises the wider question of a code or codes of administrative procedures, a matter which is dealt with in Chapter 10.

Since there is little doubt that the courts will continue to be actively

[48] See J. Stone, 'From Principles to Principles' (1981) 97 *LQR* 224.

[49] *Re Pergamon Press* [1971] Ch. 388.

involved in questions of procedural fairness, the issue is how certain intermediate steps and more constant beacons might be introduced into their judgments. One solution which appeals to administrative lawyers is to structure those judgments through guidelines in the way often seen in areas of open-ended or discretionary powers. The case for this is put well in an article by B. Dyer.[50] He argues for a structured process in deciding in each context what procedures are needed. A good example of the approach is found in the judgment of Webster J in deciding whether a prisoner should have been allowed legal representation before a Board of Visitors.[51] The judge stated a number of factors to consider: the seriousness of the charge and the penalty; whether points of law would arise; the prisoner's capacity to put his own case; whether the prisoner would be able properly to prepare his case, have adequate access to witnesses, and be able to call them at the hearing; the need for reasonable speed; and the need for fairness as between prisoners, and as between prisoners and prison officers.

A structured process of this kind does not eliminate the need for reflective judgment, incrementalism, or discretion. Its virtue is in providing factors to take into account; it is reasoned and it is open, characteristics which are, after all, the signs of a sound, practical judgment. Such judgments become precedents and may then become the basis for settled procedural rules, although in many cases it will be desirable to retain the capacity to decide on the merits without being unduly restricted by what has gone before. The focus should be, however, on developing guidelines and giving them a certain generality. We may conclude that, problematical as it may appear, the judicial involvement in issues of procedural fairness is permanent and important, and capable of being structured and principled.

11.2.4 The Judicial Construction of Procedural Fairness

How then do the courts decide whether the procedures followed by an administrator meet the demands of fairness? The courts themselves have offered some guidance on this and a good starting point is the judgment of Woolf LJ in *Lloyd* v. *McMahon*.[52] The issue was whether the district auditor had followed fair procedures in investigating the affairs of Liverpool City Council and in finding that certain losses were due to wilful misconduct of a number of councillors. The councillors made written representations to the auditor, but did not ask for and were not given an oral hearing. Amongst the various issues, the one of present interest is how Woolf LJ came to the conclusion that, even without an oral hearing, the procedures were fair.

Three factors by which to guide the assessment were identified: the

[50] B. Dyer, 'Determining the Content of Procedural Fairness' [1993] *Monash LR* 165.
[51] *R.* v. *Secretary of State, ex parte Tarrant* [1985] QB 251 at 284 ff.
[52] N. 25 above, at 663 ff.

function being performed by the official; the nature and consequences of the decision; and the matters in issue.[53] By function is meant the nature of the task, and the system of classification developed earlier may help at this first stage. Here the task was investigatory, but with a distinct adjudicative element in drawing conclusions from the investigation. Other cases may fall into other categories, such as routine administration, adjudication, or policy-based discretion. This initial classification depends on a close analysis of the statutory scheme, and is, moreover, only an initial classification which directs us to one or other grouping without revealing much about the more detailed procedures within it.

Woolf LJ did not offer a systematic analysis of the other two factors, but it is not too difficult to reconstruct their meaning. The second, the nature and consequence of the decision, partly repeats the first, but is distinctive in highlighting the consequences, presumably for those subject to it. An assessment of the consequences has two parts: first, the rights or interests at stake and, secondly, the effect an exercise of authority has on them.[54] Here the interests at stake were the reputations, livelihoods, and financial interests of the councillors, which might be severely affected by the auditor's actions. The third factor, the matter in issue, is obscure and also partly repeats aspects of the other two. But its significance may lie in referring to the powers of the authority, that is, to the precise legal standards governing its actions. If this is what is meant, then it is significant, since those standards form the basis of fair treatment and a close analysis of their meaning and scope is essential in determining what procedures are required.

In applying these factors, the auditor had to inquire into and make a finding about financial matters where important interests would be seriously affected. He advised the councillors of the evidence before him and of his provisional judgment. He received and took into consideration written representations from the councillors, but ultimately did not adopt the facts asserted in them. After considering these matters, Woolf LJ concluded that, on balance, the procedures were fair and that an oral hearing was not required. In the House of Lords, Lord Bridge added two more factors: the nature of the authority and the statutory framework,[55] although both appear to be included by implication in the factors already considered. This is one of several attempts by the courts to state the relevant factors in judging the fairness of procedures.[56] All are helpful but none is entirely satisfactory and all stop short of stating precisely why the different factors are relevant or how they are to be assessed.

[53] Ibid. 664. See also Lord Diplock in *Bushell* v. *Secretary of State for the Environment* [1981] AC at 95.

[54] This is brought out well by Lord Upjohn in his analysis in *Durayappah* v. *Fernando* [1967] 2 AC 337.

[55] N. 25 above, at 702 ff.

[56] e.g. *Russell* v. *Duke of Norfolk* [1949] 1 All ER 109 at 118; *Kioa* v. *West* (1985) 159 CLR 550, *per* Mason CJ at 584 and especially Brennan J. at 409.

To the extent that the analysis in such cases fails, it is because the underlying normative premise is not made clear. However, the premise which makes most sense of the judicial approach is exactly that put forward in my earlier analysis, namely, that each person affected by an administrative decision should be treated fairly and that the point of procedures is to lead to fair treatment. The relevant factors then help, first, to clarify what constitutes fair treatment in the particular case and then, secondly, to point to the kinds of procedures necessary. The first part is a necessary prelude to the second, for it is only by elucidating the standards of fair treatment that a judgment can be made whether the procedures are appropriate. An examination of the statutory context, of the nature and extent of the statutory powers, will help in identifying the normative standards according to which decisions should be made and activities conducted. It will also be the basis for practical judgments as to what procedures are needed for proper and accurate application of those standards. The rights and interests at issue are then relevant in assessing whether the procedures are satisfactory in holding the risk of error at the right level.[57]

Now while this approach to determine the content of fair procedures is sound in principle and generally reflects judicial attitudes, the question arises whether it works in quite that way when put into practical contexts. The suggestion is sometimes made that other variables, besides those officially declared and normatively supportable, influence judgments about procedure. One charge is that the courts do not apply the approach even-handedly, but give more procedural protection to some interests than others. Interests of a financial or property kind seem to attract more protection than interests in personal liberty or well-being. Similarly, categories of people seem to be treated differently; students, prisoners, aliens, and jockeys, have fared rather badly even when vital interests are in issue. There might be good reasons for this. The mistreatment of jockeys, for instance, might be the sign of a commitment by the courts to leave questions of procedural fairness to the sporting authorities. However, the difficulty with criticisms of this nature is that they depend on reading into judgments normative standards about how different people and groups should be treated, even though those standards play no express part in the reasoning of the judges themselves. There may well be hidden premises which affect the way courts approach procedural issues, premises based on how a person, his interests, or the group to which he belongs, should be viewed by the courts. This would not be surprising since our perceptions of different people and groups, our ranking of interests, and our understanding of what constitutes fair treatment, are deeply tied to culture and context. Considering the social attitude to prisons and prisoners,

[57] D. J. Mullan puts forward an interesting account in similar vein; he is mistaken, however, in assuming that the nature of the power will correspond to the importance of the interest. On the contrary, important interests may be affected by a highly discretionary power. See D. J. Mullan, n. 32 above, 300.

for example, or the social ambivalence about students, or the general perception of aliens as outsiders and inferiors, it isto be expected that the judicial construction of fair treatment and the procedures of fair treatment will be influenced accordingly. One of the tasks of law is to set standards which transcend cultural categories and introduce a certain universality. The different treatment of people might be taken as normal practice, with equal treatment according to general categories the exception. Whether that really is true in cases of procedural fairness, however, depends on a fuller analysis of judicial decisions than has yet been made.

We can only speculate about the effect other factors may have on the courts' approach to procedural fairness. The nature of the administrative body was mentioned as relevant by Lord Bridge.[58] He did not elaborate, but it is plausible to expect that the attitude of the court to the decisions of a minister of state, a parole board, or a tribunal will be different. Another factor might be the kind of discretion an authority has, or at least the court's characterization of that discretion; for what constitutes the proper exercise of discretion will in turn influence the shape of procedures and the dictates of fairness. These factors and others may well infiltrate the normative framework within which judgments of procedural fairness are made; but again, until a careful study is made of different areas, any conclusion must be tentative.

It has been possible in this section only to touch on a major and somewhat contentious issue in the judicial construction of procedural fairness. The discussion appears paradoxical: on the one hand, it is clearly right in principle that the fairness of procedures be assessed in the context by which an authority acts and exerts its powers; on the other hand, such an approach lends itself to the influence of extraneous factors, of invidious social and cultural categories and conventions. The paradox cannot easily be resolved; the way forward is to stand firm on the principle at issue, while at the same time trying to gain a better understanding of how procedural issues really are determined and of how extraneous and unacceptable influences can be overcome.

11.2.5 Judicial Review of the Costs and Procedures

One criticism sometimes made of the courts is that, by imposing additional procedures on administrative processes, they force agencies to spend more of their scarce resources on procedures. A hearing may be required where it was not provided for in the statute, or resources may have to be directed to supplying information or reasons. In cases like these, judicial decisions can certainly have an impact on resources, but there is little evidence as to exactly what the impact is. A study of the cases, however, suggests that the

[58] *Lloyd* v. *McMahon*, n. 25 above at 702 ff.

courts are cautious in imposing extra procedural burdens, so that the image of administrators groaning under the burden of judicially-imposed procedures is unrealistic. Where a procedure is required by the courts, the additional costs are marginal and can be accommodated by adjustments in the use of existing resources for procedures. Nevertheless, the attitude of the courts to the costs of procedures is an important matter of both principles and practice. The judges themselves sometimes make direct reference to the issue. An increase in the costs of administering the parole system was put in the scales by the Court of Appeal when considering what procedures to follow in deciding parole.[59] The House of Lords referred to the extra time and money required if prisoners, charged with offences before the Board of Visitors, were allowed legal representation.[60] Amongst the different kinds of costs that might be relevant—direct, social, and moral—the courts seem to have in mind only direct costs, the assumption being that every effort should be made to keep direct costs to a minimum. The difficulty is that in the practical world the different kinds of costs are likely to be in competition. In the light of the earlier discussion of that issue,[61] it is enough to note that a reduction in direct costs, by increasing the risk of error, is likely to increase social and moral costs. Social costs refer to the failure to achieve the goals for which the agency has been given power, while moral costs refer to the failure to treat the person fairly. When the courts say that direct costs should be taken into account, they mean that a balance has to be struck between the principle of fair treatment and the social goal of keeping down the direct costs.

The issue is a practical one, but it should be approached in a principled way. A principled approach would mean that a court should consider, first, what procedures are required for the proper application of authoritative standards, and then secondly, whether any adjustment has to be made according to the proportionality principle. Under that principle, the relative importance of different rights and interests should be taken into account and then linked to the resources available for their protection. The result may be that fewer resources are available than would be needed to ensure the proper application of standards. The levels of fair treatment then have to be scaled down to match the resources available. Any person whose interests are at stake has an initial right to such procedures as are necessary for proper application of the authoritative standards. If the resources are insufficient for that, then the right in practice has to be reduced in accordance with the principle of proportion. It follows that it is not a conclusive argument against additional procedures that they would impose extra costs on administrators. If the additions are justified within the principles above, then the person affected has rights to those procedures, the court has no discretion to deny

[59] *Payne* v. *Harris* [1981] 1 WLR 754 (CA); now overruled in *R.* v. *Secretary of State for the Home Department, ex parte Doody* [1994], AC 531 (HL).

[60] *R.* v. *Board of Visitors, ex parte Hone*, n. 30 above.

[61] See sect. 3.3.

the right, and the costs should be borne by the agency. This does not rule out considerations of economy, since society's commitment to each person is only to the minimum procedures necessary to apply the standards of fair treatment. If a less elaborate and more economical procedure is available, the courts are justified in allowing it, provided they are satisfied that it leads to proper application of the standards of fair treatment. If, for example, a hearing process based on written submissions rather than an oral hearing would be enough to secure the proper application of authoritative standards, there would be no need to incur the extra costs of an oral hearing. Indeed, one of the strengths of the present approach is that, by laying bare the ends which procedures are meant to serve, the proper role of considerations of economy in designing and judging procedures can be understood.

Whether the courts in practice deal with the costs of procedures in this way is not clear; it is not clear because they are largely silent on the matter. The silence may be attributable to their being confident that any procedures they impose are within the two principles and, therefore, are justified. The lack of a problem would explain the absence of discussion. This may be a plausible account of most cases.[62] However, when courts do occasionally raise the issue, their incautious language leaves the impression that issues of cost are being treated rather differently. The suggestion was made in *Hone* that in determining whether legal representation is required, the costs should be taken into account. If that is the right interpretation of Lord Goff's reasoning, it is incompatible with the present approach, according to which the first question to ask is whether legal representation is necessary for the proper application of standards. Costs are not relevant at this point. If the answer is that the prisoner can properly defend himself, then representation is not needed and costs are saved. But if representation is necessary for an accurate outcome, then a presumptive case based on fair treatment has been made. It is only then at the second stage that the court should consider whether the added costs of the procedures would be outside the proportionality principle. Being marginal costs, they should normally be within it. Occasionally, a claim to procedural innovation—to a full oral hearing, for example—may have to be refused for lack of resources. To approach questions of cost in this way is not only correct in principle, but also offers the courts, as well as Parliament and administrators, sound practical guidance.

11.2.6 The Courts and Statutory Procedures

The main sources of procedural rules are statutes, statutory rules by way of delegated legislation, and the informal rules of administrative bodies.[63] The

[62] Passing reference to the matter is made in some cases; see: *McInnes* v. *Onslow-Fane*, n. 36 above and *Bushell* v. *Secretary of State*, n. 53 above. For a more direct analysis of the costs of procedures, see the Australian case *Johns* v. *Release on Licence Board* (1987) 9 NSWLR 103.

[63] See the further discussion in Ch. 10.

role of the courts in relation to procedures is quite different; when they intervene in administrative processes, their task is not to design procedures afresh, but to determine whether the existing procedures meet the prescriptions of procedural fairness.[64] When the procedures are found wanting, the courts will declare so and usually the decision or act in issue will be quashed or declared invalid, and sent back for re-consideration by the administrative body.[65] The court's decision is binding only in the specific case, and while it might be hoped that such decisions will lead administrators to adapt their procedures generally, the effect of judicial pronouncements on administrative procedures is something we know little about.[66]

However, the relationship between the courts, the principle of procedural fairness, and statutory procedures raises some important issues. The general principle is that the courts will make their own assessment of statutory procedures according to their own principles of fairness. If on that test the statutory procedures fall short, a court will require that they be supplemented in whatever way is necessary.[67] Where an oral hearing or the right to legal representation, for example, is judged by the courts to be required under the fairness principle, but is not provided for in the statutory procedures, the courts will intervene. However, the courts will respect a scheme of procedures which has been expressed in detail, whether by statute, delegated legislation, or administrative rule, and they will often be persuaded to regard the scheme as adequate. Since fair treatment does not normally dictate any fixed set of procedures, but allows for variation in procedures and a significant element of judgment at the margins, it is then sensible for the courts to respect attempts by Parliament and administrators to devise a scheme of procedures and not lightly to impose their own views.[68] The final test is still whether the statutory procedures meet the common law standard of fairness, so that if a court concludes that the test is not satisfied, no matter how detailed and comprehensive the statutory scheme may be, it is likely to intervene.

Another aspect of the relationship between the courts and statutory procedures occurs when the administrative body fails to comply with the statutory rules. If the procedures are set out in the statute itself, the duty on both

[64] The principle is set out by Lord Reid in *Weiseman* v. *Borneman*, n. 27 above, at 308 and often repeated. A full discussion is contained in *R.* v. *Panel on Take-Overs and Mergers, ex parte Guinness* [1990] 1 QB 146.

[65] For a most helpful discussion, see B. Dyer, 'Determining the Content of Procedural Fairness' (1993) 1 *Monash L Rev*. 165 at 170–6.

[66] There is some discussion in C. Harlow, 'Administrative Reaction to Judicial Review' [1976] *Public Law* 116. Otherwise I know of no study of this issue. See sect. 10.2.6 for further discussion.

[67] Lord Reid in *Wiseman* v. *Borneman*, n. 27 above at 308, *Payne* v. *Harris*, n. 59 above and *Lloyd* v. *McMahon*, n. 25 above.

[68] Brennan CJ, the Australian Chief Justice, reflects this idea in suggesting that the court should not intervene if the procedure is one that 'a reasonable and fair repository of the power would adopt in the circumstances': *Kioa* v. *West*, n. 56 above, at 627.

the administrator and the courts to comply is clear. Where the procedures derive from rules made under delegated legislation, the position is still fairly clear, since delegated legislation has the force of law and binds courts and administrators. However, the position is not quite so straightforward. For example, the Prison Rules governing order and discipline in prisons are made under delegated legislation, but not all their provisions, including procedural elements, are enforceable against the prison authorities.[69] It depends on the rule in question. A court will judge whether a rule is one of weight and substance, which appears to be a way of saying that it creates rights in the prisoner. Whether rights are created is a matter of interpretation. If the rule does not create statutory rights in the party, then failure by an administrative body to follow the procedures laid down by it will be actionable only if it leads to procedural unfairness according to common law principles. Many statutory rules are likely to be treated in this way on the basis that they are technical, directory, or advisory, rather than mandatory or rights-creating. Substantial parts of the Immigration Rules governing deportation procedures are characterized in this way, so that the bindingness of any one part will be judged on whether it is a requirement of the general principle of procedural fairness.[70]

The attitude of the courts to procedural rules created by the administrative bodies rather than by Parliament gives rise to another set of issues. Such rules are usually made under express statutory authority, but in the absence of express authority, the administrator might make its own procedural rules as a necessary step to carrying out its statutory powers. Rules made under express statutory authority may be regarded by the courts as binding, but whether they are will depend on how closely they resemble delegated legislation and whether they are laid before Parliament. Rules made without express statutory authority have no clear legal status, but are likely to be considered guidelines adopted by the authority for its own benefit. The courts accept that an administrative body is entitled to draw up procedural guidelines as an incident of its statutory powers.[71] How the courts will then regard those guidelines is not straightforward, but in general they are not regarded as generating procedural rights. If self-created procedures are adequate for their purposes and for achieving fair treatment, they should be respected by the courts. If, however, self-created procedures fall short of common law principles, the courts are likely to insist that the shortfall be remedied. Failure by an administrative body to comply with procedural guidelines will have no direct legal consequences, but will be judged according to whether the procedures followed were, nevertheless, fair. One further point to note is that the guidelines will sometimes be sufficiently serious and settled for the courts to hold that expectations have been created in those

[69] *R.* v. *Hull Visitors, ex parte St. Germain* [1979] 1 QB 425.
[70] See as an example, *R.* v. *Secretary of State, ex parte Hosenball* [1976] 1 WLR 766.
[71] See e.g. *Bushell* v. *Secretary of State for the Environment*, n. 53 above.

subject to the authority's actions. If the expectation is that those procedures should be followed, the authority will be held to the procedures as laid down.[72]

11.2.7 The Impact of Judicial Review

Judicial review has in common with other forms of recourse that its primary object is to decide the specified case before the court. At the same time, however, and again in common with other forms of recourse, it has the wider dimension of influencing the administrative body in a more general way. If a court rules that a certain procedure is required in the case in hand, then the implication is that it ought to be followed in all other, similar cases. A court ruling, in other words, not only decides the particular case but may set a more general normative standard to be acted on by administrative agencies. The extent to which a ruling has general application beyond the particular case is not always easy to determine, but should be approached in accordance with normal principles of interpretation. The courts themselves express different views as to how far a judgment on procedural fairness should be extrapolated beyond the particular case. Ultimately it is a matter of interpretation in each case and some judgments at least will be the normative basis for generalized procedural standards.

Since the courts do not often make direct reference to the standard-setting aspect of judicial review, it is not always clear what part it plays in their deliberations or how much importance they attach to it. But how much importance courts attach to it in fact is not the same question as how much they should, and how much they should is a matter of principle rather than judicial discretion. If a certain procedure is held to be necessary for fair treatment in one case, then the same should hold for similar cases, and the parties involved in those similar cases should have a justified claim to the same procedure being followed.[73] Where judicial decisions create general legal standards, they create new law and new rights, in this case procedural rights. It is not then a matter for the agency to decide how it will respond to a judicial ruling; where the ruling has a generalized element, the agency has a legal obligation to comply with the law and to adjust its procedures accordingly.

While the normative principles are clear enough, the practical effects of judicial rulings on administrative procedures are largely unknown. In an early study, T. Prosser examined the impact of an important case of judicial review relating to entitlement to social security.[74] The impact was found to be mixed and complicated, but the study is important not least in dispelling

[72] See *A.G. of Hong Kong* v. *Ng Yuen Shiu*, n. 12 above.

[73] For extended discussion, see D. Maranville, 'Non-acquiescence: Outlaw Agencies, Imperial Courts, and the Perils of Pluralism' (1986) 39 *Vanderbilt L Rev*. 471.

[74] T. Prosser, 'Politics and Judicial Review: The Atkinson Case and Its Aftermath' [1983] *Public Law* 59.

any assumption that a standard laid down in judicial review will be assimilated directly into administrative practice. In a later study, based on a number of prominent judicial review cases in which ministers and departments suffered serious reverses, Sunkin and Le Sueur distinguished between the formal and the informal consequences of judicial rulings.[75] The formal consequences were to encourage departments and agencies to be more careful in drafting laws, and in that way to reduce the risk of challenge in the courts. The informal consequences related to 'the internal, informal, and private world of government departments'.[76] The threat of judicial review, the reality of which was less than imagined by agencies and departments, sparked a flurry of activity at Whitehall.

The Cabinet Office reacted by publishing a pamphlet called *The Judge Over Your Shoulder* for circulation within departments. The pamphlet alerted departments of the risks of judicial review and how to reduce them.[77] Its main aim appears to have been to propound a defensive strategy and a measure of its success must be that senior officials can now talk confidently of making administrative schemes 'judicial review-proof'. The strategy is essentially negative, but in so far as it includes greater care in drafting statutes and acting under them according to the principles of administrative law, its negative character has some merit. The government's reaction also had a positive side. The threat of judicial review may have encouraged better administration and help to improve the quality of primary decisions. Since a very small percentage of primary decisions is taken on appeal or review of any kind, any measures which improve the quality of decisions at that level are to be welcomed. Whether judicial review has that effect is more doubtful. The evidence either way is scarce, but there is little reason to doubt that Sunkin and Le Sueur are right in concluding that those who make the mass of front-line decisions are still ignorant of the most elementary legal principles.[78] If that is the case in general, then it is likely to be the case in relation to procedures.

Without more systematic study of the issue, conclusions of the kind drawn by Sunkin and Le Sueur must be tentative, but they are not surprising. The standards laid down in judicial review are external to the organizational world of a department or agency. And as important as they may be to lawyers and judges, they are but a particle in the crowded universe of the admin-

[75] M. Sunkin and A. P. Le Sueur, 'Can Government Control Judicial Review?' [1991] *Current Legal Problems* 161.

[76] Ibid. 166.

[77] The Pamphlet was not made available for sale to the public; see A. W. Bradley, 'The Judge Over Your Shoulder' [1987] *Public Law* 485. A second version of the pamphlet has now been printed and published.

[78] The gap between legal rules and primary decisions, especially in areas of mass decisions, is also shown in two recent studies: J. Baldwin, N. Whikeley, and R. Young, *Judging Social Security* (Clarendon Press, Oxford, 1993) and I. Loveland, *Housing Homeless Persons* (Clarendon Press, Oxford, 1995).

istrative official. Research into organizations has long shown how difficult it is for externally imposed norms to become internalized by those within the organization. Not only are there competing norms of greater immediacy and apparent importance, there are also the imperatives of bureaucratic structure, of scarce resources, and of political pressures from government and ministers. The communication and assimilation of information about judicial rulings is also crucial if they are to find their way into the decisions of primary administrators. To enter into that world and to have an impact must inevitably be an arduous and complex process, achieved through gradual assimilation, through such means as inclusion in manuals and handbooks, by continuing training, and by both internal and external review. Considering that the quality of decision-making often falls well below the most elementary standards, it is not surprising that the refinements offered in judicial rulings must seem remote from the day-to-day duties of an administrator.[79] This is not to suggest that judicial review is unimportant; on the contrary, the courts have a major responsibility for reflecting on the normative demands of procedural fairness and for setting appropriate standards. Nor do I wish to suggest that such standards must remain permanently external to administrative action; a principal object of administrative justice should be to ensure that principle and practice coincide. The point to note is simply that the process of internalization is hard to achieve.

[79] The annual reports of the Chief Adjudication Officer show just how poor the quality can be in social security, and presumably elsewhere.

12

The Hearing Principle

The idea that a person ought to be heard before a decision is made or action taken affecting his or her interests is often thought to be the most fundamental element of procedural fairness. The discussion in Chapter 4 shows why being heard and the sense of involvement that comes with it run so deeply in law, political theory, and psychology. We saw there not only the instrumental role a hearing has in leading to better outcomes, but also the claims made for it as something of value in its own right. This Chapter is written against that theoretical background, but my objectives now are more practical, doctrinal, and contextual. They are primarily to consider the hearing in various administrative contexts, which means examining briefly the elements of a hearing and other parts of the process, such as notice and disclosure, which are closely linked to it. Whenever possible, an attempt is made to place the doctrinal issues in context by examining the empirical studies relevant to them. The discussion then goes on to consider the hearing principle and doctrine relating to it in different administrative contexts.

12.1 GENERAL CONSIDERATIONS

12.1.1 The Notion of a Hearing

The hearing element of an administrative process refers, strictly speaking, to the presentation and examination of evidence and argument. But in order to make that part worthwhile, two other elements are normally necessary, namely, notice and disclosure. The three are so closely connected that the notion of a hearing is often taken to include all of them. Notice means telling an interested party of the impending decision and providing guidance as to what it is about and the basis on which it will be made. Disclosure means that any facts and materials relevant to the decision should be made available to interested parties. In judicial trials, disclosure refers to the exchange of information and documents between the parties, while in administrative contexts the issue is usually to what extent the authority itself should disclose to the parties information it has. Finally, the hearing element itself refers to the involvement of the parties in the decision-making process. To be heard is in some way to be involved, to be able to put one's case by presenting evidence and argument, and to be able to respond to opposing evidence and argument. These three elements taken together constitute the general sense of a hearing, although it is often more accurate to speak of 'being heard' rather than a 'hearing', since the latter suggests some form of oral hearing when in practice a lesser sense of being heard will often be adequate. Of course the ways in which a person can be heard are enormously variable. At its most formal, a hearing means an oral hearing with all the trappings of pre-hearing procedures, particularly procedures for obtaining information, for the calling of witnesses, and for cross-examination. At its most informal and minimal, the need to be heard might be satisfied by a written form, perhaps no more than an informal letter, or it might mean just the chance to present factual information.

The general point is that the notion of a hearing is open and variable, capable of being constituted by a considerable variety of procedural forms based around the three elements of notice, disclosure, and hearing. The question in each context is what combination of the three elements is needed for effective and fair decisions. That is both the main practical and normative point of a hearing, and we should be wary of suggestions that the hearing is in some sense independent and self-contained. For that reason, the highly developed procedures of a judicial trial are not necessary in most areas of administrative process; they are not necessary because decisions can be made properly and fairly on the basis of lesser forms of hearing.

12.1.2 The Hearing and Procedural Fairness

Much has already been said about the relationship between a hearing and procedural fairness. Indeed the hearing principle, with its close connection to wider ideas about participation, raises many of the most interesting questions about procedures and procedural fairness: the relationship between procedures and outcomes, between procedures and other values, the idea that procedures are simply good in themselves, and the social benefits gained from certain procedures, can all be seen in the hearing principle. Here I shall take for granted the earlier discussion of these issues and begin by briefly restating the relationship between hearings and procedural fairness.

The first virtue of the hearing principle is that it contributes to better decisions and actions, better that is, in the sense that the facts are decided accurately, the law applied properly, and any discretionary judgments reasonably made. This is so for a number of reasons. One is that the person whose situation is under scrutiny, whose past actions or present circumstances are in issue, will often be able to provide information about the situation which is not otherwise easily available. This will not always or necessarily be the case; sometimes a perfectly accurate decision can be made about a person without relying on him as a source of information. Much depends on the type of inquiry, the nature of the factual issues, and the standards to be applied. An inquiry into criminal guilt is significantly different from the decision whether to issue a driving licence. Another reason is that the person affected by a decision may be able to raise other considerations, apart from purely factual matters, which help to shape the decision and perhaps, in that way, contribute to a better outcome. The plea in mitigation at sentencing, the representations a prisoner makes in favour of his release on parole, and the aggrieved party's criticisms of a prior decision, all raise factors of an interpretive and explanatory kind which might not otherwise occur or be placed before the official. Practical judgments are, after all, a combination of interpretation, speculation, and intuition; the same matter can be looked at in different ways and usually the best results are reached after argument and deliberation. A third practical reason for valuing the hearing idea is that the involvement of an interested party may be important in exposing the weakness of the case against him, the unreliability of the evidence produced, and even the untrustworthiness of the witnesses. For while the case which withstands critical attack from those opposed to it is likely to be soundly made and worthy of confidence, the untested case, the case where only one side is heard, should be treated with scepticism. At this level the hearing is a practical procedure for achieving better outcomes. But of course it does more than that and is closely linked to fair treatment; for better outcomes mean that cases are dealt with properly according to authoritative standards and treatment according to authoritative standards is the main component of fair treatment. The hearing principle is, then, an instrument towards fair treatment. It is, however, a contingent instrument, which means that its place in an administrative process depends on its contribution to better outcomes. The right outcome might be reached without a hearing, or it may be that an equally good outcome can be achieved by another procedure which is less costly. On this approach, the hearing principle does not have a guaranteed place, but must earn it in a practical and instrumental way. It follows also that the type of hearing, ranging from the written representation to a full oral hearing, will depend on context and circumstance.

Although the hearing principle is contingent upon its contribution to outcomes, there are good reasons for adopting a general presumption in favour of the hearing.[1] This does not change its contingent nature, but gives reasons for regarding a hearing as an important part of good decision-making, unless there are equally strong countervailing considerations. The reasons for adopting such a presumption are several. The first relates to the nature of legal and administrative decision-making as enquiring, argument-

[1] See the earlier discussion in Ch. 4.

ative, and deliberative. We touched on this above, but the point is that the hearing, the opportunity to receive evidence and argument from more than one source and from more than one point of view, is an important practical device for making good decisions. The second reason for a general presumption in favour of a hearing is that individualized decisions normally require an investigation of the situation of a particular person. The specific case must be enquired into, personal actions must be examined. This gives a special focus to the process; it adds a set of data to consider, but being a decision about how a person is to be treated it adds more. The duty of respect requires attention to be paid to that person's case; it requires that such level of enquiry and consideration be made as are compatible with the interests at stake and the consequences for them, and that the final judgment take proper account of those features. The involvement of the person through the hearing principle is normally, but not inevitably, an indispensable element in securing that level of consideration. The third reason derives from the need to form a practical judgment in which we can have confidence.

In sum, hearing procedures are instrumental to and contingent upon good outcomes, while being at the same time of sufficient practical importance to support a presumption that some form of hearing will normally be required. In contributing to good outcomes, the hearing is directly linked to fair treatment. This, as we saw earlier, is the primary justification for hearing procedures in theory; it is also the basis underlying the approach of the courts and legal doctrine. However, while that is the main justification for the hearing principle, it is not the sole justification and other values may well be served. The earlier discussion revealed two further values which link the hearing to fair treatment. One is the idea that a person should be able positively to advance or defend his interests within the framework of the law.[2] This idea draws on the value of each person being actively engaged in his relationship with the state, rather than being the passive recipient of benefits or the victim of burdens. Involvement in legal and administrative processes through the hearing principle is then the most effective means of expressing that active involvement. This approach is of interest as an alternative to the instrumental-to-outcome approach. The point of involvement in the process is still to influence outcomes, but the justification for this person being heard is different; it is that his interests are at stake and he is entitled to defend them. The second alternative, or addition, to the primary justification for the hearing principle is that respect for a person requires that he be heard. The right to be heard then follows directly from the principle of respect; it is not a contingent means to some further end, but is a direct requirement of respect, since to hear a person is to show respect for him. We have seen that this is a difficult argument to make convincingly, since on close analysis, the case for the hearing principle as an expression of respect

[2] See sect. 4.3.4.

either slips into an instrumental claim or is insupportable. There is moreover scarce support for this approach in judicial statements of principle.

Each of the three approaches to the hearing principle adopts the standpoint of the person affected. Each is directed to showing that the person has a right to be heard. The first does this by claiming a right to fair treatment and then showing that the hearing principle is normally a necessary means to fair treatment. The second claims a right to defend and advance one's own interests, using the hearing principle as a means to that end, while the third claims a right to be treated with respect and that being heard is integral to the notion of respect. However, the hearing principle might be approached in another way, not in order to establish rights, but to show its value to society as a whole. The idea is that obvious social gains flow from having decisions made according to the legal standards laid down. There may also be social gains, perhaps less tangible, in having a citizenry which is active in protecting its own interests and in each being treated with respect by the whole. However, a further way in which society as a whole might benefit from the hearing principle is by seeing the principle as a useful element in developing a sense of civil society. The idea is that the person who is involved in administrative processes is likely to understand them better, to see the justification for them, and to have his support for them strengthened. This idea is related to the argument advanced above that to act in defence of one's interests in administrative processes is to be encouraged. But the present argument goes farther and suggests that the act of protection of one's own interests can become part of a wider sense of involvement as a citizen.

The difficulty with this approach is to make any informed judgment about the link between the hearing principle on the one hand, and the development of civil society on the other hand. The intuition that there must be a connection remains, in the absence of empirical evidence, merely an intuition. Moreover, even if there is a connection, it is not clear what this means for the hearing principle. The gains to a community in developing its sense of civil society through hearings are bound to be marginal. This may be another reason for the hearing principle, which on its own may have little impact on the design of procedures but, when taken together with other reasons, tips the balance in favour of a hearing. This does not exhaust the possible benefits to society of the hearing principle. It has been said that people will be more inclined to accept the outcome of a process if they have been heard, although why that should be so is not altogether clear. The hearing might also encourage people to recognize the legitimacy of the process as a whole. The chance of putting one's case and having one's say, especially in a public forum, might even make people feel good and be more contented. Claims of these kinds are rather dubious and are often shorthand ways of expressing a more complex idea, and, even if made out, the practical implications for the hearing principle are unclear.

It may be concluded that the hearing principle, like most procedural principles, can be linked to a number of goals and values. Some are directed toward the good of society as a whole, others to the protection of individuals, to the creation of rights, and to questions of fair treatment. The outstandingly important value served by the hearing principle is to ensure that people are treated according to the law and, in that sense, fairly. Let us now consider how these general considerations feature in legal doctrine.

12.1.3 The Right to be Heard: The General Judicial Approach

Of the many possible procedural issues, the hearing principle is the one most often before the courts. The normal questions which arise are: should there be a hearing at all; if so, what form should it take; has notice been given; if so, is it adequate; what material should be disclosed; is legal representation necessary. Whether a hearing was required at all used to occupy a lot of the courts' time, but happily that question is now only occasionally raised, the assumption being that the threshold test is easily met.[3] The real question now is what is needed to satisfy the hearing principle, and that in turn raises the issues just listed. The law on these matters is extensive and often technical, and I shall endeavour in this section to sketch the general framework of ideas and doctrines developed by the courts, but without providing a handbook of all the rules. The analysis begins with the general judicial approach and then moves to the application of that approach in a number of different contexts.

The general principle of English law is often stated by the highest courts to be that a person who is adversely affected by the decision or other actions of an administrative authority has a right to be heard before the decision or action is taken.[4] In the most influential modern statement of the principle, Lord Diplock considered the right to be heard one of the fundamental rights generated by the general duty on administrative officials to act fairly towards those affected by its decisions.[5] The right to be heard meant in that case learning what is alleged against the person and then having the chance to put forward an answer to it. A person is adversely affected when a right or interest of a substantial rather than trivial kind is in issue. The adverse effects may consist in losing something one already has or failing to gain a benefit or advantage for which one is eligible. The principle is not limited to any particular kind of decision or action, but applies to administrative decisions generally, subject to the qualifications set out below. The courts have expressly ruled that the distribution between administrative and judicial

[3] See sects. 11.1.1 and 11.1.2.

[4] See *Russell* v. *Duke of Norfolk* [1949] 1 All ER 109, *per* Tucker LJ at 118; *Wiseman* v. *Borneman* [1971] AC 297.

[5] *O'Reilly* v. *Mackman* [1983] 1 AC 237 at 279.

decisions is unhelpful in deciding whether the hearing principle applies.[6] It has been said that the right to be heard, at least in proceedings before a court, includes the right to have all reasonable facilities for exercising the right,[7] such as 'quiet and unobtrusive advice from another member of the public'.

The courts tend not to enter into direct discussion of why the hearing principle is a fundamental requirement of procedural fairness, but it is not difficult to construct what their reasons might be. For some judges it is simply a legal principle which is well established and for which there are many precedents. Others, however, seem to suggest that a hearing is fundamental in some deeper, pre-legal sense. Quite what that sense is remains unclear, but it might be the essentialist view that to hear a person just is to show respect for him. A third possible explanation is that, while the hearing principle is instrumental to fair treatment, a general presumption should be made that a hearing is normally required for that purpose. Now while evidence can be found for each of these explanations, the last fits best with the general nature of procedural fairness and, I suggest, is most compatible with the character of the courts' own contemporary approach. According to that approach, the guiding principle is to follow procedures which ensure fair treatment, where fair treatment consists in the proper application of authoritative standards.

The reasons for thinking that this explanation makes most sense of contemporary judicial practice are several. In the first place, the supposed principle that a person should be heard is much less secure as a general legal practice than judicial statements suggest. The courts often ask whether a hearing is necessary in the circumstances of the case to ensure fair treatment, that being the point of *McInness* v. *Onslow-Fane*,[8] where a hearing was held not to be needed in deciding on an application for a boxing manager's licence. If there really is a general legal principle requiring a hearing whenever interests are affected, the enquiry made in this case would be precluded. Secondly, support for the instrumental and contingent approach to hearings can be found by analogy with other procedural issues, such as whether legal representation or an oral hearing is required. With respect to these and other procedures, the courts consider whether in the circumstances they are necessary to guarantee fair treatment. To ask such a question is to take a contingent and instrumental approach. This leads on to the third point: with the extension of procedural fairness to diverse areas of administration, to say that there is a right to be heard is often not to say very much, for the important question is what precise form of hearing is required in the circumstances. It is understandable, however, that in such varied conditions the

[6] See *R.* v. *Commission for Racial Equality, ex parte Cotterell* [1980] 1 WLR 1580 and *R.* v. *Army Board, ex parte Anderson* [1991] ALR 297.

[7] *R.* v. *Leicester City Justices, ex parte Barrow* [1991] 3 WLR 374.

[8] [1978] 1 WLR 1520.

courts should try to assess what is needed in each context rather than begin with certain fixed procedural rules. Rather paradoxically, Lord Reid's famous dictum against hard-and-fast procedural rules would apply to the hearing rule itself as well as any other rule.[9]

These considerations suggest that the judicial approach to hearings is not as clear and certain as sometimes appears. Judicial opinions as to the basis of the hearing principle are diverse, and many of the older statements suggesting fixed rules are more apt in court-like contexts than in the varied processes of administration. Nevertheless, there is still a strong case for a presumption in administrative processes generally in favour of a hearing, not as a fundamental principle, but for the mixture of practical and value-based reasons considered above. Those reasons constitute a sound and compelling case for such a presumption, without which administrative bodies would find it all too easy and convenient to decide that in the circumstances the hearing could be dispensed with. The best approach is: (i) to have a presumption in favour of a hearing, leaving aside precisely what that may require, and (ii) to allow the presumption to be rebutted in certain conditions.

The reasons for overriding the presumption may be several. Perhaps the most important is the one just mentioned, namely, that a hearing is not necessary for fair treatment according to authoritative standards. Areas of routine administration are notable examples where even the most rudimentary hearing is unnecessary, and similar arguments might sometimes be mounted in cases of standard adjudication. In the latter case, however, where the adjudicative element is at the heart of the process, the level of protection of the presumption should be high. Indeed, cases like *McInness* v. *Onslow-Fane*, where a hearing was held to be unnecessary, are generally open to the criticism that the reasons supporting a hearing were not properly considered. A second reason which might justify rebutting the presumption of a hearing is impracticability. The example of pre-trial processes was used earlier to show the need for procedures which went beyond the adjudicative model.[10] The same examples can be used here. Some pre-trial processes, such as the constable's decision whether to arrest, although in a sense cases of standard adjudication, cannot easily be made subject to a hearing. This does not mean that the concern for fair treatment is lessened, but only that it must be secured through alternative procedures which do not rely on the hearing element. The notion of impracticability might also be extended to certain situations of emergency. A third reason for qualifying the presumption of a hearing is that precedence must sometimes be given to competing values or policies. In the famous *GCHQ* case, the interests of national security were allowed to trump the hearing principle.[11] The fourth case of rebuttal applies to decisions of general policy. The courts take the view that the procedures

[9] *Wiseman* v. *Borneman*, n. 4 above.
[10] See sect. 8.5.
[11] *Council of Civil Service Unions* v. *Minister for Civil Service* [1985] AC 374.

governing general policy decisions, whether in relation to a specific issue or by way of rule-making, should be left for Parliament to deal with by legislation. If the statute does not provide for a hearing, the courts will not insist on one. However, the justification for this approach is not entirely convincing and the courts might well revise it in the future.[12]

12.1.4 Notice and Disclosure

The idea that a person should be given notice of an impending decision is a fundamental element of the hearing principle. Notice and the chance to put one's case are often said by the courts to be the twin pillars of the first principle of natural justice, so that one without the other would be a mockery of procedural fairness.[13] The idea of notice has its origins in criminal processes and is most powerful where specific charges have to be met.[14] The idea can be extrapolated without difficulty into those areas of administration which resemble court processes. In such cases, which often relate to disciplinary matters, the courts are likely to insist on clear and precise notice being given of the matters in issue.

The point of giving notice to affected parties is to allow them to prepare their case, that is, to collect the evidence and marshal the arguments which will be relevant to the decision. The justification is that a case which is properly prepared by the party will lead to better decisions and in that way improve the likelihood of fair treatment. The context and details of notice are determined by the nature of the process and the kinds of interests at stake. In a criminal-type process, specific and detailed notice would be needed, while a rather more general outline would be adequate in matters of preliminary investigation. The nature of the interests at issue is also a relevant variable, with more important interests attracting more exacting notice.

While the importance of notice as a procedure elementary to good decision-making is not in doubt, questions may be asked, first, as to how it applies across the spectrum of individualized processes and, secondly, to what extent it is required in those contexts as a matter of law. With regard to the first of these, what does the notice rule mean where a claimant is seeking a welfare benefit, a prisoner parole, or an applicant a licence? The courts rarely have to consider such cases, but it can be presumed that a party entitled to be heard is also entitled to notice. The adjudicative element in such cases, in the sense that the decision is made about the person by applying standards to facts, lends itself to the hearing principle. The party's need to know the case he has to meet and to make in order to secure a benefit or avoid a penalty is just as important in these instances as in those of a more trial-like character.

[12] See Ch. 16.

[13] See *Wiseman* v. *Borneman*, n. 4 above.

[14] This point is well expressed in *R.* v. *Gaming Board, ex parte Benaim and Khaid* [1970] 2 QB 417 and *In re Pergamon Press* [1971] Ch. 388.

As to the second question, legal doctrine is less clear and settled than statements of general principle suggest. Administrative bodies are not under a general duty to make known the criteria on which their decisions will be made.[15] And although they often produce and make available leaflets, guides, and other forms of published material, they do not always reveal, nor are they obliged to, the more informal standards relied upon.[16] Similarly, in relation to the facts, it is not at all clear in areas of mass decision-making to what extent an authority is required by law to make known to the party the facts which must be procured. And whatever the legal duties, practice would suggest that the parties are often unclear and confused about what they are required to prove.

Closely related to notice is the disclosure by the authority to the parties of information and materials upon which it intends to base its decision and which may be adverse to the parties. Traditional formulations of the first principle of natural justice have not included disclosure, but that may only be because disclosure was seen as an element of giving notice. Now the disclosure of adverse factors is regarded as an essential element of procedural fairness. The classic situation can be seen in a decision to deport an alien without disclosing to him damaging allegations contained in a departmental report.[17] It was held that fairness required disclosure of the adverse report and that the person affected should have an opportunity of showing it to be unfounded. The underlying point is that, no matter how well-founded the adverse material may be, the party should have the chance to cast doubt on it and, in that way, give a fuller and possibly more balanced account of the facts.

12.1.5 What Kind of Hearing?

Although much attention has been paid in the cases over the years to the question whether a party was entitled to be heard, the real and practical question now is what form should the hearing take. With the extension of the right to be heard so that more or less anyone significantly affected is now entitled, attention has turned to the procedural details: should the hearing be oral or written; whether oral or written, what precise form should it take; if oral, should witnesses and cross-examination be allowed; should legal or other specialist representation be permitted? The conclusion of the Franks Committee that, with respect to tribunals, few general rules could be laid

[15] See the discussion in sect. 14.1.

[16] A contrast can be drawn with the Australian federal jurisdiction where government departments and authorities are required by statute to disclose any standards, formal or informal, on which they rely in decision-making: see Freedom of Information Act (Cth) 1975.

[17] *Kioa* v. *West* (1985) 159 CLR 550. It is interesting to compare the decision of the House of Lords in *R.* v. *Secretary of State, ex parte Abdi and Gowe* [1996] ALR 248.

down may be applied to other areas of administration. The Franks Committee urged Parliament to take responsibility for procedural issues of this kind, but questions about the form of hearing still regularly find their way to the courts.

In deciding what form a hearing should take, the courts sometimes create lines of precedents and formulate general rules, but more often their judgment is guided by practical considerations; in particular, what form of hearing is needed to ensure that the case is dealt with properly according to authoritative standards. This involves two steps: first, to clarify the standards applicable in the specific context; secondly, to make a practical judgment about the kind of hearing necessary for a reliable application of the standards. Consider some examples. In *Hone*,[18] the question was whether a prisoner should be allowed legal representation in defending a charge before the Board of Visitors. The statutory rules provided for an oral hearing, but left it to the Board to decide whether legal representation should be allowed. On an application for judicial review, the court held that, since issues before the Board were mainly factual rather than of a complex legal kind, and since the prisoner was quite able to defend himself, the case for counsel was not made. In other words the courts were confident of an accurate decision on the facts and the law without the assistance of counsel.

Another example is *R.* v. *The Army Board, ex parte Anderson*,[19] where the issue was whether an oral hearing, rather than written submissions, was necessary. Anderson was a soldier who alleged he had been discriminated against on racial grounds. His complaints were considered at various levels and finally came before the Army Board. No statutory provision was made for an oral hearing, and the request for one was refused by the Board. On an action for judicial review, the Divisional Court examined the content and decided that fairness required an oral hearing. Its reasons were: (i) even though no significance should be attached to whether the process was administrative or judicial, the present process was clearly of a judicial nature; (ii) fundamental statutory rights were at stake; (iii) substantive questions of fact were in contest with seriously conflicting evidence on each side; and (iv) the Army Board was the court of last resort (except for the possibility of judicial review). These four factors taken together made a strong case for an oral hearing.[20]

This approach is both practically sensible and theoretically sound. The right not to be discriminated against on racial grounds is a basic civil right, the importance of which indicates the need for a full and careful investigation of alleged violations. The conflict of evidence could not be resolved easily without a full oral hearing, which would normally, but not necessarily,

[18] *R.* v. *Board of Visitors, ex parte Hone* [1988] 2 WLR 177.

[19] N. 6 above.

[20] See further *Lloyd* v *McMahon* [1987] 1 AC *per* Woolf LJ and *Heatley* v. *Tasmanian Racing and Gaming Commission* (1977) 137 CLR 487.

include the calling and cross-examination of witnesses. Those two considerations, and the fact that no appeal lay from the Board's decision, point compellingly to the conclusion that an oral hearing was necessary to be confident that the process would lead to an accurate outcome. Not all cases, however, will be so clear-cut and we should not be surprised that judgments differ about whether one or other procedure is required. Such judgments are practical judgments and it is characteristic of such judgments that reasonable people may reasonably disagree. It may be that over time a body of precedents will emerge in different areas, so that the kind of assessment, which the courts had to make in the above cases, will be replaced by settled rules. There is little doubt that in future cases of the *Anderson* kind, the Army Board will allow an oral hearing. Similarly, after a spate of decisions in recent years, rules relating to hearings in parole cases by the Parole Board and ministers are beginning to emerge. Sometimes, a ruling by the courts on a procedural point may lead to a change to the statutory rules or even the statute itself. Nevertheless, the range and variety of administrative processes is so great, and the scope of the hearing principle so extensive, that in most areas the careful examination by the courts of context and the drawing of practical conclusions will continue to be necessary.

12.1.6 The Effect of a Hearing

Considering the importance in law of the right to be heard and its close connection with administrative justice, we should consider what practical effect it has on decision-making. Practical effect might be judged according to a number of different criteria, but here I shall concentrate on the role it plays in leading to better decisions, in the sense that authoritative standards are properly applied. The underlying premise is that hearing procedures can be effective instruments in leading to accurate and proper decisions. Unless hearings serve that instrumental role they risk becoming hollow forms, for whatever other ends and values may be served, they are additions to the primary instrumental role. A failure in its primary role is a fatal flaw which cannot be remedied no matter what other uses it may have.

Little empirical research appears to have been conducted into hearing procedures.[21] The research that has been done tends to concentrate on the effect of legal representation within a hearing, rather than the hearing more generally.[22] It is to be hoped that in the future research will be conducted into a variety of issues, such as: the kinds of hearings being used in different administrative contexts; the factors which influence the adoption in the first

[21] Some recent work touches on these matters: R. Sainsbury, 'Administration Justice: Discretion and Procedure in Social Security Decision-Making' in R. Hawkins, *The Uses of Discretion* and Baldwin, Wikeley, and Young, *Judging Social Security*.

[22] See sect. 13.2.2.

place of specific forms of hearing; whether those forms meet the demands of legal principle; and the influence they have on the quality of decisions. While the dearth of research on these matters makes it difficult to offer an analysis of the impact of hearings, two general observations might be advanced. One is that, while doctrines relating to notice, disclosures, and hearings are reasonably well settled in legal doctrine and are meant to apply generally to administrative processes, their application in practice is patchy. Studies of social security and housing show that, at those levels of mass decisions, the gap between legal doctrine and administrative practice is wide,[23] with the one often bearing little relation to the other. The depth of the disparity is made very apparent by research conducted into a local social welfare office in Northern Ireland.[24] Claimants were not informed of their entitlements, nor told clearly what they needed to show in order to gain benefits. The onus was put squarely on the claimants to make their claims, but often in ignorance of what benefits were available. Interviews were held, but these were concerned more with noting the information given by claimants than providing an opportunity to inquire into relevant facts and circumstances.[25] A hearing in some sense often took place, but neither in the sense required by law nor with the aim of achieving an accurate and proper outcome. Loveland makes a similar point in his study of the decisions of local authorities in providing housing for the homeless.[26] His research showed that interviews of a sort are held, but that their object is very much to allow officials to get whatever information they needed for their policy ends, rather than to contribute to good decision-making according to law.[27] The findings in these two areas are likely to be repeated elsewhere; indeed, the findings are not surprising and reasons for such a gap, between the legal conception of hearing procedures and the practical reality, are not hard to discern. The main reason is that the legal rules have not been assimilated into administrative culture, which in turn may be due to several factors: the rules might not be clear; the officials might not know about them; and even if the rules are both clear and known, they may be overshadowed by stronger forces and pressure within the organizational context.

The problem highlighted so far stems from the failure of administrative

[23] Baldwin, Wikeley, and Young, *Judging Social Security*, n. 21 above, and I. Loveland, *Housing Homeless Persons*, n. 21 above.

[24] L. E. A. Howe, 'The "Deserving" and the "Undeserving": Practice in an Urban Social Security Office' (1985) 14 *J of Soc. Policy* 49.

[25] Similar practices were found by S. Cooper, *Observations in Supplementary Benefits Offices* (Policy Studies Institute, London, 1985).

[26] For earlier work on social welfare tribunals, see M. Adler, E. Burn, and R. Johnson, 'The Conduct of Tribunal Hearings' and C. Milton, 'Appellants' Perceptions of the Tribunal Process', both in M. Adler and A. Bradley, *Justice, Discretion and Poverty* (Professional Books, London, 1975).

[27] Loveland, *Housing Homeless Persons*, n. 23 above, and Baldwin, Wikeley, and Young, *Judging Social Security*, n. 21 above, ch. 2.

bodies to adopt in practice proper notice, disclosure, and hearing procedures. A second and different issue is the effect such procedures have on decision-making when they are properly implemented. Here the question is whether the quality of decisions is improved, whether they are sounder than they would have been without a hearing. The issue is even more complicated than that because considerations of cost also have to be taken into account. The more precise question then is whether, within the constraints of the principle of proportionality, certain kinds of hearings contribute to better outcomes. Their contribution can be of various kinds: through eliciting relevant information from the person heard; by countering or questioning information derived from other sources; or in suggesting interpretations or viewpoints which influence for the good the overall judgment. These matters are unavoidably difficult to assess, especially where no reasons or no adequate reasons are given by the authority, and where no detailed analysis of the evidence is provided.[28] The need for research into these matters is all too evident; in the absence of the fuller knowledge empirical research would provide, we can do little more than resort to common sense intuition and trust that carefully designed hearing procedures will often be an important element in good and accurate decision-making.

12.2 LEGAL REPRESENTATION

One procedural aspect of a hearing which calls for closer examination is the legal representation of a party affected by administrative action. In the administrative lawyer's hall of infamy, the remark by a social administrator, that lawyers ought to be kept as far away as possible from administrative processes, has a prominent place.[29] Since we now have good empirical evidence to support the intuition that to have a lawyer improves one's chances substantially, it is fortunate that Titmuss' remark was never taken too seriously. Considering the importance of this aspect of procedures in ensuring fair treatment, we should look more closely at some of the issues raised by representation.

12.2.1 Legal Representation and Fair Treatment

Just as crime rates might drop if we each had a policeman at our elbow, so the standard of justice in administration processes should rise if all parties were assisted at each step by a lawyer. The claimant of welfare, the applicant for a licence, or the defendant against imposition of a penalty or

[28] The close connection between hearings and reasons is brought out in sect. 14.2.
[29] R. M. Titmuss, 'Welfare "Rights", Law and Discretion' (1971) 42 *Pol. Q* 113.

other burden would each surely benefit from the advice and assistance of a solicitor, barrister, or other specialist. Lawyers are trained to marshal evidence and facts, to present a case in its best light while exposing the weaknesses in someone else's, and not least to understand the law. Each of those qualities seems eminently appropriate to most aspects of administrative decision-making, for while we tend to associate lawyers with advocacy and hearings, with appeals and reviews, they are equally useful in advising and assisting at the primary decision. If it is true that at least one quarter of all decisions on the grant of supplementary benefits are mistaken,[30] then it would seem obvious that the widespread assistance of lawyers at that stage would greatly improve their quality and in turn the level of fair treatment. The awkward fact is that the great majority of people involved in administrative processes of any kind would benefit greatly from specialist advice and assistance. Here I shall concentrate on legal advice, but it should not be overlooked that advice and assistance comes from various sources, from friends and relatives, specialist groups and organizations, as well as from lawyers.

Yet the position is not so straightforward. For one thing lawyers are expensive, so that the prospect of having them available to all is about as realistic as having a personal policeman. For another thing lawyers are often thought to be a form of treatment worse than the disease; they are said to complicate matters, to introduce technicality into informal processes, and to cast over the most simple process the shadow of an adversarial contest. By a combination of those factors, administration processes can be delayed, obstructed, and made altogether less efficient. Between these two images of the lawyer's role in administration, there is perhaps a middle way. On the one hand, many administrative processes do not need lawyers, while on the other hand, many of the criticisms of lawyers are misconceived. Administrative processes and the law governing them often are complex, technical, and largely incomprehensible to the untrained. The Franks Committee urged tribunals to be informal in their procedures without perhaps fully realizing that formality and procedural complexity are natural consequences of substantive legal complexity.[31] A cursory study of any tribunal will soon bear that out. For no matter how informal a body might like to be, evidence still has to be gathered and tested, facts formed, inferences drawn, and the law understood and applied. The lawyer's complication is often no more than insistence that those tasks be done properly. The alternative to formal procedures and technical argument is often the loose and insupportable

[30] Council on Tribunals, *Annual Report* (1986, Cmnd. 9722), para. 7.

[31] The Genn study of representation before tribunals brings out this point admirably: see H. and Y. Genn, *The Effectiveness of Representation Before Tribunals* (Lloyd's of London Press, London, 1992) 112 ff. See also R. Young, 'The Effectiveness of Representation at Tribunals' (1990) 16 *Civil J Rev*. 16.

exercise of discretion, based on impression and intuition rather than hard evidence and facts.[32] Nobody would today take the view which became orthodox amongst social administrators forty years ago that the distribution of welfare was best left to discretion and lawyers should be kept out. A touch of the adversarial approach, in so far as it means that administrative officials must attend carefully to the task in hand, is not a bad thing. And in any case the concern for scrutiny, questioning, and explanation as natural instruments to better decision-making should not be confused with the negative aspects of an adversarial process.

Another possible argument against legal representation is that administrative processes generally take the form of an inquiry into the facts, followed by a decision about those facts. Much of the inquiry is conducted by the authority itself, often from resources readily available to it, and without heavy reliance on material deriving from the person affected. The primary decision, in other words, may bear no resemblance to an adversarial process where the service of a lawyer is most needed. At the appeal stage, which is usually before a tribunal, the tribunal itself may take an active role in both eliciting information and helping the applicant to make the most of his case;[33] some tribunals pride themselves on their investigative, inquisitorial role. This argument against legal representation has, fortunately, not prevailed. As the Lord Chancellor's Advisory Committee on Legal Aid recently concluded, a benevolent and helpful attitude on the part of tribunal chairmen towards applicants is no substitute for effective representation.[34] Moreover, the extent and effect of such help is easily over-stated.[35]

Against these background remarks, we should now consider three particular aspects of legal representation: first, its point and importance; secondly, its practical effect; and thirdly the approach of English law. As to the first of these, the point and importance of legal advice and representation are clear: lawyers are able to provide advice and assistance at various points in the administrative process, from the earliest beginnings until the last right of appeal has been exhausted. Lawyers can provide advice on what must be done to gain benefits or to avoid burdens; they can help in collecting evidence and presenting the facts; they can advise on the law; and they can be especially effective in examining the facts and material upon which the deciding authority proposes to act. If the matter goes to appeal, then again lawyers can provide invaluable help in assembling and presenting the case. They can also be of help in filtering out cases which have no chance of success, and in conducting informal bargaining processes

[32] Compare T. H. Marshall, *The Right to Welfare* (Heinemann, London, 1981).

[33] For discussion of this point, see *Recommendations of the Lord Chancellor's Advisory Committee on Legal Aid*, 1973/4 (24th Report), paras. 36 ff.

[34] *Ibid.*, para. 37.

[35] See the discussion in sect. 12.3.2.

with the authority.[36] The point of legal advice is to put people in a position where they are able properly to protect and advance their own interests.

Legal representation can be linked directly to fair treatment and procedural fairness. It helps to ensure that each case, whether at the initial decision or on appeal, is decided properly and accurately. The effect of legal advice in a specific case is difficult to gauge, but it is likely to increase our general confidence that decisions are being properly made. For those who value a hearing for its own sake, legal representation might be seen as a way of making it more meaningful and, in that way, enhancing dignitarian values. From the point of view of civic virtue, the role of the lawyer can also be important in providing the client with a knowledge and understanding of the process, of the matters in issue, and why they are resolved in one way rather than another. Now while legal representation is often an important element of procedural fairness, it is not always a necessary element. Like other procedures, it is contingent on whether, in any given context, it is needed to ensure that decisions are properly made. Legal representation contributes to fair treatment, but it is not always essential to fair treatment.

The difficulty lies in deciding when legal representation is necessary for fair treatment. On the one hand, the more we know about administrative processes, the clearer it is that the standard of decision-making is poor and that those subject to them would benefit from legal advice and assistance. That might not apply to all areas, nor to all people, but it is certainly the case in many areas of mass administration—social welfare, immigration, and licensing, to name a few—where at the same time the chances of having legal advice are slender. On the other hand, legal advice is costly and could only be available in such areas if provided under legal aid schemes; yet in practice legal aid is rarely allowed for administrative decisions or appeals. Indeed, even where private resources are available to provide legal representation, the law might not allow it.[37] Another cost which militates against the widespread reliance on legal representation is the cost of delay and complication which often follows from the involvement of lawyers. Quite apart from the costs of providing legal representation, the effect on efficient and expeditious administration of the parties being represented can be severe. It is not difficult to imagine that some areas would simply break down if to already slow and over-burdened administrative processes were added further demands and complications.[38] The conflict between proper advice, good decisions, and fair treatment on the one side, and reasonable efficiency and expedition in settling matters on the other side, is acute. The harsh truth is that, in order to make administrative government work, it is often necessary

[36] The various tasks are discussed more fully in Genn, n. 31 above, 116 ff.

[37] See sect, 12.3.3.

[38] There is evidence to show a correlation between legal representation and delay: Genn, n. 31 above, 157, but of course some delay might be necessary for good decision-making.

to sacrifice fair treatment, and that is especially true in relation to legal representation.

However, there are ways of mitigating the conflict between the need for legal representation and the concern to contain costs and inefficiency. The most promising approach is to seek alternative ways of achieving fair treatment, without incurring huge costs or bringing government to a halt. One alternative is for administrative bodies themselves to improve their own procedures in order to make them more open and understandable to those affected. The work of revenue authorities to simplify tax returns is a mundane but important example, the tax return of today being much easier to complete without specialist help than it was ten years ago. The same concern for intelligibility might well be copied elsewhere. Another approach is to develop advice centres which are able to give specialist help in particular areas. The creation of such centres in welfare and immigration, for example, is a notable feature of recent years. The phenomenon of the advice bureau needs a study in itself, but some of its obvious attractions are ease of access and cheapness of operation. Such bodies can provide more cheaply and effectively the assistance which might otherwise have come from lawyers and, because they specialize in a narrow area of administration, advice centres are often the best source of assistance.

In determining when legal representation is needed for fair treatment, the principal guideline should be that legal advice and representation are needed when, without them, the person affected would not be able properly to prepare and present his case. It may sometimes help to distinguish between advice on the one hand, and representation before the administrative body on the other hand, but the two go together and both are directed at enabling the person to prepare and present his case. The corollary is that, if the objective can be attained without legal representation, then it is not a requirement of fair treatment. In applying that principle, a number of more specific factors relevant in judging that issue can be suggested: (i) the complexity of the issue, where complexity might result from the facts, the law, or both; (ii) the ability of the person to prepare and present his own case; (iii) the seriousness of the issue; and (iv) the openness of the process. The first two are clear enough, but the other two call for a word of explanation. The seriousness of the issue is relevant, because the more serious it is the more important it is to guard against error, and the guidance of a lawyer may be one factor in reducing the risk of error. The fourth condition is directed to ensuring that even when administrative processes take place in private, behind closed doors, or within closed institutions, they will nevertheless be conducted properly. The police investigation of suspects, the exercise of disciplinary powers in prisons, and decisions about mentally handicapped people in institutions are all examples of where the availability of legal representation is fundamental to fair treatment.

These conditions of fairness may, however, have to compete with efficiency, cost, and expedition. On the above tests of fairness, a good case would be made out for every social welfare claimant having legal representation in dealing with the welfare agencies. Such a suggestion, of course, would be impractical considering the mass decisions in that area, but the principle remains clear: although considerations of fairness do not always prevail over expediency, fairness is compromised to that extent. Some concessions to expediency might be necessary as a matter of practical judgment, but efforts should be made to design administrative procedures so that fairness has full effect and is reduced by administrative convenience only exceptionally and marginally.

12.2.2 The Practical Effects of Legal Representation

In the above discussion, I have made a number of claims about the beneficial effects of legal representation. To some extent those claims are based on common sense and intuition, but they are also supported by empirical research, which I shall now briefly consider. The one major piece of research in the United Kingdom was recently done by H. and Y. Genn at the request of the Lord Chancellor's Department. The object was to examine the effect of representation, especially legal representation, on the proceedings of tribunals. Emphasis was put on representation at the hearing stage, but advice at earlier stages received some attention. The general conclusion reached by the researchers was that legal representation makes a significant difference to the proceedings. That is to say, the applicant's chances of a favourable outcome are improved as a direct result of legal representation. To take some examples, representation improved the applicant's chances from 30 per cent to 45 per cent in Social Security Appeal Tribunals, and from 20 per cent to 35 per cent in Mental Health Appeal Tribunals.[39] We should not assume that more favourable outcomes from the applicant's point of view necessarily mean better decisions and therefore a higher level of fair treatment; in finding for the applicant, the tribunal might on occasions be mistaken. Nevertheless, it is safe to assume that in at least some, if not most, of those cases legal representation did contribute to better and fairer decision-making. The suggestion has been made that the effects of legal representation are exaggerated in the study since it is the stronger cases which are likely to be legally represented anyhow;[40] the authors did, however, make every effort to isolate the effect of representation from other factors and succeeded in doing so.

[39] Genn, n. 31 above. The other tribunals studied were Industrial Tribunals and Immigration Adjudications.

[40] See R. Young, 'The Effectiveness of Representation of Tribunals', n. 31 above. See also J. Peay, *Tribunals on Trial* (Clarendon Press, Oxford, 1989).

A second conclusion which can be drawn from the Genn study is the importance of legal advice at earlier stages prior to the tribunal hearing.[41] Much of the work of tribunals lies in correcting the mistakes of primary decision-makers, mistakes which are often purely factual. It follows that better advice at that stage would enable the person affected to present a better application, to disclose the right evidence and facts, and generally to indicate how the case should be decided. The Genn study also noted how important legal advice can be in filtering out hopeless cases and in negotiating with an authority or tribunal the possibility of an agreed settlement. Some of these findings would be equally applicable to primary decisions and processes preliminary to them, but so far little research has been done on the effects of legal advice at the earlier stages of administrative processes.

The third major finding of the Genn study is that, notwithstanding views often expressed to the contrary, the inquisitorial character of some tribunals is not an adequate substitute for a well-presented and well-argued case by the applicant. The study makes clear that, no matter how helpful the tribunal may try to be, a well-presented case by the party is a major factor in a favourable outcome. Often it will be only with the help of a lawyer or other specialist adviser that such a case may be mounted.[42] A similar conclusion was reached by J. Peay in her study of Mental Health Review Tribunals.[43] Her results are not surprising, since even a tribunal which assumes a distinct inquisitorial approach acts under considerable pressure of time and resources, sees the situation from one point of view, and will never have the same incentive as the party itself to pursue evidence and facts. This is not to say that an enquiring, investigative approach will never be adequate; it is only to say that a properly presented case on behalf of the party has a strength and influence, the absence of which is not easily compensated for by other procedures.

12.2.3 Legal Representation in English Law

The principle of English law is that legal or other representation of a party in an administrative process is not a necessary requirement of procedural fairness. An authority must follow fair procedures, and whether representation is required as a fair procedure depends on the context.[44] Parliament often makes provision for legal representation in relation to each administrative process, and it is now the case that hearings before tribunals or any other process of a broadly judicial kind normally carry a statutory right to

[41] Genn, n. 31 above, 126 ff.

[42] See also T. Muller, 'Representation at Tribunals' (1990) 53 *MLR* 230.

[43] J. Peay, *Tribunals on Trial*, n. 40 above.

[44] These principles are often stated in the cases; see e.g. *Enderby Town F.C.* v. *Football Association* [1920] 1 QB 67; *R.* v. *Home Secretary, ex parte Tarrant* [1985] QB 251; *R.* v. *Board of Visitors, ex parte Hone*, n. 18 above.

legal representation. Where the statute is silent on the matter, the general principle is that the authority or tribunal is master of its own procedures and, in its discretion, may allow legal representation.[45] Where an authority denies representation, its decision may be challenged before the courts by judicial review. In *Tarrant*,[46] for example, the Board of Visitors of a prison refused to allow legal representation to prisoners charged with disciplinary offences. On a challenge by way of judicial review, the court held, first, that there was discretion in the Board of Visitors to allow representation; secondly, that the Board should have directed its mind to the exercise of the discretion; and thirdly, that, in doing so, it should be guided by a number of factors. It is somewhat misleading to talk of discretion here, since it is not strong discretion in the sense that, provided the authority takes into account the relevant factors, its decision will be final. The discretion is of the more limited kind which occurs in applying a fixed standard, here the standard of procedural fairness; for the question really is whether that standard points to the need for legal representation in the circumstances. The court will finally decide what the principle requires, regardless of the view taken by the authority, and the court's opinion will prevail.

The factors to be considered by a court in deciding whether procedural fairness requires legal representation are those we might expect and are broadly similar to those noted earlier in this section: (i) the seriousness of the issue for the party; (ii) whether points of law are involved; (iii) the party's capacity to present his own case; (iv) the need for reasonable speed in deciding an issue; and (v) the need for fairness as between parties, where there is more than one.[47] Notice that, in stating the relevant factors in this way, the courts do not distinguish between matters of fairness and matters of administrative expediency,[48] and so, it seems, the former might sometimes be compromised in favour of the latter. Needless to say the courts have considerable leeway in deciding whether, in the absence of statutory provision, there is a right to legal representation. In some cases, the right is well-settled, a notable example being the accused charged before the courts with a criminal offence. Other examples in which legal representation has been allowed by the courts are cases of dismissal from office, loss of livelihood, and ruination of character. In most administrative contexts, the matter is still open and, if they ever come to judicial review, cases will be decided according to the factors set out above.[49]

[45] See *Enderby* and *Tarrant*, n. 44 above.

[46] N. 44 above.

[47] This formulation is taken from Webster J in *Tarrant* ibid., and was approved in *Hone* n. 6 above; see also *R.* v. *Crown Court, ex parte Siderfin* [1994] ALR 7.

[48] See further discussion in J. Alder, 'Representation Before Tribunals' [1972] *Public Law* 278.

[49] On the related issue of having help from a friend, see *McKenzie* v. *McKenzie* [1970] 3 All ER 1034.

Disciplinary proceedings in prisons have been particularly contentious and are the subject of many of the recent judicial decisions on legal representation.[50] The courts took some time to conclude that the conditions of fairness in disciplinary proceedings might extend to legal representation, although whether it did or not had to be judged according to the circumstances of each case.[51] It is not surprising that Boards of Visitors, which until recently had disciplinary jurisdiction, tended to exercise their discretion against representation. Although strictly speaking such decisions are a matter of principle not discretion, the courts have not easily been persuaded to reverse the denial of representation at the earlier hearing. Indeed, the analysis of the House of Lords in *Hone*, as to whether a prisoner could properly represent himself, suggests that an initial refusal of representation at primary level will be hard to overturn on review. The conclusion in *Hone* is disappointing and might have been different if greater efforts had been made to understand the problems of prisons and other closed institutions. An extensive literature exists on the special characteristics of such institutions, and one might have expected the imbalance between prison and staff to have been at the centre of the court's analysis. To conclude that in the circumstances justice could be done without legal representation, without reference to the conditions and culture of a prison, is to over-simplify the issue. Nevertheless, considering that only a few years ago the prison was regarded as virtually beyond the law, the courts have made progress in a number of ways in introducing basic principles of fair treatment.[52] There is still a long way to go, and the initiative for reform in these matters has now been taken up by Parliament. Serious disciplinary offences are now tried in the normal way before a court, while lesser matters are dealt with by the governor. Offences coming before the governor range from the trivial to the fairly serious, but it is left for him to decide whether legal representation is necessary. Undoubtedly it will be refused in most cases, even where the issue is not just minor and domestic but involves a substantial penalty. So, despite some improvements the risk of procedural injustice and the resulting substantive injustice in prisons and other closed institutions is still very real.

To conclude, questions of legal representation are now generally covered by statute; where they are not, the administrative body must consider the matter and may decide to allow it. Refusal may be challenged on judicial review, and the judgment of the court will be shaped by a number of factors, all of which are clearly relevant. One major influence, however, which does not appear in the official list, is the way that different areas of administrative activity and the groups affected within them are perceived by the community.

[50] For a survey of the issues, see G. Richardson, *Law, Process, and Custody: Prisoners and Patients* (Weidenfeld and Nicolson, London, 1993), ch. 7.

[51] See Lord Goff in *Hone*, n. 18 above.

[52] See M. Loughlin and P. Quinn, 'Prisons, Rules and Courts: A Study in Administrative Law' (1993) 56 *MLR* 497.

The importance of that influence is shown in the prison cases. Another difficulty with the cases on legal representation is that no indication is given by the courts of how the claims of fairness are to be assessed against claims of expediency. This is always a difficult issue, but rather than mix the different factors together, it would be better to decide, first, what is required by fairness, and then, secondly, to what extent fairness might have to be sacrificed to expediency. By recognizing the two as separate questions, it will often be possible to respect fairness without unduly restricting administrative convenience. As Lord Atkin said, convenience and justice are often not on speaking terms,[53] but if we are clear about what each demands, it might be possible to open the dialogue. Another source of misgiving is the idea that procedural fairness, and the specific procedures required by it, are matters of discretion. When the courts speak of discretion they probably do not mean discretion in any strong sense, but to suggest that questions of procedural fairness are matters of weighing and balancing, of doing the best all things considered, is to reveal a basic misunderstanding of its nature.

12.3 THE HEARING PRINCIPLE IN DIFFERENT CONTEXTS

12.3.1 Routine Administration

The sense in which a hearing is appropriate to routine administration is minimal and should consist normally in no more than the opportunity to put before the decision-maker the facts needed for the decision. That often means little more than completing a standard form or providing straightforward information in some other way. Such information will usually be sufficient for the decision to be made and will rarely be contested—indeed the model of routine administration suggests a lack of contest. The information necessary for the decision will often be readily available to officials from sources other than the person affected. Although this is the standard case of routine administration, the position might easily become more complex: additional information might be required which might lead to an interchange between the applicant and the official; an element of disagreement and contest might appear. The basic idea, however, is that the provision of information and the decision based on it are routine matters, with no element of dispute about the facts or the rules; if an element of complexity or dispute arises, adjudication becomes the more appropriate model.

While the most important procedural issue here is whether people have proper access to the many instances of routine administration, our present interest is in the applicability of the hearing principle. Its requirements are essentially that an interested party should know what information is needed

[53] *General Medical Council* v. *Spackman* [1943] AC 627 at 638.

and should have the chance to provide it. That information will often be enough for the decision, but sometimes the official might have access to and rely upon other sources. Whether the hearing principle requires disclosure of information from such sources depends on a number of factors. If the additional sources are themselves routine and uncontentious, matters of public record for example, then the party is unlikely to want disclosure. If, however, those further sources contain information which is unknown to the party or which might be contentious, then the case for disclosure is clear. The party should then be told what the additional facts are and given the opportunity to comment on them. The hearing principle would normally be satisfied by this approach, although of course if the information is contentious, or indeed if any other aspect is disputed, then routine administration has given way to adjudication and the opportunity to be heard should be more exacting. Assuming, however, that no element of contention occurs and the case is genuinely one of routine administration, the procedural demands are few.

Cases of routine administration are unlikely to come before the courts, although it is conceivable that a challenge to a decision could be mounted on the ground that the opportunity to provide the necessary information was denied. Questions might also be raised about disclosure where information from sources other than the party is taken into account. Since failure to disclose such sources would encourage suspicion that unreliable material was being used, a general practice of disclosure would be desirable. The failure to disclose might in any event be a good ground for invoking the hearing principle, although it is in the uncontentious nature of routine administration that that would be rare. To conclude, the main focus of the hearing principle in this context is the chance to present the right information, with questions of disclosure occasionally arising.

12.3.2. Standard Adjudication

According to the earlier analysis, standard adjudication refers to the process for determining how a person is to be treated where that process is based on applying standards to the facts. It involves an enquiry into and determination of the facts, and then a judgment about the facts on the basis of authoritative standards. The structure of standard adjudication has some similarity with routine administration, but there are also differences: in adjudication the facts are likely to be more complex and possibly more difficult to settle; and while the standards are usually well-settled, there is now room for interpretation and judgment, even an element of discretion, in applying them. The similarities and the differences can be illustrated with one or two examples. Suppose that university places are no longer allocated on pure academic results, but on wider considerations, such as the applicants' educational opportunities in the past, their achievements in other fields of activity, and how well they might fit into the institution. To take a second case, suppose that, having been admitted, at some time later the student is faced with expulsion for misconduct. In both cases, authoritative standards have been laid down, but they cannot be applied by a simple, routine judgment, since they need to be interpreted to fit the case. The facts are now more complex; indeed, issues of fact are not entirely distinct from issues of characterization and judgment: how to assess previous educational opportunities, or whether the applicant will benefit from the education being offered. Questions of misconduct, moreover, inevitably carry overtones of moral and social evaluation and judgments about what sort of behaviour is acceptable.

The two examples provide a sense of standard adjudication. It is not, of course, a tight category, and varies only in degrees from routine administration; but the degree of variation is the vital element, for it connotes the need for evidence, argument, deliberation, and judgment. The need for those processes is the mark of adjudication in an elementary sense. It is also helpful here to distinguish between a decision by an official about how to treat X and a decision by an official as to how a dispute between X and Y should be resolved. Both are cases of adjudication, but each raises issues special to itself. I shall consider the hearing principle in relation to two-party adjudication in this section and in relation to three-party adjudication in the next. Two-party adjudication is the sense of adjudication which commonly occurs in administrative processes.

The importance of some form of hearing in cases of standard adjudication is easily seen; it is also easy to see why the detailed form of hearing can vary from one case to another. Since standard adjudication involves some level of inquiry into facts and circumstances directly about the particular person, his or her involvement in the process is, as a matter of common sense, an important element of good decision-making. A claim has to be made out, a set of circumstances has to be established, or a case has to be put by the person affected. Equally, as a matter of common sense it can be seen that the form the hearing takes should be responsive to the nature of the issue, the interests at stake, and the consequences for them. Where the facts are simple and the standards clear and settled, the hearing may be brief and simple, and written representations will often be adequate. In other cases, where the facts are more involved, the law more complex, or questions of interpretation more taxing, a full oral hearing might be needed.

English law has long recognized two general principles in relation to standard adjudication: first, that a hearing of some sort is a vital element of procedural fairness; and, secondly, that the nature of the hearing varies according to the criteria noted above. Evidence of the first principle can be found in cases reaching back into English legal history:[54] the barring of

[54] See the discussion in S. A. de Smith, *Judicial Review of Administrative Action* (4th edn., Stevens, London, 1980), ch. 4 and sect. 5.3 herein.

Dr Bentley from practising medicine,[55] the dismissal of Bagg the verger,[56] and the arrogant destruction of Mr Cooper's house[57] are well-known examples of the principle that a person should be heard before being adjudged to his detriment. The principle holds equally firmly in modern English law. As to the second principle, the courts now examine each process closely to determine whether the hearing provided was suitable in the circumstances. The earlier analysis of *R.* v. *Army Board, ex parte Anderson* is pertinent here.[58] There, it will be recalled, the issue was whether the Army Board should have conducted an oral hearing in adjudicating upon the allegations of racial discrimination. The court made clear that the point of the hearing was to enable the Board to consider all the relevant evidence and arguments about the evidence before reaching its conclusion; whether an oral hearing was needed then depended on whether it was necessary to satisfy that objective.[59] After considering the complexity and inconsistency of the evidence, the importance of the soldier's right not to be discriminated against, and the absence of an appeal, the court concluded that an oral hearing was essential for procedural fairness. But even where an oral hearing is necessary, further questions might arise as to what form it should take. The right to call one's own witnesses and to cross-examine opposing witnesses, for instance, does not follow automatically from the right to an oral hearing; they often go together, but an oral hearing without witnesses or cross-examination will sometimes be adequate.[60] The general point is that precisely what is required by the hearing principle and in turn by procedural fairness has to be determined according to context and circumstances, the guiding standard being in each case sound and accurate decision-making.

12.3.3 Three-party Adjudication

Three-party adjudication occurs in its clearest sense in the civil trial where two or more parties contest an issue which is finally resolved by an impartial judge according to the law. While this may be considered the paradigm of third-party adjudication, variations on it are familiar within the administrative process; they may be first-level decisions, where an official has to decide a dispute between two parties, or they may occur at the appeal level. A typical case of the latter is an appeal from a case of standard adjudication: official X decides that Y is not entitled to a benefit and Y appeals against the decision to a tribunal T. The issue is then likely to become a contest between X and Y to be judged by T. The distinctive feature in both cases, in addition

[55] *R.* v. *Chancellor & others of Cambridge University* (1765) 2 Rd Ragm. 1334.
[56] *Bagg's Case* (1615) 11 Co.Rep. 936.
[57] *Cooper* v. *Wandsworth Board of Works* (1863) 14 CB (NS) 180.
[58] N. 6 above, at 308: see sect. 12.1.5.
[59] For a similar analysis, see *R.* v. *Department of Health, ex parte Gandhi* [1991] ALR 657.
[60] See *R.* v. *Army Board, ex parte Anderson*, n. 6 above, at 310.

to the usual feature of standard adjudication, is the element of contest between the parties. The element of contest might not reach the level of intensity characteristic of adversarial adjudication, but whenever the issue becomes one between two parties some sense of contest is unavoidable.

One question that then arises is to what extent the sense of a contest between the parties should become so predominant that it pushes the process towards adversarial adjudication and the very specific form of hearing that goes with it. The administrative body or tribunal has a duty to get to the truth of the matter and to decide the issue properly according to law; it is usually entitled also to act on evidence from sources other than the parties and even in a limited way to conduct its own enquiries. None the less, once the element of contest takes hold, it is all too easy for procedural ideas developed in the judicial trial to take root in administrative processes, especially in cultures which prize the adversarial approach. The tension between an authority striving to reach the right or best decision on the one hand, and the matter being regarded as primarily a contest between two parties, on the other, can be seen in the experience of tribunals. Some tribunals, such as those dealing with welfare, are firmly committed by law or practice to an investigatory, even inquisitorial approach, especially where one of the parties is absent or unrepresented.[61] The Australian Administrative Appeals Tribunal has a duty to follow such procedures as will enable it to assess fully and fairly the merits of the case and to arrive at the decision it thinks fit.[62] It has, nevertheless, committed itself to a broadly adversarial approach, although the precise relationship between taking the steps necessary to reach the right result and allowing free rein to the adversarial contest, continues to cause difficulty.

While it would be unwise for administrative bodies or tribunals to resolve that tension too favourably towards a model of adversarial adjudication, the very sense of contest and dispute is bound to attract a form of process in which the hearing has a prominent role. Along the spectrum of hearings, it is likely to be towards the oral hearing end, together with witnesses and cross-examination. A good example of how this is reflected in the law is the case where a local authority applied under statutory powers to a magistrates' court to have a child-minder's registration cancelled.[63] The magistrates cancelled the registration on an *ex parte* application without either informing the child-minder or giving her a chance to respond to the charges. On an application for judicial review, the order was quashed on the basis of the general principle of fairness that a party so gravely affected was entitled to know the charges and to have the opportunity of answering them. Cases of

[61] See J. Beatson, and H. Matthews, *Administrative Law: Cases and Materials* (2nd edn., Clarendon Press, Oxford, 1989).

[62] See the fuller discussion in D. J. Galligan, 'Tribunals', in *Laws of Australia, Administrative Law* (Law Book Co., Sydney, 1993), 87 ff.

[63] *R.* v. *St Albans Court, ex parte Read* [1993] ALR 201.

this kind have parallels with the criminal trial, but an exacting sense of a hearing will be equally applicable to cases which lack the punitive element and resemble more closely a civil dispute. Wherever a serious item is in contest, the hearing principle in a full sense will apply.

There may be cases where the right outcome is reached without the participation of one party, but in general the party who fails to argue his case is at a serious disadvantage. For no matter how much the adversarial element is played down,[64] and no matter how hard the adjudicator tries to reach the right conclusion, it is hard for each party not to emphasize the strength of its own case. It is also hard for the adjudicator to form an entirely balanced view in the absence of an argued case from one of the parties. The party who fails to make his case, whether through absence or inability, has been shown to be clearly disadvantaged,[65] even though some tribunals, in areas of social welfare and housing, for example, emphasize their responsibility to get to the truth of the matter through their own initiative in obtaining evidence and materials.

Since the hearing principle will normally be an important aspect of procedural fairness in three-party adjudication, the practical question is what form the hearing should take. The elements of the judicial trial might be taken as a model which can then be modified in administrative contexts. The main features of the model are: preliminary procedures for the disclosure of information and documents from one party to the other, a full oral hearing with witnesses and cross-examination, legal representation, and an entirely impartial adjudicator. Administrative processes should not normally be like judicial trials, but nevertheless three-party adjudication is likely to warrant each of the elements to a greater or lesser degree, depending on the nature of the issue and the importance of what is at stake. The practical working-out of this general approach can be seen in the procedure of tribunals when provision is likely to be made for an oral hearing, either as a matter of statutory obligation or in the discretion of the tribunal.[66] An oral hearing in turn will normally include the calling and the cross-examination of witnesses, but the two are not inseparable. Provision is likely to be made for the disclosure of documents and information from one party to the other, and legal representation is commonly allowed. A similar approach with similar variations is likely to be found in other areas of three-party adjudication.

12.3.4 Policy-based Discretion

In the earlier analysis, policy-based discretion was shown to contain two elements which are not the most natural companions: one is the individualized part which is about how to treat a person, while the other part involves a

[64] See Galligan, 'Tribunals', n. 62 above.

[65] See Genn, n. 31 above.

[66] Discussion of such issues often can be found in the annual reports of the Council on Tribunals.

decision about what is best in the public interest which is to say what is the best policy to pursue in the case.[67] The first element has an affinity with the adjudicative mode, while the second gravitates towards the policy-making process and the consultative mode; the union of the two is likely in practice to be unsteady. Despite the tension between the two, the standards of fair treatment are reasonably well settled. They are threefold: first, that the facts of the case be inquired into and accurately assessed; secondly, that in deciding the discretionary part the official should consider the circumstances of the case and the consequences for it; and thirdly, that the party affected should have the opportunity to influence the policy element. The analysis can now be taken further by considering the role of the hearing principle in securing the proper application of the three standards of fair treatment.

The idea behind the first standard is that, no matter how discretionary the decision may be, it must still be based on certain facts about the person affected: has the student achieved the grades for admission; did the licence-holder break the terms of his licence; or is the applicant for welfare assistance in need? Facts such as these concerning the person and his circumstances have to be settled before a valid discretionary judgment can be made and the first object of a hearing is to ensure that they are settled accurately. The point is well illustrated in a recent case, *R.* v. *Secretary of State, ex parte Georghiades*.[68] Here a prisoner who had been recalled from parole sought fresh release. After the Parole Board refused so to recommend, judicial review was sought by the prisoner. The grounds were that prejudicial material had been relied on but not disclosed to him; and since it was not disclosed, he had no opportunity to show it was false. The substance of the material was that, years before while on parole, the prisoner had been wanted by the police for a serious crime, an allegation which is likely to have weighed heavily with the Parole Board. Since this was a matter of fact of high relevance to the Board's decision, the point of the hearing would have been to allow the prisoner to present evidence and comment which would have helped in judging its accuracy. For the Parole Board to deny the prisoner the opportunity and to run the risk of exercising its discretion on the basis of mistaken facts, would have been an unpardonable case of unfair treatment.

The second element of fair treatment concerns the discretionary judgment about the facts. It in turn has two elements, namely, the general policy being applied and the process of application in the specific case. Assuming for the moment that the policies are reasonably settled, let us concentrate on how they are applied in the particular case. Procedural fairness suggests that the party should be able to direct argument and comment towards the evaluation and judgment as to how he should be treated. If we keep in mind the image of good decision-making as not in any sense mechanical, but rather as the

[67] See sect. 9.2. [68] [1993] ALR 457.

moulding of general standards and considerations to fit the specific case, as an argumentative and dialectical process, a process for determining what is the right course of action in this case, then the involvement of the party is an important element. The point of the involvement, quite apart from helping to establish the facts, is to show how the person would be affected, what it would mean for him in the circumstances. Even policies which are apparently clear and settled must be translated into a specific context and shaped to fit the circumstances in a way which is both informed by the facts and responsive to the complexities and subtleties of the situation. The point of a hearing in its application to the discretionary element of a decision is to ensure those qualities.

The courts vary in their approach and have not always taken this view. On the one hand, the rule against fettering discretion is based on the importance of not blindly applying to specific cases policies set in advance.[69] The need to reflect on the application of the policy in each case, to change and modify policy where necessary in the light of the facts, is often stressed. Yet when it comes to the nature of the hearing in discretionary cases, the judicial attitude appears to change and the hearing rule is given a narrow interpretation. However, more recent cases suggest that the courts will now extend the hearing to the discretionary part. *R.* v. *Secretary of State, ex parte Doody*[70] is a good example. Here it was claimed by a prisoner, who was serving a life sentence, that the Secretary of State had acted unfairly in exercising his discretion about when to allow parole. In a number of policy statements, the Minister stated the procedures he would follow, which included fixing a tariff period based on retribution and deterrence which would have to be served before parole would be considered. The procedures for fixing the tariff included consultation with the trial judge and the Lord Chief Justice. In seeking judicial review, the prisoner's case was that he should have been given a chance to make representations about the length of the tariff. The court accepted this argument, holding that the Secretary of State should have told the prisoner of any information relevant to the decision and allowed him to make written submissions.[71] The fixing of the tariff period was a discretionary matter, but since it involved close examination of the prisoner's circumstances, the prisoner was held entitled to make direct submissions to the judgmental issues, to the individualization of the general policy considerations already settled by the minister. The approach in this case nicely captures the point of the hearing rule in relation to the element of judgment in a discretionary case and ought to be regarded as a model to follow.

The third element in a discretionary decision is the content of the general policy itself. Just how strong the case is for a party having the right to make

[69] See D. J. Galligan, *Discretionary Powers* (Clarendon Press, Oxford, 1986), sect. 6.2.1.
[70] [1993] ALR 93.
[71] Ibid. 107–15.

representations about the policy itself may be arguable; but, following the earlier argument that there is in principle such a right, the question now is just how far that right extends.[72] In answering that question, it is helpful to break policy down to the facts on which it is based and the element of opinion and judgment which creates the policy. Every policy is based on some set of facts, policy facts or legislative facts as they are sometimes called: policies against allowing poker machines in city centres might be refused on the grounds that they corrupt the young, or policies against giving sex offenders parole might be based on the ground that sex offenders have a high risk of re-offending. Policies like these are sound only to the extent that the facts on which they are based are accurate and reliable. How far the hearing should extend to allow representations about such facts is unclear. In a case dealing with poker machines, the court was divided, with one judge insisting on the need for hard evidence of the harmful effect on children, while the others were content to regard it as part of the policy process for which the local authority was responsible.[73] In an analogous case, *Bushell* v. *Secretary of State for the Environment*,[74] strict limits were imposed on the extent on which objectors at a public enquiry into a proposed road could challenge and try to rebut predictions about the future density of traffic. The predictions were vital to the Department's case for more roads and there were certainly grounds for suspecting they were erroneous. It was held, however, that the objectors' rights to be heard fell short of the right to bring evidence and cross-examine witnesses to prove the facts were mistaken.

This was the case of a general policy decision affecting groups and interests generally, but the same issues can arise in individualized decisions: for example should the prisoner seeking parole be allowed to challenge on the grounds of factual inaccuracy the statistical tables relied on to predict the likelihood of re-offending? Such factual matters are clearly central to the decision, yet there are reasons for limiting challenges to them in any particular case. In the first place, although the factual issue is sometimes clearly defined, often such hard facts give way to soft facts where matters of opinion, speculation and subjective judgment are integral elements. A second consideration is that the best place for examining policy facts is not in the course of an individualized decision; in other words, while policies should be based on accurate facts, the best way to ensure accuracy is through procedures for the making and scrutiny of policy.

The last point could be applied to the policy element itself, the idea being that it would be inappropriate to allow the merits of a policy to be reopened in the course of an individualized decision. A majority of the judges of the

[72] See sect. 3.2.

[73] *Sagnata* v. *Norwich* [1971] 2 QB 614. See further, D. J. Galligan, 'The Nature and Function of Policies within Discretionary Powers' [1976] *Public Law* 332. For R. M. Dworkin's analysis of this case, see *A Matter of Principle* (Clarendon Press, Oxford, 1985), 78–9.

[74] [1981] AC 75.

Australian High Court took that approach in holding that the merits of the minister's policy on parole are matters for government and should not be the object of attack in an individualized case.[75] While there is a certain good sense in that approach, several points of reservation seem warranted. First, in so far as the Australian High Court meant to rule that general policy is outside the scope of the hearing principle in discretionary adjudication, its approach is unjustifiable. It assumes far too clear a division between policy-making and policy-application, and it fails to notice the social reality of decision-making according to which general policies are not simply applied but have to be fitted to the specific context and circumstances. Secondly, it is not at all clear why the party to an individualized decision should be denied the opportunity to make representations about the policy itself, for policy-making is a dynamic process and policies are fluid and changeable, capable of responding to argument and suggestion, rather than fixed and immutable. Thirdly, we should not lose sight of the object of a hearing in this context: it is not to subject the policy element to a trial-like scrutiny, but merely to allow representations to be made about how the policy or some part of it might be improved. The mode of participation is consultative, not adjudicative. Finally, the principle of selective representation might also provide useful guidance here, for according to the principle the opportunity to be heard on the policy aspects is an individualized process and should depend on whether other opportunities have been available to that person, or by others on his behalf, at other points in the policy process.[76]

12.3.5 Informal Negotiation

The question to consider in this section is how the hearing principle applies to decisions in which authoritative standards give way to informal negotiation and agreement between the official and the party.[77] The idea behind informal negotiation is that the parties negotiate and agree on a decision or course of action which is different from that which would have resulted from applying the standards or exercising discretion. The incentive for each party, ideally, is that the negotiated outcome has advantages over alternative outcomes. In order to gain, however, each party must also surrender something; for the official the power to impose an outcome according to the statutory powers, and for the party the entitlement to be treated in accordance with authoritative standards. The process of negotiation and agreement becomes a legitimating force which replaces that which would be gained from applying

[75] *South Australia* v. *O'Shea* (1987) 73 ALR 1. The dissenting opinion of Deane J is more sympathetic to the prisoner's case and fits better with the analysis given here.

[76] For fuller description of the principle of selective representation, see Galligan, *Discretionary Powers*, n. 69 above, sect. 7.3.2.

[77] See sect. 9.4 for an introduction to informal negotiation.

authoritative standards. The legitimacy of negotiation and agreement depends on the process being fair, where fairness is judged according to three conditions: knowledge by the party of the likely outcome in the absence of agreement; willingness to enter into negotiations; and genuine negotiations.

What then is the scope of the hearing principle in this context? The party's right to know how the case would be dealt with in the absence of agreement requires disclosure of the standards which would be applied and the facts upon which the decision would be based. Elements of uncertainty may be unavoidable and in some discretionary contexts the likely outcome may be unknown. Nevertheless, disclosure of the standards, the facts, and the projected outcomes, to the extent that they are known, is the first requirement of the hearing principle. The second element of fair treatment is that the party be willing to negotiate; procedures are needed to ensure that participation in negotiations is uncoerced, but that has no direct implications for the hearing principle. The third element of fair treatment, however, is highly pertinent to the hearing. If the process is to be genuine, the need is clear for negotiations in which the party is able to participate. The party's involvement should be more than having the chance to put his case; the third element of fair treatment suggests an active process of bargaining between the parties, beginning with exploratory discussions, followed by the advancing of proposals and counter-proposals, and culminating in agreement. The procedural model to be followed here in developing the hearing principle is not that of knowing the case and being able to respond to it; the better model here is the family of procedures associated with securing agreement rather than imposing standards. Although informal negotiations are to a degree caught between the two, the main object should be to create a framework of involvement which guarantees a free and genuine process of negotiations and agreement.

It is not surprising that issues of procedural fairness in relation to informal bargaining do not often come before the courts. The very informality of the process, together with its uncertain legal status, means that the process is likely to be hidden from view and to be unquestioned by the courts. The one area where the courts have become involved is pre-trial processes where negotiations of a sort are often conducted over facts, charges, pleas, and sentences.[78] Without attempting to offer here an analysis of the voluminous case law in this area, there is good reason to conclude that, although regularly confronted with the realities of informal negotiation and agreement, the courts have not progressed far in creating a sense of procedural fairness, let alone making clear how the hearing principle is to be applied to this

[78] The leading study is J. Baldwin and M. McConville, *Negotiated Justice* (M. Robertson, London, 1977); for accounts of current practice, see A. Ashworth, *The Criminal Process* (Clarendon Press, Oxford, 1994) and A. Sanders and R. Young, *Criminal Justice* (Butterworths, London, 1994).

context. Some judges appear to cling to the notion that the formal procedures before and at the trial are the very embodiment of fairness and expunge from their minds the fact that the great majority of cases do not go to trial. Other judges more realistically acknowledge that informal negotiations are no longer to be regarded as the wanton flouting of propriety, but have not yet been impelled positively to consider the implications for procedural fairness. If this is the situation in an area of administrative process which has been not only in the glare of the public eye but under the scrutiny of a Royal Commission, then we might expect that in other, less obtrusive contexts, procedural fairness in informal bargaining goes unnoticed. The development of the hearing principle in such contexts is a major challenge for courts and administrators in the future.

12.3.6 Professional Judgments

The discussion in section 9.1 of the problems which occur in making professional judgments compatible with fair treatment and procedural fairness has already given some indication of the role and importance of the hearing principle. Here I shall add to that discussion by focusing directly on the hearing and showing how far the courts have gone in applying it in this context. We may start with the proposition that the hearing principle should apply to processes based on professional standards in the same general way as it applies to standard adjudication. The three elements of notice, disclosure, and hearing are as pertinent here as in other cases of adjudication where professional standards are not in issue. The one significant difference is that professional standards, unlike other standards, are not readily open to scrutiny by the non-expert. The question then is what that means for the hearing principle.

A useful point at which to begin is with the distinction between a process in which the professional offers an opinion to an independent decision-maker, and where the professional himself makes the decision. In the first case, the professional serves as an expert witness and the usual principles governing expert witnesses should apply. The usual position is that the expert opinion is disclosed to the person affected, the ordinary facts on which it is based are made clear, and the opportunity to test and question it is made available. The principle, which is so fundamental to a judicial trial, that an expert witness should be open to cross-examination, should apply with equal force in administrative processes.[79] The cross-examination of an expert witness is a valuable way of testing the worth and persuasiveness of testimony which inevitably will be of vital consequence to the outcome. A

[79] For a recent example, see *Land Securities* v. *Westminster City Council* [1993] 4 All ER 124 where Hoffman J, referring to an expert witness says: 'if tendered as an expert witness, would be liable to cross-examination like any other expert'. (128).

recent practice direction by the Official Solicitor on the procedures to be followed in deciding whether a minor or mentally handicapped adult should be sterilized, emphasizes the importance of cross-examination of all expert witnesses called in favour of the proposed operation.[80]

The case for applying that principle to administrative processes is strong and should prevail unless there are even weightier countervailing considerations. Where an oral hearing and cross-examination are impracticable, there should still be disclosure and an opportunity to counter the expert's opinion. Disclosure here should mean not just the opinion itself, but should include the facts and documentary records on which the opinion is based. Although those principles are fundamental to an adequate hearing and fair treatment, they are not always required under statutory schemes and the common law does not always make up the shortfall. In the mental health field, for example, the doctor's report, and the facts on which it is based, are often only partly disclosed,[81] although it is difficult to see how, except in the most exceptional cases, that practice could be justified.

A variation on this type of process occurs when the deciding authority, or a member of a deciding body or panel, himself has expert knowledge. This position is not uncommon and is often considered to be a strength of the tribunal system that membership may include someone with expert knowledge in the field. According to English law, an expert member of a court or tribunal may draw on specialized knowledge, not as a separate source of evidence, but in considering, weighing up, and assessing the evidence presented.[82] The line between the two will not be easy to draw, but more recent authority suggests that it would be a breach of natural justice if a tribunal were to use its own expertise as, in effect, a source of evidence. It is surely right in principle that the expertise of the tribunal member should be disclosed.

The other main position to consider is where an administrative decision is made by a professional directly applying his own expert knowledge. The doctor certifying that a patient is suffering from a disease or that a course of treatment is necessary; the architect or surveyor declaring that a certain state of affairs exists in a dispute over building construction; or the university finding that a thesis does not meet the grade—are common examples of experts deciding an issue by applying their own expert or professional knowledge. The courts have had difficulty in finding suitable legal categories within which to place such judgments, although they now tend to be characterized as of a judicial or adjudicative nature.[83] That characterization implies

[80] [1993] 3 All ER 222.
[81] See further, G. Richardson, *Law, Process and Custody* (Weidenfeld and Nicholson, London, 1993), 299 ff.
[82] *Wetherell* v. *Harrison* [1976] 1 QB 89.
[83] *Hickman* v. *Roberts* [1913] AC 229; *R.* v. *Boycott, ex parte Kearsley* [1939] 2 KB 651.

a duty on the professional to decide according to principles of procedural fairness, which in turn includes notice, disclosure, and hearing, before the judgment or diagnosis is made.[84] So, a medical officer deciding whether a police officer was permanently disabled on medical grounds was held to be acting in a judicial manner and was under a duty to act fairly. This meant that the materials intended to be acted on by the medical officer should have been shown to the policeman's medical adviser, and an opportunity to make representations should have been provided.

The imposition of a duty on a specialist or professional to act in a judicial manner is the courts' way of indicating that the principles of procedural fairness apply. However, it does not follow inevitably that procedural fairness includes the right to a hearing and in some contexts can be satisfied without one. An architect's decision to certify default by one of the parties to a building contract has been held not to be subject to the hearing principle,[85] with the architect being free to decide without giving the parties notice or the chance to make representations. That finding is consistent with the general principle that procedural fairness depends on what is necessary for fair treatment in the specific context; if an accurate determination can be made without a hearing then fair treatment is satisfied. A number of cases come to mind where a hearing might not seem necessary: the university examiner deciding on the merits of a thesis, an engineer certifying a technical matter, or an auditor declaring a set of accounts to be defective. Provided the professional has the right qualifications and is independent and impartial, it may be that judgments like these can be relied on as proper and accurate without a hearing. Megarry J in *Hounslow* v. *Twickenham* put the position in this way: 'it is the position of independence and skill that affords the parties the proper safeguards, and not the imposition of rules requiring something in the nature of a hearing'.[86]

Now while that approach may be persuasive in some contexts, the difficulty is to find a principled way of distinguishing between cases where a hearing is required (the medical officer diagnosing permanent disability), and where it is not (the architect certifying default under a building contract). To say that everything depends on the context is true, but not all that helpful unless we have a clear idea of what it is about different contexts that matters. This deserves a fuller treatment than I can provide here, but a few general points might be noted. The main idea is that the more completely a decision turns on the application of a professional, expert, or technical standard, where there is no doubt about the qualifications of the person applying it, then the less scope or need there is for a hearing of any sort. The

[84] In some cases, the judicial nature of the office might be varied by contract between the parties: *Panamena Europa Navigacion* v. *Frederick Leyland* [1947] AC 428.

[85] *Hounslow L.B.C.* v. *Twickenham Garden Developments* [1971] Ch. 254.

[86] Ibid. 259–60.

guarantee of quality is not the crucible of a judicial process but the warranty of a branch of scientific knowledge, properly developed, adequately organized, and reasonably applied. As sound as that general idea is, it might be compromised in a number of ways and the more serious the compromise, the stronger the case for transferring from the scientific domain to the forensic. Amongst possible compromising factors are the following: complex or contentious matters of fact being in issue; the professional standard itself being difficult to apply and requiring a substantial interpretation and judgment; and the standard itself being more than purely technical and including notions of a social or moral kind. The need to take account of factors like these, and possibly others, helps to explain the ways in which the architect's decision on a narrow technical matter is different from a complex medical judgment; it also shows why the examiner's opinion of a thesis is different from a social worker's assessment of a child's needs. The general point is that these factors provide a framework for analysing professional judgments in order to identify which elements are the proper objects of scrutiny through the hearing principle.

12.3.7 The Effectiveness of Hearings in Professional Judgments

No matter how sound a procedural approach may be in principle, its success in practice is another matter. Empirical research may help to show whether a more forensic approach to professional judgments is likely to succeed in making them more consistent with notions of fair treatment, or whether perhaps an entirely different procedural approach needs to be taken.

Although little empirical research has been made of these areas, a recent study by J. Peay of decision-making under the Mental Health Act[87] is well worth noting. In a perceptive analysis Peay shows the complex relationship between each tribunal deciding various issues relating to patients who are confined under statutory orders, and the psychiatrists who are responsible for their treatment. This is one of the few studies available of the problems encountered in bringing professional judgments within a procedural framework capable of ensuring the fair treatment of patients.

Amongst the many important points shown in the study, the following are especially interesting on procedural issues. The first point concerns the pervasive influence which the doctors, responsible for treating inmates, exert over the tribunal; the result is that the tribunal tends to follow the doctors' recommendations almost as a matter of routine.[88] In the few cases where the tribunal decided differently, it was only to take an even more cautious line about release than the psychiatrist,[89] against whose advice a patient will only

[87] J. Peay, *Tribunals on Trial*, n. 40 above.

[88] Ibid. 88, 107, 114, 209. This finding was confirmed by the Genns in *The Effectiveness of Representation Before Tribunals*, n. 31 above, 102.

[89] Peay, *Tribunals on Trial*, n . 40 above, 89.

rarely be released. Where independent psychiatric advice was put to the tribunal on behalf of the patient and conflicted with that of the responsible medical officer (RMO), the tribunal accepted almost invariably that of the latter.[90] Indeed, the presentation of independent evidence, the disclosure of the psychiatrists' reports and case notes, and the cross-examination of the experts all appear to have had little impact and rarely deflected the tribunal from following the RMO's advice. In the light of that evidence, it is difficult not to conclude that, if there is to be any real, independent assessment of the RMO's opinion, something more than the usual procedures of notice, disclosure, and an oral hearing, is required.

The second point concerns the role of the medical member of the tribunal and the difficulty of containing the influence he has over the non-medical members of the tribunal. The medical member naturally forms his own view which typically is in line with the RMO's and which usually wins the support of the lay members of the tribunal. The medical member's views are often not disclosed to the patient, or, if disclosed, are not treated as evidence and so escape the usual forms of scrutiny. Similar problems are likely to occur in other tribunals and administrative bodies where an expert is party to the decision. It is paradoxical indeed, that while the inclusion of experts in decision-making has been seen as enlightened reform, it often has the effect of putting a vital element of the decision process beyond procedural control.

The third point of interest is the difficulty of confining professional judgments to the subject matter of expertise. While the RMOs' knowledge and training relate to the treatability of patients, their statutory role often leads them into offering advice about the patient's potential dangerousness, a factor which in turn features prominently in the tribunal's decision. Psychiatrists have no special knowledge about the potential dangerousness of a detainee, nor the level of risk that society should tolerate; the consequence is that they either construct their own conceptions of dangerousness or err on the side of caution.[91] How then can the role of the expert be confined to matters of expertise? Beyond the conclusion that the hearing principle seems unlikely to have a major impact on this problem, any more positive answers are not easy to give. Part of the answer might be clearer and more precise statutory concepts and definitions, a greater awareness by the expert of the limits of his function, and more understanding on the part of the tribunal itself in distinguishing between expert opinion and moral or social judgments related to that opinion. Practical steps like these, together with procedures to give them effect, may be beneficial.

The final and most general point emerging from Peay's study of mental health is the intractable conflict between the legal process and legal values on the one hand, and the ethos and attitude of experts on the other hand. To

[90] Ibid., 87, 108. [91] Ibid., 61 ff.

borrow the metaphors of autopoiesis and systems theory,[92] each has its own logic, rationale, and view of the world, and it is not easy for one to break into the world of the other. The result is that the autopoietic nature of the psychiatrists' world has proved to be highly resistant to legal intervention. This is especially significant and somewhat ironic in mental health considering that the present statutory framework was created specifically to regulate the therapeutic environment and to protect the rights of patients.[93] The object was to impose substantive legal standards of fair treatment where previously few existed, and then to provide the procedures necessary for their proper application.[94] The undertaking has largely been a failure; the statutory procedures are followed more or less faithfully, but the outcomes have remained much the same as before, with the legal standards of fair treatment remaining unenforced and rights unprotected. A more striking example of the relationship between procedures and outcomes, and of the importance of procedures being effective in producing those outcomes, would be hard to imagine. This problem, moreover, originating in the tension between legal processes and expert systems, is likely to be endemic to any area of professional judgment. We may note in conclusion just how difficult it is to couple the legal process to expert systems so that the one regulates and channels the other. Nevertheless, the imperative of fair treatment demands that greater efforts be made to devise suitable procedures; those efforts will in turn benefit from further research into the practical workings of professional judgments in other areas.

12.3.8 Investigation and Inquiry

The idea of investigations and inquiries as distinct processes which raise distinctive issues of fair treatment and procedural fairness, was considered in section 9.3. The main standards of fair treatment are stated there and may be summarized as follows: first, that the process be conducted in a manner which respects the privacy of the person under investigation and any relevant confidential relationships or communications; and secondly that any conclusions of fact be accurate and that any critical conclusions or recommendations of further action be properly informed, made in good faith, and reasonable in their terms. In achieving those standards and taking account of the principles of adequacy and proportionality, a good case could normally be made for hearing the party being investigated. The precise form of the hearing and the degree of notice and disclosure should be responsive to

[92] See G. Teubner, *Law as an Autopoietic System* (trans. Ann Bankowska and Ruth Adler, Blackwell, Oxford: Cambridge, Mass., 1993).

[93] Peay, *Tribunals on Trial*, n. 40 above, 61 ff., 219 ff.

[94] For further discussion, see L. Gostin, *A Human Condition* (2 vols., Mind, London, 1975 and 1977) and C. Unsworth, *The Politics of Mental Health Legislation* (Clarendon Press, Oxford, 1987).

context and circumstance, and at some points in the process might sometimes justifiably be overridden by other factors. According to the principle of procedural adequacy, such a course is acceptable provided that the alternative procedures then followed ensure compliance with the standards of fair treatment.

The object now is to consider how the general principles of procedural fairness and the case for a hearing are translated into English law. Let us begin by stating three doctrines of English law which constitute the framework for more detailed analysis. The first is that English law recognizes that distinct principles of procedural fairness apply to the investigatory process. This is often provided for by the statute under which investigatory powers are conferred, and it is now accepted as a principle of general law.[95] Secondly, English law accepts that in general a person under investigation is entitled to be heard. Lord Denning has stated the principle in this way: 'The inspectors can obtain information in any way they think best, but before they condemn or criticise a man, they must give him a fair opportunity for correcting or contradicting what is said against him'.[96] The third principle is the principle of adequacy, that is to say, the precise procedures required in an investigation, and in particular the precise form of hearing, are influenced by the nature of the investigation on the one hand, and the relationship between the investigation and any subsequent decision on the other hand. Provided that, taken as a whole, fair treatment is achieved within the investigatory process, then the principle of procedural fairness is satisfied.

Within this framework, several more detailed issues can now be considered. The first concerns the initial decision of an official to undertake an investigation or inquiry into a person's affairs. The governing statute will often require that notice be given of an impending investigation and provision might also be made for the disclosure of certain materials at that stage. Much will depend on the circumstances, so that while notice and disclosure makes good sense when a formal investigation is about to be conducted under the Race Relations Act,[97] it might not be appropriate in other circumstances, where for instance the destruction of evidence would be a greater risk. However, in cases other than those where the giving of prior notice would put the inquiry at risk, a good case can be made for notice, disclosure, and hearing at this early stage. Since the very decision to investigate should be made according to sound reasons and on stated criteria, and may itself be significantly detrimental to the party involved, a hearing at this stage might show that any further inquiry is unnecessary; any further detriment could then be avoided. The common law, however, does

[95] See e.g., *In re Pergamon Press*, n. 14 above and *R.* v. *Monopolies and Mergers Commission, ex parte Elders* [1987] 1 WLR 1221 at 1232.

[96] *In re Pergamon Press*, n. 14 above. See also *R.* v. *Race Relations Board, ex parte Selvajoran* [1975] 1 WLR 1686.

[97] See *R.* v. *Commission for Racial Equality, ex parte Cottrell* [1980] 1 WLR 1580.

not appear to favour this approach. In *Norwest Holst* v. *Secretary of State*,[98] the Court of Appeal held that the decision to investigate a company under the Companies Act for wrongdoing was of an administrative nature and therefore not subject to natural justice. Ideas about what sorts of decisions attract natural justice have changed in the twenty years since that case so that its authority may now be doubted.[99] The principled approach would be to regard the initial decision to investigate as adjudicative in nature,[100] and then ask, first, whether procedural fairness points to the need for notice, disclosure, and hearing; and secondly, if it does, whether other factors, such as the destruction of evidence or the need to investigate urgently or secretly and without obstruction, should override the first.

A second procedural issue arises when the decision to investigate or inquire is joined with a decision to take some immediate action against the person involved. A familiar example is where a party is suspended—possibly a teacher,[101] senior official,[102] or pilot[103]—as a temporary measure pending further inquiry into the matter. Any decision to make the suspension final will be made after the inquiry and should be subject to notice, disclosure, and hearing, the only question being whether the prior suspension is subject to natural justice. The balance of authority is that it is not,[104] but the basis for that view is not entirely clear; according to Lord Denning, the prior action is a mere holding operation, while the majority of the Privy Council in *Furnell* thought that prior suspension was neither condemnation nor criticism. A rather different approach was taken by Schiemann J in the *Pegasus* case;[105] on his view, a decision taken prior to further investigation, but one which significantly affects the party involved, is subject to procedural fairness; what is required procedurally will then depend on the circumstances and is unlikely to be exacting.[106] In deciding what procedures are included at this point, the reasons for the prior action will be highly relevant, and where, as in *Pegasus*, it meant suspending an airline pilot on safety grounds, the procedural demands would be rather low. The approach in *Pegasus* is much to be preferred; it recognizes that preliminary decisions may involve issues of fair treatment, and it then displays a principled and structured method for determining its content.

[98] [1973] 1 Ch. 201. See also *Pearlberg* v. *Varty* [1972] 2 All ER 6.

[99] Although the idea that a worthwhile distinction can be made between administrative and judicial decisions persists: see *R.* v. *Commission for Racial Equality, ex parte Cottrell*, n. 97 above.

[100] See the analysis in Ch. 8.

[101] *Furnell* v. *Whangerai High School* [1973] AC 660.

[102] *Lewis* v. *Heffer* [1973] 1 WLR 1061. Compare *John* v. *Rees* [1970] Ch. 345 at 397.

[103] *R.* v. *Secretary of State, ex parte Pegasus* [1988] 1 WLR 990.

[104] *Furnell* v. *Whangerai High School*, n. 101 above, and *Lewis* v. *Heffer*, n. 102 above.

[105] *R.* v. *Secretary of State, ex parte Pegasus*, n. 103 above.

[106] This is closer to the approach taken by the two dissenting members of the Privy Council in *Furnell* v. *Whangerai High School*, n. 101 above.

A third procedural issue concerns the conduct of the investigation or inquiry. The basic principle is that considerations of fair treatment should be essential guiding standards. Fair treatment in turn appears here to be based on respect for privacy and the protection of confidentiality. Important analogies can be drawn with police investigations and the protections which are afforded the accused in pre-trial processes.[107] The parallels are not exact, and I shall not here attempt to give a full analysis of the investigatory process, it being enough to note that important questions of fair treatment and procedural fairness do arise. Considering how prevalent investigatory processes now are, there is a need for further study of them and particularly for empirical research into the procedural issues.

The fourth procedural question to consider here concerns the application of the hearing principle once the investigation is under way, that is to say, to the testing of evidence, the drawing of conclusions, and the making of recommendations. These three elements are often in practice taken as a single process, although each could be seen as reasonably distinct. Statutory provision is often made for some form of hearing before the final report is compiled or recommendations made; where there is no statutory provision, common law doctrine will fill the gap. According to the common law, a party should be given notice of the evidence and findings, and a hearing should be available at which the party may submit its own evidence, challenge the opposing evidence, and make representations in relation to the conclusions and recommendations proposed by the investigator. The only practical question, normally, is what kind of hearing is necessary, and the pattern in *Cottrell* is fairly typical.[108] There the Commission for Racial Equality undertook an investigation, prepared a report and recommendations, and then gave notice to the firm under scrutiny, while at the same time inviting its members to make oral and written representations. The only matter of dispute was whether members of the firm were entitled to cross-examine witnesses called by the Commission, a matter which was answered in the negative by the Court of Appeal on the ground that fair treatment was satisfied without it.

Within this general process, several subsidiary issues concerning notice, disclosure, and hearing, may occur. The notice requirement is straightforward: the party under investigation should be given notice of the findings of fact, the conclusions to be drawn, and the recommendations likely to be made. Such notice should be sufficiently detailed for the party reasonably to know the facts, to understand the reasons for what is being proposed, and to be able to present evidence and arguments by way of response. Questions of notice merge into questions of disclosure, where the issue is how extensive and detailed the disclosure of evidence and other materials should be. The

[107] For a recent account of that process, see A. Ashworth, *The Criminal Process*, n. 78 above.

[108] *R.* v. *Commission for Racial Equality, ex parte Cottrell*, n. 97 above.

guiding principle is that proposed above, namely, that the party must be told enough about the opposing case to be able to present its own case. The object behind the principle is to enable the investigation to reach a conclusion based on accurate findings of fact and on reasonable influences from them; that conclusion is likely to be reached more satisfactorily if the party has sufficient knowledge to be able properly to respond to the material adverse to it. The general principle can be difficult to apply in practice and the courts are inclined to leave it fairly much to the investigating body to decide the extent of disclosure.[109] As for the form the hearing should take, it was noted above in relation to *Cottrell* that it ought to be governed by the general principle of procedural fairness. Accordingly, the purpose is to make sure the evidence is reliable, that the facts are properly found, and that the conclusions are reasonably drawn. Procedural fairness will be satisfied by the minimum form of hearing needed for that purpose, which will normally be significantly less than that required in a judicial trial.

There is one more point to consider in relation to the disclosure of materials. While investigations are normally two-party relationships between the investigation and the party being investigated, it is not unusual for a third party to be involved. An inquiry by the Monopolies and Mergers Commission, for example, into the proposed takeover of one company by another, will require the investigation of both companies. Fairness to one company might then result in unfairness to the other. Both companies may be ordered to produce information on which the Commission's findings will be based, but disclosure to the rival company might result in detriment and unfairness; the unfairness of not disclosing relevant facts to one party will be matched by the unfairness to the other in disclosing it. However, it is not unusual to find competition between different aspects of fairness, and the general principle is that an accommodation has to be found which is principled, in the sense that it takes account of the relative importance of the competing senses of fairness and seeks to minimize the necessary restrictions on fairness by adopting suitable procedures.[110]

The last point to take account of is that the principles of procedural fairness in an investigation discussed in this section may have to compete with other considerations. Police investigations show how this can happen. For reasons of urgency or secrecy or both, it may be necessary to compromise considerations of procedural fairness at the investigatory stage. To be charged with a serious crime is a grave matter which would point to the need for significant procedural protections; but those protections will often be incompatible with an effective investigation. The solution is to ensure that

[109] *In re Pergamon Press*, n. 14 above and *R.* v. *Monopolies and Mergers Commission, ex parte Brown* [1987] 1 WLR 1235.

[110] See by way of example *R.* v. *Monopolies and Mergers Commission, ex parte Elders*, n. 95 above and *R.* v. *Monopolies and Mergers Commission, ex parte Brown*, n. 109 above.

the loss of procedural fairness at the investigatory stage is compensated for by particularly stringent mechanisms at later stages. This idea can be seen in other contexts: *ex parte* applications by one party in the absence of the other are presumptively unfair, but the unfairness can be removed by effective procedures for early challenge by the absent party.[111] The relationship between procedural fairness and the need for quick and effective administrative action is an area which has received little attention and needs to be examined more fully. However, the general principle is clear: where fairness is sacrificed to effectiveness at one stage in an administrative process, as sometimes it legitimately may be, the imbalance thereby created should be corrected by suitable procedures at a later stage.[112]

[111] For discussion of this point, see Glidewell LJ in *R.* v. *LAUTRO* [1993] ALR 573 at 591.
[112] See further *R.* v. *Secretary of State, ex parte Pegasus*, n. 103 above.

13

Recourse: Appeals, Reviews, and Other Forms

Following the earlier division of an administrative process into three stages, access, decision or other action, and recourse, the object of this Chapter is to examine the third. If the term 'recourse' sounds unfamiliar, the reader might well substitute for it appeal and review. The virtue of using recourse is that it may be taken to cover all forms of appeal and review, as well as any other processes which do not fit easily into those categories.

How then does recourse relate to procedural fairness? It is often said that the right to have a decision reviewed, or to appeal from it to a court, is of fundamental importance. Certainly extensive resources are expended in providing recourse in one form or another, yet it is not always obvious why a society should do so, or why we should think a right to recourse touches on something fundamental. The answer is simple: recourse from a decision or action by one authority to another is an element of procedural fairness and in turn of fair treatment. It is not an absolute and inflexible requirement of procedural fairness, and procedures can sometimes be fair without recourse; but, in general, the opportunity to have a decision or action re-examined by some form of appeal or review is a central part of procedural fairness. Appeals and reviews are not usually explained in this way, and it may seem particularly strange to think of judicial review as a set of procedures contributing to fair treatment; yet, like all other forms of recourse, that is what it is. This is not to say that forms of recourse serve no ends other than fair treatment; we have seen that legal forms and procedures serve various purposes as complex parts of complex social contexts. However, to consider forms of recourse as elements of procedural fairness is a most useful basis for both understanding them and seeing their justification.

13.1 RECOURSE AND PROCEDURAL FAIRNESS

13.1.1 Forms of Recourse

Once the primary decision has been made or action taken, the next and final stage of an administrative process is recourse. By recourse is meant the re-examination of the primary decision to determine whether it is wrong, whether a mistake has been made, or whether it is simply not as good, wise, or fair as it might have been. Re-examination is usually by an official or authority other than the original decision-maker, but it is not unknown or entirely incongruous for an official to be required to review his own decisions. To be more precise, recourse involves three elements: complaint, investigation, and redress. The usual pattern is that a person lodges a complaint about a decision or action; the complaint is investigated by an official, authority, or court; and then, if it is made out, some form of redress will be ordered or recommended.[1]

The usual way of initiating a form of recourse is by some form of complaint. The complaint might take various forms, from an informal letter or oral statement to a formal appeal or review procedure. It might be the complaint of a prisoner to an assistant governor about a decision of a junior prison officer; an aggrieved taxpayer might complain about his tax assessment to the local member of Parliament, who may look into the matter or send it on to the Parliamentary commissioner; while a parent may complain to the Secretary of State about the decision of an education authority in allocating places at school. On the more formal side, the complaint might take the form of an appeal to a tribunal, court, or other judicial body, or it might be an application to the superior courts for judicial review. The forms of complaint, the subjects they cover, and the range of bodies to which they can be directed, are indeed numerous. The more formal procedures for making complaints are normally governed by statute, but the more informal may be created and applied by the authority itself. Many of the complaints procedures within government departments and local authorities are of the latter kind.[2]

The main object in making a complaint is usually to draw attention to a possible defect in a decision or action, and then to have it investigated and reconsidered. Further redress will often follow, requiring perhaps that the decision be overturned or re-made, or that compensation be paid; or it might simply be that fault be admitted and an apology offered.[3] The processes of investigation and reconsideration which follow a complaint are also many and varied, as the following examples show. One group of processes is linked

[1] The literature and research on complaints and recourse is extensive. A useful, general survey is P. Birkinshaw, *Grievances, Remedies, and the State* (Sweet and Maxwell, London, 1985), while a helpful review of the research is R. Rawlings, *The Complaints Industry: A Review of Socio-Legal Research on Aspects of Administrative Justice* (ESRC, London, 1986).

[2] For a review of those procedures, see P. Birkinshaw, *Grievances, Remedies and the State*, n. 1 above.

[3] Work in social psychology draws attention to the complex nature of complaints and to the variety of outcomes that might be sought. For a helpful study of complaints about hospital treatment, see S. Lloyd-Bostock and M. Mulcahy, 'The Social Psychology of Making and Responding to Hospital Complaints: An Account Model of Complaint Processes' (1994) 16 *Law and Policy* 123.

to Parliament and includes the informal enquiries of a Member on behalf of a constituent, the more structured investigation of a select committee, or simply questions that may be asked in the House. Connected to the parliamentary process but, in practice, quite independent of it is the investigation of the Parliamentary commissioner or ombudsman, which, in cases where impropriety is established, will be followed by a recommendation to the authority at fault as to what redress should be made. With the spread of the ombudsman idea, the process of investigation and recommendation by an independent body is now available in a range of public and private spheres, such as central and local government, banking, and insurance. Another form of recourse triggered by complaints from aggrieved parties is review internal to the authority itself. Within a wide range of central and local government areas, a pattern is emerging by which, in the first instance, complaints are investigated internally. No set method is laid down by which this is done, but often a special official or unit within the department will be responsible for investigating complaints and offering suitable redress. Most claims are resolved at those lower levels, but a few complainants may go on to pursue more formal legal remedies. Special bodies are created in some areas under statutory authority to receive and investigate complaints, notable examples of which are the Commission for Racial Equality and the Civil Aviation Authority. Bodies like these are independently constituted, with power to investigate complaints across a range of public and private activities.

Appeals and reviews by courts, tribunals, or other judicial-like bodies offer another wide range of processes for dealing with complaints, although perhaps we do not always think of them in that way. Appeals and reviews differ in several ways although the categories are not watertight. Appeals are usually determined in a judicial manner and according to suitably judicial procedures, although it is not that uncommon for an appeal to lie from one administrative body to another, or even to a minister. The appeal body is still expected to act in a broadly judicial manner, but the obvious difficulties a minister faces in acting as an appeal body reinforce the good sense in confining appeals to courts, tribunals, or similar bodies. A distinction is often made between an appeal on the merits and an appeal on points of law, the first allowing the appeal body to re-make a decision where it considers the merits to have been misjudged, the second restricting the appeal to issues of law. Statutory schemes frequently allow an appeal on the merits or some aspect of the merits from a primary decision-maker to a tribunal or lower court, and then may provide for further appeals to a higher court only on points of law.

Turning to reviews, the first thing to notice is that review is not a term of art and many of the processes mentioned are forms of review. However, one distinction that is often drawn is between review on the merits and judicial review. Review on the merits can take many forms: internal review within an organization whereby one official scrutinizes the decision of another is one common form; the ombudsman's investigation and report is another; while the role of tribunals in hearing appeals might be considered a third. Special review tribunals in different areas of administration are now common in many countries, while the idea of a general administrative review tribunal has been introduced into a number of Australian jurisdictions and appears to work well.[4] Judicial review, however, is a special and exceptional form of review. It means the process by which a superior court considers whether an administrative body has exercised its powers in accordance with certain legal principles or grounds of review. The distinction between re-examining the merits of a decision and determining whether certain legal principles have been respected is fundamental to the constitutional basis of judicial review of administrative action, but the distinction is, none the less, somewhat elusive.

It is not my purpose here to undertake a full study of the many forms of complaint, of the processes which follow a complaint, or the kinds of redress that may be granted. Enough has been said to show that, while the scope and variety is considerable, a common thread runs through them: each is directed at identifying a defect or shortcoming in an earlier decision or action, and then taking some form of remedial action. Following this brief outline of forms of recourse, we must now consider the link between them and fair treatment.

13.1.2 Recourse as a Part of Procedural Fairness

Recourse from a primary decision by way of appeal or review is often an important element of procedural fairness. In order to see why this is so, we should be clear about the point of recourse: it is to scrutinize a decision or action to determine whether it has been properly made or performed. This can mean several things. The decision might be based on mistaken facts, or it may be that the law has been misunderstood or wrongly applied, or even that there is no legal authority for the decision at all. Where there is room for judgment and discretion, the complaint may be that it was not made in the right way according to the right considerations. Different forms of recourse concentrate on different kinds of defects, with the more formal avenues of recourse directed to the palpably legal defects, such as mistake of law or fact, abuse of discretion, or maladministration, while the more informal and often internal tend to be concerned with whether the decision could have been better, wiser, fairer, or more reasonable.

The claim in each case is that a binding normative standard has been breached and the point of recourse is to have that standard properly applied.

[4] For a fuller account, see D. J. Galligan, 'Tribunals' in D. J. Galligan, *The Laws of Australia: Administrative Law* (Law Book Co., Sydney, 1993).

Where the normative standards are legal, the failure to apply them means that the person has not been treated in accordance with the law. That is the consequence of mistakes of fact or law or misuse of discretion; the legal standards are misapplied in each case and the person affected is treated unfairly. Recourse by appeal or review is justified as a means for correcting the inaccuracy or impropriety and, therefore, for ensuring fair treatment in accordance with the law. It is not only clearly defined legal standards which apply to administrative action; other standards of a social or moral kind may give rise to normative expectations and so be the basis for justified complaints. The doctor, for example, who does not listen to his patient may be the subject of a complaint, not because of any legal defect, but because a social norm governing the relationship, and on which expectations are created, has been breached. Many complaints are directed at social norms of this kind and often legal procedures are created to deal with them. Breach of such standards may constitute unfair treatment but will not always do so, being more in the nature of good practice rather than creating entitlements. Such norms may be, none the less, the proper subject of complaints procedures.

Here I shall concentrate on those defects in the original process which do attract legal remedies. The main point to note is that the object of appeals and reviews is to provide a remedy so that the law is accurately and properly applied and authoritative standards are honoured. Procedures of recourse are instruments to fair treatment and an important part of fair procedures; or to put the point another way, the right to fair treatment includes the right to have decisions made properly according to law, with forms of recourse often being important elements in that process. It does not follow, however, that fair treatment always requires recourse from the original decision. The case for any procedural form has to be made by showing that the procedure in question is a necessary element in a given context. The case for recourse fits the pattern; it is contingent on showing that, in order to gain a better level of accurate decision-making, certain forms of recourseare necessary. Taken in isolation from other procedures, there is nothing inherently good or fair about recourse; but in a particular context, it may be a vital element in accurate and proper decision-making. It is also possible that in some contexts no recourse, or at least nothing beyond the barest recourse, will be needed for fair treatment.

The two guiding principles in assessing the need for recourse, and in determining the forms it should take, are the principles of adequacy and confidence. According to the principle of adequacy, procedures should be adopted which, taken as a whole, guarantee that the decisions will be properly made according to authoritative standards. Any particular procedure should be judged not in isolation, but as a whole within a given context. The case for recourse is then judged according to how effective procedures at the primary decision are likely to be in leading to accurate and proper decisions, that being a practical judgment to be made after close scrutiny of each type of administrative process. By way of example, a contrast can be drawn between two kinds of primary process. One type occurs in many areas of welfare distribution, where officials process applications under great pressure, often with only sketchy information, and without any form of hearing. Another type is of a more judicial kind, with an independent decision-maker following procedures for gathering and properly testing evidence and where some form of hearing is held. The obvious scope for a high level of errors in the first case points to a strong case for exacting forms of recourse. Errors can also occur in the second case, but the primary decision is likely to be more reliable and the forms of recourse may properly be more restricted. The principle of adequacy shows how the form of recourse required in any context is heavily influenced by the nature of the procedures at the primary level.

This leads on to the second principle, the principle of confidence. According to this principle, procedures should be adopted in each context which are sufficient for us to be confident that they will lead to accurate decisions. The application of the confidence principle usually means that, considering the imperfection of procedures in individualized processes, we should act with caution, even over-determination, in minimizing the risk of error, especially where important rights are at stake. A practical judgment has to be made as to whether a set of procedures, taken as a whole, satisfies the principle of confidence. The result in some cases might be that the primary procedures are so exacting and the risk of error so small, that no resource or only the barest minimum is warranted. The more likely conclusion, however, particularly when account is taken of empirical research into the reliability of primary decisions, is that some form of recourse allowing a reasonable opportunity for mistakes to be corrected is a necessary element of any administrative process. What constitutes a reasonable opportunity will depend on the usual factors, such as the nature of the process, the risks of error, and the rights and interests affected. Our knowledge of the high risks of error in many areas of administration would suggest the practical conclusion that, provided a threshold of seriousness is met, there ought to be a presumption in favour of some form of recourse on the merits, rebuttable only where it can be shown that the risks of error are adequately countered at the primary level.

Indeed, in practice, a presumption in favour of some form of recourse does appear generally to prevail. Legislative schemes normally include as a matter of course some form of review or appeal, or a combination of the two, from primary decisions, although some notable exceptions can still be found. Two notable exceptions in the United Kingdom are in the fields of immigration and housing where adequate appeal procedures are not provided. The absence of proper forms of recourse has been heavily criticized and the suspicion is that the levels of error and unfair treatment in these areas are high.[5] Where statutory provision is made for appeal or review, it is often supplemented by administrative bodies creating their own informal, internal methods of review. The Council on Tribunals has long argued that there ought to be as a matter of principle an appeal on the merits to a tribunal from all primary decisions of an adjudicative kind. The Council considers that to be an essential element of procedural fairness. The courts have not taken such a bold step and, despite an increasing willingness to accept procedural fairness as a dynamic principle, it has been stated that provision for an appeal from a primary administrative decision is not a necessary element of the principle.

13.2 PRACTICAL ISSUES FOR RECOURSE

13.2.1 The Effectiveness of Recourse

It is well established by a number of empirical investigations that the chances are high of a decision in many areas of administration being inaccurate or otherwise improperly made. Studies of decisions within the social welfare system make this point with unsettling regularity.[6] The reasons are understandable: administrative officers often work under such pressure that the concern for accuracy gives way to the need for speed; the procedures are often not adequate to the careful gathering and testing of evidence; and the officers themselves are not always well-trained.[7] If what is true of the social welfare system is also true of other major areas of administrative action, as is likely to be the case, then the case for providing recourse by way of appeal or review in order to improve levels of accuracy and fair treatment is powerful.

The question then is how effective appeals and reviews are likely to be in raising levels of accuracy and removing elements of impropriety at the primary level. This is a difficult matter to test. It is also a matter where generalization from one area to another must be carefully scrutinized. M. Bayles has claimed that, while the main point of an appeal is to increase accuracy, the case for thinking that accuracy will be increased is rather weak.[8] Some support for that view can be found in J. Mashaw's study of a scheme for

[5] One consequence of inadequate forms of appeal is that the number of applications for judicial review is very high compared with other areas of administrative action: see M. Sunkin, L. Bridges, and G. Mészáros, *Judicial Review in Perspective* (Public Law Project, London, 1993).

[6] Two major, recent studies are: J. Baldwin, N. Wikeley, and R. Young, *Judging Social Security* (Clarendon Press, Oxford, 1993) and I. Loveland, *Housing Homeless Persons* (Clarendon Press, Oxford, 1995).

[7] See also M. Adler, 'Justice, Discretion and Poverty: A Reappraisal' in W. Finnie *et al.* (eds.), *Edinburgh Essays in Public Law* (Edinburgh University Press, Edinburgh, 1991).

[8] M. Bayles, *Procedural Justice* (Kluwer, London, 1990), 57–8.

disability benefits in America where he concluded that appeals make a very small contribution to improving the quality of decision-making.[9] On the other hand, it has become an article of faith for the Council on Tribunals that appeals are essential in correcting errors and influencing better quality primary decision-making.[10] The experience of the mental health review system, where the tribunal rarely goes against the advice of the resident medical officer, might seem to cast a shadow over the Council's faith,[11] although a recent, detailed study of the social welfare system in the United Kingdom does give grounds for some confidence in the importance and effectiveness of appeals.[12] In judging their effectiveness on the quality of decisions, a distinction should be drawn between the effectiveness of appeals in detecting and correcting errors, and their influence in encouraging better decisions. Both are important functions of appeal and review, and both are difficult to assess. With regard to the first, an assessment of effectiveness depends on knowledge of the following matters: the proportion of decisions appealed from, the rate of success on appeal, and the ability of the appeal body to detect mistakes. It is also important in getting a sense of the worth of appeals to know what percentage of wrong decisions are not appealed against and, therefore, go undetected. That is by its nature a difficult matter to judge, but we shall see shortly that there is good reason to conclude that the levels of unappealed and unremedied mistakes are high, at least in some areas of mass decision-making.

One study which has produced valuable information about some of these issues is the social security research carried out by Baldwin, Wikeley, and Young. According to the study,[13] almost 120,000 appeals were brought in one year against decisions relating to social welfare claims. According to the department's internal practice, each appeal is first considered by the officer who made the initial decision or by another of equal rank. More than a quarter of the appeals were settled, meaning that they were decided in favour of the appellant, by this form of internal review.[14] Another 14 per cent of appeals lodged were withdrawn before the hearing, while approximately 55 per cent were heard by the tribunal. Of the appeals heard by the tribunal, just under 40 per cent went against the appellant and 18 per cent in favour. So, of the total number of appeals brought, 44 per cent were decided differently from the primary decision either on internal review or by the tribunal. This means that almost half the decisions appealed against were considered by the reviewing team to be mistaken. Whether they really were

[9] J. Mashaw, *Bureaucratic Justice* (Yale University Press, New Haven, Conn., 1983), 149.

[10] See, e.g., the Council's *Annual Reports* for 1989–90, 1990–91, and 1991–92.

[11] J. Peay, *Tribunals on Trial* (Clarendon Press, Oxford, 1989).

[12] Baldwin, Wikeley and Young, *Judging Social Security*, n. 6 above.

[13] Ibid. and N. Wikeley and R. Young, 'The Administration of Benefits in Britain: Adjudication Officers and the Influence of Social Security Appeal Tribunals' [1992] *Public Law* 238.

[14] See Wikeley and Young, 'The Administration of Benefits in Britain', n. 13 above, 240 ff.

mistaken, and whether the other half were correct, depends on the quality of the review process; but it is reasonable to assume that, subject to the possibility of occasional and extraneous factors, decisions upholding appeals were made in the main on good grounds. Whether we can have the same confidence in those dismissed is less clear. There is also evidence to suggest that the standard of primary decision-making is very poor, and that amongst the decisions not appealed against many were incorrect. If that is the case, it may seem strange that the levels of appeal were so low; the figure for 1990 is 120,000, but that is only 1 per cent of the total number of decisions. But as Wikeley and Young make clear elsewhere, there are many reasons, not least lack of understanding and advice, why aggrieved claimants do not appeal.[15]

From the facts and the inferences based on them, and assuming that other areas of decision-making follow similar patterns, the conclusion may be drawn that appeal procedures play an important part in correcting mistakes and in that way enhancing fair treatment. At the same time, however, the very low percentage of cases taken on any sort of appeal demonstrates the limitations of forms of recourse. Since the rate of appeal will probably always be low, it must not be assumed that forms of recourse can ever fully compensate for poor decision-making at the primary level; nor should the availability of appeal procedures be a reason for neglecting the importance of accuracy and propriety in the first place. From the point of view of cost, recourse is likely to be expensive and possibly more expensive than improving procedures at the primary decision. From the point of view of fair treatment, ensuring a high level of accuracy at first instance should be the main focus of procedures, especially when many claimants will not be in a position to pursue appeals. Fair treatment requires procedures which will both lead to accurate decisions in practice and be such as to engender confidence in them. That is an irreducible requirement of procedural fairness for which appeal procedures, no matter how good, are not substitutes; it is a conclusion which is plain in principle and borne out by the study of social welfare. Forms of recourse should be seen as safety devices to deal with occasional errors rather than the main device for preventing errors; if they themselves become the primary focus of procedures, something is seriously wrong.

Moving now to the second function of recourse, the influence it exerts on primary decisions, the study of Baldwin, Wikeley, and Young is again helpful. One of the main points of their research was to show the educative effect that the very existence of appeal procedures might have on the original process, a matter of special importance when only a tiny fraction of decisions are appealed against.[16] The very fewness of appeals leads one to ask how

[15] Wikeley and Young, n. 13 above, 244 ff.

[16] Less than 1% as noted above: see Wikeley and Young, 'The Administration of Benefits in Britain: Adjudication Officers and the Influence of Social Security Appeal Tribunals', n. 13 above, 241.

there could be a significant educative effect. The answer has several parts. First, a generalized educative effect is said to flow from the very existence of the appeal tribunal. This consists, presumably, in primary decision-makers knowing that their decisions might be scrutinized by an independent, external body.[17] Without questioning the reality of that effect, it should be observed that its strength is hard to measure and will depend on factors such as the likelihood of an appeal being brought, how soon it will be brought, and whether the officer deciding at the primary level will be personally responsible at the appeal level. A second aspect of the educative effect is the example set by the appeal body. The adjudicative nature of appeal procedures, the impartiality of the tribunal's members, and the concern to gather sufficient evidence and to weigh it carefully are all factors which set an example of how things should be done. The strength of education by example is again hard to judge and depends on whether primary officials really are made aware of those procedural aspects and how readily they can be assimilated into their own practices, bearing in mind the strong, countervailing pressures. This leads to the third aspect, namely, the involvement of first-level officials in the appeal process. An interesting feature displayed in the study of social security is that the adjudicating officer who made the initial decision often has to present and defend his own decision before the appeal tribunal.[18] The authors conclude that, at least in this area of decision-making, these three factors combined to give the appeal process a significant educative effect on the accuracy of primary decisions.[19]

The general conclusion to be drawn from this brief survey of empirical research is that appeal and review procedures can be valuable instruments in raising the standard of administrative processes. Forms of recourse serve the dual function of correcting mistakes in some specific cases as well as exerting a general improving influence over primary decision processes. The effectiveness of each function will depend very much on how well the two levels of process fit together. The success of the first will also be dependent on the proportion of decisions taken on appeal. One of the disconcerting facts which is so clearly revealed is the low proportion of appeals in an area of poor quality decisions, and with respect to which considerable efforts have been made to provide informal and easily accessible forms of recourse. Access to recourse and the willingness of claimants to make use of it is one of the major obstacles to more effective appeal procedures. That very experience, however, teaches a cautionary lesson and adds strength to the point that forms of recourse, no matter how accessible to claimants or effective in correcting mistakes, will always be of only limited value in improving

[17] On the educative effect, see also Loveland, *Housing Homeless People*, n. 6 above.

[18] Wikeley and Young, 'The Administration of Benefits in Britain', n. 13 above, 248 ff.

[19] The authors do note, however, that half the adjudication officers claimed they were not influenced by the tribunal; ibid. 252.

administrative processes. The main concern and the primary objective of energy and resources should be to provide high quality decisions at the primary level.

13.2.2 Kinds of Recourse

Once the general case for recourse as an element of procedural fairness has been established, questions arise as to the form it should take. The guiding test should be to create forms of recourse which are effective in correcting errors in specific cases and in influencing the general quality of decision-making at the primary level. This means in more precise terms that the various forms and levels of process, taken as a whole, should satisfy the principles of adequacy, confidence, and proportionality. The last of these is a necessary, if somewhat unwelcome, qualification on the other two, without which there would be no limit to the scope for more and better forms of recourse in striving to achieve even higher standards of decision-making. The form and extent of recourse will vary according to the nature and quality of the primary decision process; different forms may be effective in different contexts, and imaginative thinking about new forms should not be discouraged by obstinate hankering for any set pattern. A willingness in recent years on the part of governments and ministers to create novel forms of recourse has led to a variety in the creation of new offices and institutions, including tribunals, ombudsmen, and diverse forms of internal review. Little is known about the practical effectiveness of the various methods, with the possible exception of tribunals where, as the previous section shows, significant research is now being conducted.[20] Notwithstanding the diversity of both primary processes and forms of recourse, a general pattern (to which there are of course many exceptions) does seem to be emerging in respect of individualized decisions. It has the following features: a primary decision made by a department, agency, or other authority, is followed by some form of internal review; that may in turn be followed by appeal or review on the merits by a tribunal or special court, with the possibility of a further appeal on questions of law to a higher court, together with the possibility in exceptional cases of seeking judicial review for serious errors or abuses. In addition and largely external to what is in a sense a vertical progression, there are likely to be various other ways of raising complaints, including the increasingly relied-upon ombudsman with a roving commission to investigate complaints made by aggrieved parties.

Against the background of that general pattern, I shall consider a number of more detailed issues relating to forms of recourse. The first concerns the role of the tribunal. The tribunal has emerged in the United Kingdom, and

[20] For a fuller survey, although now some years out of date, see Birkinshaw, n. 1 above, and Rawlings, n. 1 above.

in a number of other jurisdictions, as a standard appeal body from individualized administrative decisions.[21] Its virtues are generally independence from the primary decision-maker, a judicial and impartial attitude, a composition which reflects the need for an understanding of the law as well as expertise in the area, an informal approach to procedures, and finally expedition in deciding cases. The powers of tribunals vary. In the United Kingdom, their main task is normally to hear appeals, in the sense that they look for errors in the primary decision, although often this in reality means reconsidering the case on its merits. In a number of Australian jurisdictions, a general administrative tribunal undertakes a fundamental review of the decision and is required to make the decision it thinks best on the merits.[22] There may not be much practical difference between the two approaches, although the British tends to provide for appeals to tribunals only when the primary decision is of an adjudicative nature, where a narrow view is sometimes taken of what that means. The principle behind the Australian system is that any administrative decision or action should be open to review by a tribunal.[23] This has led to vigorous debate about the legitimacy of an appeal tribunal reviewing matters of discretion and policy, but the worst fears of government by tribunal have proved false and the AAT must be regarded as a measured, responsible, and effective body.

The commitment to a general principle that individualized administrative decisions should be open to appeal or review by an independent tribunal or tribunal-like body would be a significant step in improving the standards of fair procedures and fair treatment. The underlying idea is that, with some exceptions, anyone subject to an administrative process ought to have the opportunity of having the decision reconsidered by an independent body. Tribunals are of course not the only bodies which might discharge that task, but, whether we call them tribunals, special courts, or something else, their strength is the capacity to reconsider, impartially and independently, primary decisions. The precise powers of such bodies might vary, sometimes being more concerned to correct identifiable mistakes, at other times having the powers to review the merits in full and to substitute its own view of what is the best decision. The Australian Administrative Appeals Tribunal represents one mode of full review which has much to commend it; in its twenty or so years, it has shown itself to be firm in examining the merits, to brook no obstruction from the administration, and yet to be responsible in respecting

[21] The literature on tribunals is extensive, but the following provide a good introduction: J. Farmer, *Tribunals* (Weidenfeld and Nicholson, London, 1974); Harlow and Rawlings, *Law and Administration*; Peay, *Tribunals on Trial,* n. 11 above.

[22] On the Australian Administrative Appeals Tribunal, see Galligan, 'Tribunals', n. 4 above.

[23] The Commonwealth Administrative Appeals Tribunal has power to review decisions, where the notion of a decision is given a wide definition: Administrative Appeals Tribunal Act 1975 (Cth), ss. 3(3) and 25.

the expertise and views of administrative officials. Although there is little empirical evidence to cite, the general impression is that the AAT has gained the confidence of the administration and that it has made a noticeable contribution to better and fairer decision-making.[24]

Whether the AAT approach of full review or something less should be adopted is a matter upon which opinions may differ and to which different answers might be given in different contexts. The most important step forward is a general commitment to provide an opportunity for independent and impartial review whatever form it takes. That commitment does not prevail in the United Kingdom. The importance of the commitment is often affirmed by bodies like the Council on Tribunals, but in practice there are areas without proper provision for appeal or review, and even in contemporary statutory schemes it is sometimes absent. In some cases, no provision is made for recourse or what is provided is inadequate, either because the scope of review is too limited or because it consists entirely in internal review. An example is the allocation of housing benefits. Under recent statutory reforms the right to appeal to a tribunal against allocation decisions was replaced by internal review by a panel consisting of three local councillors. Similarly, when the social fund was created to provide special welfare payments, the right of appeal to a tribunal gave way to a complex system of internal review.[25] It seems that in many areas of administrative decision-making, complaints procedures internal to the administrative body are either the only forms of recourse or the only forms that are regularly invoked. In prisons, for example, the two used to run in parallel, but less than 10 per cent of complaints went to the external body (the Boards of Visitors), the rest being dealt with internally.[26]

These remarks should not be taken as being unduly negative about internal review procedures. They have their strengths as well as their weaknesses. They are usually open to easy access in a way which external bodies like tribunals cannot match no matter how hard they try, and there is no reason to think that the quality of review provided is necessarily poor or in some way compromised. Serious efforts are often made within departments and agencies, the administration of the social fund being a good example, to provide effective internal review of first instance decisions. The success of the experiment in relation to the social fund will have to be judged after close monitoring over the next few years, but the study of internal review

[24] For an appraisal, see A. Mason, 'Administrative Review: The Experience of the First Timeless Years' (1989) 18 *Federal L Rev*. 122.

[25] See R. Drabble, and T. Lynes, 'The Social Fund—Discretion or Control' [1989] *Public Law* 297.

[26] The disciplining functions of Visitors have been removed, but the general point remains that internal review procedures are likely to be used much more heavily than external ones: see further C. Austin and J. Ditchfield, 'Internal Ventilation of Grievances: Applications and Petitions' in M. Maguire, J. Vagg, and R. Morgan (eds.), *Accountability and Prisons* (Tavistock, London, 1985).

procedures in other parts of social welfare shows that a good percentage of complaints, in this case 25 per cent, were settled internally in favour of the complainant.[27]

The negative aspects of internal review should also be recognized. One is the difficulty of maintaining independence between the primary decision-maker and the reviewing body. How well that can be done depends on the nature and social context of the organization, but it should not be assumed that, within the same body, different officials cannot serve different functions and, indeed, develop pride in their independence and objectivity. Another difficulty consists in the lack of openness of internal review or, more precisely, the added effort needed to make it open and capable of scrutiny. This is a special problem in countries like the United Kingdom where the resistance to openness in government and administration verges on obsession. A third difficulty concerns the level of training and experience of officials responsible for internal review. An effective review procedure requires a certain attitude of mind, an ability to assess the evidence, and a certain knowledge of and commitment to the law. It is difficult enough to guarantee those qualities in appeal tribunals, let alone within organizations where training is poor, conditions are unattractive, and the pressures of work intense. Such problems can be overcome, but the ethos of administration on the cheap, where the concern to treat each case properly and fairly is likely to be smothered by the dynamics of routine administration, can make the obstacles virtually insurmountable.

A common response to the difficulties in providing effective recourse is to offer a plurality of appeal and review procedures. Internal review might be one avenue of recourse, with further appeal to a tribunal or court, while both might be supported by an ombudsman with special responsibility to investigate complaints in the area. There may, indeed, be a whole range of other avenues of complaint, such as a letter to a Member of Parliament, to a local councillor, or to a health authority or trust. To have several forms of recourse open can be an advantage, but it also has its negative side. The initiation and pursuit of procedures for recourse is not an activity which comes naturally or easily to most aggrieved parties. Their level of knowledge and understanding of how to pursue an appeal or complaint is likely to be low and the sources of help and advice are few.[28] Even to initiate the most informal review can be a major effort for many, let alone to pursue those of a more formal kind or to have several running at once. Moreover, the discouragement of losing at the first attempt often deters the party from going any farther or from considering alternatives; appeal fatigue can be an

[27] See Wikeley and Young, 'The Administration of Benefits in Britain', n. 13 above, 240 ff.

[28] For information on this, see H. and Y. Genn, *The Effectiveness of Representation Before Tribunals* (Lord Chancellor's Department, London, 1992).

enervating condition. These are practical problems of knowledge, access, and determination, but they are, nevertheless, real obstacles to the usefulness of forms of recourse and should have a major influence on the shape and design of appeal procedures. Much remains to be learnt about how parties perceive different appeal processes, why they pursue some rather than others, and why they are so often deterred from using any at all.

13.3 THE SPECIAL CASE OF JUDICIAL REVIEW

13.3.1 Judicial Review as Fair Procedure

One of the functions of judicial review is to provide a means of recourse against primary decisions. That is by no means its only function,[29] but because it links judicial review directly to fair treatment is the one of most interest for present purposes. As a form of recourse judicial review is a special case. From a legal point of view, it is different from other forms of recourse since it looks not to the merits of a decision but to its legality, the rationale being to protect against an authority exceeding or misusing its powers. But a successful action for judicial review can be a pyrrhic victory; the authority may be required to re-make the decision, but it may be able to correct the legal defect without changing its conclusion on the merits. As well as being narrow in its objective, judicial review is also technically complex and expensive to mount. From an applicant's point of view, judicial review is likely to be seen as simply another remedy, another way of attacking the decision, perhaps an alternative to other remedies, or sometimes in practice the only remedy. Judicial review might be seen by the lawyer as a chance to vindicate high constitutional principle, but to the person aggrieved by an administrative decision, it is just another way, albeit a rather complex and costly way, of obtaining redress. Of course to most parties, judicial review is not a real option at all; the number of applications brought each year are few, and it is interesting to note its high incidence in areas such as deportation and prisons where the alternative forms of recourse are inadequate.[30] But to the millions of claimants of social welfare, for example, no matter how improper the original decision may be, the possibility of an action for judicial review is remote. As a means of recourse its practical effect in correcting errors is tiny, although its educative effect may be more significant. However, before considering these matters let us be clear about the relationship between judicial review and fair treatment.

Judicial review is linked to fair treatment in the following way: although

[29] The different functions of judicial review are well summarized in P. P. Cane, *Administrative Law* (2nd edn., Clarendon Press, Oxford 1992), 3–12.

[30] For an important recent study of the use of judicial review see Sunkin, Bridges, and Mészáros, *Judicial Review in Perspective*, n. 5 above.

concerned with the legality of a decision rather than its merits, it is directed to upholding certain normative standards. The standards are those familiar to the language of judicial review: that the authority should stay within its powers, consider the relevant matters, act reasonably, and follow certain procedures. The court has to form a judgment as to whether those standards have been sustained, but it should not concern itself with the different issue of whether the decision under review is the best or wisest or fairest that could have been made. Those last questions are at the heart of other methods of recourse, but not judicial review. What is at stake in judicial review are normative standards of different kinds, although in applying them there is inevitably a certain amount of overlap, a need to draw lines within boundaries which are inherently movable.[31] It is not especially helpful or accurate to think of judicial review as concerned with process, as if process and substance were mutually exclusive,[32] and it is a waste of energy to criticize the distinction for not being logically watertight, as if it could be, although that lesson is still to be learnt by many public lawyers. Putting these issues aside, the important point here is to note that the normative standards applied in judicial review are based on a concept of fair treatment, that is to say, fair treatment in the structured sense of treatment according to legal standards.[33] For one of the main tasks of judicial review is to uphold certain standards which channel and constrain the making of decisions by public authorities, where those standards are based on a view of what constitutes fair treatment. A decision by the Inland Revenue requiring me to pay a tax where there is no statutory basis for the decision, or where the decision was motivated by some extraneous purpose or was based on irrelevant factors, are all cases of treatment in violation of legal standards and, therefore, of unfair treatment. It is neither here nor there whether those standards are implied from the statute or from some deeper constitutional basis or simply created by the courts. What the standards should be is a constitutional issue but, once they are settled, each person is entitled to be treated by administrative bodies in accordance with them. The connection between judicial review and fair treatment is most obvious in relation to principles of procedural fairness, but the connection also applies in relation to other grounds of judicial review. Judicial review might itself well be characterized as a set of procedures for upholding certain principles of fair treatment.

[31] T. R. S. Allan brings out well this distinction between different normative spheres: T. R. S. Allan, *Law, Liberty, and Justice* (Clarendon Press, Oxford, 1993), 180 ff.

[32] Judges have become fond of putting the distinction in this way, as if process and substance are logically watertight, when of course they are not: see Hailsham LC, and others in *Chief Constable* v. *Evans* [1982] 3 A ER 141.

[33] See Ch. 2.

13.3.2 The Effectiveness of Judicial Review

Returning now to the effectiveness of judicial review as a means of recourse, the most plausible conclusion must be that it is of small effect in correcting errors. Two plain reasons for this are the cost and difficulty of bringing an action, and the limited grounds of review. As to the first, judicial review for the vast majority of those disappointed by an administrative decision is not a real option. Add to that the narrow nature of the grounds of review, confined as they are to excess or misuse of authority and procedural fairness, and the limited scope of review as a form of recourse becomes clear. The grounds of review are malleable enough and in the hands of an imaginative judge can be made quite elastic. Indeed, judges pride themselves on the way that judicial review has been developed and extended in recent years, often citing the recent history of judicial review as evidence of the dynamic and creative nature of the common law. However, these claims are easily exaggerated. Much of the purported expansion of judicial review in the United Kingdom in recent years was no more than undoing the restrictive decisions of English courts earlier this century, and extending well-established principles of review to corners of government and administration, like the prisons, which previously had been, for practical purposes, beyond the law. Both aspects of this recent history are unquestionably important, but there are still significant, self-imposed limitations on the full unfolding of the logic of judicial review.

The principles being applied in these cases are not new but, in the main, were well-established in the nineteenth century. It is hard to think of a new principle or ground of review created by the courts in recent years;[34] on the contrary, when opportunities have arisen to adopt new principles, such as proportionality or hard-look, the courts have turned their faces. The simplification of the procedures for obtaining review is perhaps the main reform of the century, but that came from Parliament not the courts. This is not to suggest that the courts should be gaily creating new grounds of review; judicial review is bound to be and is best justified as a limited form of recourse, proceeding according to a few simple and settled principles to be invoked in exceptional cases. If a hint of criticism to be entered, it is that the judges have misunderstood their own achievements, mistaking the undoing of unwarranted fetters inherited from the past for innovation and creativity.

There is an additional reason why judicial review in the United Kingdom plays a small part in correcting primary decisions. That reason is the way the courts apply the procedures for obtaining leave to bring an application for review. Under statutory rules,[35] an applicant for judicial review must first

[34] Celebrated statements of the grounds of judicial review, such as Lord Diplock's in the *GCHQ* case (*Council of the Civil Service Unions* v. *Minister for the Civil Service* [1985] AC 374) are entirely orthodox and could easily have been made by a law lord a hundred years earlier.

[35] Rules of the Supreme Court, Order 53 and Supreme Court Act 1981, s. 31.

obtain the leave of the court;[36] if leave is given, the application may then proceed to the hearing stage. The court has a discretion whether to grant leave which has been shown by recent research to be influenced by a number of policy factors.[37] These include protecting the court from being swamped by applications for review and government bodies from litigious harassment; restricting judicial review of some areas and types of administration; and ensuring that other means of recourse are first exhausted. Leave may be refused on one or other of these policy grounds even though the applicant's case on the grounds of excess or misuse of power is strong. The research by Le Sueur and Sunkin concludes that when policy factors are present, the claim to judicial review as the claim to a right to fair treatment has a minor role in the court's deliberations. Right gives way to policy; that is to say, the right to have a defect in the earlier process remedied, and the policies which point towards restricting review, are in conflict, and the latter prevail. The case for policies overriding rights is not clear. It may be justifiable to require that alternative remedies be exhausted before seeking judicial review, but to foreclose the right in the interests of a policy, such as protection of the courts from too many applications, is unjustified. The right to review is not absolute, but if a serious case is made out at the leave stage, it is difficult to see why, almost as a routine matter, it should be trumped by policy factors. The rare exception might be defensible, but to allow policy to defeat rights in routine cases is to misunderstand the nature of rights. If too many applications for judicial review are being brought, we should ask why, and if it is because alternative appeal procedures are inadequate (for which there is some evidence), then attention ought to be directed at that issue. The question clearly needs further consideration, but on the evidence available it must be concluded that the courts' present approach to the leave requirement does prevent some meritorious cases proceeding to the hearing stage, and in that way restricts the effectiveness of judicial review as a means of recourse.[38]

While the role of judicial review in correcting errors is bound to be limited to a few cases, its educative impact on administrative processes holds more promise.[39] Unlike some of the other forms of recourse, judicial review not only deals with the case in hand, but also contributes to the development of

[36] See the analysis of Donaldson MR in *R.* v. *Secretary of State, ex parte Doorga* [1990] COD 109.

[37] A. Le Sueur and M. Sunkin, 'Applications for Judicial Review: The Requirements of Leave' [1992] *Public Law* 1021.

[38] See further P. P. Craig, 'English Administrative Law—Procedure, Rights, and Remedies' (1990) 2 *Euro. R. of Public L* 425 and the Law Commission, *Administrative Law: Judicial Review and Statutory Appeals* (HMSO, London, 1993, Pam. No. 126).

[39] On the educative effect of court decisions, see P. Atiyah, *From Principles to Pragmatism* (Clarendon Press, Oxford, 1978) and D. H. Clark, 'Natural Justice: Substance and Shadow' [1975] *Public Law* 27.

general rules and principles. Individual review decisions are reasoned and often reported and, in so far as they propound general legal principles, administrative officials are bound by them. Since judicial review has been a major factor in defining the legal framework within which administration takes place, it might reasonably be expected that officials would know about and comply with it. Things are never so simple for a number of reasons. In the first place, judicial review decisions are of different kinds, with some having general application, others being specific to a particular context. The general principles governing review are themselves straightforward and most cases, even the most celebrated, merely confirm them. Judicial review decisions also have the more focused task of developing the legal principles governing a specific area of administration, such as immigration, the prisons, or social security. These are sometimes areas where the appeal procedures are unsatisfactory, so that judicial review becomes a surrogate form of recourse and a means for making specific laws applicable to that area, often in relation to procedures. A good administrator should be familiar with both the general principles governing all public bodies and the principles specific to the specific context.

This leads to the second matter, which is to ask to what extent are officials aware of and responsive to the legal principles formulated in judicial review. Do officials know that they must not fetter or abdicate their discretion, take account of irrelevant matters, follow the dictates of procedural fairness, and act reasonably according to the *Wednesbury* test? If the findings of a major study of officials dealing with homelessness are typical of other areas, then the answer is a resounding no.[40] The evidence, based on a close study of local housing officials applying the complex law governing the provision of public housing, showed that officials appeared to be ignorant of the basic legal rules and principles, including those developed by judicial review. Whether they were more familiar with rulings specific to homelessness is not made clear, but there is evidence to suggest that ignorance of the law, including the principles of judicial review, is endemic in government departments and administrative bodies.[41] The explanation is not just lack of knowledge; it is also, once again, partly the result of the conflict between administrative culture and legal norms. The norms and conventions which shape administrative culture are often in opposition to legal norms, and, being more powerful and immediate to the internal view of officials, the former tend to prevail. When considered against the mass of daily decisions made by administrators, judicial review is a rare event which many would never experience at first hand in their working lives. This need not be the case and, as we have seen elsewhere, it is both possible and imperative that legal norms should be

[40] I. Loveland, n. 6 above.

[41] M. Sunkin and A. Le Sueur, 'Can Government Control Judicial Review?' [1991] *Current Legal Problems* 161.

incorporated into the working environment of administrative officials. That takes great effort and resources, and may even require structural changes at every stage from training to operation; it certainly requires more than the circulation of notes on recent decisions, which often go unread, or the occasional training day.

Again, however, generalization has its risks and the position can vary from one authority to another and even within the same authority. To take an example from the social security system, social fund officers responsible for the initial decisions have little training in or knowledge of law, while the inspectors, who exercise a review function, are well versed in legal matters. In exercising their review function, it seems that the inspectors have adopted a set of principles similar to those of judicial review.[42] This is an interesting area in which much fuller research needs to be done in order to understand more completely the complex relationship between legal principles, whatever their source, and the internal, working environment of administrators. On the evidence available to us, it is probably safe to conclude that the educative effect of judicial review is patchy, being sometimes efficacious and at other times virtually non-existent. A new ethos of responsiveness to judicial review may have been kindled in Whitehall, but if it has, it is more likely to be tapping gently on the windows than storming the corridors. This is an important issue which deserves fuller study, and a first step in that direction would be to have more evidence of what happens across the many areas of administration; a second step then would be to develop ways of making the principles of judicial review part of the living administrative law.

13.4 APPEAL AND REVIEW IN LEGAL DOCTRINE

13.4.1 The Legal Basis of Recourse

Having seen the relationship between recourse and procedural fairness and the problems in making recourse effective, we may turn our attention in this last part of the Chapter to two legal issues: first, the general legal basis of recourse; and, secondly, the questions which arise when procedural defects in the primary decision are sought to be cured on appeal.

The first of these can despatched with a few brief comments. The basic principle is that Parliament has the primary responsibility for creating forms of appeal and review. Since statutory schemes are conceived and nurtured within government departments, it is usually there that decisions are taken about issues of appeal and review. The office of the parliamentary draftsman undoubtedly has an influence, but just how different forms of recourse are

[42] Ibid., 174 ff. and Drabble and Lynes, 'The Social Fund—Discretion or Control', n. 25 above.

decided on, and what influences are brought to bear on them, are matters we know little about. Parliament may make a contribution, but questions of recourse are unlikely to stimulate animated debate. The Council on Tribunals keeps a vigilant watch on procedural matters and argues that as a general principle an appeal should lie from any adjudicative decision to a tribunal; but that argument, as we have seen, is not universally accepted by all ministers and their departments. The growing preference within government departments for systems of internal review has strengths and weaknesses but, whatever the net balance, a strong case remains for the provision of some form of external appeal or review. Any generalizations in these matters must be ventured with caution since the science of legislation, the study of the legislative process from its earliest beginnings, both descriptive and normative, is still awaiting discovery by researchers. Until that discovery is made and until models of the administrative process are developed and tested and adopted in practice, it is not surprising that within statutory schemes the arrangements for appeal and review are haphazard.

A second source of forms of recourse is the administrative bodies themselves. Being masters of their own procedure in the absence of statutory provision, administrative bodies might create their own appeal or review procedures, although there are few examples to call on. Informal administrative appeals will tend to be internal and highly informal and may contribute to fair treatment; rarely, however, will they be a satisfactory substitute for statutory schemes.

The third body involved in creating means of recourse is the courts. The principles of judicial review and its scope are the creation of the courts. Some procedural aspects, including the requirement that leave to bring an action can be obtained, are governed by statutory rules, but even there the courts retain a significant discretion as to how the rules are applied in practice. Although the courts are very much the masters of judicial review, they cannot themselves create new forms of appeal or administrative review. In areas of administration lacking adequate forms of appeal or review, the courts may bring some pressure to bear on Parliament by commenting on the facts in cases which come before them; they might even be tempted in such areas to allow judicial review to become a kind of surrogate appeal procedure. In the two areas of immigration and deportation, and housing the homeless, notable for inadequate appeal procedures, the number of applications for judicial review are certainly high in comparison with other areas. Whether that means the courts are taking a broader view of the functions of judicial review in these areas, and whether that has had an effect on Parliament towards making better provision, on the little evidence there is seems unlikely.[43] The courts do have another form of indirect influence over

[43] See further Sunkin, Bridges, and Mészáros, *Judicial Review in Perspective*, n. 5 above.

statutory forms of recourse, namely, in deciding the scope of an appeal on matters of law, which is now provided for by statute almost as a matter of course. What constitutes a mistake of law is a complex matter which allows considerable scope for judicial creativity.[44] The exception referred to above is that the courts also provide, independently of statute, their own form of appeal on matters of law as an element of judicial review. Errors of law appearing on the record have long been within the courts' supervision, and it is not too difficult to characterize other errors of law (not appearing on the record) as errors affecting legality and, hence, open to judicial review. And, finally, it is for the courts to determine the relationship between statutory appeals and review on the one hand, and judicial review on the other hand; they decide the degree to which it is necessary to invoke other such remedies before allowing judicial review.

13.4.2 Curing Procedural Defects on Appeal or Review

The final matter to consider in this Chapter is whether a procedural error on the part of the primary decision-maker can be remedied on appeal or review. The error usually arises from a breach of the hearing principle, but the question may also arise in relation to other procedural defects. A court exercising judicial review may become involved in this question in two ways. In the first case, an application for judicial review may be countered with the defence that although a procedural defect appears in the primary decision, it made no difference to the outcome. In *Cinnamond* v. *British Airports Authority*[45] mini-cab drivers were banned from entering Heathrow Airport after a history of offences under the airport regulations. In an action brought by the drivers claiming that they should have been heard, the Court of Appeal found no breach of natural justice. The Court went on to say that, even if the drivers should have been heard as a matter of principle, the failure made no difference to the outcome. The second case occurs where the procedural defect in the primary decision is remedied on appeal. This is illustrated by the decision of the Privy Council in *Calvin* v. *Carr*.[46] A jockey who was found guilty by the stewards of a breach of the rules of racing, appealed unsuccessfully to a Committee of the Jockey Club. In proceedings for judicial review, the judge found there had been a breach of natural justice by the stewards, but that it had been cured by the appeal proceedings. The Privy Council upheld the ruling.

The issue in the first case appears to have troubled the judges. On the one side is the *Cinnamond* approach, summed up in the words of one judge as: 'no one can complain of not being given an opportunity to make

[44] From an extensive literature, see in particular J. Beatson, 'The Scope of Judicial Review for Error of Law' (1984) 4 *Oxford JLS* 22.

[45] [1980] 1 WLR 582.

[46] [1980] AC 574.

representations if such an opportunity would have availed him nothing'.[47] Despite the apparent good sense of that approach, the contrary view also has judicial support; Lord Reid put it this way: 'It is at least very doubtful whether [the fact that the breach did not affect the outcome] could be accepted as an excuse.'[48] Each view has merits: the former takes a robust view of the instrumental nature of procedures and avoids the following of useless procedures; while according to the latter view, once procedures are settled as a matter of general principle, they should not be open to an instrumental analysis in the particular case.

In forming a view about the respective units of the two approaches, guidance may be taken from consideration of both practicality and principle. The practical point is how a reviewing court can know that the procedural impropriety made no difference. Where the procedure in question is a hearing, the practical issue assumes quite serious theoretical dimensions, for how can the court know with any certainty that evidence and argument from a party would have made no difference? If by knowledge we mean justified belief, then a court can rarely know with any degree of confidence. Fact, truth, insight, and understanding all emerge from argument and discourse, and the clearest case, at the drop of a fact or the hint of an argument, can easily give way to doubt. It is hard to improve on Megarry VC's classic statement:

> the path of the law is strewn with examples of open and shut cases which, somehow, were not; of unanswerable charges which, in the event, were completely answered; of inexplicable conduct which was fully explained; of fixed and unalterable determinations that, by discussion, suffered a change.[49]

The difficulty is compounded when we take into account the special position of the courts in exercising judicial review; their task is to decide matters of legality and procedure, not to assess the merits, and although the distinction is inherently elusive, it is nevertheless important. The court faces a dilemma: to judge that a procedure would have made no difference to the original decision, it would have to put itself in the place of the decision-maker; but the more it does that, the closer it comes to an assessment of the merits. This difficulty points to an approach which is likely to be the most sensible in most cases: where they cannot know with any confidence the effects of the procedural defect, the courts would be wise to order that the procedural requirements be upheld. This need not be inflexible, and there may be

[47] Brandon LJ n. 45, at 593. Support for this view can be found in *Malloch* v. *Aberdeen Corporation* [1971] 1 WLR 1578 *per* Lord Wilberforce and *Cheall* v. *APEX* [1983] 2 AC 180. Other cases are discussed in J. Beatson and M. Matthews, *Administrative Law: Cases and Materials*, 343 ff.

[48] *Ridge* v. *Baldwin* [1964] AC 40.

[49] *John* v. *Rees* [1970] Ch. 345 at 402.

exceptions; but exceptions should need to pass a clear and compelling test, and should rarely be allowed.

Apart from the practical issues, there is also a matter of principle. It is tempting to think that so long as the primary principle is upheld by properly applying the law, no harm is done in waiving a procedural irregularity. What unfairness is there if the law has been properly applied—that after all is the justification for most procedures? This raises an important question about the relationship between procedures and the proper application of authoritative standards. My approach throughout this book has been to argue that there is nothing inherently valuable in most procedures and that there is no reason for insisting on them when the right outcome—here the application of authoritative standards—has been achieved by other means. However, to draw the conclusion that procedures are always defeasible in that way is to misunderstand the relationship. The point can be put in the language of rights: not only is there a right to the application of the primary principle, there is also a right to the procedures considered necessary to that end. The two rights are separate, closely related but separate, so that in a specific case the second is not reducible to the first. The justification for procedural rights is to ensure that outcome and non-outcome values are achieved; but in their application, procedural rights are independent of those ends.

To make this claim is not to elevate procedures into something of value in themselves; they remain of value only in so far as they serve underlying values. This feature of procedural rights is common to other rights, since we do not ask of a right whether it serves its underlying purpose in every case. The very idea of a right is a protected claim where the merits of the claim are not open for reassessment in each case. If procedures are made conditional on being necessary in each case, the very point of a right has been lost. The alternative is to consider in every case which procedures are instrumentally necessary and which are not; that would be, however, a difficult and cumbersome process, the better approach being to accept that once procedural principles are settled as generally necessary to lead to the right outcomes and to engender confidence, they should be applied consistently in each case.

There are, therefore, good reasons, both in practice and in principle, for the courts not trying to judge whether a procedural defect made any difference to the outcome, except in rare cases. The preferred approach should be to decide what procedures are needed for fair treatment in that kind of case, and then require that the procedures be followed in each instance of it. The only qualification should be that the law should not be seen to be foolish, and there may be occasions when a procedural irregularity may be overlooked. The test should be strict, allowing defects to be excused only when it can be said clearly and compellingly that they were minor, and could not logically have affected the outcome. An analogy can be drawn with appeals from criminal convictions where mistakes on evidential issues may sometimes be excused by application of the proviso.[50] The proviso is used only exceptionally, and the court, being a court of appeal, is likely to have a fuller record of the facts and evidence on which to base its judgment than a court exercising judicial review.[51]

The second situation envisaged above is where procedural defects in the primary decision are remedied on appeal. The failure of the stewards in *Calvin* v. *Carr* to provide a hearing was remedied on appeal to the committee. This issue arises when a party seeks to have an original decision quashed for procedural unfairness, and the respondent claims that the defect was cured by the appeal. It is different from the first situation considered above, for here it is not the relationship between procedures and ends that is in question, but whether it was enough that, taking the proceedings as a whole, the correct procedures have been followed. Judicial approaches again differ, but the view expressed by Wolff LJ in *Lloyd* v. *McMahon*[52] has much to commend it. According to his approach, each case depends on the governing statute and on the nature and scope of the appeal. If it is clear that the appeal goes to the merits, and if the procedures necessary to provide fair treatment are followed on appeal, then the original defect is cured. If it can be said, in other words, that the matter has been decided on its merits, according to the correct procedures, at one or other level, then the principle of adequacy has been met and fair treatment has been dispensed. If not, the procedural defect has not been cured and there has been a failure of fair treatment.

Since the object is to secure fair treatment, this approach is right in principle. The appeal is itself simply a procedural device to help in securing fair treatment; it is, indeed, a very desirable element in guaranteeing fair treatment. If it can be said with confidence that, considering the original decision and appeal process as a whole, there has been fair treatment, then the case for quashing the original decision crumbles. This differs from the first case above because here the defect at the primary level is remedied on appeal. In other words, the violation of procedural rights at the primary level is compensated for by the right of appeal, part of the point of that right being to detect and remedy the breach of procedural rights at first instance.

The only note of caution to enter is that the possibility of an appeal being brought should not be an excuse for poor procedures at the primary level. Attention has been drawn to this point several times in this Chapter: the first concern in designing procedures ought to be good quality decisions at first instance, with appeals being seen as safety devices not as alternatives. In

[50] The proviso states: 'Provided that the court may, notwithstanding that they are of the opinion that the point raised in the appeal might be decided in favour of the appellant, dismiss the appeal if they consider that no miscarriage of justice has actually occurred' (Criminal Appeal Act 1968, s. 2).

[51] See further D. H. Clark, 'Natural Justice: Substance and Shadow' [1975] *Public Law* 27.

[52] [1987] AC 625.

order to satisfy that concern it is necessary to have procedures at first instance which instil confidence that the right outcomes will be reached. The educative effect is also important. It is clearly undesirable that primary decision-makers should think that, since defects can be cured on appeal, procedural fairness at first instance does not matter. Considering the poor quality of decision-making in many areas of administration, it would be defensible for the courts to take notice of that fact and to insist on full respect for procedural standards, regardless of the possibility of cure on appeal. The insistence on procedural rights at first instance being regarded as irreducibly binding may be a significant factor in raising the educative effect of judicial review. So, to conclude, although in general it is right to allow procedural defects to be cured on appeal, there may be circumstances where a concern to improve poor quality decision-making justifies upholding full procedural rights at first instance.

14
Principles and Doctrines: Standards, Reasons, and Bias

The object of this Chapter is to examine several aspects of procedural fairness which are of particular interest and which are the basis for a number of legal principles and doctrines. The matters to be considered are: the setting of standards; the giving of reasons; and the idea of impartiality on the part of officials. They are grouped together in this Chapter for convenience rather than because of any close relationship between them. The one common factor is that all involve standards of fair treatment and raise issues of procedural fairness. It is worth observing that, of the three issues, traditionally only the rules relating to impartiality or bias have been regarded as an essential element of procedural fairness; the giving of reasons is now taken seriously but its relationship with procedural fairness is not often appreciated, while the setting of standards in administrative processes is an issue largely ignored. I shall try in this Chapter to remedy that neglect by showing not only how each is linked to notions of fair treatment, but that, understood within that relationship, their rationale and dynamic basis are both clearer and more compelling. The pattern of analysis will be: first, to show the relationship of each with fair treatment; secondly, to examine relevant contextual factors and empirical research; and thirdly, to consider legal doctrines.

14.1 SETTING STANDARDS

Several normative issues occur in relation to standards in administrative contexts: (i) to what extent administrative powers should be governed by clear and settled standards; (ii) whether such standards should be disclosed to the parties; and (iii) the degree to which an authority may impose standards upon itself. The second of these was considered in section 13.1.4 and the third has been examined at length elsewhere.[1] My intention here is to concentrate on the first, that is, on the relationship between standards and

[1] D. J. Galligan, *Discretionary Powers* (Clarendon Press, Oxford, 1986) sect. 6.2.1 and D. J. Galligan, 'The Nature and Function, of Policies Within Discretionary Powers' [1976] *Public Law* 332.

fairness.[2] The analysis will begin with an examination of that relationship followed by a brief account of contextual factors, and then move on to legal doctrines in relation to it.

14.1.1 Standards and Fair Treatment

The question here is whether fair treatment of a person by an administrative authority requires that clear and settled standards be laid down in advance as to how that case will be dealt with. In considering the issue, we should not lose sight of the point that standards can be of different degrees of specificity and bindingness, and that many do not amount to strict and binding rules or anything like it. The precise form of the standards is itself a variable which might rightly change from one context to another, depending on factors such as the nature of the interest at stake and the nature of the administrative power. I shall return to that point, but first let us examine the general relationship between standards, using the term in a broad sense, and fairness. One way of approaching the matter is to imagine areas of administrative authority which are entirely untrammelled by standards. This would amount to a case of strong discretion where neither the legislature nor the authority itself would have taken steps to formulate standards, leaving each case to be decided as the officials saw fit at the time.

When the matter is put in that way, the whole issue of discretionary powers and the values affected by it is thrown into relief. Here, however, I shall confine the analysis to considerations of fairness in relation to standards. By standards I mean to include the spectrum of norms, including rules, principles, guidelines, and factors to consider.[3] Fair treatment in its most fundamental sense relates to substantive outcomes, to whether the way those treated in the exercise of administrative powers is itself justifiable according to deeper principles of justice and fairness. How long the prisoner should serve before being released, or what kinds of social welfare relief should be offered, are both examples of the first-order principles of fairness which ought to govern the distribution of burdens and benefits. Our present interest, however, is not in first-order principles but in second-order principles of fair treatment; these are twofold: one is that people ought to know how they will be treated by those holding power over them; the other is that people ought to be treated equally in the sense that the criteria are applied generally and consistently. The formulation of standards will help in both cases to satisfy those two principles of fair treatment.

[2] The analysis here builds on *Discretionary Powers* n. 1 above, sects. 3.4.4 and 6.2.2.

[3] I shall not here offer a more detailed analysis of the different kinds of standards since the issue is well covered elsewhere: see G. Richardson *et al.*, *Policing Pollution* (Clarendon Press, Oxford, 1984, 21–6 and more generally R. Kagan, *Regulatory Justice* (Russell Sage Foundation, New York, 1978) and A. I. Ogus, *Regulation: Legal Form and Economic Theory* (Clarendon Press, Oxford, 1994).

With regard to the first principle of fair treatment, the familiar argument is that, once the rules of society have been laid down, each member of society has a good claim that the rules be observed as a matter of fairness.[4] The idea is that rules create expectations about how a person will be treated, and that then to disappoint those expectations is to act unfairly. Now while there are differences between disappointing expectations and not allowing them to arise in the first place, the similarities are sufficient for the same principle to apply to both. The principle that expectations, once created, should not be thwarted can be extended to require that stable legal relations should be fostered and expectations created. The ability to plan one's affairs with reasonable certainty and security is an important part of personal autonomy, and where serious interests are affected by administrative action, a sound case for settled standards can be made out. The case is, however, presumptive rather than absolute, and just how exacting it is and how it competes with other factors, is a matter to which we shall return shortly.

This may seem an indirect way of linking standards to fairness. Some argue that the case for standards is more direct and more basic. In his search for the inner morality of law, Lon Fuller considered the case for standards on the part of government and administration to be fundamental to the very idea of law.[5] If, as he claimed, the main point of law is to guide human behaviour, then it follows that settled standards are vital to the enterprise.[6] But the idea of guidance is not itself quite enough; to give standard-setting the centrality suggested, guidance must be placed within the relationship between the citizen and the state. Within that relationship, the idea is that the state has obligations as to how it deals with its citizens, and one of its obligations is to declare in advance through its laws the terms and conditions on which any dealings will be conducted. This should be interpreted to mean not that the state must indicate what it might or might not do, but that in all cases of authority over citizens reasonably clear standards will be proclaimed in advance. The basis for insisting on such terms and conditions is the independence and autonomy of each citizen. As independent and autonomous persons for whom state power is held in trust, we should insist on those terms and conditions as part of the trust. This is a powerful argument, provided it is not pushed too far and made to exclude all other considerations.[7] For while the setting of standards at reasonable levels of detail is a fundamental element in the citizen–state relationship and the fair treatment of persons, it is not the only element, as we shall see.

The setting of standards can be linked to fairness in a second way. Here

[4] See the discussion in Ch. 2; see also A. M. Honoré, 'Social Justice' in R. S. Summers (ed.), *Essays in Legal Philosophy* (Blackwell, Oxford, 1970).

[5] L. Fuller, *The Morality of Law* (Yale University Press, New Haven, Conn., 1964), 46–8.

[6] See further J. Raz, *The Authority of Law* (Clarendon Press, Oxford, 1983), ch. 11.

[7] The argument is taken too far in the writings of F. A. Hayek: see for instance *The Road to Serfdom* (Routledge and Sons, London, 1944).

the idea is that general standards help to ensure that people are treated according to the same considerations and, therefore, according to the principle of equal treatment. By stipulating the rules to be applied or the matters to be taken into account, general standards contribute to equal treatment. Equal treatment is a complex notion, and the substantive principles as to what constitutes equality, as to what are relevant or irrelevant differences, are much debated. Again, we need not now join in that debate; for whatever the substantive considerations are, the setting of standards in accordance with them may be a practical way of ensuring that they are respected. This is often expressed as the principle of consistency: standards help to ensure consistent treatment, and consistent treatment is an aspect of fair treatment. Now the principle of consistency can easily be overstated to suggest that consistent treatment is a good end in itself. It may be true that a kind of 'primitive equity' is satisfied when B is treated in a certain way just because that is how A was treated,[8] but consistency is best seen as one element of the wider concern that people should be treated equally in the sense that relevant considerations are applied and that pertinent similarities and differences are taken into account.[9]

It is important to see that the role of standards here is as a practical instrument to persons being treated equally. Equal treatment can still be achieved without standards, since decisions made on the merits of each case can still be based on relevant factors. (It might be argued that any context of decisions has some underlying standards, but here we are interested in whether standards of a more specific and detailed kind should be laid down.) Nevertheless, standards are generally useful instruments to equal treatment in a number of ways: they exclude certain factors from consideration; they specify what is to be taken into account; and they simplify and make easier what is a potentially complex business.[10] Standards also have their limitations since, by the very process just described, standards may over-simplify by excluding factors which ought to be considered. A sentencing system, for example, based on a few simple variables may wrongly exclude appreciation of several factors which, on a fuller view, would be relevant. Moreover, some issues are so inherently complex that any attempt at simplification through setting standards will distort the reality. There is also a risk that standards may fall out of step with the more fundamental purposes and principles governing an area of authority. The result will then be that the equal treatment gained by applying the standards is at odds with the deeper sense of equal treatment which would flow from those purposes and principles.

[8] See B. Barry, *Political Argument* (Routledge and Kegan Paul, London, 1965), 97–106.
[9] For further analysis, see M. Bayles, *Procedural Justice* (Kluwer, London, 1990), 87–9.
[10] See the discussion in Raz, *The Authority of Law*, n. 4 above, ch. 11.

14.1.2 The Level of Standards

The conclusion to be drawn from this account is that the setting of standards for the exercise of administrative powers is clearly linked to fair treatment; or, to put the point another way, fair treatment will normally be enhanced by the setting of standards. This fits well within the analysis of secondary standards given earlier in this book, with the setting of standards linked partly to outcomes but also partly to values independent of outcomes. It is, however, a somewhat tentative and contingent principle, and we must now consider its limitations. Perhaps we should start with the general observation that the issue here is not where there should or should not be standards governing administrative processes; it would be hard to quibble with the proposal that there are, and indeed should always be, some standards. The practical issue is what form the standards should take; how detailed they should be; and what normative character they should have. Once the matter is put in this way, a number of issues are opened up for debate: issues relating to the structuring of administrative powers, and about whether to adopt rules or some normatively lesser standards, such as guidelines, factors to take into account, or policy objectives. That debate is familiar enough, and I shall not embark on it here.[11] All I shall seek to do is note briefly some of the factors which are relevant to the setting of standards and to the types of standards that are most suitable for different purposes.

In determining what level of standards fair treatment requires, we should begin with the general point that it does not require an inexorable push towards strict and detailed rules. The suggestion that the creation of rules was the ideal to be aimed at can be seen in the early debate about rules and discretion,[12] but it was soon realized that fairness does not as a general principle demand strict rules. The predictability which comes with rules is only one element in the overall fair treatment of persons, and the concern for fair treatment is not always best served by rules. What then are the other elements competing with detailed rules? One is the idea that some scope should be left for each situation to be appraised on its merits. This can easily become a meaningless cliché, but it has a serious point: for there is a sense in which fair treatment is more likely to result if the standards are open-textured enough to allow a genuine consideration of the special facts of each case. The virtue of open-textured standards fits well with the earlier idea that just treatment is rarely achieved through strict and detailed rules, but is more compatible with looser and more open principles.[13] This point would

[11] See K. C. Davis, *Discretionary Justice* (Louisiana State University Press, Baton Rouge, La., 1969); my own analysis is set out in *Discretionary Powers*, n. 1 above, sect. 4.1.

[12] Davis, *Discretionary Justice*, n. 11 above, generally.

[13] See further D. J. Galligan, 'Arbitrariness and Formal Justice in Discretionary Decisions' in D. J. Galligan (ed.), *Essays in Legal Theory* (Melbourne University Press, Melbourne, 1984).

seem to indicate the need for some discretion in administrative decision-making; it also helps to counter the claim that discretion and fairness are deadly enemies. To this may be added a second point: the stricter and more detailed the rules are, the more likely there is to be an unauthorized departure from them. It is well-established, although paradoxical, that rules not only remove discretion but also create it, partly because rules have to be interpreted, but also partly because the more rules, the more opportunities there are for departing from them. That has the further consequence that such departures, being unauthorized and to a degree covert, are likely to be a greater threat to fair treatment than looser and less precise standards.

A third related point takes a different course. In some contexts, fair treatment might be better served not by rules or precise standards, but by procedures based on the representation of interests and the participation of individuals and groups. This is certainly the case where the process is itself directed at making policy and in turn setting standards, but it is also, if less obviously, the case in individualized contexts. Involvement in the latter case gives the party the opportunity to have some effect on the result, partly by presenting evidence and argument, but also partly by being involved in the social construction of the decision. Administrative decisions, as we have seen, are not simply logical processes, but are created in a social context and will reflect the influences prevailing within it. The chance to be involved through representation or participation in a context of open standards rather than closed rules may contribute to principles of fair treatment. That conclusion would be even more compelling for those who consider such involvement to be an aspect of fair treatment independently of outcomes.

The discussion so far has shown how different senses of fair treatment may apply within the one context of decision-making and that there may be an element of competition amongst them. We have seen how the senses of fairness associated with standard-setting compete with other notions of fairness which are equally important. The relationship between the various ideas of fair treatment has to be resolved within each context. This is done according to the variables within that context, guided by the aim of creating within it an equilibrium amongst different principles of fair treatment which, taken as a whole, achieves the optimum level of overall fairness. The factors which would be relevant to that process of practical judgment are: the nature of the personal interests at issue; the elements of public interest; and the objects of the power, including the levels of complexity and variability.

14.1.3 Standards in Context

When we move from the normative aspects of the relationship between fairness and standards to consider standards in their practical setting, several observations may be made. The first is that in practice decision-making in any context is normally guided by settled standards. Exceptions might occasionally occur and of course standards may be of different kinds and levels of detail; nevertheless, the tendency quickly to develop standards appears to be deeply rooted in the psychology of decision-making. The general tendency towards standards is strengthened when decisions of a similar kind are being made repeatedly. There are suggestions, indeed, that in situations of repeated decision-making the tendency will be towards detailed rules. A good example is a study of the way decisions allocating funds to families with severely handicapped children rapidly moved from open discretion to closed rules.[14] In addition to the conceptual links between decision-making and standards, other reasons for the tendency towards fixed standards, and in particular rules, are the advantages for planning and routinization and the protections they offer as shields behind which officials may take refuge.[15] However, it should not be thought that such venal factors are all that matter to the official; various researchers have drawn attention to the importance of notions of fairness and equity in the actions of administrative officials,[16] and in the case of the family fund referred to above, the connection between settled standards and the equitable treatment of claimants was a significant factor in the move away from discretion towards the creation of standards.[17]

The point to note is that the tendency for decision-makers to devise standards where none are given can have unexpected and not wholly welcome consequences. There appears to be a law of decision-making to the effect that, when standards reach a certain point of detail, a counter-force comes into play and encourages departure from them. In short, the more rules, the greater the discretion or, to put the matter in another way, while the tide of bureaucratic rationality is towards more and more detailed rules, at a certain point an opposing current, driven by a number of countervailing factors, beings to flow back towards discretion. One of the factors in these movements to and fro is likely to be a concern for fair treatment in particular cases, fair treatment, that is, which would not be achieved by blindly following the rules. The problem is that in this maelstrom of cross-currents, the behaviour of officials becomes more discretionary and unpredictable, so that the very patterns of consistency, which stimulate the concern for standards in the first place, are upset. If, from the standpoint of fair treatment, there is a point of equilibrium between settled standards and individualized

[14] J. Bradshaw, 'From Discretion to Rules: The Experience of the Family Fund' in M. Adler and A. Asquith, *Discretion and Welfare* (Heinemann Education, London, 1981).

[15] See J. Jowell, 'The Legal Control of Administrative Discretion' [1973] *Public Law* 178. Further evidence of these tendencies is demonstrated in J. Baldwin, N. Wikely, and R. Young, *Judging Social Security* (Clarendon Press, Oxford, 1993) and I. Loveland, *Housing Homeless Persons* (Clarendon Press, Oxford, 1995).

[16] K. Hawkins, *Environment and Enforcement* (Clarendon Press, Oxford, 1984) and G. Richardson, *Policing Pollution* (Clarendon Press, Oxford, 1984).

[17] J. Bradshaw, 'From Discretion to Rules: The Experience of the Family Fund', in n. 14 above, 142–3.

attention to the specific case, it may be no easy task in a complex administrative environment to achieve it. Moreover, factors other than fair treatment have a major part to play in fixing the balance between the even-handed application of standards and the more subjective exercise of discretion around them.

This leads to a third matter which concerns the relationship between officially-proclaimed standards, whether by Parliament, a minister, or the rule-making part of the authority itself, and the real but often unofficial standards being enforced in practice. The discrepancy between official and unofficial standards is an old issue in the study of decision-making. It is well-known that, even within the same organization, local units, such as a police station, a welfare office, or a local housing authority, will develop over time working rules which differ in varying ways from those officially prevailing. The reasons for this are several. One is the difficulty of assimilating external rules into the practical workings of the organization; another is the fact that the official rules often do not cope with the realities of the cases as perceived by the officials. And, finally, officials might depart from an authorized standard on the ground that it simply does not lead to the most just or even most common-sensical outcome. In her study of Mental Health Review Tribunals, Peay quotes one of the judges as saying: 'I adopt a common sense not fine detail approach to the law. If it goes against common sense then it's almost inevitably wrong.'[18] Now the substitution of one set of standards for another, which is really what is happening in these cases, is not necessarily to be deplored; the fairness element in having standards might be satisfied whether the standards are official or unofficial. The real difficulty, however, is that unofficial standards will often be very much the product of localized areas of decision-making. They will often not be disclosed indeed and the false impression of faithfully applying the official standards is likely to be fostered. The consequences for predictability and even-handedness are then all too obvious.

The fourth and final point in relation to standards is to ask just how much guidance they give anyhow to what really happens in a context of decisions. One answer would be that it depends on the standards, on how clear and detailed they are; similarly, it might reasonably be thought that the level of guidance diminishes as standards are more open-textured, inconclusive, or simply matters to take into account. While that intuitive response has much to commend it, the reality is likely to be more complex, with the level of guidance offered by standards subject to other contextual factors. One is the very complexity of decisions: the nature of the issue, the information available, and the evaluation of the situation, are amongst the variables which affect the degree of guidance which any standard is likely to give.[19] Another

[18] J. Peay, *Tribunals on Trial* (Clarendon Press, Oxford, 1989), 96.
[19] See further Richardson, *Policing Pollution*, n. 16 above, 23 ff.

contextual factor draws on a theme which appears at several points in this book, namely, the way in which standard-application is modified by informal negotiations. For instance, the way in which regulatory enforcement officers use standards, not so much as norms to be applied, but as counters to be employed in negotiations with polluters, is well documented.[20] The cost of neglecting contextual factors like these is that the qualities of standards in providing guidance to decision-making may be significantly exaggerated.

The aim of this short discussion has been once again to remind the reader of the need to take account of the social context. To demonstrate the influence of the social context on the role and guiding force of standards, to identify some of the influences and constraints deriving from that context, is not to undermine the normative connection between standards and fair treatment. Facts do not undermine norms; what facts do is alert us to the structural and procedural issues which may hinder the smooth application of normative principles. Those facts are important not only in deepening our understanding of decision-processes, but also in the practical design of institutions and procedures.

14.1.4 Doctrines in Relation to Setting Standards

The discussion of the context of standard-setting suggests that administrative decisions are normally governed by standards, whether formulated by a higher legislative authority or created by the administrative body itself. This suggestion matches the more intuitive idea that purposive, rational decision-making entails reliance on standards at some level of generality; it also corresponds with the normative principle that the articulation of standards satisfies an element of fair treatment. Moving now from context to doctrine, the present legal position is that an authority is at liberty to formulate general standards, subject to the no-fettering doctrine; however, it is not required, in the absence of a statutory duty, to do so. Where administrative powers are delegated by statute, duties may be imposed upon the authority to formulate standards, sometimes by way of formal delegated legislation, at other times in a more informal manner. This leads on to the procedures for rule-making which are considered in Chapter 15. Quite apart from that, it is not uncommon for administrative powers to be conferred on authorities without clear and settled standards, and in the absence of a duty on the authority to create its own. Discretionary powers are by nature especially prone to such an omission. The general law enters at this point, although according to the same law there is no general duty on an authority to formulate standards as to how its powers will be exercised.

The courts exercising judicial review have also been largely silent on the

[20] Hawkins, *Environment and Enforcement*, n. 16 above, ch. 2.

issue, perhaps because they consider that the matter of standards is best left either to Parliament or to the administrative bodies themselves. The suggestion may be made, however, that the scope for judicial involvement is greater than at present. A small and rather obvious step for the courts to take would be to make the connection between the issue of standard-setting and the general notion of procedural fairness. Procedural fairness is a general, background principle embracing all areas of administrative action which can be extended to generate new standards of fair treatment. The earlier claim that standards are in general an element of fair treatment seems sound, and could easily be adopted by the courts as an aspect of procedural fairness which ought to be translated into procedural doctrine. The step should be even easier to take now that the courts are developing the related doctrine requiring the disclosure of standards once formulated.[21]

It is interesting to compare the way that the issue is dealt with by the American doctrine of procedural due process. There, the question of discretionary standards is approached in two ways; one involves the formal, rule-making procedures which must be followed by federal agencies under the Administrative Procedure Act and by various state authorities under similar state law.[22] Formal rule-making broadly resembles delegated legislation in the British context. The second, more informal side, recognizes that the setting of standards is always important in the exercise of discretionary powers. Standards may derive from the terms of delegation, as in Britain, and indeed there is the federal constitutional doctrine, often reproduced at the state level, that a delegation of power must be accompanied by standards guiding its exercise. This doctrine, however, has not been enforced with any rigour in recent years, and despite occasional bursts of interest in its revival, delegations of discretion, which are subject to only the loosest standards, are likely to be upheld.[23]

An alternative approach, which is supported by K. C. Davis,[24] is for administrative authorities to be under a duty to create their own standards. This can be achieved by general statutory enactment, such as the Revised Model State Administration Procedure Act issued in 1981 which provides that each agency shall adopt rules embodying appropriate standards, principles, and procedural safeguards, which the agency is to apply in exercising its power.[25] In the absence of statutory duties, there are signs that some

[21] An alternative case for the courts involving themselves in standard-setting by administrative bodies could be based on the separation doctrine: see Galligan, *Discretionary Powers*, n. 1 above, 286–7.

[22] For an account of the American position, see B. Schwartz, *Administrative Law* (New York, 1976), ch. 4.

[23] Ibid., ch. 2.

[24] For an account of these views, see Davis, *Discretionary Justice*, n. 11 above.

[25] The terms of the Revised Model State Administrative Procedures Act 1981 are set out in K. C. Davis, *1982 Supplement to Administrative Law Treatise* (West, St. Paul, Minn., 1982), ch. 8.

American courts consider the agency to be under a common law duty to create standards, on the grounds that 'due process means that administrators must do what they can to structure and confine their discretionary powers through safeguards, standards, principles, and rules'.[26] Now even if the English courts were to follow this lead and construe standard-setting as part of procedural fairness, difficult questions would be raised as to the kinds of standards to be insisted on and how exacting they should be. It would not be just a matter of insisting on a system of detailed rules, but would mean taking account of the competing elements of fair treatment as discussed in section 14.1.1.

It seems wise that the choice of decision strategies should remain primarily in the hands of the administrative authorities, subject of course to statutory guidance. The role the courts could play would be to hedge around the administrative process a number of principles and constraints. These could be based on the idea that administrative authorities have a general duty to direct their attentions to the decision strategy to be followed, and to make public their conclusions and their reasons for them. The courts could also confirm the duty on administrative bodies to consider what fair treatment requires and to design their procedures accordingly. The duty could be made more specific in a number of ways. (i) The authority should direct itself to the issue of standards, and formulate at some level of reasonable particularity the basis upon which it will proceed in making decisions. Standards should be taken in a broad sense to include those ranging from very abstract criteria to fairly precise rules; the standards might include the specification of factors which may or must be taken into consideration, and some attempt might be made to rank them in importance. (ii) Where standards are left at a highly abstract level so that substantial discretionary assessments have to be made in individual cases, reasons should be given for adopting that approach. A complete absence of standards would never be justified, and in practice the question should be whether the standards set are sufficiently specific. An authority might have good reasons for taking an incremental approach, with an emphasis on resolving problems as they occur, and on extrapolating more general standards from actual cases rather than by advance stipulation. (iii) Once standards have been set, an authority would be expected to follow them unless it considered either that they should be modified in order to avoid an unacceptable result in a particular case, or that they were simply no longer appropriate. Any change of standards in general or departure from them in particular cases ought to be explained and justified. (iv) Where decisions are made on an incremental basis, efforts should be made to articulate the standards that implicitly are relied on and in that way to build up a system of general standards through generalizing

[26] *Historic Green Springs* v. *Beugland*, 497 F Supp. 839. (ED Va. 1980). For comment, see Davis, *1982 Supplement*, n. 25 above, 188–9.

from specific instances. Consistency from one case to another is not an overriding concern, but it is important and generally there are good reasons for linking precedents together and in that way creating standards. They need not be binding precedents, but they should be persuasive and followed unless there are good reasons for acting otherwise.

This approach might be made more exacting in one respect. Where important private interests are at stake and they are at risk of serious harm, there is a case for a presumption in favour of reasonably clear and settled standards. Interests such as personal liberty, bodily integrity, and some aspects of basic welfare, should attract the presumption.[27] The idea behind the presumption would be that, where really important interests are at risk, fairness requires that the basis on which they are at risk should be known in advance with reasonable certainty. The presumption need not be inflexible and could be modified on occasions in favour of a more incremental approach. The possible reasons for adopting an incremental approach would then include the nature of the task to be performed, the lack of experience in dealing with a matter, or because the interest in question would be better protected by procedures other than a prior formulation of standards. Some examples may be given. Where the authority can show that the complexity of a problem makes it difficult and unwise to stipulate standards in advance, an incremental approach would be acceptable, but only on condition that the parties whose interests are directly in issue would be given an indication of the approach that will be followed and an opportunity to put their cases. Again, where the very object of a discretionary power is to find a solution which constitutes an acceptable compromise amongst interests, the personal interests at stake might be better protectable through procedures which guarantee full participation in the decision. Another way of putting the point would be that where special interests are at stake or where the risk of abuse is high, the protections that are normally provided by settled standards can in special cases be secured through alternative procedures.

14.2 THE GIVING OF REASONS

14.2.1 The General Background to Reasons

To give reasons for a decision or action is to explain the basis on which it is made and then to justify that basis according to some set of standards. In a legal or administrative context that means showing the facts and how the

[27] Certain public interests might also qualify, but here I am concerned only with fair treatment in respect of personal interests: see Galligan, *Discretionary Powers*, n. 1 above, sect. 3.3.

facts were arrived at, stating the standards to be applied, and then demonstrating the reasoning process by which the standards were applied to the facts in order to reach the decision. It is a slightly loose use of language to refer to this whole process as 'giving reasons', but the usage is now settled and no harm is done provided we remember what is meant. The degree of detail of any set of reasons can of course vary from a very full account of each step taken, on the one hand, to a rather loose and general account, where the aim is to give the gist rather than the detail, on the other hand. This makes it difficult to formulate any uniform standard of adequacy, since what is adequate depends so much on the context and on the purpose for which reasons are given. The only generalization we might tender is that in legal and administrative contexts the main purpose of reasons is to show that the decision has been properly made according to the relevant authoritative standards. What precisely that means will itself change according to different kinds of processes.

While the giving of reasons is a vital part of open administrative government and fair treatment, the difficulties inherent in the very idea of providing reasons for action should not be ignored. A moment's reflection on the matter stimulates a series of questions: what does it mean to give reasons for one's actions; can we assume that the agent himself is able to give reasons for his own actions; how can reasons be tested in order to judge their accuracy? If reason-giving by officials is to meet the expectations we have of it, then legal research should concern itself with these issues. Here I shall make a small move in that direction by drawing attention to a few elementary points. The first point to make clear is that to give reasons is to offer an explanation for an action or decision. It is not an attempt to state the causes for acting as one did, but rather to reveal the plan one had in mind and the purposes one sought to achieve.[28] Harré and Secord put the point in this way: 'A man is capable of initiating action, action that may take place only after deliberation and with a more or less clear end in view.'[29] For the administrative official, we might add that the ends, the purposes, and the plans, are set by the statutory context.

Secondly, we might ask why it should be assumed that the agent acts for reasons and is able to identify and report those reasons. That we do act for reasons is a fundamental tenet of notions of personal identity and responsibility and may be taken for granted. But whether we are able accurately to report our reasons for acting is more problematical. A distinction should be drawn between being able and being willing. Any official is under a natural temptation to give reasons which satisfy the prevailing standards, whether or not the reasons given are the real reasons. The disparity between the two is

[28] See further R. Harré and P. F. Secord, *The Explanation of Social Behaviour* (Blackwell, Oxford, 1972), 40–2.

[29] Ibid. 40.

often a serious problem in legal contexts, although empirical research can assist in showing that the reasons given are not the reasons acted upon.

That problem is serious enough, but even more serious is the suggestion that the actors themselves, even when acting in good faith, are likely to portray an inaccurate picture of their reasons. Research by psychologists shows that the reasons people give for their actions can be significantly different from the actual reasons.[30] The disparity may be due partly to the sheer difficulty people have in understanding and explaining their own actions, partly to the heavy burden that intuition, hunch, or instinct may play in decision-making, and partly to an inherent, subconscious tendency to rationalize one's past actions according to what is considered to be acceptable and expected.[31] By careful empirical analysis of decision-making, researchers have been able to reveal this disparity between the actor's account of his actions after the event, and the reasons which actually make sense of those actions as they are done. These problems relating to the giving of reasons should not be taken as arguments against the principle that reasons ought to be given. The point of raising the difficulties is to draw attention to the fact that reason-giving is not a simple or unproblematical process. Indeed, this is a good example of the contribution social science can make to our understanding of the law. An apparently straightforward and normatively compelling legal practice is shown by the work of social scientists to be a rather more complex social process. The insights gained from social science research can then be used to help overcome the problems, so that reason-giving serves the role meant for it. The consequence in practical terms is simply that in order to achieve that end officials must be instructed and trained in giving reasons.

14.2.2 Reasons, Fair Treatment, and Procedural Fairness

Moving now to the relationship between reasons, fair treatment, and procedural fairness, three aspects of the relationship warrant particular attention. The first aspect relates to the quality of the decision-process itself; here the idea is that the need to give reasons for a decision may have a beneficial effect on the quality of the decision. A good example of this can be seen in relation to the duties imposed on police officers to give and record their reasons for taking certain decisions with respect to the arrest, detention, and questioning of suspects.[32] A similar, although rather more implicit, assumption partly explains the growing practice of imposing statutory duties on

[30] See e.g. R. Nisbett and L. Ross, *Human Inference: Strategies and Shortcomings of Social Judgment* (Prentice Hall, N.J., 1980).

[31] For further discussion see S. Lloyd-Bostock, *Law in Practice* (British Psychological Society and Routledge, London, 1988), ch. 4.

[32] The details can be seen in The Police and Criminal Evidence Act 1984 and the *Codes of Practice*.

officials to provide, either as a matter of course or on request, reasons for their actions.[33] The assumption behind practices like these is that the official who knows that his decisions will have to be explained and justified will try to make better decisions. And since better decisions mean decisions which are more accurate as to the facts and more reliable in the application of standards and the exercise of judgment, the result is that parties are more likely to be treated properly according to authoritative standards and, therefore, fairly. Better decisions in that sense generally mean fairer decisions.

The second part of the relationship between reasons and fairness refers not to the making of the decision, but to providing the basis on which others may understand and critically appraise the decision. This has two elements: one is that reasons provide the basis for knowing how the decision was made and for judging whether it was properly made; the other is that if an error appears, the reasons help in seeking recourse to have the decision corrected. Notice that on this account the value of reasons is not in making the primary decision itself better and fairer in any sense; rather, the link with fairness is in providing the basis for checking whether the decision has been properly made and, if not, for pursuing some form of redress. The giving of reasons is, therefore, closely connected to the protection of rights and is an indispensable instrument to that end. For without reasons, it is harder to judge whether a decision is correct and, as a result, errors are then more likely to escape undetected and unremedied. The importance of reasons as part of a wider set of procedures and practices for protecting rights, and indeed as an element of the rule of law, is widely recognized. Modern legislation tends as a matter of course to require administrative officials to give reasons for their actions, mainly, it seems, in order to allow parties to be satisfied that they were properly performed and to seek recourse where they were not. The courts often talk of the importance of reasons in mounting an appeal or review of a decision, although, as we shall see in the next section, they have never regarded it as a basic element of procedural fairness. For present purposes, it is important to see that in facilitating recourse reasons contribute directly to parties being properly treated and their rights protected.

The giving of reasons on this approach is a means for helping to determine whether a power has been properly exercised. The underlying principle of fair treatment is that a party be treated according to authoritative standards, and the giving of reasons is a means to that end. A procedural right to reasons is justified on that basis. The analysis, however, can be taken one step farther; there is, I suggest, a stronger claim to reasons based on a second principle of fair treatment. In order to understand the principle, let us begin with the idea that any administrative decision should be based on good reasons and that any party affected has a right that it be so. That may

[33] The Australian Administrative Appeals Tribunal Act 1975 is a good example.

seem to be merely another way of saying that a person has a right to be treated according to authoritative standards, since good reasons here means reasons deriving from those standards. Now while of course that is the touchstone of good reasons, the claim can be taken further to demand not only that there be good reasons, but that they be stated and made known to the party affected. The idea is that, given the imperfections of decision-processes and the fallibility of decision-makers, the statement and revelation of reasons is so closely tied to the existence of good reasons, that the right to a decision made for good reasons also supports a right to be given those reasons. The rationale for this is simple: without a statement of reasons the party affected or indeed anyone else could never know whether there were in fact good reasons. The standard of fair treatment is, in other words, not only that there be good reasons, but also that the reasons be given. The basis for these additional standards is then partly as an instrument to ensure that there are good reasons, but also partly a less contingent and irreducible idea that a party should be able to see for himself that the exercise of authority over him is justified.[34]

This approach helps us to understand better the idea that the giving of reasons is a way of providing satisfaction to the parties. Now what makes a person feel satisfied is a complex issue of psychology and is not necessarily connected to fair treatment. However, one very particular form of satisfaction is that which comes from being able to see that one's case has been dealt with properly according to authoritative standards. The satisfaction lies in being treated fairly; fair treatment is the normative principle, the satisfaction that follows a psychological state.[35] Other satisfactions may also derive from the receipt of reasons, but they have nothing to do with fairness.

This leads on to the third aspect of the relationship between reasons and fairness. Of the two accounts so far given, the first is blatantly instrumental to good outcomes, and the second is partly instrumental to testing the consistency of outcomes but also partly a non-instrumental value of worth for itself. The third way of expressing the relationship is different again: here the idea is that it just is fair to give a person reasons for an action which affects him. The basis for the idea is that to explain and justify an action taken in the exercise of authority is to show respect for the person, and in that sense to treat him fairly; the standard of fair treatment is to be treated with respect. The giving of reasons does not lead on to anything further, but is itself an expression of respect and, so, of fair treatment. In the earlier discussion of arguments of these kinds, we saw how opinions divide sharply

[34] The analysis here derives from an earlier essay; D. J. Galligan, 'Judicial Review and the Textbook Writers' [1982] 2 *Oxford JLS* 257. See also the further development of the idea in G. Richardson, 'The Duty to Give Reasons: Potential and Practice' [1986] *Public Law* 437.

[35] Compare Richardson, 'The Duty to Give Reasons: Potential and Practice', n. 34 above, 445 where reference is made to 'fairness or the provision of satisfaction to the parties' as if they were the same thing.

over the very coherence of the idea that procedures can express respect for persons; we also considered the practical issue of whether the case for procedures as expressing values can ever be strong enough to justify procedures which would not otherwise be warranted on instrumental grounds. The arguments need not be repeated here except to make one point: when we ask in what sense the giving of reasons expresses respect, it is difficult not to fall back on the idea that reasons enable the person to understand the decision and to see whether it has been properly made. But that is the essence of the second account given above; if there is some other sense in which the provision of reasons expresses respect without collapsing in this way into something else, it is not easy to see what it is.

The point of this discussion has been to demonstrate the relationship between reasons, fair treatment, and procedures. The approach has been the familiar one of identifying the principles of fair treatment and then showing how the giving of reasons relates to them. The fundamental principle that people should be dealt with according to authoritative standards constitutes a good strong case for procedures requiring reasons. That principle should be supplemented by the notion that a person is entitled to a reasoned decision being made and the reasons being disclosed. The precise terms of the second principle, and whether there is a third principle based on respect, are subject to some debate. But perhaps the most important point of the discussion here is to show that, whatever other justification there might be for providing reasons, the case based on fair treatment is coherent and compelling.

14.2.3 The Law Relating to Reasons

The law relating to the giving of reasons is dependent partly on statute and partly on the common law as expressed in judicial review. Where statutory provisions are laid down, they typically require a general statement of reasons, and then leave it for the courts to decide on their adequacy;[36] where there are no statutory provisions, the issue is left entirely to the common law. Statutory requirements regarding reasons are to be found either in statutes applying generally to classes of authorities or types of decisions, or in the specific statutes under which administrative powers are confirmed. One example of the first is the Tribunals and Inquiries Act 1949 in Britain, which covers the decisions of most tribunals and inquiries; another example is the Australian Administrative Appeals Tribunal Act 1975 which enables a person whose interests are affected by certain types of discretionary decisions to require a statement setting out: (a) the findings on material matters

[36] On the adequacy of reasons where there is a statutory duty to disclose, see *Re Poyser and Mills' Arbitration* [1964] 2 QB 467, *Mountview Court Properties* v. *Devlin* (1970) 21 P&CR 689, and *Elliott* v. *Southwark LBC* [1976] 1 WLR 499.

of fact; (b) the evidence or other material on which the findings are based; and (c) giving reasons for the decision.[37]

Apart from these statutes of more general application, various specific statutes can be found imposing more or less exacting duties as to the giving of reasons. However, many areas of administration remain relatively exempt from statutory requirements, the penal process being a notable example. Despite the continued existence of such areas of exemption, evidence can be seen of an increasingly strong and widespread commitment to the provision of reasons as an integral part of good administration. The annual reports of the Council on Tribunals, for example, regularly restate the case for the giving of reasons to be extended across a wide range of administrative areas. The Council has urged that, save where a case is made out for an exception in special circumstances, reasons should be given in writing by all tribunals for all their decisions. This is likely in time to become an axiom applied to all administrative decisions, unless there are clear and established policies in specific contexts against revelation as, for example, in matters of national security.

Turning now to the approach of the courts in judicial review, the principle is well settled that there is no general duty to give reasons for administrative decisions in the sense that failure to do so would be a ground of invalidity. Now while the courts continue to restate the absence of a general duty to give reasons,[38] they are sounding more and more like Mark Antony at Caesar's funeral: saying one thing and meaning another.[39] In recent cases the courts have with one breath said there is no general duty and in the next breath that in that particular case there is a duty.[40] The explanation for what seems a very odd method of approach is that, despite their protestations to the contrary, the courts have made a fundamental shift in the way they view the issue. Instead of asking the question whether there is a general duty on officials to give reasons, as if it were a general policy matter, and then answering that negatively, the courts now perceive the issue as a matter of procedural fairness.[41] In characterizing the question in that way, the courts open up a new logic and a new form of discourse; for we are now in the territory of rights, where the rights at stake are rights to fair treatment and the question is what procedures are needed to ensure fair treatment.

[37] For an account of the requirement of reasons under the AAT Act, see D. J. Galligan, 'The Administrative Appeals Tribunal' in D. J. Galligan (ed.), *The Laws of Australia: Administrative Law* (Law Book, Sydney, 1993).

[38] *R.* v. *Civil Service Board, ex parte Cunningham* [1991] IRLR 297 (CA) and *Doody* v. *Secretary of State* [1993] 3 All ER 92 (HL).

[39] The extent to which the absence of a general duty to give reasons is being eroded by a multitude of exceptions is well analysed in P. P. Craig, 'The Common Law, Reasons and Administrative Justice' (1994) 53 *Camb. LJ* 282.

[40] See for instance, *R.* v. *Mayor, Commonalty and Citizens of the City of London, ex parte Matson* [1996] ALR 49. Compare *R.* v. *Royal Borough of Kensington and Chelsea, ex parte Grillo* (1996) ALR 165.

[41] See the important judgment of Lord Donaldson in *Cunningham*, n. 38 above.

This is the key to understanding the perceptive reasoning of Lord Mustill in a recent decision of the House of Lords, *Doody* v. *Secretary of State*,[42] which marks a turning point in the approach of the English courts. The question was whether a prisoner serving a mandatory life sentence was entitled to know the Home Secretary's reasons for fixing the length of the penal element of the sentence, and, in particular, for not following the recommendations of the trial judge on that point. It should be observed that, in a case like this, the giving of reasons for the decision becomes mixed up with giving notice of the case the person has to meet. Since both are connected to fair treatment, it should not matter whether an issue is characterized as one or the other, but here the courts emphasized the reason-giving aspects. Reasons were linked to fair treatment in two ways. One was the recognition that, in order for the minister's decision to be good and fair, it ought to take into account the proper consideration of the prisoner's case, which in turn meant hearing and deliberating upon any representations he might make. But in order for the prisoner to be able to make sensible and relevant representations, he must know the minister's reasons for deciding or proposing to decide the penal element.[43] The idea seems to be that, even if the minister first decided and then gave reasons, the prisoner could still make representations directed to changing the minister's mind. On this approach, the need for disclosure of reasons is directly instrumental to achieving the underlying standards of fair treatment. The other reason the court gave relates more clearly to the giving of reasons after a final decision has been made. Here the emphasis was on reasons as evidence which might reveal errors in the way the decision was made and, therefore, provide the means for deciding whether recourse by way of judicial review would be open. This is a good example of the general principle that reasons are usually essential in revealing possible errors, and thus in facilitating recourse, the object of which is to correct the error and to ensure the person is treated according to the relevant standards of fairness.

When the issue is approached in this way, the case for reasons will usually be irresistible. Without a statement from the minister showing how the penal element of the sentence was arrived at, the decision process is flawed and the result thrown into doubt, especially in discretionary contexts where process and outcome tend to merge into each other. Similarly, once the decision has been made, the failure to provide reasons jeopardizes the detection of error and the chance of having it remedied through some form of recourse. The only form of recourse available here was judicial review, but the same reasoning would apply to other forms of review or appeal; all

[42] N. 38 above. But compare *R.* v. *Higher Education Funding Council, ex parte Institute of Dental Surgery* [1944] 1 WLR 242.

[43] Here reasons relate to the disclosure of the criteria of decision-making in *advance*; that is rather different from a statement of reasons after the decision has been made: see further Galligan, *Discretionary Powers*, n. 1 above, sects. 6.1 and 6.2.

are devices for correcting different kinds of errors in the original decision and, in that way, ensuring fair treatment of the prisoner.

The approach of the House of Lords in this case to reasons is now in line with the general approach of the courts to procedural fairness. According to that approach, the first step is to identify the standards of fair treatment, and the second step is to ascertain what procedures will ensure proper treatment within the standards. Particular procedures are contingent upon and instrumental to achieving that objective. However, one point of reservation should be made about this approach to reasons. On the basis of the idea that reasons are necessary as a means for detecting errors, the conclusion might be drawn that reasons will always be a necessary requirement of fairness. The basis for the conclusion would be partly that we would normally have no way of assessing the correctness and propriety of a decision without reasons, and partly that the giving of reasons is itself expressive of the non-instrumental value of showing that the decision has been properly made. A case can be made, in other words, for regarding the giving of reasons as such a vital aspect of procedural fairness that it should not be regarded in the contingent and instrumental way suggested in recent cases. That idea might already be implicit in the logic of the judicial approach so that, in practice, it will be difficult not to conclude that, in virtually every context, a statement of reasons is a requirement of procedural fairness. As the force of that logic becomes more apparent, it will be easy for the courts to give it full effect; and as the force of that logic becomes more compelling, all reference to the supposed general principle that reasons need not be given can quietly be dropped.[44]

The argument presented here is that recent judicial decisions mark a fundamentally new approach to the giving of reasons. If the new approach succeeds, so that generally a statement of reasons for an administrative decision will be regarded as an element of procedural fairness, then various devices invented in the past in order to allow the consequences of a refusal of reasons to be taken into account will gradually lose their significance.

14.3 IMPARTIALITY IN ADMINISTRATIVE PROCESSES

14.3.1 The Nature of Bias and Loss of Independence

That a judge or other official should act impartially in making decisions is often said to be one of the most elementary requirements of fair treatment. Indeed, the rule against bias stands with the hearing rule as one of the twin

[44] The justices of the Australian High Court, so forward-looking in other respects, might also in time feel able to bury their own unfortunate decision in *Public Service Board* v. *Osmond* (1986) 63 ALR 559.

pillars of the common law concept of procedural fairness. And, as M. Bayles points out, the repugnance felt towards biased decision-makers is widely reflected in constitutions, international conventions, and administrative law codes.[45] While naturally wishing to join the chorus of condemnation, we should pause to consider just what it is that is so offensive about a public official who is motivated by bias or prejudice, lacks impartiality, or displays a loss of independence in any other way. The task in this section is to consider the various flaws and to examine their relationship to procedural fairness.

Let us begin by being clear about the nature of the defect. The family concept is impartiality; within the family, the two main ways of ceasing to be impartial are being biased or losing one's independence. To be biased means broadly to have an inclination or predisposition towards one side rather than the other; it might also have the stronger connotation of being prejudiced. The idea of prejudice as pre-judgment brings out well the core idea that to be biased is in some way to have judged the issue beforehand or to have judged it for reasons which are not the right reasons. The inclination, predisposition, or prejudice may result from a number of causes, and it may help in our understanding of the nature of bias to divide the causes into three groups. The first group may be referred to as personal bias, since it emphasizes factors personal to the official. It includes personal preferences or feelings; a personal interest, whether financial or emotional; or a personal connection to the matter through the interests of family or friends. This list is illustrative rather than comprehensive, and the guiding test should be whether, because of some such factor, the judge or other official has prejudged or is rendered incapable of properly judging or deciding the issue. Personal bias is the category most familiar to lawyers, and while it will normally be difficult to prove, the law is strict and tends to regard any signs of bias as sufficient evidence of a serious risk of bias.

The second category of bias is often referred to as systemic bias.[46] By systemic bias is meant those inclinations and predispositions which each person has, not because of a personal interest or by a deliberately adopted attitude or stance, but as a result of belonging to a social class or coming from a certain kind of background or working within a particular organizational context. The idea is that, within any such social milieu, certain distinctive attitudes will prevail and will influence the actions and views of anyone within it. D. A Wood puts the point in this way:

[45] Bayles, *Procedural Justice*, n. 9 above, ch. 2.

[46] See D. A. Wood, 'Judicial Fairness and Systemic Bias' in S. Parker and C. J. G. Sampford (eds.), *Legal Ethics and Legal Practice: Contemporary Issues* (Clarendon Press, Oxford, 1995). Much of the discussion has been about judges, but the same analysis can be applied to administrative officials; see further: Canadian Judicial Council, *Commentaries on Judicial Conduct* (Quebec, 1991) and S. Cooney, 'Gender and Judicial Selection: Should There Be More Women on the Courts?' (1993) 19 *Melb. UL Rev.* 20.

> Individuals are to a large extent creatures of their backgrounds and life-experiences. They have a natural affinity towards other individuals from similar backgrounds and with similar life-experiences. If not consciously and overtly, then unconsciously and tacitly, individuals tend to favour such persons.[47]

Indeed, systemic bias goes beyond such notions of background and experience; it may also be the product of organizations and of the attitudes which develop within them. The attitude of the police to certain kinds of offenders or offences, the welfare officers' classification of claimants for benefits as genuinely needy or unscrupulous exploiters,[48] the housing committee's judgment of applicants as deserving or undeserving, and the approach of officials to different categories of immigrants are all notable examples of the dangers of systemic bias within organizations. Systemic bias is hard to prove and generally escapes the attention of the law, for the person who alleges systemic bias is throwing down a challenge in the face of which legal standards and legal remedies are largely ineffective. There might occasionally be sufficient traces of systemic bias in the actions or judgments of an official for the law to act in that case; but systemic bias is by its very nature so ingrained in social and cognitive understandings that it can be removed or reduced only by critical change to the system itself. The alleged preferences of judges for men over women, the deep-seated racism of some police officers, or the moralistic stereotyping of welfare claimants is each likely to be alleviated only by fundamental reforms in the education and training of those making the judgments. But to concede that systemic bias is deep-seated in the social fabric is not to allow that it is in some degree inevitable or tolerable. Its effect is the same as more blatant forms of personal bias; it distorts legal and administrative processes by introducing illegitimate reasons. Its very insidiousness, however, makes it an even more serious threat than more blatant forms of bias to the fair treatment of those affected.

The third category of bias may be referred to as cognitive bias. Here the idea is that, within the processes of decision-making, certain assumptions are made, certain steps are taken, which are unjustified and which have the effect of leading to false conclusions. The work of social psychologists into the complexities of decision-making provides the background. Their researches show that, although decision-making is inherently complex, we develop ways of simplifying the task.[49] Time, knowledge, and costs, are all reasons for 'pruning the tree—or in other words, of cutting down the number of alterations considered'.[50] However, in doing so, there is a risk of introducing cognitive biases of several kinds: for example, we are inclined to

[47] N. 46 above, at 4.

[48] Baldwin, Wikeley, and Young, *Judging Social Security*, n. 15 above, 34.

[49] See e.g. V. Konecni and E. Ebbesen, *The Criminal Justice System: A Social Psychological Analysis* (Freeman, San Francisco, Calif., 1982).

[50] S. Lloyd-Bostock, *Law in Practice*, n. 31 above, 67.

attribute behaviour to easily identified personal factors rather than more complex situational ones; we tend to conclude rather too readily that our own view of an issue is widely shared; and when we believe variables to be related to each other, we will hold them to be related even when they are not.[51] These are instances of numerous common errors which usually go unnoticed in decision-processes. They are in a sense simple errors of reasoning, but they have the effect of producing false outcomes; they are, therefore, as devastating as personal or systemic bias to the cause of fair treatment. Much of the work on cognitive bias has been in relation to sentencing,[52] but there is good reason to think that similar problems arise in administrative decision-making generally.[53]

It is evident from this brief account that bias in its various senses in administrative processes is an interesting problem which has not yet gained a firm foothold in empirical studies. Considering its serious impact, it should become a basic concept in future research.[54] But bias is only one branch of the family of partiality, the other branch being loss of independence. The line between loss of independence and bias is not always easy to draw, but the emphasis in the case of the former is on the official surrendering his independence of thought and judgment in such a way that he is unable to deal with the case on its merits and according to the relevant standards. The strongest cases are bribery and duress, where one agrees, in the first case for profit and the second out of fear, to decide an issue in a certain way regardless of its merits. In less striking cases, an official's independence might be lost through excessive reliance on the opinion of another official, through blind compliance with a superior's directions, or even by unduly self-fettering of his own judgment in advance. Attacks have been mounted against administrative officials on the ground of 'departmental bias', by which is meant that, since a policy-view or similar approach has already been settled on, the official does not approach each specific case with an independent mind. Such attacks on predetermined policy have not usually been successful, not least because they strike at the very basis of effective administrative government. Nevertheless, it can be seen just how problematical and uncertain the concept of loss of independence is. Bias is usually easier to deal with than loss of independence: once certain signs of bias are detected, the process is considered to be tainted; while loss of independence

[51] These cognitive factors are discussed at length in C. Fitzmaurice and K. Pease, *The Psychology of Judicial Sentencing* (Manchester UP., Manchester, 1986), ch. 2.

[52] See Lloyd-Bostock, *Law in Practice*, n. 31 above, and Fitzmaurice and Pease, *The Psychology of Judicial Sentencing*, n. 51 above.

[53] Some evidence for this can be seen in A. Lovegrove, 'The Listing of Criminal Cases as an Administrative Discretion' [1984] *Crim. L Rev.*, 738 and K. Hawkins, 'Discretion in Making Legal Decisions' (1987) 43 *Washington and Lee L Rev.*, 1161.

[54] Studies such as Baldwin, Wikeley, and Young, *Judging Social Security*, n. 15 above, and Loveland, *Housing the Homeless*, n. 15 above, touch on notions of systemic and cognitive bias.

is rather more difficult to ascertain and in any case its role in administrative processes is less precise. As we shall see in the next section, a number of legal doctrines try to settle the criteria for determining loss of independence.

14.3.2 Impartiality and Fair Treatment

Returning now to the relationship between loss of impartiality and fair treatment, we can see why the one undermines the other. To lack impartiality means being willing to decide a matter for reasons which are unrelated to legitimate reasons. The judge who allows his personal feelings towards a party to intrude on his deliberations, or the licensing justice who takes into account his own financial interest in the licence being refused, are both acting out of bias and have surrendered their impartiality. The personal feelings of the judge and the financial interests of the justice are reasons which should be excluded from their decisions. They are improper reasons because they are unrelated to the authoritative standards by which the cases should be decided. The judge is supposed to decide between the two parties according to the principles of civil law, while the justice should determine licensing applications according to the statutory criteria. Where there is discretion so that the judge or the justice has to settle for himself at least some of the standards to apply, it would be equally illegitimate to adopt standards based on personal feelings or financial interest. Any choice which discretion allows does not include the selection of standards based on personal feelings or financial interest.

Once the link is made between loss of impartiality and the process of reasoning which an official is required to follow, the relationship between bias and fairness can be seen. For the official who acts for improper reasons fails to apply authoritative standards correctly or to exercise discretion properly; as a consequence, the person affected is not treated in accordance with those standards and, therefore, is treated unfairly. This does not undermine the idea that reasons do not come ready-made or branded as good or bad; reasons, of course, are constructed out of a social context, guided, but not closely constricted, by given legal standards. The present argument claims merely that whatever reasons are good reasons, those displaying bias will never be amongst their number. We can now see why loss of impartiality is roundly condemned: the unseemliness of prejudice or personal interest influencing the holder of a public office is evidence of the deeper principle rather than the principle itself. We can also see that, being an attack on the idea that in any legal context there are authoritative standards to apply, the absence of impartiality is a fundamental flaw which renders the process illegitimate.

14.3.3 The Problems of Proof

While there may be no doubt that where partiality is demonstrated the process is improper, it is by nature often difficult to prove. The prejudice or personal preference which often constitutes bias can easily be concealed from outside scrutiny. For that reason, the object in legal contexts is often to watch for and act on the signs of partiality rather than insist on proof of actual partiality. What the signs are and how well they must be proved are matters to be judged in different contexts; but, for the purposes of the law, any external signs which show a real risk of internal impropriety in judges or other officials are generally enough to condemn the process. In some contexts the signs of partiality might be present without there being actual loss of impartiality; a judge might have an interest of a personal or pecuniary kind in a matter and yet be capable of not allowing such matters to affect his judgment. Since it will be difficult to know whether the judge is able to put aside such personal factors and decide impartially, the law sensibly declines to take the risk. Legal doctrine tends, therefore, to regard the signs of bias as enough to condemn the process.

While the main concern here is with the relationship between loss of impartiality and fair treatment, it should be noted that there are other reasons for not allowing the signs of partiality to pass without sanction. The point is often made that to do so, whether or not there is actual bias, might bring the system into disrepute. The external signs of bias raise suspicions of real bias which must either be shown to be unfounded or be regarded as adequate grounds for invalidating the process. To ignore the signs would be to augment the misgivings an observer as well as a participant might have that, where justice is not seen to be done, the chances are it is not being done. Whether well-founded or not, such misgivings cast a shadow over the whole process and undermine the public interest in having a legal and administrative system which earns the respect of its citizens.

The final matter to consider in this section is how these general ideas about impartiality apply to the administrative system. Many of the ideas have developed with particular reference to courts where a judge is required to decide impartially between the parties according to authoritative standards. The adversarial nature of the court process and the idea of it being a contest between the parties renders any hint of bias especially odious. The same idea can readily be applied to administrative processes which involve an adjudicative element; it might be adjudication in the three-party sense, although it should extend to the element of judgment in applying standards to particular cases. Bias on the part of the administrative official in applying settled standards to specific cases is as fatal as in any more trial-like context.

The more difficult issue is to determine under what conditions an official's independence of mind is so diminished that the canons of impartiality are violated. A distinction should be made here between factors of a personal kind, which will often have connotations of corruption, and factors which have no such connotations but relate to the official as official. An example of the first would be the official who is bribed or threatened with blackmail, while examples of the second occur where one official is allowed to follow the directions of another, or to bind himself by policy rules in advance of specific cases, or to form firm views about a matter before properly considering it. The difficulties in defining what constitutes loss of independence in this second sense are considerable. The explanation for the difficulties is that, while bias directly undermines certain undisputed standards of fair treatment, the standards against which loss of independence is to be judged are themselves to a degree unsettled and problematical.

Consider some examples. Suppose a minister, who has a statutory duty to consult interested parties about a policy issue, has already formed a firm view of what the policy should be. Or suppose that one minister, who has to take a policy decision on an issue, indicates that he will follow the policies adopted by another minister. Another example occurs where an official with statutory or common law powers of his own is instructed to exercise it in a certain way or according to certain guidelines. The last kind of case often occurs in large administrative organizations where officials are greatly constrained by the internal rules, standards, and conventions in the way they handle cases. These examples amply demonstrate the issues that arise and how different views might easily be taken as to whether or not they amount to a loss of independence. On the one hand are the realities and practicalities of administrative institutions and processes, which are enormously variable, and where the lines between policy and implementation, between a sense of continuity and fair dealing in the particular case, between effective administration and keeping an open mind, are often hard to draw. On the other hand are the normative principles dictating that administrative authorities come to each case with a mind which is in some sense open and independent. What is at stake, then, are the standards by which each case should be judged and that is a matter on which opinions can reasonably differ. In practice, within a legal system, the legislature and the courts will be responsible for setting the standards; in English law, for example, we are familiar with doctrines against fettering discretion, against abdicating one's statutory powers to another or accepting dictation from another. These are, however, often troublesome doctrines, the application of which in practice requires the making of practical judgments which may be highly debatable.

While doctrines of the kind mentioned are reasonably settled, they do point to a deeper concern about the loss of independence of officials in fulfilling their statutory duties. Attention has been drawn to the pressures under which officials work in areas of mass decisions, such as the social welfare area, with the result that quantity and turnover overshadow the proper adjudication of each case.[55] Misgivings have also been expressed about appeal procedures where there is no real independence between those who originally decide and those who hear the appeal. A procedure which provides for an appeal to a superior authority from primary decision-makers, who are applying guidelines set by the superior, is not designed to inculcate an independence of mind on the part of the latter.[56] These are just two examples of how difficult it can be to achieve the barest levels of independence and detachment which are necessary conditions for the proper assessment of a case, and in turn of fair treatment. They are problems which very much derive from the organization, structure, and dynamics of administrative bodies and they are likely to be alleviated only by careful attention being paid to those matters. Legal remedies might also have a contribution to make, but the present state of administrative law has little to offer; its notion of bias has originated in a judicial culture and the courts have been tactful in not clumsily treating administrative processes as lesser forms of a judicial trial. While a policy of restraint on the part of the courts is clearly sensible, it has at the same time meant that the courts have not become involved in developing, through administrative law principles, a culture of administrative independence which reaches down to the lowest and least visible rungs of the administrative ladder.

To sum up, the analysis here has shown why the lack of impartiality is a fundamental flaw in legal and administrative processes. The explanation is that, by introducing illegitimate reasons, a lack of impartiality on the part of the decision-maker prevents a decision being made in accordance with legitimate reasons and, therefore, in accordance with authoritative standards of fair treatment. Within the general principle of impartiality, two reasonably distinct strands can be separated, one based on bias, the other on loss of independence in making decisions. The application of the bias principle is straightforward, the only practical question being what signs of possible bias are sufficient to act on. The independence principle is rather more difficult to apply since the standards as to what is acceptable administrative practice are themselves to a degree arguable. It is usual within a legal system for doctrines to be developed which reflect a particular view of the appropriate standards.

14.3.4 Impartiality in Legal Doctrine

The issue which has most occupied the courts is what test should be used in deciding whether certain signs of bias, without proof of actual bias, are

[55] Baldwin, Wikeley, and Young, *Judging Social Security*, n. 15 above, 207 and Loveland, *Housing Homeless Persons*, n. 15 above. See also R. Sainsbury, 'Social Security Appeals' in Finnie (ed.), *Edinburgh Essays in Public Law* (Edinburgh University Press, Edinburgh, 1991).

[56] See C. Reid, E. Scobie, and C. Barker, *Community Charge Registration and Appeals* (1990) and the comment by Maloney and Young, 10 *Civil JQ*, 208.

enough to invalidate a legal or administrative process.[57] The claim of bias is frequently made in a great variety of situations and, because bias has such fatal consequences for an administrative process, getting the test right is of considerable importance. Perusal of recent cases of judicial review shows just how varied those situations can be; they include such matters as coroners and juries, planning committees and ministers, judges and licensing authorities. In a sea of decisions, judicial reasoning at both its best and its worst is displayed, with some rising to the heights of legal sophistication, others portraying an abysmal sophistry. However, in a number of recent decisions, culminating in a lucid and authoritative pronouncement by Lord Goff in the House of Lords, much of the old learning has been swept away and legal doctrine has been given a firm and compelling foundation.[58]

The facts in *R.* v. *Gough* nicely illustrate the way issues of bias occur. At the end of a criminal trial, a juror suddenly realized that the brother of the accused was her next-door neighbour. The brother was not on trial, but the charge against the accused was that he had conspired with his brother to commit robbery; naturally much of the trial concerned the relations between the two. Upon realizing who the brother was, the juror informed the court; the trial judge considered that he had no power to reopen the case, so judicial review was brought to quash the proceedings. The question was whether on the facts there was an appearance of bias sufficient to taint the trial. After an analysis of the authorities, Lord Goff, on behalf of the court, propounded an approach along the following lines: the test to apply is whether, in all the circumstances, there is a real danger of bias on the part of the official or member of a court or tribunal (in this case the juror). By bias is meant that the official or member 'might unfairly regard with favour or disfavour the case of a party to an issue under consideration'.[59]

The logic of the argument may be displayed more fully: (i) bias on the part of an authority taints its decisions; (ii) if actual bias is shown, that is an end of the matter; (iii) but given the difficulties in most situations of knowing whether there is real bias, a decision will be tainted whenever there is a genuine risk of bias. The difficult part in practice is to determine when the external signs of possible bias are grave enough to conclude that there is a real or genuine risk of actual bias. Terms such as real danger or real possibility are ways of indicating just how grave the risk must be; but language can never be entirely adequate in itself and must be regarded as merely a guide to the kind of practical judgment that has to be made. The

[57] Detailed discussion of the cases can be seen in standard textbooks on administrative law: H. W. R. Wade, *Administrative Law* (6th edn., Clarendon Press, Oxford, 1992), and P. P. Craig, *Administrative Law* (3rd edn., Sweet and Maxwell, London, 1994). A concise account is Franklin, 'The Rule Against Bias' in Galligan, *Laws of Australia: Administrative Law*, n. 37 above.

[58] *R.* v. *Gough* [1993] 2 WLR 724. See also *R.* v. *Wilson and Sprason* [1996] ALR 1.

[59] Ibid. 737.

underlying principle is that a biased decision is an unfair decision; Lord Goff does not expressly say, but being implicit in his analysis might well have said, that the decision is unfair because the wrong reasons have been relied on. Where the wrong reasons are relied on the decision is unauthorized and the person dealt with on the basis of an unauthorized decision is dealt with unfairly. The legal test formulated in *Gough* not only removes the need for the tortuous analysis of many earlier cases; by insisting that what is important is whether there is a serious risk of bias, the Law Lords have given authoritative recognition to the direct line between bias and unfair treatment.

Two final points on bias should be noted. One is that where the risk of bias derives from a personal interest on the part of the judge or official, it will be enough, in order to invalidate the process, simply to demonstrate the interest.[60] The ideas behind this stem from common sense rather than deep principle. A personal interest, whether financial, proprietary, or based on a special human association, automatically creates a powerful risk of bias which is likely to have an insidious influence on the decision-maker, no matter how hard he strives to overcome it. It would be difficult to persuade an observer of the process that the effect of such an interest had been neutralized.[61] This leads on to the second idea that the confidence of the public in the propriety of legal and administrative processes should be maintained. Confidence in the system might to some degree rightly be considered a separate element of the public interest, separate, that is, from questions about the link between bias and unfairness. Since public perception can be fickle, it might be that the slightest hint of bias will be enough to dint general confidence. In general, however, it is better that public confidence should be based on the recognition that the crucial concern is that parties in the system should be treated fairly according to authoritative standards. If legal doctrine and practical experience are such that we can be reasonably satisfied of that object being attained, then we should have confidence in and respect for the system.

Turning now from issues of bias to questions of independence of mind, it should be noted that current legal doctrines are less certain and settled. The reasons, as suggested in the preceding section, are that the very concept of independence of mind on the part of administrative officials is problematical. It is problematical in the sense that the standards as to what constitutes fair and proper treatment of the parties are to some degree uncertain and unsettled. That legal doctrine should also be uncertain and unsettled is not surprising. Moreover, it appears that the growth of doctrine has been retarded by the persistent practice of characterizing the issue as one of bias, rather than recognizing that the different issues as to what standards ought

[60] *R.* v. *Gough*, n. 58 above, 729.

[61] Another principle often introduced here is that a person should not be a judge in his own cause.

to govern the way officials, themselves enmeshed in an administrative and sometimes political context, approach specific cases. Once legislators and courts direct their minds to that issue, the ground will be laid for the growth of a normative foundation of a sound administrative culture.

There is evidence to suggest that some progress has been made in that direction. The first and possibly most important is the tendency for the courts to ask what does procedural fairness require in each context. To approach the issue in that manner opens the way for direct enquiry into the standards of fair treatment, which in turn means reflecting on the nature of administrative government. The significance of this can be seen in a fairly recent case, *R.* v. *Amber Valley District Council, ex parte Jackson*.[62] The question was whether a local planning committee, the Labour majority of which had declared in advance its being in favour of granting planning permission, had acted properly. In a perceptive judgment, Woolf J characterized the matter as one of procedural fairness and then analysed the underlying standards in order to determine what they were and whether they were properly served in this case. This led the judge to examine the nature of local government, the context of planning decisions, and the role of party politics within them. Woolf J concluded that, in that context, the prior expression of their policy views favouring the application did not so preclude members of the Labour majority from considering the objections that might be raised as to invalidate the process. To be 'politically predisposed' in that way did not constitute a loss or surrender of independence of mind in that context.[63]

A second development in recent cases follows on from the first: various doctrines relating to fettering, abdicating, or acting under dictation, which have always appeared to be free-floating without clear purpose, can now be anchored to notions of fair treatment. At one level they might be viewed as examples of good administrative practice, but at another level it should be realized that what that means depends largely on what constitutes fair treatment in different administrative contexts. For example, the doctrine against fettering in advance the way in which powers will be used is an attempt to reconcile the character of administrative government with the need to consider properly each case. It is also, therefore, an expression of what constitutes fair treatment and a delineation of the scope of administrative independence. This approach has promise, not only in giving more secure foundations to established doctrines, but also in opening the way to a better understanding of what independence means in administrative contexts. That may in time lead the legislature, the courts, and the administrators themselves to tackle more vigorously the need for more and better standards of administrative independence.

[62] A good example is the analysis of Woolf J; see [1985] 1 WLR 298.
[63] See Woolf J's analysis, ibid. 307–8.

PART V

Policy Formation and Rule-Making

Introduction

Much of the discussion so far in this book has concentrated on administrative processes of an individualized nature. In this final part, the focus will be on the policy-making aspects of administration. The distinction between the two activities is neither exact nor strictly logical since policy-making may occur as part of an individualized process. Where there is discretion as to how particular cases should be dealt with, it may first be necessary to formulate some policy guidelines. Although policy-making in that context has been touched on elsewhere, much of the analysis in this part will also be applicable to it, since the object here is to consider issues of procedural fairness in relation to policy-making wherever it occurs.

This part divides into two chapters. In the first, the policy process is examined and a number of different models of policy-making are proposed and scrutinized. Some of the contextual factors which shape policy are identified, but the main objective is to explore the relationship between the policy process and fair procedures. This is done by examining the standards of fair treatment which prevail or which arguably ought to prevail, and then showing what kinds of procedures are needed to uphold those standards. In the second chapter, the aim is to move from the contextual and normative levels to consider how questions of procedural fairness in relation to policy-making are dealt with in law. The legal system of the United Kingdom is the main point of discussion, with some interesting comparisons being drawn with Australia and the United States.

15
Procedural Fairness in the Policy Process

The object of this Chapter is to examine those administrative processes the main point of which is to settle or to make recommendations about matters of policy. This can be contrasted with individualized processes, where the issue is how a particular person or situation should be dealt with. The distinction between the two is not always clear or precise, and indeed individualized processes may involve elements of policy, including sometimes matters of high policy. Nevertheless, it is useful to maintain a general, working distinction between the two and, to the extent that policy matters are incidental to individualized processes, they are dealt with in other chapters. The emphasis in this chapter is on the general policy process, whatever the context in which it occurs. By general policy I mean issues such as whether a new motorway should be built and, if so, what route it should take, or the formulation of policies governing the release of prisoners on licence, or what rules should govern the admission of children to different schools.

The Chapter divides into two parts. The first part contains an account of the main features of policy-making. Different forms of policy-making are identified and efforts are made to place the process in a wider context. Some of the main influences are noted, with particular attention being paid to the informal nature of administrative policy-making and to the important role of interest groups and the policy communities which form around them. In the second part of the Chapter, attention moves from the descriptive features of the policy-process to the normative standards which guide it. The main objective here is to develop a notion of procedural fairness in relation to administrative policy-making, which in turn depends on articulating the standards of fair treatment of persons and groups. This is an area of procedural fairness which has not been the subject of close study at either the theoretical or the empirical level, and so the discussion of principles of fair treatment and procedural standards is somewhat tentative. The relationship between the citizen and the state in this context can be expressed in different ways and according to different normative understandings. My suggestion is that, of the three main normative models which can be constructed, one of them best expresses the more fundamental political principles of a democratic society. This standard model is then made the basis for the analysis of policy-making and from that model more specific standards of procedural fairness are drawn. In the last section of the Chapter, the practical reality of administrative policy-making and the principles of fair treatment and fair procedures are brought together.

15.1 THE POLICY PROCESS

15.1.1 General Nature of the Policy Process

Administrative bodies often have to decide matters of policy since policy issues occur at all levels of decision-making by officials, sometimes openly and explicitly, at other times by implication and interpretation. A decision of policy is one where the authority has to draw on general considerations of a social, economic, or ethical kind in deciding an issue, where the decision is likely to affect a range of groups and interests. It generally means that different possible courses of action are open and that the official has some freedom in deciding which to take. In the strongest case, the authority may be given an issue and asked to decide on a way of dealing with it, where a range of matters will need to be taken into account and all sorts of influences and constraints to be accommodated; but in the end the authority may decide as it thinks best. The strongest case, however, is not the only case, and lesser elements of policy may occur at various points in decision-making. Where there is discretion, there is policy, and discretion occurs not only in the absence of standards, but also in interpreting them, determining their normative force, and in deciding whether to depart from or modify them. It has been aptly remarked, indeed, that policy-making is not one process but a series of sub-processes.[1] Policy decisions are sometimes contrasted with decisions of principle, where by the latter is meant that there are settled standards to apply and someone has a right that they be applied.[2] In that case, the task is to apply the standard according to the interpretation that seems best, while part of the point of a policy decision is that there are no authoritative standards, or at least that they are unsettled enough to allow wider considerations to count. This distinction, however, should not be drawn too strictly, for matters of principle may have a place in wider issues of policy.

The primary policy-maker is Parliament in its legislative role, although the real centre of policy-making is cabinet and its departmental advisers. Any piece of legislation, by the time it has entered the statute book, will be

[1] J. J. Richardson and A. G. Jordan, *Governing Under Pressure* (M. Robertson, Oxford, 1979), 153.

[2] This distinction lies at the heart of R. M. Dworkin's theory of adjudication: see *Taking Rights Seriously* (Duckworth, London, 1978), ch. 4.

the result of a long course of policy-making. However, not all matters can be dealt with by Parliament, and it is common practice to delegate important issues of policy to executive and administrative bodies at different levels and in different forms. At the highest levels, cabinet ministers, other ministers, and their senior advisers and officials determine policy issues, while at the lower levels, administrative officers may discover pockets of policy in implementing statutory schemes. Some aspects of policy-making are open and responsive to public participation, but many others are hidden from the public and resolved without reference to it. When members of the public do become involved in the policy-process it is usually by organizing as interest groups, and in the course of this Chapter the activities of such groups are shown to have a vital role in policy-making.

It is important in understanding the policy-making process to realize that in Britain and other European countries (and probably elsewhere) most policy is made through informal procedures and networks which often evolve over a long period and which often have no formal legal basis. These informal procedures and networks provide the arena for interest-group activity, and within them practices become settled and understandings established between groups and government agencies. In some areas of policy-making more formal procedures are laid down. One example in Britain is the public inquiry; another is the rule-making process. The public inquiry may itself take various forms, but it usually means that a special board or official is given the task of inquiring into an issue, and either deciding it or making a recommendation to a minister for a final decision. Public enquiries are a common feature of British administration, ranging from such local matters as whether planning permission should be granted for development in a village, to truly national issues, such as the future of the nuclear energy industry. Rule-making is another form of policy-making familiar in modern government. It usually consists in a minister or other authority formulating the rules to regulate an area of activity. The processes through which this form of policy is made are variable and diverse, the public inquiry itself sometimes being an important part of it. The legal character of rule-making also ranges from formal, delegated legislation expressly authorized by statute with set procedures to be followed, to informal rule-making by an authority in the exercise of its discretion.

Policy-making in these different settings raises issues of procedural fairness. The main concern in deciding policy should be to act for the common good, although that is itself a complex notion which needs to be examined further. At the outset, however, the general point may be that, while the interests and claims of individuals and groups are ingredients to be added to the cauldron of policy-making, the final decision should reach beyond particular concerns to a broader sense of the interests of all. If the general aim is to make policy for the public good, the question then is whether duties are owed to persons and groups as to how that aim should be achieved; in other words, what are the standards of fair treatment of persons and groups in the policy process? In order to identify those standards, we need to examine the relationship between the citizen and the state in its application to policy-making; the nature and content of the standards of fair treatment will then point the way to fair procedures.

An initial objection might be raised that there simply are no principles of procedural fairness in policy-making. Since policy-making bodies act under authority delegated by Parliament, the argument would be that, in a democratic system based around a representative and responsible parliament, any principles of procedural fairness should be confined to participation in the macro-political process. Parliament takes its authority from that process and although it might delegate parts of its policy-making authority to other bodies, each remains accountable to it. Such an argument draws some support from the centrality of Parliament and the principles of ministerial accountability to Parliament, but ultimately it is far from persuasive. Many areas of governmental policy-making are in practice largely free of the checks and controls of the political system. The parliamentary system remains at the centre of the policy process and provides a system of scrutiny and account, but it is not able in practice to cover all policy-making, whatever its forms and wherever it occurs.

In order to provide a more complete system of accountability and responsiveness, the political, parliamentary system needs to be supplemented by other principles and processes. It is important, therefore, to consider the normative framework within which policy-making occurs and to identify the standards of fair treatment within it. On the basis of those standards good and fair procedures can be devised, which will help in turn to regulate the policy process and make it legitimate. We should be careful, nevertheless, not to claim too much for procedural fairness in its more specifically legal forms. The political process itself is based on a notion of how government ought to work and of the place for participation by citizens, which itself constitutes a framework of normative standards of fair treatment. The very notion of democratic participation includes a notion of what is fair treatment and what procedures should be built on it. Many issues of fair treatment are best treated at the political level, and it should not be thought that every shortcoming of the political system should be corrected by a legal form of remedy. Indeed, the policy process straddles the boundaries between the political process and the legal, and one of the difficulties is to know whether an issue is suitable for legal treatment or best left to the political process. With this note of caution in mind, I shall now go on to examine the policy process in more detail and then consider the meaning of fair treatment and procedural fairness within it.

15.1.2 The Context of Policy-Making

First, a brief word should be said about the legal categories of policy-making. General policy decisions can be divided into two broad legal categories according to the nature of the outcome of each. The first is where an issue has to be decided by considering the best course of action in the circumstances. Whether to build a new road or perhaps close an old one; whether to grant a licence to broadcast or to operate another service, such as an airline or nuclear-power generator, where the consequences for the public are considerable, are typical examples of decisions involving matters of general policy. They require attention to considerations of a social and economic kind, where there is clearly no right answer, where opinions may differ sharply, and where a number of possible solutions might be both open and defensible. The other category of policy decisions is different. Here the object is not to decide a specific issue in that sense, but to formulate a set of standards which will be the basis for deciding particular cases and issues in the future. In order to set the general standards, which I shall refer to as rules (loosely speaking), policy choices have to be taken, again often of a far-reaching social and economic kind. And while Parliament and the executive acting through Parliament are the principal rule-makers, a host of other bodies is involved in the rule-making process; in short, rule-making by subordinate authorities is an integral part of modern government.

Rule-making itself can be divided into two categories: the more formal process of delegated legislation, on the one hand, and the informal processes which result in guidelines, policy statements, circulars, etc., on the other hand. These categories are not to be taken too strictly, since it will not always be clear whether a rule falls within one or the other. The first category, which I shall call formal rule-making, means rules which are made under parliamentary authority and which are required to be laid before Parliament and to be subject to its scrutiny. The duty to lay may arise under the general provisions of the Statutory Instruments Act or by express provision in the parent statute. The duty to lay delegated rules before Parliament arises under the Statutory Instruments Act if the parent statute states that the rules should be made by way of statutory instrument.[3] Independently of that general provision, a statute which delegates the power to make rules also may provide that they should be laid before Parliament. The second category of rules I shall refer to as informal rules. These are rules made by administrative bodies under powers delegated by Parliament, but which are not normally subject to the laying requirements. The parent statute might delegate expressly the power to make rules, but often the administrative

[3] For more detail on the laying requirements, see J. Beatson and M. A. Matthews, *Cases and Materials on Administrative Law* (2nd edn., Clarendon Press, Oxford, 1989).

body, assuming it has the authority to do, simply draws up rules and guidelines about how it will exercise its powers. In the latter case, the process followed in making the rules is often left to the administrator's discretion, and, like the rules themselves, may escape both statutory controls and scrutiny by Parliament. Around each of these categories, numerous variations can be found, with some rules falling somewhere between the very formal processes and the very informal.

The different contexts within which rule-making (particularly informal rule-making) occurs, and the different kinds of standards resulting have been much discussed in recent years. K. C. Davis was one of the first to advocate the structuring of discretion through the setting of general standards of varying normative categories, including guidelines, policy statements, directives, and expressions of intention.[4] Other writers, stimulated by Davis' ideas, have attempted to give a fuller analysis of the different types of standards. R. Baldwin and J. Houghton offer a comprehensive taxonomy,[5] while the work of C. Diver has been important in matching different kinds of standards to different tasks and contexts.[6] Writers like these have made a significant contribution in showing that the rules in rule-making are actually of various kinds and that each can have distinct and specific functions according to its context: sometimes strict rules are appropriate, while at other times a set of looser guidelines is more suitable.[7] However, while keeping in mind the fluid nature of rule-making and the variety of rules which results, it is enough for present purposes to have in mind a clear case of the two main processes, one where rules are made in a structured legal environment, the other operating in the twilight of discretion and in the virtual absence of legal constraints.

The institutions and officials responsible for policy-making are also many and varied in their characters and powers. In addition to cabinet and ministers of state, who are at the centre of the process, policy is made by a diverse range of statutory agencies and regulatory bodies. Notable examples are such bodies as the Gaming Board, the Health and Safety Executive, and the Office of Fair Trading. Each had distinct policy-making functions, sometimes with ministerial supervision and control, at other times with substantial autonomy.[8] Recent studies of agencies in the financial services industry[9] and

[4] K. C. Davis, *Discretionary Justice* (Louisiana State University Press, Baton Rouge, La., 1969).

[5] R. Baldwin and J. Houghton, 'Circular Arguments: Status and Legitimacy of Administrative Rules' [1986] *Public Law* 239.

[6] C. Diver, 'Policy-Making Paradigms in Administrative Law' (1981) 95 *Harvard L Rev.* 393.

[7] See further J. Black, 'Which Arrow? Rule-Type and Regulatory Policy' in D. J. Galligan (ed.), *Socio-Legal Readings in Administrative Law* (Clarendon Press, Oxford, 1996), and Galligan, *Discretionary Powers*, (Clarendon Press, Oxford, 1986), sect. 4.1.

[8] Case studies of these agencies are set out in R. Baldwin and C. McCrudden (eds.), *Regulation and Public Law* (Weidenfeld and Nicholson, London, 1987).

[9] J. Black, *Regulators as Rule-Makers* (Clarendon Press, Oxford, forthcoming).

of the Civil Aviation Authority[10] have provided interesting accounts of such matters as the kinds of authorities involved in policy, the relationship between an authority and its policy tasks, the influences which shape policy, and the relationship between such agencies and government. The idea that only ministers make policy, or that only ministers should make policy, has long been abandoned as unrealistic in practice and uncompelling in principle. Indeed, there are often good reasons for delegating policy-making to subordinate bodies; a certain distance from the political process can itself be an advantage, and the need for expert and specialist knowledge, which administrative bodies often have, can be good reasons for policy-making at administrative levels.

Whether policy-making can be separated clearly from policy-implementation is another issue upon which opinions differ. The established view is that any such line is bound to be artificial, that even the clearest rules bring with them a web of discretion, and that where there is discretion there is also policy. A recent attempt to challenge that view, and to revive the distinction between making policy and implementing it, is at the centre of the trend towards the fragmentation of government by the creation of the Next Steps Agencies. The claim behind this trend is that ministers should make policy and agencies should implement it.[11] However, the distinction is difficult to sustain, the better view being that elements of policy occur at all levels of government and administration, whether it be in the making of primary legislation or subordinate rules, or their implementation.[12] The distinction does, however, have advantages not least in drawing attention to the fact that administrative institutions are concerned in general with the implementation of legislation where the greater policy issues have already been settled at the political level.

Issues of implementation, it has been said, are mainly concerned with detail, technique, and administration;[13] although what is a matter of detail or technique from one point of view can have significant consequences from another, and it would be wrong to underestimate the importance of policy issues at the implementation level. Moreover, while the big issues of policy are difficult to influence, specific groups and interests are often closely affected by policy details and may have a real chance of shaping the implementation process.[14] The main responsibility for implementation usually lies

[10] R. Baldwin, *Regulating the Airlines* (Clarendon Press, Oxford, 1985).

[11] On Next Steps Agencies see P. Greer, 'The Next Steps Initiative: An Examination of the Agency Framework Document' [1990] *Public Administration* 89 and P. Kemp, *Beyond Next Steps* (Social Market Foundation, London, 1993).

[12] Further discussion can be found in W. Grant, *Pressure Groups, Politics and Democracy in Britain* (Philip Allan, London, 1989), 63–4; J. J. Richardson and A. G. Jordan, *Governing Under Pressure* n. 1 above, 137–53; J. L. Pressman and A. Wildavsky, *Implementation* (University of California Press, Berkeley, Calif., 1973).

[13] S. E. Finer, *Anonymous Empire* (2nd edn., Pall Mall Press, London, 1966).

[14] See S. A. Walkland, *The Legislative Process in Great Britain* (Allen & Unwin, London,

with the departments and agencies, which in practice have substantial autonomy from Parliament and cabinet, and sometimes even from the responsible ministers. The departments and agencies will normally have well-established relationships with interest groups, and issues about implementation normally will be settled within those networks.

Turning to the forms and procedures for making policy, we at once confront a considerable diversity. The choice for American lawyers in formal policy-making is between the procedures associated with rule-making and trial-type adjudication. That means a choice between notice-and-comment procedures and the procedures directed at settling policy issues in the course of a trial-type procedure about how to decide a specific issue.[15] Notice and comment procedures are based on giving notice of the terms of the proposed rule, including information about the material and evidence being relied on, and the method of analysis employed. The public should be invited to make representations, which the agency must in turn deal with in its statement of reasons for the final form of the rule.[16] Trial-type procedures, on the other hand, mix together policy-making and adjudication. Here the procedures are those of the adversarial trial, with parties, evidence, examination, and argument, where the object is to settle both the cases in question and a wider policy issue. The policy made in one case will then apply in later cases. Both these procedural forms are frequently used and their respective merits are much debated.

The procedures followed in making policy in the United Kingdom are less clearly defined. On the one hand the notice-and-comment approach is often adopted in one form or another, while on the other hand the public inquiry into a specific issue tends to become adversarial and trial-like. In the absence of a general code of procedures, everything depends on the relevant statute and it is not unusual to find significant variations around the two dominant forms.[17] It is difficult to discern a set procedural pattern with respect to such matters as the giving of notice, the imparting of information about policy proposals, the means and extent of consultation with interested parties, and the nature of the reasons given.[18] It is also common enough, particularly in statutory agencies, to find policy being made in the course of adjudicative procedures; but again the procedures, while broadly trial-type, vary from one context to another,[19] and, it ought to be noted that the distinction

1968), ch. 5; G. C. Moodie and G. Studdart-Kennedy, *Opinions, Public and Pressure Groups* (Allen & Unwin, London, 1970), 74–7.

[15] Administrative Procedure Act 1946, s. 4.

[16] See M. Asimow, 'Delegated Legislation: United States and United Kingdom' (1983) 3 *Oxford JLS* 253.

[17] A fuller account of those variations can be seen in G. Ganz, *Administrative Procedures* (Sweet and Maxwell, London, 1974).

[18] Some of that variety can be seen in the case studies contained in Baldwin and McCrudden, n. 8 above.

[19] R. Baldwin's study of the Civil Aviation Authority's licensing decisions is a good example of trial-type procedures: Baldwin, *Regulating Airlines*, n. 10 above, 143 ff.

between notice-and-comment and trial-type procedures has never been as important in the United Kingdom as in the United States.

The debate about the respective merits and demerits of those two forms of policy-making can be linked to deeper currents in the literature and to wider theoretical issues.[20] The image of the policy-making authority collecting information, analysing the problem, considering possible solutions, and then arriving at a conclusion reflects the idea of comprehensive planning.[21] There the assumption is that the social world can be fully comprehended and general standards to deal with problems formulated. Social realities are in practice rather more unruly than this idea allows, so that grander versions of comprehensive planning have to be modified to take account of inadequate knowledge, overbearing complexity, and imperfect judgment. The idea of being able rationally and effectively to deal with an issue through general standards nevertheless remains firmly at the hub of policy-making. An alternative, which also runs deeply in administrative theory and practice, is incrementalism, that is, the step-by-step approach dealing with specific issues as they arise, deciding only those issues, and in this way, over time, developing a stream of policy. Cautiousness, responsiveness to concrete issues, and the flexibility it leaves for the future are said to be the strengths of incrementalism. Its natural link to the adjudicative approach and the trial-type procedure is clear to see. While examples can be found of them both, the very informal nature of administrative policy-making in the United Kingdom usually means that some form of notice-and-comment is preferred to trial-type procedures, with the former often themselves being highly informal and variable.

15.1.3 The Role of Interest Groups

Policy-making is at the heart of government and administration, whether it be the major legislative issues debated in Parliament or the relatively minor and sometimes technical matters settled in the lower echelons of administrative bodies. Wherever it occurs, policy is finally for determination by government or administration, in a manner which is responsive to the needs and wishes of the community. The question which then begins to take shape is how the concern for effective policy-making can be matched with the equally important concern that the process be responsive to the community generally and to those affected by it in particular. This leads us on to consider the normative principles which ought to govern the policy-process and to the procedures suitable for giving effect to them. Such processes would include the means for gaining information about what is proposed, for allowing those with an interest or concern to put their point of view, and to

[20] For a fuller account, see Galligan, *Discretionary Powers*, n. 7 above, 117 ff.

[21] See further J. Black, *Regulators as Rule-Makers*, n. 9 above.

have some influence on outcomes; they should also include processes by which the policy choice would be explained with reasons and facts. Inherent in this image is an acceptance that most issues of policy cannot be settled by popular consensus but that hard choices have to be made; it is at the same time a rejection of the notion that the citizen's influence on policy should begin and end with the occasional vote.

Before examining these normative and procedural issues, it is important to take account of the major impact of interest-groups' activity on the policy process. It has two main elements: the first is to give certain groups and interests an advantage by belonging to policy communities from which others are excluded; the second is the creation of an environment in which policy is settled by informal negotiations between interest groups and administrative authorities. In order to understand these two elements, we must briefly explore the role of interest groups.

Interest groups play a major role at all levels of politics and administration; the lone individual may still through his efforts exert some influence, but a more accurate image of modern societies is one which puts interest groups rather than individuals at the centre of policy-making. The idea is that organized groups, whose interests are likely to overlap and conflict, compete for status and influence across the policy process.[22] The very point of interest groups is to influence the policy process, and their influence is such that the efforts of individuals are normally most effective if directed through them. Interest groups are many and varied, with several thousands operating in the United Kingdom, including voluntary organizations and charities, trades unions, companies and firms, churches, professional bodies, and consumer-protection groups. Bodies such as the Church of England, the Institute of Economic Affairs, the Royal Automobile Club, and the Cats' Protection League have little in common except that each represents a group of people with certain interests, each trying in its own sphere of concerns to influence government policy. Interest groups have numerous aims, but the one common to all is their concern to influence policy.

Amongst the various methods of classifying interest groups, the distinction between sectional groups and cause groups is especially useful.[23] Sectional groups represent members of the community with a common interest, which is typically but not inevitably of an economic kind. Groups of employers and employees are common examples, as are various trade and professional bodies. Cause groups, on the other hand, advocate a set of beliefs or principles; they have a cause to advance, whether religious, ethical, charitable, or

[22] The literature on interest groups is enormous, but the following are especially helpful on their role in the UK: Moodie and Studdart-Kennedy, *Opinions, Policies and Pressure Groups*, n. 14 above, and G. K. Wilson, *Interest Groups* (Blackwell, Oxford, 1990). On the European dimension, see C. Harlow, 'A Community of Interests: Making the Most of European Law' (1992) 55 *MLR* 331.

[23] See the discussion by W. Grant, n. 12 above.

environmental. The membership of different groups may overlap and any one person is likely to be a member of several. The division between sectional groups and cause groups is not watertight, since a sectional group may also seek to advance a cause, and a cause group might include sectional interests. But generally any group will fall clearly within one category or the other.

Another useful distinction relevant to policy-making is between insider and outsider groups.[24] As W. Grant has put it:

> Insider groups are regarded as legitimate by government and are consulted on a regular basis. Outsider groups either do not wish to become enmeshed in a consultation relationship with officials or are unable to gain recognition. Another way of looking at them is to see them as protest groups which have objectives that are outside the mainstream of political opinion.[25]

In short, insider groups, which may be sectional or cause groups, are part of the network within which policy issues are resolved; they have a close and complex relationship with a department or administrative agency, and are likely to influence policy directly and regularly. Their interests will be well-known to departmental officials, and the inter-relationship between groups and departmental officials will ensure that the interests of the former are taken seriously.

Indeed, the notion of a policy community sums up the relationship between administrative agencies and interest groups.[26] Government and administration divide into a set of policy-making arenas or committees, each with a department or agency at its centre around which a number of insider or client groups cluster. Within each policy community, policy-making is a co-operative enterprise between interest groups and the administration. There may be competition and tension between interest groups within a policy community, and the department or agency may finally have to decide amongst competing views; but any insider group can be confident of an active role, a sympathetic reception, and a degree of influence.[27] Being an inside group means, as Grant puts it, the 'four Cs': (i) consultation by the policy-maker; (ii) a desire on the part of the policy-maker to get their consent to policy proposals; (iii) close co-operation between groups and the department; and (iv) continuing involvement of the group in policy issues.[28] Groups on the outside have few of these benefits. They find it difficult to get involved in the policy process, let alone influence it, since the dynamics of the process do not include their interests. There can be movement both into and out of a

[24] W. Grant, n. 12 above, 14–21.

[25] Ibid. 14–15.

[26] See Richardson and Jordan, *Governing Under Pressure*, n. 12 above, 174.

[27] See further Moodie and Studdart-Kennedy, *Opinions, Public and Pressure Groups*, n. 14 above, 71–7.

[28] Grant, *Pressure Groups, Politics and Democracy in Britain*, n. 23 above, 65.

policy community, and outsider groups are in general naturally keen to win entry. Insider groups equally naturally are likely to offer resistance, since the admission of others may dilute their own positions of influence and increase the competition over policy.

As powerful as the notion of a policy community is, it is not the only influence on policy, and other avenues should not be overlooked, not least because they may be more accessible to outsider groups and individual persons. Parliament itself can be used as an instrument of influence on departmental or agency policy. Individual Members of Parliament may act on behalf of interest groups and, once enlisted, the Parliamentarian has open to him a host of ways of bringing pressure to bear on a responsible minister, or in having the issue raised in the House or in a select committee. Resort may even be had to a private Member's Bill, or to a system of lobbying, or to bringing influence to bear within the committee structure of the political parties. And if an interest group can mobilize the support of the media, its efforts on these various fronts may be more successful.

One of the results of interest-group activity, and the policy communities which form around them, is that informal negotiations become a major feature of the policy-making process. Since we know from empirical studies that informal negotiation between the administrative body and the person affected is likely to occur at many points throughout the administrative system, it is no surprise that it is strikingly present in policy-making.[29] Within the context of a policy-community, informal negotiation directed towards reaching agreement amongst the member groups, and between them and the administrative authority, is the natural procedural mode. The tension between the negotiatory mode and more formal procedures is likely to be acute.

Interest groups have a major role in policy-making and any attempt to understand the process without including them would be seriously defective. My present purpose is not to debate whether they are good or bad; they are a fact of political life and their role must be taken into account in constructing standards of fair treatment and fair procedures. Nevertheless, one or two general comments might be made. The first is that there are certain advantages to be gained from interest-group activity. Interest groups bring influence to bear on government and they foster scrutiny of its proposals where otherwise there would be little of either. Membership of a group can provide individual citizens with an opening to the policy process which otherwise would be unavailable or unattainable. However, interest groups also have a negative side. They are unequal in their bargaining power and

[29] For examples of informal negotiations, see B. Hutter, *The Reasonable Arm of the Law* (Oxford Socio-Legal Monographs, Oxford, 1988); K. Hawkins, *Environment and Enforcement* (Clarendon Press, Oxford, 1984); I. Ramsay, 'The Office of Fair Trading: Policing the Consumer Market Place' in Baldwin and McCrudden, n. 8 above.

the more powerful insider groups can exert disproportionate influence. This may encourage a corporatist rather than pluralistic approach to policy-making.[30] Some groups, moreover, become the instruments of their leaders, a powerful medium for advancing their own views, rather than a conduit for the views of their members. Another negative factor is the tendency for interest groups to depreciate individual endeavour by making it difficult for voices lacking the support of a group to be heard. Interest groups may create the impression that, beyond the boundaries of group activity, there are no other legitimate interests or sources of information.[31] These negative factors need to be taken into account in creating standards of fair treatment and procedural fairness.

15.2 THE NORMATIVE FOUNDATION OF POLICY-MAKING

15.2.1 Three Normative Models

The next matter to consider is the normative framework within which the policy-making process ought to be conducted. The normative framework, which will enable us to identify the standards of fair treatment in policy-making should be realistic in taking account of how policy is made in practice, without being simply a mirror of existing practices; for the normative framework should provide standards as to how policy should be made and, where the two diverge, it should be the basis for changing practice. Normative principles and practical policy-making closely influence each other, so that our very conception of the standards which ought to apply may be conditioned by what happens in practice, while practice may be conditioned by deeper ideas of fair treatment. Once an acceptable normative context has been devised, more particular standards of fair treatment can be drawn from it; the emphasis here will be on showing what fairness means in the policy process.

An immediate difficulty is in finding a base from which to begin to construct a normative approach to policy-making. Normative standards should be imbued with the values of a society, but it is not always clear what those values are and it is not unusual to find quite different understandings of what they should be. This problem is acute in analysing the policy process where contrasting accounts of the underlying standards are apparent. Participation by interested parties is clearly one of the main values, but views about

[30] The closer the relationship between particular groups and government, the more a society becomes corporatist, so that the centres of effective power are located within that relationship. For a recent account of corporatism, see D. Held, *Models of Democracy* (Polity Press, Cambridge, 1987), 201–5, 214–20.

[31] See further Moodie and Studdart-Kennedy, *Opinions, Public and Pressure Groups*, n. 14 above, 95–6.

the point and worth of participation are themselves notoriously divergent. Some of the issues relating to participation are considered in Chapter 5, and the reader may find it useful to refer back to that discussion. Here, however, my approach will be different. Instead of concentrating on the principle of participation, I shall begin with the notion of the common good, in the sense that the aim of policy is to achieve what is good for the society as a whole. An analysis of the common good soon reveals several different conceptions of what it means and what processes are suited to achieving it. Here I shall outline three such models and then argue for one of them as the standard case to be preferred.

The first model of the common good is the most familiar, the one likely to be most in evidence in a modern society. It means the good of the community, all things considered. It carries the connotation that the policy-maker defines the issue, examines the evidence and facts, identifies the different courses open, and then decides as appears best for the overall good. The good of the community is the governing criterion, but that means more than simply the policy-maker's view of what is good; it means that the policy-maker will be guided by a framework of values which has two layers. One layer consists of the timeless precepts of practical reasonableness:[32] the policy maker's approach should be rational, coherent, and consistent; and there should be no arbitrary preferences among courses of action or among persons. We might add that the policy-maker should be well informed, should know the advantages and disadvantages of different options, and should realize that much can be learnt from consulting the people affected. And, finally, the policy-maker's decision should be reasoned and reasonable. The other layer consists of the values specific to the community. Policy is made for the common good when it is made in accordance with the settled, public values of the society, with its charter of principles.[33] The charter of principles does not provide direct answers, but it constitutes the context within which policies must be determined; and in deciding what is best within that context, the official should take guidance from the consequences which different courses of action would have for different parts of the community.

The second normative model of policy-making shows less faith in a notion of the common good as anything more than the accommodation of conflicting interests. The term, 'the common good' might still be appropriate, but it means no more than the outcome which best satisfies competing interests, since beyond that competition and resolution, there is no further sense of the common good. This approach to policy-making is often linked to versions of pluralism which view society as an arena of competing

[32] J. Finnis, *Natural Law and Natural Rights* (Clarendon Press, Oxford, 1980), ch. 5.

[33] See J. Rawls, *A Theory of Justice* (Clarendon Press, Oxford, 1971), 5, and the discussion in sect. 4.4.3.

interests.[34] The task of law and politics is then to resolve conflicts and to satisfy as many of those interests as possible.[35] There are numerous variations, and not all take quite such a minimalist view of social order and the common good; but the idea in its simplest form has had a major influence on writings in public law and politics, especially in the American literature.[36] We need not here go into the many refinements of this version of pluralism, nor subscribe to any particular variation on it, but simply note that the image of competing interests represents one major approach to policy-making. This approach I shall refer to as competing interests approach; within it the main point of procedures is to see that all interests are able to compete in the political market-place, and that the choice of policy reflects and accommodates as many of those interests as possible.[37]

The third approach to policy-making shares with the first the idea that there is a common good to be sought, and that the object of procedures is to lead to that end; it also shares the idea that the common good embraces the interests of those affected, while going beyond them. Indeed, the striking feature of this approach is the belief that the members of a society should be able to agree on what the common good requires in specific situations. That agreement is reached through procedures which encourage discussion, which are open and transparent, and within which popular participation is given special importance. On this approach to policy-making, which is closely associated with both proceduralism and strong democracy,[38] the central claim is that through meetings, discussions, and close involvement, people can reach a higher level of understanding and tolerance; they can also grasp a full understanding of the social order within which their own interests are important but not dominant, being elements of an organic whole rather than self-contained and individualistic.[39] This version of policy-making also draws

[34] There is evidence that this approach continues to flourish in Whitehall: see Richardson and Jordan, *Governing Under Pressure*, n. 12 above, 172 ff.

[35] A good and comprehensive account of pluralism is found in P. P. Craig, *Public Law and Democracy* (Clarendon Press, Oxford, 1990), chs. 3–6.

[36] For a review of the literature, see ibid.

[37] A literature critical of the approach is ever-growing. Some of the more telling criticisms are seen in R. Stewart, 'The Reformation of Administrative Law' (1974–5) 88 *Harvard L Rev.* 1667; G. Frug, 'The Ideology of Bureaucracy in American Law' (1984) 97 *Harvard L Rev.* 1276; and C. Sunstein, 'Beyond the Republican Revival' (1988) 97 *Yale LJ* 1539.

[38] Amongst the many texts which espouse a sense of strong democracy and, consequentially, a view of the common good through agreement, the most noteworthy are B. Barber, *Strong Democracy: Participatory Politics for a New Age* (University of California Press, Berkeley, Cal., 1984) and C. Pateman, *Participation and Democratic Theory* (Cambridge University Press, Cambridge, 1970). The strongest version of the common good through agreement is probably that based around the idea of communicative action put forward by J. Habermas in *Theory of Communicative Action* (Beacon Press, London, 1984). For a helpful account of the theory, see A. Brand, *The Force of Reason* (Allen and Unwin, Sydney, 1990). On proceduralism, see secs. 1.2.4 and 1.3.4.

[39] One practical example which comes close to the consensual model is the British Advisory Conciliation and Arbitration Service in its rule-making capacity: see L. Dickens, 'The Advisory Conciliation and Arbitration Service: Regulation and Voluntarism in Industrial Relations' in Baldwin and McCrudden, n. 8 above.

on a view of citizenship: the real citizen is not only interested in his own good, but wants genuinely to understand what is for the good of all, and to act accordingly. Participation and involvement are directed partly to finding the common good, but they are also partly a process of learning for the participant. It is through participation, through hearing the other side, and through the cross currents of debate, that citizens come to see beyond their own interests and develop a sense of the good of all. This approach will be referred to as policy-making through consensus.

15.2.2 The Respective Merits of the Three Models

Although there are important differences between the first model and the third, they share much common ground, since both have a view of the common good as going beyond narrow sectional interests. The main differences between them are twofold. One is that, while the third version insists on consensus as to outcome, the first version accepts that people of goodwill, guided by the two layers of values, may still disagree on what should be done, so that the need for a decision by someone in authority is essential. Such decisions can be accepted as authoritative and for the common good even by those who would have preferred a different course, provided that the decisions are made in accordance with certain standards and principles. The other point of difference between the first and third versions of the common good lies in procedures. The role of procedures on the first model is to ensure that the official makes a decision which best advances the common good, all things considered, but where at the same time the interests and concerns of the community and the various groups within it are the elements from which a conception of the common good is constructed. The common good is realized, in other words, through a structured process which enables the spectrum of interests and opinion to be revealed through involvement and participation, and which ensures that the spectrum is properly reflected in the outcome. The role of procedures on the third model builds on the first but is much more exacting, for procedures here are inextricably and indispensably linked to the process of reaching agreement. The participation by citizens is, on this account, the engine of transformation for both citizens and the society, and since agreement depends on that transformation, participatory procedures are essential to it.

Each of these three models contains a view of the relationship between the citizen and the state in policy-making. It also contains a view of the relationship among citizens who are, in a sense, competing against each other in the policy process. From that foundation, more particular normative standards can be devised for each model, and in turn from those standards, which include ideas of fair treatment, guidance can be taken in developing procedures. But before building on that foundation, a brief comment should be made on the respective merits of the three approaches. Of the three, the common good as competing interests is the least attractive. It rests on a view of society as a market place of competing interests and yet offers no normative basis for choosing amongst them. The result is that either the more powerful interests prevail or the decision-maker covertly appeals to some external principle. The former offers an unsatisfactory basis for ordering society, while to adopt the latter by relying on an external standard would be to introduce a view of the common good which goes beyond competing interests and so undermines the model itself. Threadbare as the first model is, however, it often accurately reflects what happens in practice, so that one of the enduring problems for administrative agencies is to prevent the most powerful groups dominating the policy process.

At the other end of the spectrum, the sense of seeking the common good through agreement appeals to noble ideals: it has a vision of participatory democracy and citizenship; it offers a solution to the most acute problems of social order, to the alienation of groups and individuals from government and policy; and it shows how the instinct always to advance and prefer our own interests might be overcome. There are, however, difficulties with this approach. Some of these were considered earlier, but perhaps the major drawback is that this splendid vision, which is suited to a society much simpler than our own, when placed in the harsh and complex conditions of modern societies, soon fades. It fades because it cannot cope, and even if it could, we might be reluctant to accept that social order should depend entirely on the momentary consensus of shifting alliances. This is not to say that more discussion, participation, and agreement are to be shunned. On the contrary, they should be encouraged and many of the procedural features of the third model could usefully be transferred to the standard model and might well enhance it.

This leaves the standard model, the idea that policies should be for the common good, where the common good is achieved through authoritative judgments formed in a structured environment. The model is both attractive and realistic. It is realistic in the sense that policy-makers in practice do try to justify their decisions by appeal to the common good; no matter how distorted their understanding of the notion may sometimes be. Some notion of the common good remains the touchstone of legitimacy and authority. The model is also attractive because, while recognizing that the common good is the guiding light, it acknowledges that final agreement may be impossible and that a decision has to be made by someone in authority. Far from being a mere act of will based on the power of the official, each policy decision is formed in a crucible of values and principles, and within that crucible the interests of those affected are recognized as both obligatory and legitimate materials from which to mould the common good. Without the cynicism of the second model or the naïve idealism of the third, the standard model responds to the true conditions of a society which is mixed in composition and yet which seeks to develop some sense of unity and coherence. For these reasons, the standard model is the most normatively compelling of the three, and so will receive most attention in the following discussion.

15.3 FAIR TREATMENT IN POLICY-MAKING

Within the normative context of the standard model of policy-making, the task is to consider how groups and individual persons should be treated. That means examining further the notion of the common good in order to understand that part of it which refers to the rights of persons in the policy-process; such an enquiry is in turn another way of asking what are the standards of fair treatment of persons in administrative policy-making. Once the standards of fair treatment have been identified, more specific procedural principles can be formulated. It is interesting to note that the issue of procedural fairness or due process in policy-making has received little attention, even though groups and individuals can be seriously affected in their rights and interests.[40] The decision to build a major new road, or to change the rules for distributing social welfare or the allocation of resources within the health services, or the policies governing parole, are a few instances of the innumerable ways in which marginal changes of policy may wash across a pool of rights, interests, and concerns, where the consequences for those affected can be direct, immediate, and serious. Here I shall begin the enquiry into what procedural fairness means in these contexts, while recognizing, however, that there is ample scope for a much fuller study in the future.

15.3.1 Standards of Fair Treatment

One way of approaching the issue is to ask what are the expectations a person or group might reasonably have as to how the policy process should proceed and how the person or group should be treated within it. The first principle likely to emerge is that while everyone naturally hopes for an outcome most favourable to them, such an outcome cannot normally be regarded as something to which one is entitled. The very idea of a policy choice is that different interests are likely to be in competition, where the claim of one has no priority over the claim of another, and where the policy-maker has to form a judgment as to what is best, all things considered. Hard choices have to be made from which some will gain and others will lose. The

[40] An important recent book which deals with some of the issues of procedural fairness in policy-making is R. Baldwin, *Rules and Government* (Oxford Socio-Legal Studies, Oxford, 1995).

first principle, then, is that people affected by a policy have no right that the policy should have any particular content.

The first principle, however, is not unqualified. For although it is unlikely that anyone will have rights to the content of a policy in general terms, policies should be formed to ensure the rights deriving from other sources are respected. The sources of such rights might be constitutional, legislative, deriving from common law, or, increasingly in the United Kingdom, from European law or the European Convention on Human Rights. To take some examples, policies about the running of a prison must respect the prisoners' rights to communicate with their solicitors; policies about the retirement age of women must comply with legal principles of equal treatment; and policies restricting the payment of unemployment benefits to students must be subject to any rights they have under statute. Once we think of examples like these, it becomes clear that policy-making, especially at the administrative level, is subject to a great range of legal restrictions. A fundamental principle of fair treatment is, accordingly, that policy-making shows respect for rights arising under such rules and principles, unless the policy-maker has the authority to alter them. This idea may be extended beyond principles of creating legal rights to principles of a general moral kind. Ideas about liberty, fairness, and equality, about respect for persons in areas concerning privacy and just compensation, are examples of the deeper foundation of principles which informs and qualifies policy-making. Such principles might not have the status of legal principles and, therefore, questions about their precise role in policy-making may be difficult to answer. They are, however, vital in developing the idea of a charter of basic standards with reference to which all policy is made. We may conclude that the first principle of fair treatment should be modified to include respect not only for legal rights, but also for other important moral or social principles prevailing in the society.

While the first principle is primarily a source of restrictions on policy-making, there is a second principle of fair treatment which applies directly and positively to the formulation of policy itself. The second principle is reached by asking how we may move from the general idea that the interests and opinions of individuals and groups should be elements in the policy process to formulating one or more standards of fair treatment. Drawing on my earlier discussion,[41] I suggest that the general idea here can be expressed in three more specific principles: the first that the interests and opinions of all should be considered, the second that all should have opportunities to participate in the policy process, and the third that the process should be open. These three principles are still open-textured, but they constitute the normative boundaries within which more detailed principles can be devised in different contexts. They also constitute the three basic principles of fair

[41] In particular, the right to consideration is discussed in sect. 3.2.4, the right to participation in 4.4.

treatment in policy-making.[42] The main rationale of the principles of participation and consideration is that citizens are given the opportunity of influencing political events, a rationale which holds good for many issues of general policy. A second, stronger basis for citizens being involved in the policy process is also contained in my earlier discussion: participation in particular is closely linked not just to influencing specific policies, but also to the social and moral principles which constitute the normative context of policy-making. Participation is concerned with the development of those principles, and in being satisfied that policies comply with them. This approach to participation is especially important in developing a sense of the common good, since, by being involved, the citizen learns to judge policies against a framework of principles, rather than against sectional interests.

It follows that the principles of consideration and participation carry great weight in the policy process. It might seem that the case for the two principles rests on the advantages it brings to the overall society, rather than on a principle of fair treatment of persons. However, on close inspection, it can be seen to rest on both. The advantages to society are clear: by taking account of the interests and concerns of citizens and, by allowing the involvement of citizens in the policy process, better policies may result. Although the relationship between involvement and outcomes can be complex and hard to assess, one of the qualities of a good outcome is simply that it takes account of and is influenced by the views of citizens. In addition to the gains to society collectively, there is also a dimension of fairness to individuals: the citizen has a claim of right to be considered and to be involved, and the basis for the claim is the opportunity to help shape the laws and policies of the society. The opportunity need not be taken, but the right to do so is fundamental; it is an expression of the idea that each of us is an autonomous and moral agent, an idea which carries with it the right to mould our lives, to live as we think best, not only in the private sphere but also in the public. The opportunity to shape the public sphere through influencing both the moral framework of society and its specific policies is a direct emanation of that right. For these reasons, the failure to consider the interests and concerns of citizens, or the denial of involvement in the political process, would be unfair to the person as well as a loss to society.

While the principles of consideration and participation express the two main standards of fair treatment, there is a third principle which is closely associated with the first two, but which is sufficiently central to fair treatment to warrant special attention. The normative idea here is that policy-making should be an open process, by which is meant citizens should know about it and have access to it; it should be conducted in public so far as possible, with relevant evidence and other information readily available, and a proper explanation and justification given for the course of action chosen.

[42] See sect. 4.4.3.

15.3.2 Fair Treatment in Context

The principles of participation, consideration, and openness constitute the foundational standards of fair treatment in policy-making. They create rights in citizens with respect to the policy process, although the rights are general and abstract and need to be made more specific and precise in different contexts. The next question to consider is how those rights can be made more specific in different contexts and at different levels of policy-making. My analysis so far has been based on the idea that each person has certain rights in the policy process as a citizen; in presenting that analysis, the image may have been created of the policy process as a series of discrete decisions in which citizens could participate as they wish. We must now try to relate these general ideas more closely to the realities of policy-making by taking account of several factors: to the extent that citizens become involved in the policy process, it is generally through group activity; groups vary in the nature of the interests they have in the policy process; and policy-making occurs at different levels in government and administration.

The first of these draws attention to the fact that, while the lone campaigner is still a familiar sight, involvement in the policy process is usually through group activity. The nature of groups is itself an interesting issue, but in this context it may be taken to mean the combination of individual persons in order to pursue a common cause. Each person combining in this way brings whatever rights he has as a citizen to be involved in the policy process and in a sense transfers them to the group; the group for its part has no rights other than those brought by its members.[43] The second factor to build into the policy process is that groups have different interests and the interests they have vary as to their importance. The notion of an interest is notoriously difficult to analyse satisfactorily. One distinction is between interests in the sense of goods that are valued, and interests in the sense of things one is interested in. In the first sense, I have an interest in receiving an increase in salary which is different from my interest (in the second sense) in an area of natural beauty not being destroyed by the construction of a road. The distinction is similar to that made earlier between groups acting for sectional interests and for cause, although in both cases one sense of interest may become difficult to separate from the other.

If we accept that the interests people have are enormously diverse in their nature and importance, the next question is how that affects rights to participation and consideration. The answer is again complex, but one or two

[43] This is not to say that groups never have rights which are distinctively group-rights; it is only to suggest that with respect to interest-group activity, the rights to participation and consideration normally derive from the rights of the individual persons constituting the group. For discussion, see A. M. Honoré, 'Groups, Laws and Obedience' in A. W. B. Simpson (ed.), *Oxford Essays in Jurisprudence* (Clarendon Press, Oxford, 1993).

general principles can be suggested. The first principle is that a person's right as a citizen to participation and consideration in the policy process does not depend on having particular interests. Each person has such a right *qua* citizen without having to show more; while the policy-maker for its part must hear and consider all interests. The nature and importance of the different interests at issue will naturally affect the way that the policy-maker considers them, but at this general level there is no need for differentiation of procedures on the basis of interests. The second principle is that a person or group may have interests affected by a policy proposal which warrant special consideration and which give them rights to fair treatment in addition to their general rights as citizens. The claim now is that, since this person will be affected in a direct and significant way, his or her relationship with the policy-maker has a special character. The idea is familiar in law where the person who has a special interest compared with the rest of the community is often accorded a special status and consideration.[44]

What amounts to a special interest and whether the consequences are serious enough may be difficult to state in the abstract, but generally in practice the distinction is fairly apparent. The farmer whose land is about to disappear under a reservoir, the child whose school is on the verge of closing, or the prisoner who sees his hopes of imminent release on parole dashed by a change of policy, all have a special interest. The special interest in turn creates a special duty of fair treatment which goes beyond the citizen's right to be involved. Now while this seems correct intuitively, the reasons for according more exacting rights of fair treatment to those with a special interest is not always clear. The most satisfactory justification appears to derive from the principle of equal treatment: the person with an interest which is additional to that of people generally and which is vulnerable in the face of changes of policy faces a risk of special loss. To ignore that special interest and the potential harm to it, to treat that person in the same way as others in deciding on the common good, would be to demonstrate a lack of equal concern for all.[45] If this is a convincing reason for special treatment, and I suggest it is, the next question is what exactly is the special treatment that ought to be provided. The answer is not that further principles of fair treatment should be added to the three given above, but rather that their application should be more clearly focused on the special case and more exacting in considering it. The principles remain the same, but their meaning and content, and the procedures for implementing them, become more stringent.

[44] A striking example is the law relating to injunctions against public authorities, where a special interest over and above that of others has to be shown. Whether the legal distinction between a person's general and special rights is sound in principle requires careful consideration, but I shall not pursue the issue here.

[45] French administrative law well illustrates how this idea can be applied in practice; see N. Brown and J. S. Bell, *French Administrative Law* (4th edn., Clarendon Press, Oxford, 1993).

The third matter is to relate these ideas to the fact that policy-making occurs at different levels of government and administraton. At the highest levels of policy-making, a wide range of factors and interests needs to be taken into account, while at lower levels of administrative policy-making, the issues are more narrowly focused and the range of relevant interests much reduced. To take an example, the formulation of general policy about what conditions should govern the viability of small schools, and when they might sensibly be closed, should attract representations from a wide range of groups and interests. When it comes to deciding whether a particular school should be closed policy issues may still occur, but they are now focused on local factors and the circle of relevant interests is much reduced. Here the principle of selective representation becomes important;[46] it means that groups which have had ample opportunity to make their case at one level of policy-making will not necessarily be entitled to participate at other, more focused levels. The lines should not be drawn too strictly, but as a matter of practical judgment they are not normally too difficult to draw. With reference to the example of school closure, groups with an interest in general educational policy, which have been able to express their views in one forum, have a weak claim to participation in the decision whether a particular village school should be closed. Conversely, a local parents' group which has probably had no involvement in the wider policy debate has a direct and significant interest in the local issue.

It has been possible here to sketch only in broad outline the way that the three factors—involvement through groups, diversity of interests, and different levels of policy-making—help in making more specific the general rights to participation and consideration. The last matter to consider in this section is to give an idea of how the principles of fair treatment would apply to the other two models of policy-making, namely, the common good as competing interests and the common good as agreement. Since the common good in the first consists in the accommodation of competing interests, the main standard of fair treatment is to be able to join in the competition. The parties affected have no claims to particular outcomes, but only that the interests of each should feature in reaching an outcome. Whether fair treatment goes further is difficult to say because the normative foundation of this approach is itself unclear. One possible extension would be that all interests should be treated on an equal footing; if so, procedures would be needed to control the more powerful and support the less powerful. Moreover, since the active involvement of parties in the market place of interests is the main component of this model, the procedural requirements should be that parties are able to put their claims and counter the claims of others, where the decision-maker is impartial and concerned only to reach a decision which provides the best accommodation of the competing claims. This suggests

[46] The principle is explained in Galligan, *Discretionary Powers*, n. 7 above, sect. 7.3.2.

also that the process should be open and that the policy-maker should give reasons which show how interests have been assessed and a policy formulated. The final point about this approach is that there is no room for distinguishing between the general principle of political participation and the principle of consideration; they appear to merge into the single principle that an interested party should be able to compete and to have his interests counted, while the person without interests in the particular issue would have no reason to intervene.

The third model of policy-making, according to which policy should be reached by agreement, also imports its own variations on fair treatment. The central idea is that agreement as to the common good is reached through the involvement of citizens in the process. Involvement is of crucial importance, first because it is the means by which outcomes are reached, and secondly because individuals must themselves be transformed from being inward-looking and selfish to being outward-looking and social. Ideas of citizenship and participation are uppermost, while the usual urge to advance one's own interests is largely overcome. The principle of equal participation provides the basic principles of fair treatment, but its connotations here are wider and richer than on the standard model. Involvement and participation should now be comprehensive enough to lead to consensus, and the object of procedures should be to cultivate an environment in which such a full sense of involvement could be realized.

To conclude, the point in this section has been to identify the standards of fair treatment in relation to the policy process. There are three: consideration, participation, and openness. The three principles vary greatly in their application to specific contexts, depending on whether a person's claim is as a citizen or as the bearer of a special interest, where the latter is more exacting than the former. There may be other values, such as privacy, which are also relevant to the policy process. The emphasis here has been on the role of these three principles within the standard model of policy-making, but brief comments have been made about their application within the other two models. Now that we have a normative framework within which to develop standards of fair treatment, the next task is to link them through procedures to the practical workings of the policy process as outlined earlier.

15.3.3 Designing Procedures

The principles of fair treatment identified in the last section provide the basis for designing and evaluating procedural standards. Such standards should be directed to applying in the various contexts of policy-making the principles of consideration, participation, and openness. The object of this section is to offer some general remarks about the design of procedures, while in the next section consideration will be given to ways of overcoming the problems posed by interest-group activity, by the tendency to lack of openness, and by informal negotiations between groups and policy-makers. The way is then clear for a study in the next chapter of how these general ideas are applied in a number of legal systems.

In considering the translation of each of the three principles of fair treatment into practical procedures, two questions have to be answered: first, what exactly does each principle require in a given context and, secondly, what procedures are needed to meet those requirements. At an abstract level, the answer to the first question is straightforward: consideration means that the interests and concerns of individuals and groups should be taken into account; participation means that they should have the opportunity to be involved in the policy process, in the sense of being able to submit evidence and present arguments with a view to influencing the outcome; while openness for its part suggests that notice be given, that the proceedings be accessible, that information be available, and that reasons be given. The first and rather obvious point to note is that each principle can be made more or less exacting. Participation may range from the informal written submission to the trial-like procedures of a public inquiry. Consideration might begin with the duty to read the evidence and submissions and end with a full analysis of how each set of materials has been dealt with, how much weight has been placed on them, and why one course of action has been preferred to another. Similarly, openness might be taken at several levels.

The second point to note is that the interpretation of the three principles in specific contexts should be guided by a number of factors, such as the nature of the policy issue in the sense of its seriousness and its effects, the range of parties with an interest in it, the nature of those interests, and the level at which the policy decisions are being made. In giving meaning and content to the three principles at the administrative level, the notion of selective representation will be a source of guidance. The notion, it will be recalled, captures the idea that the principle of participation, and indeed the principle of consideration also, can be satisfied in various ways and at various levels. The determination of what the principles require at one level of policy-making depends on viewing the full picture, including the opportunities available at other points in the policy process. A policy issue which has broad and general consequences would normally warrant widespread involvement: whether to consent to nuclear energy, fundamental reforms of the legal profession, or radical reform of the law governing the press are good examples. When matters like these are delegated to administrative bodies, even if only to investigate and report on them, the principle of participation applies with force. Where matters are more local or limited in their interest, the general principle is more easily met. Whether a local primary school should be closed or new development be allowed on the edges of a village are hardly matters on which the citizenry in general, as opposed to those in the locality, would be expected to intervene. Between these two sets of examples, a range and diversity of policy issues are possible, although the general approach should be clear whatever the issue: application of the general principles is to be gauged by examining the nature of the policy issue and its place in the overall policy process.

Once the content of the general principle has been settled for the policy matter in issue, the second question is how to devise suitable procedures. This means developing procedures which meet the demands of the general principles for the policy matter in issue, while at the same time being economical. The variety of possible procedures is considerable. Sometimes they might follow a trial-like approach,[47] but more commonly the principles will be served by informal and piecemeal methods of notice, consultation, and deliberation. Sometimes an oral proceeding might be necessary, but in many cases consultation through written representations, informal discussions, or investigation by the authority will be enough. The forms and methods are many and the point to stress is that the three principles of fair treatment do not dictate particular procedures but can be satisfied in various ways, according to various procedural regimes. The principle of participation will not normally require a full-scale hearing, but in some of the more important and complex cases it might be the most effective and economical means of resolving an issue. The guiding concern in each area of policy-making should be to enable interested parties, including those with special interests, to have the chance to put their evidence and arguments. The principle of consideration, for its part, points to the need for procedures which guarantee proper attention being paid to the evidence and arguments submitted to the policy-maker. That guarantee will often be best provided through procedures deriving from the principle of openness, since one of the main reasons for openness is to enable the participant and the observer to see how the deliberative process is being conducted. The giving of reasons, which is another aspect of the openness principle, is also instrumental in showing how the different arguments have been dealt with; it also shows how the concerns of different groups have been taken into account and why some have carried more weight than others.

15.3.4 Overcoming the Obstacles to Procedural Fairness

The reader will have noticed that the two currents running through this chapter appear to flow in different directions. On the one hand, a normative view of how administrative policy should be made has been proposed, while on the other hand policy-making in practice seems to have a quite different

[47] The Civil Aviation Authority is one agency which tends to develop policy through trial-type procedures: see R. Baldwin, 'Civil Aviation Regulation: From Tribunal to Regulatory Agency' in Baldwin and McCrudden, n. 8 above.

basis. The normative view, moreover, may appear to be based on a vision of society as a collection of independently-minded individuals, while the true engine of policy-making is the interaction between government and interest groups. The question now to consider is how the two might be brought together; that is to say, how interest-group activity, together with the lack of openness and the tendency to informal negotiations which follow in its wake, can be accommodated within the standard normative model of policy-making. The task of bringing the two together is not easy; interest-group activity is a fact of administrative government which cannot be ignored and must be assimilated into a normative approach. At the same time the practice of interest groups should not itself dictate the normative standards which ought to prevail. Each affects the other but we should not expect any perfect reconciliation of the two. The interesting issue to consider here is just how far the two diverge and to what extent adjustments can be made to bring them closer together.

Let us begin by asking exactly what is the relationship between the standard normative model and the realities of policy-making. The first point to note in answering the question is that many aspects of interest-group activity are compatible with at least two of the three principles of fair treatment, namely, participation and consideration. Participation operates at two levels: individual persons participate in interest groups, which in turn participate in the policy process. Individual involvement is one step removed from the policy process, but provided each group is accessible and conducts its affairs democratically, that is not itself a major disadvantage. Provided also that the interest group is able to win its place in a policy community, its involvement in policy-making is likely to be extensive; for not only will it be consulted at many points in the development of policy, it will also influence the agenda in determining what the policy issues are. The principle of consideration is also likely to be satisfied, since abundant evidence exists to show that the views and concerns of interest groups really do count in the formation of policy, from the earliest inkling of a policy issue to its final realization in practice.[48] It is a fact of political life that, in order to develop policies which will be regarded as legitimate and which will be implemented, policy-makers have no choice but to consult interest groups and to be responsive to their views;[49] indeed, it is often necessary for the administrative policy-maker to go beyond consultation and actually obtain their agreement and consent.

The conclusion that participation and consideration are well served by interest-group activity rests on a rather ideal view of how the policy process works; in relating the idea to the reality, we must now propose a number of

[48] The full and rich sense in which interest groups influence policy is well brought out in Grant, *Pressure Groups, Politics and Democracy in Britain*, n. 23 above, and Richardson and Jordan *Governing Under Pressure*, n. 1 above.

[49] See further S. E. Finer, *Anonymous Empire* n. 13 above.

qualifications. The first is that not all groups with an interest in an area of policy are able to participate in its formation. Since the consultative process is highly informal, the group must first gain entry into the policy community in order to be involved. The usual practice is for the administrative body to give preference to sectional groups over cause groups, and even among the former some will find it harder to gain access than others. Groups representing powerful and tangible interests of an economic or financial nature are likely to find entry into the policy community relatively easy and, once admitted, will exercise considerable influence.[50] Two practical points may be drawn from this imbalance amongst groups: first, procedures are needed to open up access to policy communities to all interest groups; secondly, the traditional preference for sectional groups over cause groups is difficult to sustain. Cause groups represent interests and concerns which are central to the policy process and which should not be regarded as necessarily of lesser concern. The environmental impact of a proposal is as relevant to good policy as is its economic consequences; similarly, policies relating to the export of live animals should respond to the concerns of groups dedicated to the welfare of animals, as well as to those of the exporters.

A second qualification relates to the principle of consideration. The conclusion to be drawn from studies of interest-group activity is that membership of a policy community not only secures access to the policy-process, but also guarantees that proper account is taken of the views held by each of the groups within it. The corollary is that outsider groups experience difficulty in having their views properly considered, partly because access may not be available, and partly because even if formal legal procedures make provision for access, such groups may be heard but not listened to. For whatever the formal legal procedures, the substantive issues of policy are likely to be greatly influenced, if not determined by, a different set of informal processes. In other words, the provision of legal forms which open participation to a wider range of groups will not in itself guarantee that their views are properly considered. Procedural innovation should include wider participation, but it must go farther and provide the procedures for ensuring that the views of all interest groups really are taken into account. The gulf between the reality of policy-making networks and the normative standards according to which all groups should properly be considered is wide and not easily bridged. There are, however, practical measures to be taken: processes of consultation can be formalized to enable all groups to participate; the very process of consultation can be made more public and transparent without undermining confidentiality (where it should be preserved); the range of information about policy options provided by the authority to interest groups could be

[50] The influence will sometimes be so great that it amounts to capture of the agency, although the position in the UK appears to be that the influence of groups usually falls short of capture.

extended and made more open; and, finally, the policy-maker could be required to explain how the preferred option has been arrived at and the reasons for it. Measures like these may not entirely remove the gap between normative principles about how policy should be made and the practical reality, not least because of the strength of policy networks and the strong attraction they hold for those within them. Nevertheless, procedures which are responsive to the dynamics of policy-making can have a significant effect in directing them towards a more acceptable approach.

A third matter to consider is the tension between the idea that administrative authorities should listen but then decide, and the natural tendency for the participants within a policy community to negotiate amongst themselves and agree on an outcome. On the one hand the government and its authorities should govern, while on the other hand negotiation and agreement amongst select groups are not only natural responses, but may also add to the authority of the policy-outcome and increase the likelihood of its being implemented. Why then should we be concerned about a high level of negotiation and agreement, since consensus between the government and the governed might be seen as a superior form of social ordering, superior certainly to policy simply being dictated. The reality, however, is neither so obvious nor so simple. Negotiation and agreement in policy-making have a negative side: the more powerful groups will have greater bargaining power; sectional groups are likely to have more weight than cause groups; bargaining amongst select groups often tends towards a corporatist relationship with governments which is distant from the views and concerns of the wider populace; and finally the bargaining process is likely to be informal and hidden from public view.

The tension between the notion that the government and its agencies should determine policy and the reality of informal negotiation and agreement within policy networks is readily apparent but less readily resolved. One response would be to urge the case for better procedures: if the principles of participation and consideration are being overshadowed by negotiation and agreement between administrative agencies and select groups, then the current procedures, or indeed lack of procedures, are not achieving their purpose and should be amended. The logic of this view is that, since informal negotiation is encouraged by the lack of more formal procedures, the introduction of the practical procedural measures proposed earlier would help to reinstate proper regard for the principles of participation and consideration. Such a response is unlikely to satisfy completely the sceptic whose rejoinder might well be that the social factors which foster informal negotiation and agreement will not be tamed by new and better procedures. Procedural changes are easily made, but there is no guarantee that they will harness the deeper social forces at work. This of course touches on the issue of how laws and procedures can ever effectively regulate social practice; but without now entering into what is a vexed and complex issue, my suggestion is that we need not be overly sceptical of the capacity of legal procedures to regulate the policy-process. Once procedural standards and the institutions necessary to oversee them are in place, they themselves become part of the social context and their influence on it will soon be felt. It may be that elements of informal negotiation and agreement will never be completely eradicated; it may be, indeed, that at some level they should be regarded as desirable elements in policy-making, the object of procedures being to harness the process rather than eliminate it. My suggestion is, however, that a commitment to procedural formality, to openness and transparency, to the disclosure of information, and to the need for explanation for and justification of the course chosen, could have a marked influence on policy-making and bring it more into line with the principles of participation and consideration. Here the principle of openness is especially important, since policy communities thrive in an atmosphere which is informal and secretive, which allows relationships between the members to develop incrementally and at various levels, and which encourages diversity and flexibility in approach. The principle of openness poses a direct challenge to that atmosphere of informality.

It is now time to take stock. My purpose in this Chapter has been to identify the principles of fair treatment and fair procedures in policy-making. It soon became clear in the course of the analysis that different understandings can be held about the nature of the process, about its objectives, and about the relationship between the citizens and the state as it applies to policy-making. From those different understandings, which are linked to more fundamental differences about the nature of society and the political principles which ought to govern it, three main models were formulated. Taking the standard model as the most compelling of the three, I then went on to isolate the standards of fair treatment within it. The standards of fair treatment are threefold, namely, participation, consideration, and openness. An outline was then given of how the three principles apply in policy-making and of the procedures needed for their application, the underlying idea being that procedural fairness consists in upholding the principles of fair treatment. Variations in the standards of fair treatment for the other two approaches were then briefly noted. The next stage was to move from the level of abstract models and general principles to consider how they apply in reality, and how the practice of administrative policy-making can be brought into line with normative principles. The task for the next chapter is to examine the legal approaches of policy-making, but with reference to reforms in other jurisdictions, especially the United States and Australia.

16

Legal Approaches to the Policy Process

Now that the context of policy-making, whether on a specific issue or in making rules, has been considered and standards of procedural fairness identified, the purpose of this Chapter is to examine the legal approaches to rule-making within several jurisdictions. The emphasis will be on the policy process in English law, but extensive reference will be made to important variations in the USA and Australia. The method to be followed here is partly descriptive of what the legal approach is in each case, but it is also partly critical and evaluative in judging how well the law meets the requirements of fair treatment and fair procedures. The analysis concentrates on rule-making, both formal and informal, while little is said about policy-making on specific issues. Although the latter does raise interesting issues of procedural fairness, they are similar in principle to rule-making, and in order not to lengthen unduly an already long book, I have left the detailed study of policy-making on specific issues for another occasion.

16.1 FORMAL RULE-MAKING IN THE UNITED KINGDOM

16.1.1 Formal and Informal Rules: A Note on the Distinction

In the following discussion, administrative policy issues are divided into three categories: formal rule-making, informal rule-making, and policy-making on a specific issue. The distinction between formulating rules and deciding a specific policy issue was made earlier,[1] but a word of explanation ought to be offered about the distinction between formal and informal rule-making. The distinction relates not to the content of the rules, but to the legal authority by which they are made and to their legal status once made. Formal rules are made by a minister or administrative body under statutory authority, or possibly in the exercise of prerogative powers, while informal rules are made without express authority, simply as part of an administrative power. Formal rules include various forms of delegated legislation and are

[1] Ch. 15.

usually subject to certain procedures, including laying before Parliament, while it is unusual to find statutory procedures governing the making of informal rules. The two kinds of rules also vary as to legal status: formal rules are binding legal rules, while informal rules are not and have a lesser status. Indeed, it is contrary to administrative law principles to allow informal rules, made in the exercise of an administrative power, to be treated as binding legal rules.[2] Informal rules usually take the form of guidelines, directives, or statements of intention, but they do have some legal consequences. In particular, informal rules may create expectations about how cases will be dealt with and an authority which departs from them may have to extend procedural rights to the parties affected.[3] Although there are significant legal differences between the two rules, the two categories are neither clearly defined nor always easily separated.

16.1.2 Rule-making Procedures

To the observer of the British approach to the making of statutory rules by ministers or administrative bodies under delegated powers from Parliament, two main features stand out. One is that while statutory rules are made by various subordinate bodies, final responsibility rests with Parliament. Exceptions to the principle can be found, but in general Parliament has the power to scrutinize and veto delegated legislation. The other main feature is that no general and systematic procedure exists for the making of subordinate legislation. The constitutional focus is on Parliament, on its powers to delegate rule-making authority and to control it after the rules have been made, not on the rule-making process. After examining these two features more closely, I shall consider the legal constraints on the rule-making process itself. Whether the system as a whole meets the requirements of procedural fairness can then be examined.

In delegating legislative powers to administrative bodies, Parliament has complete authority and may impose whatever procedures it wishes. Once subordinate legislation has been made, Parliament has wide powers to examine it, to require that changes be made, or through its powers of veto to declare it null. Its role in exercising the power of veto has been much discussed.[4] The normal practice is that delegated legislation should be laid before both Houses of Parliament for a certain number of days before coming into effect in order to give members the opportunity to scrutinize its terms and possibly move for reference back or even a veto. The laying

[2] *British Oxygen* v. *Minister of Technology* [1971] AC 610.

[3] For a fuller discussion, see G. Ganz, *Quasi-Legislation* (Sweet and Maxwell, London, 1987) and R. Baldwin and J. Houghton, 'Circular Arguments; The Status and Legitimacy of Administrative Rules' [1986] *Public Law* 239.

[4] A useful survey is J. Beatson, 'Legislative Control of Administrative Rulemaking: Lessons from the British Experience?' (1979) 12 *Cornell Int. LJ* 199.

requirements were introduced in the nineteenth century and, with the increase in delegated legislation, have been developed and extended through a series of statutory and internal parliamentary measures,[5] the object in each case being to increase Parliament's control. Without here looking into the history and detail of those measures, it is enough to note the main features of current procedures. First, most rules are required to be laid before the Houses of Parliament so that Members may raise issues about them.[6] Secondly, the Joint Scrutiny Committee considers all delegated legislation to see whether or not it has been laid before Parliament. Matters within the exclusive jurisdiction of the House of Commons, usually matters of a financial kind, are examined by a select committee. Scrutiny by these committees is largely confined to matters of form and technique. Thirdly, a standing committee, known as the Merits Committee, was recently introduced to review and report on the merits of statutory rules. Fourthly, in general, either House of Parliament may annul delegated legislation which had been laid before it.

These procedures taken together appear to invest Parliament with an impressive system of scrutiny and control of delegated legislation. The reality, however, is less impressive, with the full use of Parliament's powers being hindered by a number of factors: rules are not generally published in advance of being laid; little, if any, consultation occurs between the administrators and departments making the rules and Parliament; and, finally, the sheer volume of rules being produced makes effective scrutiny of both form and merits difficult.[7] It is hard enough for the committees to master the material; it is even harder to get matters before the House for debate. The committees have no power of annulment of their own and can only recommend and propose to the House; indeed, neither the committees charged with technical matters nor the Merits Committee appear to have realized their potential as effective forms of scrutiny.

Moving now to the process for making rules, the first thing one notes is the absence of a general and systematic legal framework. Rules are made by ministers and their departments and by a number of other administrative and statutory bodies. The power to make formal statutory rules depends entirely on the parent statute, which also in the main dictates the procedures to be followed. The general provisions for publication apply to most rules,[8] while the laying requirement is also of fairly general application. Beyond that, matters of procedure in making rules are left to the parent statute.[9]

[5] For a detailed account of the measures, see ibid.

[6] There is no general laying requirement, but it is usual for provision to be made in the parent statute.

[7] For further discussion, see H. W. R. Wade, *Administrative Law* (6th edn., Clarendon Press, Oxford, 1992).

[8] Statutory Instruments Act 1946.

[9] An interesting case study of rule-making in the form of a code can be seen in C. McCrudden, 'Codes in a Cold Climate' (1988) 51 *MLR* 408.

Some statutes conferring legislative power impose no procedures to govern its exercise, and leave the matter to the discretion of the administration. However, modern statutes usually specify the procedures to be followed, and while the procedural variation is extensive, certain distinctive patterns can be detected.[10] One is that where a group is directly affected, provision is often made for objections to be lodged against draft rules. Once objections are made, different courses might be followed: the minister might be required to take the objections into account, or the objections might be the trigger for a public inquiry, or some other form of hearing where interested parties may put their views. An alternative pattern appears where the minister is required to consult certain interests before drafting the legislation, although he will normally have discretion as to whom he consults. This often means consulting the representatives of special groups or organizations or advisory bodies, such as the Law Society, the United Synagogue, or the British Medical Association, although there may also be scope for individuals to make their views known. Consultation is often informal, although different elements of formality may be introduced, one of the more common of which is some form of hearing. Less common patterns of procedure occur where the legislative rules are initially drafted by a special advisory or representative body, with power in the minister to amend; alternatively, the minister may draft the regulations and then submit them to a special body for its comments and recommendations. Such special bodies in turn have various ways of consulting interests and ascertaining public opinion. Within each of these patterns, considerable scope for procedural variation and differences of emphasis is still possible. It is interesting to note that a recent report of a committee of the Hansard Society stresses the importance of consultative procedures in relation to the working of delegated legislation and proposes a set of guidelines which would apply to both primary and delegated legislation.[11]

Where the parent statute fails to specify the procedures to be followed in rule-making, the subordinate authority must proceed as it thinks best. It might adopt procedures which include the publication of working papers, the opportunity for notice and comment, consultations, and the taking of expert advice. There is no set pattern, however, with different rule-making bodies proceeding largely according to their own lights. Some procedures are reasonably formal, while others are entirely informal, reflecting the rule-maker's attitudes and preferences rather than systematic principles. Here the informal networks, which we have seen are deeply ingrained in the

[10] See J. A. G. Griffith and H. Street, *Introduction to Administrative Law* (5th edn., Pitman, London, 1973), 126–35.

[11] Report of Hansard Society Committee, *Making the Law* (Hansard Society, London, 1992), 40–2.

British system, play a major role in the creation of legislative rules. Some argue that these networks work well, although how that is known in the absence of hard evidence is another matter. The claim is often made that informality, pragmatism, and the ability to tap currents of opinion are characteristic of British public life and its special genius. It is often added, moreover, that overall the system works well.[12] The earlier analysis of interest-group activity and the closed nature of policy networks gives good cause for questioning those claims, although it is clearly a matter on which more empirical evidence is needed. In any event, the perception that the British system of informality works well appears to have been sufficiently strong to warrant its transplantation to other parts of the world.

16.1.3 The Role of the Courts

The role of the courts in the procedures of rule-making is severely limited. In accordance with constitutional principle, subordinate legislation may be reviewed by the courts on the ground that it falls outside the scope of statutory authority.[13] There is also scope for review on the grounds of bad faith, improper purposes, and unreasonableness,[14] while the position relating to procedural fairness is less clear or settled. Where statutory procedures are laid down for rule-making, the courts may be asked to decide whether the authority has complied with them. If, after examining the statute, the court concludes that the procedures are mandatory, it will insist on compliance and may then have to determine whether there has been compliance. So, where the statute requires consultation, the court may have to decide whether the procedures followed have been sufficient within the terms of the statute.[15] If the question of who should be consulted is left to the rule-maker's discretion, the court should satisfy itself that the discretion has been exercised according to legal principles. The guiding principle for the courts in doing so is that they are interpreting and giving effect to the governing statute. Where no statutory provision is made for rule-making procedures, the courts must look to the common law.

The common law in this regard is rather threadbare, since the courts have been unwilling to develop a jurisprudence of procedural fairness in rule-making. Lord Reid gave the lead in *Ridge* v. *Baldwin* in distinguishing

[12] This appears to be the attitude not only of commentators, but of the professional rule-makers themselves. See M. Asimow, 'Delegated Legislation: United States and United Kingdom' (1983) 3 *Oxford JLS* 253 at 262.

[13] For the general approach of the courts; *McEldowney* v. *Forde* [1971] AC 632; *Kruse* v. *Johnson* [1898] 2 QB 91.

[14] *Kruse* v. *Johnson* n. 13 above; *Re Toohey, ex parte Northern Land Council* (1981) 38 ALR 439.

[15] e.g. *R.* v. *Secretary of State for Social Services, ex parte Association of Metropolitan Authorities* [1986] 1 WLR 1.

between individualized decisions and general policy decisions, with the primary question in the former being how a person should be treated and in the latter what should be done in the public interest, all things considered. The policy-maker will have 'to consider all manner of questions of public interest, and, it may be, a number of alternative schemes'.[16] Nothing in Lord Reid's words suggests an intention to deny the need for procedural fairness in rule-making, his only point being that the rules of natural justice, which evolved in relation to individualized decisions, should not simply be transferred to the policy sphere. Policy-making raises its own issues of procedural fairness to which careful consideration should be given, without being overly influenced by the rules applicable in individualized cases. But while the way was left open for developing doctrines of procedural fairness in rule-making, the courts have not ventured down it. Instead, the scope for creating a jurisprudence of procedural fairness in this context seems to have been foreclosed altogether. In the later case of *Bates* v. *Hailsham*,[17] Megarry J thought that, in the absence of statutory provisions, there was no 'implied right to be consulted or to make objections'.[18] If this is meant to signal a denial of any right to fair procedures in rule-making, the judge gave no reasons to support his view; he gave no reasons why, as a matter of principle, an individual person, who is interested in or affected by a new rule, should have no right to fair treatment and fair procedures. If this is indeed what Megarry J meant, his view is not only unsupported but is unsupportable for the reasons given in the preceding chapter.

While the conclusion in *Bates* v. *Hailsham* appears to be that individuals and groups have no rights to fair treatment in rule-making, it is difficult to find other cases where the courts consider the matter.[19] Indeed, the courts might take one or other of two approaches: one would be that there are no principles of fair treatment in rule-making, the other that, whether or not there are, legislative processes are beyond the proper scope of judicial supervision.[20] Although the courts do not always separate the two approaches as clearly as they might,[21] and since there are no cases in which a full analysis is offered as to what fairness means in rule-making, it may be

[16] [1964] AC 40.

[17] [1972] 1 WLR 1373.

[18] That view appears to have been confirmed as correct by Lord Oliver in *Leech* v. *Governor of Parkhurst* [1988] 2 WLR 290 at 321.

[19] A majority of the Australian High Court touched on the issue in a case dealing with policy matters relating to a parole decision: *South Australia* v. *O'Shea* (1987) 73 ALR 1. The issue there is analogous but not exactly the same.

[20] This distinction is well made in a helpful article by G. Craven: 'Legislative Action by Subordinate Authorities and the Requirement of a Fair Hearing' (1988) 16 *Melb. ULR* 569 at 570–7.

[21] Consider the reasoning in the following Australian cases: *Salemi* v. *Mackellar (No 2)* (1977) 137 CCR 396; *FAI Insurances* v. *Winneke* (1982) 151 CCR 342, and *Kioa* v. *West* (1985) 159 CCR 550. Discussion of the issue in the English cases is virtually non-existent.

concluded that the main reason for declining to intervene is that matters of fairness in that context are for Parliament, not the courts. If this is the most plausible explanation of the judicial approach, then we should pause to consider the deference to Parliament argument.

The deference to Parliament argument has clearly weighed heavily on the courts in their choosing to play a minor role in relation to rule-making procedures. The argument really has two parts: one is that as a matter of constitutional authority, Parliament ought to provide for rule-making procedures; the other part is of a functional kind and rests on the idea that the courts are unsuited to the task of designing rule-making procedures. Both parts taken together constitute a convincing basis for Parliament (and on occasions administrative bodies acting under delegation) being responsible for procedures; but, at the same time, it does not follow from acceptance of the argument that the courts should be excluded altogether. It is interesting to note that a similar argument can be used, and indeed was used earlier in the century, to restrict judicial review of administrative actions generally.[22] Fortunately the argument did not hold sway and judicial review of administrative action has become a dynamic area of judicial creativity, not least in relation to procedural fairness. Similarly, the objection should not be accepted as a legitimate barrier to judicial involvement in rule-making, for there is no good reason why the courts should not be able to develop principles of fair treatment in this context and translate them into suitable procedures. One of the benefits of the courts doing so would be that such principles would reflect back on Parliament and its advisers and influence the initial design of statutory schemes.

On the assumption that the courts have a legitimate role in relation to fair procedures in rule-making, the next question is what their role should be. One approach would be to accept, first, that Parliament is responsible for the initial design of procedures and, secondly, that since the policy issues inherent in rule-making are close to the political process, any procedural scheme formulated by Parliament should carry a presumption of adequacy. The presumption should apply particularly to the principle of participation where the object is to provide access to the policy process for individuals and groups on a broadly equal footing. The principle could be satisfied through various procedural approaches, and it is best that the procedures be devised and imbalances corrected within the political process itself. But even here there may be clear and serious cases where it becomes apparent that a person or group has been unfairly excluded from participation in the process; it is hard to see any persuasive reason why in such cases the courts should not declare the exclusion to be unfair.[23]

[22] See the discussion in D. J. Galligan, *Discretionary Powers* (Clarendon Press, Oxford, 1986), 220–8.

[23] The courts already have experience in interpreting statutory provisions dealing with

In deciding when to intervene by way of judicial review for denial of participation, the courts might take some guidance from the distinction between persons or groups with a special interest in the issue and those who seek to be involved simply as citizens. Since it is only persons or groups with a special interest (using the term to include cause as well as sectional interests) who normally want to be involved, this distinction may not be all that helpful in practice. But while the courts might sensibly take the view that questions of general participation as citizens are best left to Parliament, that reason is less compelling when a person or group with a special interest appears before them. The courts are then in familiar territory and the case for judicial scrutiny is strong. The English courts have not so far entered into this issue, but a ray of light, albeit a flickering ray, can be seen in the Australian experience. In their general approach to procedural fairness in rule-making, the Australian courts are close to the English in tending to leave such matters to the legislature.[24] However, they have taken a step towards recognizing that a special interest might attract judicial protection. In *Bread Manufacturers* v. *Evans*,[25] the High Court considered whether an association representing the manufacturers of bread was entitled to be consulted prior to an order being made by the Prices Commission regulating the price of hamburger buns. Whether the decision is better classified as one of rule-making or deciding a point of general policy is not important; the issue for the court was whether the manufacturers' association had such a special interest that it ought to have been consulted. The court found the association's interests no greater than that of various others affected by the order, and concluded that it had no right to be consulted in any special manner.

In its recognition that the courts should be involved in issues of procedural fairness in rule-making and general policy, the decision is a step forward.[26] Its less appealing aspect is the requirement that the special interest must be over and above that of anyone else. The restriction is unjustified, and the better approach would have been to hold that anyone with a special interest was entitled to be consulted. It is difficult to see a good reason for insisting that, in order to be heard, the special interest of one must be greater than that of another. For this reason *Evans* is only a chink in the courts' traditional approach, but it does at least open the way to judicial review for lack of procedural fairness and the restriction it imposes could easily be shed. Even if that step were taken, it would only be the beginning with

consultation in rule-making; they are also used to enforcing undertakings to consult before making rules or other decisions of general policy. An example is *R.* v. *Liverpool City Council, ex parte Liverpool Taxi Drivers' Association* [1972] 2 QB 299.

[24] See *Salemi* v. *Mackellar (No. 2)*, n. 21 above, at 45; and *Kioa* v. *West*, n. 21 above, at 620.

[25] (1981) 56 ALJR 89.

[26] See also the New Zealand case: *Licensed Victuallers' Association* v. *Price Tribunal* [1959] NZLR 167.

questions such as what constitutes a special interest and what level of participation would be required for different interests, still to be considered.[27]

If the courts were to involve themselves in issues of participation in rule-making, the extension of review based on the principles of consideration and openness would follow easily. The basic idea of consideration is that the arguments and interests of those affected should be taken into account: it does not mean that their views will prevail, but only that proper attention should be paid to them. That is a task for which the courts appear well suited. It involves scrutiny of the rule-making process to see what evidence has been presented, what arguments have been submitted, and then how they have been dealt with by the rule-maker in reaching its decisions. The courts' scrutiny of consideration would be facilitated in turn by the principle of openness, for openness ensures that disclosure is made of the evidence and materials relied on, and that a reasoned account is given by the rule-maker showing how the information and arguments have been dealt with. The main reservation about judicial scrutiny of these matters is that the courts risk being embroiled in the very substance and merits of policy issues. Once they begin to delve into the procedures of rule-making, the distinction between procedure and substance soon disappears, leaving the courts stranded in a landscape where there are few features by which to plot their proper course. A lesson might be learnt from the American courts, which, having entered that landscape, experienced difficulty in stopping short of almost dictating the result.[28] But while it is important to be warned of the risks, that is not itself a sufficient reason for the courts' deciding to enter into the rule-making process. Judicial review of administrative action of any kind forces courts to draw lines based as much on common sense and political realism as on principle. Rule-making processes may be one step closer to the heart of government, but it is not clear why our faith in the courts being able to cope with the clash of law and political reality in administrative contexts generally should be lost when they turn to administrative rule-making.[29]

16.1.4 Procedural Fairness on the British Model

How well does the British approach meet the requirements of procedural fairness? The claim that it does so adequately rests on two main pillars. The first relies on the idea that Parliamentary democracy is the basis of the British constitution and that rule-making under delegated powers, being subject to final scrutiny and rejection by Parliament, fits neatly within that

[27] For a thorough analysis of these issues, see G. Craven, 'Legislative Action by Subordinate Authorities', n. 20 above.

[28] The American experience is considered in sect. 16.2.

[29] The example of *Bushell* v. *Secretary of State* [1981] AC 75 demonstrates well the capacity of the courts to navigate their way through politically-charged waters.

idea. Since Parliament always has the power to call for the amendment of formal rules or even to reject them, the procedures by which they are made are relatively unimportant. Different versions of parliamentary democracy are available, but in the British version legislative rules made by subordinate authorities draw their legitimacy from Parliament, in the sense that Parliament confers such powers and then oversees their exercise. But while the principle of parliamentary democracy is a potent source of legitimacy, it does not connect directly with procedural fairness. In order to make the connection, it would have to be assumed that Parliament would only approve subordinate rules which had been made according to sound procedural principles. The discussion of parliamentary scrutiny makes clear that any such assumption would be largely unwarranted. Since the principle of parliamentary democracy does not itself guarantee procedural fairness, we must invoke a second argument, namely, that in practice attention has been paid to the rule-making process, and in an informal and piecemeal way, ideas of participation through consultation, consideration, and openness, have become integral to the system. Formal legal and constitutional recognition may be lacking, but the reality is that a fuller and more exacting notion of participatory democracy has quietly crept into the system.

The argument is, in other words, that by a mixture of law, practice, and convention, rather than according to a comprehensive legal framework, the legitimacy of delegated legislation is no longer based just on its link to parliamentary democracy, but also draws on wider notions of democracy, citizenship, and participation. The idea is implicit in administrative rule-making that those affected by policy decisions should have their interests taken into account, and that the policy process should be open, intelligible, and capable of reasoned explanation and defence. A reasonably strong case could then be made for concluding that the combination of parliamentary scrutiny and the procedures followed in rule-making, diverse and unpatterned though they be, satisfies the requirements of procedural fairness. If the test is that, in realizing a sense of the common good, the interests and claims of those concerned and affected should be properly taken into account, then the British model could be regarded as reasonably successful. Advocates of the interest representation model would find unsettling the diversity of British practice and the hit-and-miss approach to representation, since the success of that model turns on all relevant interests having ready access to the decision-process and on there being a carefully structured framework for representation. Similarly, those in the strong democracy camp, where full and unhindered participation is essential, would also find much wanting in the unco-ordinated basis of the British approach. On the standard model, however, such criticisms are less telling; all that is needed there is that the voices of concerned citizens and interested parties be heard, by whatever means, and properly considered. The evidence of policy-making by administrative bodies lends some support to the claim that overall the British system, for all its informality and diversity, achieves just that.

On closer scrutiny, however, the British approach to procedural fairness in rule-making displays several shortcomings. The lack of system and co-ordination is one, which means that there is no guarantee of any of the elements of procedural fairness being met in a particular case. Whether particular groups or interests are consulted can be a matter of chance, and the informality of the system may lead to consultation being selective and partial. The result often is that instead of being open and public, rules are made behind closed doors and in secret. Since administrators do not have to explain or justify the rules they make, we cannot always be sure that the range of opinions and the various interests are properly taken into account. Informality and diversity are commendable, provided the rule-making process takes place within a clear framework of basic laws and principles, while the absence of such a framework is a serious defect. If we add to that the imbalances which follow from intense interest-group activity and the formation of policy communities, the absence of a general and systematic framework for rule-making compounds the inadequacies of the present system. A second defect, related but more serious, is an apparent lack of interest in the very idea of procedural fairness. One can search in vain for clear public recognition that rule-making by administrative bodies is an integral part of modern government, that it is at least one step removed from the parliamentary process, and that it raises issues different from that of parliamentary legislation. Parliament in its watchdog role takes little interest in how the rules are made and, in general, the courts consider rule-making to be outside the common law principles of procedural fairness, so that any initiative to extend the principles to rule-making must come from Parliament. Often Parliament does take the initiative in respect of particular statutes, but the process is haphazard. The rule-makers themselves may have a good sense of procedural fairness, but in the absence of a suitable legal framework, their main concerns will naturally be to make the rules as quietly and efficiently as possible, and the additional costs of additional procedures will not readily or voluntarily be assumed. The British approach certainly falls short of the procedural standards which a commitment to the standard model would entail.

16.2 RULE-MAKING IN THE UNITED STATES

16.2.1 The General Approach

Anyone who considers the British system altogether too informal and haphazard will find the American approach a welcome relief. For although rule-making procedures across the federal and state systems are diverse, they occur within a structured legal framework. Here I shall concentrate on federal rule-making, but the same approach applies in many of the states. The due process clauses of the Federal Constitution do not apply to rule-making,[30] but the federal Administrative Procedure Act 1946 sets out a statutory scheme of procedures. The scheme is complicated and provides for numerous options, amongst which the notice-and-comment procedure of section 553 is of most interest for the present discussion.[31] Under this procedure, notice of the proposed rule must be published and interested parties given an opportunity to comment. These are minimum requirements which are often supplemented by more exacting standards in specific statutes. They are at the same time general standards which can usually be satisfied by a diversity of procedural arrangements, such as consultations and conferences, presentations and inquiries.[32] Sometimes an oral hearing is held, but that is unusual. The Administrative Procedure Act does not attempt to dictate uniformity, and its minimum standards may be added to by the parent statute or by agency practice. An agency has discretion to dispense with the standards if it has good reason to think they are impractical, unnecessary, or contrary to the public interest, although it appears that the dispensing power is rarely used.[33] The notice-and-comment procedure does not apply to certain kinds of rules, including interpretative rules, general statements of policy, and rules of agency organization and practice. Some argue that the exemptions are unwarranted, since there is no satisfactory way of distinguishing between rules which are exempted and those which do attract the notice-and-comment procedure.[34]

Notice-and-comment procedures are often referred to as informal, and are distinguished from formal procedures. Formal procedures, which are sometimes required for rule-making under the Administrative Procedure Act, mean a trial-type hearing closely modelled on court adjudication. Since the American usage of these terms does not correspond to the British, I shall

[30] See note, 'The Judicial Role in Defining Procedural Requirements For Agency Rule-making' (1974) 87 *Harvard L Rev.* 782.

[31] Americans distinguish between informal and formal rule-making, but it does not match the way these terms are sometimes used elsewhere. The distinction in America turns on the procedure to be followed. Informal rule-making refers to the notice-and-comment procedure, while formal rule-making is reserved for those relatively few cases where rules are made by following an adjudicative procedure. Notice-and-comment is the normal procedure; the adjudicative process must be followed only if so stated by the parent statute. For discussion, see K. C. Davis, *Administrative Law Treatise* (West Publishing, New York, 1979), i, ch. 6.

[32] For further discussion of the procedural diversity, see ibid. A good summary of rule-making procedures is in W. F. Fox, *Understanding Administrative Law* (2nd edn., Binder, New York, 1992), ch. 7.

[33] See note, 'The Judicial Role in Defining Procedural Requirements for Agency Rule-Making', n. 30 above.

[34] For a comprehensive analysis, see M. Asimow, 'Public Participation in the Adoption of Interpretive Rules and Policy Statements' (1977) 75 *Michigan L Rev.* 520.

use the fuller titles notice-and-comment and trial-type procedures. The parent statute, under which an agency takes its powers, determines which of the two types of procedure is to be followed, while the relative merits of the two types have been the subject of prolonged debate.[35] In practice, notice-and-comment is the procedure most commonly used.

In order to bring out the distinctiveness of American rule-making, it is necessary to go beyond this skeletal account of the statutory procedures and examine some of the background factors. In the first place, rule-making tends to take place within administrative agencies which are very different from the British ministerial department or statutory body. The American agency is a creation of statute and takes its powers from statute, but it is well removed from direct control by the executive or the legislature. The agency is not accountable to either for the rules it makes, and within the scope of its powers is a genuinely independent legislator. The assumption made in Britain that rule-making is an adjunct to Parliament's functions and takes place under its supervision, is absent from the American experience. American agencies are not only relatively independent bodies, but they often have to decide more important issues of policy than their British counterparts. For these reasons, there has been a greater concern to formalize the procedures of American agencies. A second factor is that the American courts generally play a more active role in government and administration than in Britain. This is reflected in rule-making, both in the way that procedures tend to reflect the judicial trial, and in the interventionist role of the courts in exercising judicial review. Judicial activism in this context can be attributed partly to the existence of a general procedural framework and to the statutory standards it contains; it is also partly because American courts generally take a more active role in public law. They are at their most vigilant when the formal, trial-type procedures are used in rule-making, but judicial supervision also extends to notice-and-comment procedures. Here the aim of judicial review is to see that notice has been given and that interested parties have had the opportunity to comment. The courts are vigilant in ensuring that the right of citizens to participate in rule-making under section 553 of the Administrative Procedure Act are upheld.[36] Some commentators argue, however, that the courts ought to go beyond this minimum requirement and devise a more complete sense of procedural due process in rule-making.[37]

[35] See e.g. H. Friendly, 'Some Kind of Hearing' (1975) 123 *U Pa. L Rev.* 1267 and M. Shapiro, 'The Choice of Rule-Making or Adjudication in the Development of Agency Policy' (1983) 92 *Yale LJ* 1487.

[36] For a fuller account of the judicial role, see D. J. Gifford, *Administrative Law: Cases and Materials* (Anderson, U.S.A., 1992), ch. 7.

[37] E. R. Sinaiko, 'Due Process Rights of Participation in Administrative Rule-Making' (1975) 63 *Calif. LR* 886, 907 ff; R. Stewart, 'The Development of Administrative and Quasi-Constitutional Law' (1977) 62 *Iowa LR* 720, 731 ff.

A third factor in comparing the American approach with the British concerns the respective roles of interest groups. The impression is often given that American interest groups are more powerful and better organized, and have a greater impact on rule-making than the British. America, after all, is the home of a pluralist vision of government based on ideas of competing interest groups. Many a writer, moreover, is haunted by the spectre of powerful interests capturing a defenceless agency. Whether interest groups do exert a greater influence on policy-making in America than Britain is not at all clear on the evidence;[38] nor is it easy to generalize about the respective extent of agency capture. Interest groups in America are certainly active in overtly pursuing their interests within administrative agencies, and appear only too willing to challenge unfavourable outcomes in the courts. If it is true that agency rule-making in the United States deals with bigger issues of policy than ministerial departments or administrative bodies in Britain, it would follow that interest-group influence on rule-making and policy is likely to be both more direct and more substantial. Subordinate rule-making in Britain does tend to be concerned mainly with detail, technique, and administration, with the important policy issues being settled in cabinet and Parliament.[39] Interest groups still have their influence on the big issues, but often in the informal and covert ways described. On the basis of these three factors, it can be seen that there are marked differences between rule-making in the two systems.

16.2.2 Procedural Fairness on the American Approach

The American approach under the Administrative Procedure Act gives clear but limited recognition to the rights of citizens to be involved in rule-making.[40] The underlying principle of notice-and-comment procedures is that anyone interested can know what rules are proposed and have a chance to make submissions in relation to them. The agency has the final choice of policy, but it is expected to hear and to consider the views of interest groups. At a deeper level, commentators are divided about how agencies should approach their tasks, with some arguing they should aim at the best accommodation of competing interests (the interest representation model), others that they should seek a wider sense of the common good (the standard model). Both models include as a basic standard of fair treatment the requirement that the views of all interested parties should be taken into account and considered on an equal basis. Indeed, it is the concern for equal consideration that explains the dread of more powerful interests exerting

[38] See the analysis by G. K. Wilson, *Interest Groups* (Blackwell, Oxford, 1990).

[39] See S. A. Walkland, *The Legislative Process in Britain* (Allen & Unwin, London, 1968), ch. 4.

[40] See generally E. Gellhorn and S. O. Robinson 'Rulemaking "Due Process": An Inconclusive Dialogue' (1981) 48 *U of Chicago L Rev.* 201.

undue influence over the process. Some commentators urge greater reliance on procedural measures, including more judicial review, as ways of removing any such imbalance. The general idea that all groups should have their views taken into account can be expressed more fully in the two principles of participation and consideration, while both can be made more effective through the principle of openness. Much discussion can be found of the precise scope of these principles in rule-making, and of their relationship with wider notions of political participation.[41] Judge Skelly Wright has likened participation in rule-making to voting, while both participation and consideration are often viewed as aspects of the general principle of political participation.[42] It is also interesting to note that, while American writers emphasize the importance of interest group activity in rule-making, the justification given for such practices is expressed in terms of the rights of individuals, interest groups being simply collections of individuals.

How well then do the notice-and-comment procedures satisfy the three principles of fair treatment? The need for knowledge and access is well met: knowledge of rule-making procedures is available to anyone interested and access is open to all. The relative informality of the process means that interested parties can put their views to the agency in whatever form they wish. The public nature of the notice provisions and the invitation to comment guarantee a certain level of openness, although an agency has no duty beyond that to hold any form of hearing or other proceeding in public. The practice of agencies varies, but the deliberative process for considering and evaluating the evidence and arguments is normally left to the discretion of the agency. The material is not normally examined in an open forum, and since the notice-and-comment procedure does not require a reasoned explanation of how the decision was made, there is no way of knowing whether the parties' submission has been seriously considered. As a result, the initial concern for openness is not carried through to the stages of deliberation and decision-making. The impartiality principle also has a problematical role in rule-making. The general issue of impartiality is taken up in Chapter 12, but it is useful to note here some of the difficulties in relation to rule-making. One difficulty is how an agency can reconcile its own commitment to certain policies with the duty to take into account interests and arguments which point in a different direction. Another aspect of impartiality applies to the way the agency deals with competing interests and raises the question of how it can deal with them in an even-handed manner. This aspect of impartiality is especially important on the interest-representation approach, since

[41] As examples, see Sinaiko, 'Due Process Rights of Participation in Administrative Rule-Making', n. 37 above and R. Stewart, 'The Development of Administrative and Quasi-Constitutional Law in Judicial Review of Environmental Decision-Making: Lessons from the Clean Air Act' (1977) 62 *Iowa L Rev*. 720.

[42] See also Asimow, 'Public Participation in the Adoption of Interpretive Rules and Policy Statements, n. 34 above.

favourable treatment of one group or interest is an unwarranted interference in the competition between competing interests. Bias in this sense is also important on the standard model because partiality towards an interest may distort the concern to realize the common good.

The aspect of procedural fairness which appears most problematical in notice-and-comment procedures is the level of consideration. Notice-and-comment procedures guarantee the chance to make submissions, but do not guarantee that they will be taken into account and given due weight. Without that guarantee, the participation of interested parties may be a hollow form. How best to overcome that risk and to secure genuine consideration is not easily solved and has been much debated. One drastic solution would be to adopt trial-type hearings; evidence and argument could be submitted, witnesses examined and cross-examined, findings made, and reasons given. The merits of such an approach have been the subject of spirited debate, although the preponderance of opinion appears to be against it.[43] The main argument in favour is that trial-type proceedings are ideal for examining an issue in all its detail, exposing its advantages and disadvantages and allowing parties a real involvement. The principal argument against is that policy decisions, being complex and many-faceted, are unsuited for resolution by adjudicative procedures. A second argument is that trial-type proceedings are likely to be costly. The trial-type process is used for some forms of rule-making,[44] but, for the reasons given, it is unlikely to become the standard form.

An alternative would be to adopt a middle course between notice-and-comment and trial-type procedures. According to this approach, which is sometimes referred to as a paper hearing,[45] the duties on an agency would be: to give the grounds for its actions in detail; to provide a reasoned elaboration of its decision; to respond in its decision to criticisms and evidence to the contrary given by participants; and to include the documentary evidence and written argumentation in the materials it considers. The effect would be to create a full record of proceedings and to open the way for intense judicial scrutiny. The case for pursuing this middle course is that it has many of the advantages of the trial-type adversary approach, but without the costs in resources and time of oral proceedings. While a fuller analysis of the different approaches is warranted, it is enough for present purposes to note the shortcomings of the existing notice-and-comment procedures and to see that alternative approaches could be taken. The main shortcoming is that the procedures do not adequately serve the principle of consideration

[43] See e.g. G. O. Robinson, 'The Making of Administrative Policy' (1970) 118 *U. Pa L Rev.* 485.

[44] See Fox, *Understanding Administrative Law*, n. 32 above, ch. 7.

[45] R. Stewart, 'The Development of Administrative and Quasi-Constitutional Law in Judicial Review of Environmental Decision-Making', n. 41 above.

which is a fundamental standard of fair treatment; a failure of fair treatment is in turn a failure of procedural fairness.

The final procedural element of fair treatment relates to forms of recourse, that is, the opportunity a party has to challenge a rule. A dissatisfied party may have recourse to the political process to try to win a change or reversal, but the American system has nothing equivalent to Parliamentary scrutiny; once the rules are made by the agency, they will normally be final. One consequence of such limited political scrutiny is that judicial review as a form of recourse assumes a special importance. Part of the courts' supervisory role is simply to uphold the statutory requirements of notice-and-comment; the other part consists in the courts, putting their own stamp on rule-making procedures and in developing procedural doctrines in order to gain better protection of the principles of fair treatment. The legal basis for imposing more exacting procedures on the rule-making process might be the arbitrary and capricious standard, or the general principles against abuse of discretion. More extensive judicial review would mean going beyond the formalities of notice-and-comment procedures and examining the agency's reasoning process. One of the main objects of such review would be for the courts to satisfy themselves that evidence and arguments are more fully considered and that the representations of interested parties are taken into account.[46]

In practice, the scope of judicial review of rule-making has fluctuated. At one period, the Federal Court of Appeal took bold steps to advance the scope of review, claiming that an agency must show through its procedures and its reasoning how it had considered the different interests.[47] In some cases, the courts, acting pursuant to the hard-look doctrine, went farther and took the view that an agency must show that the course taken was the most rationally defensible on the evidence and material before it.[48] Following the Supreme Court's decision in *Vermont Yankee*,[49] it is not now open to the courts to extend the scope of review in this way.[50] The consequence for rule-making is that, in the absence of specific statutory authority, the courts are not entitled to go beyond ensuring compliance with notice-and-comment procedures. An agency which misuses its powers or abuses its discretion will of course be subject to judicial review on the usual grounds provided for in the Administrative Procedure Act, but under present law, the deeper levels of the decision-process itself are exempt from scrutiny by the courts.

[46] This would mean forcing the agency to go beyond the notice-and-comment procedures and adopt hybrid procedures, as they are often called.

[47] See Fox, *Understanding Administrative Law*, n. 32 above, ch. 7.

[48] *Citizens to Preserve Overton Park* v. *Volpe* 401 US 402 (1971) gives an idea of the exacting levels of review being imposed.

[49] *Vermont Yankee Nuclear Power* v. *Natural Resources Defense Council* 435 US 519 (1978).

[50] For comment, see S. Breyer, 'Vermont Yankee and the Court's Role in the Nuclear Energy Controversy' (1978) 91 *Harv. L Rev*. 1833.

To conclude, the American approach to rule-making contrasts sharply with the British. It is based around a settled legal framework, at the centre of which is the notice-and-comment procedure, which in turn is an expression of the importance of procedural fairness in rule-making. However, the system is far from perfect. The notice-and-comment procedure goes only part of the way to ensuring that parties and their interests are properly considered; it guarantees the opportunity to know and to be heard, but it stops short of insisting that the agency show just what consideration there has been and how it can be defended. Similarly, the principle of openness is only partially satisfied, and despite an active and dynamic approach to judicial supervision, the courts have recently drawn back from offering a depth of review which could have insisted on a higher standard of fair treatment of interested parties. However, we must be careful not to oversimplify what is a complex and diverse system. The notice-and-comment procedures are often supplemented by additional statutory requirements, and around the bare bones of the law an informal but organic administrative process flourishes and, in practice, involves interested parties in rule-making to a greater degree than the law requires.

Nevertheless, the American approach, encapsulated in the notice-and-comment procedure, is a half-way house. It sits uneasily between the policy-based nature of rule-making and the trial-type hearing of formal adjudication. Interested parties are guaranteed a limited involvement, but not to the extent of being involved in the actual decision-process or entitled to a full account of how it was conducted. From the agency's point of view, this approach is defensible; it makes sure that by having the submissions of interested parties before it, a full view of the public interest can be taken, without unduly trammelling its discretion finally to decide policy issues as it thinks best. It is important from that point of view to recognize that such decisions cannot properly be forced into the tighter harness of a trial. The point of view of the interested party is understandably different. From that standpoint, the flaw in the process is that notice-and-comment procedures fail to follow through to the decision itself, and so do not guarantee that the process will be rational and defensible. The idea that that further step should be taken lies behind the paper-hearing model considered above. The agency would then need to show exactly how the material had been dealt with and how the decision was reached. It would be an attempt to introduce more exacting standards of reasoning and reasonableness; in doing so, it would open up the decision-process and provide a fuller basis for judicial review. Its final effect would be considerably to enhance the principles of procedural fairness.

16.3 INNOVATION IN AUSTRALIA

16.3.1 Statutory Schemes for Rule-Making

Australian federal and state jurisdictions have traditionally followed the British approach. In the absence of a general legal framework for rule-making, it was left to the parliament of each jurisdiction to make provisions in each parent statute as to the procedures to be followed. Practice varied, with some statutes imposing detailed procedures for consultation, others leaving it to the discretion of the rule-makers. Judicial review was restricted to ensuring that delegated legislation was within the terms of the parent statute and that mandatory procedures were followed. Questions of procedural fairness were not normally dealt with in the parent statute, and so did not come before the courts. Australian judges in general share the view of the British courts that common law principles of procedural fairness should not be imposed on the rule-making process; parliament ought to deal with such matters, and if it does not, the courts can offer no help.

While the courts have maintained this stance, several legislatures have recently introduced a different and highly innovative approach. The states of Victoria and New South Wales, together with the Commonwealth, have adopted a general legal framework governing rule-making,[51] the most interesting features of which can be summarized as follows. The general approach is to place on the minister responsible a number of duties to be performed before a rule is made.[52] In the first place, the minister must not proceed with a proposed rule unless what is to be achieved is made clear; it is also necessary to show that the benefits to the community would outweigh the costs. Costs here include the adverse effects the rule might have on the economy and on various groups and interests in the community. In discharging this general duty, the minister's task is facilitated by a second duty to prepare a regulatory impact statement.[53] A regulatory impact statement should specify the objectives of the rules and the reasons for them; it should include an analysis of the various ways those objects might be achieved, an assessment of the costs and benefits of each, where that includes social as well as economic costs, and, finally, a statement of the consultation programme envisaged. The Minister's third duty is to consult 'appropriate representatives of the consumers, the public, relevant interest groups, and any sector of industry or commerce likely to be affected by the rule'. Finally, the minister is required to give public notice of the proposed rule, stating its objects, advising where a copy of the rule and the accompanying regulatory

[51] Here I shall use an example of the new style legislation, the Subordinate Legislation Act (NSW) 1989.

[52] S. 4 and Sched. 1.

[53] See Sched. 2.

impact statements can be obtained, and inviting comments and submissions from interested parties. Once these duties have been discharged, the minister may make the new rule. The final ministerial duty is to forward to the Regulation Review Committee (RRC) (which is a committee of parliament) the proposed rules, the regulatory impact statement, and the written comments and submissions received on them.[54] The RRC is then responsible for ensuring that the various duties on the minister have been carried out and that the procedures arising under the statute have been followed. Any failure in these matters on the part of the minister should be reported by the RRC to parliament.

This is an interesting and innovative approach. The underlying idea is to introduce into rule-making a more exacting set of procedures and to encourage a higher level of reasoning and deliberation. The idea is also to guarantee that the public interest in general, and the interests of special groups in particular, are properly considered. Implicit in the scheme is a sense of the common good, which includes the welfare and concerns of diverse groups, not just those with strong financial or proprietory interests. The scheme proceeds on the assumption that the welfare and concerns of the community can properly be ascertained only through listening to those affected. Notice that the scheme goes beyond simple notice-and-comment; it enjoins the rule-maker to defend publicly the proposed rules in the light of the representations from interested parties. The final decision whether a rule meets the statutory conditions is left to the minister (a feature which might seem to be a weakness); but the main point of the scheme is primarily to create a set of procedures the effects of which are to make the minister give a reasoned justification for the choice of rules.

Another feature of the scheme is that breach of the statutory duties imposed on rule-making does not result in invalidity. The scheme for making rules is directory and advisory, a set of guidelines, where recourse for breach is to parliament through the RRC, rather than to the courts. The non-justiciable nature of the duties on rule-makers is consistent with the object of raising the standard of rule-making and providing the greater scope for consultation, while at the same time preserving the traditional principle that rule-making is a policy-based, legislative process which is best conducted under the eye of parliament and subject to its sanctions. The statutes make no provision for judicial supervision of rule-making, but it is not out of the question that the courts might be persuaded that some issues arising under the statute are justiciable. It is probably safe to predict, however, that the courts will not see themselves as having a significant role in the new statutory scheme.

[54] The RRC was created under an earlier statute, Regulatory Review Act (NSW) 1987.

16.3.2 Procedural Fairness on the Australian Approach

The new statutory schemes for rule-making show a commitment to the idea that ministers and agencies should take seriously the impact which rules will have on the community as a whole and on groups and individuals in particular. It recognizes that regulatory action is truly in the common good only if it is based on knowing and taking proper account of the likely impact. The approach retains the basic principle that the final decision as to what is best for the common good is a matter of judgment which rightly belongs within the political, policy-making process. The object of the new schemes is not to change that basic principle, but rather to channel and structure the process so that those affected can see how the public interest is advanced, while at the same time being reassured that their interests have been considered, even if the outcome is not what they wished. Fair treatment for those affected by new legislative rules is at the heart of the statutory innovation.

The procedures to be followed in implementing the new schemes appear to be effective in recognizing the centrality of fair treatment. The notice provisions ensure that parties know of the proposals and have an opportunity to participate through consultation. The precise form of consultation is left to the minister, but what form it is to take must be made clear in the regulatory impact statement. From the statement of objectives contained in the regulatory impact statement and the various possible ways of achieving them, an interested party will know exactly what the issues are and should then be able to make relevant submissions. The concern to state clearly the issues to be resolved in making a set of rules should enhance the value and effectiveness of consultation. The importance of openness in rule-making is also clearly recognized in the notice provisions and the publication of a regulatory impact statement. The statute does not require, however, that a public hearing or proceeding of any kind be held, but leaves the matter to the discretion of the rule-maker. A public hearing of some kind might become normal practice, but it is more likely that written submissions will be the usual method of consultation, leaving the rule-maker to deliberate in private. The risk that the open aspects of the process will be undermined by the private deliberation of the rule-maker is to some extent offset by the onerous duties on the minister to justify the proposed rules in the regulatory impact statement. Since the various policy options must be stated, and since any proposal must be defended as the best course of action open, the level of reasoning and explanation should be high. In the course of examining costs and benefits, the minister is expected to show that competing considerations, such as those put forward by interested parties, have been taken into account; the impact statement should also make clear why they have not prevailed.

The principle of impartiality is dealt with later, but we should note here that the elaborate procedures for requiring the rule-maker to justify the course of action proposed should go some way to reducing the risk of bias. As for the principle of recourse, we have seen that the scheme is oriented towards parliament, and the committees of parliament, rather than the courts. To the extent that the provisions relating to notice, participation, and reasons create rights in individuals and groups (and there is good reason to think that they do), recourse for any breach is likely to be confined to the parliamentary process. The character of the statutory scheme suggests that, on such matters, there should be no access to the courts, or to other review bodies, such as the Ombudsman or special tribunals. This may mean that a person aggrieved by non-compliance with the scheme has no effective recourse. A complaint could be made to the RRC, which might in turn recommend to the minister that remedial action be taken, in default of which parliament could be asked to invalidate the rules. It is difficult to predict how parliament would react, but when the occasion arises it will be a good test of how seriously it takes its own commitment to procedural fairness. At this early stage in the history of the new schemes, it appears likely that parliament will intervene only in the strongest cases.

What conclusions can be drawn? The imaginative schemes for rule-making adopted in several Australian jurisdictions are marked improvements on the British approach. By creating a general statutory scheme, parliament in each case has proclaimed not only a real concern to advance the common good through rule-making, but has also made a commitment to the principle of fair treatment of persons. The commitment is in turn put into practice through a set of detailed and exacting procedures. The new schemes also ensure a level of consideration and explanation which goes beyond that required by the American notice-and-comment procedures. Some shortcomings in the new schemes have been identified, but these may turn out in practice to be relatively minor. The most potentially serious is the limited recourse available for breach of procedural rights, in particular the absence of statutory provision for recourse to the courts. It is possible that, despite the silence of the statutes, Australian courts will assume jurisdiction to protect the rights created in the statute through the normal avenues of judicial review. In the hands of American courts with a stronger tradition of intervention, such provisions would be bound to attract judicial review; Australian courts, being closer in attitude to their British counterparts, may well decide that the rule-making process is still outside their competence.

16.4 INFORMAL RULES

16.4.1 The Nature of Informal Rules

The clearest cases of informal rules are where, first, they are made without express statutory authority and, therefore, without statutory guidance as to their content or as to the procedures for making them. A second characteristic follows from the first: in the absence of express statutory authority for their creation, informal rules are unlikely to be subject to any of the normal procedures for parliamentary supervision. Administrative rules of any kind can be drawn to the attention of Parliament in a variety of ways: questions may be raised by Members of either House; a ministerial statement might be called for; a select committee might take it upon itself to examine the rules and practices of government departments or administrative authorities; or the parliamentary commissioner might investigate a complaint in relation to them. Through these various means, any legislative or administrative rule about which a complaint is raised may be brought to the attention of Parliament; but the process is haphazard and piecemeal, with most informal rules escaping any form of parliamentary scrutiny.

The reality is that, throughout the administrative process, rules are made which greatly influence the way statutory powers are exercised, while being largely outside both the knowledge and the scrutiny of Parliament. Such rules are sometimes deliberately formulated, while at other times they emerge from the practical need for an authority to deal with the policy elements which occur in individualized cases. Administrative bodies usually assume that a grant of authority from Parliament to act or to decide a range of matters carries with it the power to formulate policy, to generalize about how things should be done, or to bring an open discretion within an acceptable structure of standards and guidelines. To call these various standards rules is itself misleading. Some exhibit the qualities of a binding rule and might be regarded as rules by the authorities themselves. However, there are legal limits on the extent to which an administrative body may impose rules upon itself without statutory authority.[55] Such rules should not be regarded as rules strictly so called; they are more likely to be presented as guidelines, policy statements, open standards, expressions of intention, or matters to take into account. In administrative practice, the distinction between rules and something less than rules is often ignored, and even in law can be tantalisingly subtle. It is convenient in any case to continue to refer to these various standards as rules to indicate that they have at least some qualities of generality and bindingness.[56]

[55] For an analysis of these limits, see D. J. Galligan, 'The Nature and Function of Policies within Administrative Powers' [1976] *Public Law* 322.

[56] A more complete description of the legal status of informal rules can be seen in P. P.

Informal rules are of interest because they are such a familiar part of administrative processes and because they involve decisions of policy. In that sense informal rule-making is a form of legislative activity. It is important, therefore, to understand how informal rules are made and to examine the issues of procedural fairness in relation to them. But first it may be helpful to give more examples of the kind of rules in question.[57] Perhaps the most common are rules setting out how a statutory power will be exercised. This involves an element of interpretation and a degree of stipulation. Having settled on an understanding of its powers, an authority might then devise criteria for applying that understanding to specific cases. Rules stating the criteria might themselves branch in two directions, one set being for the guidance of those subject to the authority, the other being for the guidance and control of the officials themselves. That is common enough practice; it is also common practice for one set of the rules to be openly available, the other remaining confidential within the bureaucracy.[58] The rules of interpretation and criteria may be surrounded by a variety of lesser rules serving different ends, rules within rules, as they have been called. Such rules can be evidential, setting out how an issue will be approached; they may be directory and recommendatory, showing what should be done by a party in order to satisfy a statutory requirement—how to treat a detainee, or how to satisfy health and safety standards. There may be rules about when the authority will waive the statutory conditions or depart from a settled policy. Such dispensing rules are commonly found in the areas of taxation where the revenue authorities may grant exemptions and concessions from statutory requirements. On the other side of the same coin are rules about the selective enforcement of a power, a device often resorted to by police, prosecutors, and immigration officials. In one sense, these are rules of interpretation and clarification, but they are worth special mention because they are often kept secret within the organization. Another noteworthy category includes rules for the smooth and efficient running of an organization, such as a prison, which in one sense may be very much rules of convenience, but which in another sense thinly veil issues of policy.

These are examples of rule-making rather than an exhaustive list. They show that administrative rules have different functions, are addressed to groups inside and outside the organization, and derive from various sources. Their prevalence suggests that informal administrative rules are an integral

Craig, *Administrative Law* (3rd edn., Sweet and Maxwell, London, 1994), and R. Baldwin, *Rules and Government* (Oxford Socio-Legal Studies, Clarendon Press, Oxford, 1995).

[57] The following classification is based to a great extent on the classification of R. Baldwin and J. Houghton in 'Circular Arguments: The Status and Legitimacy of Administrative Rules' [1986] *Public Law* 239.

[58] C. Harlow and R. Rawlings, *Public Law and Administration* (Weidenfeld and Nicholson, London, 1984), 545.

part of administrative processes. Much has been written about the role of informal rules, and it is worth mentioning in passing the main reasons for them.[59] One reason is the need to develop criteria for exercising discretionary powers or even for exercising powers which are not on their face discretionary. Quite apart from the obvious practical reasons for doing so, it is a basic feature of decision-making in any context that we try to relate specific decisions to general standards. Organizational aspects are another reason, since general rules are ways of controlling and regulating the way officials make decisions within an administrative authority. Rules not only contribute to bureaucratic rationality, but are also instruments of centralized control. A third set of reasons derives from the relationship between the administrative body and those who are subject to its actions. The development of general standards about how a person will be treated is linked to fair treatment, and although the relationship between the two is quite complex, one sense of fairness is clearly served by having decisions made according to settled standards. In addition to these three sets of reasons, there is a fourth which is most relevant to our present concerns; it is that, in the implementation of any statutory power, issues of policy are likely to arise and need to be settled. The scope for policy and the nature of the policies in issue vary according to the administrative context; some are narrow and technical, but others, such as the Home Secretary's power to set the guidelines for parole, raise substantive issues. It might be expected that the most important issues will be settled either at the level of statute or at least by way of statutory rules; but whether or not it is sound constitutional practice, many issues are left for determination through informal rule-making.

16.4.2 Procedures for Making Informal Rules

The first point to note is that informal rules may emerge from two different sources: one is a procedure by which rules are formulated to deal with a certain subject matter; the other is where rules develop in the course of individualized decision-making. With regard to the first, policy-making leading to informal rules has the same characteristics as policy-making generally. The process is likely to be marked by a high level of interest-group activity, by the formation of policy communities, and by negotiations amongst administrative bodies and interest groups. Interest groups will be concerned to influence the content of policies, and it is of little moment to them whether that content is expressed in statute, statutory rules, or informal guidelines.

When we turn from the reality of informal rule-making to the legal framework, it should be no surprise to find little guidance as to how the process should be conducted. There are no general statutory standards and

[59] Examples are Ganz, *Quasi-Legislation*, n. 3 above, and Baldwin, *Rules and Government*, n. 56 above.

the parent statute is itself normally silent. The formal provisions for parliamentary supervision do not apply, and it is unlikely that procedures will be specified in the parent statute. Within this informal setting, consultation with interest groups will often take place, but it is likely to be reactive, depending more on political factors and the importance of certain interests than a commitment to fair treatment by ensuring that all groups have their views considered. Since procedural matters are generally left to the discretion of the administrative body making the rules, practice varies greatly as to whether any form of notice is given to those with an interest; practice also varies as to whether informal rules are ever made public. It can be seen from this brief description that the procedures for making informal rules are themselves normally highly informal.

While some informal rules are developed as guidelines in advance, others emerge from a course of individualized decisions. The policy issue might first appear when the administrative body begins to consider how to exercise a discretion in a specific case. Decisions must be made and there may be no time or opportunity for consideration of the broader issues or for consultation with interests beyond those directly involved in the process. Policy-making through individualized decisions is a common feature of the administrative process, with clear policies gradually emerging over a course of decisions. This is policy-making at its most informal, and here it is especially difficult to inject into the process the barest notions of procedural fairness to anyone other than the parties themselves.

16.4.3 Procedural Fairness

In considering the standards of fair treatment and fair procedures, we ought to begin with two background considerations, one an issue of principle, the other a practical matter. The issue of principle is that major policy issues should have been settled at the earlier stages of primary or delegated legislation, so that, by the time it reaches the level of informal rule-making, the scope of the policy is likely to be circumscribed and the range of interests narrow. Through the involvement of groups and interests at earlier stages in the policy process, much of the force of the principles of participation and consideration will have been spent. This is not invariably the case, so that on occasions, important and far-reaching elements of policy are left to informal rule-making. But that is neither the usual pattern nor should it be considered desirable. It should be urged on legislators and administrators that significant issues of policy should be dealt with at the higher levels of administrative government. The second more practical point is that the difficulties of providing for the involvement of a wide range of groups and interests at the level of informal rule-making are considerable. Informal rule-making often occurs in the course of individualized decisions, and although the wise administrator should try to foresee in advance and make plans for the issues which will arise, it is not always possible to do so.

Against these two background factors, we may consider briefly the implications for fair treatment and fair procedures. The guiding principles are that those who have an interest in the policy issues with which formal rule-making is concerned ought to be treated in accordance with the principles of participation and consideration. The two principles can be satisfied by different procedural approaches, and an agency might argue with some justification that the informal policy networks provide ample opportunity for interested parties to be heard and to be considered. An agency might also feel that, over a continuing course of decision-making and through regular contact with interested parties, it acquires a good knowledge and understanding of their attitudes and approaches so that any more formal procedures would serve little purpose beyond adding substantive burdens on time and resources. The argument is, in other words, that informal rule-making is one area in which highly informal procedures work well and satisfy the demands of fair treatment.

While there is force in this approach, we should be careful not to endorse too readily practices which tend to be of low visibility, conducted well away from outside scrutiny, and at the same time occupying a major part of administrative processes. In order to take account of these factors, a rather different approach on the following lines may be suggested. On the assumption that informal rules do play a vital role in administrative processes, and that their role in structuring discretion serves important values, it is difficult to see why they should not be made according to sound and established procedures. The premise on which this alternative approach is based is that the more processes veer towards inherent secrecy, informality, and low visibility, the more open they are to abuse and the stronger the case for a more formalized procedural approach. Empirical research into formal rule-making is scarce, but the evidence from more general studies of the administrative process points to a tendency within administrative agencies towards developing informal rules and standards, which are often not made public, and which tend to be made without proper consultation or consideration.[60]

If that is an accurate empirical basis on which to proceed (and the need for more research is clear), then a more exacting approach to the procedures for making informal rules is warranted. The starting point for such an approach would be the principle that informal rules can be acted upon by the authority only if the are first published in accessible places. This principle was introduced some years ago into the new administrative law in various Australian jurisdictions and appears to work well.[61] It does not directly relate

[60] See e.g. I Loveland, *Housing Homeless Persons* (Clarendon Press, Oxford, 1995).
[61] See Australian Administrative Tribunals Act (Cwth, 1975).

to the making of informal rules, but, by requiring publicity, sets a certain tone which should in turn be reflected in the procedures themselves. It is surely elementary, moreover, that where informal rules are being relied on they should be made known. As for the procedures for making rules, it is equally elementary that parties with an interest, whether of a sectional or cause nature, who have not had reasonable opportunities at earlier stages to make representations and to have their interests considered, ought to be able to do so at this level. A procedure similar to the American practice of notice-and-comment with respect to proposed rules would normally be adequate, although on more important issues of policy an additional duty on the rule-maker to give a brief explanation and justification for the rule would be warranted.

One objection to this approach might be that any move towards more formal procedures will be costly. While that is undoubtedly true, the rejoinder may be made that notice-and-comment procedures can themselves be simple, informal, and inexpensive to operate. It might also be added that the application of principles of fair treatment unavoidably incurs some costs, but that provided they are commensurate with the relative importance of the interests at issue and the nature of the administrative power, they are justified costs. To declare that procedures impose costs is not itself an argument one way or the other; it is a statement of fact from which we must then go on to consider whether the cost is justified as a matter of principle. One final point is to note that a distinction should be made between informal rules which really do involve issues of policy and those which are genuinely concerned with detail or technique. Rules of the latter kind do not raise issues of fair treatment, or at least not in the same way as those involving elements of policy; my suggestions here are confined to rules of the former kind.[62]

In the discussion so far, it has been assumed that informal rules are made prior to and separately from decision-making in individualized cases. That distinction is in practice more difficult to sustain. Policy issues can arise and need to be settled in the course of deciding how to deal with a specific case, and the most conscientious agency may find that no matter how well it has planned for the future by devising informal standards and guidelines, the peculiarity of cases will uncover issues previously unforeseen. Some agencies might even take the view that informal rules are best developed incrementally as issues arise in real situations. It is more common, however, for administrative agencies to take a middle course, where forward planning and incrementalism both have a place. On the occasions that policy does have to be made incrementally in the course of a decision, an uneasy balance holds between the circumstances of the case and the wider questions of policy. On the one hand a decision has to be made in that case, while on the other hand it will usually be difficult and inconvenient to try in the course of

[62] Compare the approach taken in Craig, *Administrative Law*, n. 56 above.

the decision to consult groups who may have an interest in the policy aspects. There is no easy or single solution to this dilemma. Sometimes the decision might not be urgent and could be postponed to allow for wider consultation. Another approach, which has been adopted in Australia, is to restrict the agency in each case to those informal rules which have already been formulated and published. This has the advantage of encouraging agencies to decide issues of policy and to devise guidelines in advance of their deciding cases. An approach on these lines might conflict with the duty on an authority to decide each case on its merit and not to fetter itself in advance. That problem could be overcome by allowing the authority to make an exemption in that case in order to do justice to the party; the incremental departure, however, should not become a general standard unless it were first submitted to the procedures for making informal rules and then published.

16.4.4 The Role of the Courts

The last matter to consider is the contribution the courts have made in extending ideas of procedural fairness to informal rule-making. An initial distinction should be made between two different matters: one concerns judicial doctrines in relation to the rule-making process, the other the legal consequences following from informal rules once made. Here we are interested in the first of these questions, although it is to be noted that the courts have created various doctrines in relation to the latter, some of which are highly relevant to the fair treatment of parties to whom informal rules are applied.[63] The rule-making process itself is the focus of our present interest and here the courts take the same general approach as that set out in relation to formal rule-making:[64] either fair treatment does not apply to rule-making or, if it does, Parliament rather than the courts should be responsible for it. Although that is the general approach, some differences both as to doctrine and principle can be seen in judicial attitudes to informal rule-making.

The courts have followed this general approach to rule-making to the extent that they have not created general doctrines of procedural fairness in informal rule-making. The general principles of participation, consideration, and openness have not been applied by the courts to this context. However, the courts have created a number of doctrines which indirectly bear on informal rule-making. The first derives from the idea that informal rules should not be so fixed that they preclude the capacity on the part of the administration to take account of the circumstances in a specific case.[65] This could mean only that the possibility should be kept open of making an exception to the rule in the particular case, but the statements made by

[63] See sect. 14.1.

[64] See sect. 16.1.3.

[65] This is part of the justification for the no-fettering doctrine: see D. J. Galligan, 'The Nature and Function of Policies Within Discretionary Powers', n. 55 above.

judges suggest the stronger idea that the administrator should positively consider whether to change the rule.[66] The odd thing is, however, that the doctrine stops short of imposing a duty on the administrative body to hear representations from the party as to what changes might be made. The most the party can hope for is that the opportunity will arise as part of a general right to be heard in individualized cases, although even then the administrator is not bound to disclose details as to the basis for the rule or even to make known its full terms. This doctrine must be regarded as making the very slightest advance, if any at all, towards procedural fairness in informal rule-making.

A second doctrine is in a sense opposite to the first: where informal rules have been made and made known, the authority is under a duty to apply the rules in specific cases, unless it first follows certain procedures which include giving notice to the party affected and inviting representations against change.[67] The reasoning behind the doctrine is that informal rules create expectations in parties as to how their cases will be dealt with, and while that is not enough to prevent the rules being changed it is enough to justify the imposition of certain procedures. Whether the authority is obligated to disclose its rules in the first place to allow expectations to arise is not clear. Again, however, this doctrine makes only a slight contribution to procedural fairness in informal rule-making.

The third doctrinal development is the clearest and most direct of the three: where an administrative body gives an undertaking to consult a party before changing the informal rules governing a matter, the undertaking will be regarded as binding.[68] While an express undertaking to consult parties clearly attracts application of the doctrine, an implicit undertaking should also be sufficient. A link can be made with the second doctrine since the very formulation and notification of informal rules may be taken as an implicit undertaking that they will be followed; it is then a short step to holding that they may be departed from only after consultation. To sum up, each of these doctrines is of interest and each makes a slight dent in the idea that informal rule-making is beyond common law doctrine and judicial supervision. However, even taken together, the doctrines fall far short of a systematic approach to procedural fairness.

Apart from the specific doctrines developed by the courts, a more general issue is whether the case for judicial supervision of informal rule-making is stronger than in the case of formal rule-making. The general view appears to be that since the courts leave the procedures of formal rule-making to Parliament, they should apply the same attitude to informal rules. There

[66] See e.g. *British Oxygen* v. *Minister of Technology* [1971] AC 610 and *R.* v. *Torquay Licensing Justices, ex parte Brockman* [1951] 2 KB 784.

[67] *R.* v. *Secretary of State, ex parte Khan* [1985] 1 All ER 40.

[68] *R.* v. *Liverpool Corporation, ex parte Liverpool Taxi Fleet Operators' Association* [1972] 2 QB 299.

are, however, good reasons for the courts taking a contrary view and being more activist in relation to informal rules. The basis for that approach would be, first, that informal rule-making is likely to be of low visibility and conducted away from the outside gaze and, secondly, that any procedural constraints Parliament might place on formal rule-making will probably not apply to informal rules. The conclusion we might draw from these two factors is that, in the likely absence of adequate parliamentary supervision, the courts should have a useful role to play in developing at least minimal standards of procedural fairness.

Bibliography

ABEL, R. L., *The Politics of Informal Justice* (Academic Press, New York, 1982), i and ii.

ABERCROMBIE, N., HILL, S., and TURNER, B. S., *The Dominant Ideology Thesis* (Allen and Unwin, London, 1980).

ADLER, M., 'Justice, Discretion and Poverty: A Reappraisal' in Finnie *et al.*, *Edinburgh Essays in Public Law* (Edinburgh University Press, Edinburgh, 1991).

—— and ASQUITH, S., *Discretion and Welfare* (Heinemann, London, 1981).

—— and BRADLEY, A., *Justice, Discretion and Poverty* (Professional Books, London, 1975).

—— BURN, E. and JOHNSON, R., 'The Conduct of Tribunal Hearings' in Adler, M. and Bradley, A., *Justice, Discretion and Poverty* (Professional Books, London, 1975).

ALDER, J., 'Representation Before Tribunals' [1972] *Public Law* 278.

ALLAN, T. R. S., *Law, Liberty and Justice* (Clarendon Press, Oxford, 1993).

ANONYMOUS, 'Specifying the Precedence Required by Due Process: Towards Limits on the Use of Interest Balancing' (1978) 88 *Harv. L Rev.* 1510.

ARTHURS, H., 'Rethinking Administrative Law: A Dicey Business' (1979) *Osgoode Hall LR* 1.

—— *Without the Law* (University of Toronto Press, Toronto, 1985).

ASHWORTH, A., *The Criminal Process* (Clarendon Press, Oxford, 1994).

ASIMOW, M., 'Public Participation in the Adoption of Interpretive Rules and Policy Statements' (1977) 75 *Michigan LR* 520.

—— 'Delegated Legislation: United States and United Kingdom' (1983) 3 *OJLS* 253.

ASTOR, H. and CHINKIN, C. M., *Dispute Resolution in Australia* (Butterworths, Sydney, 1990).

ATIYAH, P. S., *From Principles to Pragmatism* (Clarendon Press, Oxford, 1978).

AUSTIN, C. and DITCHFIELD, J., 'Internal Ventilation of Grievances: Applications and Petitions' in Maguire, M., Vagg, J., and Morgan, R. (eds.), *Accountability and Prisons* (Tavistock, London, 1985).

BALDWIN, J. and MCCONVILLE, M., *Negotiated Justice* (Martin Robertson, London, 1977).

BALDWIN, J., WIKELEY, N., and YOUNG, R., *Judging Social Security* (Clarendon Press, Oxford, 1993).

BALDWIN, R., *Regulating the Airlines* (Clarendon Press, Oxford, 1985).

—— 'Civil Aviation Regulation: From Tribunal to Regulatory Agency' in Baldwin, R. and McCrudden, C., *Regulation and Public Law* (Weidenfeld and Nicolson, London, 1987).

BALDWIN, R., *Rules and Government* (Oxford Socio-Legal Studies, Clarendon Press, Oxford, 1995).

BALDWIN, R. and HOUGHTON, J., 'Circular Arguments: the Status and Legitimacy of Administrative Rules' [1986] *Public Law* 239.

—— and MCCRUDDEN, C. (eds.), *Regulation and Public Law* (Weidenfeld and Nicolson, London, 1987).

BARBER, B., *Strong Democracy: Participatory Politics for a New Age* (U. of California P., Berkeley, Cal., 1984).

BARRON, A. and SCOTT, C., 'The Citizen's Charter Programme' (1992) 55 MLR 526.

BARRY, B., *Political Argument* (Routledge and Kegan Paul, London, 1965).

BAUMANN, Z., *Modernity and the Holocaust* (Polity Press, London, 1989).

BAYLES, M., *Procedural Justice* (Kluwer, London, 1990).

BEAN, P., *Rehabilitation and Deviance* (Routledge and Kegan Paul, London, 1976).

BEATSON, J., 'Legislative Control of Administrative Rule-making: Lessons from the British Experience?' (1979) 12 *Cornell Int. LJ* 199.

—— 'The Scope of Judicial Review for Error of Law' (1984) 4 *OJLS* 22.

—— and Matthews, M. H., *Administrative Law: Cases and Materials* (2nd edn., Clarendon Press, Oxford, 1989).

BEDDARD, R., *Human Rights in Europe* (Sweet and Maxwell, London, 1992).

BENNET, W. L. and FELDMAN, M. S., *Reconstructing Reality in the Courtroom* (Tavistock, London, 1981).

BIRKINSHAW, P., *Grievances, Remedies and the State* (Sweet and Maxwell, London, 1985),

BLACK, J., 'Which Arrow? Rule-Type and Regulatory Policy' in Galligan, D. J., *A Reader on Administrative Law* (Clarendon Press, Oxford, 1996).

—— *Regulators as Rule-Makers* (Clarendon Press, Oxford, forthcoming).

BLACKBURN, R. and TAYLOR, J. (eds.), *Human Rights for the 1990s* (Mansell, London, 1991).

BLACKSTONE, W., *Commentaries on the Laws of England* (W. Strahan, T. Cadell, D. Prince (eds.), 9th edn., T. Cadell and W. Davies, London, 1809).

BLOCH, R. H., *Medieval French Literature and Law* (U. of California P., Berkeley, Cal., 1977).

BRADLEY, A. W., 'The Judge Over Your Shoulder' [1987] *Public Law* 485.

—— 'Sachsenhausen, Barlow Clowes and Then' [1992] *Public Law* 353.

BRADSHAW, J., 'From Discretion to Rules: the Experience of the Family Fund' in Adler, M. and Asquith, S., *Discretion and Welfare*

BRAND, A., *The Force of Reason* (Allen and Unwin, Sydney, 1990).

BREYER, S., 'Vermont Yankee and the Court's Rule in the Nuclear Energy Controversy' (1978) 91 *Harvard LR* 1833.

BROWN, N. and BELL, J. S., *French Administrative Law* (4th edn., Clarendon Press, Oxford, 1993).

BRUDNO, B., 'Fairness and Bureaucracy: The Demise of Procedural Due Process for Welfare Claimants' (1979) 25 *Hastings LJ* 813.

CALVINO, I., 'A Judgment' in *Adam, One Afternoon* (Picador, London, 1957).

CALVINO, I., 'Why Read the Classics' in *The Literature Machine* (Picador, London, 1989).

CANADIAN JUDICIAL COUNCIL, *Commentaries on Judicial Conduct* (Quebec, 1991).

CANADIAN LAW REFORM COMMISSION, *Working Paper on Commissions of Inquiry* (Ottawa, 1977).

CANE, P., *An Introduction to Administrative Law* (2nd edn., Clarendon Press, Oxford, 1992).

CARLTON, W., *In Our Professional Opinion: The Primacy of Clinical Judgments in our Moral Choice* (Notre Dame, Indiana, 1978).

CARNEY, T., 'Cloaking the Bureaucratic Dagger: Administrative Law in the Welfare State' [1989] *Canberra B of PA* 123.

CHAYES, A., 'The Role of the Judge in Public Law Litigation' (1976) 89 *Harv. LR* 1281.

CHEAPER, M., 'Compromise and Litigation' in Pennock, J. R. and Chapman, J. W. (eds.), *Compromise in Ethics, Law and Politics* (Nomos xxi, New York University Press, New York, 1979).

CLARK, D. H., 'Natural Justice: Substance and Shadow' [1975] *Public Law* 27.

COKE, SIR E., *The First Part of the Institutes of the Laws of England* (3 vols., E and R. Brooke, London, 1628),

COLLINS, H., *Justice in Dismissal: the Law of Termination of Employment* (Clarendon Press, Oxford, 1992).

COMMITTEE ON SUPREME COURT PRACTICES AND PROCEDURES, *Report*, Cmnd. 8573 (HMSO, London, 1973).

COONEY, S., 'Gender and Judicial Selection: Should There be More Women on the Courts?' (1993) 19 *Melb ULR* 20.

COONS, J., 'Approaches to Court-induced Compromise—the Uses of Doubt and Reason' (1964) 58 *Northwestern ULR* 750.

COOPER, S., *Observations in Supplementary Benefits Offices* (Policy Studies Institute, London, 1985).

COOTE, A. (ed.), *The Welfare of Citizens: Developing New Social Rights* (Rivers Oram Press, London, 1992).

COTTERRELL, R., *The Sociology of Law* (Butterworth, London, 1984).

CAVADINO, M., 'Commissions and Codes: A Case Study in Law and Public Administration' [1993] *Public Law* 333.

CRAIG, P. P., *Public Law and Democracy* (Clarendon Press, Oxford, 1990).

—— 'English Administrative Law—Procedure, Rights, and Remedies' (1990) 2 *Euro. Rev. Public L.* 425.

—— 'Legitimate Expectations and Procedural Fairness: A Conceptual Analysis' (1992) 108 *LQR* 79.

—— *Administrative Law* (3rd edn., Sweet and Maxwell, London, 1994).

—— 'The Common Law, Reason, and Administrative Justice' (1994) 53 *Camb. LJ* 282.

CRAVEN, G., 'Legislative Action by Subordinate Authorities and the Requirement of a Fair Hearing' (1988) 16 *Melb. ULR* 569.

DAMASKA, M., 'Evidentiary Barriers to Conviction: Two Models of Criminal Procedure' (1973) 121 *U. Penn. LR* 506.

—— 'Structures of Authority and Comparative Criminal Procedure' (1975) 84 *Yale LJ* 480.

—— *The Faces of Justice and State Authority* (Yale University Press, New Haven, Conn., 1986).

Davis, K. C., *Discretionary Justice* (Louisiana State University Press, Baton Rouge, La., 1969).

—— *Administrative Law Treatise* (West Publishing, New York, 1979), i.

—— *1982 Supplement to Administrative Law Treatise* (West Publishing, St. Paul, Minn., 1982).

Davis, P. C., 'Law, Science, and History' (1988) 86 *Michigan LR* 1096.

Dennis, I. (ed.), *Criminal Law and Justice* (Sweet and Maxwell, London, 1987).

Devlin, P., *Trial by Jury* (Stephens and Sons, London, 1988).

Detmold, M., *Courts and Administrators* (Weidenfeld and Nicolson, London 1989).

Dicey, A. V., 'The Development of Administrative Law in England' (1915) 31 *LQR* 148.

—— *The Law of the Constitution* (E. C. S. Wade (ed.) Macmillan, London, 1961).

Dickens, L., 'The Advisory Conciliation and Arbitration Service: Regulation and Voluntarism in Industrial Relations' in Baldwin, R. and McCrudden, C., *Regulation and Public Law* (Weidenfeld and Nicolson, London, 1987).

Diver, C., 'Policy-Making Paradigms in Administrative Law' (1981) 95 *Harv. LR* 393.

Dostoevsky, F. *Crime and Punishment* (trans. by Constance Garrett, Bantam Books, Toronto; New York, 1981).

Drabble, R. and Lynes, T., 'The Social Fund—Discretion and Control' [1989] *Public Law* 297.

Duff, A., *Trials and Punishments* (Cambridge University Press, Cambridge, 1986).

Dumont, M. (ed.), *A Thesis on Judicial Evidence, Judicial Procedure and Rationale of Judicial Evidence* (London, 1825).

Dunham, W. H., 'Magna Carta and British Constitutionalism' in Thorne, S., Dunham, W., Kurland, P., and Jennings, I., *The Great Charter: Four Essays on Magna Carta and the History of our Liberty* (Pantheon, New York, 1968).

Dunleavy, P., 'The Architecture of the British Central State' (1989) 67 *Public Admin* 249.

Durkheim, E., *The Division of Labour in Society* (trans. by G. Simpson, The Free Press, New York; Collier-Macmillan Ltd., London, 1964).

Dworkin, R. M., *Taking Rights Seriously* (Duckworth, London, 1978).

—— 'The Forum of Principle' (1981) 56 *New York ULR* 469.

—— 'Principle, Policy, Procedure' and *passim*, *A Matter of Principle* (Clarendon Press, Oxford, 1985).

—— *Law's Empire* (Fontana, London, 1986).

Dyer, B., 'Determining the Content of Procedural Fairness' (1993) *Monash LR* 165.

Easterbrook, F., 'Substance and Due Process' [1982] *Sup. Ct. Rev.* 85.

Eggleston, R., 'What is Wrong with the Adversary Process' (1974) 49 *Australian LJ* 428.

Eisenberg, M. A., 'Private Ordering Through Negotiation: Dispute-Settlements and Rule-Making' (1976) 89 *Harv. LR* 637.

Eisenberg, T. and Yeazell, S. L., 'The Ordinary and the Extraordinary in Institutional Litigation' (1980) 93 *Harv LR* 465.

Elias, N., *The Nature of African Customary Law* (Manchester U.P., Manchester, 1956).

FARMER, J. A, 'A Model Code of Procedure for Administrative Tribunals—An Illusory Concept' (1970) 4 *NZUL Rev.* 105.

—— *Tribunals and Government* (Weidenfeld and Nicolson, London, 1974).

FELDMAN, D., *Civil Liberties and Civil Rights* (Clarendon Press, Oxford, 1993).

FINER, S. E., *Anonymous Empire* (2nd edn., Pall Mall Press, London, 1966).

FINNIE, W., *et al.* (eds.), *Edinburgh Essays in Public Law* (Edinburgh U.P., Edinburgh, 1991).

FINNIS, J. M., *Natural Law and Natural Rights* (Clarendon Press, Oxford, 1980).

FISHER, R., and URY, W., *Getting to Yes* (Penguin, London, 1981).

FISS, O. M., 'The Forms of Justice' (1979) 93 *Harv. LR* 1.

—— 'Against Settlement' (1984) 93 *Yale LJ* 1073.

FITZMAURICE, C. and PEASE, K., *The Psychology of Judicial Sentencing* (Manchester U.P., Manchester, 1986).

FLOUD, J. and YOUNG, G., *Dangerousness and Criminal Justice* (Heinemann, London, 1981).

FLOWER, C. T., *Public Works in Medieval Law* (Selden Society, London, vol., 1, 1915; vol. 2, 1923).

FLYNN, G., *et al.*, 'Symposium on Improving Management in Government' (1980) 66 *Public Administration* 429.

FOX, W. F., *Understanding Administrative Law* (2nd edn., Binder, New York, 1992).

FRANKLIN, N., 'The Rule Against Bias' in Galligan, D. J., *The Laws of Australia: Administrative Law* (Law Book Co., Sydney, 1993).

FRIEDMAN, K., 'Realization of Ombudsmen Recommendations', *4th International Ombudsmen Conference* (1988).

FRIENDLY, H., 'Some Kind of Hearing' (1975) 123 *U. Pa. LR* 1267.

FRUG, G., 'The Ideology of Bureaucracy in American Law' (1984) 97 *Harv. LR* 1276.

FULLER, L., *The Morality of Law* (Yale University Press, New Haven, Conn., 1964).

—— 'Mediation' (1970–1) 44 *S. Calif. LR* 305.

—— 'The Forms and Limits of Adjudication' (1978) 92 *Harv. LR* 353.

—— and EISENBERG, M., *Basic Contract Law* (3rd edn., West, St. Paul, Minn., 1972).

GALLIGAN, D. J., 'The Nature and Function of Policies within Administrative Powers' [1976] *Public Law* 332.

—— 'Judicial Review and the Textbook Writers' (1982) 2 *OJLS* 257.

—— 'Arbitrariness and Formal Justice in Discretionary Decisions' and *passim*, Galligan, D. J. (ed.), *Essays in Legal Theory* (Melbourne U.P., Melbourne, 1984).

—— *Discretionary Powers: A Legal Study of Official Discretion* (Clarendon Press, Oxford, 1986).

—— 'Rights, Discretion, and Procedure' in Galligan, D. J. and Sampford, C., *Law, Rights, and the Welfare State* (Croom Helm, London, 1986).

—— 'Regulating Pre-trial Decisions' in Dennis, I. (ed.), *Criminal Law and Justice* (Sweet and Maxwell, London, 1987),

—— 'The Right to Silence Reconsidered' [1988] *Current Legal Problems* 69.

—— 'Procedural Rights in Social Welfare' in Coote, A. (ed.) *Citizens' Rights in the Modern Welfare State* (Rivers Oram Press, London, 1992).

—— 'Tribunals' and *passim*, *The Laws of Australia: Administrative Law* (Law Book Co., Sydney, 1993).

GALLIGAN, D. J., 'Procedural Fairness' in Birks, P. B. H. (ed.), *The Frontiers of Liability* (Oxford, 1994).

—— *A Reader in Administrative Law* (Clarendon Press, Oxford, 1996).

—— and SAMPFORD, C. (eds.), *Law Rights and the Welfare State* (Croom Helm, London, 1986).

GANZ, G., *Administrative Procedures* (Sweet and Maxwell, London, 1974).

—— *Quasi-Legislation* (Sweet and Maxwell, London, 1987).

GARTH, B., 'The Movement Towards Procedural Informalism in North American and Western Europe: A Critical Survey' in Abel, R. L., *The Politics of Informal Justice* (Academic Press, New York, 1982).

GELLHORN, E., and ROBINSON, S. O., 'Rulemaking "Due Process": an Inconclusive Dialogue' (1981) 48 *U. of Chicago LR* 201.

GENN, H., *Hard Bargaining* (Oxford Socio-Legal Studies, Clarendon Press, Oxford, 1990).

GENN, H. and Y., *Representation Before Tribunals* (Lord Chancellor's Department, London, 1992).

GEWIRTH, A., 'The Epistemology of Human Rights' (1984) 1 *Social Philosophy and Policy* 1.

GIFFORD, D. J., *Administrative Law: Cases and Materials* (Anderson, USA, 1992).

GLUCKMAN, M., *The Judicial Process Among the Barotse of Northern Rhodesia* (2nd edn., Manchester University Press, Manchester, 1973).

GOLDBERG, S. B., GREEN, E. D., and SANDER, F. E. A., *Dispute Resolution* (Little, Brown, London, 1985).

GOLDING, M. P., 'Comment on Mashaw: Process and Psychology' (1987) 39 *Florida LR* 445.

GOSTIN, L., *A Human Condition* (2 vols., Mind, London, 1975 and 1977).

GRACE, C. and WILKINSON, P., *Sociological Inquiry and Legal Phenomenon* (Collier, Macmillan, London, 1978).

GRAHAM, C. and PROSSER, T., 'Rolling Back the Frontier: The Privatization of State Enterprises' in Graham, C. and Prosser, T. (eds.), *Waiving the Rules* (Open University Press, Milton Keynes, 1988).

GRANT, W., *Pressure Groups, Politics and Democracy in Britain* (Philip Allan, London, 1989).

GRAY, T. C., 'Procedural Fairness and Substantive Rights' in Pennock, J. and Chapman, J., *Due Process* (Nomos xvii, New York University Press, New York, 1977).

GREER, P., 'The Next Steps Initiative: An Examination of the Agency Framework Document' [1990] *Public Administration* 89.

GRIFFITH, J., 'Ideology in Criminal Procedure or a Third Model of the Criminal Process' (1970) 79 *Yale LJ* 359.

—— and STREET, H., *Principles of Administrative Law* (5th edn., Pitman, London, 1967).

GROSS, M. R., 'The American Advantage: The Value of Inefficient Litigation' (1987) 85 *Michigan LR* 734.

HABERMAS, J., *Theory of Communicative Action* (vol. 1, Heinemann, London, 1984; vol. 2, 3rd edn., Beacon, Boston; Polity, Cambridge, 1987).

HACKER, J., 'Hart's Philosophy of Law ' and *passim* in Hacker, J., and Raz, J. (eds.), *Law Morality and Society* (Clarendon Press, Oxford, 1977).

HAMPSHIRE, S., *Innocence and Experience* (Blackwell, Oxford, 1990).

HANDLER, J., 'Controlling Official Behaviour in Welfare Administration' (1966) 54 *Calif. LR* 479.

—— *The Conditions of Discretion: Autonomy, Community, Bureaucracy* (Russell Sage Foundation, New York, 1986).

HANSARD SOCIETY COMMITTEE, *Making the Law* (Hansard Society for Parliamentary Government, London, 1992).

HARDEN, I. and LEWIS, N., *The Noble Lie* (Hutchinson, London, 1986).

HARLOW, C., 'Administrative Reaction to Judicial Review' [1976] *Public Law* 116.

—— 'A Community of Interests: Making the Most of European Law' (1992) 55 *MLR* 331.

—— and RAWLINGS, R., *Public Law and Administration* (Weidenfeld and Nicolson, London, 1984).

HARRÉ, R., and SECORD, P. F., *The Explanation of Social Behaviour* (Blackwell, Oxford, 1972).

HART, H. L. A., *The Concept of Law* (Clarendon Press, Oxford, 1961).

—— *Law, Liberty, and Morality* (Clarendon Press, Oxford, 1963).

—— *Punishment and Responsibility* (Clarendon Press, Oxford, 1968).

HARTLEY, T. C., *The Foundations of European Community Law* (3rd edn., Clarendon Press, Oxford, 1993).

HAWKINS, K., *Environment and Enforcement* (Clarendon Press, Oxford, 1984).

—— 'Discretion in Making Legal Decisions' (1986) 43 *Washington Lee LR* 1161.

—— (ed.), *The Uses of Discretion* (Clarendon Press, Oxford, 1992).

HAYEK, F. A., *The Road to Serfdom* (Routledge and Sons, London, 1994).

HAZARD, G. C., 'Rationing Justice' (1965) 8 *J. of Law and Econ.* 1.

HEINZ, A. M., 'Precedence over Consequences: Experimental Evidence of Preference for Procedural and Distributive Justice' in Talarico, S. M. (ed.), *Courts and Criminal Justice* (8th edn., Butterworths, London, 1995).

HELD, D., *Models of Democracy* (Polity Press, Cambridge, 1987).

HERZ, M., 'Parallel Universes: NEPA Lessons for the New Property' (1993) 93 *Columbia LR* 1668.

HOLDSWORTH, W., *A History of English Law* (16 vols., 7th edn., Methuen and Co., London, 1956).

HONORÉ, A. M., 'Social Justice' in Summers, R. (ed.), *Essays in Legal Philosophy* (Basil Blackwell, Oxford, 1968).

—— 'Groups, Laws and Obedience' in Simpson, A. W. B., (ed.), *Oxford Essays in Jurisprudence* (Clarendon Press, Oxford, 1973),

HOWE, L. E. A., 'The "Deserving" and the "Undeserving": Practice in an Urban Social Security Office' (1985) 14 *J. of Soc. Policy* 49.

HUTTER, B., *The Reasonable Arm of the Law* (Oxford Socio-Legal Monographs, Clarendon Press, Oxford, 1988).

JACOB, J. I. M., *The Fabric of English Civil Justice* (Stevens and Sons, London, 1981)

—— *The Reform of Civil Procedure Law* (Sweet and Maxwell, London, 1982).

JACOB-GUILLAMOD, D., 'Rights Related to Good Administration of Justice' in Mac-

Donald, R. St J., *et al.*, *The European System for the Protection of Human Rights* (Martinus Nijhoff, Dordrecht; London, 1993).

JAFFE, L. L., and HENDERSON, E. G., 'Judicial Review and the Rule of Law' (1956) 72 *LQR* 345.

JANIS, M. and KAY, R., *European Human Rights Law* (The University of Connecticut Law School Foundation Press, 1990).

JENNINGS, I., *The Law and the Constitution* (4th edn., University of London Press, London, 1952).

JOLOWICZ, J. A., 'On the Nature and Purpose of Civil Procedure Law' in Scott, I. R. (ed.), *International Perspectives on Civil Justice* (Sweet and Maxwell, London 1990).

JOWELL, J., 'The Legal Control of Administrative Discretion' [1973] *Public Law* 178.

—— and LESTER, A., 'Beyond Wednesbury: Substantive Principles of Administrative Law' [1987] *Public Law* 368.

JUROW, K., 'Untimely Thoughts: A Reconsideration of the Origins of Due Process of Law' (1975) 19 *American J. of Legal History* 265.

KADISH, S., 'Methodology and Criteria in Due Process Adjudication: A Survey and Criticism' (1957) 66 *Yale LJ* 319.

KAFKA, F., *The Trial* (trans. by W. and E. Muir, Secker and Warburg, London, 1968).

KAGAN, R., *Regulatory Justice* (Russel Sage Foundation, New York, 1978).

KAPLAN, B., 'Civil Procedure—Reflection on the Comparison of Systems' (1959–60) 9 *Buffalo LR* 409.

KEIR, D. L., *The Constitutional History of Modern Britain 1485–1951* (6th edn., A. and C. Black, London, 1960).

KEITH, K. J., *A Code of Procedures for Administrative Tribunals* (Legal Research Foundation, New Zealand, 1974).

KEMP, P., *Beyond Next Steps* (Social Market Foundation, London, 1993).

KONECHI, V., and EBBESEN, E. (eds.), *The Criminal Justice System: A Social Psychological Analysis* (Freeman, London, 1982).

KRITZER, H., *Let's Make a Real Bargain: Understanding the Negotiation Process in Ordinary Litigation* (University of Wisconsin Press, Madison, Wis., 1991).

LACEY, N., 'The Jurisprudence of Discretion: Escaping the Legal Paradigm' in Hawkins, K. (ed.), *The Uses of Discretion* (Clarendon Press, Oxford, 1992).

LANGBEIN, J. H., 'The German Advantage in Civil Procedure' (1985) 52 *U. Chicago LR* 823.

LAW COMMISSION, *Administrative Law: Judicial Review and Statutory Appeals* (HMSO, London, 1993, Pam. No. 126).

LEMPERT, R., 'Discretion in a Behavioural Perspective: The Case of the Housing Eviction Board' in Hawkins, K. (ed.), *The Uses of Discretion* (Clarendon Press, Oxford, 1992).

LE SUEUR, A., and SUNKIN, M., 'Applications for Judicial Review: The Requirements of Leave' [1992] *Public Law* 1021.

LEWIS, N., 'Reviewing Change in Government: New Public Management and Next Steps' [1994] *Public Law* 105.

LIND, E. A., *et al.*, *The Perception of Justice* (Institute for Civil Justice, Rand Corporation, Santa Monica, Cal., 1989).

LINTON, R., *The Tanala: A Hill Tribe in Madagascar* (Field Museum of National History, Chicago, Ill., 1933).

LLOYD-BOSTOCK, S., *Law in Practice* (British Psychological Society and Routledge, London, 1988).

—— and MULCAHY, L. 'The Social Psychology of Making and Responding to Hospital Complaints: An Account Model of Complaint Processes' (1994) 16 *Law and Policy* 123.

LOMASKY, L. E., *Persons, Rights, and the Moral Community* (Clarendon Press, Oxford, 1987).

LONGLEY, D., *Public Law and Health Service Accountability* (Open University Press, Milton Keynes 1993).

LOUGHLIN, M., 'Procedural Fairness; A Study of the Crisis in Administrative Law' (1978) 28 *University of Toronto LJ* 215.

—— *Local Government in the Modern State* (Sweet and Maxwell, London, 1986).

—— and QUINN, P., 'Prisons, Rules and Courts: A Study in Administrative Law' (1993) 56 *MLR* 497.

LOVEGROVE, A., 'The Listing of Criminal Cases as an Administrative Discretion' [1984] *Crim. LR* 738.

LOVELAND, I., *Housing Homeless Persons* (Clarendon Press, Oxford, 1995).

LUCAS, J. R., 'The Phenomenon of Law' in Hacker, J., and Raz, J., *Law, Morality, and Society* (Clarendon Press, Oxford, 1977).

—— *On Justice* (Clarendon Press, Oxford, 1978).

LUSTGARTEN, L., *The Governance of Police* (Sweet and Maxwell, London, 1986).

McBarnett, D. J., *Conviction: Law, the State and the Construction of Justice* (Macmillan, London, 1983).

MCCORMICK, N., 'Rights in Legislation' in Simpson, A. W. B. (ed.) *Oxford Essays in Jurisprudence* (Clarendon Press, Oxford, 1973).

MCCRUDDEN, C., 'Codes in a Cold Climate' (1988) 51 *MLR* 408.

MACDONAGH, O., 'Delegated Legislation and Administrative Discretion in the 1850s: A Particular Study' [1958] *Victorian Studies* 29.

—— 'The Nineteenth-Century Revolution in Government: A Reappraisal' (1958) 1 *Historical Journal* 52.

MACDONALD, R. ST. I. *et al.* (eds.), *The European System for the Protection of Human Rights* (Martinus Nijhoff, Dordrecht: London, 1993).

MCILWAIN, C. H., 'Due Process of Law in Magna Carta' (1914) 14 *Columbia LR* 27.

MACKAY, A. W., 'Mandates, Legal Foundations, Powers and Conduct of Commissions of Inquiry' (1989–90) 12 *Dalhousie LJ Commissions of Inquiry* 29.

MALONEY, T. and YOUNG, R., 'Community Charge Appeals: A Major Problem?' (1991) 10 *Civil Justice Q* 206.

MARANVILLE, D., 'Non-acquiescence: Outlaw Agencies, Imperial Courts, and the Perils of Pluralism' (1986) 39 *Vanderbilt LR* 471.

MARSHALL, T. H., *The Right to Welfare* (Heinemann, London, 1981).

MASHAW, J. L., *Bureaucratic Justice* (Yale University Press, New Haven, Conn., 1983).

—— *Due Process in the Administrative State* (Yale University Press, New Haven, Conn., 1985).

MASON, A., 'Administrative Review: The Experience of the First Twelve Years' (1989) 18 *Fed LR* 122.

MAUSS, M., *The Gift: Forms and Functions of Exchange in Archaic Societies* (Cohen and West, London: New York, 1954).

MELVILLE, H., *Billy Bud: Sailor* (ed. by A. Robert Lee, Everyman, London, 1993).

MENKEL-MEADOW, C., 'Towards Another View of Legal Negotiations: The Structure of Problem Solving' (1983–4) 31 *UCLA LR* 754.

—— 'Lawyer Negotiations: Theories and Realities' (1993) 56 *MLR* 366.

MICHELMAN, F., 'Formal and Associational Aims in Procedural Due Process' in Pennock, J., and Chapman, J., *Due Process* (Nomos xvii, New York University Press, New York, 1977).

MILL, J. S., *Utilitarianism* (ed. by M. Warnock, Fontana, London, 1962).

—— *Considerations on Representative Government* (ed. by C. V. Shields, New York, 1988).

MILSOM, S. F. C., *Historical Foundations of the Common Law* (2nd edn., Butterworths, London: Boston, 1981).

MILTON, C., 'Appellants' Perceptions of the Tribunal Process' in Adler, M., and Bradley, A., *Justice, Discretion and Poverty* (Professional Books, London, 1975).

MNOOKIN, R. and KORNHAUSER, L., 'Bargaining in the Shadow of the Law: The Case of Divorce' (1979) 88 *Yale LJ* 950.

MONAGHAN, H. D., 'Of "Liberty" and "Property"' (1977) 62 *Cornell LR* 405.

MOODIE, G. C. and STUDDART-KENNEDY, G., *Opinions, Public and Pressure Groups* (Allen and Unwin, London, 1970).

MOORE, S. F., *Law as Process: An Anthropological Approach* (Routledge and Kegan Paul, London, 1978).

MULLAN, D. J., 'Fairness: The New Natural Justice' (1975) 25 *U. Toronto LJ* 281.

MULLER, T., 'Representation at Tribunals' (1990) 53 *MLR* 230.

MYERS, R. S., 'The End of Substantive Due Process' (1988) 45 *Washington Lee LR* 557.

NELSON, W. N., *Justifying Democracy* (Routledge, London, 1980).

—— 'The Very Idea of Procedural Justice' (1980) 90 *Ethics* 502.

NISBETT, R. and ROSS, L., *Human Interference: Strategies and Shortcomings of Social Judgment* (Prentice Hall, 1980).

NONET, P. and SELZNICK, A., *Law and Society in Transition* (U. of California P., Berkeley, Ca., 1978).

NORTHROP, F. S. C., *The Complexity of Legal and Ethical Experience: Studies in the Method of Normative Subjects* (Little, Brown, Boston, Mass., 1959).

Note, 'The Judicial Role in Defining Procedural Requirements for Agency Rule-Making' (1974) 87 *Harv. L.R.* 782.

NOWAK, J., ROTUNDA, R., and YOUNG, J., *Constitutional Law* (3rd edn., West, St Paul, Minn., 1986).

OGUS, A. I., *Regulation: Legal Reform and Economic Theory* (Clarendon Press, Oxford, 1994).

OSBORNE, G., 'Inquisitorial Procedure in the Administrative Appeals Tribunal—A Comparative Perspective' (1982) 13 *Fed. LR* 151.

PACKER, H., *The Limits of the Criminal Sanction* (Stanford University Press, Stanford, CA, 1969).

PARDOE, A., 'Investigation by the Commission for Racial Equality' [1982] *NLJ* 670.
PARRY, G., *Participation in Politics* (Manchester University Press, Manchester, 1972).
PATEMAN, C., *Participation and Democratic Theory* (Cambridge University Press, Cambridge, 1970).
PEAY, J. *Tribunals on Trial: A Study of Decision-Making under the Mental Health Act 1983* (Clarendon Press, Oxford, 1989).
PENNOCK, J. and CHAPMAN, J. (eds.), *Participation in Politics* (Nomos xvi, Lieber-Atherton, New York, 1977).
—— and —— (eds.) *Due Process* (Nomos xvii, New York University Press, New York, 1977).
—— and —— (eds.), *Compromise in Ethics, Law and Politics* (Nomos xxi, New York University Press, New York, 1979).
PINCOFFS, E. L., 'Due Process, Fraternity, and a Kantian Injunction', in Pennock, J. and Chapman, J., *Due Process* (Nomos, xvii, New York University Press, New York, 1977).
PLUCKNETT, T. F. P., 'Bonham's Case and Judicial Review' (1926) 40 *Harv. LR* 30.
—— *A Concise History of the Common Law* (Butterworths, London, 1956).
POLLOCK, F., *Essays in the Law* (Macmillan, London, 1922).
—— and MAITLAND, F., *History of English Law* (Cambridge University Press, Cambridge, 1888).
POSNER, R., 'An Economic Approach to Legal Procedure and Judicial Administration' (1973) 2 *J. of Legal Studies* 399.
POSTEMA, G., *Bentham and the Common Law Tradition* (Clarendon Press, Oxford, 1988).
PRESSMAN, J. L. and WILDAVSKY, A., *Implementation* (Berkeley, Cal., 1973).
PROSSER, T., 'Poverty, Ideology and Legality' (1977) 4 *Brit. J. of Law and Society* 39.
—— 'Politics and Judicial Review: The Atkinson Case and Its Aftermath' [1983] *Public Law* 59.
—— *Nationalized Industries and Public Control* (Basil Blackwell, Oxford, 1986).
RAMSAY, I., 'The Office of Fair Trading: Policing the Consumer Market Place' in Baldwin, R. and McCrudden, C. (eds.), *Public Law and Regulation* (Weidenfeld and Nicolson, London, 1987)
RAWLINGS, R., *The Complaints Industry: A Review of Socio-Legal Research on Aspects of Administration Justice* (ESRC, London, 1986).
RAWLS, J., *A Theory of Justice* (Clarendon Press, Oxford, 1971).
RAZ, J., 'Promises and Undertakings' in Hacker, J. and Raz, J. (eds.), *Law, Morality and Society* (Clarendon Press, Oxford, 1977).
—— *The Authority of Law* (Clarendon Press, Oxford, 1983).
—— 'On the Nature of Rights' (1984) xciii *Mind* 184.
—— 'Legal Rights' (1984) 4 *OJLS* 1.
REDISH, M. J. and MARSHALL, L. C., 'Adjudicatory Independence and the Values of Procedural Due Process' (1986) 95 *Yale LJ* 455.
REICH, R., 'The New Property' (1964) 73 *Yale LJ* 733.
—— 'Individual Rights and Social Welfare: The Emerging Legal Issues' (1965) 74 *Yale LJ* 1245.
REID, C., SCOBIE, E., and BARKER, C., *Community Charge Registration and Appeals*.
RESNICK, J., 'Managerial Judges' (1982) 96 *Harvard LR* 376.

RESNICK, J., 'Tiers' (1984) 57 *S. Cal. LR* 837.

—— 'Due Process: A Public Dimension' (1987) 39 *Florida LR* 405.

RHODES, G., *Committees of Inquiry* (Allen and Unwin for the Royal Institute of Public Administration, London, 1975).

RICHARDSON, G., 'The Duty to Give Reasons: Potential and Practice' [1986] *Public Law* 437.

—— *Law, Process, and Custody: Prisoners and Patients* (Weidenfeld and Nicolson, London, 1993).

—— OGUS, A., and BURROWS, P., *Policing Pollution* (Clarendon Press, Oxford, 1984).

RICHARDSON, J. and JORDAN, A. G., *Governing Under Pressure* (Martin Robertson, Oxford, 1979).

RICHARDSON, S. and GENN, H. (eds.), *Administrative Law and Government Action* (Clarendon Press, Oxford, 1994).

RIGGS, R. E., 'Substantive Due Process in 1791' [1990] *Wisconsin LR* 941.

ROBARDET, P., 'Should We Abandon the Adversarial Model in Favour of the Inquisitorial Model?' in 12 *Dalhousie LJ Commissions of Inquiry*.

ROBERTS, S., 'Mediation in Family Matters' (1983) 46 *MLR* 537.

ROBINSON, G. O., 'The Making of Administrative Policy' (1970) 118 *U. Pa. LR* 485.

RUBIN, E. 'Due Process and the Administrative State' (1984) 72 *Calif. LR* 1044

SAINSBURY, R., 'Social Security Appeals' in Finnie, W., *et al.* (eds.), *Edinburgh Essays in Public Law* (Edinburgh University Press, Edinburgh, 1991).

—— 'Administrative Justice: Discretion and Procedure in Social Security Decision-Making' in Hawkins, K., *The Uses of Discretion* (Clarendon Press, Oxford, 1992).

—— 'Internal Reviews and the Weakening of Social Security Claimants' Rights of Appeal' in Richardson, G. and Genn, H., *Administrative Law and Government Action* (Clarendon Press, Oxford, 1994).

SANDERS, A. and YOUNG, R., *Criminal Justice* (Butterworths, London, 1994).

SAPHIRE, R. B., 'Specifying Due Process Values: Towards a More Responsive Approach to Procedural Protection' (1978) 127 *U. Penn. LR* 111.

SCAFF, L. A., *Fleeing the Iron Cage* (UCLA Press, Berkeley, Cal., 1989).

SCANLON, T., 'Due Process' in Pennock, J., and Chapman, J., *Due Process* (Nomos xvii, New York University Press, New York, 1977).

SCHERMERS, H., 'The Right to a Fair Trial under the European Convention on Human Rights' in Blackburn, R. and Taylor, J., *Human Rights for the 1990s* (Mansell, London, 1991).

SCHWARZ, B., *Administrative Law* (Little, Brown, Boston, Mass., 1976).

SCOTT, I. R. (ed.), *International Perspectives on Civil Justice: Essays in Honour of Sir Jack I. H. Jacob* (Sweet and Maxwell, London, 1990).

SCOTT, W., *Waverley* (ed. and with introduction by A. Hook, Penguin, Harmondsworth, 1972).

SEARCHINGER, T., 'The Procedural Due Process Approach to Administrative Discretion: The Court's Inverted Analysis' (1986) 95 *Yale LJ* 1017.

SEIDMAN, L. M., 'Factual Guilt and the Burger Court: An Examination of Continuity and Change in Criminal Procedure' (1980) 80 *Columbia LR* 436.

SELDEN SOCIETY, *Select Cases in the Council of Henry VII* (ed. by C. G. Bayne and W. H. Dunham, B. Quaritch, London, 1958).

SENEVIRATNE, M., *Ombudsmen in the Public Sector* (Open University Press, Milton Keynes, 1994).
SHAPIRO, M., 'Compromise and Litigation' in Pennock, J. and Chapman, J. (eds.), *Compromise in Ethics, Law and Politics* (Nomos xxi, New York University Press, New York, 1979).
—— 'The Choice of Rule-Making on Adjudication in the Development of Agency Policy' (1983) 92 *Yale LJ* 1487.
SHKLAR, J., *The Faces of Injustice* (Yale University Press, New Haven, Conn., 1990).
SIMPSON, A. W. B. (ed.), *Oxford Essays in Jurisprudence* (Clarendon Press, Oxford, 1973).
SINAIKO, L. R., 'Due Process Rights of Participation in Administrative Rule-Making' (1975) 63 *Calif. LR* 886.
DE SMITH, S. A. and EVANS, T., *de Smith's Judicial Review of Administrative Action* (4th edn., Stevens, London, 1980).
SMITH, M. B. E., 'The Value of Participation' in Pennock, J. and Chapman, J. (eds.), *Participation in Politics* (Nomos xvi, Lieber-Atherton, New York, 1977).
SNYDER, F. E., 'Crime and Community Mediation' [1978] *Wisconsin LR* 737.
STAVROS, S., *The Guarantees for Accused Persons under Article 6 of the European Convention on Human Rights* (Martinus Nijhoff, Dordrecht, 1992).
STEPHEN, J. F., *The History of the Criminal Law* (Macmillan, London, 1883).
STEWART, 'The Development of Administrative and Quasi-Constitutional Law in Judicial Review of Environmental Decision-Making: Lessons from the Clean Air Act' (1977) 62 *Iowa LR* 720.
STEWART, R., 'The Reformation of Administrative Law (1974–5) 88 *Harv. LR* 1667.
STONE, J., 'From Principles to Principles' (1981) 97 *LQR* 224.
STRONG, F., *Substantive Due Process of Law* (Carolina Academic Press, Durham, N.C., 1986).
SUBRIN, S. N. 'How Equity Conquered Common Law: The Federal Rules of Civil Procedure in Historical Perspective' (1987) 135 *U. Penn. LR* 909.
SUMMERS, R. (ed.), *Essays in Legal Philosophy* (Basil Blackwell, Oxford, 1968).
—— 'Evaluating and Improving Legal Procedure: A Plea for Process Values' (1974) 60 *Cornell LR* 199.
SUNKIN, M., BRIDGES, L., and MÉSZÁROS, G., *Judicial Review in Perspective* (Public Law Project, London, 1993).
—— and LE SUEUR, A. P., 'Can Government Control Judicial Review?' (1991) *Current Legal Problems* 161.
SUNSTEIN, C., 'Beyond the Republican Revival' (1988) 97 *Yale LJ* 1539.
TALARICO, S. M. (ed.), *Courts and Criminal Justice* (8th edn., Butterworths, London, 1995).
TAPPER, C. F. H., *Cross and Tapper on Evidence* (6th edn., Butterworths, London, 1985).
TERREL, T. P., 'Rights and Wrongs in the Rush to Response: on the Jurisprudence and Dangers of Authoritative Dispute Resolution' (1987) 36 *Emory LJ* 541.
TUEBNER, G., 'Substantive and Reflexive Elements in Modern Law' (1983) 17 *Law and Society Rev.* 239.

TUEBNER, G., *Law as an Autopoietic System* (Blackwell, Oxford, 1993).
THIBAUT, J. and WALKER, L., *Procedural Justice* (Erebaum, New Jersey, 1975).
—— and —— 'A Theory of Procedures' (1978) 66 *Calif. LR* 540.
THOMAS, M. W., *The Early Factory Legislation* (Thomas Bank, Leigh-on-Sea, 1948).
THOMPSON, F., *Magna Carta: Its Role in the Making of the English Constitution 1300–1629* (University of Minnesota Press, Minneapolis, Minn., 1948).
THORNE, S., Dunham, W., Kaarland, P., and Jennings, I., *The Great Charter: Four Essays on Magna Carta and the History of Our Liberty* (Pantheon, New York, 1968).
TITMUSS, R. M., 'Welfare "Rights", Law and Discretion' (1971) 42 *Political Q*. 113.
TRIBE, L., *American Constitutional Law* (2nd edn., Foundation Press, New York, 1988).
TURNER, B. S., 'Prolegomena to a General Theory of Social Order' in Turner, B. S. (ed.), *Citizenship, Civil Society and Social Cohesion* (University of Essex, Colchester, 1986).
TWEEDIE, J., 'Rights in Social Programmes: The Case for Parental Choice of School' [1986] *Public Law* 407.
TWINING, W., *Theories of Evidence: Bentham and Wigmore* (Weidenfeld and Nicolson, London, 1986).
TYLER, T. R., 'Procedural Justice Research' (1987) 1 *Social Justice Research* 41.
—— 'What Is Procedural Justice?' (1988) 22 *Law and Society Rev*. 103.
—— *Why People Obey the Law* (Yale University Press, New Haven, Conn., 1990).
UNSWORTH, C., *The Politics of Mental Health Legislation* (Clarendon Press, Oxford, 1987).
VAN ALSTYNE, W., 'Cracks in the "New Property": Adjudicative Due Process in the Administrative State' (1977) 62 *Cornell LR* 445.
VAN DIJK, P., 'Access to Court' in MacDonald, R. St J., *et al.*, *The European System for the Protection of Human Rights* (Martinus Nijhoff, Dordrecht: London, 1993).
VERKUIL, P., 'A Study of Informal Adjudication Procedures' (1976) 43 *U. of Chicago LR* 739.
WADE, H. W. R., *Administrative Law* (6th edn., Clarendon Press, Oxford, 1992).
WALKLAND, S. A., *The Legislative Process in Great Britain* (Allen and Unwin, London, 1968).
WATSON, A., *Legal Transplants: An Approach to Comparative Law* (2nd edn., University of Georgia Press, Athens, Ga., 1993).
WEBB, S. and B., *English Local Government: From the Revolution to the Municipal Corporation Act: The Parish and the County* (Longmans, London, 1906).
WEBER, M., *Economy and Society* (ed. by Roth, G. and Wittich, C., U. of California Press, Berkeley, Cal., 1978).
WEILER, P., 'Two Models of Judicial Decision-Making' (1968) 46 *Canadian B. Rev.* 406.
WHEARE, K. C., *Government by Committee* (Clarendon Press, Oxford, 1955).
WIKELEY, N. and YOUNG, R., 'The Administration of Benefits in Britain: Adjudication Officers and the Influence of Social Security Appeal Tribunals' [1992] *Public Law* 238.
WILSON, G. K., *Interest Groups* (Blackwell, Oxford, 1990).

WOOD, D. A., 'Judicial Fairness and Systematic Bias' in Parker, S. and Sampford, C. J. G. (eds.), *Legal Ethics and Legal Practice: Contemporary Issues* (Clarendon Press, Oxford, 1995).

WRAITH, R. and HUTCHINON, P., 'Administrative Tribunals' (Allen and Unwin, London, 1973).

YOUNG, R., 'The Effectiveness of Representation at Tribunals' (1990) 16 *Civil J. Rev*. 16.

ZUCKERMAN, A. A. S., 'Interlocutory Remedies in Quest of Procedural Fairness' (1993) 56 *MLR* 325.

—— 'Quality and Economy in Civil Procedure' (1994) 14 *OJLS* 353.

—— 'Public Interest Immunity—A Matter of Prime Judicial Responsibility' (1994) 57 *MLR* 703.

ZWEIGERT, K. and KOTZ, H., *An Introduction to Comparative Law* (Clarendon Press, Oxford, 1987).

Author Index

Subject Index